Year	GDP*	Consumption	Investment	Government Purchases	Net Exports**	Real GDP in billions of chained 2005 dollars	Percentage Change from Previous Year		
							Real GDP	Consumer Price Index	Unemployment Rate
1970	1039	648	152	234	4	4270	0.2	5.6	4.9
1971	1127	702	178	246	1	4413	3.4	3.3	5.9
1972	1238	770	208	263	−3	4648	5.3	3.4	5.6
1973	1382	852	245	282	4	4917	5.8	8.7	4.9
1974	1500	933	249	318	−1	4890	−0.5	12.3	5.6
1975	1638	1034	230	358	16	4880	−0.2	6.9	8.5
1976	1825	1151	292	383	−2	5141	5.3	4.9	7.7
1977	2030	1278	361	414	−23	5378	4.6	6.7	7.1
1978	2294	1428	438	454	−25	5678	5.6	9.0	6.1
1979	2562	1591	493	501	−23	5856	3.2	13.3	5.8
1980	2789	1756	479	566	−13	5840	−0.2	12.5	7.1
1981	3127	1940	572	628	−13	5987	2.5	8.9	7.6
1982	3253	2076	517	680	−20	5871	−1.9	3.8	9.7
1983	3535	2289	564	733	−52	6136	4.5	3.8	9.6
1984	3931	2501	736	797	−103	6577	7.2	3.9	7.5
1985	4218	2718	736	879	−115	6849	4.1	3.8	7.2
1986	4460	2897	747	949	−133	7087	3.5	1.1	7.0
1987	4736	3097	785	999	−145	7313	3.4	4.4	6.2
1988	5100	3350	822	1039	−110	7613	4.1	4.6	5.5
1989	5482	3595	875	1101	−88	7886	3.5	4.6	5.3
1990	5801	3836	861	1182	−78	8034	1.9	6.1	5.6
1991	5992	3980	803	1236	−27	8015	−0.2	3.1	6.8
1992	6342	4237	865	1274	−33	8287	3.4	2.9	7.5
1993	6667	4484	953	1295	−64	8523	2.9	2.7	6.9
1994	7085	4751	1097	1330	−93	8871	4.1	2.7	6.1
1995	7415	4987	1144	1374	−91	9094	2.5	2.5	5.6
1996	7839	5274	1240	1421	−96	9434	3.7	3.3	5.4
1997	8332	5571	1389	1474	−101	9854	4.5	1.7	4.9
1998	8794	5919	1511	1526	−162	10,284	4.4	1.6	4.5
1999	9354	6342	1642	1631	−262	10,780	4.8	2.7	4.2
2000	9952	6830	1772	1731	−382	11,226	4.1	3.4	4.0
2001	10,286	7149	1662	1846	−371	11,347	1.1	1.6	4.7
2002	10,642	7439	1647	1983	−427	11,553	1.8	2.4	5.8
2003	11,142	7804	1730	2113	−504	11,841	2.5	1.9	6.0
2004	11,868	8285	1969	2233	−619	12,264	3.5	3.3	5.5
2005	12,638	8819	2172	2370	−723	12,638	3.1	3.4	5.1
2006	13,399	9323	2327	2518	−769	12,976	2.7	2.5	4.6
2007	14,078	9826	2289	2677	−714	13,254	2.1	4.1	4.6
2008	14,441	10,130	2136	2883	−708	13,312	0.4	0.1	5.8
2009	14,256	10,089	1629	2931	−392	12,987	−2.4	2.7	9.3

* Numbers may not add up because of rounding.
** From 1929–1937, 1942, 1954, and 1959 net exports were less than ± $0.5 billion.
Source: www.bea.gov

The McGraw-Hill Series

Economics

Macroeconomics

TENTH EDITION

Stephen L. Slavin

Union County College
Cranford, New Jersey

The New School University
New York City

McGraw-Hill
Irwin

MACROECONOMICS

Published by McGraw-Hill/Irwin, a business unit of The McGraw-Hill Companies, Inc., 1221 Avenue of the Americas, New York, NY, 10020. Copyright © 2011, 2009, 2008, 2005, 2002, 1999, 1996, 1994, 1991, 1989 by The McGraw-Hill Companies, Inc. All rights reserved. No part of this publication may be reproduced or distributed in any form or by any means, or stored in a database or retrieval system, without the prior written consent of The McGraw-Hill Companies, Inc., including, but not limited to, in any network or other electronic storage or transmission, or broadcast for distance learning.

Some ancillaries, including electronic and print components, may not be available to customers outside the United States.

This book is printed on acid-free paper.

1 2 3 4 5 6 7 8 9 0 WDQ/WDQ 1 0 9 8 7 6 5 4 3 2 1 0

ISBN 978-0-07-731719-5
MHID 0-07-731719-X

Vice president and editor-in-chief: *Brent Gordon*
Publisher: *Douglas Reiner*
Director of development: *Ann Torbert*
Managing development editor: *Christina Kouvelis*
Vice president and director of marketing: *Robin J. Zwettler*
Senior marketing manager: *Jen Saxton*
Vice president of editing, design, and production: *Sesha Bolisetty*
Project manager: *Dana M. Pauley*
Senior buyer: *Carol A. Bielski*

Lead designer: *Matthew Baldwin*
Senior photo research coordinator: *Jeremy Cheshareck*
Photo researcher: *Keri Johnson*
Lead media project manager: *Kerry Bowler*
Senior media project manager: *Ron Nelms*
Typeface: *10/12 Times*
Compositor: *Aptara®, Inc.*
Printer: *Worldcolor*

Library of Congress Cataloging-in-Publication Data

Slavin, Stephen L.
    Macroeconomics / Stephen L. Slavin.—10th ed.
        p. cm.—(The McGraw-Hill series economics)
    Includes index.
    ISBN-13: 978-0-07-731719-5 (alk. paper)
    ISBN-10: 0-07-731719-X (alk. paper)
    1. Macroeconomics. I. Title.
HB172.5.S554 2011
339—dc22

                                        2010026975

Photo Credits

Page 5 National Portrait Gallery, Smithsonian Institute/ Art Resource, NY
Page 6 The Granger Collection, New York
Page 8 National Portrait Gallery, Smithsonian Institute/ Art Resource, NY
Page 10 Franklin D. Roosevelt Library
Page 26 © Bettmann/Corbis
Page 30 © Bettmann/Corbis
Page 51 Historical Pictures/Stock Montage
Page 61 Historical Pictures/Stock Montage
Page 110 Historical Pictures/Stock Montage
Page 112 © Roger Ressmeyer/Corbis

Page 113 (top) © Frank Carrere
Page 113 (bottom) 1993 Susan Muniak
Page 155 Brown Brothers
Page 255 Historical Pictures/Stock Montage
Page 267 © Walter Stoneman/Samuel Bourne/Getty Images
Page 382 Collections of the Library of Congress
Page 418 The Granger Collection, New York
Page 446 1993 Susan Muniak
Page 447 © Time & Life Pictures/Getty Images
Page 474 © Roger-Viollet
Page 505 © Jeanne Strongin

About the Author

Photo credit: Leontine Temsky

Stephen L. Slavin received his BA in economics from Brooklyn College and his MA and PhD in economics from New York University. He has taught at New York Institute of Technology, Brooklyn College, St. Francis College (Brooklyn), and in the MBA program at Fairleigh Dickinson University, at the New School University in New York City, and at Union County College in Cranford, New Jersey.

He has written eight other books: *The Einstein Syndrome: Corporate Anti-Semitism in America Today* (University Press of America); *Jelly Bean Economics: Reaganomics in the Early 1980s* (Philosophical Library); *Economics: A Self-Teaching Guide, All the Math You'll Ever Need, Math for Your First- and Second-Grader, Quick Business Math: A Self-Teaching Guide* (all four published by John Wiley & Sons); *Chances Are: The Only Statistics Book You'll Ever Need* (University Press of America); and *Everyday Math in 20 Minutes a Day* (Learning-Express). He is the coauthor of four other Wiley books, *Practical Algebra, Quick Algebra Review, Precalculus,* and *Geometry.* In addition he is also the coauthor of *Basic Mathematics,* a text published by Pi r squared Publishers.

Dr. Slavin's articles have appeared in *Studies in Family Planning, Economic Planning, Journal of BioSocial Science, Business and Society Review, Bankers Magazine, Education for Business, Public Management, Better Investing, Northwest Investment Review, U.S.A. Today Magazine, Patterns in Prejudice, Culturefront,* and *Conservative Review.* In addition, he has written more than 500 newspaper commentaries on public policy, demographic economics, politics, urban economics, international trade, investments, and economics fluctuations.

Preface to the Instructor

As an undergraduate economics student, I never imagined writing a textbook—let alone one going into its tenth edition. Back in those good old days, economics texts were all stand-alone books without any supplements, and seldom cost students more than five dollars. While we certainly need to keep up with the times, not all change is for the good. Surely not when our students are paying $150 for textbooks they barely read.

Why not write a book that students would actually enjoy reading and sell it at a price they can afford? Rather than serving up the same old dull fare, why not just have a conversation with the reader, illustrating various economic concepts anecdotally?

Economics can be a rather intimidating subject, with its extensive vocabulary, complicated graphs, and quantitative tendencies. Is it possible to write a principles text that lowers the student's anxiety level without watering down the subject matter? To do this, one would need to be an extremely good writer, have extensive teaching experience, and have solid academic training in economics. In this case, two out of three is just not good enough.

Why did I write this book? Probably my moment of decision arrived more than 25 years ago when I mentioned to my macro class that Kemp-Roth cut the top personal income tax bracket from 70 percent to 50 percent. Then I asked, "If you were rich, by what percentage were your taxes cut?"

The class sat there in complete silence. Most of the students stared at the blackboard, waiting for me to work out the answer. I told them to work it out themselves. I waited. And I waited. Finally, someone said, "Twenty percent?"

"Close," I replied, "but no cigar."

"Fourteen percent?" someone else ventured.

"No, you're getting colder."

After waiting another two or three minutes, I saw one student with her hand up. One student knew that the answer was almost 29 percent—*one* student in a class of 30.

When do they teach students how to do percentage changes? In high school? In middle school? Surely not in a college economics course.

How much of *your* time do you spend going over simple arithmetic and algebra? How much time do you spend going over simple graphs? Wouldn't you rather be spending that time discussing economics?

Now you'll be able to do just that, because all the arithmetic and simple algebra that you normally spend time explaining are covered methodically in this book. All you'll need to do is tell your students which pages to look at.

The micro chapters offer scores of tables and graphs for the students to plot on their own; the solutions are shown in the book. Learning actively rather than passively, your students will retain a lot more economics.

As an economics instructor for more than 30 years at such fabled institutions as Brooklyn College, New York Institute of Technology, St. Francis College (Brooklyn), and Union County College, I have used a variety of texts. But each of their authors assumed a mathematical background that the majority of my students did not have. Each also assumed that his graphs and tables were comprehensible to the average student.

The biggest problem we have with just about any book we assign is that many of our students don't bother to read it before coming to class. Until now, no one has written a principles text in plain English. I can't promise that every one of your students will do the readings you assign, but at least they won't be able to complain anymore about not understanding the book.

Distinctive Qualities

My book has six qualities that no other principles text has.

1. **It reviews math that students haven't done since middle school and high school.**

2. **It's an interactive text, encouraging active rather than passive reading.** Students are expected to solve numerical problems, fill in tables, draw graphs, and do economic analysis as they read the text.

3. **It's a combined textbook and workbook.** Each chapter is followed by workbook pages that include multiple-choice and fill-in questions, as well as numerical problems.

4. **It costs substantially less than virtually every other text on the market.** And it has a built-in study guide.

5. **It's written in plain English without jargon.** See for yourself. Open any page and compare my writing style with that of any other principles author. This book is written to communicate clearly and concisely with the students' needs in mind.

6. **It is written with empathy for students.** My goal is to get students past their math phobias and fear of graphs by having them do hundreds of problems, step-by-step, literally working their way through the book.

Special Features

Four special features of the book are its integrated coverage of the global economy, its extra help boxes, its advanced work boxes, and its end-of-chapter current issues.

The Global Economy

Until the early 1970s our economy was largely insulated from the rest of the world economy. All of this changed with the oil price shock of 1973, our subsequent growing appetite for fuel-efficient Japanese compact cars, as well as for TVs, DVD players, cell phones, personal computers, and other consumer electronics made in Asia. As our trade deficits grew, and as foreigners bought up more and more American assets, every American became quite aware of how integrated we had become within the global economy.

The tenth edition has three chapters devoted entirely to the global economy—Chapter 18 (International Trade), Chapter 19 (International Finance), and Chapter 8 (The Export-Import Sector). Chapter 8 is part of the sequence (C, I, G, and X_n) leading up to the chapter on GDP (Chapter 9). In addition, we have integrated a great deal of material dealing specifically with the global economy throughout the text.

Here are some of the things we look at:

- Shipbreaking (Ch. 3, p. 57)
- The "Isms": Capitalism, Communism, Fascism, and Socialism (Ch. 3, pp. 63–67)
- The Decline of the Communist System (Ch. 3, p. 66)
- The American Consumer: World-Class Shopper (Ch. 5, p. 116)
- Why Did Incorporation Come So Late to Islamic Middle-Eastern Nations? (Ch. 6, pp. 128–129)
- Foreign Investment in the United States (Ch. 6, p. 133)
- Are We Giving Away the Store? (Ch. 7, p. 151)
- Trillion Dollar Economies (Ch. 9, p. 205)
- Comparative Unemployment Rates (Ch. 10, p. 229)
- Surplus or Deficit as Percentage of GDP, Selected Countries (Ch. 12, p. 297)
- Economic Growth during the Last Millennium (Ch. 16, p. 400)

Extra Help Boxes

Students taking the principles course have widely varying backgrounds. Some have no problem doing the math or understanding basic economic concepts. But many others are lost from day one.

I have provided dozens of Extra Help boxes for the students who need them. They are especially useful to instructors who don't want to spend hours of class time going over material that they assume should be understood after one reading.

Of course these boxes can be skipped by the better prepared students.

Here are some of the topics covered in the Extra Help boxes:

- Finding the Opportunity Cost (Ch. 2, p. 36)
- How Changes in Demand Affect Equilibrium (Ch. 4, p. 76)
- How Changes in Supply Affect Equilibrium (Ch. 4, p. 78)
- Price Ceilings, Price Floors, Shortages, and Surpluses (Ch. 4, p. 82)
- How Did We Get an Average Tax Rate of 15%? (Ch. 7, p. 154)
- Calculating Percentage Changes (Ch. 9, p. 200)
- Read Only if You're Not Sure How to Calculate the Unemployment Rate (Ch. 10, p. 227)
- Finding Percentage Changes in the Price Level (Ch. 10, p. 235)
- Finding Equilibrium GDP (Ch. 11, p. 270)
- Finding the Multiplier (Ch. 12, p. 286)
- Does Printing More Money Increase Our Money Supply? (Ch. 14, p. 352)
- Finding the Percentage of Income Share of the Quintiles in Figure 1 (Ch. 17, p. 429)
- Interpreting the Top Line in Figure 5 (Ch. 19, p. 498)

Advanced Work Boxes

There are some concepts in the principles course that many instructors will want to skip. (Of course, if they're not included in principles texts, this will make other instructors quite unhappy.) These boxes are intended for the better prepared students who are willing to tackle these relatively difficult concepts.

Here is a sampling of my Advanced Work boxes:

- Post-World War II Recessions (Ch. 1, p. 12)
- The Law of Increasing Costs (Ch. 2, p. 34)
- APCs Greater than One (Ch. 5, p. 99)
- Nominally Progressive, Proportional, and Regressive Taxes (Ch. 7, p. 156)
- Should Cigarettes Be Taxed? (Ch. 7, p. 160)
- Why NDP Is Better than GDP (Ch. 9, p. 196)
- Calculating Per Capita Real GDP (Ch. 9, p. 206)

- The Paradox of Thrift (Ch. 12, p. 287)
- Money versus Barter (Ch. 13, p. 315)
- Three Modifications of the Deposit Expansion Multiplier (Ch. 14, p. 345)
- Rational Expectations versus Adaptive Expectations (Ch. 15, p. 385)
- The Malthusian Theory of Population (Ch. 16, p. 419)

Current Issues

Students often ask, "How does any of this affect me?" Or, "Why do I have to study economics?" The Current Issues provide answers to those questions. Each is a practical application of at least one of the concepts covered in the chapter.

What's New and Different in the Tenth Edition?

One substantial change is the doubling of the number of practical applications, which appear at the end of each chapter. These enable your students to solve real world problems using what they have learned in each chapter.

At the end of nearly each chapter, you'll now find one or two Web activities which will reinforce what your students have learned. There's a world of information on the Web, and the key to using it effectively is knowing where to look.

A third major change is a thorough discussion of the causes and effects of the Great Recession. This takes place not just in the chapters on fiscal and monetary policy, but is integrated into most of the macro chapters as well as some of the micro chapters.

The advent of the Great Recession brought Keynesian economics back into fashion. Indeed, the massive stimulus programs enacted by the United States, China, and other leading economic powers were lifted directly from Keynes' *General Theory*. If you look back at the previous nine editions, you'll see that Slavin's *Economics* covered Keynesian analysis more extensively than any other principles text. Now, in the tenth edition, we discuss how Keynesian policy prescriptions were used to fight the Great Recession.

Finally, seven new "Chapter Issues" have been added—including "Should Ben Bernanke Have Been Given a Second Term?" (Chapter 14). This feature helps make economics more relevant to students.

Content and data updates have been made throughout the book to reflect currency. In addition, many of the examples have been updated, with a focus on examples that connect to current events such as the financial crisis and the Great Recession of 2007–2009. A more thorough listing of chapter-by-chapter changes is supplied below.

- **Chapter 1:** New Section: "The Great Recession."
- **Chapter 5:** Combined sections: "The Average Propensity to Consume and Save" as well as "The Marginal Propensity to Consume and Save." New graph: Figure 10: "Consumption as a Percentage of GDP, 1980–2010." New section: "The Wealth Effect."
- **Chapter 9:** Added subsection: "Volunteer Work" to "Production That Is Excluded" (from GDP) section.
- **Chapter 12:** Added Figure 5, "Hypothetical Business Cycles," showing how the automatic stabilizers smooth the business cycle to Part III, "The Automatic Stabilizers." New part: Part VI: "The Economic Stimulus Package of 2009." Sections: "The Economic Stimulus Act of 2009"; "How Effective Was the Stimulus Package?"; "Was the Deficit Too Big?"; "The Chinese Stimulus Plan." Added Figure 11, "Percentage of National Debt Publicly Held and Held by U.S. Government Agencies" to Part IX, "The National Debt." New Current Issue 1: "A Jobless Recovery?" Current Issue 2: "Trillion-Dollar Deficits as Far as the Eye Can See": Now includes

more on effects on deficit of efforts to deal with the Great Recession and the financial crisis.

- **Chapter 13:** Revised box: "Are Credit Cards and Debit Cards Money?" Deleted subsection of "Modern Banking: Internet Banking" from "Modern Banking" section. Added Figure 5: U.S. Bank Failures, 2000–2009 to "The Federal Deposit Insurance Corporation" section. Deleted section, "Walmart Bank?" Expanded Current Issue: "Overdraft Privileges."

- **Chapter 14:** Deleted box, "Check Clearing." Deleted section, "Fiscal and Monetary Policies Should Mesh." as well as "Who Controls Our Interest Rates?" Changed "The Housing Bubble, the Subprime Mortgage Mess, and the Financial Crisis of 2008" from Current Issue to regular section of chapter. Added subsection, "Paying Interest on Reserves" to section, "The Tools of Monetary Policy." Added new section: "Restoring a Normally Functioning Financial System," with these subsections: "The $700,000,000,000 TARP Bailout" and "Stopping Mortgage Foreclosures." New Chapter Issue: "Should Ben Bernanke Have Been Given a Second Term?"

- **Chapter 15:** Doubled size of section, "The Economic Behaviorists" by adding four paragraphs summarizing some of the key points made by Richard Thaler and Cass Sunstein in their book, *Nudge*. Section, "Conventional Macropolicy to Fight Recessions": now contains a new subsection, "Fighting the Great Recession." Current Issue: Changed from, "Is George W. Bush a Supply-Sider or a Keynesian?" to "True Believers."

- **Chapter 16:** New section: "Our Inefficient Transportation System." Split section, "Rising Health Care Costs and the Shift to a Service Economy" into two sections. Expanded new section, "Our Bloated Health Care System."

- **Chapter 18:** Part I: "A Brief History of U.S. Trade": added section, "The Effect of the Great Recession on Our Balance of Trade." Section: "What Are the Causes of Our Trade Imbalance": Added subsection: "(6) Our Shrinking Manufacturing Base." Added second Current Issue: "Globalization."

- **Chapter 19:** Deleted Advanced Work box, "The Yuan vs. the Dollar."

The Supplement Package

The *Economics* supplement package has been streamlined and updated for the tenth edition. All supplements are available at www.mhhe.com/slavin10e. In addition to updated online quizzes, the Test Bank is tagged for Learning Objectives, AACSB categories, and Bloom's Taxonomy. Also, the PowerPoint presentations for each chapter have been revised to increase relevance and clarity.

Instructor's Manual

This provides instructors with ideas on how to use the text, includes a description of the text's special features, a chapter-by-chapter discussion of material new to the tenth edition, and a rundown of chapter coverage to help them decide what they can skip. Also found here are the answers to the workbook questions and questions for thought and discussion at the end of each chapter of the text, as well as chapter worksheets and worksheet solutions.

Mark Maier, who has used the text for several editions, took over the Instructor's Manual in the sixth edition, and has included sections on chapter objectives, ideas for use in class, and homework questions and projects (including scores of very useful websites) for each chapter. The Instructor's Manual provides a rich source of interesting ideas of classroom activities and discussions involving concepts and issues included in the text.

Test Bank

The test bank includes over 9,000 multiple-choice questions, fill-in questions, and problems tagged to Learning Objectives, AACSB categories, and Bloom's Taxonomy. My thanks to Jerry Dunn and Ralph May from Southwestern Oklahoma State University, who have kept the test bank current, culling outdated questions and adding new ones.

Computerized Testing

A comprehensive bank of test questions is provided within a computerized test bank powered by McGraw-Hill's flexible electronic testing program EZ Test Online (www.eztestonline.com). EZ Test Online supplies instructors with the capability to create tests or quizzes in this easy to use program!

Instructors can select questions from multiple McGraw-Hill test banks or author their own, and the either print the test for paper distribution or supply it online. This user-friendly program allows instructors to sort questions by format; edit existing questions or add new ones; and scramble questions for multiple versions of the same test. You can export your tests for use in WebCT, Blackboard, and PageOut. Sharing tests with colleagues, adjuncts, TAs is easy! Instant scoring and feedback is provided and EZ Test's grade book is designed to easily export to your grade book.

PowerPoint Presentations

PowerPoint presentations are available and can be customized by the professor for length and level. Deborah M. Figart and Ellen Mutari of Richard Stockton College of New Jersey have done a great job updating and revising these presentations to highlight the most important concepts from each chapter.

Digital Image Library

All the graphs from the text are available in chapter-specific files for easy download. These images will aid in classroom presentations and the student's understanding.

Videos

A selection of videos is available to adopters, including both tutorial lessons and programs that combine historical footage, documentary sequences, interviews, and analysis to illustrate economic theory. A series of videos produced by Paul Solman, business and economics correspondent for the Lehrer News Hour and WGBH Boston, covers the core topics in economics.

Book Website
www.mhhe.com/slavin10e

Some of the text's unique qualities are incorporated in a dynamic new website. Updated online multiple-choice quizzes, emphasize the chapter Learning Objectives and offer further reinforcement of important chapter concepts.

McGraw-Hill *Connect*™ *Economics*

Less Managing. More Teaching. Greater Learning.

 McGraw-Hill *Connect*™ *Economics* is an online assignment and assessment solution that connects students with the tools and resources they'll need to achieve success.

McGraw-Hill *Connect*™ *Economics* helps prepare students for their future by enabling faster learning, more efficient studying, and higher retention of knowledge.

McGraw-Hill *Connect*™ *Economics* features

 *Connect*™ *Economics* offers a number of powerful tools and features to make managing assignments easier, so faculty can spend more time teaching. With *Connect*™ *Economics,* students can engage with their coursework anytime and anywhere, making the learning process more accessible and efficient. *Connect*™ *Economics* offers the features as described here.

Simple Assignment Management

With *Connect*™ *Economics,* creating assignments is easier than ever, so you can spend more time teaching and less time managing. The assignment management function enables you to:

- Create and deliver assignments easily with selectable end-of-chapter questions and test bank items.
- Streamline lesson planning, student progress reporting, and assignment grading to make classroom management more efficient than ever.
- Go paperless with the eBook and online submission and grading of student assignments.

Smart Grading

When it comes to studying, time is precious. *Connect*™ *Economics* helps students learn more efficiently by providing feedback and practice material when they need it, where they need it. When it comes to teaching, your time also is precious. The grading function enables you to:

- Have assignments scored automatically, giving students immediate feedback on their work and side-by-side comparisons with correct answers.
- Access and review each response; manually change grades or leave comments for students to review.
- Reinforce classroom concepts with practice tests and instant quizzes.

Instructor Library

- The *Connect*™ *Economics* Instructor Library is your repository for additional resources to improve student engagement in and out of class. You can select and use any asset that enhances your lecture.

Student Study Center

The *Connect*™ *Economics* Student Study Center is the place for students to access additional resources. The Student Study Center:

- Offers students quick access to lectures, practice materials, eBooks, and more.
- Provides instant practice material and study questions, easily accessible on the go.

Student Progress Tracking

Connect™ *Economics* keeps instructors informed about how each student, section, and class is performing, allowing for more productive use of lecture and office hours. The progress-tracking function enables you to:

- View scored work immediately and track individual or group performance with assignment and grade reports.
- Access an instant view of student or class performance relative to learning objectives.
- Collect data and generate reports required by many accreditation organizations, such as AACSB.

Lecture Capture

Increase the attention paid to lecture discussion by decreasing the attention paid to note taking. For an additional charge Lecture Capture offers new ways for students to focus on the in-class discussion, knowing they can revisit important topics later. Lecture Capture enables you to:

- Record and distribute your lecture with a click of a button.
- Record and index PowerPoint presentations and anything shown on your computer so it is easily searchable, frame by frame.
- Offer access to lectures anytime and anywhere by computer, iPod, or mobile device.
- Increase intent listening and class participation by easing students' concerns about note-taking. Lecture Capture will make it more likely you will see students' faces, not the tops of their heads.

McGraw-Hill *Connect*™ *Plus Economics*

McGraw-Hill reinvents the textbook learning experience for the modern student with *Connect*™ *Plus Economics*. A seamless integration of an eBook and *Connect*™ *Economics*, *Connect*™ *Plus Economics* provides all of the *Connect*™ *Economics* features plus the following:

- An integrated eBook, allowing for anytime, anywhere access to the textbook.
- Dynamic links between the problems or questions you assign to your students and the location in the eBook where that problem or question is covered.
- A powerful search function to pinpoint and connect key concepts in a snap.

In short, *Connect*™ *Economics* offers you and your students powerful tools and features that optimize your time and energies, enabling you to focus on course content, teaching, and student learning. *Connect*™ *Economics* also offers a wealth of content resources for both instructors and students. This state-of-the-art, thoroughly tested system supports you in preparing students for the world that awaits.

For more information, please visit www.mcgrawhill connect.com, or contact your local McGraw-Hill sales representative.

Tegrity Campus: Lectures 24/7

Tegrity Campus is a service that makes class time available 24/7 by automatically capturing every lecture in a searchable format for students to review when they study and complete assignments. With a simple one-click start-and-stop process, you capture all computer screens and corresponding audio. Students can replay any part of any class with easy-to-use browser-based viewing on a PC or Mac.

Educators know that the more students can see, hear, and experience class resources, the better they learn. In fact, studies prove it. With Tegrity Campus, students quickly recall key moments by using Tegrity Campus's unique search feature. This search helps students efficiently find what they need, when they need it, across an entire semester of class recordings. Help turn all your students' study time into learning moments immediately supported by your lecture.

To learn more about Tegrity watch a 2-minute Flash demo at http://tegritycampus.mhhe.com

McGraw-Hill Customer Care Contact Information

At McGraw-Hill, we understand that getting the most from new technology can be challenging. That's why our services don't stop after you purchase our products. You can e-mail our Product Specialists 24 hours a day to get product-training online. Or you can search our knowledge bank of Frequently Asked Questions on our support website. For Customer Support, call **800-331-5094**, e-mail hmsupport@mcgraw-hill.com, or visit www.mhhe.com/ support. One of our Technical Support Analysts will be able to assist you in a timely fashion.

Assurance of Learning Ready

Assurance of learning is an important element of many accreditation standards. *Macroeconomics,* 10e is designed specifically to support your assurance of learning initiatives.

Each chapter in the book begins with a list of numbered learning objectives, which appear throughout the chapter, as well as in the end-of-chapter Workbook. Every test bank question is also linked to one of these objectives, in addition to level of difficulty, Bloom's Taxonomy level, and AACSB skill area. EZ Test and EZ Test Online, McGraw-Hill's easy-to-use test bank software, along with *Connect*™ *Economics* allow you to search the test bank by these and other categories, providing an engine for targeted Assurance of Learning analysis and assessment.

AACSB Statement

The McGraw-Hill Companies is a proud corporate member of AACSB International. Understanding the importance and value of AACSB accreditation, *Macroeconomics,* 10e has sought to recognize the curricula guidelines detailed in AACSB standards for business accreditation by connecting selected questions in the test bank to the general knowledge and skill guidelines found in the AACSB standards.

The statements contained in *Macroeconomics,* 10e are provided only as a guide for the users of this text. The AACSB leaves content coverage and assessment within the purview of individual schools, the mission of the school, and the faculty. While *Macroeconomics,* 10e and the teaching package make no claim of any specific AACSB qualification or evaluation, we have, within *Macroeconomics,* 10e labeled selected questions according to the six general knowledge and skills areas.

Acknowledgments

Over the years since the first edition, hundreds of people have helped in large and small ways to shape this text. I especially wish to thank past editors Gary Nelson, Tom Thompson, Paul Shensa, and Doug Hughes.

Anne Hilbert, the developmental editor, saw this project through from the first reviews, the chapter-by-chapter revisions, and the dozens of deadlines that we met, to the time the book finally went into production. Anne was great at keeping all the plates spinning, dealing with a diverse group of personalities, making sure that all the pieces fit, and seeing to it that the text and the supplements were ready to go.

Project manager Dana Pauley, with whom I worked day to day, managed the copyediting, artwork, and page proofs, and saw to it that we stayed not just on schedule, but ahead of schedule. Karen Nelson did a very thorough copyediting job, finding errors and inconsistencies, some of which originated in earlier editions. Also, special thanks to proofreader Nym Pedersen for exceptional attention to detail. Matt Baldwin oversaw the design of the book from cover to cover. Rakhshinda Chishty, the project manager at Aptara Corporation delivered an attractive and accurately composed text. Senior buyer Carol Bielski made the printing process seamless and effortless. Senior media project manager Kerry Bowler made sure the supplement production process went smoothly.

Brent Gordon, the Vice President and Editor-in-Chief, Douglas Reiner, the executive editor, and Anne Hilbert and

Christina Kouvelis, the developmental editors, were all involved from start to finish. Once the book was well into production, Anne became a sales rep in the Washington, D.C. area, so she is now selling the book she edited. In addition to making sure that the text and all the supplements were printed on schedule, Christina is looking forward to hearing suggestions from instructors using the text. Jennifer Saxton, the senior marketing manager, and Jennifer Jelinski, the marketing specialist, have been working to help the book reach an even wider audience than the ninth edition.

Every economist knows that no product sells itself. Without major sales and marketing efforts, my text could not sell very well. Most of the credit goes to all the McGraw-Hill/Irwin sales reps for all their efforts to sell my book. And I would especially like to thank the reps in Dubuque, Iowa, who have personally accounted for about a quarter of our sales.

Thomas Parsons (Massachusetts Bay Path Community College), Ronald Picker (St. Mary of the Woods College), Tom Andrews (West Chester State University), Christine Amsler (Michigan State), Cal Tamanji (Milwaukee Area Technical College), Kelly Whealan George (Embry Riddle University), Khalid Mehtabdin (The College of St. Rose), and Jim Watson (Jefferson College) very generously provided numerous suggestions which greatly improved the text. I also want to thank Ellen Mutari for her thorough accuracy check of all the in-text problems. You may have been wondering who took that great photo of me on the author's page. The photographer is Leontine Temsky, who happens to be my sister. She also found a great website, www.zillow.com, which tells you instantly how much your house is worth. You'll find dozens of useful websites listed throughout the text.

I'd also like to thank the many reviewers who helped improve this text.

Sindy Abadie, *Southwest Tennessee Community College*
Shawn Abbott, *College of the Siskiyous (California)*
Kunle Adamson, *DeVry College of New Jersey*
Carlos Aguilar, *El Paso Community College*
Ercument Aksoy, *Los Angeles Valley College*
Rashid B. Al-Hmoud, *Texas Tech University*
Ashraf Almurdaah, *Los Angeles City College*
Nejat Anbarci, *Florida International University*
Guiliana Campanelli Andreopoulos, *William Patterson University*
Thomas Andrews, *West Chester University*
Jim Angus, *Dyersburg State Community College (Tennessee)*
Lee Ash, *Skagit Valley College*
John Atkins, *Pensacola Junior College*
Lyndell L. Avery, *Penn Valley Community College (Missouri)*
James Q. Aylsworth, *Lakeland Community College*
John Baffoe-Bonnie, *Pennsylvania State University*

Mohsen Bahmani-Oksooee, *University of Wisconsin, Milwaukee*

Kathleen Bailey, *Eastern Arizona College*

Kevin Baird, *Montgomery Community College*

Gyanendra Baral, *Oklahoma City Community College*

Patrick Becker, *Sitting Bull College*

David Bennett, *Ivy Tech (Indiana)*

Derek Berry, *Calhoun Community College*

John Bethune, *Barton College (North Carolina)*

Anoop Bhargava, *Finger Lakes Community College*

Robert G. Bise, *Orange Coast College*

John Bockino, *Suffolk County Community College*

Van Bullock, *New Mexico State University*

James Burkard, *Nashville State Community College*

Gerard A. Cahill, *Florida Institute of Technology*

Joseph Calhoun, *Florida State University*

Joy Callan, *University of Cincinnati*

Tony Caporale, *University of Dayton*

Perry A. Cash, *Chadwick University (Alabama)*

Andrew Cassey, *University of Minnesota*

Jannet Chang, *Northwestern University*

Michael Cohik, *Collin Community College*

Steve Cole, *Bethel College*

Ana-María Conley, *DeVry Institute of Technology—Decatur*

Dave Cook, *Western Nevada Community College*

James Cover, *University of Alabama, Tuscaloosa*

Andre Crawford, *Virginia Polytechnic Institute and State University*

Debra Cummings, *Fort Scott Community College (Kansas)*

Rosa Lea Danielson, *College of DuPage*

Ribhi Daoud, *Sinclair Community College*

Bill Demory, *Central Arizona College*

Craig Depken II, *University of Texas, Arlington*

Thomas O. Depperschmidt, *University of Memphis*

Sowjanya Dharmasankar, *Waubonsee Community College*

Amrik Singh Dua, *Mt. San Antonio College*

Ronald Dunbar, *MATC Truax*

Swarna Dutt, *University of West Georgia*

Faruk Eray Duzenli, *Denison University*

Angela Dzata, *Alabama State University*

Stacey Edgington, *San Diego State University*

Deborah M. Figart, *Richard Stockton College (New Jersey)*

Daniel Fischer, *University of Arizona*

Russell L. Flora, *Pikes Peak Community College*

Jack Foley, *Blinn College*

Diana Fortier, *Waubonsee Community College*

Charles Fraley, *Cincinnati State Technical and Community College*

Arthur Friedberg, *Mohawk Valley Community College*

Harold Friesen, *Friends University*

Yoshikazu Fukasawa, *Midwestern State University*

Marilyn Fuller, *Paris Junior College (Texas)*

Alejandro Gallegos, *Winona State University*

Frank Garland, *Tricounty Technical College (South Carolina)*

Eugene Gendel, *Woodbury University*

Kelly George, *Florida Community College of Jacksonville*

Kirk Gifford, *Brigham Young University, Idaho*

Adam Gifford, *Lake-Sumter Community College*

Scott Gilbert, *Southern Illinois University, Carbondale*

Michael Goode, *Central Piedmont Community College*

Jay Goodman, *Southern Colorado University*

Cindy Goodyear, *Webster University*

Mehdi Haririan, *Bloomsburg University (Pennsylvania)*

Charles W. Harrington Jr., *Nova Southeastern University (Florida)*

Virden Harrison, *Modesto Junior College; California State University, Stanislaus, Turlock*

Tina Harvell, *Blinn College*

Gail Hawks, *Miami Dade Community College*

Sanford B. Helman, *Middlesex County College*

Carol Hogan, *University of Michigan, Dearborn*

Jim Holcomb, *The University of Texas at El Paso*

Lora Holcomb, *Florida State University*

Jack W. Hou, *California State University, Long Beach*

Nancy Howe-Ford, *Hudson Valley Community College*

Calvin Hoy, *County College of Morris*

Won-jea Huh, *University of Pittsburgh*

Scott Hunt, *Columbus State Community College*

Janet Hunter, *Northland Pioneer College (Arizona)*

Robert Jakubiak, *Milwaukee Area Technical College*

Danny Jeftich, *Ivy Tech (Indiana)*

Mark G. Johnson, *Lakeland Community College*

Roger Johnson, *Messiah College*

Paul Jorgensen, *Linn-Benton Community College*

George Jouganatos, *California State University, Sacramento*

Lillian Kamal, *Northwestern University*

Brad Kamp, *University of South Florida*

Tim Kane, *University of Texas, Tyler*

Janis Kea, *West Valley College*

Elizabeth Sawyer Kelly, *University of Wisconsin, Madison*

James Kelly, *Rio Hondo College*

M. Moosa Khan, *Prairie View A&M University (Texas)*

Kenneth E. Kimble, *Sinclair Community College*

Kamau Kinuthia, *American River College*

Sara Kiser, *Judson College*

Jack Klauser, *Chaminade University of Honolulu*

Wayne Klutarits, *Jefferson College*

Shawn Knabb, *Western Washington University*

Harry Kolendrianos, *Danville Community College*

Michael J. Kuryla, *SUNY-Broome Community College*

Sungkyu Kwak, *Washburn University*

Larry LaFauci, *Johnson and Wales University*

Helen C. Lafferty, *University of Pittsburgh*

Rose LaMont, *Modesto Junior College*

Quan Vu Le, *Seattle University*

Jim Lee, *Texas A&M University, Corpus Christi*

Raymond Lee, *Benedict College*

Alan Levinsohn, *SUNY-Morrisville*

Hui Li, *Eastern Illinois University*

Stephen E. Lile, *Western Kentucky University*

Paul Lockard, *Black Hawk College*

Marty Ludlum, *Oklahoma City Community College*

Brian Lynch, *Lake Land College, Illinois*

Alyson Ma, *University of San Diego*

Y. Lal Mahajan, *Monmouth University*

Mark H. Maier, *Glendale Community College (California)*

Kelly Manley, *Gainesville State College*

Eddi Marlow, *Dyersburg State Community College (Tennessee)*

Jane Mattes, *The Community College of Baltimore City*

Koula Matzouranis, *Broward Community College, South*

Fred May, *Trident Technical College*

Steven B. McCormick, *Southeastern Illinois College*

Christopher R. McIntosh, *University of Minnesota, Duluth*

Kevin McWoodson, *Moraine Valley Community College*

Steven Medema, *University of Colorado, Denver*

Kimberly Mencken, *Baylor University*

Evelina Mengova, *California State University, Fullerton*

Lewis Metcalf, *Lake Land College, Illinois*

Arthur Meyer, *Lincoln Land Community College*

John E. Michaels, *University of Phoenix*

Green Miller, *Morehead State University*

David Mitchell, *University of South Alabama, Mobile*

Daniel Morvey, *Piedmont Technical College*

Thaddaeus Mounkurai, *Daytona Beach College*

Todd Myers, *Grossmont College*

Charles Myrick, *Dyersburg State Community College (Tennessee)*

Sung No, *Southern University A&M College*

Bill Nook, *Milwaukee Area Technical College*

Louise Nordstrom, *Nichols College*

Gerald Nyambane, *Davenport University Career Center*

Ronan O'Beirne, *American Institute of Computer Sciences (Alabama)*

Joan O'Brien, *Quincy College*

David O'Hara, *Metropolitan State University*

Albert Okunade, *University of Memphis*

Alannah Orrison, *Saddleback College*

Michael L. Palmer, *Maple Woods Community College (Missouri)*

Craig Parmley, *Ivy Tech (Indiana)*

Thomas R. Parsons, *Massachusetts Bay Path Community College*

Louis A. Patille, *University of Phoenix*

Ronald Picker, *St. Mary of the Woods College (Indiana)*

Ray Polchow, *Zane State College*

Robert Posatko, *Shippensburg University of Pennsylvania*

George Radakovic, *Indiana University of Pennsylvania*

Eric Rahimian, *Alabama A&M University*

Farhad Rassekh, *University of Hartford*

Mitchell Redlo, *Monroe Community College*

Helen Roberts, *University of Illinois, Chicago*

Judith K. Robinson, *Massachusetts Bay Path Community College*

S. Scanlon Romer, *Delta College*

Brain Rosario, *American River College*

Michael Rosen, *Milwaukee Area Technical College*

Rose M. Rubin, *University of Memphis*

Sara Saderion, *Houston Community College, SW*

David Schutte, *Mountain View College*

Mourad Sebti, *Central Texas College*

W. H. Segur, *University of Redlands*

L. Guillermo Serpa, *University of Illinois, Chicago*

Dennis Shannon, *Southwestern Illinois College*

Mehdi S. Shariati, *Kansas City Kansas Community College*

Rimma Shiptsova, *Utah State University*

Stephen Shmanske, *California State University, East Bay*

Nancy Short, *Chandler-Gilbert Community College*

Barry Simpson, *University of South Alabama, Mobile*

Garvin Smith, *Daytona Beach College*

Noel Smith, *Palm Beach Community College*

John Somers, *Portland Community College*

Don M. Soule, *University of Kentucky*

Karen Spellacy, *SUNY-Canton*

Rob Steen, *Rollins College*

Bruno Stein, *New York University*

Stephen Steller, *University of Phoenix*

Daniel Stern, *South Hills School of Business (Pennsylvania)*

Edward Stevens, *Nebraska College of Business*

Gary Stone, *Winthrop University*

Arlena Sullivan, *Jones County Junior College*

Denver O. Swaby, *Columbia Union College (Maryland)*

Max Tarpley, *Dyersburg State Community College (Tennessee)*

Henry Terrell, *University of Maryland*

Bette Lewis Tokar, *Holy Family College (Pennsylvania)*

Brian Trinque, *University of Texas, Austin*

Mark Tyrpin, *John Wood Community College*

Jose Vasquez, *University of Illinois at Urbana-Champaign*

Jim Watson, *Jefferson College, Missouri*

Jim Watson, *Jefferson College (Missouri)*

Christian Weber, *Seattle University*

Simone Wegge, *CUNY-Staten Island*

Marc Weglarski, *Macomb Community College*

Steven White, *Glendale Community College (California)*

J. Christopher Wreh, *North Central Texas College*

Elaine Gale Wrong, *Montclair State College*

Linda M. Zehr, *Chandler-Gilbert Community College*

Sandy Zingo, *Rogers State University (Oklahoma)*

Finally, to all adopters of the past nine editions, thank you. Your comments and suggestions have helped to make this the best edition yet.

—*Stephen L. Slavin*

Preface to the Student

What have you heard about economics? That it's dull, it's hard, it's full of undecipherable equations and incomprehensible graphs? If you were to read virtually any of the introductory economics textbooks, that's exactly what you would find.

How is this book different from all other books? Reading this book is like having a conversation with me. I'll be right there with you, illustrating various points with anecdotes and asking you to work out numerical problems as we go along.

Are you a little shaky about the math? Your worries are over. If you can add, subtract, multiply, and divide (I'll even let you use a calculator), you can do the math in this book.

How do you feel about graphs? Do you think they look like those ultramodern paintings that even the artists can't explain? You can relax. No graph in this book has more than four lines, and by the time you're through, you'll be drawing your *own* graphs.

In nearly every chapter you'll find one or two boxes labeled "Extra Help." Sometimes you can master a concept when additional examples are given. Don't be too proud to seek extra help when you need it. And when you don't need it, just skip the boxes.

Unlike virtually every other economics text, this one includes a built-in workbook. Even if your professor does not assign the questions at the end of each chapter, I urge you to answer them because they provide an excellent review.

I can't guarantee an "A" in this course, but whether you are taking it to fulfill a college requirement or planning to be an economics major, you will find that economics is neither dull nor all that hard.

—*Stephen L. Slavin*

Contents in *Brief*

Expanded Contents

Chapter 1

A Brief Economic History of the United States

More than two centuries ago, some Americans believed it was "manifest destiny" that the 13 states on the eastern seaboard would one day be part of a nation that stretched from the Atlantic to the Pacific. Was it also our manifest destiny to become the greatest economy in the history of the world?

LEARNING OBJECTIVES

After reading this chapter you should be able to:

1. Summarize America's economic development in the 19th century.
2. Describe the effect of the Great Depression on our economy and evaluate the New Deal measures to bring about recovery.
3. Discuss the impact of World War II on our economy.
4. List and discuss the major recessions we have had since World War II.
5. Summarize the economic highlights of each decade since the 1950s.
6. Differentiate the "new economy" from the "old economy."
7. Assess America's place in history.

Introduction

"May you live in interesting times," reputedly an ancient Chinese curse, could well describe the economic misfortunes which overtook us in late 2007 and continued for the next couple of years.

- Our worst economic downturn since the Great Depression.
- The bursting of the housing bubble.
- A financial crisis requiring over $2.5 trillion in loans by the Federal Reserve and the U.S. Treasury.
- The mortgage crisis, threatening some 7 million American families with foreclosure.
- Over 15 million Americans officially unemployed.

Our economy is a study in contrasts. We have poverty in the midst of plenty; we have rapidly expanding industries like computer software and medical technology, and dying industries like shipbuilding, textiles, and consumer electronics; we won the cold war against communism, but we may be losing the trade war against China.

Which country has the largest economy in the world, the United States, China, or Japan? Believe it or not, our national output is much greater than that of China and Japan combined.

America is the sole superpower and has one of the highest standards of living in the world. Communism—at least the version that was practiced in the Soviet Union and Eastern Europe—to borrow a phrase from Karl Marx, has been "swept into the dustbin of history."

The baby-boom generation has earned higher incomes than any other generation in history. Indeed, Americans once considered it their birthright to do better than their parents. But that ended about 35 years ago, and a lot of young people are worrying about their futures.

In the decade of the 1990s our economy generated more than 22 million new jobs. But there were fewer Americans working in early 2010 than there were 10 years earlier.

To sum up the good and the bad: We have the world's largest economy, and one of the world's highest standard of living, and, even though our recent economic performance has been less than stellar, most Americans have decent jobs paying decent wages. But there's the downside:

The economic downside

- Our federal budget deficit is at a record high and will remain high in the foreseeable future.
- Our trade deficit has averaged nearly $650 billion over the last 5 years.
- We are borrowing nearly $2 billion a day from foreigners to finance our trade and budget deficits.
- Unless Congress acts soon, our Social Security and Medicare trust funds will run out of money well before you reach retirement age.
- When you graduate, you may not be able to get a decent job.
- Our savings rate has averaged less than 3 percent a year since the new millennium.
- The real hourly wage (after inflation) of the average worker is lower today than it was in 1973.

In these first four chapters, we'll be looking at how our economy uses its basic resources, at the workings of the law of supply and demand, and at how capitalism and other economic systems work. But first we need to ask how we got here. After all, the American economic system evolved over nearly four centuries.

> Those who cannot remember the past are condemned to repeat it.
>
> –George Santayana–

What did the great philosopher mean by this? Perhaps he meant that those who do not learn enough history the first time around will be required to repeat History 101. But whatever he meant, it is clear that to understand our economy today, we need to know how it developed over the years.

Did you see *Back to the Future?* You may have seen parts 1, 2, and 3, but let's stick with just part 1. Imagine being sent back to the 1950s. The way people lived then was very different from the way we live today—and the 1950s represented life in the fast lane compared to daily existence during the first decade of the 20th century. So before we worry about today's economy, we'll take a few steps back and look at life in this country about 200 years ago.

The American Economy in the 19th Century

Agricultural Development

America has always had a large and productive agricultural sector. At the time of the American Revolution, 9 out of every 10 Americans lived on a farm; 100 years later, however, fewer than 1 out of every 2 people worked in agriculture. Today just 1 out of every 500 Americans is a full-time farmer. But our farms not only feed America but also produce a huge surplus that is sold abroad.

Unlike Europe, 200 years ago America had an almost limitless supply of unoccupied fertile land. The federal government gave away farmland—usually 160-acre plots (one-quarter of a square mile)—to anyone willing to clear the land and farm on it. Although sometimes the government charged a token amount, it often gave away the land for free.

America had an almost limitless supply of land.

The great abundance of land was the most influential factor in our economic development during the 19th century. Not only did the availability of very cheap or free land attract millions of immigrants to our shores, but it also encouraged early marriage and large families, since every child was an additional worker to till the fields and handle the animals. Even more important, this plenitude of land, compared to amount of labor, encouraged rapid technological development.

When George Washington was inaugurated in 1789, there were about 4 million people living in the United States. By the time of the War of 1812, our population had doubled. It doubled again to 16 million in 1835 and still again by 1858. Our numbers continued to grow, but at a somewhat slower pace, reaching the 100 million mark in 1915 and the 200 million mark in 1968, and 300 million in 2006.

Although all regions of the United States remained primarily agricultural in the years following the Civil War, New England, the Middle Atlantic states, and the Midwest—with their already well-established iron, steel, textile, and apparel industries—were poised for a major industrial expansion that would last until the Great Depression. In contrast, the South, whose economy was based on the cash crops of cotton, tobacco, rice, and sugar, as well as on subsistence farming, remained primarily an agricultural region well into the 20th century. The South continued to be the poorest section of the country, a relative disadvantage that was not erased until the growth of the Sun Belt took off in the 1960s. (See the box titled "Two Economic Conflicts Leading to the Civil War.")

Southern economic development remained agricultural.

Southern agriculture developed very differently from agriculture in the other regions of the nation. We know, of course, that most of the labor was provided by slaves whose ancestors had been brought here in chains from Africa. On the average, Southern farms were

Two Economic Conflicts Leading to the Civil War

In the decades before the Civil War, the economic interests of the North and South came into sharp conflict. Northern manufacturers benefited from high protective tariffs, which kept out competing British manufacturers. The Southern states, which had only a small manufacturing sector, were forced to buy most of their manufactured goods from the North and to pay higher prices than they would have paid for British goods had there been no tariff.*

As the nation expanded westward, another conflict reached the boiling point: the expansion of slavery into the new territories. In 1860, when Abraham Lincoln had been elected president, most of the land between the Mississippi River and the Pacific Ocean had not yet been organized into states. As newly formed territories applied for membership in the Union, the big question was whether they would come in as "free states" or "slave states." Lincoln—and virtually all the other leaders of the new Republican Party—strenuously opposed the extension of slavery into the new territories of the West.

The Southern economy, especially cotton agriculture, was based on slave labor. The political leaders of the South realized that if slavery were prohibited in the new territories, it would be only a matter of time before these territories entered the Union as free states and the South was badly outvoted in Congress. And so, as Abraham Lincoln was preparing to take office in 1861, 11 Southern states seceded from the Union, touching off the Civil War, which lasted four years, cost hundreds of thousands of lives, and largely destroyed the Southern economy.

The two major consequences of the war were the freeing of 4 million black people who had been slaves and the preservation of the Union with those 11 rebel states. It would take the nation more than a century to overcome the legacies of this conflict.

---

*Tariffs are fully discussed in the chapter on international trade.

American Agricultural Technology

In the 19th century, a series of inventions vastly improved farm productivity. In the late 1840s, John Deere began to manufacture steel plows in Moline, Illinois. These were a tremendous improvement over the crude wooden plows that had previously been used.

Cyrus McCormick patented a mechanical reaper in 1834. By the time of the Civil War, McCormick's reaper had at least quadrupled the output of each farm laborer. The development of the Appleby twine binder, the Marsh brothers' harvesting machine, and the Pitts thresher, as well as Eli Whitney's cotton gin, all worked to make American agriculture the most productive in the world.

The mechanization of American agriculture, which continued into the 20th century with the introduction of the gasoline powered tractor in the 1920s, would not have been possible without a highly skilled farm workforce. Tom Brokaw described the challenge that farmers faced using this technology:

> Farm boys were inventive and good with their hands. They were accustomed to finding solutions to mechanical and design problems on their own. There was no one else to ask when the tractor broke down or the threshing machine fouled, no 1-800-CALLHELP operators standing by in those days.*

*Tom Brokaw, *The Greatest Generation* (New York: Random House, 1999), p. 92. The "greatest generation" was the one that came of age during the Great Depression and won World War II.

large. By 1860, four-fifths of the farms with more than 500 acres were in the South. The plantation owners raised commercial crops such as cotton, rice, sugar, and tobacco, while the smaller farms, which were much less dependent on slave labor, produced a wider variety of crops.

In the North and the West, self-sufficient, 160-acre family farms were most common. Eventually, corn, wheat, and soybeans became important commercial crops. But in the years following the Civil War, increasing numbers of people left the farms of the North to take jobs in manufacturing.

Bad times for agriculture

Times were bad for agriculture from the end of the Civil War until the close of the century. The government's liberal land policy, combined with increased mechanization, vastly expanded farm output. The production of the nation's three basic cash crops—corn, wheat, and cotton—rose faster than did its population through most of that period. Why did production rise so rapidly? Mainly because of the rapid technological progress made during that period. (See the box titled "American Agricultural Technology.") This brings

Supply and demand

us to supply and demand, which is covered in Chapter 4 and explains why times were bad for agriculture despite expanded output. If the supply of corn increases faster than the demand for corn, what happens to the price of corn? It goes down. And this happened to wheat and cotton as well. Although other countries bought up much of the surpluses, the prices of corn, wheat, and cotton declined substantially from the end of the Civil War until the turn of the century.

The National Railroad Network

The completion of the transcontinental railroads

The completion of a national railroad network in the second half of the 19th century made possible mass production, mass marketing, and mass consumption. In 1850, the United States had just 10,000 miles of track, but within 40 years the total reached 164,000 miles. The transcontinental railroads had been completed, and it was possible to get virtually anywhere in the country by train. Interestingly, however, the transcontinental lines all bypassed the South, which severely retarded its economic development well into the 20th century.

In 1836, it took travelers an entire month to get from New York to Chicago. Just 15 years later, they could make the trip by rail in less than two days. What the railroads did, in effect, was to weave the country together into a huge social and economic unit, and eventually into the world's first mass market (see the box titled "Mass Production and Mass Consumption").

Mass Production and Mass Consumption

Mass production is possible only if there is also mass consumption. In the late 19th century, once the national railway network enabled manufacturers to sell their products all over the country, and even beyond our shores, it became feasible to invest in heavy machinery and to turn out volume production, which, in turn, meant lower prices. Lower prices, of course, pushed up sales, which encouraged further investment and created more jobs. At the same time, productivity, or output per hour, was rising, which justified companies in paying higher wages, and a high-wage workforce could easily afford all the new low-priced products.

Henry Ford personified the symbiotic relationship between mass production and mass consumption. Selling millions of cars at a small unit of profit allowed Ford to keep prices low and wages high—the perfect formula for mass consumption.

So we had a mutually reinforcing relationship. Mass consumption enabled mass production, while mass production enabled mass consumption. As this process unfolded, our industrial output literally multiplied, and our standard of living soared. And nearly all of this process took place from within our own borders with only minimal help from foreign investors, suppliers, and consumers.

After World War II, the Japanese were in no position to use this method of reindustrialization. Not only had most of their plants and equipment been destroyed by American bombing, but also Japanese consumers did not have the purchasing power to buy enough manufactured goods to justify mass production of a wide range of consumer goods. And so the Japanese industrialists took the one course open to them: As they rebuilt their industrial base, they sold low-priced goods to the low end of the American market. In many cases they sold these items—textiles, black-and-white TVs, cameras, and other consumer goods—at half the prices charged in Japan.

Japanese consumers were willing to pay much higher prices for what was often relatively shoddy merchandise, simply because that was considered the socially correct thing to do. Imagine American consumers acting this way! Within a couple of decades, Japanese manufacturers, with a virtual monopoly in their home market and an expanding overseas market, were able to turn out high-volume, low-priced, high-quality products. We will look much more closely at Japanese manufacturing and trade practices in the chapter on international trade.

John Steele Gordon describes the economic impact of the railroads:

> Most East Coast rivers were navigable for only short distances inland. As a result, there really was no "American economy." Instead there was a myriad of local ones. Most food was consumed locally, and most goods were locally produced by artisans such as blacksmiths. The railroads changed all that in less than 30 years.[1]

Before railroads, shipping a ton of goods 400 miles could easily quadruple the price. But by rail, the same ton of goods could be shipped in a fraction of the time and at one-twentieth of the cost.

The Age of the Industrial Capitalist

The last quarter of the 19th century was the age of the industrial capitalist. The great empire builders—Carnegie (steel), Du Pont (chemicals), McCormick (farm equipment), Rockefeller (oil), and Swift (meat packing), among others—dominated this era. John D. Rockefeller, whose exploits will be discussed in the chapter on corporate mergers and antitrust, built the Standard Oil Trust, which controlled 90 percent of the oil business. In 1872, just before Andrew Carnegie opened the Edgar Thomson works, the United States produced less than 100,000 tons of steel. Only 25 years later, Carnegie alone was turning out 4 million tons, almost half of the total American production. Again, as supply outran demand, the price of steel dropped from $65 to $20 a ton.

The industrial capitalists not only amassed great economic power, but abused that power as well. Their excesses led to the rise of labor unions and the passage of antitrust legislation.[2]

---

[1]John Steele Gordon, "The Golden Spike," *Forbes ASAP*, February 21, 2000, p. 118.
[2]See the chapters on labor unions and antitrust in *Economics* and *Microeconomics*.

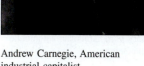

Andrew Carnegie, American industrial capitalist

The Development of the Automobile Industry

Nothing is particularly hard if you divide it into small jobs.

–Henry Ford–

Who was the first automobile manufacturer to use a division of labor and an assembly line? Was it Henry Ford? Close, but no cigar. It was Ransom E. Olds,* in 1901, when he started turning out Oldsmobiles on a mass basis. Still another American auto pioneer, Henry Leland, believed it was possible and practical to manufacture a standardized engine with interchangeable parts. By 1908, he did just that with his Cadillac.

Henry Ford was able to carry mass production to its logical conclusion. His great contribution was the emphasis he placed on an expert combination of accuracy, continuity, the moving assembly line, and speed, through the careful timing of manufacturing, materials handling, and assembly. The assembly line speeded up work by breaking down the automaking process into a series of simple, repetitive operations.

When Ford introduced a moving assembly line— the first ever used for large-scale manufacturing—this innovation reduced the time it took to build a car from more than 12 hours to just 30 minutes. It was inspired by the continuous-flow production methods used in breweries, flour mills, and industrial bakeries, as well as in the disassembly of animal carcasses in Chicago's meat-packing plants. By installing a moving conveyer belt in his factory, Ford enabled his employees to build cars one piece at a time, instead of one car at a time. The new technique allowed individual workers to stay in one place and perform the same task repeatedly on multiple vehicles that passed by them.

Back in 1908, only 200,000 cars were registered in the United States. Just 15 years later, Ford built 57 percent of the 4 million cars and trucks produced. But soon General Motors supplanted Ford as the country's number one automobile firm, a position it continues to hold. In 1929, motor vehicle production peaked at 5.3 million units, a number that was not reached again until 1949.

*In earlier editions I mistakenly attributed these feats—as well as the introduction of the moving assembly line—to Henry Olds. A student, who carefully researched these questions, found that it was Henry Ford who introduced the moving assembly line.

One of the most important changes in our industrial history took place late in the 19th century, with the transition from private electric generators to centralized, utility-based power production. Freed of the need to invest in expensive electric generators, companies could secure as much electric power as they needed through a simple power-line hookup. Now even the smallest start-up manufacturers could compete with the great industrial capitalists.

The American Economy in the 20th Century

On the world's technological cutting edge

By the turn of the century, America had become an industrial economy. Fewer than 4 in 10 people still lived on farms. We were among the world's leaders in the production of steel, coal, steamships, textiles, apparel, chemicals, and agricultural machinery. Our trade balance with the rest of the world was positive every year. While we continued to export most of our huge agricultural surpluses to Europe, increasingly we began to send the countries of that continent our manufactured goods as well.

We were also well on our way to becoming the world's first mass-consumption society. The stage had been set by the late-19th-century industrialists. At the turn of the 20th century, we were on the threshold of the automobile age (see the box titled "The Development of the Automobile Industry"). The Wright brothers would soon be flying their plane at Kitty Hawk, but commercial aviation was still a few decades away.

American technological progress—or, if the South can forgive me, Yankee ingenuity— runs the gamut from the agricultural implements previously mentioned to the telegraph, the telephone, the radio, the TV, and the computer. It includes the mass-production system perfected by Henry Ford, which made possible the era of mass consumption and the high living standards that the people of all industrialized nations enjoy today. America has long been on the world's technological cutting edge, as well as being the world's leader in manufacturing.

This technological talent, a large agricultural surplus, the world's first universal public education system, and the entrepreneurial abilities of our great industrialists combined

Henry Ford, American automobile manufacturer

to enable the United States to emerge as the world's leading industrial power by the time of World War I. Then, too, fortune smiled on this continent by keeping it out of harm's way during the war. This same good fortune recurred during World War II; so, once again, unlike the rest of the industrial world, we emerged from the war with our industrial plant intact.

America's large and growing population has been extremely important as a market for our farmers and manufacturers. After World War II, Japanese manufacturers targeted the American market, while the much smaller Japanese market remained largely closed to American manufactured goods. Japan—with less than half our population and, until very recently, much less purchasing power than the United States—has largely financed its industrial development with American dollars. (See again the box titled "Mass Production and Mass Consumption.")

The Roaring Twenties

World War I ended on November 11, 1918. Although we had a brief depression in the early 1920s, the decade was one of almost unparalleled expansion, driven largely by the automobile industry. Another important development in the 1920s was the spreading use of electricity. During this decade, electric power production doubled. Not only was industrial use growing, but by 1929 about two out of every three homes in America had been wired and were now using electrical appliances. The telephone, the radio, the toaster, the refrigerator, and other conveniences became commonplace during the 1920s.

The postwar boom

The spreading use of electricity

Between 1921 and 1929, national output rose by 50 percent and most Americans thought the prosperity would last forever. The stock market was soaring, and instant millionaires were created every day, at least on paper. It was possible, in the late 1920s, to put down just 10 percent of a stock purchase and borrow the rest on margin from a stockbroker, who, in turn, borrowed that money from a bank. If you put down $1,000, you could buy $10,000 worth of stock. If that stock doubled (that is, if it was now worth $20,000), you just made $10,000 on a $1,000 investment. Better yet, your $10,000 stake entitled you to borrow $90,000 from your broker, so you could now own $100,000 worth of stock.

How to become a millionaire in the stock market

This was not a bad deal—as long as the market kept going up. But, as they say, what goes up must come down. And, as you well know, the stock market came crashing down in October 1929. Although it wasn't immediately apparent, the economy had already begun its descent into a recession a couple of months before the crash. And, that recession was the beginning of the Great Depression.

...the chief business of the American people is business.
—President Calvin Coolidge

Curiously, within days after the crash, several leading government and business officials—including President Hoover and John D. Rockefeller—each described economic conditions as "fundamentally sound." The next time you hear our economy described in those terms, you'll know we're in big trouble.

The 1930s: The Great Depression

> Once upon a time my opponents honored me as possessing the fabulous intellectual and economic power by which I created a worldwide depression all by myself.
>
> –President Herbert Hoover–

By the summer of 1929, the country had clearly built itself up for an economic letdown. Between 1919 and 1929, the number of cars on the road more than tripled, from fewer than 8 million to nearly 27 million, almost one automobile for every household in the nation. The automobile market was saturated. Nearly three out of four cars on the road were less than six years old, and model changes were not nearly as important then as they are today. The tire industry had been overbuilt, and textiles were suffering from overcapacity. Residential construction was already in decline, and the general business investment outlook was not that rosy.

The August 1929 recession

Had the stock market not crashed and had the rest of the world not gone into a depression, we might have gotten away with a moderate business downturn. Also, had the federal government acted more expeditiously, it is quite possible that the prosperity of the 1920s, after a fairly short recession, could have continued well into the 1930s. But that's not what happened. What did happen completely changed the lives of the people who lived through it, as well as the course of human history itself.

Prices began to decline, investment in plant and equipment collapsed, and a drought wiped out millions of farmers. In fact, conditions grew so bad in what became known as the Dust Bowl that millions of people from the Midwest just packed their cars and drove in caravans to seek a better life in California. Their flight was immortalized in John Steinbeck's great novel *The Grapes of Wrath,* which was later made into a movie. Although most of these migrants came from other states, they were collectively called Okies, because it seemed at the time as if the entire state of Oklahoma had picked up and moved west.

There had been widespread bank failures in the late 1920s and by the end of 1930, thousands of banks had failed and the generally optimistic economic outlook had given way to one of extreme pessimism. From here on, it was all downhill. By the beginning of 1933, banks were closing all over the country; by the first week in March, every single bank in the United States had shut its doors.

When the economy hit bottom in March 1933, national output was about one-third lower than it had been in August 1929. The official unemployment rate was 25 percent, but official figures tell only part of the story. Millions of additional workers had simply given up looking for work during the depths of the Great Depression, as there was no work to be had. Yet according to the way the government compiles the unemployment rate, these people were not even counted since they were not actually looking for work.[3]

The Depression was a time of soup kitchens, people selling apples on the street, large-scale homelessness, so-called hobo jungles where poor men huddled around garbage-pail fires to keep warm, and even fairly widespread starvation. "Are you working?" and "Brother, can you spare a dime?"[4] were common greetings. People who lived in collections of shacks made of cardboard, wood, and corrugated sheet metal scornfully referred to them as Hoovervilles. Although President Herbert Hoover did eventually make a few halfhearted attempts to get the economy moving again, his greatest contribution to the economy was apparently his slogans. When he ran for the presidency in 1928, he promised "two cars in every garage" and "a chicken in every pot." As the Depression grew worse, he kept telling Americans that "prosperity is just around the corner." It's too bad he didn't have Frank Perdue in those days to stick a chicken in every pot.

While most Americans to this day blame President Hoover for not preventing the Depression, and then, doing too little to end it, perhaps the single biggest cause of the Depression was that the Federal Reserve let the money supply fall by one-third, causing deflation. And to make things still worse, it did nothing to prevent an epidemic of bank failures, causing a credit crisis.

Why did the downturn of August 1929 to March 1933 finally reverse itself? Well, for one thing, we were just about due. Business inventories had been reduced to rock-bottom levels, prices had finally stopped falling, and there was a need to replace some plants and equipment. The federal budget deficits of 1931 and 1932, even if unwillingly incurred, did provide a mild stimulus to the economy.[5]

Clearly a lot of the credit must go to the new administration of Franklin D. Roosevelt, which reopened the banks, ran large budget deficits, and eventually created government job programs that put millions of Americans back to work (see the box titled "The New Deal"). Recognizing a crisis in confidence, Roosevelt said, "The only thing we have to fear is fear itself." Putting millions of people back to work was a tremendous confidence builder. A 50-month expansion began in March 1933 and lasted until May 1937. Although output did finally reach the levels of August 1929, more than 7 million people were still unemployed.

Margin notes

The Dust Bowl and the "Okies"

The bank failures

Hitting bottom

Herbert Hoover, thirty-first president of the United States

Herbert Hoover and the Depression

Why did the downturn reverse itself?

I see one-third of a nation ill-housed, ill-clad, ill-nourished.
—Franklin D. Roosevelt
Second Inaugural Address,
January 1937

---

[3]How the Department of Labor computes the unemployment rate is discussed in the chapter on economic fluctuations in *Economics* and *Macroeconomics.* In Chapter 2, we'll be looking at the concept of full employment, but you can grasp intuitively that when our economy enters even a minor downturn, we are operating at less than full employment.

[4]"Brother, Can You Spare a Dime?" was a depression era song written by Yip Harburg and Jay Gorney.

[5]In Chapter 12 of *Economics* and *Macroeconomics* we'll explain how budget deficits stimulate the economy.

The New Deal

When Franklin D. Roosevelt ran for president in 1932, he promised "a new deal for the American people." Action was needed, and it was needed fast. In the first 100 days Roosevelt was in office, his administration sent a flurry of bills to Congress that were promptly passed.

The New Deal is best summarized by the three Rs: relief, recovery, and reform. Relief was aimed at alleviating the suffering of a nation that was, in President Roosevelt's words, one-third "ill-fed, ill-clothed, and ill-housed." These people needed work relief, a system similar to today's workfare (work for your welfare check) programs. About 6 million people, on average, were put to work at various jobs ranging from raking leaves and repairing public buildings to maintaining national parks and building power dams. Robert R. Russell made this observation:

> The principal objects of work-relief were to help people preserve their self-respect by enabling them to stay off the dole and to maintain their work habits against the day when they could again find employment in private enterprises. It was also hoped that the programs, by putting some purchasing power into the hands of workers and suppliers of materials, would help prime the economic pump.*

The economic recovery could not begin to take off until people again began spending money. As these 6 million Americans went back to work, they spent their paychecks on food, clothing, and shelter, and managed to pay off at least some of their debts. The most lasting effect of the New Deal was reform. The Securities and Exchange Commission (SEC) was set up to regulate the stock market and avoid a repetition of the speculative excesses of the late 1920s, which had led to the great crash of 1929. After the reform, bank deposits were insured by the Federal Deposit Insurance Corporation (FDIC) to prevent future runs on the banks by depositors, like those experienced in the early 1930s. Also, an unemployment insurance benefit program was set up to provide temporarily unemployed people with some money to tide them over. The most important reform of all was the creation of Social Security. Although even today retired people need more than their Social Security benefits to get by, there is no question that this program has provided tens of millions of retired people with a substantial income and has largely removed workers' fears of being destitute and dependent in their old age.

The New Deal was a much greater success in the long run than in the short run. While New Deal spending programs did not end the Depression, the reforms it put in place laid the foundation for unprecedented economic growth and broadly shared prosperity in the years after World War II.

---

*Robert R. Russell, *A History of the American Economic System* (New York: Appleton-Century-Crofts, 1964), p. 547.

By far, the most important reason for the success of the New Deal's first four years was the massive federal government spending that returned millions of Americans to work. This huge infusion of dollars into our economy was just what the doctor ordered. In this case, the doctor was John Maynard Keynes, the great English economist, who maintained that it didn't matter *what* the money was spent on—even paying people to dig holes in the ground and then to fill them up again—as long as enough money was spent. But in May 1937, just when it had begun to look as though the Depression was finally over, we plunged right back into it again.

What went wrong? Two things: First, the Federal Reserve Board of Governors, inexplicably more concerned about inflation than about the lingering economic depression, greatly tightened credit, making it much harder to borrow money. Second, the Roosevelt administration suddenly got that old balance-the-budget-at-all-costs religion. Government spending was sharply reduced—the budget of the Works Progress Administration was cut in half—and taxes were raised. The cost of that economic orthodoxy—which would have made sense during an economic boom—was the very sharp and deep recession of 1937–38. Tight money and a balanced budget are now considered the right policies to follow when the economy is heating up and prices are rising too quickly, but they are prescriptions for disaster when the unemployment rate is 12 percent.[6]

The recession of 1937–38

The ensuing downturn pushed up the official unemployment count by another 5 million, industrial production fell by 30 percent, and people began to wonder when this depression would ever end. But there really *was* some light at the end of the tunnel.

---

[6]These policies will be discussed in Chapters 12 and 14 of *Economics* and *Macroeconomics*.

Franklin D. Roosevelt, thirty-second president of the United States

In April 1938, both the Roosevelt administration and the Federal Reserve Board reversed course and began to stimulate the economy. By June, the economy had turned around again, and this time the expansion would continue for seven years. The outbreak of war in Europe, the American mobilization in 1940 and 1941, and our eventual entry into the war on December 7, 1941, all propelled us toward full recovery.

When we ask what finally brought the United States out of the Great Depression, there is one clear answer: the massive federal government spending that was needed to prepare for and to fight World War II.

For most Americans the end of the Depression did not bring much relief, because the nation was now fighting an all-out war. For those who didn't get the message in those days, there was the popular reminder, "Hey, bub, don't yuh know there's a *war* goin' on?"

The country that emerged from the war was very different from the one that had entered it less than four years earlier. Prosperity had replaced depression. Now inflation had become the number one economic worry.

The 1940s: World War II and Peacetime Prosperity

Just as the Great Depression dominated the 1930s, World War II was the main event of the 1940s, especially from the day the Japanese bombed Pearl Harbor until they surrendered in August 1945. For the first time in our history, we fought a war that required a total national effort. Although the Civil War had caused tremendous casualties and had set the South back economically for generations, we had never before fought a war that consumed over one-third of our nation's total output.

At the peak of the war, more than 12 million men and women were mobilized and, not coincidentally, the unemployment rate was below 2 percent. Women, whose place was supposedly in the home, flocked to the workplace to replace the men who had gone off to war. Blacks, too, who had experienced great difficulty finding factory jobs, were hired to work in the steel mills and the defense plants in the East, the Midwest, and the West.

America's industrial might

No more than 2 or 3 percent of the defense plant workers had any experience in this area, but thanks to mass production techniques developed largely by General Motors and Ford, these workers would turn out nearly 300,000 airplanes, over 100,000 tanks, and 88,000 warships. America clearly earned its title, "Arsenal of Democracy."

Between 1939 and 1944, national output of goods and services nearly doubled, while federal government spending—mainly for defense—rose by more than 400 percent. By the middle of 1942, our economy reached full employment for the first time since 1929. To hold inflation in check, the government not only instituted price and wage controls but also issued ration coupons for meat, butter, gasoline, and other staples.

During the war, 17 million new jobs were created, while the economy grew 10 or 11 percent a year. Doris Kearns Goodwin attributed "a remarkable entrepreneurial spirit" not only to the opportunity to make huge wartime profits but to a competitiveness "developed within each business enterprise to produce better than its competitors to serve the country." A sign hanging in many defense plants read: "PLEDGE TO VICTORY: The war may be won or lost in this plant."[7]

It was American industrial might that proved the decisive factor in winning World War II. Essentially our production of ships, tanks, planes, artillery pieces, and other war matériel overwhelmed the production of the Germans and the Japanese.

Globally, we were certainly at the top of our game. With just 7 percent of the world's population, we accounted for half the world's manufacturing output, as well as 80 percent of its cars and 62 percent of its oil. Our potential rivals, Japan, Germany, France, and the United Kingdom, would need at least 15 years to repair their war-damaged industrial plant and begin competing again in world markets.

The United States and the Soviet Union were the only superpowers left standing in 1945. When the cold war quickly developed, we spent tens of billions of dollars to prop up

---

[7]Doris Kearns Goodwin, "The Way We Won: America's Economic Breakthrough during World War II," *The American Prospect,* Fall 1992, p. 68.

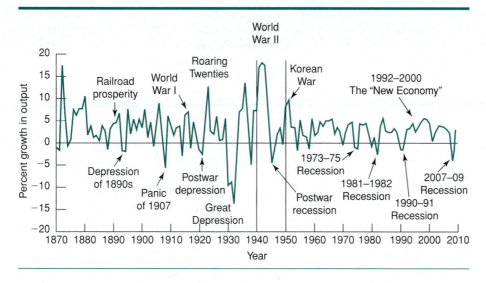

Figure 1

Annual Percentage Growth of U.S. Output of Goods and Services, 1870–2009

Although there were plenty of ups and downs, in most years, output grew at a rate of between 2 and 5 percent. What stands out are the booms during World War I, the Roaring Twenties, the abortive recovery from the Great Depression (in the mid-1930s), World War II, and the relative prosperity since the beginning of World War II. The two sharpest declines in output occurred during the Great Depression and after World War II. The drop after World War II was entirely due to a huge cut in defense spending, but our economy quickly reconverted to producing civilian goods and services, so the 1945 recession was actually very mild.

Sources: U.S. Department of Commerce, and AmeriTrust Company, Cleveland.

the sagging economies of the nations of Western Europe and Japan, and we spent hundreds of billions more to provide for their defense. In the four decades since the close of World War II we expended 6 percent of our national output on defense, while the Soviet Union probably expended at least triple that percentage. This great burden certainly contributed to the collapse of the Soviet Union in 1990–91, and our own heavy defense spending continues to divert substantial resources that might otherwise be used to spur our economic growth.

Figure 1 provides a snapshot of U.S. economic growth since 1870. You'll notice that our economy has been pretty stable since the end of World War II. The latter half of the 1940s was largely a time of catching up for the American economy. For years we had gone without, first during the Great Depression, and then, because so much of our resources had been diverted to the war effort. Wartime government posters urged us to:

> Use it up,
> Wear it out,
> Make it do,
> Or do without.

Once the war was over, there was a huge increase in the production of not just housing and cars, but refrigerators, small appliances, and every other consumer good that had been allowed to wear down or wear out.

Within a year after the war ended, some 12 million men and several hundred thousand women returned home to their civilian lives. Very little housing had been built during the war and the preceding depressed period, so most veterans lived in overcrowded houses and apartments, often with three generations under one roof. The first thing veterans wanted was new housing.

The federal government obligingly facilitated this need for new housing by providing Veterans Administration (VA) mortgages at about 1 percent interest and often nothing down to returning veterans. The Federal Housing Administration (FHA) supplemented the VA program with FHA mortgages to millions of other Americans. Where were these houses built? In the suburbs. By 1945, little land was available in the cities, so suburbanization was inevitable.

The suburbanization of America

Post–World War II Recessions

Since the closing months of World War II, the United States has had 12 recessions of varying length and severity. The longest and most severe was from December 2007 to June 2009 (although we do not yet have official word that the recession ended in that particular month).

February 1945–October 1945

November 1948–October 1949

July 1953–May 1954

August 1957–April 1958

April 1960–February 1961

December 1969–November 1970

November 1973–March 1975 This one was set off by a fourfold increase in the price of oil engineered by the OPEC nations (which we'll talk a lot more about in the chapter on economic fluctuations in *Economics* and *Macroeconomics*). Simultaneously, there was a worldwide shortage of foodstuffs, which drove up food prices. To make matters worse in this country, we struck a deal to export about one-quarter of our wheat and other grains to the Soviet Union. Output fell about 5 percent, and, to make matters still worse, the rate of inflation remained unacceptably high.

January 1980–July 1980 A doubling of oil prices by OPEC and a credit crunch set off by the Federal Reserve Board of Governors, which had been alarmed by an inflation rate that had reached double-digit levels, pushed us into a very brief, but fairly sharp, recession. When interest rates rose above 20 percent, the Federal Reserve allowed credit to expand and the recession ended.

July 1981–November 1982 This downturn was also set off by the Federal Reserve, which was now determined to wring inflation out of our economy. By the end of the recession—which now held the dubious distinction of being the worst downturn since the Great Depression—the unemployment rate had reached almost 11 percent. But the inflation rate had been brought down, and in late summer 1982, the Federal Reserve once again eased credit, setting the stage for the subsequent recovery. At the same time, the federal government had been cutting income tax rates, further helping along the business upturn.

July 1990–March 1991 After the longest uninterrupted peacetime expansion in our history, a fairly mild downturn was caused by a combination of sharply rising oil prices (due to Iraq's invasion of Kuwait in August 1990 and the ensuing Persian Gulf War), tight money, and a deficit-cutting budget agreement between President George Bush and Congress in October. President Bush himself termed the recovery "anemic," and its slow pace was largely responsible for his loss of the 1992 election to Bill Clinton.

March 2001–November 2001 By mid-2000, it had become apparent that many high-tech stocks in telecommunication, Internet, and computer software companies were over-valued, and consequently, investment in these industries began to sink very rapidly. Excess capacity needed to be worked off before investment would revive. What was very unusual for a recession was that consumer spending, buoyed by low interest rates, mortgage refinancing, and massive federal tax cuts, actually continued to rise throughout the recession. Then, just when recovery seemed likely, the terrorist attacks of 9/11 provided an additional economic shock, depressing the demand for air travel and hotel rooms. To counter the effects of the recession as well as to aid in the recovery from the attacks, the Bush administration pushed through Congress not only a major tax cut and tax refunds, but increased government spending. The recession was one of the mildest on record, and output began to rise in the fourth quarter of 2001.

December 2007–June 2009* Throughout the book I refer to the recession of 2007–2009 as the Great Recession. The worst economic downturn since the 1930s, its effects were expected to linger well into 2011. To avert a financial meltdown and to stimulate the economy, the Federal Reserve and the Treasury poured trillions of dollars into the economy.

Tens of millions of Americans had been using their homes like ATMs, taking out hundreds of billions of dollars every year in home equity loans to finance spending on new cars, vacation trips, shopping sprees, paying their children's college expenses, or just filling up their gas tanks. When the housing bubble burst in early 2007, it became increasingly difficult for them to keep borrowing. And the less they could borrow, the less they could spend.

The decline in housing prices had an even more direct economic effect. Hundreds of thousands of construction workers, real estate agents, mortgage brokers, financial service workers, and others with jobs in these economic sectors were thrown out of work.

During 2008 and 2009 employment fell by 8.4 million. In fact, even though our economy began growing in the second half of 2009, employment continued falling through the end of the year. In mid-2010, most economists expected a weak recovery with continued high unemployment through 2011.

---

*In early June 2010, it appeared to many economists, including myself, that the recession had ended exactly one year earlier. The Business Cycle Dating Committee of the National Bureau of Economic Research, however, had not yet decided on an official date.

Levittown, U.S.A.

No man who owns his own house and lot can be a communist.

–William Levitt–

Levittown, Long Island, a tract development of 17,000 nearly identical homes, was built right after World War II, largely for returning veterans and their families. These 800-square-foot, prefabricated homes sold for $8,000 with no down payment for veterans. William Levitt described the production process as the reverse of the Detroit assembly line:

> There, the car moved while the workers stayed at their stations. In the case of our houses, it was the workers who moved, doing the same jobs at different locations. To the best of my knowledge, no one had ever done that before.*

Levittown became the prototype of suburban tract development, and the Levitts themselves built similar developments in New Jersey, Pennsylvania, and Maryland. In 1963, civil rights demonstrations targeted William Levitt's housing development in Bowie, Maryland.

Levitt admitted he had refused to sell houses to black families, because, he said, integrating his developments would put him at a competitive disadvantage. Levitt's discriminatory sales policy was no different from most other developers, who did not relent until well into the 1960s, when government pressure forced them to do so.

Of course racism was hardly confined to developers like Levitt. James T. Patterson, a historian, wrote that the Federal Housing Administration "openly screened out applicants according to its assessment of people who were 'risks.'"[†] These were mainly blacks, Hispanics, Asians, Jews, and other "unharmonious racial or nationality groups." In so doing, FHA enshrined residential segregation as a public policy of the United States government.

In New York and northern New Jersey, fewer than 100 of the 67,000 mortgages insured by the GI Bill supported home purchases by nonwhites.

*Eric Pace, "William J. Levitt, 86, Pioneer of Suburbs, Dies," *New York Times,* January 29, 1994, p. A1.

†James T. Patterson, *Grand Expectations* (New York: Oxford University Press, 1997), p. 27.

And how would these new suburbanites get to work? By car. So more highways were needed. Once again, the federal government stepped in. Before long a federally subsidized interstate highway network was being built, along with thousands of state and local highways, parkways, and freeways, as well as local streets and roads.

Hence the late 1940s and the 1950s were one big construction boom. Highway building and home construction provided millions of jobs. The automobile industry, too, was prospering after a total shutdown during the war. In the postwar era, we not only supplied all the new suburbanites with cars, but we also became the world's leading auto exporter.

The returning veterans had a lot of catching up to do. Couples had been forced to put off having children, but after the war the birthrate shot up and stayed high until the mid-1960s. This baby boom and low gasoline prices added impetus to the nation's suburbanization. Why continue to live in cramped urban quarters when a house in the suburbs was easily affordable, as it was to most middle-class and working-class Americans (see the box titled "Levittown, U.S.A.")?

In 1944 Congress passed the GI Bill of Rights, which not only offered veterans mortgage loans, as well as loans to start businesses, but also provided monthly stipends for those who wanted help with educational costs. By 1956, when the programs ended, 7.8 million veterans, about half of all who had served, had participated. A total of 2.2 million went to college, 3.5 million to technical schools below the college level, and 700,000 to agricultural schools. The GI Bill made college affordable to men from working-class and lower-middle-class backgrounds and was almost entirely responsible for enrollments more than doubling between 1940 and 1949.

The GI Bill of Rights

The 1950s: The Eisenhower Years

The economy was further stimulated by the advent of television in the early 1950s, as well as by the Korean War. It didn't really matter what individual consumers or the government spent their money on, as long as they spent it on something.

The Consequences of Suburbanization

Suburbanization was the migration of tens of millions of middle-class Americans—nearly all of them white—from our nation's large central cities to newly developed suburban towns and villages. Instead of getting to work by public transportation, these commuters now went by car. Truck transport replaced railroads as the primary way to haul freight. Millions of poor people—the large majority of whom were black or Hispanic—moved into the apartments vacated by the whites who had fled to the suburbs.

Suburbanization left our cities high and dry. As middle-class taxpayers and millions of factory jobs left the cities, their tax bases shrank. There were fewer and fewer entry-level jobs for the millions of new arrivals, largely from the rural South. Throughout the 1950s, 1960s, and 1970s, a huge concentration of poor people was left in the cities as the middle-class workers—both black and white—continued to flee to the suburbs. By the mid-1970s, the inner cities were rife with poverty, drugs, and crime, and had become socially isolated from the rest of the country.

Still other consequences of suburbanization were our dependence on oil as our main source of energy and eventually, our dependence on foreign sources for more than half our oil. Indeed, America's love affair with the automobile has not only depleted our resources, polluted our air, destroyed our landscape, and clogged our highways but also has been a major factor in our imbalance of trade.*

---

*The damage we are doing to our nation's environment and to that of our planet is alarming, but discussing it goes beyond the scope of this book. However, in the chapter on international trade, we do have a lengthy discussion of our trade imbalance and how our growing oil imports have contributed to it.

Eisenhower would end the war and end the inflation.

General Dwight D. Eisenhower, one of the great heroes of World War II, made two key promises in his 1952 campaign for the presidency: He would end the war in Korea, and he would end the inflation we had had since the close of World War II. Eisenhower made good on both promises. Although three recessions occurred during his eight years in office, economic growth, although not as fast as it had been in the 1940s, was certainly satisfactory (see the box titled "The Consequences of Suburbanization").

What may be most significant about the Eisenhower years is what *didn't* happen rather than what did. Eisenhower made no attempt to undo the legacies of the New Deal such as Social Security, unemployment insurance, or the regulatory reforms that had been instituted. The role of the federal government as a major economic player had become a permanent one. By the end of the decade America was well on its way to becoming a suburban nation. In a sense we had attained President Herbert Hoover's 1928 campaign promise of a car in every garage and a chicken in every pot. But we did him one better. In 1950 just 10 percent of all homes had a TV; by 1960 87 percent of all American homes had at least one set.

The Soaring Sixties: The Years of Kennedy and Johnson

When John F. Kennedy ran for president in 1960, the country was mired in the third Eisenhower recession. Kennedy pledged to "get the country moving again." The economy *did* quickly rebound from the recession and the country embarked on an uninterrupted eight-year expansion. An assassin shot Kennedy before he could complete his first term; he was succeeded by Lyndon Johnson, who in his first speech as president stated simply, "Let us continue." A major tax cut, which Kennedy had been planning, was enacted in 1964 to stimulate the economy. That and our growing involvement in the Vietnam War helped bring the unemployment rate down below 4 percent by 1966. But three major spending programs, all initiated by Johnson in 1965, have had the most profound long-term effect on the economy: Medicare, Medicaid, and food stamps.

Our rapid economic growth from the mid-1940s through the late 1960s was caused largely by suburbanization. But the great changes during this period came at a substantial price (see the box titled "The Consequences of Suburbanization"). Whatever the costs and benefits, we can agree that in just two and a half decades, this process made America a very different place from what it was at the close of World War II.

The Sagging Seventies: The Stagflation Decade

The 1970s brought Americans crashing back to economic reality. In 1973, we were hit by the worst recession since the 1930s. This came on the heels of an oil price shock: The Organization of Petroleum Exporting Countries (OPEC) had quadrupled oil prices in the fall of 1973, and by then, too, we were mired in double-digit inflation, an annual rate of increase in prices of at least 10 percent. About the only good thing during this period was that we were able to add a new word to our vocabularies—*stagflation*. The first part of this word is derived from stagnation. Our economic growth, which had been fairly rapid for 25 years after World War II, had slowed to a crawl. Usually when this happened, prices would stop rising or at least would slow their rate of increase. But now the opposite had happened: We had a bad case of inflation, which gave us the second part of the word *stagflation*.

Stagnation + inflation = stagflation

The president who seemed to have the worst economic luck of all was Jimmy Carter. He presided over mounting budget deficits that, coupled with a rapid growth of the money supply, pushed up the inflation rate to nearly double-digit levels. And then suddenly, in 1979, the Iranian revolution set off our second oil shock. Gasoline prices went through the ceiling, rising from about 70 cents a gallon to $1.25.

Jimmy Carter's economic problems

Alarmed at the inflation rate, which had nearly doubled in just three years, the Federal Reserve literally stopped the growth of the money supply in October 1979. By the following January we were in another recession, while the annual rate of inflation reached 18 percent. Talk about stagflation!

The 1980s: The Age of Reagan

Ronald Reagan, who overwhelmingly defeated incumbent Jimmy Carter in the 1980 presidential election, offered the answers to our most pressing economic problems. For too long, he declared, we had allowed the federal government to "tax, tax, tax, spend, spend, spend." Big government was not the answer to our problems. Only private enterprise could provide meaningful jobs and spur economic growth. If we cut tax rates, said Reagan, people would have more incentive to work, output would rise, and inflation would subside. After all, if inflation meant that too many dollars were chasing too few goods, why not produce more goods?

This brand of economics, supply-side economics, was really the flip side of Keynesian economics. Both had the same objective: to stimulate output, or supply. The Keynesians thought the way to do this was to have the government spend more money, which, in turn, would give business firms the incentive to produce more. The supply-siders said that if tax rates were cut, people would have more of an incentive to work and would increase output.

Supply-side economics

Personal income taxes were cut by a whopping 23 percent in 1981 (stretched over a three-year period), and business taxes were also slashed. This was the heart of the supply-side program. As it happened, most of the tax cuts went to the wealthy.

In January 1981, it was Ronald Reagan's ball game to win or lose. At first he seemed to be losing. He presided over still another recession, which, by the time it ended, was the new postwar record holder, at least in terms of length and depth. The second-worst recession since World War II had been that of 1973–75. But the 1981–82 recession was a little longer and somewhat worse.

By the end of 1982, the unemployment rate reached nearly 11 percent, a rate the country had not seen since the end of the Depression. But on the upside, inflation was finally brought under control. In fact, both the inflation and unemployment rates fell during the next four years, and stagflation became just a bad memory.

The recession of 1981–82

Still, some very troubling economic problems surfaced during the period. The unemployment rate, which had come down substantially since the end of the 1981–82 recession, seemed stuck at around 6 percent, a rate that most economists consider to be unacceptably high. A second cause for concern were the megadeficits being run by the federal government year after year. Finally, there were the foreign trade deficits, which were getting progressively larger throughout most of the 1980s.

In 1988, George H. W. Bush, who had served as Reagan's vice president for eight years and claimed to be a convert to supply-side economics, made this famous campaign promise: "Read my lips: No new taxes." Of course, the rest is history. Bush won the election, and a couple of years later, in an effort to reduce the federal budget deficit, he agreed to a major tax increase. Not only did his words come back to haunt him when he ran for reelection in 1992, but the deficit continued to rise. And to completely ruin his party, we suffered a lingering recession that began in the summer of 1990 and from which we did not completely recover until the end of 1992, with the unemployment rate still hovering above 7 percent.

The State of American Agriculture

Fewer farmers feeding more people

The story of American agriculture is the story of vastly expanding productivity. The output of farm labor doubled between 1850 and 1900, doubled again between 1900 and 1947, and doubled a third time between 1947 and 1960. In 1800 it took 370 hours to produce 100 bushels of wheat. By 1960 it took just 15 hours. In 1820 one farmer could feed 4.5 people. Today that farmer could feed over 100 people.

One of the most dramatic agricultural advances was the mechanical cotton picker, which was introduced in 1944. In an hour, a laborer could pick 20 pounds of cotton. The mechanical picker could pick one thousand pounds of cotton in the same length of time. Within just four years, millions of the Southern rural poor—both black and white—were forced off the farms and into the cities of the South, the North, and the Midwest.

While agriculture is one of the most productive sectors of our economy, only about 4.5 million people live on farms today, and less than half of them farm full time. Of 2.2 million working farms, just half produce more than $5,000 worth of agricultural products. Despite hundreds of billions of dollars in price-support payments to farmers for crops in the years since World War II, the family farm is rapidly vanishing. This is certainly ironic, since the primary purpose of these payments has been to save the family farm. During the more than seven decades that this program has been in operation, 7 out of every 10 family farms have disappeared, while three-quarters of the payments go to large corporate farms. One by one, the dairy farmers, the poultry farmers, the grain growers, and the feedlot operators are being squeezed out by the huge agricultural combines.

While we have lingering images of family farms, large farms—those with more than $250,000 in sales—now account for more than three-quarters of all agricultural sales. In the mid-1980s, their share was less than half. To keep costs down, especially when growing corn, wheat, and soybeans, a farmer needs a lot of expensive equipment and, consequently, must plant on a huge acreage.[8] In other words, you've got to become big just to survive.

Senator Dick Lugar, who owns a farm in Indiana that grows corn and soybeans, has long been a critic of huge agricultural subsidies. In a *New York Times* op-ed piece,[9] he blamed the federal government for creating and perpetuating the huge and growing mess in agriculture:

> Ineffective agricultural policy has, over the years, led to a ritual of overproduction in many crops and most certainly in the heavily supported crops of corn, wheat, cotton, rice, and soybeans and the protected speciality products like milk, sugar, and peanuts. The government has provided essentially a guaranteed income to producers of these crops. So those farmers keep producing more crops than the market wants, which keeps the price low—so low that these farmers continually ask the government for more subsidies, which they get.

The farm bill of 2002

President George W. Bush signed a 10-year $190 billion farm bill in 2002 providing the nation's largest farmers with annual subsidies of $19 billion. In 2009 the producers of corn, soybeans, wheat, rice, and cotton received almost $15 billion in subsidies. The law's defenders point out that the European Union gives its farmers $60 billion in annual subsidies, and that to compete in world markets, we need to keep our prices down. So

---

[8]The average farm has gone from 139 acres in 1910 to 435 acres today.
[9]Dick Lugar, "The Farm Bill Charade," *The New York Times*, January 21, 2002, p. A15.

what we and the Europeans are doing is subsidizing the overproduction of agricultural commodities so that we can compete against each other.

American farms are so productive that we often export more than one-third of our corn, wheat, and other crops. And yet millions of Americans go to bed hungry every night. Back in the depths of the Great Depression, hungry Americans resorted to soup kitchens for their only meals. Today some 37 million Americans make use of food pantries, soup kitchens, and other emergency food distribution programs.

on the web

The Environmental Working Group lists the subsidies paid to grain farmers by name and by zip code on its website. If you're interested in how much individual farmers are collecting, go to www.ewg.org, and click on Farming, select Farm Subsidies, and then on Farm Subsidy Database.

The "New Economy" of the Nineties

What exactly *is* the "new economy"? And is it really all that new? It is a period marked by major technological change, low inflation, low unemployment, and rapidly growing productivity. Certainly that is a fair description of the 1990s, but one may ask if other decades—the 1920s and the 1960s—might be similarly described. Perhaps judging the appropriateness of the term "new economy" might best be left to the economic historians of the future. But new or not new, the 1990s will surely go down in history as one of the most prosperous decades since the founding of the republic.

The new economy could trace its beginnings back to the late 1970s when the federal government began an era of deregulation, giving the market forces of supply and demand much freer reign. In the 1980s federal income tax rates were slashed, allowing Americans to keep much more of their earnings, thereby providing greater work incentives.

As the decade of the 1990s wore on, the economic picture grew steadily brighter. The federal deficit was reduced each year from 1993 through the end of the decade, by which time we were actually running budget surpluses. Inflation was completely under control, and an economic expansion that began in the spring of 1991 reached boom proportions toward the end of the decade. Optimism spread as the stock market soared, and by February 2000, the length of our economic expansion reached 107 consecutive months—an all-time record. This record would be extended to 120 months—exactly 10 years—before the expansion finally ended in March 2001.

The 1990s was the decade of computerization. In 1990 only a handful of households were on the Internet; by the end of 2000, about 40 percent were connected. Much more significant was the spread of computerization in the business world. Indeed, by the millennium there was a terminal on almost every desk. Planes, cars, factories, and stores were completely computerized. All this clearly has made the American labor force a lot more efficient. Economists, as well as ordinary civilians, believe that our rapid economic growth has been largely the result of computerization of the workplace.

California's Silicon Valley became a hotbed of entrepreneurial innovation. New companies, financed by local venture capitalists, sprang up to perform new economic roles—eBay, Amazon.com, Netscape, Google, Yahoo, and Excite! to name just a few. As these companies went public, their founders became not just millionaires, but often instant billionaires.

Back in 1941, Henry Luce, the founder of *Life Magazine,* wrote an editorial titled "The American Century." History has certainly proven Luce right. Not only had American soldiers and economic power won World Wars I and II, but we also contained communism from the mid-1940s through the 1980s. With the collapse of the Soviet Union, we were the only military and economic superpower left standing.

Just as no man is an island, there are no longer any purely national economies. As we've seen, the United States, which began as 13 English colonies, expanded across the continent, attracted tens of millions of immigrants, and eventually became an economic superpower, importing and exporting hundreds of billions of dollars of goods and services. Over the last three decades, our economy has become increasingly integrated with the global economy.

We've never been better off, but can America keep the party going?
—Jonathan Alter, *Newsweek,* February 7, 2000

The American Century

First there was an exodus of jobs making shoes, cheap electronics, toys, and clothing to developing countries. Next to go were jobs in steel, cars, TV manufacturing, and furniture-making. Then simple service work like writing software code and processing credit card receipts was shifted from high-wage to low-wage countries.

Now white-collar jobs are being moved offshore. The driving forces are digitization, the Internet, and high-speed data networks that span the globe. In the 1990s, hundreds of thousands of immigrants helped ease our shortage of engineers, but now, we are sending routine service and engineering tasks to nations like India, China, and Russia where a surplus of educated workers are paid a fraction of what their American counterparts earn.

The Ominous 00s

From good times to bad

A decade that began with a recession and ended with the worst economic downturn since the Great Depression cannot be called the best of times. Over 15 million people entered our labor force during the decade, but we ended that period with virtually the same number of jobs as we had in 2000.

The new economy of the 1990s gave way to the bursting of the dot-com bubble in 2000 and a mild recession in 2001. The subsequent recovery was slow, taking two and a half years for total employment to reach the level it had been at before the recession. But inflation was low and economic growth fairly brisk for the next few years. From the fall of 2005 through the end of 2007 the unemployment rate was at or below 5 percent.

The American consumer had been largely responsible for keeping our economy growing during the 2001–2007 economic expansion. Much of that spending was financed by hundreds of billions of dollars a year in home equity loans. Real estate prices were rising rapidly, home construction was booming, and mortgage brokers had relaxed their standards to the degree that they were not even checking the incomes of half the people to whom they granted mortgages. The federal government, which had been running budget surpluses began running budget deficits. Two large tax cuts and the financing of wars in Iraq and Afghanistan were largely responsible for moving us from surplus to deficit. These deficits, like consumer spending, helped spur economic growth.

As long as housing prices were rising, banks and other lenders were willing to extend larger and larger home equity loans. But when the housing bubble burst in mid-2006 and home prices began to decline, lenders were less willing to extend these loans. In addition, foreclosures began to rise very rapidly, and millions of homeowners discovered that their homes' market value had sunk below what they owed on their mortgages. Hundreds of thousands just walked away from their homes, mailing their keys to their mortgage brokers.

In December 2007 we entered the twelfth recession since the Great Depression. Largely because of the bursting of the housing bubble, our economy had begun to slow during the second half of the previous year. The ranks of the unemployed increased steadily and over 8 million people lost their jobs in 2008 and 2009. In April of 2009, the recession, then 17 months old, was the longest economic downturn since the 1930s. And when all the analysis was finally completed, the Great Recession[10] would almost surely be considered the worst recession in seven decades.

In mid-2010, when our economy was a full year into recovery, there was still a lingering concern that we could slip back again into recession. The housing market was still in the doldrums, unemployment remained very high, and the nation's output of goods and services had not yet gotten back up to the level it had been at the end of 2007 when the recession began.

In late July of 2010 it become increasingly apparent that the the economic recovery had begun to falter. More than three-quarters of the economic stimulus money had been spent, and Congressional Republicans, spurred on by millions of Tea Party members, were blocking any further major spending programs. Work on the 2010 Census was ending, and hundreds of thousands of census workers were being let go. To make matters still worse,

---

[10]Perhaps the first person to call this "the Great Recession" was Diana Furchtgott-Roth, a former chief economist at the U.S. Department of Labor, in an article, "The Great Recession of 2008?" in *The American*, December 21, 2007, www.american.com/archive/2007/december-12-07/the-great-recession-of-2008.

state and local governments, facing combined budget deficits of some $200 billion, were planning to lay off tens of thousands of teachers, police officers, and other civil servants.

There was a growing fear that the recession was not yet over. Indeed, some economists were suggesting that we were in the midst of a *double dip recession.* Although it had been widely believed that the Great Recession ended in the summer of 2009, our level of economic activity had not re-attained its pre-recession peak. In other words, we had not yet made a full recovery. So what if, say in the third and fourth quarters of 2010, out output of goods and services once again began to decline? Very likely, then we would be in the second downward phase of a double dip recession.

I've already gone out on a limb by stating in the box on page 12—and in later chapters—that the recession ended in June 2009. That's my estimate, for what it's worth. If we sink back into recession, then I'll have some egg on *my* face. Still, in late July 2010, a double dip recession was still not that likely. But only you will know for sure whether I was right or wrong.

Current Issue: America's Place in History

America, America
God shed his grace on thee

–From the song, "America the Beautiful," by
Katherine Lee Bates–

In the early years of the 20th century, the United States emerged as the world's leading industrial power, with the largest economy and the largest consumer market. By the end of World War I, we had become the greatest military power as well.

Our economic and military roles grew during the next two decades, and by the close of World War II, the United States and the Soviet Union were the world's only military superpowers. Although Western Europe and Japan eventually recovered from the devastation of the war, the United States continued to be the world's largest economy. Henry Luce was certainly correct in calling the 20th century "The American Century."

At the end of that century, although some economic problems had emerged—namely our huge budget and trade deficits—we were clearly at the top of our economic game. The dot-com bubble had not yet burst, the new economy was in full flower, and most Americans were confident that the party would go on forever. Just 10 years earlier the Soviet Union had dissolved, its Eastern European empire largely allied itself with the West, and even the most ardent militarists agreed that the costly arms race was finally over.

Back in the 19th century, the sun never set on the British Empire, but the drain of two world wars compelled the British to give up their empire. By the mid-20th century, American military bases dotted the globe, and today we have become, to a large extent, the world's policeman. Many observers believe we are overstretched both militarily and economically, and that, consequently, we will be compelled to cut back on these commitments.

Now, in the wake of the dot-com crash, the attacks on 9/11, the wars in Afghanistan and Iraq, the rising budget deficit, a lagging job market, and, of course, a near financial meltdown, the Great Recession, we may well wonder if the 21st, like the 20th, will be an American century. We wonder if Social Security and Medicare will even be there when we retire. And in the meanwhile, will we be able to live as well as our parents did?

I wish I could answer these questions, but as Benjamin Franklin once said, "A question is halfway to wisdom." As you continue reading, each of these questions will be raised again, and hopefully, we'll get closer to their answers.

Questions for Further Thought and Discussion

1. Describe, in as much detail as possible, the impact of the Great Depression on the lives of those who lived through it. If you know anyone who remembers the 1930s, ask him or her to describe those times.

2. What were the main agricultural developments over the last two centuries?

3. How have wars affected our economy? Use specific examples.

4. Inflation has been a persistent problem for most of the 20th century. What were some of its consequences?

5. In what ways were the 1990s like the 1920s, and in what ways were the two decades different?

6. When our country was being settled, there was an acute shortage of agricultural labor. Over the last 100 years millions of Americans have left the farms. How have we managed to feed our growing population with fewer and fewer farmers?

7. Today America has the world's largest economy as well as a very high standard of living. What factors in our economic history helped make this possible?

8. List the main ways the "new economy" (since the early 1990s) differs from the "old economy."

Workbook for Chapter 1

Mc Graw Hill connect | ECONOMICS

Name _____   Date _____

Multiple-Choice Questions

Circle the letter that corresponds to the best answer.

1. Which statement is true? (LO2)
   a) Twenty-five million Americans were officially unemployed in 1933.
   b) Our economy expanded steadily from 1933 to 1945.
   c) Once the Great Depression began in 1929, our economy moved almost steadily downhill until the beginning of 1940.
   d) None of the above.

2. In the early 19th century, the United States suffered from a scarcity of _____. (LO1)
   a) land and labor
   b) land—relative to labor
   c) labor—relative to land
   d) neither land nor labor

3. Which statement is false? (LO4, 5)
   a) President Eisenhower presided over three recessions.
   b) Our economy has not had an unemployment rate below 5 percent since the early 1940s.
   c) There were six straight years of economic expansion under President Reagan.
   d) None of the above. (All of the above are true.)

4. Which statement is true? (LO4, 5)
   a) There was a great deal of stagflation in the 1970s.
   b) We had full employment for most of the 1980s.
   c) We have had seven recessions since World War II.
   d) None of the above.

5. Each of the following were elements of the New Deal except _____. (LO2)
   a) relief, recovery, reform
   b) a massive employment program
   c) unemployment insurance and bank deposit insurance
   d) a balanced budget

6. Which of these best describes the post-World War II recessions in the United States? (LO4, 5)
   a) They were all very mild, except for the 1981–82 recession.
   b) They were all caused by rising interest rates.
   c) None lasted more than one year.
   d) Each was accompanied by a decline in output of goods and services and an increase in unemployment.

7. At the time of the American Revolution, about _____ of every 10 Americans lived on a farm. (LO1)
   a) one   c) five   e) nine
   b) three   d) seven

8. Between 1939 and 1944, federal government spending rose by more than _____. (LO3)
   a) 100%   c) 300%   e) 500%
   b) 200%   d) 400%

9. Each of the following was a year of high unemployment except _____. (LO4)
   a) 1933   c) 1944   e) 1982
   b) 1938   d) 1975

10. The year 2009 could be described as having had a relatively _____ unemployment rate and a relatively _____ rate of inflation. (LO6)
    a) low, low   c) high, low
    b) high, high   d) low, high

11. Between 1929 and 1933, output fell _____. (LO2)
    a) by about one-tenth   c) by about one-half
    b) by about one-third   d) by about two-thirds

12. The inflation rate declined during the presidency of _____. (LO5)
    a) both Eisenhower and Reagan
    b) neither Eisenhower nor Reagan
    c) Reagan
    d) Eisenhower

13. Which of the following would be the most accurate description of our economy since the end of 2007? (LO6)
    a) We have had virtually no economic problems.
    b) We experienced the worst economic mess since the Great Depression.
    c) Aside from the federal budget deficit, we have no major economic problems.
    d) Our unemployment and inflation rates have generally been relatively low.

14. The transcontinental railroads completed in the 1860s, 1870s, and 1880s all bypassed the _____. (LO1)
    a) Northeast   d) mountain states
    b) Midwest   e) Far West
    c) South

15. Compared to our economic history between 1870 and 1945, our economic history since 1945 could be considered _____. (LO4, 5)
    a) much more stable   c) much less stable
    b) about as stable

16. The longest economic expansion in our history began in _____. (LO5)
    a) the spring of 1961
    b) the winter of 1982
    c) the spring of 1991
    d) the fall of 1993

17. The age of the great industrial capitalists like Carnegie, Rockefeller, and Swift was in the _____. (LO3)
    a) second quarter of the 19th century
    b) third quarter of the 19th century
    c) fourth quarter of the 19th century
    d) first quarter of the 20th century
    e) second quarter of the 20th century

18. _____ completely changed the face of the United States in the 25 years following World War II. (LO5)
    a) Almost constant warfare
    b) Suburbanization
    c) Welfare spending
    d) The loss of jobs to Japan, India, and China

19. Medicare and Medicaid were inaugurated under the administration of _____. (LO5)
    a) Franklin D. Roosevelt
    b) Harry S. Truman
    c) Dwight D. Eisenhower
    d) John F. Kennedy
    e) Lyndon B. Johnson

20. Most of the recessions since World War II lasted _____. (LO4)
    a) less than 6 months
    b) 6 to 12 months
    c) 12 to 18 months
    d) 18 to 24 months
    e) 24 to 36 months

21. Which statement is true? (LO5)
    a) President Eisenhower attempted to undo most of the New Deal.
    b) There was a major tax cut in 1964.
    c) The federal budget deficit was reduced during President Lyndon Johnson's administration.
    d) None of the above.

22. There was a major tax cut in _____. (LO5)
    a) both 1964 and 1981
    b) neither 1964 nor 1981
    c) 1964, but not in 1981
    d) 1981, but not 1964

23. Our economic growth began to slow markedly _____. (LO5)
    a) in the early 1940s
    b) in the early 1960s
    c) in the early 1970s
    d) between 1982 and 1985

24. During World War II most of the people who got jobs in defense plants were _____ who had _____ experience building planes, tanks, and warships. (LO3)
    a) men, substantial
    b) men, no
    c) women, substantial
    d) women, no

25. In the 1970s, our economy suffered from
_____. (LO5)
   a) inflation but not stagnation
   b) stagnation but not inflation
   c) inflation and stagnation
   d) neither inflation nor stagnation

26. There were no recessions during the administration of
_____. (LO4, 5)
   a) Dwight D. Eisenhower
   b) Ronald Reagan
   c) Bill Clinton
   d) George W. Bush

27. Our longest uninterrupted economic expansion took
place mainly in the decade of the _____. (LO5)
   a) 1940s   c) 1960s   e) 1980s
   b) 1950s   d) 1970s   f) 1990s

28. In the 1990s our economy has generated more than
_____ million additional jobs. (L05, 6)
   a) 5   b) 10   c) 15   d) 20

29. What set off the Great Recession? (LO4, 6)
   a) The bursting of the housing bubble.
   b) The sharp decline in oil prices.
   c) The escalation of the war in Iraq.
   d) A surge in imports from China.

30. Which statement is the most accurate? (LO2)
   a) The South had some very substantial economic
      grievances against the North in the years
      immediately preceding the Civil War.
   b) The South seceded from the Union when President
      Lincoln proclaimed that he was freeing the slaves.
   c) Aside from slavery, southern and northern
      agriculture were very similar.
   d) Most of the nation's industries were relocated
      from the North and Midwest to the South in the
      years immediately following the Civil War.

31. The massive shift of population and industry out of
the large central cities from the late 1940s through
the 1960s was caused by _____. (LO5)
   a) wars
   b) the mechanization of agriculture
   c) suburbanization
   d) immigration
   e) fear of nuclear war

32. Each of the following was a major contributing factor
to suburbanization except _____. (LO5)
   a) low-interest federal loans
   b) a federal highway building program
   c) the pent-up demand for housing
   d) the baby boom
   e) federal subsidies for public transportation

33. Which statement is true? (LO2, 6)
   a) Although our economy was not performing well,
      college graduates from the classes of 2009 and
      2010 received more job offers than any other
      graduating class in history.
   b) The economic downturn that began in
      December 2007 is the longest since the 1930s.
   c) Until the time of the Great Depression, the United
      States was primarily an agricultural nation.
   d) There were no recessions during the presidency of
      Bill Clinton (January 1993–January 2001).

34. Who made this statement? "Once upon a time my
opponents honored me as possessing the fabulous
intellectual and economic power by which I created a
worldwide depression all by myself." (LO2)
   a) Franklin D. Roosevelt
   b) Herbert Hoover
   c) John F. Kennedy
   d) Ronald Reagan
   e) Bill Clinton

35. Which statement is the most accurate? (LO6)
   a) The 21st century will almost definitely be another
      "American Century."
   b) The 21st, rather than the 20th, will be called
      "The American Century."
   c) The 21st century will definitely not be an
      "American Century."
   d) Although we got off to a rocky start, this century
      may well turn out to be another "American
      Century."

36. Our most rapid job growth was in the period from
_____. (LO5, 6)
   a) 2000 to 2005
   b) 1995 to 2000
   c) 1978 to 1983
   d) 1953 to 1958

37. If you could blame just one person or group of people that caused the Great Depression, which one of the following would you choose? (LO1)
    a) President Herbert Hoover
    b) President Franklin Roosevelt
    c) the Federal Reserve Board
    d) the bankers

38. Each of the following happened during the Great Recession *except* _____. (LO6)
    a) a financial crisis
    b) the loss of more than 8 million jobs
    c) a sharp rise in the inflation rate
    d) a sharp decline in our output of goods and services

39. Which of the following is the most accurate statement? (LO7)
    a) Like the 20th century, the 21st century will definitely be "the American Century."
    b) Although we have had some recent problems, our economy is strong enough to continue to support our present global military commitments indefinitely.
    c) The United States is a fading economic and military power, and will soon be overtaken by its rivals.
    d) It is far too soon to say whether or not the 21st century will be another "American century."

Fill-In Questions

1. The low point of the Great Depression was reached in the year _____. (LO2)

2. In 1790, about _____ of every 10 Americans lived on farms. (LO1)

3. The worst recession we had since World War II occurred in _____. (LO4)

4. The country with the world's largest output is _____. (LO1)

5. In 1933, our official unemployment rate was _____%. (LO2)

6. Bills providing for Medicare and Medicaid were passed during the administration of President _____. (LO5)

7. Today one full-time American farmer feeds about _____ people. (LO5)

8. During President Dwight D. Eisenhower's two terms, there were _____ recessions. (LO4, 5)

9. Rapid technological change in agriculture during the first half of the 19th century was brought on mainly by _____. (LO1)

10. The main factor in finally bringing us out of the Great Depression was _____. (LO2, 3)

11. Since the end of World War II there have been _____ recessions. (LO4)

12. The quarter century that was completely dominated by the great industrialists like Andrew Carnegie and John D. Rockefeller began in the year _____. (LO1)

13. Passage of the _____ in 1944 enabled nearly 8 million veterans to go to school. (LO3)

14. The _____ century was termed "The American Century." (LO6)

Chapter 2

Resource Utilization

Economics is defined in various ways, but scarcity is always part of the definition. We bake an economic pie each year, which is composed of all the goods and services we have produced. No matter how we slice it, there never seems to be enough. Some people feel the main problem is how we slice the pie, while others say we should concentrate on baking a larger pie.

LEARNING OBJECTIVES

After reading this chapter you should be able to:

1. Define economics.
2. Identify the central fact of economics and explain how it relates to the economic problem.
3. Name the four economic resources and explain how they are used by the entrepreneur.
4. Explain and apply the concept of opportunity cost.
5. Describe and distinguish among the concepts of full employment, full production, and underemployment.
6. Describe the concept of the production possibilities curve and how it is used.
7. Identify and explain the three concepts upon which the law of increasing costs is based.
8. Define and explain productive efficiency.
9. Identify and explain the factors which enable an economy to grow.

Economics Defined

Economics is the efficient allocation of the scarce means of production toward the satisfaction of human wants. You're probably thinking, What did he say? Let's break it down into two parts. The scarce means of production are our resources, which we use to produce all the goods and services we buy. And why do we buy these goods and services? Because they provide us with satisfaction.

The only problem is that we don't have enough resources to produce all the goods and services we desire. Our resources are limited while our wants are relatively unlimited. In the next few pages, we'll take a closer look at the concepts of resources, scarcity, and the satisfaction of human wants. Keep in mind that we can't produce everything we'd like to purchase—there's scarcity. This is where economics comes in. We're attempting to make the best of a less-than-ideal situation. We're trying to use our resources so efficiently that we can maximize our satisfaction. Or, as François Quesnay put it back

Economics is the efficient allocation of the scarce means of production toward the satisfaction of human wants.

Economics is the science of greed.

—F. V. Meyer

in the 18th century, "To secure the greatest amount of pleasure with the least possible outlay should be the aim of all economic effort."[1]

The Central Fact of Economics: Scarcity

Scarcity and the Need to Economize

Most of us are used to economizing; we save up our scarce dollars and deny ourselves various tempting treasures so we will have enough money for that one big-ticket item—a new car, a sound system, a trip to Europe. Since our dollars are scarce and we can't buy everything we want, we economize by making do with some lower-priced items—a Cadillac instead of a Rolls Royce, chicken instead of steak, or an education at a state university rather than at an Ivy League college.

If there were no scarcity, we would not need to economize.

If there were no scarcity, we would not need to economize, and economists would have to find other work. Let's go back to our economic pie to see how scarcity works. Most people tend to see scarcity as not enough dollars, but as John Maynard Keynes[2] pointed out more than 70 years ago, this is an illusion. We could print all the money we want and still have scarcity. As Adam Smith noted in 1776, the wealth of nations consists of the goods and services they produce, or, on another level, the resources—the *land, labor, capital,* and *entrepreneurial ability*—that actually produce these goods and services.

The Economic Problem

John Kenneth Galbraith, American economist and social critic

In the 1950s, John Kenneth Galbraith coined the term *the affluent society,* which implied that we had the scarcity problem licked. Americans were the richest people in the world. Presumably, we had conquered poverty. But within a few years, Michael Harrington's *The Other America*[3] challenged that contention.

The economic problem, however, goes far beyond ending poverty. Even then, nearly all Americans would be relatively poor when they compared what they have with what they would like to have—or with what the Waltons, Gateses, Buffetts, Allens, and Ellisons have.

Human wants are relatively limitless. Make a list of all the things you'd like to have. Now add up their entire cost. Chances are you couldn't earn enough in a lifetime to even begin to pay for half the things on your list.

The Four Economic Resources

We need four resources, often referred to as "the means of production," to produce an output of goods and services. Every society, from a tiny island nation in the Pacific to the most complex industrial giant, needs these resources: *land, labor, capital,* and *entrepreneurial ability.* Let's consider each in turn.

Land

As a resource, land has a much broader meaning than our normal understanding of the word. It includes natural resources (such as timber, oil, coal, iron ore, soil, and water) as well as the ground in which these resources are found. Land is used not only for the extraction of minerals but for farming as well. And, of course, we build factories, office buildings, shopping centers, and homes on land. The basic payment made to the owners of land is rent.

Labor

Labor is the work and time for which employees are paid. The police officer, the computer programmer, the store manager, and the assembly-line worker all supply labor. About two-thirds of the total resource costs are paid to labor in the form of wages and salaries.

Capital

Capital is "man"-made goods used to produce other goods or services. It consists mainly of plant, equipment, and software. The United States has more capital than any other country

---

[1]François Quesnay, *Dialogues sur les Artisans,* quoted in Gide and Rist, *A History of Economic Doctrines,* 1913, pp. 10–11.

[2]Keynes, whose work we'll discuss in later chapters of *Economics* and *Macroeconomics,* was perhaps the greatest economist of the 20th century.

[3]Michael Harrington, *The Other America* (New York: Macmillan, 1962).

in the world. This capital consists of factories, office buildings, and stores. Our shopping malls, the Empire State Building, and automobile plants and steel mills (and all the equipment in them) are examples of capital. The return paid to the owners of capital is interest.

Entrepreneurial ability is the least familiar of our four basic resources. The entrepreneur sets up a business, assembles the needed resources, risks his or her own money, and reaps the profits or absorbs the losses of this enterprise. Often the entrepreneur is an innovator, such as Andrew Carnegie (U.S. Steel), John D. Rockefeller (Standard Oil), Henry Ford (Ford Motor Company), Steven Jobs (Apple Computer), Bill Gates (Microsoft), and Sam Walton (Walmart).

Entrepreneurial ability

We may consider land, labor, and capital passive resources, which are combined by the entrepreneur to produce goods and services. A successful undertaking is rewarded by profit; an unsuccessful one is penalized by loss.

In the American economy, the entrepreneur is the central figure, and our long record of economic success is an eloquent testimonial to the abundance of our entrepreneurial talents. The owners of the over 30 million businesses in this country are virtually all entrepreneurs. The vast majority either work for themselves or have just one or two employees. But they have two things in common: Each runs a business, and each risks his or her own money.

Sometimes entrepreneurs cash in on inventions—their own or someone else's. Alexander Graham Bell and Thomas Edison were two of the more famous inventors who *did* parlay their inventions into great commercial enterprises. As you know, tens of billions of dollars were earned by the founders of America Online, Amazon, eBay, Yahoo!, Google, and the thousands of other so-called dot-coms when they went public. These folks were all entrepreneurs. But have you ever heard of Tim Berners-Lee, the creator of the World Wide Web? Berners-Lee worked long and hard to ensure that the Web remained a public mass medium in cyberspace, an information thoroughfare open to all. He came up with the software standards for addressing, linking, and transferring multimedia documents over the Internet. And most amazing, Tim Berners-Lee did not try to cash in on his years of work.

Is this man an entrepreneur? Clearly he is not. He is an inventor of the first rank—like Bell and Edison—but the act of invention is not synonymous with being an entrepreneur.

Perhaps nothing more typifies American entrepreneurial talent than the Internet, which *The New York Times* termed the "Net Americana." Steve Lohr observed that "all ingredients that contribute to the entrepreneurial climate in the United States—venture capital financing, close ties between business and universities, flexible labor markets, a deregulated business environment, and a culture that celebrates risk-taking, ambition, and getting very, very rich"—fostered the formation of the Internet.[4]

What factors explain why so many of the world's greatest innovations have originated in the United States? Thomas Friedman produces a summation:

> America is the greatest engine of innovation that has ever existed, and it can't be duplicated anytime soon, because it is the product of a multitude of factors: extreme freedom of thought, an emphasis on independent thinking, a steady immigration of new minds, a risk-taking culture with no stigma attached to trying and failing, a noncorrupt bureaucracy, and financial markets and a venture capital system that are unrivaled at taking new ideas and turning them into global products.[5]

Resources are scarce because they are limited in quantity. There's a finite amount of land on this planet, and at any given time a limited amount of labor, capital, and entrepreneurial ability is available. Over time, of course, the last three resources can be increased.

Our economic problem, then, is that we have limited resources available to satisfy relatively unlimited wants. The reason why you, and everyone else, can't have three cars, a town house and a country estate with servants, designer clothing, jewelry, big screen TVs in each room, and a $50,000 sound system is that we just don't have enough resources to produce everything that everyone wants. Therefore, we have to make choices, an option we call opportunity cost.

---

[4]Steve Lohr, "Welcome to the Internet, the First Global Colony," *The New York Times,* January 9, 2000, Section 4, p. 1.

[5]Thomas Friedman, "The Secret of Our Sauce," *The New York Times,* March 7, 2004, Section 4, p. 13.

Opportunity Cost

There was an accounting professor nicknamed "the phantom," who used to dash from his last class to his car, and speed off to his office. During tax season, he was almost never seen on campus, and certainly not during his office hours. One day a student managed to catch him in the parking lot. Big mistake. As he climbed into his car, the professor asked scornfully, "Do you realize how much money you're costing me?"

Unknowingly, the phantom was illustrating the concept of opportunity cost. "Every minute I waste answering your questions could be spent in my office earning money. So if I spend five minutes with you, that just cost me $10." Perhaps if the student had handed him a ten dollar bill, he could have bought a few minutes of his professor's time.

Because we can't have everything we want, we must make choices. The thing we give up (that is, our second choice) is called the opportunity cost of our choice. Therefore, *the opportunity cost of any choice is the forgone value of the next best alternative.*

> The opportunity cost of any choice is the forgone value of the next best alternative.

Suppose a little boy goes into a toy store with $15. Many different toys tempt him, but he finally narrows his choice to a Monopoly game and a magic set, each costing $15. If he decides to buy the Monopoly game, the opportunity cost is foregoing the magic set. And if he buys the magic set, the opportunity cost is foregoing the Monopoly game.

In some cases the next best alternative—the Monopoly game or the magic set—is virtually equal no matter what choice is made. In other cases, there's no contest. If someone were to offer you, at the same price, your favorite eight-course meal or a Big Mac, you'd have no trouble deciding (unless, of course, your favorite meal *is* a Big Mac).

> *Even children learn in growing up that "both" is not an admissible answer to a choice of "which one?"*
> —President Warren G. Harding

If a town hires an extra police officer instead of repaving several streets, the opportunity cost of hiring the officer is not repaving the streets. To obtain more of one thing, society foregoes the opportunity of getting the next best thing.

Today, as we all know, people are living longer. This has set the stage for an ongoing generational conflict over how much of our resources should be devoted to Medicare, Social Security, nursing homes, and old age homes, and how much to child care, Head Start, and, in general, education. If we are to be a humane society, we must take care of our aging population. But if our economy is to be competitive in the global economy, we need to devote more dollars to education.

What are some of the opportunity costs *you* have incurred? What is the opportunity cost of attending college? Owning a car? Or even buying this economics text? There's even an opportunity cost of studying for an exam. How would you have otherwise spent those precious hours?

What is the opportunity cost of the wars in Iraq and Afghanistan? Because the conduct of the wars costs taxpayers about $150 billion a year, the opportunity cost of the wars is how that money might have otherwise been spent. Possibilities include reducing the federal budget deficit, a tax cut, more students loans, research for a cure for breast cancer, and a high speed rail system between pairs of major cities.

I'm sure you can think of at least a few other examples of the opportunity cost of the wars in Iraq and Afghanistan. My *own* preference would be to spend some of these resources on the reconstruction of New Orleans. It seems inconceivable that it is somehow more important to rebuild Baghdad than to rebuild that great American city.

If you'd like to read what I *really* think about our neglect in helping New Orleans to rebuild, go to www.tucsoncitizen.com/ss/opinion/41952.php.

Full Employment and Full Production

Everyone agrees that full employment is a good thing, even if we don't all agree on exactly what full employment means. Does it mean that every single person in the United States who is ready, willing, and able to work has a job? Is *that* full employment?

The answer is no. There will always be some people between jobs. On any given day thousands of Americans quit, get fired, or decide that they will enter the labor force by finding a job. Since it may take several weeks, or even several months, until they find the "right" job, there will always be some people unemployed.

If an unemployment rate of zero does not represent full employment, then what rate does? Economists cannot agree on what constitutes full employment. Some liberals insist that an unemployment rate of 4 percent constitutes full employment, while there are conservatives who feel that an unemployment rate of 6 percent would be more realistic.

If economists were laid end to end, they would not reach a conclusion.
—George Bernard Shaw

Similarly, we cannot expect to fully use all our plant and equipment. A capacity utilization rate of 85 or 90 percent would surely employ virtually all of our usable plant and equipment. At any given moment there is always some factory being renovated or some machinery under repair. During wartime we might be able to use our capacity more fully, but in normal times 85 to 90 percent is the peak.

In a global economy, not only has it become increasingly difficult to define which goods and services are made in America and which originate abroad, but one may even question the relevance of a plant's location. If our steel industry were operating at full capacity, we could get still more steel from Germany, Japan, South Korea, Brazil, and other steel-producing nations. In the context of the global economy, our capacity utilization ratio is clearly much less important than it was just a few decades ago.

As long as all available resources are fully used—given the constraints we have just cited—we are at our production possibilities frontier. A few additional constraints should also be considered because they too restrict the quantity of resources available. These are institutional constraints, the laws and customs under which we live.

The so-called blue laws restrict the economic activities that may be carried out in various cities and states, mainly on Sundays. Bars and liquor stores must be closed certain hours. In some places, even retail stores must be closed on Sundays.

State and federal law carefully restricts child labor. Very young children may not be employed at all, and those below a certain age may work only a limited number of hours.

Traditionally, Americans dislike working at night or on weekends, particularly on Sundays. Consequently, we must leave most of our expensive plant and equipment idle except during daylight weekday hours. We don't consider that plant and equipment unemployed, nor do we consider those whose labor is restricted by law or custom unemployed. All of this is already allowed for in our placement of the location of the production possibilities frontier (shown in Figure 1 in the next section).

By full production, we mean that our nation's resources are being allocated in the most efficient manner possible. Not only are we using our most up-to-date technology, but we are using our land, labor, capital, and entrepreneurial ability in the most productive way.

Full production: Our nation's resources are being allocated in the most efficient manner possible.

We would not want to use the intersection of Fifth Avenue and 57th Street in Manhattan for dairy farming, nor would we want our M.D.s doing clerical work. But sometimes we do just that.

Until very recently in our history blacks, Hispanics, and women were virtually excluded from nearly all high-paying professions. Of course, this entailed personal hurt and lost income; this discrimination also cost our nation in lost output. In the sports world, until 1947, when Brooklyn Dodger owner Branch Rickey defied baseball's "color line" and signed Jackie Robinson for the team, major league baseball was played by whites only (see the box titled, "The Jackie Robinson Story"). At that time, only a tiny handful of Hispanic players were tolerated. Today there are several black and Hispanic players on every team. Today, professional basketball would hardly be described as a "white man's sport." Nor, for that matter, would the National Football League be accused of discrimination, at least at the level of player personnel. But until the late 1940s, blacks were almost entirely banned from those professional sports.

Employment discrimination

As late as the 1950s, only a few stereotypical roles were available to blacks in the movies and on TV. And, except for Desi Arnaz (Ricky Ricardo of "I Love Lucy"), there were virtually no Hispanic Americans in these entertainment media. That was America not all that long ago, when employment discrimination was the rule, not the exception.

Until recently only a tiny minority of women employed in the offices of American business were not typists or secretaries. In the 1950s and even into the 1960s, virtually every article in *Fortune* was written by a man and researched by a woman. What a waste of labor potential!

The Jackie Robinson Story

Blacks had always been banned from professional sports, but most notoriously by the "American sport"—major league baseball. For decades there was a parallel association for blacks called the Negro leagues. Finally, the color barrier was broken in 1947 when Jackie Robinson began playing for the Brooklyn Dodgers.

Looking back, then, to all those years when black ballplayers were not permitted to play major league baseball (and basketball and football), we see that hundreds of athletes were underemployed. Not only did they suffer economically and psychologically, but the American public was deprived of watching innumerable talented athletes perform.

Jackie Robinson

In 1991 I met a few of the men who played in the Negro leagues when I was visiting Kansas City, where the Negro League Baseball Museum is located. They all knew Satchel Paige, a legendary pitcher whose fastball was so fast, the batters often couldn't even see it, let alone hit it. Sometimes Paige would wind up and pretend to throw a pitch. The catcher pounded his glove and the umpire called a strike. Then the catcher, who had the ball all along, threw it back to Paige. As great as he was, Satchel Paige didn't play in the major leagues until the twilight of his career, when he was in his late forties.

I can still picture one ad that appeared in several business magazines back in the 1950s. Four or five young women were on their knees on an office carpet sorting through piles of papers. This was an advertisement for a collator. The caption read, "When your office collator breaks down, do the girls have to stay late for a collating party?"

This ad said a great deal about those times. Forget about political correctness! Every woman (but almost no men) applying for office jobs was asked, "How fast can you type?" because those were virtually the only jobs open to women in corporate America—even to college graduates. Typing, filing, and other clerical positions were considered "women's work." The high-paying and high-status executive positions were reserved for men. So when the collator broke down, it seemed perfectly logical to ask the "girls" to stay late for a "collating party."

These are just a few of the most blatant examples of employment discrimination, a phenomenon that has diminished but has not yet been wiped out. Employment discrimination automatically means that we will have less than full production because we are not efficiently allocating our labor. In other words, there are millions of Americans who really should be doctors, engineers, corporate executives, or whatever but have been condemned to less exalted occupations solely because they happen not to be white Protestant males.

But, in the words of Bob Dylan, "the times, they are a' changin'." The civil rights revolution of the 1960s and the women's liberation movement a decade later did bring millions of blacks and women into the economic mainstream. Elite business schools began admitting large numbers of women in the mid-1970s, and today there are hundreds of women occupying the executive suites of our major corporations.[6]

We have certainly come a long way since President Franklin Roosevelt appointed Labor Secretary Frances Perkins as the first woman cabinet member in history, and, some three decades later, when President Lyndon Johnson made Housing Secretary Warren Weaver the first black cabinet member. It would be a fair description to say that the presidential administrations of George W. Bush and Barack Obama represent the face of America a whole lot better than those of presidential administrations just one generation ago.

Using the best technology

Finally, there is the question of using the best available technology. Historically, the American economy has been on the cutting edge of technological development for almost

---

[6]There is an additional discussion of employment discrimination near the end of the chapter on Labor Markets and Wages in *Economics* and *Microeconomics*.

200 years; the sewing machine, mechanical reaper, telephone, airplane, automobile, assembly line, and computer are all American inventions.

Now it's the computer software industry. Not only are we on the forefront in this rapidly expanding industry, but we produce and export more software than the rest of the world combined. Microsoft, Cisco, Oracle, and a host of other American companies are household names not just in the United States but all across the globe.

Let's tie up one more loose end before moving on to the main focus of this chapter, the production possibilities frontier. We need to be clear about distinguishing between less than full employment and underemployment of resources.

Full employment and underemployment

If we are using only 70 percent of our capacity of plant and equipment, as we do during some recessions, this would be a case of our economy operating at less than full employment of its resources. Anything less than, say, an 85 percent utilization rate would be considered below full employment.

More familiarly, when the unemployment rate is, say, 10 percent, there is clearly a substantial amount of labor unemployed. But how much *is* full employment? We never really answered that one.

As a working definition, we'll say that an unemployment rate of 5 percent represents full employment. Why not use 4 percent, as the liberal economists suggest, or the 6 percent figure favored by the conservatives? Because 5 percent represents a reasonable compromise. So we'll be working with that figure from here on, but keep in mind that not everyone agrees that a 5 percent unemployment rate represents full employment.

Unemployment means that not all our resources are being used. Less than 95 percent of our labor force is working, and less than 85 percent of our plant and equipment is being used. It also means that our land and entrepreneurial ability are not all being used.

Was our economy at full employment in 2009? Hardly. For most of that year our unemployment rate was over 9 percent while our capacity utilization rate was below 70 percent and that is exactly what you would expect during a very severe recession.

What is underemployment of resources? To be at full production, not only would we be fully employing our resources, we would also be using them in the most efficient way possible. To make all women become schoolteachers, social workers, or secretaries would grossly underuse their talents. Equally absurd—and inefficient—would be to make all white males become doctors or lawyers and all black and Hispanic males become accountants or computer programmers.

Similarly, we would not want to use that good Iowa farmland for office parks, nor would we want to locate dairy farms in the middle of our cities' central business districts. And finally, we would certainly not want to use our multimillion-dollar computer mainframes to do simple word processing.

During 2009 and 2010 perhaps the hardest hit were those Americans under 25, one quarter of whom were unemployed. But among recent college graduates who *were* employed, half were in positions not requiring college degrees. So your immediate prospects in the job market may well be either unemployment or underemployment.

These are all examples of underemployment of resources. Unfortunately, a certain amount of underemployment is built into our economy, but we need to reduce it if we are going to succeed in baking a larger economic pie.[7]

The production possibilities frontier represents our economy at full employment and full production.

This brings us, at long last, to the production possibilities curve. As we've already casually mentioned, the production possibilities frontier represents our economy at full employment and full production. However, a certain amount of underemployment of resources is built into our model. How much? Although the exact amount is not quantifiable, it is fairly large. But to the degree that employment discrimination has declined since the early 1960s, underemployment of resources may still be holding our output to 10 or 15 percent below what it would be if there were a truly efficient allocation of resources.

[7]Sometimes the news media refers to the underemployment rate, which is found by adding the unemployment rate to the percentage of people in the labor force who are working part-time, but would prefer to work full-time. But in this text we'll consider underemployment the less than efficient use of our resources.

The Production Possibilities Curve

Since scarcity is a fact of economic life, we need to use our resources as efficiently as possible. If we succeed, we are operating at full economic capacity. Usually there's some economic slack, but every so often we *do* manage to operate at peak efficiency. When this happens, we are on our production possibilities frontier (or production possibilities curve).

Often economics texts cast the production possibilities curve in terms of guns and butter. A country is confronted with two choices: It can produce only military goods or only civilian goods. The more guns it produces, the less butter and, of course, vice versa.

If we were to use all our resources—our land, labor, capital, and entrepreneurial ability—to make guns, we would obviously not be able to make butter at all. Similarly, if we made only butter, there would be no resources to make any guns. Virtually every country makes *some* guns and *some* butter. Japan makes relatively few military goods, while the United States devotes a much higher proportion of its resources to making guns.

You are about to encounter the second graph in this book. This graph, and each one that follows, will have a vertical axis and a horizontal axis. Both axes start at the origin of the graph, which is located in the lower left-hand corner and is usually marked with the number 0.

In Figure 1 we measure units of butter on the vertical axis. On the horizontal axis we measure units of guns. As we move to the right, the number of guns increases—1, 2, 3, 4, 5.

The curve shown in the graph is drawn by connecting points A, B, C, D, E, and F. Where do these points come from? They come from Table 1. Where did we get the numbers in Table 1? They're hypothetical. In other words, I made them up.

Table 1 shows six production possibilities ranging from point A, where we produce 15 units of butter and no guns, to point F, where we produce 5 units of guns but no butter. This same information is presented in Figure 1, a graph of the production possibilities curve. We'll begin at point A, where a country's entire resources are devoted to producing butter. If the country were to produce at full capacity (using all its resources) but wanted to make some guns, they could do it by shifting some resources away from butter. This would move them from point A to point B. Instead of producing 15 units of butter, they're making only 14.

Guns and butter

Figure 1

Production Possibilities Curve
This curve shows the range of possible combinations of outputs of guns and butter extending from 15 units of butter and no guns at point A to 5 units of guns and no butter at point F.

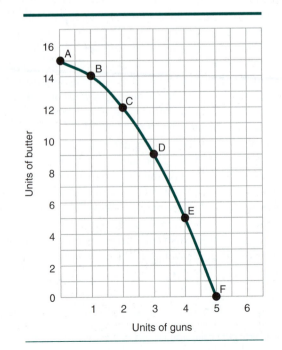

Units of butter

Units of guns

TABLE 1	Hypothetical Production Schedule for Two-Product Economy	
Point	Units of Butter	Units of Guns
A	15	0
B	14	1
C	12	2
D	9	3
E	5	4
F	0	5

Before we go any further on the curve, let's go over the numbers at points A and B. We're figuring out how many guns and how much butter are produced at each of these points. Starting at the origin, or zero, let's check out point A. It's directly above the origin, so no guns are produced. Point A is at 15 on the vertical scale, so 15 units of butter are produced.

Now we'll move on to point B, which is directly above 1 unit on the guns axis. At B we produce 1 unit of guns and 14 units of butter (shown vertically). Incidentally, to locate any point on a graph, first go across, or horizontally, then up, or vertically. Point B is 1 unit to the right, then 14 units up.

Now locate point C: 2 units across and 12 up. At C we have 2 guns and 12 butters. Next is D: 3 across and 9 up (3 guns and 9 butters). At E: 4 across and 5 up (4 guns and 5 butters). And finally F: 5 across and 0 up (5 guns and no butter).

The production possibilities curve is a hypothetical model of an economy that produces only two products—in this case, guns and butter (or military goods and civilian goods). The curve represents the various possible combinations of guns and butter that could be produced if the economy were operating at capacity, or full employment.

> The production possibilities curve represents a two-product economy at full employment.

Since we usually do not operate at full employment, we are seldom on the production possibilities frontier. So let's move on to Figure 2, which shows, at point X, where we generally are. Sometimes we are in a recession, with unemployment rising beyond 8 or 9 percent, represented on the graph by point Y. A depression would be closer to the origin, perhaps shown by point Z. (Remember that the origin is located in the lower left-hand corner of the graph.)

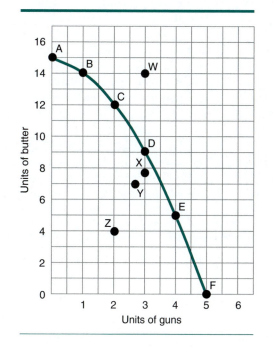

Figure 2

Points Inside and Outside the Production Possibilities Curve Since the curve represents output of guns and butter at full employment, points X, Y, and Z, which lie inside or below the curve, represent output at less than full employment. Similarly, point W represents output at more than full employment and is currently unattainable.

The Law of Increasing Costs

The production possibilities curve below reproduces Table 1. You may notice that, as we shift production from guns to butter, we have to give up increasing units of guns for each additional unit of butter. Or, shifting the other way, we would have to give up increasing units of butter for each additional unit of guns we produce.

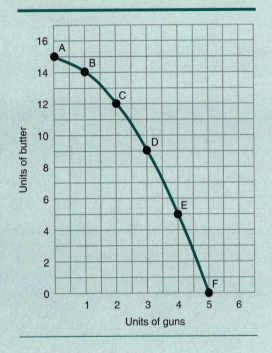

Note that as you move from A to B you produce an extra gun at the expense of 1 unit of butter, but when you move from E to F, you produce an extra gun at the expense of 5 units of butter.

We will be calling this "the law of increasing costs." Stated formally, this law says that *as the output of one good expands, the opportunity cost of producing additional units of this good increases.* In other words, as more and more of a good is produced, the production of additional units of this good will entail larger and larger opportunity costs.

The law of increasing costs is based on three concepts: (1) the law of diminishing returns, (2) diseconomies of scale, and (3) factor suitability. We've already alluded to factor suitability when we talked about using our resources in the most efficient way possible. One example was to use

our computer mainframe for sophisticated data analysis rather than for simple word processing.

The law of diminishing returns, which we'll take up more formally in a later chapter, is defined this way: *If units of a resource are added to a fixed proportion of other resources, eventually marginal output will decline.* Suppose one farmer working with one tractor can produce 100 bushels of wheat on one acre of land. Two farmers, working together, can produce 220 bushels. And three, working together, can produce 350.

The marginal output of the first farmer is 100. (In other words, the first farmer added 100 bushels to output.) The marginal output of the second farmer is 120. And the marginal output of the third farmer is 130. So far, so good. We call this increasing returns.

If we keep adding farmers, do you think we'll continue to enjoy increasing returns? Won't that single acre of land start getting a little crowded? Will that one tractor be sufficient for four, five, and six farmers? Suppose we did add a fourth farmer and suppose output rose from 350 to 450. By how much did marginal output rise?

It rose by only 100. So marginal output, which had been rising by 120 and 130, has now fallen to 100. We call this diminishing returns.

Diseconomies of scale is a new term. As a business firm grows larger, it can usually cut its costs by taking advantage of quantity discounts, the use of expensive but highly productive equipment, and the development of a highly specialized and highly skilled workforce. We call these *economies of scale.* But as the firm continues to grow, these economies of scale are eventually outweighed by the inefficiencies of managing a bloated bureaucracy, which might sometimes work at cross-purposes. Most of the day could be spent writing memos, answering memos, and attending meetings. Labor and other resources become increasingly expensive, and not only are quantity discounts no longer available, but now suppliers charge premium prices for such huge orders. As costs begin to rise, diseconomies of scale have now overcome economies of scale.*

Let's look at some increasing costs. We have already seen how we have had to give up the production of some guns to produce more butter and vice versa. We'll now take this a step further. To produce additional units of guns—one gun, two guns, three guns—we will have to give up

Table A Production Shifts from Butter to Guns

Shift from Point to Point	Change in Gun Production	Change in Butter Production
A to B	+1	−1
B to C	+1	−2
C to D	+1	−3
D to E	+1	−4
E to F	+1	−5

increasing amounts of butter. Similarly, to produce additional units of butter, we will have to give up increasing numbers of guns.

How many units of butter would we have to give up to produce each additional gun? This is shown in the table above, which is derived from the figure in this box, or, if you prefer, from Table 1 earlier in this chapter.

In the table above, as we begin to switch from butter to guns, we move from point A to point B. We give up just one unit of butter in exchange for one unit of guns. But the move from B to C isn't as good. Here we give up two butters for one gun. C to D is still worse: We give up three butters for one gun. D to E is even worse: We give up four units of butter for one gun. And the worst trade-off of all is from E to F: We lose five butters for just one gun.

This is why we call it the law of increasing relative costs. To produce more and more of one good, we have to give up increasing amounts of another good. To produce each additional gun, we have to give up increasing amounts of butter.

There are three explanations for the law of increasing relative costs. First, there's diminishing returns. If we're increasing gun production, we will need more and more resources—more land, more labor, more capital, and more entrepreneurial ability. But one or more of these resources may be relatively limited. Perhaps we will begin to run out of capital—plant and equipment—or perhaps entrepreneurial ability will run out first.

Go back to our definition of the law of diminishing returns. *If units of a resource are added to a fixed proportion of other resources, eventually marginal output will decline.* Had we been talking about farming rather than producing guns, the law of diminishing returns might have

set in as increasing amounts of capital were applied to the limited supply of rich farmland.

A second explanation for the law of increasing costs is diseconomies of scale. By shifting from butter to guns, the firm or firms making guns will grow so large that diseconomies of scale will eventually set in.

The third explanation, factor suitability, requires more extensive treatment here. We'll start at point A of Table A where we produce 15 units of butter and no guns. As we move to point B, gun production goes up by one, while butter production goes down by only one. In other words, the opportunity cost of producing one unit of guns is the loss of only one unit of butter.

Why is the opportunity cost so low? The answer lies mainly with factor suitability. We'll digress for a moment with the analogy of a pickup game of basketball. The best players are picked first, then the not-so-good ones, and finally the worst. If a couple of players from one side have to go home, the game goes on. The other side gives them their worst player.

If we're shifting from butter to guns, the butter makers will give the gun makers their worst workers. But people who are bad at producing butter are not necessarily bad at making—or shooting—guns.

When all we did was make butter, people worked at that no matter what their other skills. Even if a person were a skilled gun maker, or a gun user, what choice did he have? Presumably, then, when given the choice to make guns, those best suited for that occupation (and also poorly suited for butter making) would switch to guns.

As resources are shifted from butter to guns, the labor, land, capital, and entrepreneurial ability best suited to guns and least suited to butter will be the first to switch. But as more resources are shifted, we will be taking resources that were more and more suited to butter making and less and less suited to gun making.

Take land, for example. The first land given over to gun making might be terrible for raising cows (and hence milk and butter) but great for making guns. Eventually, however, as nearly all land was devoted to gun making, we'd be giving over fertile farmland that might not be well suited to gun production.

---

*Economies and diseconomies of scale are more fully discussed in the chapter on Cost in *Economics* and *Microeconomics*.

Finding the Opportunity Cost

Figure A shows us how many apples and oranges we can produce. The more apples we produce, the fewer oranges we can produce. Similarly, the more oranges we produce, the fewer apples we can produce.

Opportunity cost tells us what we must give up. So if we increase our production of oranges by moving from point B to point C, how many apples are we giving up?

We are giving up 1 apple. Next question: If we move from point F to point D, how many oranges are we giving up?

We are giving up 2 oranges. Now, let's take it up a notch. What is the opportunity cost of moving from A to D?

It's 3 apples, because at point A we produced 5 apples, but at point D we're producing only 2. One more question: What is the opportunity cost of moving from E to B?

It's 6 oranges, because at E we produced 10 oranges and at B, only 4.

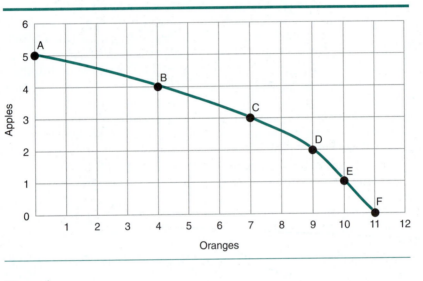

Figure A

What if we were at the origin? What would that represent? Think about it. What would be the production of guns? How about the production of butter? They would both be zero. Is that possible? During the Great Depression in the 1930s, the U.S. economy sank to point Z, but no economy has ever sunk to the origin.

Move back to the production possibilities curve, say, at point C, where we are producing 2 units of guns and 12 units of butter. Is it possible to produce more guns? Certainly. Just move down the curve to point D. Notice, however, that we now produce fewer units of butter.

At D we have 3 units of guns and 9 units of butter. When we go from C, where we have 2 guns, to D, where we have 3, gun production goes up by 1. But at the same time, butter production declines from 12 at C to only 9 at D (a decline of 3).

If we're at point C, then, we can produce more guns, but only by sacrificing some butter production. The opportunity cost of moving from C to D (that is, of producing 1 more gun) is giving up 3 units of butter.

Let's try another one, this time moving from C to B. Butter goes up from 12 to 14—a gain of 2. Meanwhile, guns go down from 2 to 1, a loss of 1. Going from C to B, a gain of 2 butters is obtained by sacrificing 1 gun. The opportunity cost of producing 2 more butters is 1 gun. If you need a little more practice, please work your way through the accompanying Extra Help box.

Except at point A, we can go somewhere else on the production possibilities curve and increase our output of butter. Similarly, anywhere but at point F, we can go somewhere else on the curve and raise our output of guns. It is possible to increase our output of *either* guns *or* butter by moving somewhere else on the curve, but there is an opportunity cost involved. The more we produce of one (by moving along the curve), the less we produce of the other. It is not possible, then, if we are anywhere on the curve, to raise our production of both guns *and* butter. Of course, over time it is possible to produce beyond our current production possibilities curve as our economy grows. We'll get to economic growth in a few minutes.

What if we're somewhere inside the production possibilities curve? Would it be possible to produce more guns *and* more butter? The answer is yes. At point Z we have an output of 2 guns and 4 butters. By moving to point D we would have 3 guns and 9 butters. Or, by going to point E, output would rise to 4 guns and 5 butters.

We are able to increase our output of both guns and butter when we move from Z to D or E because we are now making use of previously unused resources. We are moving from depression conditions to those of full employment. But when we go from C to D, we stay at full employment. The only way we can produce more guns is to produce less butter, because resources will have to be diverted from butter to gun production. As we divert increasing amounts of resources to gun production, we will be able to understand the law of increasing costs (see the box titled "The Law of Increasing Costs").

Productive Efficiency

So far we've seen that our economy generally falls short of full production. Now we'll tie that failure in to our definition of economics.

At the beginning of this chapter, we defined economics as *the efficient allocation of the scarce means of production toward the satisfaction of human wants.* The scarce means of production are our resources, land, labor, capital, and entrepreneurial ability. So how efficiently do we use our resources?

An economy is efficient whenever it is producing the maximum output allowed by a given level of technology and resources. *Productive efficiency is attained when the maximum possible output of any one good is produced, given the output of other goods.* This state of grace occurs only when we are operating on our production possibilities curve. Attainment of productive efficiency means that we can't increase the output of one good without reducing the output of some other good.

> Productive efficiency is attained when the maximum possible output of any one good is produced, given the output of other goods.

As we've seen, our economy rarely attains productive efficiency, or full production. We have managed this state of grace from mid-1997 through mid-2001, when the unemployment rate dipped below 5 percent. And then, from October 2005 through February 2008, it never rose above 5 percent. The previous time our economy actually operated on its production possibilities frontier was during the Vietnam War, in 1968 and 1969.

Economic Growth

If the production possibilities curve represents the economy operating at full employment, then it would be impossible to produce at point W (of Figure 2). To go from C to W would mean producing more guns *and* more butter, something that would be beyond our economic capabilities, given the current state of technology and the amount of resources available.

Every economy will use the best available technology. At times, because a country cannot afford the most up-to-date equipment, it will use older machinery and tools. That country really has a capital problem rather than a technological one.

> The best available technology

As the level of available technology improves, the production possibilities curve moves outward, as it does in Figure 3. A faster paper copier, a more smoothly operating assembly line, or a new-generation computer system are examples of technological

The Production Possibilities Frontier during World War II

World War II was a classic case of guns and butter, or, more accurately, guns *or* butter. Almost two years before we became actively involved in the war, we began increasing our arms production and drafting millions of young men into the armed services. Did this increase in military goods production mean a decrease in the production of consumer goods?

Gee, that's a very good question. And the answer is found when you go from point A to point B on the first figure shown here.

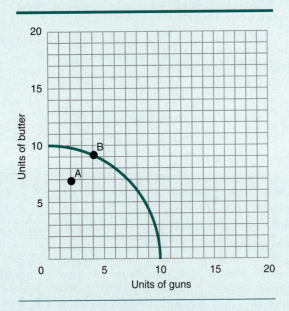

How were we able to increase the production of both guns and butter in 1940 and 1941? Because there was still a great deal of economic slack in those years. It was the tail end of the Great Depression described in Chapter 1, and there were still millions of people out of work and a great deal of idle plant and equipment that could be pressed into use.

Now we're in the war, and we're at point B in the first figure. Is it possible to further expand our output of both guns and butter? Think about it.

Is there any way we could do it? How about if there's economic growth? In the second figure shown here, we went from point B to point C by moving to a higher production possibilities curve. Is this *possible?* Over a considerable period of time, yes. But in just a couple of years? Well, remember what they used to say: There's a *war* going on. So a move from point B to point C in just a couple of years is possible during a war.

Now we're really going to push it. How about a move from point C to point D in the second figure? Is *this* move

possible? Can we raise our production of both guns *and* butter to a point beyond our production possibilities frontier without jumping to a still higher production possibilities curve?

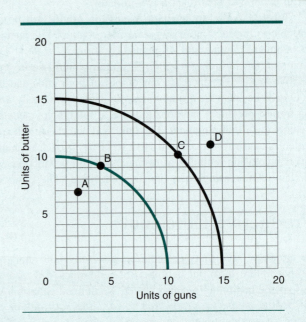

Well, what do *you* think? Remember, there's a war going on. The answer is yes. In 1942, 1943, and 1944 we did push our official unemployment rate under 3 percent, well below the 5 percent rate we would consider full employment today. Employers were so desperate for workers that they would hire practically anybody, and people who wouldn't ordinarily be in the labor market—housewives, retired people, and teenagers—were flocking to the workplace.

Meanwhile, business firms were pressing older machinery and equipment into use, because it was almost impossible to get new machinery and equipment built during the war. And so we were operating not only at full capacity but well beyond that point.

How long were we able to stay at point D? Only as long as there was a war going on. Point D represents an output of guns and butter that our economy can produce temporarily if it operates beyond its production possibilities curve. It's almost like bowling 300. You can't expect to go out and do it every night.*

---

*One can argue that we were temporarily operating on a higher production possibilities curve, and, at the end of the war, we returned to the lower production possibilities curve.

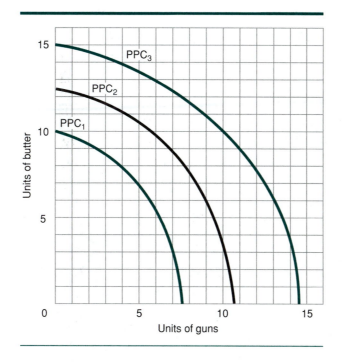

Figure 3
Production Possibilities Curves
A move from PPC$_1$ to PPC$_2$ and
from PPC$_2$ to PPC$_3$ represents
economic growth.

advances. And increasingly, industrial robots and bank money machines are replacing human beings at relatively routine jobs.

As you know, recent advances in information technology (or, IT, as it's often called) has boosted output per worker and cut costs. It costs FedEx $2.40 to track a package for a customer who calls by phone, but only four cents for one who visits its website. FedEx now gets about 3 million online tracking requests a day, compared with only 30,000 or 40,000 by phone.

Our economic capacity also grows when there is an expansion of labor or capital. More (or better trained) labor and more (or improved) plant and equipment would also push the production possibilities curve outward. This is illustrated in Figure 3, as we go from PPC$_1$ to PPC$_2$, and from PPC$_2$ to PPC$_3$.

Imagine that in 1991 a hypothetical nation had two choices. It could either produce a preponderance of consumer goods or a preponderance of capital goods. Which choice would lead to a faster rate of growth?

On the left side of Figure 4 we see what would have happened to the nation if it had chosen to concentrate on producing consumer goods; on the right side we see what would have happened if it had concentrated on producing capital goods. Obviously by concentrating on capital goods production, that nation would have had a much faster rate of economic growth.

The main factors spurring growth are an improving technology, more and better capital, and more and better labor. Using our resources more efficiently and reducing the unemployment of labor and capital can also raise our rate of growth. This topic is discussed more extensively in Chapter 16 of *Economics* and *Macroeconomics*.

Current Issue: Will You Be Underemployed When You Graduate?

Every spring newspaper reporters ask college placement officials about the job prospects of that year's graduating class. During good years corporate recruiters are lining up to interview the new grads. But in bad years, it's the other way around. The years 2006 and 2007 were pretty *good* and, 2008, 2009, and 2010, quite bad.

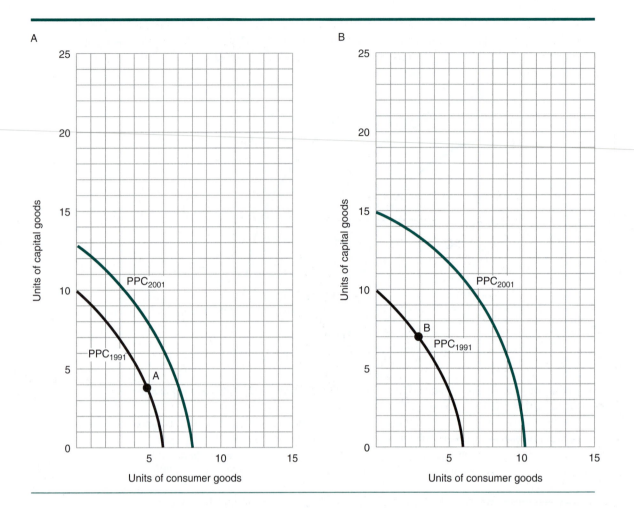

Figure 4

Recent college graduates, when they can find work at all, are settling for jobs at places like Starbucks, Gap, and the post office (where 12 percent of the employees have college degrees). Half of college graduates under 25 are in positions that do not require college degrees. Which may leave a lot of parents wondering why they shelled out all that money for their children's education.

I happened to graduate during a *bad* year. My only job offer was from the recruiter from Continental Baking Company to drive a bakery truck. "But how will I use my economics?" He told me I could economize on the gasoline.

Had I taken the truck-driving job, I would have been underemployed. When you graduate, you may face the same problem. It turns out that one in five college graduates ends up in a job that does not require a college degree. In addition, many employers require a degree just as a credential. So when you start interviewing, ask yourself, "I need a degree to do *this*?"

There are millions of college grads who are asking themselves this very question. Some 37 percent of all flight attendants hold bachelor's degrees, as do 19 percent of the theater ushers, lobby attendants, and ticket takers. In addition, 13 percent of all bank tellers and 14 percent of all typists and word processors are college graduates.[8]

From time to time you'll hear reports of PhD's driving cabs, lawyers typing their own briefs, and doctors bogged down in paperwork. Perhaps there's some degree of

---

[8]Louis Uchitelle, "College Still Counts, Though Not as Much," *The New York Times,* October 2, 2005, Section 10, p. 4.

underemployment in almost everyone's future. All you can really do is avoid taking a job in which you are clearly underemployed. So when you're interviewing with prospective employers at your college placement office and that guy with the bakery truck shows up, just say no.

Questions for Further Thought and Discussion

1. If you were in a position to run our economy, what steps would you take to raise our rate of economic growth?

2. Under what circumstances can we operate outside our production possibilities curve?

3. Give an example of an opportunity cost for an individual and a nation.

4. Would it be harder for a nation to attain full employment or full production? Explain.

5. Could a nation's production possibilities curve ever shift inward? What might cause such a shift to occur?

6. What is the opportunity cost you incurred by going to college?

7. Although the U.S. is one of the world's wealthiest nations, some of the federal government's budget decisions are severely constrained by scarcity. Can you think of one such decision that was in the recent economic news?

8. Why is scarcity central to economics?

9. Can you think of any decisions you have recently made that incurred opportunity costs?

10. Do you know any entrepreneurs? What do they do?

11. Why is entrepreneurship central to every business firm?

12. Explain the law of increasing costs, using a numerical example.

13. Discuss the three concepts on which the law of increasing costs is based.

14. *Practical Application:* Underemployment of college graduates is a growing problem. If you were appointed to the board of trustees of your college, what measures would you suggest to alleviate this problem for the graduates of your school?

Workbook for Chapter 2

Name _____

Date _____

Multiple-Choice Questions

Circle the letter that corresponds to the best answer.

1. The word that is central to the definition of economics is _____. (LO1)
   a) resource
   b) wants
   c) scarcity
   d) capital

2. We would not need to economize if _____. (LO2)
   a) the government printed more money
   b) there was no scarcity
   c) there was less output of goods and services
   d) everyone received a big pay increase

3. Human wants are _____. (LO1)
   a) relatively limited
   b) relatively unlimited
   c) easily satisfied
   d) about equal to our productive capacity

4. Which of the following is an economic resource? (LO3)
   a) gold
   b) scarcity
   c) labor
   d) rent

5. Each of the following is an example of capital except _____. (LO3)
   a) land
   b) an office building
   c) a computer system
   d) a factory

6. The opportunity cost of spending four hours studying a review book the night before a final exam would be _____. (LO4)
   a) the cost of the review book
   b) missing four hours of TV
   c) a higher grade on the exam
   d) the knowledge gained from studying

7. An economy operating its plant and equipment at full capacity implies a capacity utilization rate of _____. (LO5)
   a) 40 percent
   b) 70 percent
   c) 85 percent
   d) 100 percent

8. The full-production level of our economy implies _____. (LO5, 8)
   a) an efficient allocation of our resources
   b) zero unemployment
   c) our plant and equipment being operated at 100 percent capacity
   d) a high unemployment rate

9. Underemployment means _____. (LO5)
   a) the same thing as unemployment
   b) underutilization of resources
   c) a recession
   d) slow economic growth

10. The production possibilities curve represents _____. (LO6, 8)
    a) our economy at full employment but not full production
    b) our economy at full production but not full employment
    c) our economy at full production and full employment

11. If we are operating inside our production possibilities curve _____. (LO6)
    a) there is definitely a recession going on
    b) there is definitely not a recession going on
    c) there is definitely less than full employment
    d) there is definitely inflation

12. The closer we are to the origin and the farther away we are from the production possibilities curve _____. (LO6)
    a) the more unemployment there is
    b) the less unemployment there is
    c) the more guns we are producing
    d) the more butter we are producing

13. Economic growth will occur if any of the following occur except _____. (LO9)
    a) a better technology becomes available
    b) the level of consumption rises and the savings rate falls
    c) more capital becomes available
    d) more labor becomes available

14. To attain a higher rate of economic growth, we need to devote _____. (LO9)
    a) a higher proportion of our production to capital goods and a lower proportion to consumer goods
    b) a higher proportion of our production to consumer goods and a lower proportion to capital goods
    c) a higher proportion of our production to both consumer goods and capital goods
    d) a lower proportion of our production to both consumer goods and capital goods

15. Which is the most accurate statement? (LO3)
    a) Nearly every major economic innovation originated abroad and was then applied in the United States.
    b) The United States provides a poor environment for innovation.
    c) Freedom of thought, a risk-taking culture, and a noncorrupt bureaucracy have made the United States very hospitable to innovation.
    d) Although the United States was once the world's leading innovator, since we lost most of our manufacturing base, we are no longer a major innovator.

16. Which is the most accurate statement? (LO5)
    a) Most Americans are underemployed.
    b) Employment discrimination causes underemployment of labor.
    c) It is impossible for an economy to operate outside its production possibilities curve.
    d) There is no longer employment discrimination.

17. Statement 1: The old Negro leagues provide an example of underemployment.
    Statement 2: Underemployment means basically the same thing as unemployment. (LO5)
    a) Statement 1 is true and statement 2 is false.
    b) Statement 2 is true and statement 1 is false.
    c) Both statements are true.
    d) Both statements are false.

18. Employment discrimination is most closely related to _____. (LO5)
    a) specialization   c) unemployment
    b) technology   d) underemployment

19. Miranda Bowman, a Harvard MBA, is almost definitely _____ if she is working as a secretary. (LO5)
    a) unemployed   b) underemployed
    c) both unemployed and underemployed
    d) neither unemployed nor underemployed

20. On the following list, the most serious problem facing today's college graduate is _____. (LO5)
    a) outsourcing of jobs to foreign countries
    b) employment discrimination
    c) unemployment
    d) underemployment

21. Which statement is true? (LO2, 3)
    a) America has always had a shortage of entrepreneurs.
    b) Our economic problem is that we have limited resources available to satisfy relatively unlimited wants.
    c) America has less economic resources today than we had 40 years ago.
    d) Aside from a few million poor people, we have very little scarcity in the United States.

22. Suppose you had $1,000 to spend. If you spent it on a vacation trip rather than on new clothes, your second choice, or 1,000 lottery tickets, your third choice, what was your opportunity cost of going on a vacation trip? (LO4)
    a) $1,000
    b) the vacation trip itself
    c) not buying the new clothes
    d) not buying the lottery tickets
    e) missing out on the $10 million lottery prize

23. Which of the following best describes the role of an entrepreneur? (LO3)
    a) the inventor of something with great commercial possibilities
    b) anyone who made a fortune by purchasing stock in a dot-com before its price shot up
    c) inventors who parlay inventions into commercial enterprises
    d) any employee earning at least $200,000 at a Fortune 500 company

24. As we produce increasing amounts of a particular good, the resources used in its production _____. (LO7)
   a) become more suitable
   b) become less suitable
   c) continue to have the same suitability

25. The law of increasing costs is explained by each of the following except _____. (LO7)
   a) the law of diminishing returns
   b) diseconomies of scale
   c) factor suitability
   d) overspecialization

26. As a firm grows larger, _____. (LO7)
   a) economies of scale set in, then diseconomies of scale
   b) diseconomies of scale set in, then economies of scale
   c) economies of scale and diseconomies of scale set in at the same time
   d) neither economies of scale nor diseconomies of scale set in

27. The law of increasing costs states that, as _____. (LO7)
   a) output rises, cost per unit rises as well
   b) the output of one good expands, the opportunity cost of producing additional units of this good increases
   c) economies of scale set in, costs increase
   d) output rises, diminishing returns set in

28. If Figure 1 shows our production possibilities frontier during World War II, at which point were we operating? (LO6)
   a) point A
   b) point B
   c) point C
   d) point D

29. If Figure 1 shows our production possibilities frontier during the Great Depression, at which point were we operating? (LO6)
   a) point A
   b) point B
   c) point C
   d) point D

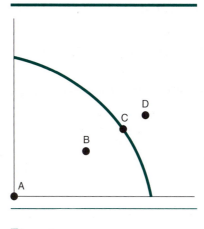

Figure 1

30. Which one of the following is the most accurate statement? (LO6, 9)
   a) Our economy was at full employment in 2008 and 2009.
   b) Our economy operated outside of its production possibilities curve in 2009 and 2010.
   c) Our economy is currently operating on its production possibilities curve.
   d) Our economy is currently operating inside its production possibilities curve.

31. Which statement is true? (LO6)
   a) As our economy recovers from a recession, it moves closer to its production possibilities curve.
   b) When an economy moves into a recession, it slides along its production possibilities curve.
   c) We have never operated outside our production possibilities curve.
   d) There is no way to represent a bad recession or a depression on a graph of the production possibilities curve.

32. Which one of the following statements is the most accurate? (LO6)
   a) Half of all college graduates under 25 are unemployed.
   b) Half of all college graduates under 25 are underemployed.
   c) Half of all high school dropouts are underemployed.
   d) Despite the recession, nearly all college graduates of the class of 2010 found jobs commensurate with their training and educational backgrounds.

Fill-In Questions

1. A PhD driving a cab would be considered _____. (LO5)

2. The central fact of economics is (in one word) _____. (LO2)

3. Human wants are relatively _____, while economic resources are relatively _____. (LO2, 3)

4. The law of increasing costs states that, as the output of one good expands, _____. (LO7)

5. The law of diminishing returns, diseconomies of scale, and factor suitability each provide an explanation for the law of _____. (LO7)

6. If you went into a store with $25 and couldn't decide whether to buy a pair of jeans or a jacket, and you finally decided to buy the jeans, what would be the opportunity cost of this purchase? _____. (LO4)

7. Full employment implies an unemployment rate of about _____ percent. (LO5)

8. List some constraints on our labor force that prevent our fully using our plant and equipment 24 hours a day, seven days a week. (LO5)

    (1) _____;

    (2) _____;

    and (3) _____.

9. Employment discrimination results in the _____ of our labor force. (LO5)

10. When we are efficiently allocating our resources and using the best available technology, we are operating on our _____. (LO6, 8)

11. Most of the time our economy is operating _____ its production possibilities frontier. (LO6)

12. Economic growth can be attained by: (LO9)

    (1) _____ and

    (2) _____.

Problems

1. If we were at point C of Figure 2 below, could we quickly produce substantially more houses *and* more cars? (LO6, 9)

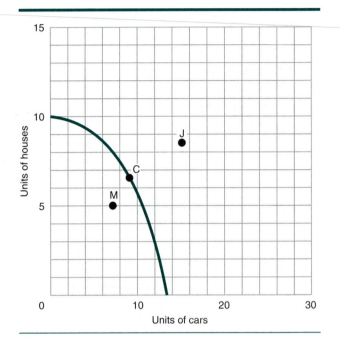

Figure 2

2. If we were at point M of Figure 2, could we quickly produce substantially more houses *and* more cars? (LO6, 9)

3. If we were at point C on Figure 2, could we quickly go to point J? (LO6, 9)

4. Fill in the following points on Figure 3. (LO6)

   Point X: where our economy generally operates

   Point Y: a serious recession

   Point Z: a catastrophic depression

   Point W: economic growth

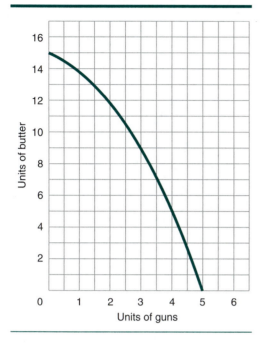

Figure 3

5. In Figure 4, fill in a new production possibilities frontier representing substantial economic growth. (LO6, 9)

6. In Figure 4, place point M where there is 100 percent unemployment. (LO6)

Figure 4

7. Fill in the following points on Figure 5. (LO6)

   Point A: an unemployment rate of 100 percent

   Point B: an unemployment rate of 20 percent

   Point C: an unemployment rate of 2 percent

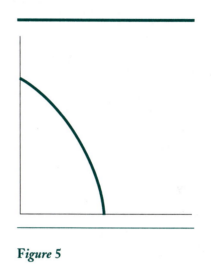

Figure 5

8. Given the information in Table 1, below, what is the opportunity cost of going from point B to point C? And of going from point D to point C? (LO4)

TABLE 1	Hypothetical Production Schedule for Two-Product Economy

Point	Units of Butter	Units of Guns
A	15	0
B	14	1
C	12	2
D	9	3
E	5	4
F	0	5

9. Use Figure 6 to answer these questions: (LO6, 4)

a) What is the opportunity cost of going from point B to point C?

b) What is the opportunity cost of going from point D to point C?

c) What is the opportunity cost of going from point B to point A?

d) What is the opportunity cost of going from point C to point D?

10. Use the data in Figure 6 to illustrate the law of increasing costs numerically. (Hint: Start at point E and move toward point A.) (LO6, 7)

11. Put an X on Figure 7 to represent where our economy operated in 2010. (LO6)

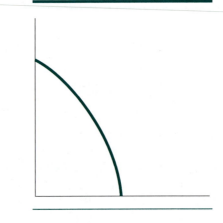

Figure 7

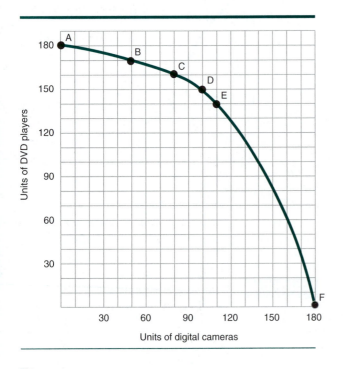

Figure 6

Chapter 3

The Mixed Economy

Ours is a mixed economy because there is a private sector and a public sector. Close to 90 percent of our goods and services originate in the private sector, although the government co-opts some of this production for its own use. China also has a mixed economy; the public sector produces about one-third the goods and services. Every economic system needs to put bread on the table, clothes on people's backs, and a roof over their heads. The question is how resources are used to attain these goods and services.

LEARNING OBJECTIVES

After reading this chapter you should be able to:

1. List and explain the three questions of economics.
2. Explain the concepts of the profit motive, the price mechanism, competition, and capital.
3. Analyze the circular flow model.
4. Describe and illustrate market failure and externalities.
5. Describe and explain government failure.
6. Discuss the economic role of capital and its importance.
7. Define and describe the "isms": capitalism, fascism, communism, and socialism.
8. Summarize and explain the decline and fall of the communist system.
9. Discuss the economic transformation of China.

The Three Questions of Economics

Because every country in the world is faced with scarce (limited) resources, every country must answer three questions: (1) What shall we produce? (2) How shall these goods and services be produced? (3) For whom shall the goods and services be produced? We'll take up each in turn.

What Shall We Produce?

In the United States, most of our production is geared toward consumer goods and services. About 5 percent goes toward defense. In the former Soviet Union, a much higher proportion was devoted to armaments, with a proportionately smaller percentage devoted to consumer goods and services. Japan has concentrated on building up its plant and equipment but devotes just 1 percent of its production to defense.

Military, consumption, or capital goods?

Who makes these decisions? In the United States and Japan there is no central planning authority, but rather a hodgepodge of corporate and government officials, as well as individual consumers and taxpayers. The Soviets *did* have a central planning authority. In

Figure 1

Sector Employment as
Percentage of Total
Employment, 1940–2010
The service sector, which accounted
for less than half the jobs in our
economy in 1940, now accounts for
82 percent.

Source: U.S. Census Bureau, *Statistical
Abstract of the United States*, 2010.

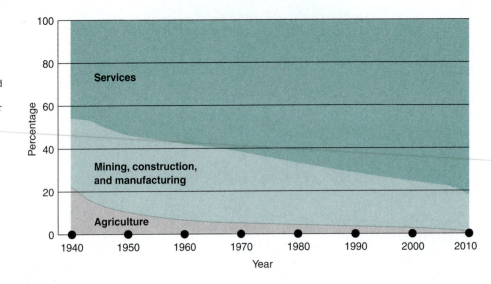

fact, every five years the Soviet government used to come up with a new plan that set goals for its economy in numbers of cars, TVs, factories, and bushels of wheat and corn to be produced.

As a nation matures, its economy shifts from agricultural to manufacturing, and then to services. This shift is reflected in employment (see Figure 1). Until about 150 years ago, most Americans worked on farms. But today, only 1 in 500 still farms full time. Today, four out of every five workers produce services.

How Shall These Goods and Services Be Produced?

In our country—and in most others as well—nearly everything is produced by private businesses. Not only are all the goods and services that consumers purchase produced by businesses, but so are most of what the government purchases. For example, when our astronauts landed on the moon, a long list of contractors and subcontractors was released. It read like a who's who in American corporations.

In socialist countries, of course, the government is the main producer of goods and services. But even in a communist country, China, there is still a substantial role for private enterprise.

For Whom Shall the Goods and Services Be Produced?

For whom shall the goods be produced?

Economics may be divided into two parts: production, which we dealt with in the first two questions, and distribution. In the first question, we asked what the economic pie should be made of; in the second, we talked about how the pie would be made. Now we are ready to divide up the pie.

Our distribution system is a modified version of one dollar, one vote. In general, the more money you have, the more you can buy. But the government also has a claim to part of the pie. Theoretically, the government takes from those who can afford to give up part of their share (taxes), spends some of those tax dollars to produce various government goods and services, and gives the rest to the old, the sick, and the poor. (Nevertheless, the rich reap a major share of the subsidies to airlines, shipping companies, defense contractors, and agriculture.)

Henry Fairlie has come up with a capitalist credo: From each according to his gullibility. To each according to his greed.

In theory, the Soviets' distributive system was diametrically opposed to ours. The communist credo "From each according to his ability, to each according to his needs" was something the Soviet leaders claimed to follow, and it does have a nice ring to it. But in actuality, their income distribution system, with its jerry-built structure of wage incentives, bonus payments, and special privileges, was probably no more equitable than our own.

To Sum Up

In a mixed economy, both the government and the market have roles in answering: (1) What shall we produce? (2) How shall these goods and services be produced? (3) For whom shall these goods and services be produced? In nearly all mixed economies the government plays a relatively minor role in production, but may play a relatively strong role in distribution.

The Invisible Hand, the Price Mechanism, and Perfect Competition

We have just set the stage for a comparison between our economic system and those of several other countries. We'll start with the competitive economic model, and then talk about the economic roles of government and of capital. These concepts, common to all economies, need to be understood before we can make comparisons among the economies of different nations.

The Invisible Hand

Adam Smith, Scottish professor of philosophy

When Adam Smith coined this term in 1776, he was thinking about an economic guidance system that always made everything come out all right. He believed that if people set out to promote the public interest, they will not do nearly as much good as they would if they pursued their own selfish interests. That's right! If all people are out for themselves, everyone will work harder, produce more, and we'll all be the richer for it. And that premise underlies the free-enterprise system.

Smith said that the entrepreneur is motivated by self-interest:

> He generally, indeed, neither intends to promote the public interest, nor knows how much he is promoting it. By preferring the support of domestic to that of foreign industry, he intends only his own gain, and he is in this, as in many other cases, led by an invisible hand to promote an end which was no part of his intention. . . . By pursuing his own interest he frequently promotes that of the society more effectually than when he really intends to promote it.[1]

Whenever a businessperson runs for public office, he or she invariably brings up the fact that his or her opponent never met a payroll. This businessperson, motivated solely by a quest for profits, provided jobs for perhaps hundreds, or even thousands, of people. His or her firm produced some good or service so desirable that buyers were willing to pay for it. And so, this aspiring politician, who went into business solely to make money, now claims credit for creating jobs and promoting the public interest. And not a word of thanks to the invisible hand.

Some 20 years ago, about one-third of the food in the Soviet Union was produced on just 2 percent of the land under cultivation. That 2 percent was made up of small, privately owned plots; the other 98 percent was in the form of large collective farms. Obviously, the same farmers worked much harder on their own land than on the land whose produce was owned by the entire society. As Adam Smith said, a person pursuing his own interest "frequently promotes that of society more effectively than when he really intends to promote it."

Greed makes the world go round.

The invisible hand is really the profit motive.

---

[1]Adam Smith, *The Wealth of Nations,* Book IV (London: Methuen, 1950), chap. II, pp. 477–78.

The Chinese communists, too, forced hundreds of millions of peasants to work on huge collective farms, and like the Soviet agricultural experiment, it had disastrous results. Robert Shiller wrote about the first American experiment in collective ownership:

> When they arrived in the New World, in 1620, the Pilgrims of Plymouth Colony tried communal ownership of the land. It didn't work: crops were not well cared for and the result was a severe food shortage. So in 1623 each family was given a private plot of land along with responsibility for maintaining it. This worked much better. As William Bradford, the second governor of Plymouth Colony, recounted in *Of Plymouth Plantation,* people worked harder when they had private plots, and the crop yield was much higher. The moral of this story—at least according to the proponents of private ownership who like to quote from it—is simple: people take better care of things they own individually than of things they hold in common.[2]

The Price Mechanism

It is often said that everyone has a price, which means that nearly all of us, for a certain sum of money, would do some pretty nasty things. The key variable here is *price*. Some of us would do these nasty things for $100, others for $1,000, others perhaps only for $1 million.

Not only does every*one* have a price, but every*thing* has a price as well. The price of a slice of pizza or a gallon of gasoline is known to all consumers. Although they vary somewhat, gas prices rarely fall below $2.00 and hardly anyone would pay $10 for a slice of pizza.

Prices send signals to producers and consumers.

Just as prices send signals to consumers, they also signal producers or sellers. If pizza goes up to $10 a slice, I'll put an oven in my living room and open for business the next day.

When consumers want more of a certain good or service, they drive the price up, which, in turn, signals producers to produce more. If the price rise is substantial and appears permanent, new firms will be attracted to the industry, thereby raising output still further.

During the 1970s, when we experienced some of the worst inflation in our history, many people called for price controls. These were very briefly and halfheartedly instituted by President Nixon, and their results in controlling inflation were decidedly mixed. Critics of controls believe they interfere with our price mechanism and the signals that mechanism sends to producers and consumers. Others, most notably John Kenneth Galbraith, have argued that the prices of our major products are administered or set by the nation's largest corporations rather than in the marketplace. What this disagreement boils down to is whether our economic system is basically competitive, with millions of buyers and sellers interacting in the marketplace, or whether our economy is dominated by a handful of corporate giants who have subverted the price system by setting prices themselves.

Competition

Competition makes the price system work.

What is competition? Is it the rivalry between Burger King and McDonald's? GM and Ford? Walmart and Target? Most economists will tell you that to have real competition, you need many firms in an industry. How many? So many that no firm is large enough to have any influence over price. So, by definition, an industry with many firms is competitive.

When Philip Morris or R. J. Reynolds announces its new prices, *those* are the prices for cigarettes. Of course, when Microsoft talks about the price of its latest version of Windows, everyone listens. No ifs, ands, or buts. No give-and-take in the marketplace. And the price mechanism? It just doesn't apply here.

To allow the price mechanism to work, we need many competing firms in each industry. There are entire industries—autos, computer software, oil refining, pharmaceuticals, retail bookstores, breakfast cereals, and long distance phone calls—which are dominated by no more than three or four firms.

---

[2]Robert J. Shiller, "American Casino," *The Atlantic Monthly,* March 2005, p. 33.

If large sectors of American industry are not very competitive, then the price system doesn't work all that well, and the invisible hand becomes even more invisible. However, even without a perfectly competitive economic system, we can't just toss the price mechanism out the window. The forces of supply and demand, however distorted, are still operating. With all their price manipulation, even the largest corporations must guide themselves by the wishes of their consumers. In conclusion, then, let's just say that we have an imperfectly functioning price system in a less than competitive economy that is guided by a not too vigorous invisible hand.

Trust

You'll find the saying, "IN GOD WE TRUST," printed on the back of our currency. Some cynic made up another saying, "In God we trust; all others pay cash"—which means, we suspect that your check might bounce, so we insist on being paid right now in cash.

But despite our cynicism, capitalism is based on trust. Lenders expect borrowers to pay them on time and in full. Sellers ship goods or provide services in advance of payment. And although all businesses guard against theft, the presumption is that the people you deal with are not out to steal from you. Indeed, we build up business relationships over time, and those relationships are based largely on trust.

Capitalism is based on trust.

Because of that underlying trust, business flows smoothly in virtually all capitalist societies. Although the parties to major transactions are bound by formal legal contracts, day-to-day business is usually conducted in person, by phone, by fax, or by e-mail.

Imagine doing business in a socialist or communist economy. You need to order a pencil. So you make out a purchase order, hand it to your supervisor, the purchase order goes up through five more levels of authority, and is then sent to a government purchasing agency where it might sit for several months before some bureaucrat gets around to taking the necessary action. If you're lucky, you'll have your pencil by the end of the year.

Of course government agencies are not all so inefficient, but the reason they are often so bound by rules and regulations is the presumption that bureaucrats can't be trusted to make any business decisions on their own. Under capitalism, we assume that individuals will do the right thing, and because most people are quite trustworthy, the system works very efficiently.

Equity and Efficiency

Under our economic system, most of the important decisions are made in the marketplace. The forces of supply and demand (that is, the price system) determine the answers to the three basic questions we raised at the beginning of the chapter: What? How? And for whom? Most economists would agree that this system leads to a very efficient allocation of resources, which, incidentally, happens to conform to our definition of economics: *Economics is the efficient allocation of the scarce means of production toward the satisfaction of human wants.*

So far, so good. But does our system lead to a fair, or equitable, distribution of income? Just look around you. You don't have to look far to see homeless people, street beggars, shopping-bag ladies, and derelicts. Indeed, there are about 37 million Americans whom the federal government has officially classified as "poor." Later in this chapter, we'll see that one of the basic functions of our government is to transfer some income from the rich and the middle class to the poor. Under the capitalist system, there are huge differences in income, with some people living in mansions and others in the streets. One of the most controversial political issues of our time is how far the government should go in redistributing some of society's income to the poor.

Is our income distributed fairly?

Very briefly, the case for efficiency is to have the government stand back and allow everyone to work hard, earn a lot of money, and keep nearly all of it. But what about the people who don't or can't work hard, and what about their children? Do we let them starve to death? The case for equity is to tax away some of the money earned by the relatively well-to-do and redistribute it to the poor. But doing so raises two questions:

(1) How much money should we redistribute? and (2) Won't this "handout" just discourage the poor from working? We'll discuss this further in the chapter on income distribution and poverty toward the end of the book.

The Circular Flow Model

In Chapter 2 we talked about the four basic resources—land, labor, capital, and entrepreneurial ability. Who owns these resources? We all do. Nearly all of us sell our labor, for which we earn wages or salaries. In addition, many people own land or buildings for which they receive rent. A landlord may have just one tenant paying a few hundred dollars a month, or she may own an office building whose rent is reckoned by the square foot.

We also may receive interest payments for the use of our funds. Since much of the money we put into the bank is borrowed by businesses to invest in plant and equipment, we say that interest is a return on capital.

Finally, there are profits. Those who perform an entrepreneurial function (that is, own and run a business) receive profits for income.

What do people do with their incomes?

The question we are asking here is: What do people *do* with their incomes? What happens to the tremendous accumulation of rent, wages and salaries, interest, and profit? Mostly, it is spent on consumer goods and services, which are produced by private businesses.

This is the essence of what economists call the *circular flow model*. A model is usually a smaller, simplified version of the real thing. (Think of a model plane, a model ship, a map, or a globe.) An economic model shows us how our economy functions, tracing the flow of money, resources, and goods and services. Let's take the circular flow model step by step.

First we have some 117 million households receiving their incomes mainly from the business sector. A household may be a conventional family—a father, mother, and a couple of children—it may be a person living alone, or it may be two cohabiting adults. Any combination of people under one roof—you name it—is defined as a household.

Who owns our resources? It is not the employer who pays wages—he only handles the money. It is the product that pays wages.

—Henry Ford

We diagram the household income stream in Figure 2. Businesses send money income (rent, wages and salaries, interest, and profits) to households. We've ignored the government sector (that is, Social Security checks, welfare benefits, food stamps) and the foreign trade sector.

In Figure 3 we show where this money goes. It goes right back to the businesses as payment for all the goods and services that households buy. In sum, the households provide business with resources—land, labor, capital, and entrepreneurial ability—and use the income these resources earn to buy the goods and services produced by these same resources.

In effect, then, we have a circular flow of resources, income, goods and services, and payments for these goods and services. By combining Figures 2 and 3, we show this circular flow in Figure 4.

There are two circular flows.

We can distinguish two circular flows in Figure 4. In the inner circle, we have resources (land, labor, capital, and entrepreneurial ability) flowing from households to business firms. The business firms transform these resources into goods and services, which then flow to the households.

The outer circular flow is composed of money. Households receive wages and salaries, rent, interest, and profits from business firms. This money is spent on goods and services, so it is sent back to business firms in the form of consumer expenditures.

Thus we have two circular flows: (1) money and (2) resources, and goods and services. These two flows represent the economic activities of the private sector. Whenever any transaction takes place, someone pays for it, which is exactly what *does* happen whenever we do business.

Although the circular flow model may appear fairly complex, it actually oversimplifies the exchanges in our economy by excluding imports, exports, and the government sector. I leave it to your imagination to picture the additional flow of taxes, government purchases, and transfer payments such as unemployment and Social Security benefits. We shall now look at the government's economic role, but our analysis will be separate from our analysis of the private sector.

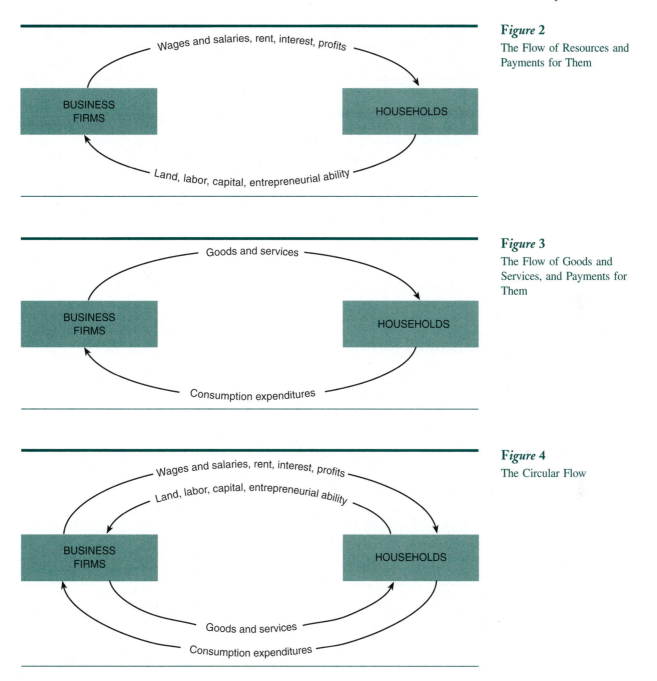

Figure 2
The Flow of Resources and Payments for Them

Figure 3
The Flow of Goods and Services, and Payments for Them

Figure 4
The Circular Flow

The Economic Role of Government

The government under our federal system has three distinct tiers. At the top is the federal, or national, government, which we generally refer to as "the government." There are also 50 state governments and tens of thousands of local governments.

Each of these units of government collects taxes, provides services, and issues regulations that have a profound effect on our economy. By taxing, spending, and regulating, the government is able somewhat to alter the outcome of the three questions: What? How? and For whom?

The government provides the legal system under which our free enterprise economy can operate. It enforces business contracts and defines the rights of private ownership. Our legal system works so well that bribery is the very rare exception, rather than the rule, as it is in so many other countries, especially in Asia and Africa.

The government also maintains our competitive system and ensures the relatively unfettered operation of the law of supply and demand. Barriers to competition are sometimes broken down by the government, particularly when a few large firms attempt to squeeze their smaller competitors out of a market. We'll discuss those efforts more fully in the chapter on corporate mergers and antitrust in *Economics* and in *Microeconomics*.

Some of what we produce is done in response to government demand for roads, schools, courthouses, stamp pads, and missile systems. Government regulations have prevented business firms from producing heroin, cyclamates (from the mid-1960s to the late 1970s), and alcoholic beverages (from 1920 to 1933), as well as prostitutes' services (except in part of the state of Nevada, where they are legal).

How things are produced is also influenced by child labor laws, health and safety regulations, and pollution control. And finally, the government, by taking over $3 trillion away from wage earners in taxes, redistributes some of these funds to the old, the disabled, and the poor, thus strongly altering the outcome of the question "For whom?"

The government must provide the infrastructure for a market system to function efficiently. In addition to ensuring that competition flourishes, the government must see that information flows freely, that property rights are protected, and that unpleasant side effects such as pollution are minimized.

Market Failure

Markets don't always provide the most desirable economic outcomes. For example, we assume a great deal of competition among firms, but what happens when some firms grow larger and larger, driving out their smaller competitors? What if one giant firm like Microsoft corners almost the entire market? In the chapter on corporate mergers and antitrust in *Economics* and *Microeconomics,* we'll see how the government has intervened to preserve competition.

When our resources are not allocated efficiently, we have market failure. So while we might prefer to leave as much as we can to the forces of demand and supply, it is sometimes necessary for the government to take action.

We'll examine three basic classes of market failure: externalities, environmental pollution, and the lack of public goods and services. Each provides the government with the opportunity to improve on the work of Adam Smith's invisible hand.

Externalities

Your own property is at stake when your neighbor's house is on fire.

–Horace (Roman poet)–

When you drive to school, how much does your ride cost you? Once you figure in the cost of gas, oil, insurance, and the depreciation on your car, you might come up with a figure of, say, 35 cents a mile. We call that 35 cents the *private cost* of driving to school.

External cost

But there's also an *external cost.* You cause a certain amount of pollution and congestion, and we could even factor in the cost of highway construction and maintenance. It would be hard to actually come up with a monetary figure, but there is no question that your drive to school imposes a definite social, or external, cost on society.

You probably never thought that driving to school was such a terrible thing, especially if there is no convenient public transportation. But you will be happy to know that you are capable of doing many socially beneficial things as well. If you paint your house and plant a beautiful garden in your front yard, you will not only add to the beauty of your neighborhood, but you will also enhance its property values. So now you are providing an *external benefit.*

External benefit

Let's define *external cost* and *external benefit. An external cost occurs when the production or consumption of some good or service inflicts costs on a third party without compensation. An external benefit occurs when some of the benefits derived from the production or consumption of some good or service are enjoyed by a third party.*

Definition of external cost and benefit

Shipbreaking

When ships grow too old and expensive to run—usually after about 25 or 30 years—their owners sell them on the international scrap market, where the typical freighter may bring a million dollars for the weight of its steel. Are the ship owners behaving in an environmentally correct manner, like those of us who return our soda cans to the grocery or deposit them in recycling bins? It turns out that they are not.

About 90 percent of the world's annual crop of 700 condemned ships are sailed right up on the beaches of China, Pakistan, India, and Bangladesh, where they are dismantled. Predictably, these once pristine beaches have become an environmental wasteland. In an *Atlantic Monthly* article, William Langewiesche describes the risks to which the workers are exposed: "falls, fires, explosions, and exposure to a variety of poisons from fuel oil, lubricants, paints, wiring, insulation, and cargo slop. Many workers are killed every year."*

What the United States and other industrial nations have done is exported our environmental problems to the less developed countries of the world. Langewiesche explains how this came about:

Shipbreaking was performed with cranes and heavy equipment at salvage docks by the big shipyards of the United States and Europe until the 1970s, when labor costs and environmental regulations drove most of the business to the docksides of Korea and Taiwan. Eventually, however, even these entrepreneurial countries started losing interest in the business and gradually decided they had better uses for their shipyards. This meant that the world's shipbreaking business was again up for grabs. In the 1980s enterprising businessmen in India, Bangladesh, and Pakistan seized the initiative with a simple, transforming idea: to break a ship they did not need expensive docks and tools; they could just wreck the thing—drive the ship up onto a beach as they might a fishing boat, and tear it apart by hand.†

---

*William Langewiesche, "The Shipbreakers," *The Atlantic Monthly,* August 2000, p. 34.

†Ibid., p. 33.

The private market, governed solely by the forces of supply and demand, does not take into account external costs and external benefits. This is market failure. When the market failure imposes a high cost on society, we demand that the government do something about it.

Basically, the government can take three types of action. If you are doing something that provides an external benefit, such as running a family farm, the government may provide you with a subsidy to encourage you to continue farming. As we saw back in Chapter 1, although the federal government has paid out hundreds of billions of dollars in farm subsidies since the 1930s, not only have most family farms disappeared, but huge corporate farms have gotten most of the subsidies.

If you are incurring external costs, the government can discourage these activities in two ways. It can tax you, or it can impose stringent regulations.

Let's consider what the government can do about air and water pollution. It could tax these activities highly enough to discourage them. A hefty tax on air pollution will force the biggest offenders to install pollution-abatement equipment. What about the disposal of nuclear waste? Do we let nuclear power plants dump it into nearby rivers but make them pay high taxes for the privilege? Hardly. The federal government heavily regulates nuclear plants.

Basically, we want to encourage activities that provide external benefits and discourage those that incur external costs. One method now used in many states is the five-cent deposit on cans and bottles. Millions of people have a monetary incentive to do the right thing by returning these bottles and cans for recycling.

A major part of the external costs of manufacturing and commerce affect our environment. Obvious examples include strips of tires along the highways, abandoned cars, acid rain, and toxic waste. The accompanying box discusses an international example of external costs—shipbreaking.

Air pollution and water pollution are perhaps the two greatest external costs of industrial economies. Let's see how the government can curb pollution.

Curbing Environmental Pollution

The incentive to pollute is much stronger than the incentive to curb pollution.

Left to its own devices, private enterprise creates a great deal of pollution. After all, it's a whole lot easier—and cheaper—to dump waste products into nearby rivers and streams, or send them up a smokestack. The government, most notably the federal Environmental Protection Agency, has taken two types of measures to lower pollution levels—command-and-control regulations and incentive-based regulations.

Command-and-Control Regulations   Automobile fuel-burning emissions are a major cause of air pollution. The federal government has imposed three regulations which have substantially reduced these emissions—mandating the use of catalytic converters on all new vehicles, fuel economy standards for all new cars, and a ban on leaded gasoline. Overall, these regulations have greatly reduced air pollution from motor vehicles. However, fuel economy standards were supposed to be raised periodically (more miles per gallon), but these increases have been periodically postponed. Furthermore, these standards are applied just to new cars, exempting minivans and sports utility vehicles (SUVs), which are classified as light trucks, and not subject to the fuel standards. Today cars are just half of all new passenger vehicles.

Since the passage of the Clean Air Act in 1972, which requires companies to reduce air pollution, there has been a marked improvement in air quality throughout much of the United States. During the decade of the 1990s alone, concentrations of sulfur dioxide and carbon monoxide decreased by 36 percent, and lead by 60 percent.

Do command-and-control regulations work? Clearly they do. But can we do better? Nearly all economists would agree we can do better using incentive-based regulations.

Incentive-Based Regulations   How can we give people an incentive to cause less air pollution? Why don't we raise gasoline taxes to the same levels as in Western Europe? Can you guess why we don't? Imagine that you are a member of Congress getting ready to vote on raising the federal tax on gasoline to $4 a gallon. Your constituents back home would not be very happy campers, and, if you were planning any kind of political future, you would not vote for this tax increase.

Emissions rights trading

Perhaps the most promising approach to incentive-based regulations is emissions rights trading, which originated as a result of the 1990 Amendments to the Clean Air Act. The government determines the permissible level of pollution and issues permits to each polluting firm. These permits allow up to a certain level of pollution, and the firms are allowed to buy or sell the permits.

What level of pollution is acceptable to you? Would you be willing to give up driving to reduce auto emissions to zero? Would you be willing to use a lot less electricity to curb emissions of electrical power plants? In general, would you be willing to accept a substantially lower standard of living if that would result in substantially less pollution? I think it's a pretty safe bet that your answer is "No!" to all three questions.

You can check out the pollution problems in your own neighborhood at www.epa.gov/epahome/commsearch.htm.

Lack of Public Goods and Services

A wide range of goods and services is supplied by our federal, state, and local governments. These include national defense; a court system; police protection; the construction and maintenance of streets, highways, bridges, plus water and sewer mains; environmental protection; public parks; and public schools. Few of these would be supplied by private enterprise because entrepreneurs would not be able to make a profit.

Interestingly, many of these goods and services *were* once supplied by private enterprise. The nation's first toll road, Pennsylvania's Lancaster Turnpike, was built two centuries ago. Private toll bridges were constructed all over the country. Even today, there are more than twice as many people who work in private security ("rent-a-cops," store and hotel detectives, building security, campus security, and private investigators, for example) than there are city and state police. Our national rail lines were once privately owned, with such fabled names as the Pennsylvania (or Pennsy) Railroad; the Baltimore and Ohio (you'll still find the B&O on the Monopoly board); the Seaboard; the Southern; the Great Northern; the New York Central; the New York, New Haven, and Hartford; the Boston and Maine; the Southern Pacific; and the storied Atchison, Topeka, and the Santa Fe.

Let's talk about the difference between *public* goods and *private* goods. Private goods are easy. You buy a car. It's your car. But a public good is something whose consumption by one person does not prevent its consumption by other people. Take our national defense. If you want to pay to have your home defended from nuclear attack, then everyone on your block is defended as well, even though they don't chip in a cent. Or, if your block association hires a private security firm to patrol your neighborhood, even your neighbors who were too cheap to pay their dues are protected.

Difference between public and private goods

Not everything produced by the public sector is a public good. We mentioned defense as a public good—something whose consumption by one person does not prevent its consumption by other people. What about a ride on a public bus? Or driving on the Jersey Turnpike? These are not public goods because only those who pay get to ride.

Public goods and services have two defining characteristics. First, they are *nonexcludable,* which means that once it exists, everyone can freely benefit from it. You can benefit from unpolluted air whether or not you helped pay for it. Second, public goods and services are *nonrivalrous,* which means that one person's benefiting from it does not reduce the amount of it available for others. Police protection for you does not prevent others from also enjoying that protection.

The two defining characteristics of public goods and services

Public goods tend to be indivisible; they usually come in large units that cannot be broken into pieces for purchase or sale in private markets. Often there is no way they can be produced by private enterprise because there is no way to exclude anyone from consuming the goods even if she or he did not pay for them. National defense is a classic example. Could you imagine putting *that* service on a pay-as-you-go basis? "I think this year I'll just skip being defended." We can't exactly move the nuclear umbrella away from my house while continuing to shield those of all my neighbors.

Not everyone favors an expansion of public goods. Aristotle observed that "What is common to many is taken least care of, for all men have a greater regard for what is their own than for what they possess in common with others." Public property is often not as well maintained as private property, because, as Aristotle noted, people will take better care of their own property than of property held in common.

Government Failure

Just as the market sometimes fails us, so does the government. Below is a short list of some of the more blatant forms of government failure. Keep in mind, however, that in most cases the government performs its functions reasonably well, so these failures should be considered exceptions and not the norm.

Let's start with an obvious failure—our complex and confusing federal tax code. It costs taxpayers (in accounting fees as well as in the value of their own time) about $150 billion a year to complete their tax returns.[3] According to the Internal Revenue Service it takes 28 and a half hours to complete an average tax return with itemized deductions. The present system is so complicated that about 60 percent of all taxpayers rely on professionals to do their taxes. Even the simplest form, 1040EZ, takes on average 3 hours and 43 minutes to fill out.

Closely related are the forms the government sends all large and most medium-sized companies. It takes hundreds of hours a year to fill out these monthly, quarterly, and

The United States is the only country where it takes more brains to figure your tax than to earn the money to pay it.
—Edward J. Gurney

The hardest thing in the world to understand is the income tax.
—Albert Einstein

---

[3]It costs business firms an additional $125 billion to comply with our tax code.

annual forms. The government compiles copious statistics on the economy, which it then publishes in thousands of monthly, quarterly, and annual reports. I enjoyed dropping in to my local federal bookstore to peruse these publications and would usually buy a few. But the stores were closed in 2003 to save money. Question: Wouldn't it then have made sense to cut down on the number of these publications? And maybe not collect so much data, thereby freeing up tens of thousands of corporate employees?

Another abject government failure is its agricultural price support program, which currently costs the taxpayers $19 billion a year, and, since its inception more than seven decades ago, has cost hundreds of billions of dollars. What is the main purpose of this program? Ostensibly the purpose is to save the family farm. But since the 1930s millions of family farms have gone out of business; most of the payments now go to huge corporate farms.

A society should be judged largely by how it treats its children. Of the 39 million Americans living in poverty, more than half are children. In the 1960s President Lyndon Johnson declared a massive war on poverty, and some 30 years later came the Welfare Reform Act of 1996. And yet, today, one of every six American children is growing up poor.

Our public education system, once the envy of the world, is now the laughingstock. While we still have some of the finest schools of higher education, our elementary, middle, and high schools have been deteriorating for decades. The fact that we need to teach the three r's—reading, writing, and arithmetic—to millions of college students pretty much says it all. While all the blame for our failing educational system cannot be placed on the government's doorstep, the fact remains that getting a decent education has become a difficult challenge for most children. I am old enough to remember when high school graduates could actually read, write, and do some algebra and geometry.

Hurricane Katrina is still fresh enough in our memory that if I asked you to grade the government's response, I'm sure you would have a pretty strong opinion. You might give a failing grade to the state and local authorities, to the federal government, or to all three. But regardless of how the blame is apportioned, Hurricane Katrina provides a very clear example of government failure.

Millions of Americans helped the hurricane victims, directly or indirectly. But these private efforts were directed at ameliorating the suffering, rather than preventing it. In hindsight, New Orleans and its suburbs should have been fully evacuated, and once the flooding took place, those left behind should have been quickly rescued. Those were not jobs for individuals, voluntary organizations, or business firms, but mainly for the federal government.

Local and state officials, as well as the Army Corps of Engineers, knew only too well that New Orleans' levees would not be able to hold back the floodwaters produced by a major hurricane. Once the city began to flood, only federal agencies such as FEMA (Federal Emergency Management Agency) had the resources to deal with a catastrophe of this magnitude. While there are plenty of places to spread the blame of the slow and halting rescue and recovery effort, maybe someone should have sent President Bush a copy of the placard President Harry Truman kept on his desk. It read: "The buck stops here."

Like you, I have a pretty strong opinion of which government officials should be blamed. Dealing with hurricanes, other natural disasters, as well as terrorist attacks is very clearly a government function. In late August and early September of 2005 our government very badly failed the people on the Gulf Coast. Will our government be better prepared when the next disaster strikes?

In contrast to government failure, large companies such as Walmart, Home Depot, and FedEx were the first responders in the wake of Hurricane Katrina. The October 3, 2005 issue of *Fortune* sings the praises of these companies, which had, as our army generals like to say, boots on the ground. While the government took precious days to act, these and other large companies made plans days in advance, and put them into effect hours after the hurricane made landfall.

Just by staying open for business, these and other companies provided a lifeline to hurricane victims. Jessica Lewis, the co-manager of the Waveland, Mississippi Walmart, had to deal with two feet of water and tons of damaged stock. Here is an account of what she saw and how she reacted:

> As the sun set on Waveland, a nightmarish scene unfolded on Highway 90. She saw neighbors wandering around with bloody feet because they had fled their homes with no shoes. Some wore only underwear. "It broke my heart to see them like this," Lewis recalls. "These were my kid's teachers. Some of them were *my* teachers. They were the parents of the kids on my kid's sports teams. They were my neighbors. They were my customers."
>
> Lewis felt there was only one thing to do. She had her stepbrother clear a path through the mess in the store with a bulldozer. Then she salvaged everything she could and handed it out in the parking lot. She gave socks and underwear to shivering Waveland police officers who had climbed into trees to escape the rising water. She handed out shoes to her barefoot neighbors and diapers for their babies. She gave people bottled water to drink and sausages, stored high in the warehouse, that hadn't been touched by the flood. She even broke into the pharmacy and got insulin and drugs for AIDS patients. "This is the right thing to do," she recalls thinking. "I hope my bosses aren't going to have a problem with that."[4]

While all Walmart managers might not have acted as altruistically as Jessica Lewis, the company made a major difference simply by staying open, keeping their stores stocked with food and water, and, in keeping with their slogan, charging low, everyday prices. Unlike price gougers who drove into the disaster area to sell portable generators for $1,500, Walmart sold theirs at their regular $300 price.

Finally, let's talk about the Medicare drug prescription plan, which was rammed through Congress in 2005 by President George W. Bush and Republican Congressional leaders and has caused mass confusion among senior citizens, pharmacists, doctors, nursing home administrators, and the dozens of participating insurance companies. When the new plan went into effect in January 2006, hundreds of thousands of senior citizens were turned away by their pharmacies when they came in to have their prescriptions filled. It would be charitable to say that the system had some glitches that needed to be worked out. Writing in *The New York Times,* Jane Gross described some of the complexities of the drug prescription plan, and the problems they have caused:

> Even those who received their new prescription drug cards on time are not home free. Each person has an ID number, an Issuer number, an Rx Bin number, an Rx PCN number and an Rx Group number. Type one digit wrong when ordering medications and the computer flashes an error message.
>
> …
>
> Each plan also has tiered subplans, labeled bronze, silver or gold. And each of those has its own formulary, the list of drugs that are covered, and its own appeals process for those that are not. But search the plans' websites looking for instructions for appeals. "Sorry, the document you request doesn't exist," comes the mannerly reply.[5]

Capital

Capital is the crucial element in every economic system. Karl Marx's classic *Das Kapital* examined the role of capital in the mid-19th-century industrializing economy of England. According to Marx, the central figure of capitalism is the capitalist, or business owner, who makes huge profits by exploiting his workers. Capital consists mainly of plant, equipment, and software. Marx said that whoever controlled a society's capital controlled that society.

Furthermore, Marx observed that one's social consciousness was determined by one's relationship to the means of production. Inevitably, he believed, there would be a clash between the capitalists and the workers, leading to an overthrow of capitalism and the establishment of a communist society. Then the workers would own the means of

Karl Marx, German economist, historian, and philosopher

---

[4]Devin Leonard, "The Only Lifeline Was the Wal-Mart," *Fortune,* October 3, 2005, p. 75.

[5]Jane Gross, "Nursing Homes Confront New Drug Plan's Hurdles," *The New York Times,* January 15, 2006, p. 16.

Where Capital Comes From

The following hypothetical situation will illustrate the value of capital. Suppose it takes a man 10 hours to make an optical lens, while someone working with a machine can make one in just 5 hours. Let's assume that it would take 1,000 hours to build such a machine.

Assume, however, that a person working 10 hours a day is barely able to support himself and his family. (Karl Marx observed that, in most working-class families, not only did wives work, but they didn't have to worry about day care centers or baby-sitters for the children because factories employed six- and seven-year-olds.) If he could not afford to spend 100 days (1,000 hours) building the machine, he still had two choices. He could cut back on his consumption—that is, lower his family's standard of living—by working nine hours a day on the lenses and one hour a day on building the machine. Or he could work, say, an extra hour a day on the machine.

In either case, it would take 1,000 days to build the machine. If he cut back on his consumption *and* worked an extra hour a day, it would take him 500 days to build the machine.

Once he had the machine, he'd *really* be in business. He could double his daily output from one lens a day to two a day (remember that a person working with a machine can turn out a lens in just 5 hours).

Each day, if he held his consumption to the same level, he would produce two lenses and sell one for food, rent, and other necessities. The other lens he'd save. At the end of just 100 days, he'd have saved 100 lenses. Those 100 lenses represent 1,000 hours of labor, which is exactly the same amount of labor that went into building a machine. He would probably be able to buy another machine with those 100 lenses.

Now he's *really* a capitalist! He'll hire someone to run the second machine and pay him a lens a day. And in another 100 days, he'll have a surplus of 200 lenses, and he'll be able to buy two more machines, hire a foreman to run his shop, retire to a condominium in Miami Beach at the age of 36, and be the richest kid on the block.

---

production. In the Soviet Union, incidentally, the means of production *were* owned by the workers, but the ruling elite, the top Communist Party officials, had real economic and political control.

Capital consists of plant and equipment.

The central economic role of capital

The role of capital in the production process is central to why our country is rich and most of the rest of the world is poor. The reason an American farmer can produce 10 or 20 times as much as a Nigerian farmer is that the American has much more capital with which to work—combines, tractors, harvesters, and reapers. And the reason the American factory worker is more productive than the Brazilian factory worker is that our factories are much better equipped. We have a tremendous stock of computers, assembly lines, warehouses, machine tools, and so on.

Take the example of the word processor and its successor, the personal computer. In the past, a lot of business letters had to be personally or individually typed, although they were really only form letters. Today we have a PC that can be programmed to print identical texts with different addresses at the rate of one letter every couple of seconds.

Our stock of capital enables us to turn out many more goods per hour of labor than we could produce without it. Much backbreaking as well as tedious labor has been eliminated by machines. Without our capital, we would have the same living standard as that of people living in the poorer countries of Asia, Africa, and Latin America.

Where did capital come from?

Where did capital come from? Essentially from savings. Some people would set aside part of their savings, go into business, and purchase plant and equipment (see the box, "Where Capital Comes From"). But we're really skipping a step.

Initially there was no capital, except for some crude plows and other farm tools. People worked from sunrise to sunset just to produce enough food to put on the table. But a few farmers, a little more prosperous than their neighbors, were able to spare some time to build better farm tools. Or they might have had enough food stored away to employ someone to build these tools. Either way, some productive resources were diverted from producing consumer goods to producing capital goods.

The factory conditions of the 19th-century England that Marx described in *Das Kapital* were barbaric, but the end result was that a surplus of consumer goods was produced. The factory owner, by paying his workers meager wages, was able to use this surplus to buy more capital goods. These enabled his factory to be more productive, creating still greater surpluses that were used to purchase still more plant and equipment.

Under Joseph Stalin, the Russians devoted a large part of their production to capital goods, literally starving the Russian population of consumer goods. To this day there is a great shortage of consumer goods in the former Soviet Union. But this shortage is no longer due to diversion of resources from production of consumer goods to the production of capital goods. It is due to the inefficiencies of the economic system itself—something we'll be looking at more closely in the closing pages of this chapter.

In the years following World War II, Japan and the countries of Western Europe, struggling to rebuild their shattered economies, held down their consumption as they concentrated on building new plant and equipment. The South Koreans and Taiwanese later followed this model of building capital.

The world's developing nations face nearly insurmountable obstacles—rapidly growing populations and very little plant and equipment. The experience of the industrializing nations in the 19th century was that, as people moved into cities from the countryside and as living standards rose, the birthrate invariably declined. But for industrialization to take place, capital must be built up. There are two ways to do this: Cut consumption or raise production. Unfortunately, most developing nations are already at subsistence levels, so no further cuts in consumption are possible without causing even greater misery. And production cannot easily be raised without at least some plant and equipment.

With the exception of the OPEC nations, which have been able to sell their oil in exchange for plant and equipment, the poorer nations of Africa, Asia, and Latin America have little hope of rising from extreme poverty. A supposed exchange of letters that took place between Mao Tse-tung and Nikita Khrushchev when China and the Soviet Union were allies in the early 1960s illustrates the futility of a third way out—foreign aid.

Mao: Send us machinery and equipment.
Khrushchev: Tighten your belts.
Mao: Send us some belts.

Capital is past savings accumulated for future production.

—Jackson Martindell

Capital is the key to our standard of living.

The "Isms": Capitalism, Communism, Fascism, and Socialism

Q: What is the difference between capitalism and socialism?
A: Under capitalism, man exploits man. Under socialism, it's just the opposite.

–Overheard in Warsaw–[6]

Property is the exploitation of the weak by the strong.
Communism is the exploitation of the strong by the weak.

–Pierre-Joseph Proudhon–[7]

During the 20th century, perhaps no three opprobriums have been hurled more often at political opponents than those of Communist! Capitalist! and Fascist! Let's compare the four great economic systems. Capitalism, as we've already seen, is characterized by private ownership of most of the means of production—that is, land, labor, capital, and entrepreneurial ability. Individuals are moved to produce by the profit motive. Production is also guided by the price system. Thus, we have millions of people competing for the consumer's dollar. The government's role in all of this is kept to a minimum; basically, it ensures that everyone sticks to the rules.

Capitalism

Since the early 1980s there has been a huge swing throughout much of the world towards capitalism. First capitalism took root in China, and a decade later in the former Soviet Union and in what had been its satellite empire in Eastern Europe as well. Today the great preponderance of the world's output of goods and services is produced under capitalism.

---

[6]Lloyd G. Reynolds, *Microeconomic Analysis and Policy,* 6th ed. (Burr Ridge, IL: Richard D. Irwin, 1988), p. 435.
[7]Pierre-Joseph Proudhon, *What Is Property?* chap. V, Part II.

Capitalism is often confused with democracy. A democracy has periodic elections in which the voters freely choose their rulers. Most capitalistic nations—for example, the United States, Japan, and the members of the European Union—are democracies.

On the opposite end of the political spectrum is the dictatorship, under which the rulers perpetuate themselves in power. Their elections do not have secret ballots, so predictably the rulers always win overwhelmingly. Indeed, Saddam Hussein received 100 percent of the vote in Iraq's 2002 presidential election.

Sometimes capitalistic dictatorships evolve into capitalistic democracies. Taiwan, South Korea, Indonesia, the Philippines, and Chile are recent examples. The Soviet Union, which has been going through a painful conversion from communism to capitalism, now holds relatively free elections, and could be considered a democracy. There are hopes that China will also evolve into a democracy. But the leaders of the Communist Party, who have handed power down from one generation to the next, show no signs of allowing free elections.

"The theory of the Communists may be summed up in the single sentence: Abolition of private property," declared Karl Marx and Friedrich Engels in *The Communist Manifesto*. Who would own everything? The state. And eventually the state would wither away and we would be left with a workers' paradise.

In the Soviet version of communism, under which the state had evidently not yet withered away, most of the capitalist roles were reversed. Instead of a guidance system of prices to direct production, a government planning committee dictated exactly *what* was produced, *how* it was produced, and *for whom* the goods and services were produced. After all, the state owned and operated nearly all of the means of production and distribution.

All of the resources used had to conform to the current five-year plan. If the goal was 2 million tractors, 100 million tons of steel, 15 million bushels of wheat, and so on, Soviet workers might have expected to be putting in a lot of overtime.

The big difference between the old Soviet economy and our own is what consumer goods and services are produced. In our economy, the market forces of supply and demand dictate what gets produced and how much of it gets produced. But a government planning agency in the Soviet Union dictated what and how much was made. In effect, central planning attempted to direct a production and distribution process that works automatically in a market economy.

How well did the Soviet communist system work? Remember the chronic shortages of consumer goods we mentioned earlier in the chapter? Although Soviet president Mikhail Gorbachev went to great lengths to shake up the bureaucracy and get the economy moving again, his efforts were futile. To raise output, he found he needed to somehow remove the heavy hand of bureaucracy from the economic controls. But as he stripped away more and more of the Communist Party's power, he found that his own power had been stripped away as well.

If the Soviet Union did not exemplify pure communism, then what country did? In the box, "Real Communism," you'll read that we have had pure communism right under our noses for many years.

One of the fundamental economic problems with *any* economy that attempts to substitute government planning for the price system (or to replace the law of demand and supply with government decrees) is that changes in price no longer help producers decide what and how much to produce. In a capitalist country, higher microwave oven prices would signal producers to produce more microwave ovens. But in the Soviet Union, there was very little inflation even though there were widespread shortages of consumer goods. In fact, the Soviets came up with a great cure for inflation. Just let everyone wait in line.

The entire Soviet economy was a Rube Goldberg contraption[8] of subsidies, fixed prices, bureaucratic rules and regulations, special privileges, and outright corruption. Had Gorbachev not acted, the entire Soviet system might well have come apart by itself over another couple of generations.

A joke that circulated in the late 1980s went like this: Under communism your pockets are full of money, but there isn't anything in the stores you can buy with it. Under capitalism, the stores are full, but you have no money in your pockets.

Communism

Communism doesn't work because people like to own stuff.
—Frank Zappa, Musician

Communist: A fellow who has given up all hope of becoming a capitalist.
—Orville Reed

They pretend to pay us, and we pretend to work.
—Polish folk definition of communism

Communism was a great system for making people equally poor.
—Thomas Friedman

---
[8]Such a device is designed to accomplish by complex means what seemingly could be done simply.

Real Communism

Several years ago, I knew a history professor at St. Francis College in Brooklyn who loved to shock his students by telling them that he had been a communist. As a young man, he had joined a Catholic religious order, lived in a commune, and shared all his possessions with his fellow seminarians. "What could be more communist than living in a commune with no private property?" he asked his students.

And so we may ask whether what they had in the Soviet Union and in Eastern Europe was really communism. How would Karl Marx have reacted to those huge bureaucratic dictatorships? Marx had foreseen "the withering away of the state," until all that was left was a society of workers who followed his credo "From each according to his ability; to each according to his needs." This sounds a lot more like that history professor's seminary than what was passing for communism in the old Soviet empire.

The Soviet regime collapsed not just because of its bureaucratic inefficiencies but also because it supported a huge military establishment that claimed between one-fifth and one-quarter of its resources and national output.

In 1922 Benito Mussolini took power in Italy, leading the world's first fascist government. "Fascism should more appropriately be called corporatism, because it is the merger of state and corporate power," he declared. In effect, then, fascism turned large corporations into extension of government, while centralizing governmental authority in one person. Although Mussolini's Italy followed this model, it was Hitler's Germany, a decade later, that truly placed power in the hands of an absolute dictator.

Fascism

Fascism hasn't been in vogue since Hitler's defeat in 1945, but it does provide another model of an extreme. In Nazi Germany the ownership of resources was in private hands, while the government dictated what was to be produced.

The problem with describing the fascist economic model is that there really *is* no model. The means of production are left in private hands, with varying degrees of governmental interference. Generally those in power are highly nationalistic, so a high proportion of output is directed toward military goods and services.

Fascists have been virulently anticommunist but have also been completely intolerant of any political opposition. The one-party state, suppression of economic freedom, and a militaristic orientation have been hallmarks of fascism.

The early 1940s were evidently the high-water mark of fascism. Although from time to time a fascist state does pop up, it appears to be a temporary phenomenon. With the possible exception of Hitler's Germany, which did put most Germans back to work after the Great Depression, albeit largely at military production, most fascist states have been economic failures that apparently collapsed of their own weight.

Socialism

Socialism has not gotten the bad press that capitalism, fascism, and communism have received, perhaps because those who dislike the socialists prefer to call them communists. In fact, even Soviet government officials used to refer to themselves as socialists and their country, the U.S.S.R., was formally called the Union of Soviet Socialist Republics, although President Ronald Reagan referred to the Soviet Union as the evil empire. And the countries with socialist economies were our military allies.

It is a socialist idea that making profits is a vice; I consider the real vice is making losses.
—Winston Churchill

The economies of such countries as Sweden, Canada, Great Britain, and, recently, France and Greece have been described as socialist, not only by government officials in those countries but by outside observers as well. In general, these economies have three characteristics: (1) government ownership of some of the means of production; (2) a substantial degree of government planning; and (3) a large-scale redistribution of income from the wealthy and the well-to-do to the middle class, working class, and the poor.

One of the most familiar characteristics of socialist countries is cradle-to-grave security. Medical care, education, retirement benefits, and other essential needs are guaranteed to every citizen. All you need to do is be born.

The vice of capitalism is that it stands for the unequal sharing of blessings; whereas the virtue of socialism is that it stands for the equal sharing of misery.
—Winston Churchill

Where does the money to pay for all of this come from? It comes from taxes. Very high income taxes and inheritance taxes fall disproportionately on the upper middle class and the rich. In Israel several years ago, a joke went around about a man who received an unusually large paycheck one week. He couldn't figure out what had happened until his wife looked at his check stub and discovered that he had been sent his deductions by mistake. Only the very wealthy must give the government more than half their pay in socialist countries, but the story *did* have a ring of truth to it.

Rather than allow the market forces to function freely, socialist governments sometimes resort to very elaborate planning schemes. And since the government usually owns the basic industries and provides the basic services, this planning merely has one hand directing the other.

Swedish socialism

Sweden is often considered the archetypal socialist country, although perhaps 90 percent of the country's industry is privately owned. It is the government's massive intervention in the private economy that gives Swedish society its socialist tone. Not only has the Swedish government kept the unemployment rate generally below 3 percent for several decades by offering industry and workers a series of subsidies and incentives, but it provides one of the most elaborate cradle-to-grave programs in the world. The government doles out $100 monthly allowances for each child and provides day care centers, free education from nursery school through college, free medical care, and very generous unemployment and retirement benefits. Women may take a year off work after the birth of a child while receiving 80 percent of their pay.

Norwegian socialism

But Sweden's brand of socialism pales in comparison to that of Norway, its Scandinavian neighbor. In addition to free day care, subsidized housing and vacations, and free medical care, Norwegians receive annual stipends of more than $1,600 for every child under 17, retirement pay for homemakers, and 44 weeks of fully paid maternity leave. How do they pay for all of this? Not only does Norway have the world's highest income tax rates, but it has a 23 percent sales tax and a gasoline tax of about $5 a gallon. Hallmarks of Norwegian society are a great disdain for the trappings of wealth and power and a profound sense of equality, which militate against a wide disparity in pay.

Perhaps this joke, which has made its rounds on the Internet, may best sum up the four isms:

Socialism: You have two cows. State takes one and gives it to someone else.
Communism: You have two cows. State takes both of them and gives you milk.
Fascism: You have two cows. State takes both of them and sells you milk.
Capitalism: You have two cows. You sell one and buy a bull.

The Decline and Fall of the Communist System

Under Joseph Stalin and his successors, from the late 1920s through the 1960s, Soviet economic growth was very rapid, as government planners concentrated on building the stock of capital goods, largely neglecting consumer goods. The government purposely set prices on consumer goods very low, often not changing them for decades. They wanted even the poorest people to be able to afford the basic necessities.

By the late 1970s, China began reforms, very gradually evolving into a market economy. However the Soviet Union, through the 1980s, continued to stagnate, devoting most of its talent and capital to its military establishment. Most of its armed forces served, basically, as an army of occupation in Eastern Europe. By the time that army was withdrawn, in 1989, and defense expenditures slashed, the Soviet Union was in political turmoil. Within two years the communists, along with the huge central planning apparatus, were gone, and the Soviet Union was dismembered into 15 separate nations, the largest of which was Russia.

Transformation in China

For decades before they attained power, the Chinese communists depicted themselves as agrarian reformers who would provide hundreds of millions of landless peasants with their own farms. But soon after attaining power they abolished virtually all private property and forced about 90 percent of the population to live and work on huge collective farms.

The communists came to power in 1949, taking over one of the world's poorest nations. For the first three decades, largely under Mao Tse-tung (his friends called him Chairman

Mao, and he liked the rest of the Chinese to refer to him as "the Great Helmsman"), the Chinese economy was dominated by Soviet-style central planning. Even though the economy absorbed two extremely disruptive setbacks—the Great Leap Forward (1958–60), during which perhaps 30 million people starved to death, and the Cultural Revolution (1966–75), both of which Mao used to consolidate power—economic growth may have averaged 9 or 10 percent a year. China was pulled up from a backward country plagued by periodic famine to one in which everyone had enough to eat and many could afford to buy TVs, refrigerators, cameras, and some of the other amenities we in the United States take for granted. In 1978 there were 1 million TV sets in China; by 1998 there were nearly 300 million. Today China leads the world with more than 800 million cellphone users.

In China, as in the former Soviet Union, the big boss of a province, or of the entire country, has held the modest title of First Secretary of the Communist Party. Back in 1978 a man named Zhao Ziyang was the First Secretary in Szechuan province, which was becoming world famous for its wonderful cuisine. Until 1978, the highly centralized Chinese planning system had slowed economic growth. Zhao issued an order that year freeing six state-owned enterprises from the control of the central planners, allowing the firms to determine their own prices and output, and even to keep any profits they earned. In just two years some 6,600 firms had been cut loose, Zhao had become the Chinese head of state, and China was well on its way to becoming a market, or capitalist, economy.

The shift toward capitalism

The farmers employed by the huge collective farms had little incentive to work hard. As John McMillan noted, "It made little difference whether a farmer worked himself to exhaustion or dozed all day under a tree. Either way, the amount he took home to feed his family was much the same."[9]

Beginning in 1979 many provincial leaders across China, independent of the central authorities in Beijing, shifted the responsibility of operating huge collective farms to the families that lived on the farms. Although each family was given a production quota to meet, any additional output could be sold at a profit. By 1984 more than 90 percent of China's agricultural land was farmed by individual households. In just six years food output rose by 60 percent.

In the late 1970s and early 1980s, reform began to take hold in the industrial sector as well. State firms were free to sell any surplus output, after having met their quotas. Simultaneously millions of tiny family-run enterprises were springing up all across the land, ranging from street peddlers, owners of tiny restaurants, and bicycle repair shops, to large factories and international trading companies. By the late 1980s, many of these large private factories were at least partially owned by Chinese businessmen from Hong Kong and Taiwan, as well as by investors from Japan, other Asian countries, and even some from Western Europe and the United States. China's southern provinces, and especially her coastal cities, have become veritable "export platforms," sending out a stream of toys, consumer electronics, textiles, clothing, and other low-tech products mainly to consumers in Japan, Europe, and North America. Between 1978 and 2000, Chinese exports rose from $5 billion to more than $200 billion, and by 2007 to $1.2 trillion. In 2009 its export surplus with the United States was $227 billion.

The agricultural and industrial reforms diluted the ideological purity that had marked the first 30 years of communist rule. In 1984 the Communist Party's Central Committee went so far as to depart from the traditional communist credo "From each according to his ability, to each according to his needs." The new slogan was "More pay for more work; less pay for less work." What this did, implicitly, was to say to budding entrepreneurs, "It's OK if you get rich—you worked hard for your money."

To get rich is glorious.
—Deng Xiaoping

Although average family income has at least quintupled since 1978, China remains a relatively poor agricultural nation with two-thirds of its population living in rural areas. But it has 1.3 billion people (one out of every five people on this planet lives in China), and it has become a world class industrial power. Already the world's largest exporter, China passed Japan in 2009 to become the number one automobile producer.

China today, despite its lip service to following the precepts of communism, has a basically capitalist economy. Although a couple of hundred large state enterprises

---

[9]John McMillan, *Reinventing the Bazaar* (New York: W. W. Norton, 2002), p. 94.

continue to spew out industrial goods, about three-quarters of the nation's output is produced by privately owned firms. Today more Chinese have stock brokerage accounts than are members of the communist party.

Current Issue: The Bridge to Nowhere

If the quest for profits motivates business owners, then what motivates members of Congress? They want to get reelected. And they're quite good at it: Over 98 percent of our representatives get reelected every two years.

The most effective campaign issue of every member of Congress is that they can bring home the bacon. They can point to the highways, bridges, rapid transit systems, military bases, and courthouses for which the federal government shelled out hundreds of millions of dollars. Never mind that, in the process, we have been running record federal budget deficits. The important thing is that your representative delivers.

Every member of Congress has a very strong incentive to bring home as much federal money as possible. So we have 435 Congressional districts competing for this money. It doesn't matter whether the projects are good or bad as long as the money is being spent. So what we have here is systematic government failure.

A handful of states, Alaska among them—are so sparsely populated that they have just one member of the House of Representatives. Alaska, for example, the third least populated state, is represented by Don Young, who happened to be the chairman of the House Committee on Transportation and Infrastructure. So perhaps it was no coincidence that when the Transit Act of 2005 was passed, Alaska got $941 million, the fourth largest amount received by any state. The two key projects funded were $231 million for a bridge near Anchorage called the "bridge to nowhere" and $233 million for another bridge connecting the tiny village of Ketchikan to an island with 50 inhabitants.

The "bridge to nowhere," to be formally called "Don Young's Way," would connect Anchorage with a swampy undeveloped port. The Ketchikan bridge would carry an estimated 100 cars a day, saving them a seven-minute ferry ride. So if the federal government would foot the bill, Alaska would take the money and run.

In 2006, in response to the widespread ridicule of this dubious project, Congress removed the federal earmark for the bridge, but allowed Alaska to use the money for other transportation projects. Among them was a $25 million "road to nowhere," which was built on the island—actually an access road to the nonexistent bridge. Faithful to its name, virtually no one among the island's 50 residents seems to make use of this road.

Questions for Further Thought and Discussion

1. The circular flow model is a simplified version of our economy. Describe how this model works.

2. What are the three basic economic questions that all economies must answer? Describe the differences in the ways capitalism and socialism answer these questions.

3. What was Adam Smith's invisible hand, and what economic function did it serve?

4. What are the two basic classes of market failure? What would be an example of each?

5. Can you think of any other government failures in addition to those listed in the chapter?

6. How far has China evolved into a market economy? To what degree has this evolution contributed to China's economic growth?

7. For many years Americans referred to the People's Republic of China as "Communist China." Why would that label be misleading today?

8. Explain why you would prefer to live in a socialist or a capitalist country.

9. *Practical Application:* Conduct your own investigation of government waste. Go to Google.com, type in "government waste," and compile a list of wasteful spending projects.

Workbook for Chapter 3

Name _____   Date _____

Multiple-Choice Questions

Circle the letter that corresponds to the best answer.

1. We have a mixed economy because
   _____. (LO1)
   a) we produce guns and butter
   b) we consume domestically produced goods as well as imports
   c) we consume both goods and services
   d) there is a private sector and a public sector

2. Which does not fit with the others? (LO2)
   a) competition
   b) government planning and regulation
   c) the invisible hand
   d) the price mechanism

3. Adam Smith believed the best way to promote the public interest was to _____. (LO2)
   a) have the government produce most goods and services
   b) let people pursue their own selfish interests
   c) wait for individuals to set out to promote the public interest
   d) get rid of the price mechanism

4. Our economy does a very good job with respect to _____. (LO2)
   a) both equity and efficiency
   b) equity, but not efficiency
   c) efficiency, but not equity
   d) neither equity nor efficiency

5. Which is the most accurate statement? (LO1, 9)
   a) No country could be classified as having a communist economic system.
   b) It could be argued that every nation has a mixed economy.
   c) The United States is basically a socialist economy.
   d) The Chinese economy is evolving away from capitalism and toward pure communism.

6. Adam Smith believed people are guided by all of the following except _____. (LO2)
   a) the profit motive
   b) self-interest
   c) the public good
   d) the invisible hand

7. The price system is based on _____. (LO2)
   a) government regulation (i.e., the government sets most prices)
   b) the individual whim of the businessperson who sets it
   c) the feelings of the individual buyer
   d) supply and demand

8. Which one of the following would be the best public policy? (LO4)
   a) Zero tolerance for pollution.
   b) Allow private business firms to curb their own pollution.
   c) Provide business firms with incentives to curb their pollution.
   d) Hold economic growth to a minimum until pollution levels are reduced substantially.

9. In the United States, nearly all resources are owned by _____. (LO1)
   a) the government
   b) business firms
   c) individuals
   d) foreigners

10. The pilgrims who settled Plymouth, Massachusetts, concluded that _____. (LO2)
    a) only a social society of collective ownership would make economic sense
    b) a capitalist society with large industrial corporations would make economic sense
    c) private ownership worked better than collective ownership
    d) from each according to his ability to each according to his wants was the best course to follow

11. Wages, rent, interest, and profits flow from _____. (LO3)
    a) business firms to households
    b) households to business firms
    c) business firms to the government
    d) the government to business firms

12. Private ownership of most of the means of production is common to _____. (LO7)
   a) capitalism and communism
   b) capitalism and fascism
   c) capitalism and socialism
   d) fascism and communism

13. The price mechanism is least important under _____. (LO2, 7)
   a) capitalism
   b) socialism
   c) fascism
   d) communism

14. The five-year plan had been the main economic plan of _____. (LO7, 8)
   a) the United States
   b) Sweden
   c) Nazi Germany
   d) the Soviet Union

15. Fascism peaked in the _____. (LO7)
   a) 1920s
   b) 1930s
   c) 1940s
   d) 1950s

16. The strongest criticism of Sweden's economic system has been that _____. (LO7)
   a) it provides too many benefits
   b) its taxes are too high
   c) its taxes are too low
   d) it doesn't provide enough benefits

17. The strongest indictment of the capitalist system was written by _____. (LO7)
   a) Adam Smith
   b) John Maynard Keynes
   c) Rose D. Cohen
   d) Karl Marx

18. Karl Marx said that _____. (LO7, 8)
   a) whoever controlled a society's capital controlled that society
   b) in the long run, capitalism would survive
   c) the U.S.S.R.'s communist system was "state capitalism"
   d) capitalists and workers generally had the same economic interests

19. The main reason the American farmer can produce more than the farmer in China is that he _____. (LO1, 6)
   a) has more land
   b) has more capital
   c) has more labor
   d) is better trained

20. Capital comes from _____. (LO2, 6)
   a) gold
   b) savings
   c) high consumption
   d) the government

21. An individual can build up his/her capital _____. (LO2)
   a) by working longer hours only
   b) by cutting back on consumption only
   c) by both cutting back on consumption and working longer hours
   d) only by borrowing

22. Which is the most accurate statement about shipbreaking? (LO4)
   a) It is generally done in a manner that is environmentally sound and that minimizes dangers to workers.
   b) It is an extremely profitable activity that is sought after by the world's largest shipbuilders.
   c) Ship owners whose boats have grown too old and expensive to run usually abandon them at sea or sink them.
   d) The United States and other industrial nations have exported their environmental problems like shipbreaking to less developed countries such as India, Bangladesh, and Pakistan.

Fill-In Questions

1. The invisible hand is generally associated with (a) the _____ and (b) _____. (LO2)

2. Adam Smith believed that if people set out to promote the public interest, they will not do nearly as much good as they will if they _____. (LO2)

3. Defense spending and police protection are examples of _____. (LO4, 5)

4. Painting the outside of your house and planting a garden in your front yard are _____ to your neighbors. (LO4)

5. When you drive, rather than walk or take public transportation, you incur social costs such as _____. (LO4)

6. _____ could be described as a merger of state and corporate power. (LO6)

higher prices the suppliers are willing and able to sell larger and larger quantities, while the buyers are willing to buy smaller and smaller quantities. Similarly, as price declines, buyers are willing to buy more and sellers are willing to sell less. But we're getting a little ahead of ourselves, since you haven't yet been formally introduced to a supply schedule. So first check out Table 2, and then Figure 2, which is a graph drawn from the numbers in the table.

What happens, then, to quantity supplied as the price is lowered? It declines. It's as simple as that.

In our definitions of demand and supply, we talked about a schedule of quantities of a good or service that people are willing and able to buy or sell at different prices. But what if some buyers just don't have the money? Then those buyers are simply not counted. We say that they are not in the market. Similarly, we would exclude from the market any sellers who just don't have the goods or services to sell. I'd *love* to sell my services as a $600-an-hour corporate lawyer, but quite frankly, I just don't have those services to sell.

That brings us to a second factor not included in our definitions of supply and demand. The supply and demand for any good or service operates within a specific market. That market may be very local, as it is for food shopping; regional, as it is for used cars; national, as it is for news magazines; or even international, as it is for petroleum.

TABLE 2	Hypothetical Daily Supply for Coach Seats on Round-Trip Weekday Flights between Denver and Chicago
Price	Quantity Supplied
$500	62,000
450	59,000
400	54,000
350	48,000
300	40,000
250	30,000
200	16,000
150	7,000
100	2,000

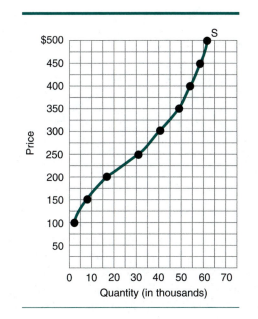

Figure 2

Hypothetical Daily Supply for Coach Seats on Round-Trip Weekday Flights between Denver and Chicago

Equilibrium

You've heard a lot about supply and demand—or is it demand and supply? It doesn't matter whether you put demand or supply first. What *does* matter is placing them together on the same graph. Look at Figure 3.

Can you find the equilibrium price? Did you say $250? Good! And how much is equilibrium quantity? Right again! It is 30,000.

Let's step back for a minute and analyze what we've just done. We've figured out the equilibrium price and quantity by looking at the demand and supply curves in Figure 3. So we can find equilibrium price and quantity by seeing where the supply and demand curves cross.

Equilibrium price is the price at which quantity demanded equals quantity supplied.

What is equilibrium price? It's the price at which quantity demanded equals quantity supplied. What is equilibrium quantity? It's the quantity sold when the quantity demanded is equal to the quantity supplied.

Surpluses and Shortages

Is the actual price, or market price, always equal to the equilibrium price? The answer is no. It could be higher and it could be lower. Suppose the airlines were selling tickets for $400. How many tickets would be demanded? Look back at Table 1 or, if you prefer, Figure 1 or Figure 3.

A total of 7,000 tickets would be demanded. And at a price of $400, how many tickets would be supplied?

Figure 3

Hypothetical Demand and Supply Curves

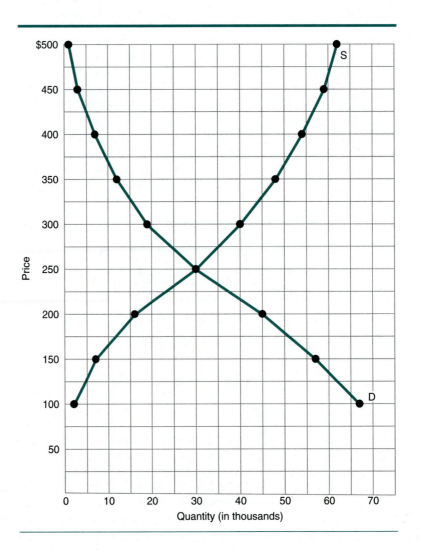

The quantity supplied would be 54,000. What we've got here is a surplus. This occurs when the actual price, or the market price, is greater than the equilibrium price. How much is that surplus? You can measure it by finding the horizontal distance between quantity demanded and quantity supplied in Figure 3. Or, you can subtract the quantity demanded that you found in Table 1 (at a price of $400) from the quantity supplied in Table 2 (also at a price of $400). Either way, the surplus comes to 47,000.

A surplus occurs when the market price is above the equilibrium price.

The quantity that sellers are willing and able to sell (54,000) is much greater than the quantity buyers are willing and able to buy (7,000). This difference (54,000 − 7,000) is the surplus (47,000). The amount that sellers can sell is restricted by how much buyers will buy.

What happens when there's a surplus? The forces of demand and supply automatically work to eliminate it. In this case, some of the airlines, which would be very unhappy about all those empty seats, would cut their prices. If the market price fell to $300, would there still be a surplus?

A glance at Figure 3 tells us that there would be. And how much would that surplus be?

It would be 21,000 seats. So *then* what would happen?

Some of the airlines would cut their prices to $250, and the buyers would flock to them. The other airlines would have no choice but to cut their price—or stop flying the Denver–Chicago route altogether. At $250, we would be at the equilibrium point. There would be no tendency for the price to change.

What if the market price were below equilibrium price? Then we'd have a shortage. How much would that shortage be if the market price in Figure 3 were $200?

A shortage occurs when the market price is below the equilibrium price.

At a price of $200, quantity demanded would be 45,000, while quantity supplied would be just 16,000. So the shortage would be 29,000.

This time the buyers would be disappointed, because they would be quite happy to pay $200 for a round-trip ticket, but most would be unable to get one without waiting for months. Many of the buyers would be willing to pay more. So what do you think would happen?

You guessed it! The market price would rise to $250. At that price—the equilibrium price—quantity demanded would equal quantity supplied, and the shortage would be eliminated.

Thus we can see that the forces of demand and supply work together to establish an equilibrium price at which there are no shortages or surpluses. At the equilibrium price, all the sellers can sell as much as they want and all the buyers can buy as much as they want. So if we were to shout, "Is everybody happy?" the buyers and sellers would all shout back "yes!"

Shifts in Demand and Supply

So far we've seen how the forces of demand and supply, or the price mechanism, send signals to buyers and sellers. For example, the surplus that resulted from a price of $400 sent a clear signal to sellers to cut their prices. Similarly, a price of $200 was accompanied by a shortage, which made many buyers unhappy. And sellers quickly realized that they could raise their price to $250 and *still* sell all the tickets they wanted to sell.

Now we'll see how shifts in supply curves and shifts in demand curves change equilibrium price and quantity, thereby sending new sets of signals to buyers and sellers. Figure 4 has a new demand curve, D_2. This represents an increase in demand because it lies entirely to the right of D_1, the original demand curve. There has been an increase in demand if the quantity demanded is larger at every price that can be compared.

Why did the demand for airline tickets increase? Let's say that newer planes were introduced that cut travel time by 30 percent.

I'd like you to find the new equilibrium price and the new equilibrium quantity. When you do, please write down your answers.

The new equilibrium price is $300, and the new equilibrium quantity is 40,000. So an increase in demand leads to an increase in both equilibrium price and quantity.

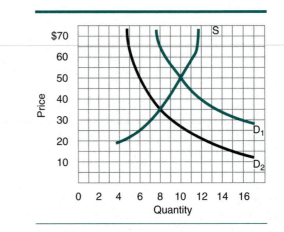
How Changes in Demand Affect Equilibrium

If demand falls and supply stays the same, what happens to equilibrium price and equilibrium quantity? To answer those questions, sketch a graph of a supply curve, S, and a demand curve, D_1. Then draw a second demand curve, D_2, representing a decrease in demand. I've done that in this figure.

The original equilibrium price was $50, and the original equilibrium quantity was 10. Equilibrium price fell to $35, and equilibrium quantity fell to 8. So a decrease in demand leads to a decrease in equilibrium price and quantity.

What would happen to equilibrium price and equilibrium quantity if demand rose and supply stayed the same? Equilibrium price and quantity would rise.

Figure 4

Increase in Demand

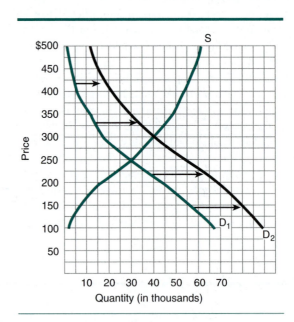

Next question: What would happen to equilibrium price and quantity if there were a decrease in demand?

There would be a decrease in both equilibrium price and quantity. Need a little extra help? Then see the box, "How Changes in Demand Affect Equilibrium."

OK, one more set of shifts and we're out of here.

Figure 5 shows an increase in supply. You'll notice that the new supply curve, S_2, is entirely to the right of S_1. There has been an increase in supply if the quantity supplied is larger at every price that can be compared.

Why did supply increase? Let's assume that the cost of jet fuel fell by 50 percent. In response, the airlines scheduled more flights. Please find the new equilibrium price and quantity, and write down your answers.

An increase in supply lowers equilibrium price and raises equilibrium quantity.

The new equilibrium price is $200, and the new equilibrium quantity is 45,000. So an increase in supply lowers equilibrium price and raises equilibrium quantity. One last question: If supply declines, what happens to equilibrium price and equilibrium quantity?

Figure 5
Increase in Supply

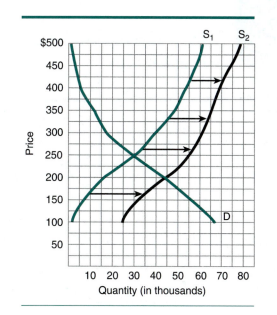

Now let's work out a couple of problems. First, look at Figure 6 and write down your answers to this set of questions: (*a*) If the supply curve is S_1, how much are the equilibrium price and quantity? (*b*) If supply changes from S_1 to S_2, does that represent an increase or decrease in supply? (*c*) How much are the new equilibrium price and quantity?

Here are the answers: (*a*) $13; 275; (*b*) decrease; and (*c*) $14; 225.

Figure 6

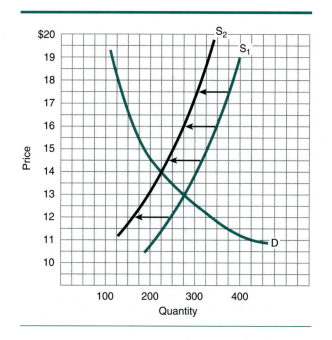

When supply declines, equilibrium price rises and equilibrium quantity declines. As you make your way through this text, supply and demand graphs will pop up from time to time. In every case you'll be able to find equilibrium price and quantity by locating the point of intersection of the demand and supply curves. If you need extra help, see the box, "How Changes in Supply Affect Equilibrium."

Next problem: Use Figure 7 to answer these questions: (*a*) If the demand curve is D_1, how much are the equilibrium price and quantity? (*b*) If demand changes from D_1 to D_2, does that represent an increase or decrease in demand? (*c*) How much are the new equilibrium price and quantity?

EXTRA
HELP

How Changes in Supply Affect Equilibrium

If supply rises and demand stays the same, what happens to equilibrium price and equilibrium quantity? Again, to answer those questions, sketch a graph of a demand curve, D_1, and a supply curve, S_1. Then draw a second supply curve, S_2, representing an increase in supply. I've done that in this figure.

The original equilibrium price was $12, and the original equilibrium quantity was 20. Equilibrium price fell to $9, and equilibrium quantity rose to 26. So an increase in supply leads to a decrease in equilibrium price and an increase in equilibrium quantity.

What happens to equilibrium price and equilibrium quantity if supply falls and demand stays the same? Equilibrium price rises and equilibrium quantity falls.

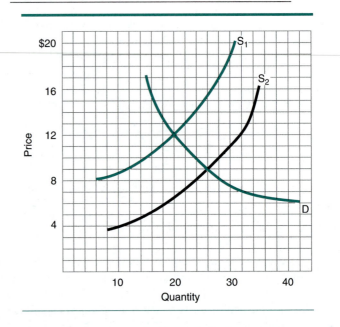

Figure 7

Here are the answers: (*a*) $26; 120; (*b*) decrease; and (*c*) $24.50; 100.

OK, you're taking an exam, and here's the first question: Demand rises and supply stays the same. What happens to equilibrium price and quantity? Just sketch a graph (like the one in Figure 4). Then you'll see that an increase in demand raises equilibrium price and quantity.

What happens to equilibrium price and quantity when there's a decrease in demand? Again, just sketch a graph, and you'll see that a decrease in demand lowers equilibrium price and quantity.

Next question: What happens to equilibrium price and quantity when there's an increase in supply? If your sketch looks like the one in Figure 5, you'll see that an increase in supply leads to a lower equilibrium price and a higher equilibrium quantity.

And finally, how does a decrease in supply affect equilibrium price and quantity? A decrease in supply leads to a higher equilibrium price and a lower equilibrium quantity.

Now let's return to that exam. When you're asked: How does an increase or decrease in demand affect equilibrium price and quantity, what do you do?

You just sketch a graph of a demand curve and a supply curve, and then another demand curve representing an increase or decrease in demand. Similarly, if you're asked how an increase or decrease in supply affects equilibrium price and quantity, just draw a sketch. It leads you to the right answers.

Price Ceilings and Price Floors

One of the most popular sayings of all time is "You can't repeal the law of supply and demand." Maybe not, but our government sure has a lot of fun trying. Price floors and price ceilings, which Washington has imposed from time to time, have played havoc with our price system. And taxes on selected goods and services have also altered supply and demand.

You can't repeal the law of supply and demand.

What's the difference between a floor and a ceiling? If you're standing in a room, where's the floor and where's the ceiling? As you might expect, economists turn this logic upside down. To find floors, we need to look up. How high? Somewhere above equilibrium price. And where are ceilings? Just where you'd expect economists to place them. We need to look down, somewhere below equilibrium price. A *price floor* is so named because that is the lowest the price is allowed to go in that market. Similarly, a *price ceiling* is the highest price that is allowed in that market.

Figure 8 illustrates a price floor. Equilibrium price would normally be $10, but a price floor of $15 has been established. At $15 businesses are not normally able to sell everything they offer for sale. Quantity supplied is much larger than quantity demanded. Why? At the equilibrium price of $10, sellers are willing to sell less while buyers are willing to buy more.

At a price of $15, there is a surplus of 30 units (quantity demanded is 20 and quantity supplied is 50). The government has created this price floor and surplus to keep the price at a predetermined level. This has been the case for certain agricultural commodities, most notably wheat and corn. It was hoped that these relatively high prices would encourage family farms to stay in business. That the bulk of farm price support payments has gone to huge corporate farms has not discouraged Congress from allocating billions of dollars a year toward this end.

Floors and surpluses

The way the government keeps price floors in effect is by buying up the surpluses. In the case of Figure 8, the Department of Agriculture would have to buy 30 units.

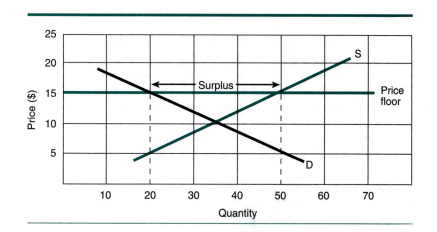

Figure 8

Price Floor and Surplus
The price can go no lower than the floor. The surplus is the amount by which the quantity supplied is greater than the quantity demanded.

Another important price floor is the minimum wage. As of July 24, 2009 the vast majority of Americans are guaranteed a minimum of $7.25 an hour. On that date the minimum hour wage is scheduled to increase from $6.55. Unless your job is not covered under the Fair Labor Standards Act, you are legally entitled to at least this wage rate.

Price ceilings are the mirror image of price floors. An example appears in Figure 9. Price ceilings are set by the government as a form of price control. "No matter what," the government tells business firms, "don't charge more than this amount."

Ceilings and shortages

A ceiling prevents prices from rising. The last time we had widespread price ceilings was during World War II. Because ceilings cause shortages, a rations system was worked out to enable everyone to obtain their "fair share" of such commodities as butter, meat, and sugar.

I remember World War II. I remember the ration books and the coupons you'd tear out when you went to the store. But chances are, even your parents don't remember the war, with its attendant shortages and rationing.

Ceilings and gas lines

Those over 35 may remember the gas lines we had in 1979, and real old-timers even recall the ones we had back in 1973. If not, imagine waiting a couple of hours in a line of cars six blocks long just to fill up your tank. What was the problem? In 1973 it was the Arab oil embargo, while the crisis in 1979 was set off by the Iranian Revolution.

How shortages are eliminated

In both cases, there was ostensibly an oil shortage. But according to the law of supply and demand, there can't really *be* any shortages. Why not? Because prices will rise. For example, in Figure 9, at a price of $25, there's a shortage. But we know the price will rise to $30 and eliminate that shortage. Why? Who drives it up? The dissatisfied buyers (the people who would rather pay more now than wait) drive it up because they are willing to pay more than $25. Note that as the price rises, the quantity demanded declines, while the quantity supplied rises. When we reach equilibrium price, quantity demanded equals quantity supplied, and the shortage is eliminated.

Figure 9

Price Ceiling and Shortage
The price can go no higher than the price ceiling. The shortage is the amount by which quantity demanded is greater than quantity supplied.

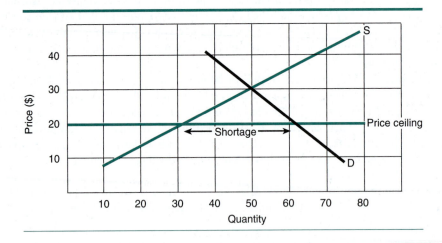

Now, I left you back in that gas line, and I know you don't want to wait two hours until it's your turn at the pump. Wouldn't you be willing to pay a few cents more if that meant you didn't have to wait? Let's suppose the gas station owner posted a higher price. What would happen? Some people would get out of line. What if he posted a still higher price? Still more people would leave the line. And as gas prices rose, more stations would miraculously open, and the others would stay open longer hours. What would happen to the gas lines? They'd disappear.

Who actually caused the shortages?

So now, let's ask the obvious question: What *really* caused the gasoline shortages? Who was the *real* villain of the piece? You guessed it! It was the federal government, which had set a ceiling on gasoline prices.

Let's return once more to Figure 9, the scene of the crime. What crime? How could you forget? Our government was caught red-handed, trying to violate the law of supply and demand.

In Figure 9, when a ceiling of $20 is established, there is a shortage of about 30 units. Had price been allowed to stay at the equilibrium level of $30, there would have been no shortage. However, at this lower price, business firms would be willing to sell about 18 units fewer than they'll sell at equilibrium, and consumers would demand about 12 units more than they would at equilibrium. This explains the shortage.

One way the market deals with a government-imposed shortage is to create what is known as a black market. Products subject to the price ceiling are sold illegally to those willing to pay considerably more. During World War II there was an extensive black market.

Two important price ceilings are rent control laws (see the box, "Rent Control: The Institution People Love to Hate") and usury laws, which put a ceiling on interest rates. Usury laws go back to biblical times when the prophets debated what, if anything, was a "fair" rate of interest. This same debate was carried on more than two millennia later by Christian scholars. And to this day we ask whether it is "moral" to charge high interest rates.

Usury laws put a ceiling on interest rates.

Rent Control: The Institution People Love to Hate

I grew up in a rent-controlled apartment and still believe that rent control worked very well at the time it was instituted. Very little new housing had been built during the 1930s because of the Great Depression and during the first half of the 1940s because of World War II. If rents had been allowed to rise to their market value in the late 1940s, my family, and hundreds of thousands—if not millions—of other families would have been forced out of their apartments.

Rent control is an institution that landlords, economists, libertarians, and nearly all good conservatives just love to hate. In fact, about the only folks who still seem to support rent control are the tenants whose rents are below what the market would have set and the politicians who voted for these laws in the first place.

Rent controls establish ceilings for how much rent may be charged for particular apartments and how much, if at all, these rents may be raised each year. The case for rent control is that it keeps down housing costs for the poor and the elderly. Actually, it keeps down housing costs for a lot of middle-class and rich people as well. Because the rent ceiling is established for each apartment regardless of who is living there, many people are paying a lot less than they could afford.

One of the perverse effects of rent control is to reduce vacancy rates. First, those paying low rents don't want to move. Second, real estate developers are reluctant to build apartment houses if their rents will be subject to controls. Still another perverse effect has been the large-scale abandonment of apartment buildings, especially in the inner cities, when landlords find that it makes more sense to walk away from their buildings than to continue losing money. These landlords had been squeezed for years by rising maintenance costs and stagnant rent rolls.

Richard Arnott has noted that "Economists have been virtually unanimous in their opposition to rent control." Why? Arnott provides a full list of reasons:

There has been widespread agreement that rent controls discourage new construction, cause abandonment, retard maintenance, reduce mobility, generate mismatch between housing units and tenants, exacerbate discrimination in rental housing, create black markets, encourage the conversion of rental to owner-occupied housing, and generally short-circuit the market mechanism for housing.*

After rent control was imposed in New York City in 1943, many landlords stopped taking care of their buildings and eventually walked away from 500,000 apartments.

Today nearly 200 cities, mostly in New York, New Jersey, and California, have some form of rent control. It is clear that this price ceiling has kept rents well below their equilibrium levels and consequently has resulted in housing shortages.

From a policy standpoint, do we want to eliminate rent controls? Would skyrocketing rents drive even more families into the ranks of the homeless? Perhaps a gradual easing of rent controls and their eventual elimination in, say, 10 or 15 years would send the right message to builders. But because these are local laws, only local governments can repeal them. And because the name of the political game is getting reelected, it is unlikely that many local politicians will find it expedient to repeal these popular laws.

---

*Richard Arnott, "Time for Revisionism on Rent Control?" *Journal of Economic Perspectives,* Winter 1995, p. 99.

Price Ceilings, Price Floors, Shortages, and Surpluses

Let's look at Figure 1. See if you can answer these three questions: (1) Is $10 a price ceiling or a price floor? (2) Is there a shortage or a surplus? (3) How much is it?

Let's look at Figure 2. We see that the quantity demanded is 75 and the quantity supplied is 45. The shortage is equal to quantity demanded less quantity supplied (75 − 45 = 30).

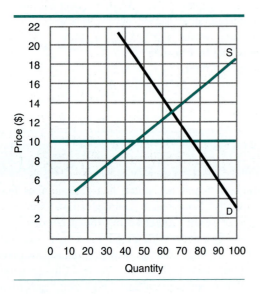

Figure 1

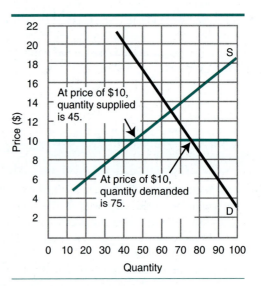

Figure 2

Solution: (1) $10 is a price ceiling because it is below equilibrium price: The ceiling is holding the market price *below* equilibrium price. (2) There is a shortage because quantity demanded is greater than quantity supplied. (3) The shortage is 30.

One dictionary definition of usury is "an unconscionable or exorbitant rate or amount of interest."[1] Many states have usury laws that prohibit banks, savings and loan associations, and certain other financial institutions from charging above specified rates of interest. What effect, if any, do these laws have?

Until the late 1970s interest rates were well below their legal ceilings. But then came double-digit inflation rates, sharply rising interest rates, and, as these interest rates reached their legal ceilings, a full-fledged credit crunch. In other words, these interest rate ceilings created a shortage of loanable funds—which is exactly what one would expect to happen when a price ceiling is set below the market's equilibrium price. In this case we're talking about the market for loanable funds and their price, the interest rate.

The confusion over the location of price floors and ceilings on the graph may be overcome by considering what the government is doing by establishing them. Normally, price would fall to the equilibrium level, but a price floor keeps price artificially high.

---
[1]*Webster's Collegiate Dictionary*, 10th ed., p. 1302.

Moving right along, answer these three questions with respect to Figure 3. (1) Is $40 a price ceiling or a price floor? (2) Is there a shortage or a surplus? (3) How much is it?

Let's look at Figure 4. We see the quantity supplied is 130 and quantity demanded is 80. The surplus is equal to quantity supplied less quantity demanded ($130 - 80 = 50$).

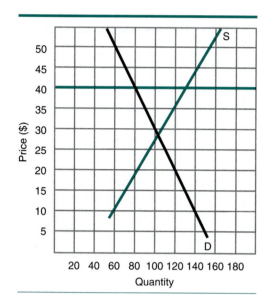

Figure 3

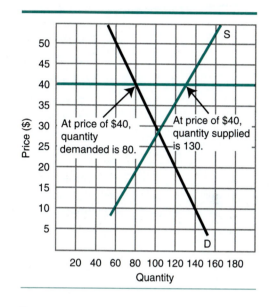

Figure 4

Solution: (1) $40 is a price floor because it is above equilibrium price: The floor is holding market price *above* equilibrium price. (2) There is a surplus because quantity supplied is greater than quantity demanded. (3) The surplus is 50.

Think of a floor holding price above equilibrium; therefore, a price floor would be located above equilibrium price.

By the same logic, a price ceiling is intended to keep price *below* equilibrium. If not for that ceiling, price would rise. Therefore, an effective price ceiling must be located below equilibrium to keep price from rising to that level.

Keep in mind, then, that the normal tendency of prices is to move toward their equilibrium levels. A price ceiling will prevent prices from rising to equilibrium, while a price floor will prevent prices from falling to equilibrium. If you need more information about ceilings, floors, shortages, and surpluses, see the box, "Price Ceilings, Price Floors, Shortages, and Surpluses."

Let's summarize: When the government sets a price floor above equilibrium price, it creates a surplus. That surplus is the amount by which the quantity supplied exceeds the quantity demanded. When the government sets a price ceiling below equilibrium price, it creates a shortage. That shortage is the amount by which the quantity demanded exceeds the quantity supplied.

Applications of Supply and Demand

Throughout this book we encounter many applications of supply and demand—so many, in fact, that I'm going to give you a quiz. But it will be an extremely easy quiz. There's just one answer to all these questions. Are you ready?

1. Interest rates are set by _____.
   Did you answer "supply and demand"? Good.

2. Wage rates are set by _____.

3. Rents are determined by _____.

4. The prices of nearly all goods are determined by _____.

5. The prices of nearly all services are determined by _____.

We may conclude, then, that the prices of nearly everything are determined by demand and supply.

Occasionally, however, government intervention interferes with the price mechanism and imposes price floors (or minimums) or price ceilings (or maximums). This gets economists very upset because it not only prevents the most efficient allocation of resources. It also makes it much harder to read our supply and demand graphs.

Interest Rate Determination

Let's take a closer look at the determination of the interest rate. I want to state right up front that there is no "interest rate" but rather scores of interest rates, such as mortgage rates, commercial loan rates, and short-term and long-term federal borrowing rates, as well as the interest rates paid by banks, credit unions, and other financial intermediaries. Figure 10 shows a hypothetical demand schedule for loanable funds and a corresponding hypothetical supply schedule.

We can see that $600 billion is lent (or borrowed) at an interest rate of 6 percent. In other words, the market sets the price of borrowed money at an interest rate of 6 percent. What would happen to the interest rate and to the amount of money borrowed if the supply of loanable funds increased?

Figure 10

Hypothetical Demand for and Supply of Loanable Funds

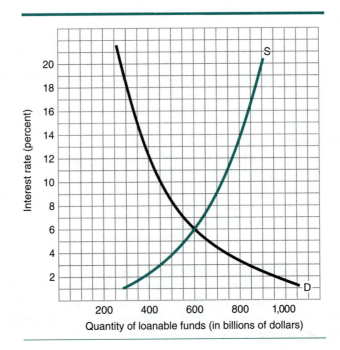

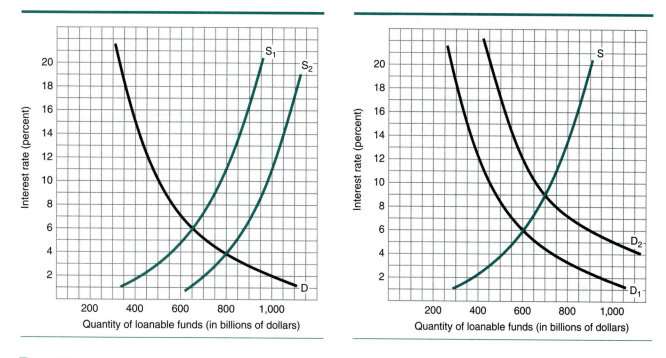

Figure 11
Hypothetical Demand for and Supply of Loanable Funds

Figure 12
Hypothetical Demand for and Supply of Loanable Funds

Did you figure it out? If you did, then you can confirm your answers by glancing at Figure 11. A rise in the supply of loanable funds leads to a decrease in the interest rate to 4 percent and an increase in the amount of money borrowed to $800 billion.

One more question: What happens to the interest rate and to the amount of money borrowed if the demand for loanable funds rises?

Did you say that the interest rate would rise and the amount of money borrowed would also rise? Good. Then what you must have done was to have sketched a graph like the one shown in Figure 12. The interest rate rose to 9 percent, and the amount of money borrowed rose to $700 billion.

College Parking

One of the big complaints on college campuses is the scarcity of parking spots for students—which means that, if you get to school after 9 o'clock, you may have to walk a half mile or even more to get to class.

Is parking free at your school? Although you may well believe it should be, let's look at the consequences of free parking. The school has set the price of parking at zero. That's a price ceiling of zero. We may conclude that this price ceiling has caused a shortage of available parking spots.

Suppose that the college administration decided to charge $25 a semester to students, faculty members, administrators, and other employees (and eliminated reserved parking as well). Would this fee eliminate the parking shortage? Surely it would cut down on the quantity of parking spots demanded. But if the shortage were not completely eliminated, perhaps a fee of $50 might do the trick. Or even $100. In short, if the price of parking were set high enough, the parking shortage would disappear.

Should parking be free at your school?

The Rationing Function of the Price System

If gasoline went up to $8 a gallon, would you cut back on your driving? Maybe you would try to do all your shopping in one trip instead of in two or three. And if gasoline went still higher, maybe you would even agree to join a car pool.

The price system is constantly sending buyers and sellers thousands of signals. The price of *this* service has gone through the roof. *That* product is on sale. *This* good is over-priced and *that* one is a bargain. When something becomes very expensive, we generally cut back. We do this not because the government ordered us to do so or because it issued ration coupons entitling everyone to only three gallons a week, but because the price system itself performed this rationing function.

Think of how most people behave at all-you-can-eat buffets. They certainly eat a lot more than they would in a regular restaurant. *Why?* The price system signals to them: This appetizer will cost them another $4.50, or that slice of pie will cost them another $3.75. At the buffet there's nothing to get them to ration how much they eat—except possibly a very full stomach. But in a regular restaurant the price system performs its rationing function so well that they end up eating less.

At the beginning of Chapter 2, economics was defined as *the efficient allocation of the scarce means of production toward the satisfaction of human wants.* In a free-market, private-enterprise economy such as ours, we depend on the price mechanism, or the forces of supply and demand, to perform that job.

The advent of the Internet has made the workings of supply and demand even more efficient. Before the Internet, we bought nearly all of our books in bookstores. Now we buy them online from a variety of sellers. If you want to buy a bestseller, your local bookstore will charge you full price. But chances are, you could find a seller online offering that same book at a steep discount. See for yourself by going to the websites that follow.

on the web

Check the price charged at your local bookstore for a couple of bestsellers and then go to these sites to see how much money you could save: www.amazon.com; www.barnesand-noble.com; www.halfprice.com; and www.ebay.com.

Last Word

We talked earlier of how the government sometimes interferes with the free operation of markets by imposing price floors and price ceilings. But the government may also ensure the smooth operation of markets by protecting property rights, guaranteeing enforcement of legal contracts, and issuing a supply of money that buyers and sellers will readily accept. Economist John McMillan has emphasized the historic importance of property rights:

Mohammed on supply and demand and property rights

> The prophet Mohammed was an early proponent of property rights. When a famine in Medina brought sharp price increases, people implored him to lessen the hardship by fixing prices. He refused because, having once been a merchant himself, he believed the buyers' and sellers' free choices should not be overridden. "Allah is the only one who sets the prices and gives prosperity and poverty," he said. "I would not want to be complained about before Allah by someone whose property or livelihood has been violated."[2]

So while governmental interference with the market system can have adverse effects, the government does have a substantial supportive role to play in a market economy. In the previous chapter we considered the role of government under economic systems ranging from capitalism to communism.

Current Issue: High Gas Prices: Something Only an Economist Could Love

On the Labor Day weekend of 2005, gas prices reached nearly $6 in some parts of the South. Customers groused about "price gouging," and many even limited their purchases to "just" $30 or $40, rather than filling their tanks.

---

[2]John McMillan, *Reinventing the Bazaar* (New York: W. W. Norton, 2002), p. 90.

What drove prices so high—*besides* the greed of the sellers? As you may remember, Hurricane Katrina, in addition to devastating New Orleans and its neighboring Gulf Coast communities, also temporarily shut down offshore oil wells which accounted for 25 percent of our domestic oil production. The storm also briefly put about 10 percent of our refineries out of commission.

What we had was a sudden drop in supply. When that happens, of course, price will go up sharply. Which is exactly what happened.

So what is there to love about high gas prices? Consider the alternative. Back in 1973 and 1979 we had similar supply problems, when shipments from the Middle East were curtailed. Although prices rose sharply, there were gas lines, sometimes six or eight blocks long. In 1979, various states imposed odd and even days to buy gas. If your license plate ended with an even number, you could buy gas on Monday, Wednesday, and Friday. If it ended with an odd number, then you were a Tuesday, Thursday, Saturday buyer.

The government's solution to the gasoline shortage in the 1970s was to restrict purchases and to hold down price increases. One unintended consequence was two- and three-hour waits on gas lines. But in 2005, the government basically took a hands-off attitude to the gasoline shortage. Prices certainly *did* go up, but there were few gas lines. Everyone was able to buy as much gas as they wanted, albeit at perhaps $3.50 or $3.75 a gallon. So the price system performed its rationing function very, very well. Although there were widespread complaints about prices, nearly everyone was much happier to pay, say, a dollar a gallon more, and not have to wait in line for an hour or two to buy gas.

Most economists believe price ceilings do more harm than good. In the short run, at least we don't have to wait in gas lines. Furthermore, because of high prices since the summer of 2005, some people cut back on their driving. In the long run, if gas prices stay high, some of them will trade in their SUVs for more gas efficient cars. Also, higher prices encourage greater exploration for oil, as well as the development of alternative energy sources. To sum up, rather than impose price controls, we should let the market forces of supply and demand reduce the shortage of gasoline.

Questions for Further Thought and Discussion

1. a. If market price is above equilibrium price, explain what happens and why.
   b. If market price is below equilibrium price, explain what happens and why.

2. a. As the price of theater tickets rises, what happens to the quantity of tickets that people are willing to buy? Explain your answer.
   b. As the price of theater tickets rises, explain what happens to the quantity of tickets that people are willing to sell. Explain your answer.

3. Where is a price ceiling with respect to equilibrium price? What will be the relative size of quantity demanded and quantity supplied?

4. How is equilibrium price affected by changes in (*a*) demand and (*b*) supply?

5. What are the two ways to depict a demand schedule? Make up a demand schedule for some good or service you often buy.

6. What is equilibrium? Why is it advantageous for the market price to be at equilibrium?

7. If you were a landlord, why would you be against rent control? A shortage occurs when the market price is below the equilibrium price.

8. *Practical Application:* How would the abolition of rent control reduce the housing shortage in some cities? Explain in terms of supply and demand.

9. *Practical Application:* Urban highways are usually very congested during morning and evening commuting times. Using supply and demand analysis, what simple step could be taken to greatly reduce congestion?

Workbook for Chapter 4 connect |ECONOMICS

Name _____   Date _____

Multiple-Choice Questions

Circle the letter that corresponds to the best answer.

1. When demand rises and supply stays the same, _____. (LO3)
   a) equilibrium quantity rises
   b) equilibrium quantity declines
   c) equilibrium quantity stays the same

2. When supply rises and demand stays the same, _____. (LO3)
   a) equilibrium quantity rises
   b) equilibrium quantity falls
   c) equilibrium quantity stays the same

3. At equilibrium price, quantity demanded is _____. (LO3)
   a) greater than quantity supplied
   b) equal to quantity supplied
   c) smaller than quantity supplied

4. When quantity demanded is greater than quantity supplied, _____. (LO3)
   a) market price will rise
   b) market price will fall
   c) market price will stay the same

5. What happens to quantity supplied when price is lowered? (LO3)
   a) It rises.
   b) It falls.
   c) It stays the same.
   d) It cannot be determined if it rises, falls, or stays the same.

6. What happens to quantity demanded when price is raised? (LO3)
   a) It rises.
   b) It falls.
   c) It stays the same.
   d) It cannot be determined if it rises, falls, or stays the same.

7. When market price is above equilibrium price, _____. (LO3)
   a) market price will rise
   b) equilibrium price will rise
   c) market price will fall
   d) equilibrium price will fall

8. At equilibrium, quantity demanded is _____ equal to quantity supplied. (LO3)
   a) sometimes
   b) always
   c) never

9. Market price _____ equilibrium price. (LO3)
   a) must always be equal to
   b) must always be above
   c) must always be below
   d) may be equal to

10. A demand schedule is determined by the wishes and abilities of _____. (LO1)
    a) sellers
    b) buyers
    c) buyers and sellers
    d) neither sellers nor buyers

11. In Figure 1, if market price were $110, there would be _____. (LO5, 6)
    a) a shortage
    b) a surplus
    c) neither a shortage nor a surplus

12. In Figure 1, if market price were $140, there would

    be _____. (LO5, 6)
    a) a shortage
    b) a surplus
    c) neither a shortage nor a surplus

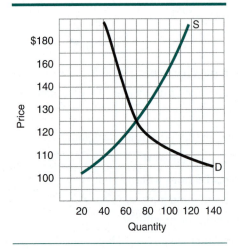

    Figure 1

13. Market price may not reach equilibrium if there

    are _____. (LO5, 6)
    a) both price ceilings and price floors
    b) neither price ceilings nor price floors
    c) only price ceilings
    d) only price floors

14. Gas lines in the 1970s were caused

    by _____. (LO5, 6)
    a) price floors
    b) price ceilings
    c) both price floors and price ceilings
    d) neither price floors nor price ceilings

15. Statement 1: Price ceilings cause shortages. (LO5, 6)
    Statement 2: Interest rates are set by supply and
    demand, but wage rates are not.
    a) Statement 1 is true and statement 2 is false.
    b) Statement 2 is true and statement 1 is false.
    c) Both statements are true.
    d) Both statements are false.

16. If the equilibrium price of corn is $3 a bushel, and the
    government imposes a floor of $4 a bushel, the price

    of corn will _____. (LO5, 6, 7)
    a) increase to $4
    b) remain at $3
    c) rise to about $3.50
    d) be impossible to determine

17. Usury laws tend to _____. (LO5, 6)
    a) create a shortage of loanable funds
    b) create a surplus of loanable funds
    c) make it easier to obtain credit
    d) have no effect on the amount of loanable funds
       available

18. If the price system is allowed to function without
    interference and a shortage occurs, quantity

    demanded will _____ and quantity

    supplied will _____ as the price rises to its

    equilibrium level. (LO5, 6)
    a) rise, rise
    b) fall, fall
    c) rise, fall
    d) fall, rise

19. Which statement is true? (LO5, 6)
    a) A price floor is above equilibrium price and
       causes surpluses.
    b) A price floor is above equilibrium price and
       causes shortages.
    c) A price floor is below equilibrium price and
       causes surpluses.
    d) A price floor is below equilibrium price and
       causes shortages.

20. An increase in supply while demand remains

    unchanged will lead to _____. (LO3)
    a) an increase in equilibrium price and a decrease in
       equilibrium quantity
    b) a decrease in equilibrium price and a decrease in
       equilibrium quantity
    c) an increase in equilibrium price and an increase in
       equilibrium quantity
    d) a decrease in equilibrium price and an increase in
       equilibrium quantity

21. A decrease in demand while supply remains unchanged will lead to _____. (LO3)
    a) an increase in equilibrium price and quantity
    b) a decrease in equilibrium price and quantity
    c) an increase in equilibrium price and a decrease in equilibrium quantity
    d) a decrease in equilibrium price and an increase in equilibrium quantity

22. As price rises, _____. (LO1, 2)
    a) quantity demanded and quantity supplied both rise
    b) quantity demanded and quantity supplied both fall
    c) quantity demanded rises and quantity supplied falls
    d) quantity demanded falls and quantity supplied rises

23. When quantity demanded is greater than quantity supplied, there _____. (LO5, 6)
    a) is a shortage
    b) is a surplus
    c) may be either a shortage or a surplus
    d) may be neither a shortage nor a surplus

24. When quantity supplied is greater than quantity demanded, _____. (LO3)
    a) price will fall to its equilibrium level
    b) price will rise to its equilibrium level
    c) price may rise, fall, or stay the same, depending on a variety of factors

Use Figure 2 to answer questions 25 and 26.

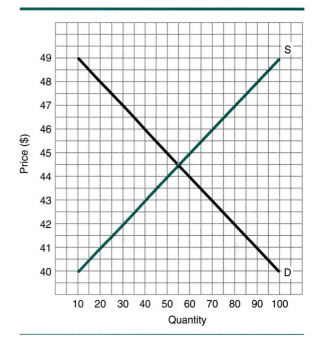

Figure 2

25. At a market price of $47, there is _____. (LO5, 6)
    a) a shortage
    b) a surplus
    c) both a shortage and a surplus
    d) neither a shortage nor a surplus

26. At a market price of $42, there is _____. (LO5, 6)
    a) a shortage
    b) a surplus
    c) both a shortage and a surplus
    d) neither a shortage nor a surplus

27. If the government set a price ceiling of 25 cents for a loaf of bread, the most likely consequence would be _____. (LO5, 6, 7)
    a) a surplus of bread
    b) no one would go hungry
    c) most Americans would put on weight
    d) a shortage of bread

28. Usury laws and rent control are examples of
    _____. (LO5, 6)

    a) price floors
    b) price ceilings
    c) rationing
    d) the law of supply and demand

29. The best way to eliminate gas lines would be to
    _____. (LO7)

    a) impose government price ceilings
    b) impose government price floors
    c) allow the forces of supply and demand to function
    d) put price gougers into jail

Fill-In Questions

1. If demand falls and supply stays the same,
   equilibrium price will _____, and equilibrium
   quantity will _____. (LO3)

2. If supply rises and demand stays the same,
   equilibrium price will _____, and equilibrium
   quantity will _____. (LO3)

3. If quantity supplied were greater than quantity
   demanded, market price would _____. (LO3)

4. Equilibrium price is always determined by
   _____ and _____. (LO3)

5. As price is lowered, quantity supplied
   _____. (LO3)

6. Shortages are associated with price _____;
   surpluses are associated with price
   _____. (LO5, 6)

7. If supply falls and demand remains the same,
   equilibrium price will _____, and equilibrium
   quantity will _____. (LO3)

8. Price floors and price ceilings are set
   by _____. (LO5, 6)

9. Interest rates are set by _____ and
   _____. (LO3, 7)

10. What happens to interest rates when the demand for
    money rises? _____. (LO3, 7)

11. When the supply of money falls, interest rates
    _____. (LO7)

Use Figure 3 to answer questions 12 through 15.

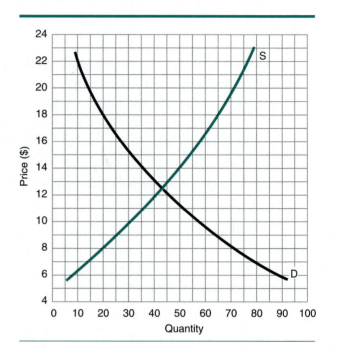

Figure 3

12. Equilibrium price is about $ _____. (LO3)

13. Equilibrium quantity is about _____. (LO3)

14. If price were $20, there would be a (shortage or
    surplus) _____ of _____ units of
    quantity. (LO5, 6)

15. If price were $8, there would be a (shortage or
    surplus) _____ of _____ units of
    quantity. (LO5, 6)

16. Price floors keep prices _____ equilibrium
    price; price ceilings keep prices _____
    equilibrium price. (LO5, 6)

Problems

1. In Figure 4, find equilibrium price and quantity (in dollars and units, respectively). (LO3)

2. Draw in a new demand curve, D$_1$, on Figure 4, showing an increase in demand. What happens to equilibrium price and quantity? (LO4)

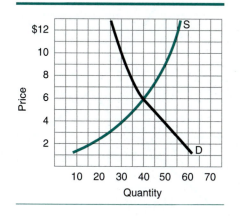

Figure 4

3. In Figure 5, find equilibrium price and quantity (in dollars and units, respectively). (LO3)

4. Draw in a new supply curve, S$_1$, on Figure 5, showing a decrease in supply. What happens to equilibrium price and quantity? (LO4)

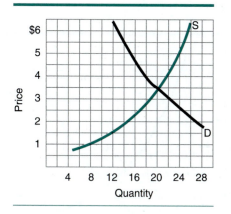

Figure 5

5. a) In Figure 6, if the demand curve is D$_1$, how much are equilibrium price and quantity? b) If demand changes from D$_1$ to D$_2$, does that represent an increase or decrease in demand? c) How much are the new equilibrium price and quantity? (LO3, 4)

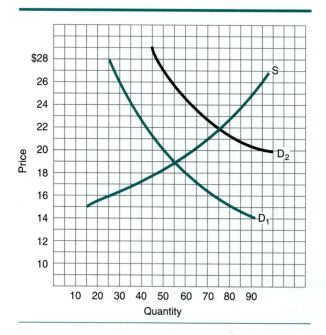

Figure 6

6. a) In Figure 7, if the supply curve is S_1, how much are equilibrium price and quantity? b) If the supply changes from S_1 to S_2, does that represent an increase or decrease in supply? c) How much are the new equilibrium price and quantity? (LO3, 4)

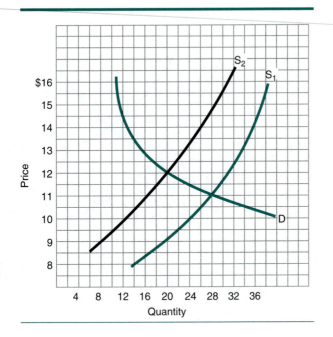

Figure 7

7. Given the information in Figure 8: a) Is $12 a price ceiling or a price floor? b) Is there a shortage or a surplus? c) How much is it (in units of quantity)? (LO5, 6)

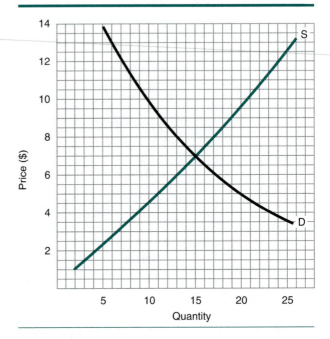

Figure 8

8. Given the information in Figure 9: a) Is $16 a price ceiling or a price floor? b) Is there a shortage or a surplus? c) How much is it (in units of quantity)? (LO5, 6)

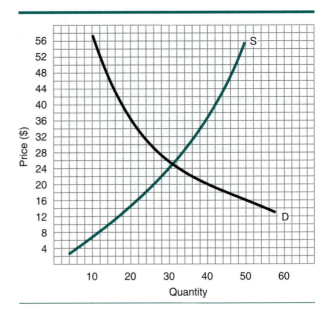

Figure 9

The Household-Consumption Sector

C hances are you've never been to the South Street Seaport Museum in New York City, a combination museum-shopping center, with some great shops and restaurants. When it opened in 1983, Christopher Lowrey, its director, said, "The fact is that shopping is the chief cultural activity in the United States." So the next time you want to sop up some culture, instead of attending a concert or play, just head over to the mall.

Anyone who says money doesn't buy happiness doesn't know where to shop.

—Anonymous

In this chapter we begin our examination of the four sectors of gross domestic product (GDP): C (consumption), I (investment), G (government spending), and X_n (net exports). We look at consumption: why people spend money, what they buy, and why they save so little of their incomes. We will also introduce graphing techniques as a tool for macroeconomic analysis, which will be covered in Chapters 11 and 12.

LEARNING OBJECTIVES

After reading this chapter you should be able to:

1. Define and compute the average propensity to consume and the average propensity to save.
2. Define and compute the marginal propensity to consume and the marginal propensity to save.
3. Explain the consumption function.
4. Explain the savings function.
5. Calculate autonomous and induced consumption.
6. List and discuss the determinants of consumption.
7. Interpret and assess the permanent income hypothesis.
8. Explain why we spend so much and save so little.

GDP and Big Numbers

Consumption, investment, and government spending are the three main sectors of GDP. But what, exactly, is GDP? Gross domestic product is a term that you'll find quite frequently in the financial section of your newspaper, as well as in *The Wall Street Journal, BusinessWeek, Fortune,* and other financial publications. Gross domestic product, which is the subject of Chapter 9, is the *nation's expenditure on all the final goods and services produced during the year at market prices.*

I'm going to be throwing very large numbers at you—millions, billions, and trillions. Most of the numbers you'll come across in the next ten chapters will be stated in billions and trillions. 1 trillion = 1,000 billion.

In 2009 our GDP was about $14.3 trillion, or $14,300 billion. If we wanted to take the time, we could also express that number like this: $14,300,000,000,000.

What's the difference between mathematics and economics? Mathematics is incomprehensible; economics just doesn't make sense.

Consumption in 2009 was $10.089 trillion, or $10,089 billion. That number could also be expressed as 10 trillion, 89 billion dollars.

Consumption

The average American spends virtually all of her income after taxes. The total of everyone's expenditures is consumption, designated by the letter C. The largest sector of GDP, C, now accounts for 7 out of every 10 dollars.

Consumers spend 67.7 percent of their disposable income on services such as medical care, gasoline, eating out, video rentals, life insurance, and legal fees. The rest is spent on durable goods, such as television sets and furniture, or on nondurable goods, such as food and gasoline. All consumption falls into one of the two categories of goods or services.

> The consumption function states that as income rises, consumption rises, but not as quickly.

Until the late 1990s, consumption was usually between 90 and 95 percent of disposable income. John Maynard Keynes (pronounced "canes") noted that consumption is a stable component of income. His theory, called the consumption function, states that *as income rises, consumption rises, but not as quickly.*[1] For example, if a country's disposable income rises by 300 (from 2,000 to 2,300), its C will rise, but by less than 300. If C were 1,800, it might rise by 250 to 2,050.

The consumption function is illustrated by the hypothetical figures in Table 1. We'll start with a disposable income of $1,000 billion, or $1 trillion, and consumption of $1,400 billion. Now let's move up to a disposable income of $2,000 billion and a C of $2,200 billion. So an increase of $1,000 billion in disposable income (from $1,000 billion to $2,000 billion) pushed up C by just $800 billion (from $1,400 billion to $2,200 billion). This relationship remains the same as we raise disposable income by increments of $1,000 billion to $3,000 billion, $4,000 billion, and $5,000 billion. Each $1,000 billion increase in disposable income induces an $800 billion increase in C.

So, as disposable income rises in increments of 1,000, C rises in increments of 800, which conforms to the consumption function: *As income rises, consumption rises, but not as quickly.*

When we say, then, that consumption is a function of disposable income, we mean that it *varies* with disposable income. When disposable income goes up, so does consumption, though by a smaller amount. And when disposable income declines, so does consumption, but again, by a smaller amount.

TABLE 1 Consumption and Disposable Income
(in billions of dollars)

Disposable Income	Consumption
1,000	1,400
2,000	2,200
3,000	3,000
4,000	3,800
5,000	4,600

---

[1]His exact words were, "Men are disposed, as a rule and on the average, to increase their consumption as their income increases, but not by as much as the increase in their income."

Individual Saving

Saving is simply not spending. Since the early 1990s our savings rate seems to be performing its own version of the limbo. In answer to the question, "How low can you go?" you'll see by glancing at Figure 1 that it fell from 10.5 in 1984 to below 5 in the late 1990s. In the third quarter of 2005 our savings rate actually turned negative—for the first time in 73 years. Indeed we had not experienced a negative savings rate since the depths of the Great Depression in 1932 and 1933.

During the depression many families had little or no income. They survived by digging into their savings, borrowing, and receiving private and public assistance. So their negative savings was no great surprise. But in these times of relative prosperity, Americans are spending more than they're earning. Unlike during the 1930s, when people spent most or all of their incomes just to put some food on the table and a roof over their heads, today Americans are buying a lot of things they want, but don't necessarily need. Our spending seems driven by a pervasive sense of entitlement.

> *When one has had to work so hard to get money, why should he impose on himself the further hardship of trying to save it?*
>
> —Don Herold

> *Live within your income, even if you have to borrow money to do so.*
>
> —Josh Billings

Figure 1

Savings as a Percentage of Disposable Personal Income, 1984–2009

Our savings rate fell quite steadily from the early 1980s into the new millennium. In 2005 and 2007, savings rate dipped below 2 percent.

Source: Economic Report of the President, 2010; *Survey of Current Business,* March 2010.

How does our saving rate stack up against those of other leading developed economies? As you can see from a glance at Figure 2, we are near the bottom of the heap. Savings rates in virtually all these countries have fallen sharply over the last 10 years.

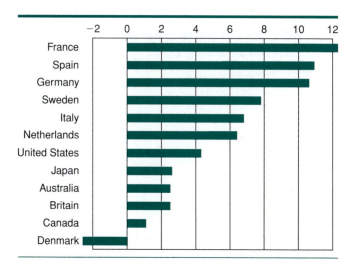

Figure 2

Household Saving as a Percentage of Disposable Income, 2009
Source: OECD.

If our savings rate is negative, does that mean that nobody saves any money? Not at all! While tens of millions of Americans live well beyond their means, there are also tens of millions who regularly save substantial parts of their earnings. Many of them are putting money away for their children's educations, a down payment on a new home, furniture, a medical procedure, a wedding, or for their retirement.

The higher your income, the more you are likely to save. While the poor are forced into debt just trying to make ends meet, the rich generally have more money than they wish to spend.

Two other factors that influence our savings rate are interest rates and inflation. If you can earn a high rate of interest on your savings, you will be more likely to save than if you could earn just one or two percent. When there's a high rate of inflation, people tend to spend their money on consumer goods and services, before prices rise still more. So a high inflation rate tends to discourage saving. After all, would *you* want to just hold your money while it loses its value?

Our nation's saving includes not just saving by individuals, but also by business firms and government. Near the end of this chapter we'll talk about our total national saving, and its decline over the last 25 years.

You can check our personal savings rate monthly by going to www.bea.gov. Then click on "Personal, Income and Outlays." The big question is whether our personal savings rate will be above or below 0.

Average Propensity to Consume and Average Propensity to Save

$$APC = \frac{Consumption}{Disposable\ income}$$

The average propensity to consume is the percentage of disposable income spent. Using the data in Table 2, let's calculate the APC.

To find the percentage of disposable income spent, we need to divide consumption by disposable income.

$$APC = \frac{Consumption}{Disposable\ income} = \frac{\$30,000}{\$40,000} = \frac{3}{4} = 0.75$$

Let's review how this is done. We use the three-step method of solving this problem. First, write the formula. Then, substitute the numbers into the formula. Finally, solve the formula.

The APS is the mirror image of the APC. It is the percentage of disposable income saved. Using the data in Table 2, calculate the APS.

Use the same three-step method we used to calculate the APC: (1) Write the formula, (2) plug in your numbers, and (3) solve. Do it right here.

TABLE 2	
Disposable Income	Consumption
$40,000	$30,000

ADVANCED WORK

APCs Greater than One

Is it possible to have an APC greater than one? You bet it is! How much would your APC be if you had a disposable income of $10,000 and your consumption was $12,000? Figure it out:

$$APC = \frac{Consumption}{Disposable\ income} = \frac{\$12,000}{\$10,000} = \frac{12}{10} = 1.2$$

Where would this extra $2,000 come from? Let's round up the usual suspects. You might take money out of the bank, borrow on your credit cards, take out a car loan or a home equity loan, or buy on the installment plan. The bottom line is that many people find it quite easy to spend more than they earn year after year, whether by drawing down their savings, borrowing money, or some combination thereof.

Incidentally, if your APC *were* 1.2, how much would your APS be? Work it out right here:

$$APS = \frac{Saving}{Disposable\ income} = \frac{-\$2,000}{\$10,000} = \frac{-2}{10} = -0.2$$

Is it possible to have a negative APS? If your savings happens to be negative (that is, you spend more than your income), then your APS will definitely be negative. And you'll notice that your APC (1.2) plus your APS (−0.2) add up to 1.0.

Now we'll check your work. The formula is:

$$APS = \frac{Saving}{Disposable\ income}$$

Next we'll substitute into the formula. You already know from Table 2 that disposable income is $40,000. How much is saving? It's not in Table 2, but since consumption is $30,000, we can find saving by subtracting consumption from disposable income: $40,000 − $30,000 = $10,000. Now we can complete the problem.

$$APS = \frac{Saving}{Disposable\ income} = \frac{\$10,000}{\$40,000} = \frac{1}{4} = 0.25^2$$

Note that the APC and the APS add up to 1. Let's work out another one, using the data in Table 3.

TABLE 3

Disposable Income	Saving
$20,000	$1,500

Use the space below to calculate the APC and the APS.

Solutions:

$$APC = \frac{Consumption}{Disposable\ income} = \frac{\$18,500}{\$20,000} = \frac{185}{200} = \frac{37}{40} = 0.925$$

$$APS = \frac{Saving}{Disposable\ income} = \frac{\$1,500}{\$20,000} = \frac{15}{200} = \frac{3}{40} = 0.075$$

---

[2]To convert ¼ into a decimal, we must divide the bottom number, 4, into the top number, 1.

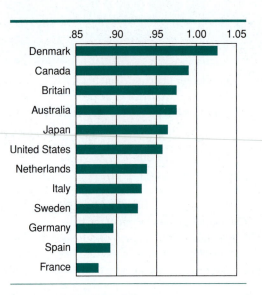

APC + APS = 1

Note that once again APC (.925) and APS (.075) add up to 1. This is your check to ensure that you haven't made a mistake in your calculations. (But can the APC ever be greater than 1? See the box, "APCs Greater than One.")

Now that we've done all this work, what does it mean to say that a person has an APC of .925 and an APS of .075? Think about the APC and the APS as percentages of disposable income. A person with an APC of 0.925 spends 92.5 percent of her disposable income and saves 7.5 percent of it. Go back to the formulas for the APC and the APS.

Just two more questions: How much is the current APC for the United States? How much is the country's APS? For the last 3 years it's averaged just over 0.99. In other words, Americans spend over 99 percent of their disposable incomes and save less than 1 percent.

How does our APC compare with those of other countries? As you can see at a glance from Figure 3, we're in the middle of the pack. Before our savings rate rose during the Great Recession, ours was one of the lowest among the economically advanced nations.

Marginal Propensity to Consume and Marginal Propensity to Save

When income changes, so does consumption. When income rises, consumption also rises, but by less than does income. This is the consumption function, introduced at the beginning of the chapter.

The formula for calculating the MPC is:

$$\text{MPC} = \frac{\text{Change in C}}{\text{Change in income}}$$

$$\frac{\text{Change in C}}{\text{Change in income}}$$

TABLE 4		
Year	Disposable Income	C
2000	$30,000	$23,000
2001	40,000	31,000

Using the data in Table 4, calculate the MPC in the space below.

Solution:

$$\text{MPC} = \frac{\text{Change in C}}{\text{Change in income}} = \frac{\$8,000}{\$10,000} = \frac{8}{10} = 0.8$$

When income changes, not only does consumption change, but so does saving. When income rises, both consumption and saving will rise. Similarly, when income falls, both consumption and saving fall.

The formula for calculating the MPS is:

$$\text{MPS} = \frac{\text{Change in saving}}{\text{Change in income}}$$

$$\text{MPS} = \frac{\text{Change in saving}}{\text{Change in income}}$$

Using Table 4 again, calculate the MPS. (Note: Remember how to find saving when you have disposable income and consumption.)[3]

Solution:

$$\text{MPS} = \frac{\text{Change in saving}}{\text{Change in income}} = \frac{\$2,000}{\$10,000} = \frac{2}{10} = 0.2$$

I must confess that in the last few pages I pulled something of an economic slight of hand. What I did was shift the discussion from a macroeconomic viewpoint to a microeconomic viewpoint. That is, instead of continuing to look at large economic aggregates, like total saving and total consumption, you were asked to work out a bunch of problems that involved finding an individual's APC, APS, MPC, and MPS.

So you did all these calculations using relatively small and easily managed numbers. But a little later in this chapter you'll get to apply the MPC formula to solve problems involving trillions of dollars.

Graphing the Consumption and Saving Functions

Reading a Graph

The key to reading economic variables from a graph is knowing where to look for them; so before we even look at graphs, let's just talk about them for a moment. There is a vertical line on the left side of every graph called the *vertical scale,* and there is a

---

[3]From Table 4: Disposable income − Consumption = Savings
        (2000) $30,000 − $23,000 = $7,000
        (2001) $40,000 − $31,000 = $9,000

Figure 4

Disposable Income and Expenditures

The 45-degree line equates expenditures and disposable income. For example, when disposable income is 4,000, expenditures are 4,000. Expenditures in subsequent graphs over the next four chapters will include consumption, investment, government spending, and net exports.

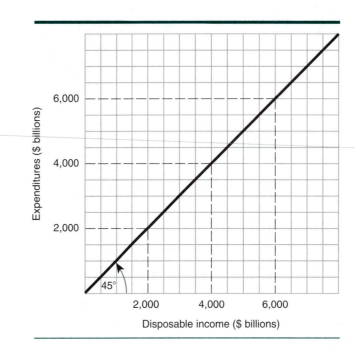

Disposable income ($ billions)

Expenditures are measured on the vertical scale and disposable income along the horizontal scale.

horizontal line on the bottom side of every graph called the *horizontal scale*. Take a peek at Figure 4 to see what I'm talking about.

Every graph you will ever see in an economics text will have these two dimensions: the horizontal and the vertical. The vertical scale is almost always measured in dollars. In Figure 4 we have an expenditures scale with the numbers 2,000, 4,000, and 6,000, which represent expenditures of $2 trillion, $4 trillion, and $6 trillion, respectively. Note that the distances between each of the successive numbers are equal. The horizontal axis in Figure 4 measures disposable income, also in units of 2,000, 4,000, and 6,000. This graph has only one line: a 45-degree line. This line has one purpose: to equate the horizontal scale with the vertical scale, that is, expenditures with disposable income.

Note the dotted line rising from a disposable income of 2,000. It meets the 45-degree line and then moves horizontally to the left to the vertical scale. For a disposable income of 4,000, there is another dotted line rising to the 45-degree line and then moving straight across to the vertical scale. The same pattern occurs at a disposable income of 6,000.

The Consumption Function

Now we're ready to graph the consumption function. First we'll review it: *As income rises, consumption rises, but not as quickly.* How should it look on a graph? It is represented by the C line in Figure 5.

Now we're ready to read the graph in Figure 5. How much is consumption when disposable income is $3 trillion? This question is so easy, you should be able to answer it by just glancing at the graph.

When disposable income is $3 trillion, consumption is also $3 trillion. You'll notice that the C line and the 45-degree line cross at that point. To answer the question, just follow the dotted lines. Move up vertically from a disposable income of $3 trillion to the 45-degree line. Then move horizontally to the left to a consumption of $3 trillion on the vertical axis.

Next question: How much is consumption when disposable income is $6 trillion? The answer is $4.5 trillion. Again, go straight up from $6 trillion on the horizontal axis to the C line, and then straight across to the left to $4.5 trillion on the vertical axis.

Last question: How much is consumption when disposable income is $1 trillion?

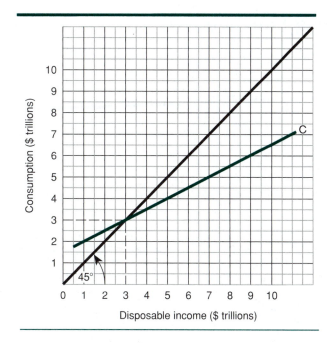

Figure 5
The Consumption Schedule
At a disposable income of $3 trillion the C line crosses the 45-degree line. So consumption expenditures are equal to disposable income at $3 trillion.

C is $2 trillion. How can our nation have a disposable income of just $1 trillion and manage to consume $2 trillion worth of goods and services? We can dig into our savings and we can borrow from banks and other lenders. And as a nation, we can borrow from foreigners.

Moving right along, let's use Figure 5 to find the nation's marginal propensity to consume and its average propensity to consume. See if you can do it on your own beginning with the MPC formula. Do your work right here:

Solution:

Let's say that disposable income rises from $3 trillion to $5 trillion. By how much does C rise?

At a disposable income of $3 trillion, C = $3 trillion. At a disposable income of $5 trillion, C = $4 trillion. So when disposable income rises from $3 trillion to $5 trillion, C rises by $1 trillion.

Now we can substitute numbers into the MPC formula and solve:

$$\text{MPC} = \frac{\text{Change in consumption}}{\text{Change in disposable income}} = \frac{\$1 \text{ trillion}}{\$2 \text{ trillion}} = \frac{1}{2} = 0.5$$

Now find the average propensity to consume when disposable income is $5 trillion.

Solution:

$$\text{APC} = \frac{\text{Consumption}}{\text{Disposable income}} = \frac{\$4 \text{ trillion}}{\$5 \text{ trillion}} = \frac{4}{5} = 0.8$$

The Saving Function

Figure 6, which illustrates the saving function, is derived from Figure 5. For example, if you look back at Figure 5, you'll see that at a disposable income level of $3 trillion, consumption is also $3 trillion. Therefore, saving would be 0. That gives us one of the points in Figure 6.

Figure 6
The Saving Schedule

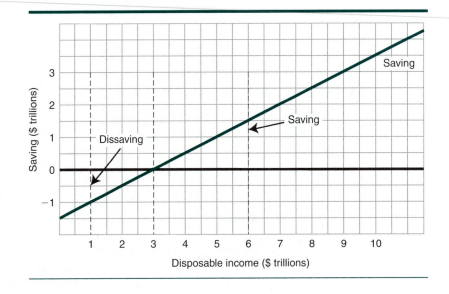

You'll notice in Figure 6 that when the disposable income is less than $3 trillion, saving is negative. We call saving below 0 dissaving. You'll also notice that as disposable income rises, so too does saving.

The saving function is almost the same as the consumption function: *As income rises, saving rises, but not as quickly.*

The following equation summarizes some very basic relationships:

$$\text{Disposable income} = \text{Consumption} + \text{Saving}$$

If disposable income is $12 trillion and savings is $2 trillion, how much is consumption?

Consumption is $10 trillion. If disposable income is $5 trillion and consumption is $8 trillion, how much is saving?

Saving is −$3 trillion. Remember that disposable income ($5 trillion) = consumption ($8 trillion) + saving (−$3 trillion). When savings is negative, we call it "dissaving."

Let's turn back again to Figure 5 and find how much this nation saves at various levels of disposable income. Here's an easy one: How much is saving when disposable income is $3 trillion?

You can see that it's zero, because at the intersection of the C line and the 45-degree line, consumption = disposable income. Next, find savings when disposable income is $9 trillion.

Saving is $3 trillion. It's measured by the vertical distance between the C line and the 45-degree line. Incidentally, how much is C when disposable income is $9 trillion?

C is $6 trillion. To prove your answers, just substitute them into the formula:

$$\text{Disposable income} = \text{Consumption} + \text{Saving}$$
$$\text{\$9 trillion} \quad = \quad \text{\$6 trillion} \quad + \text{\$3 trillion}$$

Now find consumption and savings when disposable income is $2 trillion.

Finding Consumption, Savings, the MPC, and the APC on a Graph

See if you can find savings and consumption when disposable income is $8 trillion in Figure A.

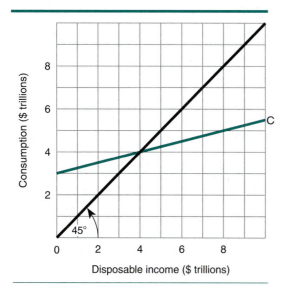

Figure A

Consumption is $5 trillion and savings is $3 trillion. Note that consumption ($5 trillion) and savings ($3 trillion) = disposable income ($8 trillion).

Now do this three-part problem by filling in the table below:

	Disposable income	Consumption	Savings
(a)	$2 trillion		
(b)	$4 trillion		
(c)	$6 trillion		

Solution:

(a) Disposable income ($2 trillion) = C ($3.5 trillion) + saving (−$1.5 trillion)

(b) Disposable income ($4 trillion) = C ($4 trillion) + saving (0)

(c) Disposable income ($6 trillion) = C ($4.5 trillion) + saving ($1.5 trillion)

Now find the MPC.

Solution:

We'll go from a disposable income of $4 trillion to one of $8 trillion. When disposable income is $4 trillion, C is $4 trillion. When disposable income is $8 trillion, C is $5 trillion.

$$MPC = \frac{\text{Change in consumption}}{\text{Change in disposable income}} = \frac{\$1 \text{ trillion}}{\$4 \text{ trillion}}$$

$$= \frac{1}{4} = 0.25$$

One more problem: Find the APC when disposable income is $6 trillion.

Solution:

$$APC = \frac{\text{Consumption}}{\text{Disposable income}} = \frac{\$4.5 \text{ trillion}}{\$6 \text{ trillion}} = \frac{9}{12} = 0.75$$

Solution:

Disposable income = Consumption + Saving

$2 trillion = $2.5 trillion + (−$0.5 trillion)

$2 trillion = $2.5 trillion − $0.5 trillion

How are you doing? If you're getting the right answers, then you're ready to tackle autonomous consumption and induced consumption. But if you'd like a little more practice finding consumption, saving, and the MPC and APC by reading a graph, please work your way through the accompanying Extra Help box.

Autonomous Consumption and Induced Consumption

Autonomous consumption is our level of consumption when disposable income is 0. It is called autonomous consumption because it's autonomous, or independent, of changes in the level of disposable income. People will spend a certain minimum amount on the necessities of life—food, clothing, and shelter—even if they have low incomes or no incomes. Whether they have to beg, borrow, or steal, people will spend some minimum amount.

In Figure 7, can you find the level of autonomous consumption? Write down your answer.

Autonomous consumption is $2 trillion. Even if disposable income is 0, consumption will be $2 trillion. Therefore, when disposable income is 0, autonomous consumption is equal to total consumption.

It's very easy to spot autonomous consumption on a graph. It's the level of C when the C line is touching the vertical axis. Of course, when the C line *is* touching the vertical axis, disposable income is 0.

Induced consumption is that part of consumption which varies with the level of disposable income. As disposable income rises, induced consumption also rises; when disposable income falls, induced consumption also falls. Changes in the level of disposable income induce changes in the level of consumption.

We had said that when disposable income is 0, autonomous consumption is equal to total consumption. A disposable income level of 0 cannot induce any consumption.

$$\text{Consumption} = \text{Autonomous consumption} + \text{Induced consumption}$$

The consumption function tells us that as income rises, consumption rises, but not as quickly. If consumption rises and autonomous consumption (by definition) stays the same, then what happens to induced consumption?

Obviously, it rises. In fact we can make two stronger statements: When consumption rises, induced consumption rises by the same amount; when consumption falls, induced consumption falls by the same amount.

Figure 7

Finding Autonomous Consumption and Induced Consumption

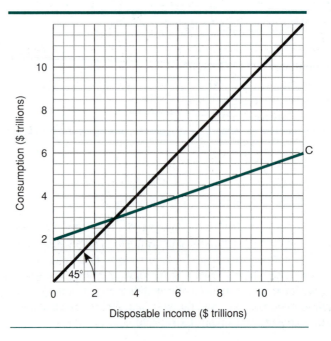

OK, let's go to the graph in Figure 7. For disposable income levels of $3 trillion, $6 trillion, and $9 trillion, find autonomous consumption and induced consumption. Write your answers here:

Solution:

We know that autonomous consumption is $2 trillion. That's the level of consumption when disposable income is 0. So at disposable income levels of $3 trillion, $6 trillion, and $9 trillion, autonomous consumption remains $2 trillion.

When disposable income is $3 trillion, C is $3 trillion. We know that autonomous consumption is $2 trillion. Therefore, induced consumption must be $1 trillion:

Consumption = Autonomous consumption + Induced consumption
$3 trillion = $2 trillion   + $1 trillion

When disposable income is $6 trillion, C = $4 trillion.

Consumption = Autonomous consumption + Induced consumption
$4 trillion = $2 trillion   + $2 trillion

When disposable income is $9 trillion, C = $5 trillion.

Consumption = Autonomous consumption + Induced consumption
$5 trillion = $2 trillion   + $3 trillion

What the Consumer Buys

A century ago Americans spent 43 percent of their incomes on food and another 14 percent on clothing. Today we spend just 13.8 percent on food and 3 percent on clothing. So what *do* we spend our money on?

Consumption is traditionally divided into three categories: durables, nondurables, and services. Durables are things that last a while—say, at least three years. Nondurables, such as food, gasoline, and children's clothing, don't last long. (In fact, a case could be made that the clothing worn by fashion-conscious adults doesn't last either, although the reason it doesn't last is that fashions change rather than that it wears out.)

The consumer buys durables, nondurables, and services.

Durable goods include personal computers, TVs, household appliances, cars, and furniture. They last—or, at least, they're supposed to last for at least three years. The big change in our economy since World War II has been in the service sector, which now produces over half of what consumers buy. Medical care, education, legal and financial services, and entertainment are some of the fields that have grown rapidly in the last five decades.

Figure 8 summarizes where the consumer's dollar went in 1955 and where it went in 2009. There has been a huge shift from expenditures on durables and nondurables to expenditures on services.

In 1955 Americans spent only 36 cents out of every consumer dollar on services; but today 67.7 cents goes toward services. Why this massive shift? For one thing, Americans are spending a much larger part of their incomes on medical care than they did in the 1950s. This trend has been reinforced as our population grows older. More Americans are going to college, eating out, travelling, and suing one another than ever before. Computer services, financial services, and personal services have expanded rapidly. Basically, we're paying people to do things for us that we either did for ourselves in the 1950s or didn't do at all.

Do you bring your lunch to school every day? Do you know anyone who does? Had you gone to college in the 1950s, the chances are you would have brown-bagged it. How does a homemade lunch go into GDP? It goes into the category of nondurable goods. But the lunch you buy in the cafeteria or at Burger King is classified as a service. Similarly, if you buy lettuce, tomatoes, carrots, and other raw vegetables, cut them up at home, and eat a salad, the components of that salad classify as nondurables. But if you stop at a

Figure 8

Consumer Spending, 1955 and
2009

The major change in consumer
spending has been a massive shift
from nondurables to services.

Source: Survey of Current Business,
March 2010.

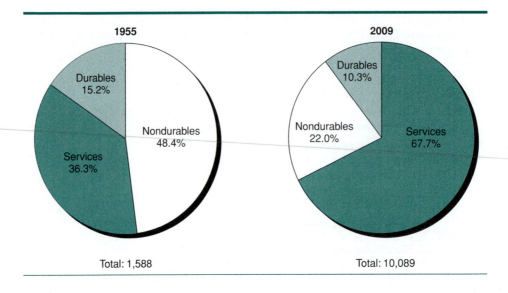

salad bar and buy the identical components, which have been cut up for you—and pay
about 10 times as much per pound—then this expenditure would count as a service.[4]

The U.S. Department of Commerce has found that the average American family
spends nearly three-quarters of its income on housing, transportation, food and beverages,
and medical care (see Figure 9). Overall, we spent over $10 trillion on consumer goods
and services in 2009.

Figure 9

Expenditures of the Average
American Household, 2009

Source: U.S. Bureau of Economic
Analysis, www.bea.gov

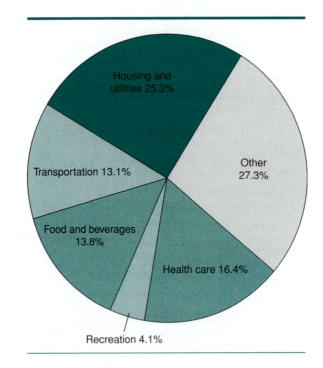

If you glance back at Figure 1, you'll see again the downward trend in saving as a
percentage of disposable income. This will come as no surprise, then, that we should find an
upward trend in consumption as a percentage of GDP. As you can see in Figure 10, between
1982 and 2009, it rose from 62 percent to about 70 percent.

---

[4]In 1955 about one-quarter of the average household's food budget was spent outside the home. Today it's
more than one-half. Did someone say McDonald's?

Figure 10

Consumption as a Percentage of GDP, 1980–2010

Since 1982 there has been a steady upward trend in consumption as a percentage of GDP.

Source: U.S. Bureau of Economic Analysis, www.bea.gov

Determinants of the Level of Consumption

You can't have it all. Where would you put it?

–Ann Landers–

Why do people spend money? Some people hate to spend a penny, and others spend every penny they can lay their hands on. The aphorism, "If you don't have it, you can't spend it," is especially relevant to any discussion of the determinants of consumption. The six basic determinants are listed below. (As we shall see, however, a person's level of spending is determined largely by how much money he or she has.)

A budget tells us what we can't afford, but it doesn't keep us from buying it.

—William Feather

1. Disposable income.
2. Credit availability.
3. Stock of liquid assets in the hands of consumers.
4. Stock of durable goods in the hands of consumers.
5. Keeping up with the Joneses.
6. Consumer expectations.
7. The wealth effect.

The Level of Disposable Income

Many factors influence how much money people spend; by far the most important is disposable income. As illustrated with the consumption function, as income rises, consumption rises, but not as quickly.

The most important determinant of consumption is the level of disposable income.

At very low income levels, people not only don't save, they actually dissave. That is, their saving is negative. Suppose, for example, you lose your job. Do you simply stop spending money? If you did, you'd sure lose a lot of weight. How do you get by? If you collect unemployment benefits, then that's your disposable income. But the chances are, you would spend more each week than your unemployment checks, especially if you support a family. You still have to pay rent, car payments, other installment payments, utilities, and food bills, as well as the cost of looking for another job.

To manage all this you might borrow—if you can get credit—and you will go into your savings. So, at very low levels of income, you tend to spend more than your disposable income.

I don't think you can spend yourself rich.

—George Humphrey, Treasury Secretary in Eisenhower Administration

The more you've got, the more you spend. Or, alternatively, if you ain't got it, you can't spend it. So you can be sure that the working-class family spends more than the poor family. And that the upper-middle-class family spends more than the working-class family. Almost every family spends most of its income, so clearly the level of disposable income largely determines the level of consumption.

The main point here is that rich people spend a lot more money than do poor people. Why? Because they *have* more money. What is the most important determinant of consumption? Disposable income.

Credit Availability

Remember when people worried about how much it took to buy something, instead of how long?
—Earl Wilson

Never spend your money before you have it.
—Thomas Jefferson

You can't borrow money if you don't have credit. The most popular ways of borrowing are credit cards, especially VISA and MasterCard. Bank loans, home mortgages, home equity loans, and auto loans are other ways of borrowing. When credit is eased, people tend to borrow more.

For example, suppose a furniture store, which had been asking its customers to put down 50 percent of their purchases in cash and pay out the balance in six months, now offered new terms: nothing down and two years to pay. Many more people would buy furniture on these terms. This is not to say that everyone stretches his or her credit to the limit, although some people do.

Credit availability varies inversely with the level of consumer debt. That is, the more you owe, the less credit available. If your credit card limit is $5,000 and you already owe $4,900, you have only $100 of credit available. Furthermore, people who owe a great deal are somewhat reluctant to take on still more debt.

The most valuable asset held by most American families is their home. And as tens of millions of these families have discovered through the 1990s and the first six or seven years of this decade, their homes can be turned into virtual ATMs when they take out second mortgages. During the housing boom that ended in 2006, banks were happy to extend home owners hundreds of billions of dollars a year in home equity loans. As long as housing prices were rising, there was little worry about these loans being repaid. In the meanwhile, all this borrowing helped finance consumer spending, which managed to rise even during the 2001 recession. But when housing prices began to fall in 2006, the process was reversed. Bankers became increasingly reluctant to extend home equity loans, and this consequently put a big crimp in consumer spending.

Stock of Liquid Assets in the Hands of Consumers

The chief enjoyment of riches consists in the parade of riches.
—Adam Smith

People own things that can be quickly turned into cash. These are called liquid assets. Prime examples include government and corporate bonds, corporate stocks, savings accounts, bank certificates of deposit (CDs), and money market funds.

In the United States today, people hold a stock of liquid assets of a few trillion dollars. This makes some people feel rich. Suppose, for example, you hold 1,000 shares of IBM stock and the price of that stock rises $2. You are $2,000 richer (at least on paper). This may induce you to go out and spend some of that money you just made.

Economists estimate that consumers cut back spending by about 4 cents for every dollar's worth of wealth they lose in the market, so a $1 trillion stock market plunge would cause about a $40 billion drop in annual consumption, or less than one-half of one percent of total spending. Of course, if the market were to continue to rise, we would see a corresponding *increase* in consumption.

In addition to *feeling* rich, if your liquid assets rise, you do indeed have more money to spend. That is, you can quickly convert some of these assets into money, then go out and spend it. Economists have found that there is some correlation between consumption and the amount of liquid assets held. The reasoning here is that if you don't have it, you can't spend it, and if you do have it, you will spend some of it.

Stock of Durable Goods in the Hands of Consumers

In 1929, radios, phonographs, toasters, vacuum cleaners, waffle irons, and other appliances were relatively new because most of the country had been electrified only over the

Thorstein Veblen, American sociologist and economist

last decade and a half. More than 95 percent of the cars on the road were less than 10 years old. By 1930, the market for consumer durables was temporarily saturated.

When few people own items such as personal computers, DVD players, flat screen TVs, or video games, sales will rise. But when the market is saturated (and people own relatively late models), it will be some time before sales pick up again.

Consumer durables are now a relatively small part of total consumption—only 10.3 percent of all goods and services sold to consumers in 2009. However, their sales are somewhat erratic, largely because they vary inversely with the stock of consumer durables in the hands of consumers. When people hold a large stock of consumer durables, consumer durable sales tend to be low; when that stock is low, sales tend to be high.

Keeping Up with the Joneses

Most of us, at least a few times in our lives, have been guilty of showing off our expensive clothes, our jewelry, our cars, or even our Florida tans. And most of us have been tempted to keep up with our neighbors, relatives, and friends. When the Joneses buy something, we have to go out and buy one, too—even if we can't afford it—because if we don't buy it, we won't be keeping up.

Why do some people spend $10,000 on a wristwatch, $200 for a pair of sneakers, or $5,000 for an evening gown? To a large degree, they're showing off. I have so much money, they seem to be saying, that I can afford these indulgences.

Almost a century ago Thorstein Veblen coined the term *conspicuous consumption*. In a marvelous book titled *The Theory of the Leisure Class*, Veblen stated, "Conspicuous consumption of valuable goods is a means of reputability to the gentleman of leisure." He went on to say, "With the exception of the instinct of self-preservation, the propensity for emulation is probably the strongest and most alert and persistent of the economic motives proper."[5]

Wealth has never been a sufficient source of honor in itself. It must be advertised, and the normal medium is obtrusively expensive goods.

—John Kenneth Galbraith, *The Affluent Society*

Conspicuous consumption

I shop. Therefore I am.

—Anonymous

Maintaining a "Basic" Standard of Living

What do you need to maintain a "basic," no-frills standard of living? What do you need besides food on the table, clothes on your back, and a roof over your head? Do you need a cell phone, a PC with high-speed Internet access, an iPod, cable TV, and an Xbox? Even unemployed 25-year-olds, still living with their parents, would consider all of the above basic necessities. What do *you* think?

Back in 1950 just one family in 10 owned a small-screen black and white TV. Today over 80 percent of all households have more than one large-screen color TV with cable or alternative access (such as satellite). We have more cars on the road than licensed drivers. Poor Americans live better today than middle-class Americans did just a few decades ago. What was a luxury a few years ago is now a basic. The bar keeps rising.

Consumer Expectations

When people expect inflation, they often buy consumer durables before prices go up. On the other hand, when they expect recession, they tend to reduce their purchases of such big-ticket items as cars, furniture, and major appliances. Many people fear being laid off or having their income reduced because of recessions, so they tend to postpone major purchases until times get better.

If you take another look at Figure 1 near the beginning of the chapter, you'll see that during and/or immediately after the recessions of 1990–1991, 2001, and 2007–2009, our savings rate turned upward. So during bad economic times, people tend to cut back on consumption until they see that the economy is improving.

The Wealth Effect

When the value of your home rises, or the prices of the stocks you own go up, you perceive yourself as being wealthier. A Federal Reserve model estimates that for every $1,000 that

[5]Thorstein Veblen, *The Theory of the Leisure Class,* Chapters 4 and 5.

your wealth rises, you will spend an additional $37.50—which comes to exactly 3.75 percent of your gain in wealth. Not surprisingly, economists call this the *wealth effect*.

During the run-up of housing prices between 2000 and 2006—which was accompanied by rising stock prices—consumption rose rapidly. Indeed, the APS fell below 1 percent. But as they say, what goes up must come down. And as housing prices and stock prices fell through 2007 and 2008, Americans sustained a loss of some $13 trillion—on paper. Quite reasonably, they perceived themselves as poorer, and cut their consumption accordingly.

The Permanent Income Hypothesis

Milton Friedman, winner of Nobel Prize, 1976, for work on monetary theory

According to Milton Friedman, a prominent conservative economist, the strongest influence on consumption is one's estimated average lifetime income. No one knows what his or her average lifetime income will actually be, but people can generally figure out if they are earning more or less than that average.

If a factory worker earning $35,000 a year expects to remain a factory worker, she can estimate her future earnings until she retires. According to Friedman, people gear their consumption to their expected earnings more than to their current income.

Suppose someone's income temporarily contracts, say, because of a factory lay-off. Would the person cut back very sharply on her consumption? No, she would not, says this theory, since she knows she will be back on the job within a few months. She has to continue paying her rent, meeting her car payments, and eating three times a day.

Earnings tend to rise until late middle age (about 55 or so) and then decline. Therefore the permanent income hypothesis would predict that most people's consumption is greater than their income until their mid- or late 20s. From the late 20s to the early 60s, current disposable income is usually greater than consumption. In old age, the relationship between consumption and current disposable income is again reversed, so consumption is greater than income.

Thus, our consumption is determined by our average expected income, or permanent income. That income is a constant; consumption is a constant percentage of that income. Suppose that you expected your average lifetime income to be around $35,000 a year. Some years it would be much higher than $35,000 and some years, much lower. But year after year, according to the permanent income hypothesis, you would still consume pretty much the same amount—say, $34,000.

According to Friedman's hypothesis, if you suddenly win the lottery, you will spend *some* of it because it will raise your permanent income, but you will spend only a small part of it. Is this how most lottery winners have handled their windfalls? Certainly not. But even though the permanent income hypothesis does not always hold true, it is still useful in predicting lifetime spending patterns.

Is the Consumer Really King?

Before we even receive our paychecks today, nearly all those dollars already have someone else's name on them. *Think* about it. How much of *your* family's paychecks goes toward paying off your mortgage, credit card debt, your cars, school tuition, insurance, medical bills, and home repair? Of course you would have had a lot more to spend if the government hadn't already taken *its* share of your pay before you even saw your paycheck.

Let's start with what is, by far, our most important purchase—a home. Once that purchase is made, you're committed to making mortgage payments, real estate taxes, heating bills, homeowner's insurance, upkeep, and repairs. Back in 1949, the average 30-year-old head of household needed to spend just 14 percent of his paycheck to make the payments on his home. By 1970 it took more than 21 percent of his paycheck to pay for that home. And today the average 30-year-old has to shell out almost 40 percent of his take-home pay.

The American dream has gradually become a financial nightmare. I recently asked my students how many cars their families owned. The majority owned three or four.

Suburban sprawl has almost completely obviated the use of mass transit. The trip to work, to school, to the store, to little league practice, and to virtually anywhere else must be made by car. The cost of car payments, insurance, gas, maintenance, and repairs takes another large chunk—often more than 20 percent—out of the typical suburban family's income. So it's no wonder that most households depend on two full-time incomes, and often one or two additional part-time incomes as well.

Elizabeth Warren and Amelia Warren Tyagi maintain that most middle-class families with children are caught in *The Two-Income Trap*. Even with two wage earners, families today are worse off than families supported by just one wage earner 30 years ago.

Elizabeth Warren and Amelia Warren Tyagi

> The average two-income family earns far more today than did the single-breadwinner family of a generation ago. And yet, once they have paid the mortgage, the car payments, the taxes, the health insurance, and the day-care bills, today's dual-income families have *less* discretionary income—and less money to put away for a rainy day—than the single-income family of a generation ago.[6]

What happened between the early 1970s and today? Warren and Tyagi explain that millions of stay-at-home moms were compelled to enter the labor force to ensure that their children would live in safe neighborhoods and go to decent schools. A bidding war for housing in desirable suburban neighborhoods drove up the price of housing by 70 percent after allowing for inflation. So even though the two-wage-earner families today are bringing home 75 percent more than what one-wage-earner families brought home 30 years ago, they have less discretionary income. Nearly three-quarters of their income is earmarked for fixed expenses—mortgage, child care, health insurance, car(s), and taxes. Back in the early 1970s, the single-income family devoted just 54 percent of its income to fixed expenses, leaving the rest for discretionary spending. In addition, the stay-at-home mom spent a lot more time with her children.

Who was better off, ask Warren and Tyagi, the one-wage-earner family of the early 1970s or the two-wage-earner family today?

> A generation ago, a single breadwinner who worked diligently and spent carefully could assure his family a comfortable position in the middle class. But the frenzied bidding wars, fueled by families with two incomes, changed the game for single-income families as well, pushing them down the economic ladder. To keep Mom at home, the average single-income family must forfeit decent public schools and preschools, health insurance, and college degrees, leaving themselves and their children with a tenuous hold on their middle-class dreams.[7]

Today's family needs at least two paychecks just to maintain yesterday's standard of living.

—John J. Sweeney
President, AFL–CIO

So what do *you* think? Were families better off in the good old days back in the early 1970s than they are today? How well off are *your* parents compared to their own parents 35 years ago?

Why Do We Spend So Much and Save So Little?

> It may sometimes be expedient for a man to heat the stove with his furniture. But he should not delude himself by believing that he has discovered a wonderful new method of heating his premises.
>
> –Ludwig von Mises, early 20th-century Austrian economist–

Americans have been on a spending binge these last 30 years. In fact, the national motto might well be "Buy now, pay later," "Shop till you drop," or "We want it all,

Murray Weidenbaum, President Reagan's first chief economic advisor

---

[6]Elizabeth Warren and Amelia Warren Tyagi, *The Two-Income Trap* (New York: Basic Books, 2003), p. 8. In December 2008, Elizabeth Warren was appointed the Chair of the Congressional Oversight Panel, which was given the task of making sure that the $700 billion financial bailout was being spent in the interest of the taxpayers. This topic will be covered in Chapter 14.

[7]Warren and Tyagi, *op. cit.*, p. 9.

and we want it now!" The "me generation" has had a fascination for every conceivable type of electronic gadget, has had to buy new wardrobes every six months as the fashions change, and has had to drive the latest-model, fully loaded luxury foreign car. In fact, much of what we buy is made by foreigners. Murray Weidenbaum, who served as President Ronald Reagan's first chief economic advisor, summed up our profligacy this way:

> As citizens of the United States, we are consuming more than we are producing, borrowing more than we are saving, and spending more than we are earning. We are rapidly approaching the time when we will have to pay the piper.

The federal government has actually underwritten our spending binge. Mortgage interest and property taxes are fully deductible. So buy a home and charge part of your costs to Uncle Sam. And if you need to borrow still more money, just take out a second mortgage and use this money to finance your ever-growing consumption expenditures.

The tremendous expansion of bank credit cards, installment credit, and consumer loans has further fueled the consumer binge of the last dozen years. Every day Americans are offered millions of credit cards, whether they asked for them or not. In fact, from 1990 to 2000 household debt doubled to $7 trillion and doubled again to $14 trillion in 2008. Some people call credit cards "mall money."

Our saving rate might not have been so low were it not for two factors that have become increasingly important over the last five decades—Social Security and widespread home ownership. Most Americans do not feel the pressing need to save for their old age because they will receive Social Security benefits, not to mention private pensions. Similarly, home ownership is seen as a form of saving, especially during a period of rising real estate prices.

Bruce Steinberg, a Merrill Lynch economist, takes a contrarian view, by claiming that the savings rate is badly biased downward. His view was summarized by *BusinessWeek*:[8]

> In calculating the rate, he notes, the government inconsistently subtracts capital-gains taxes from income while failing to count as income the gains on which those taxes are paid.
>
> If realized capital gains were counted as income (which is how most people see them), Steinberg figures the current savings rate would be 10 percent—close to its historic level. In other words, people have not been dipping into their unrealized capital gains, as some charge.

Before we are *too* critical of our spendthrift ways, we need to ask ourselves *what* are we consuming. For example, how much of *your* income, not to mention that of your parents, goes toward your education? Although spending on education is classified as consumption, wouldn't it make sense to classify it instead as an investment (one of the main topics of the next chapter)?

So if we consider all of these mitigating factors, we may conclude that while our savings rate is quite low, it is not really as low as it looks. Which may be a lot like saying, Mrs. Jones, your son failed all his exams, but on each one he did manage to score in the mid-fifties.

How *have* we been able to put off paying the piper for so long? By borrowing. As individual consumers, we borrow; as giant corporations, we borrow; and as the federal government, we borrow. And who lends us this money? Increasingly, the answer is foreigners.

So far I've described the American consumer as someone who leaves the mall only to work and sleep. But most middle-class Americans, especially couples with children, are hard-pressed to make ends meet. They might have a nice suburban house and a couple of cars, but they may have a real struggle to make ends meet. And so we ask, Is the consumer really king?

Finally, let's consider the effect of recessions on saving. If you look ahead to Figure 11, you notice that personal savings as a percentage of GDP rose during each of the recessions since 1960 (indicated by the shaded areas). During the Great Recession of 2007–2009, the APS (which is slightly higher than personal saving as a percent of GDP), rose from an

It seems a lot of trouble if, instead of having to earn money and save it, you can just go and borrow it.
—Winston Churchill

Nobody goes to the mall anymore because they're too crowded.
—Standard retail industry joke

A penny saved is a penny earned.
—Benjamin Franklin

---

[8]"Are Americans Spendthrifts?" *BusinessWeek,* November 22, 2000, p. 18.

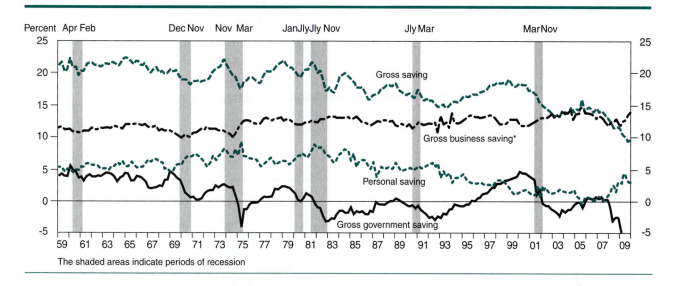

Figure 11

Savings as Percentage of GDP, 1959–2009

Personal saving has been on the decline since the mid-1980s, while government saving (by the federal, state, and local governments), which was negative for most of the 1980s and 1990s, became positive in the late 1990s when the federal government went from huge budget deficits to huge surpluses. Now, as the federal budget deficits mount, government saving is −7.5 percent of GDP. By far, the most important component of national saving is business saving.

Source: Survey of Current Business, March 2010.

annual rate of just 1.2 percent in the first quarter of 2008 to 5.4 percent in the second quarter of 2009. Does this increase indicate a reversal of the long-term downward trend in personal savings? Probably not. As the economic recovery took hold in the second half of 2009 and early 2010, the savings rate had begun to fall.

Total Saving: Individual Saving + Business Saving + Government Saving

Every economy depends on saving for capital formation. That saving is the total of individual saving, business saving, and government saving.[9] We've seen that individual saving has dwindled in recent years. Businesses set aside savings in the form of depreciation allowances and retained earnings, while our local, state, and federal governments save by running surpluses and dissave by running deficits.

As you can see in Figure 11, the decline in household saving between 1993 and 2000 was offset by a sharp rise in government saving and business saving. But since 2001, while personal savings continued its decline, government saving fell too. Indeed, both government and personal saving were both negative in 2005, dragging down the gross savings rate.

Until the recession of 1981–82, as a nation we generally saved about 20 percent of our Gross National Product. Except for a surge in gross saving in the mid-to-late 1990s, it has trended downward. By 2009 our gross saving rate was just over 10 percent. This was not nearly enough to fund business investment needs as well as to finance the federal budget deficit. Since Americans were not saving enough, we have needed to borrow almost $2 billion a day from foreigners. But what if some day foreigners refuse to lend us any more money? Clearly we cannot continue spending more than we earn, whether as individuals or as a nation.

---

[9]Government saving = federal surplus (or deficit) + state and local surplus.

Current Issue: The American Consumer: World-Class Shopper

How does our consumption spending compare with that of the citizens of other countries? You won't be too surprised to learn that as consumers, we are in a league of our own. While consumption accounts for just over 70 cents of every dollar of our GDP, in most other industrial countries consumption spending accounts for substantially less (see Figure 12).

Figure 12

Private Consumption as percentage of GDP, Selected Countries 2008
Sources: CEIC; OECD; World Bank.

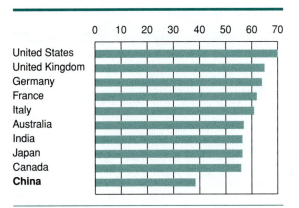

There is no question but that the American consumer is the prime mover not just of our economy, but of the world economy as well. As any business owner will tell you, you can't run a business without buyers for your goods or services. So despite all the terrible things I've said about the spendthrift American consumer in this chapter—Born to shop, Shop till you drop—it's the consumer who makes our economy go.

The level of consumer spending was especially important during 2010 as our economy recovered from the 2007–2009 recession. In the late spring of that year, it was not yet clear if consumers would spend enough to boast economic growth and substantially reduce unemployment. As you read these words, you will have a much better idea if the American consumer came through.

Because the United States has the largest consumer market in the world, it has been targeted by foreign sellers, especially the Japanese and Chinese. Selling to America made possible the Japanese economic miracle in the decades after World War II, when Japanese industry was being rebuilt and its home market had relatively low purchasing power. Japan was able to sell us black and white TVs, then color TVs, cameras, VCRs, stereos, and cars. The American consumer helped finance the Japanese recovery.

China, which had maintained a growth rate of about 10 percent over the last 25 years, also hitched its economic wagon to the American market. Again, it was the American consumer buying microwave ovens, TVs, apparel, shoes, toys, personal computers, and consumer electronics that enabled China to lift itself by its own bootstraps. Today, the Chinese run such huge trade surpluses with us that they can finance most of our federal budget deficit.[10]

So while all this spending may be putting us more and more into the debt of foreigners, it is doing wonders for China, Japan, South Korea, Canada, Mexico, and other countries running large trade surpluses with the United States. Were you to ask economists in these nations about the level of consumption spending in the United States, most of them would probably say it is just fine, thank you.

---

[10] There will be a much more extensive discussion of our trading relationships with Japan and China in the next-to-last chapter of this book.

Questions for Further Thought and Discussion

1. Explain the relationship between consumption and saving.

2. Explain the difference between autonomous consumption and induced consumption.

3. Explain how the stock of consumer durables in the hands of consumers and credit availability each affect the level of consumption.

4. Since the 1950s a massive shift in consumption patterns with respect to nondurable goods and services has taken place. What is this shift and how can it be explained?

5. How little do Americans save? Why do they save so little?

6. How is it possible for a nation's consumption to sometimes exceed its disposable income?

7. The marginal propensity to consume (MPC) for a nation is .85. Explain what this means.

8. Why is the demand for consumer nondurable goods more stable than that for consumer durable goods?

9. How much was our APC and APS in 2009? (Hint: Look at Figure 1 near the beginning of this chapter.)

10. *Practical Application:* If you had the power to write laws, how would you provide incentives to encourage Americans to save more?

Workbook for Chapter 5 McGraw Hill connect |ECONOMICS

Name _____   Date _____

Multiple-Choice Questions

Circle the letter that corresponds to the best answer.

1. Since 1955 Americans have been spending _____. (LO3)
   a) a larger percentage of their incomes on services
   b) a smaller percentage of their incomes on services
   c) about the same percentage of their incomes on services

2. When the C line crosses the 45-degree line, saving is _____. (LO3, 4)
   a) positive
   b) negative
   c) zero
   d) impossible to calculate because there is not enough information to know

3. When disposable income is zero, _____. (LO5)
   a) autonomous consumption is equal to induced consumption
   b) autonomous consumption is equal to total consumption
   c) induced consumption is equal to total consumption

4. The minimum amount that people will spend even if disposable income is zero is called _____ consumption. (LO5)
   a) autonomous
   b) induced
   c) total

5. According to the permanent income hypothesis, if a person received a windfall of $100,000, he would spend _____ that year. (LO7)
   a) some of it   c) nearly all of it
   b) most of it   d) all of it

6. As disposable income rises, _____. (LO5)
   a) autonomous C rises   c) induced C rises
   b) autonomous C falls   d) induced C falls

7. The largest component of GDP is _____. (LO3)
   a) net exports   c) consumption
   b) investment   d) government purchases

8. The largest component of C is _____. (LO3)
   a) durable goods
   b) services
   c) nondurable goods

9. The consumption function tells us that, as income rises, consumption _____. (LO3)
   a) declines
   b) remains the same
   c) rises more slowly than income
   d) rises more quickly than income

10. When income levels are very low, C is _____. (LO3)
    a) zero
    b) lower than income
    c) higher than income

11. When income is equal to consumption, saving is _____. (LO3, 4)
    a) negative
    b) zero
    c) positive
    d) impossible to calculate because there is insufficient information

12. Which of the following relations is *not* correct? (LO1, 2)
    a) MPC + MPS = 1   d) 1 − APS = APC
    b) APC + APS = 1   e) 1 − MPC = MPS
    c) MPS = MPC + 1

13. Induced consumption expenditures _____. (LO5)
    a) fall as income rises
    b) are always equal to autonomous consumption expenditures

c) plus saving equals total consumption expenditures

d) represent consumption that is independent of income

e) are influenced mainly by income

14. Autonomous consumption expenditures are

_____. (LO5)

a) equal to induced consumption expenditures

b) proportional to disposable income

c) not influenced by income

d) influenced primarily by the saving function

15. The average propensity to save _____. (LO1)

a) is disposable income divided by savings

b) is a measure of the additional saving generated by additional income

c) is negative at very high income levels

d) varies directly with income; as income rises, the APS rises

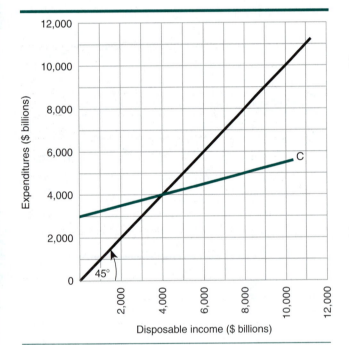

Figure 1

Use the data in Figure 1 to answer questions 16–18.

16. Savings is equal to zero at a disposable income of

_____. (LO4)

a) 0

b) $2,000 billion

c) $4,000 billion

d) $6,000 billion

e) $8,000 billion

17. Consumption is equal to 5,000 at a disposable income

of _____. (LO3)

a) $2,000 billion

b) $4,000 billion

c) $6,000 billion

d) $8,000 billion

e) $10,000 billion

18. When disposable income is $2,000 billion,

consumption is _____. (LO3)

a) −$3,500 billion

b) 0

c) $2,000 billion

d) $3,500 billion

e) $4,000 billion

19. Which is the most accurate statement? (LO8)

a) The American personal savings rate would be higher if we counted capital gains as income which is not spent.

b) An average propensity to save of .02 means that only 2 percent of the population is saving any of their income.

c) Our low savings rate is not considered a problem by many economists.

d) Our government savings rate is always negative.

20. Our consumption spending tends to rise as the stock of liquid assets in the hands of consumers

_____ and credit availability

_____. (LO6)

a) rises, rises

b) falls, falls

c) rises, falls

d) falls, rises

21. Boyd and Dianne Call earn $100,000 a year. They went deeply into debt after paying $75,000 for their daughter Chelsea's wedding and $50,000 for their daughter Kaylynne's sweet sixteen party. Their behavior might best be described by

_____. (LO6, 7, 8)

a) Milton Friedman

b) John Maynard Keynes

c) Bruce Steinberg

d) Thorstein Veblen

22. As a nation's income falls, induced consumption

_____. (LO5)

a) rises

b) falls

c) remains the same

23. Twenty years from now our disposable income will rise from $30 trillion to $31 trillion. What would your best guess be as to how much consumption will rise? (LO8)

    a) $50 billion   c) $950 billion

    b) $500 billion   d) $1.05 trillion

24. Which one of the following statements is the most accurate? (LO6, 8)

    a) The American consumer was largely responsible for Japan's economic resurgence since World War II.

    b) China, as the world's most populous country, has the world's largest consumer market.

    c) Although there are some who call the American consumer a world-class shopper, most Americans save substantial parts of their incomes.

    d) Since we import most of our goods, the American economy has only a small impact on the world's other large economies.

25. Which statement is true? (LO1, 8)

    a) Americans save much more of their incomes than they did 20 years ago.

    b) In 2009, our APC was a little below 1.0.

    c) Although the U.S. does not have the highest saving rate in the world, Americans save more money than the citizens of every other country.

    d) Our APS has been negative since the early 1990s.

26. Which statement is true? (LO6)

    a) Consumption spending accounts for about 60 percent of our GDP.

    b) The basic long-term trend in consumption spending as a percentage of GDP has been downward.

    c) The wealth effect accounts for some additional consumption when people perceive themselves to be wealthier.

    d) Were it not for the wealth effect, most Americans, especially those who owned homes and corporate stock, would have cut back on their consumption even more, making the Great Recession more severe.

Fill-In Questions

1. About _____ percent of what Americans spend on consumption is spent on services. (LO1, 3)

2. The average propensity to consume is found by dividing _____ by _____. (LO1)

3. The APS + the APC = _____. (LO1)

4. The consumption function states that _____. (LO3)

5. Dissaving takes place when _____. (LO5)

6. Induced consumption is induced by _____. (LO5)

7. According to the saving function, as disposable income rises, _____. (LO4)

8. The most important determinant of the level of consumption is _____. (LO6)

9. The average propensity to consume in the United States today is about _____. (LO1)

10. 1 − MPS = _____. (LO2)

11. When the C line crosses the 45-degree line, saving is equal to _____. (LO3, 4)

Problems

1. Given the information shown in Table 1, calculate the APC and the APS. (LO1)

TABLE 1

Disposable Income	Consumption
$10,000	$8,400

2. Given the information shown in Table 2, calculate the MPC and MPS. (Assume disposable income rises from $35,000 to $37,000.) (LO2)

TABLE 2

Year	Disposable Income	Saving
2002	$35,000	$4,600
2003	37,000	5,300

3. Using the information in Figure 2, how much are consumption and saving when disposable income is: (LO3, 4)

	C	Saving
a) 1,000	_____	_____
b) 2,000	_____	_____
c) 3,000	_____	_____

4. Using your answers from question 3a, calculate the APC and the APS. (LO1, 6)

5. Using your answers from questions 3a and 3b, calculate the MPC and the MPS when disposable income rises from $1,000 billion to $2,000 billion. (LO2)

6. Using the data in Figure 2, how much is autonomous consumption? (LO5)

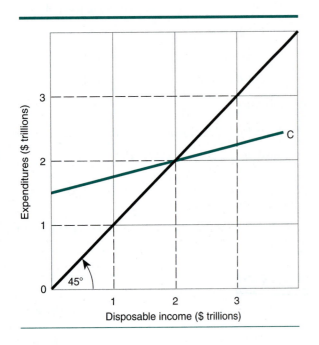

Figure 2

7. Using the data in Figure 2, determine induced consumption when disposable income is: (LO5)
   a) $1 trillion
   b) $2 trillion
   c) $3 trillion

8. If C is $4 trillion, disposable income is $5 trillion, and autonomous consumption is $3 trillion: (LO5)
   a) How much is saving?
   b) How much is induced consumption?
   c) How much is the APS?
   d) If the APS falls by .01, how much (in dollars) does saving fall?

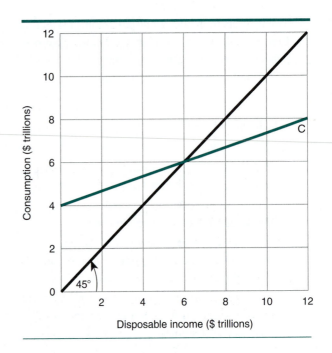

Figure 3

Use the data in Figure 3 to answer questions 9–12.

9. Determine induced consumption when disposable income is: (LO5)
   a) 0
   b) $6 trillion
   c) $12 trillion

10. When disposable income is $9 trillion: (LO3, 4)
    a) How much is autonomous consumption?
    b) How much is total consumption?
    c) How much is saving?

11. When disposable income is $12 trillion: (LO1)
    a) How much is the APC?
    b) How much is the APS?

12. In problem 11: (LO2)
    a) How much is the MPC?
    b) How much is the MPS?

Chapter 6

The Business-Investment Sector

Are you ready for two very easy questions? (1) Which country produces more goods and services than any other? (2) Which country has more capital than any other country? The answer to each question is the United States. Do you think there's some kind of connection between our having the most capital and producing the most output? The connection is very simple: The main reason we are able to produce so much is because we have so much capital.

Unlike in Vietnam, Cuba, North Korea, and dozens of other communist and socialist nations, most investment in the United States is carried out by private business firms rather than by the government. That investment consists of the production of new plant and equipment, residential housing, and additions to our inventories.

LEARNING OBJECTIVES

After reading this chapter you should be able to:

1. List the three types of business firms and discuss their advantages and disadvantages.
2. Define investment and identify its main components.
3. Show how savings gets invested.
4. Distinguish between gross investment and net investment.
5. Explain how capital is accumulated.
6. List and discuss the determinants of the level of investment.
7. Analyze the graph of the C + I line.

Proprietorships, Partnerships, and Corporations

There are three types of business firms in the United States. Proprietorships are owned by individuals and are almost always small businesses. Partnerships, which are also usually small, are owned by two or more people. There are relatively few large businesses in our country, and virtually all of them are corporations. Most corporations, like most businesses, are small.

Most businesses are small.

The Proprietorship

A typical proprietorship would be a grocery, a barbershop, a candy store, a restaurant, a family farm, or a filling station. Chances are, nearly all of the places in the neighborhood where you shop are proprietorships.

To start a proprietorship, a person simply decides to go into business, either opening a new firm or taking over an existing one. With a proprietorship, there are fewer legal complications than with any other form of business organization. Another advantage is that you are your own boss. You don't have to consult with other owners, partners, or stockholders. Finally, there are tax advantages. A proprietor's income is taxed only once—when she or he pays personal income tax. But if the same firm were to incorporate, its income would be taxed twice—once as the income of the firm (the corporate income tax) and again as the personal income of the owner.

A proprietorship has three disadvantages. First, the entire burden of running the company falls on one person's shoulders. Second, the owner may be sued for everything she has if the business is sued. And third, it's a lot harder for one person, rather than two or more people, to raise capital.

The Partnership

Advantages of a partnership

Two or more people can form a partnership. Although the typical partnership has two people, some law and accounting firms have hundreds of partners. Two key advantages of forming a partnership are being able to raise more capital and to divide the work and responsibility of running the business.

A typical division of labor between partners would be production and sales, or, in the parlance of business, inside and outside. The advantages of forming a partnership must be weighed against two basic disadvantages. The first is that the partnership must be dissolved when one of its members dies or wants to leave the business. A second disadvantage is that of unlimited liability.

Disadvantages of a partnership

Both proprietors and partners are liable for all debts incurred by their businesses. For example, if the firm is sued for negligence, the owners are personally liable to pay the amount awarded if the firm cannot do so. If one partner absconds with funds, the other partners may lose their homes and cars even though they were innocent victims. The way to avoid ever having to face this dilemma is to incorporate.

The Corporation

The main advantage to incorporating is limited liability.

The key advantage of the corporation is limited liability. That is, each owner's liability is limited to the amount of money he has invested in the business. If there's a negligence suit or someone absconds with funds, the most you can lose is your investment. No one can touch your house, car, or any other personal property.

Corporation: An ingenious device for obtaining individual profit without individual responsibility.

—Ambrose Bierce,
The Devil's Dictionary

A corporation is a legal person. As such, it can sue and be sued. What is significant about this attribute is that the people who own the corporation—the stockholders—cannot be sued no matter how grievous the transgressions of the corporation. However, the courts have, on occasion, found stockholders liable (for example, when stockholders form a corporation for fraudulent purposes).

A second advantage of a corporation is its potentially perpetual life. While a partnership must be dissolved when one of the partners leaves the business, a corporation can continue indefinitely: The stock owned by the principal who wants to pull out is purchased by someone else. In the case of large, publicly held corporations, such transactions take place routinely at the major stock exchanges.

A third advantage is paying lower federal personal income tax. If you're a small business owner making at least $40,000, says Judith McQuown, author of *Incorporate Yourself,*[1] you can actually save on your taxes by incorporating.[2] You can find all of this spelled out in McQuown's book, and, if you decide to incorporate, you'll want to hire an accountant to calculate your tax savings.

Still another advantage of incorporating is that the company can sell stock to the public to raise more money. Because the owners have limited liability and the firm itself

---

[1]Judith McQuown, *Inc. Yourself: How to Profit by Setting Up Your Own Corporation,* 9th ed. (New York: Broadway Books, 1999).

[2]In 2003 Congress passed a law which largely eliminated "double taxation" of corporate profits (until then corporate profits were subject to the federal corporate income tax and the federal personal income tax).

Small Corporations

The typical corporation is very small, like the old North American Uniform Cap Corporation. Although the company had a rather impressive name, its officers were Jonas Lewy, president; Nadja Lewy, vice president; and their son, Henry Lewy, secretary-treasurer. They ran their business out of a tiny loft in Manhattan's garment district, sewing up work caps, military caps, and what are now called "gimme caps." They had about a half-dozen sewing machines, and Henry's parents—the president and the vice president—operated two of them.

During the "busy season," they hired another three or four operators.

The North American Uniform Cap Corporation never grew into a large enterprise, although the Lewys were always waiting for that one big order—like maybe a few million caps for the Chinese Peoples Liberation Army. But the big order never came, and, like 85 percent of all corporations, North American Uniform Caps never managed to do a million dollars worth of business in a single year.

TABLE 1	The Top Ten in U.S. Sales, 2008	
RANK 2008		(in billions of $)
1	**ExxonMobil**	443
2	**Walmart Stores**	406
3	**Chevron**	263
4	**ConocoPhillips**	231
5	**General Electric**	183
6	**General Motors**	149
7	**Ford Motor**	146
8	**AT&T**	124
9	**Hewlett-Packard**	118
10	**Valero Energy**	118

Source: www.fortune.com

has ongoing life, the corporation is in a better position than the proprietorship or partnership to go to the public to raise funds.

Of course, only a tiny fraction of all corporations ever go public. Nearly all are relatively small businesses that are completely owned by a few individuals. (See the box, "Small Corporations.")

Most corporations are small firms.

The largest 10 corporations are shown in Table 1. Who's number one? It's Exxon-Mobil, with sales of $443 billion.

How do the largest American firms stack up against the largest firms in the world? As you can see in Table 2, ExxonMobil is number two, right behind Royal Dutch Shell, and overall, there are three American firms among the top ten.

There are two disadvantages to incorporating. First, you have to have papers drawn up and pay a fee for a charter. The expense of doing this varies, but most states charge filing fees of less than $200. A second disadvantage is that you will have to pay federal, and possibly state, corporate income tax. Although the rates are very low for small corporations, those with profits of more than $10 million must pay 35 percent of anything above that amount to the Internal Revenue Service.[3] Because most corporations are very small, 60 percent paid no corporate income tax in 2007.

Two disadvantages to incorporating

The box titled, "The Hybrid Varieties" describes companies that are a cross between partnerships and corporations.

---

[3]Corporations earning smaller profits pay lower rates.

The Hybrid Varieties

Some companies seem to fall into the cracks between partnerships and corporations. There are limited partnerships, which not only avoid paying corporate income taxes but, as their name implies, also minimize legal risk to their investors. There are S corporations—named after the subchapter of the Internal Revenue Code that authorizes them—which offer their shareholders limited liability and pay no corporate income tax. Since 1988, the Internal Revenue Service has also authorized limited liability companies, which have the legal insulation of a corporation and the preferred tax treatment of a limited partnership.

You can also form a limited liability company, or limited liability partnership, to protect your personal assets if your business is sued. A suit can place only the assets of your business at risk. Between 1992 and 1994 more than 40 states—with California a prominent exception—passed limited liability legislation. A limited liability company carries the same benefits as the S corporation, with taxes assessed solely at the individual level; the owners pay personal income tax on their profits but do not have to pay corporate income tax.

But all of this said, these are still the exceptions that prove the rule. The vast majority of businessowners incorporate to secure limited liability, and are then subject to paying corporate income taxes. The hybrid entities do provide loopholes, but so far only a small minority of businessowners have crawled through.

TABLE 2	The Top Ten in World Sales, 2008	
RANK 2008		(in billions of $)
1	**Royal Dutch Shell** Britain/Netherlands	458
2	**ExxonMobil** U.S.	443
3	**Walmart Stores** U.S.	406
4	**BP** Britain	367
5	**Chevron** U.S.	263
6	**Total** France	235
7	**ConocoPhillips** U.S.	231
8	**ING Group** Netherlands	227
9	**Sinopec** China	208
10	**Toyota Motor** Japan	204

Source: www.fortune.com

Given the advantages of incorporating, one may ask (as I did in the accompanying box), "Why Did Incorporation Come So Late to Islamic Middle-Eastern Nations?" As you'll see, the reasons may be traced back many centuries.

How easy is it to form a corporation? In most states it can be done in a matter of days and might cost a few hundred dollars. But in Austria, setting up any new business takes about six months and costs nearly $12,000 in official fees. In Mexico, it takes "only" four months and costs about $2,500. And in Egypt and Bolivia, the cost of setting up a business adds up to more than double the per capita income, while in Chad it's triple that figure.

It takes about five days to register and launch a new business in the United States, but considerably longer in most poorer nations. For example, it takes an average of 79 days in Belarus, 146 days in Angola, and an average of 203 days in Haiti. And once a business has managed to open, the regulatory burdens that poor countries have in place make it difficult to get credit, register property, or hire and fire employees. So despite our governmental reputation for red tape, you *ain't* seen nothing until you try starting a business in Chad, Burkina Faso, or Bangladesh.

on the web

Fortune, which compiles both sales and profits, updates its top 500 list every July. You can find the full list at www.fortune.com. Click on "Fortune 500."

Stocks and Bonds

Stockholders are owners of a corporation. Bondholders lend money to a company and are therefore creditors rather than owners. This distinction becomes important when we consider the order in which people are paid off when the corporation is doing well and when it goes bankrupt.

There are two types of corporate stock: common and preferred. The advantage of owning preferred is that you will receive a stipulated dividend, say 6 percent of the face value of your stock, provided there are any profits out of which to pay dividends. After you are paid, if some profits remain, the common stockholders will be paid.

Two types of stock

Why bother to own common stock? Mainly because only common stockholders may vote on issues of concern to the corporation as well as on who gets to run the corporation. Both preferred and common stockholders own the corporation, or hold equity in the company, but only common stockholders vote.

Bondholders are creditors rather than owners of a corporation. Like the preferred stockholders, they must be paid a stipulated percentage of the face value of their bonds, say 8 percent, in the form of interest, but they must be paid whether or not the company makes a profit. In fact, the interest they receive is considered one of the costs of doing business. And should a company go bankrupt, the bondholders, as creditors, have to be paid off before the owners of preferred and common stock see any money.

Bondholders are creditors—not owners.

Capitalization and Control

A corporation's total capital, or capitalization, consists of the total value of its stocks and bonds. For example, a $4 billion corporation may have $1 billion in bonds, $500 million in preferred stock, and $2.5 billion in common stock. Similarly, a corporation with $200 million in bonds, $100 million in preferred stock, and $300 million in common stock would be capitalized at $600 million.

One might ask how much money would be needed to gain control of a large corporation. Let's consider a corporation that's capitalized for $500 million—$300 million in bonds, $120 million in preferred stock, and $80 million in common stock. Theoretically, you would need slightly over $40 million, or 50 percent plus one share of the common stock.

But most large corporations are rather widely held; that is, there are many stockholders with only a few holding even 1 percent. Furthermore, many stockholders either don't bother to vote their shares or they give proxies to others who will. Usually, then, holding about 5 percent of the common stock of a company will be sufficient for control. So, in this case, by holding $4 million worth of common stock (5 percent of $80 million), you should be able to control this $500 million corporation.

Now let's work out a problem testing your knowledge of capitalization and control: If the XYZ corporation has $4 billion in preferred stock, $6 billion in common stock, and $3 billion in bonds: (*a*) How much is its capitalization? (*b*) Theoretically, how much would it take to control it? (*c*) Practically speaking, it may take only about how much to control it?

Work out your answers here:

Solutions: (*a*) $4 billion + $6 billion + $3 billion = $13 billion
(*b*) $6 billion × .50 = $3 billion, or, technically speaking, $3 billion + $1
(*c*) $6 billion × .05 = $300 million

Why Did Incorporation Come So Late to Islamic Middle-Eastern Nations?

While the corporation is the dominant form of enterprise in the industrialized world, it is a very new development in the Islamic Middle East, where small and very temporary partnerships have been the dominant business form for centuries. This raises two questions: (1) Why did corporations develop earlier in Western Europe and North America? (2) What have been the consequences of these very different histories?

The rules set forth by Islamic lawmakers for forming and executing partnerships were shaped by the needs of the mercantile class during the 7th to 10th centuries. These rules strongly affected Middle-Eastern economic development—or the lack thereof—over the next millennium. Timur Kuran explained this long-lasting effect:

> [T]he Islamic jurists treated the needs of the mercantile community as fixed. Given the sacredness of Islamic law the presumption of fixity meant that while several generations of merchants left their mark on Islamic commercial law, later generations were effectively prevented from revising the corpus of that law in accordance with changing economic conditions.*

Because every Islamic partnership ended with the death of any of its members, after each death a new partnership had to be negotiated. As Kuran noted, "Every additional partner raised the risk of premature liquidation by increasing the probability of a partner dying before the termination of the contract period. This situation obviously fostered [an] incentive to keep partnerships small."[†]

Such a firm would have great difficulty hiring employees, borrowing money, or raising capital from its partners. And so, the typical Islamic partnership consisted of just two members, who pooled their resources for perhaps a single trade mission. This tradition continued throughout most of the Middle East until well into the 20th century.

By the 13th century, Italian financiers were forming partnerships that lasted for many years, and did not dissolve with the death of a member. Between the 16th and 18th centuries, the great European trading organizations evolved from large and durable partnerships into joint-stock companies, the forerunners of the modern corporation.

Large accumulations of wealth were channeled into large European corporations. These accumulations were made possible by the inheritance laws of Western Europe. Let's see how Islamic and Western inheritance laws differed.

The Koran specified that at least two-thirds of an estate be divided among the deceased's spouse, sons and daughters, parents and grandparents, brothers and sisters, and possibly even distant blood relatives. This led to an equalization of wealth. On the downside, it

---

Many economists believe that you really need to hold about 10 percent of the common stock to be assured of control. In *that* case, we have: $6 billion × .10 = $600 million. So to be fair, we would have to accept an answer to question (c) of either 5 percent of the common stock or 10 percent of the common stock. Or, for that matter, any percentage between 5 and 10.

The Business Population

There are over 30 million business firms in the United States—almost one business for every ten people. As you'll notice in panel (*a*) of Figure 1, 72 percent of all American businesses are proprietorships. In panel (*b*), you'll see that corporations account for 82 percent of sales.

Investment

Investment is really the thing that makes our economy go. When we have prosperity, investment is high and rising. And when we're in a recession, it is low and falling. Let's define investment and then see how it varies.

hindered efforts to keep property intact over time, and also prevented great accumulations of wealth, which might have been channeled into capital formation.

Although there was a wide diversity of inheritance rules throughout pre-modern Europe, Timur Kuran wrote that these rules differed from the Islamic system in two critical respects.

First, none define the family as broadly as did the Koran; usually they limited the legal heirs to the kinship group now known as the nuclear family. Second, because Christian canon law did not standardize the law of inheritance, practices were easier to modify, and attempts at reform were less likely to be challenged as sacrilegious. Consequently, barriers to keeping estates intact across generations were considerably lower in relation to the Middle East. From the Middle Ages to recent times, the un-Islamic—and un-modern—devices of primogeniture (the preference in inheritance given to the oldest son) and ultimogeniture (the preference given to the youngest son) enjoyed legal recognition in broad stretches of Europe.‡

Islamic inheritance laws were consistent with the economic realities of that time. Most wealth was in the hands of traders and nomads, whose possessions consisted of movable and relatively easily partitioned goods, such as animal herds and cash. These could be quickly and easily divided among the heirs. By contrast, Roman and Germanic law developed in heavily agricultural societies, whose members sought to keep land in units of sufficient size to sustain a family. Indeed, it was the quest for farmland that drove millions of Europeans to America, especially during the 19th century.

Basically, the very different histories of economic development in the Middle East and in Western Europe and North America can be largely explained by the development of very different economic institutions. As we've seen, the inheritance laws of the West enabled the accumulation of large fortunes, which were then invested in corporate capital. In the Middle East, while the inheritance laws encouraged economic equality, they discouraged the accumulation of capital. In addition, the Islamic laws governing partnerships discouraged the formation of large business enterprises and prevented the advent of corporations until well into the 20th century. In Western Europe and the United States, unfettered by such laws, the corporation became the dominant form of business enterprise by the second half of the 19th century. It was the large corporation that became the engine of economic growth and the facilitator of the economy of mass production and mass consumption.

---

*Timur Kuran, "The Islamic Commercial Crisis: Institutional Roots of the Delay in the Middle East's Economic Modernization," Research Paper No. C01–12, University of Southern California Law School, Center for Law, Economics, and Organization Research Paper Series, March 2001, p. 7 (http://papers.ssrn.com/abstract_id=276377).

†Ibid., pp. 12–13.

‡Ibid., pp. 29–30.

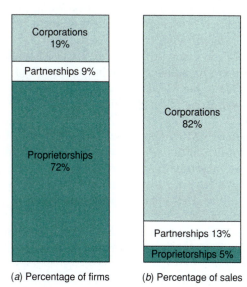

(a) Percentage of firms   (b) Percentage of sales

Figure 1

The Business Population and Shares of Total Sales, 2009

Source: Statistical Abstract of the United States, 2010.

TABLE 3	Hypothetical Inventory Levels of General Motors
Date	Level of Inventory
January 1, 2021	$120 million
July 1, 2021	145 million
December 31, 2021	130 million

TABLE 4	Hypothetical Inventory Levels of Shell Oil
Date	Level of Inventory
January 1, 2024	$230 million
May 15, 2024	215 million
September 1, 2024	240 million
December 31, 2024	220 million

Investment Defined

Investment is any new plant, equipment, additional inventory, computer software, or residential housing.[4] Plant includes factories, office buildings, department and other retail stores, and shopping malls. Examples of equipment are assembly lines, machine tools, display cases, cash registers, computer systems, and office furniture—as long as businesses purchase them. For example, if you buy a car for your personal use, it's a consumption expenditure. But if Shell Oil buys a car for its executives to ride around in (on company business), then it's an investment. The key question we must ask is whether the purchase adds to a company's plant, equipment, or inventory. If not, then it's not investment. What if your town buys a new police car or a new PC or puts up a new school? Is this investment? Close, but no cigar. When the government makes these purchases, it's government spending rather than investment. This may sound arbitrary, but it's part of the rules of national income accounting, which we discuss fully in Chapter 9.

What if you were to purchase 100 shares of Intel stock? Would that be investment? Does that add (directly) to Intel's plant, equipment, or inventory? It doesn't? Then it isn't investment. It's merely a financial transaction. When Intel uses those funds to buy plant, equipment, or inventory, *then* it's investment.

Inventory includes goods on store shelves waiting to be sold, cars in a showroom or car lot, finished goods in a factory waiting to be shipped, and even parts of a product ready to be assembled. Business firms do not want to hold more inventory than they need because that inventory ties up money and also incurs storage costs. Suppose you owned a toy store and had sales of $10,000 a week. Would you want to carry an inventory of $100,000 in toys? Today, with inventory computerization, many firms use the just-in-time method of inventory control. Faster delivery systems—think of UPS and FedEx—also help companies to keep their inventories lower. Stores and factories, many tied to the Internet, have found they can cut costs by shrinking the warehouses where they store the materials they use in production or the goods they sell later to consumers.

Calculating inventory investment is a little tricky. We include only the net change from January 1 to December 31 of a given year. For example, how much was inventory investment for General Motors in 2021 (using the figures in Table 3)?

How much was GM's inventory investment in 2021? $25 million? Nope. $395 million? Nope. The answer is $10 million. All you have to do is look at the levels of inventory on January 1 and December 31 and calculate the difference.

Let's try another one. Using the data in Table 4, calculate the inventory investment for Shell Oil in 2024.

Your answer should be −$10 million. Between the first day of the year and the last day of the year, the level of Shell's inventory went down by $10 million. In other words, inventory investment was negative.

The fact that we can have negative inventory investment is significant. Because investment is one sector of GDP, declining inventories will be a drag on GDP. That's what happens during recessions.

A glance at Figure 2 shows just how unstable inventory investment has been over the last 50 years. In fact, you've probably never been on a roller coaster that had as many steep

You are investing if you are adding to your firm's plant, equipment, or inventory.

How to calculate inventory investment

---

[4]Residential construction does not properly belong in a chapter on business investment, but I am prepared, just this once, to dispense with propriety, because I don't know where else to put it.

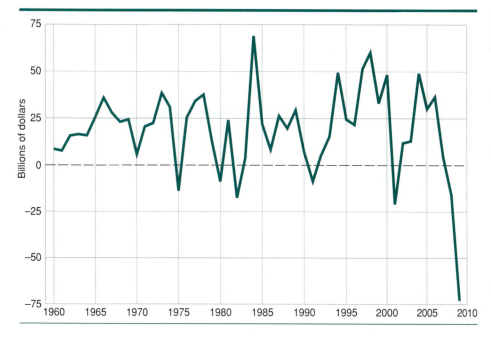

Figure 2

Inventory Investment, 1960–2009
(in billions of 1987 dollars)
This is the most volatile sector of
investment. Note that inventory
investment was actually negative
during recessions in 1975, 1980,
1982, 1991, and 2001. Notice how
pronounced the drop was in 2001.
*Source: Economic Report of the
President,* 2010; *Economic Indicators,*
March 2010.

ups and downs as inventory investment. Most of the steep drops are associated with recessions, and the years of negative investment (when inventories were being depleted) all occurred during recession years—1975, 1980, 1981–82, 1990–91, 2001, and 2007–2009.

Investment in plant and equipment, or capital spending, represents the total cost of all the new factories and office buildings, machinery, software, computers, and other equipment that companies acquire to produce their goods and services. In the year 2007, capital spending was over $1.3 trillion, almost 60 percent higher (in 2007 dollars) than it had been just 10 years earlier. It fell sharply during the ensuing recession. Almost half of today's fixed investment is in information processing equipment and software, in contrast to less than 10 percent in the mid-1980s.

Investment in plant and equipment, while it has its ups and downs, is more stable than inventory investment. Unlike inventory investment, even in a bad year companies will still invest a substantial amount in new plant and equipment, mainly because old and obsolete factories, office buildings, and machinery must be replaced. This is the depreciation part of investment.

A second reason for the stability of plant and equipment investment is that most of it is planned years ahead and will be carried out on schedule regardless of what phase the business cycle is in. Since this plant and equipment is being built to meet the needs of the years ahead, little would be gained by postponing construction for the duration of a recession.

A final reason for carrying out capital investment during a recession is that interest rates tend to come down at that time. As the cost of borrowing money is a major part of construction costs, it can be advantageous to carry out construction projects during times of recession. Other resources, too, would tend to be available at lower costs. Each of these factors places a floor under investment spending during recessionary years.

The three reasons for the stability of investment during business downturns were overwhelmed by the general economic collapse of the Great Depression. Why replace worn-out or obsolete plant and equipment when your plant is half idle? Why carry out long-term investment plans when your firm may not survive the next few weeks? Why bother to borrow at low interest rates when your expected rate of profit is negative?

Investment in plant and equipment plummeted over 70 percent between 1929 and 1933. While some people believe another depression could happen at any time, we shall see in subsequent chapters the country has several safeguards built into its economy to prevent a collapse of such proportions. Nevertheless, investment remains the loose cannon on our economic deck, a destabilizing element that tends to push our economy to its highs and lows.

For a majority of American families, their home is, by far, their largest asset. Not only is it their largest purchase, but they spend, on average, about 40 percent of their income on mortgage payments, real estate taxes, heating fuel, repairs, and upkeep.

Residential construction involves replacing our aging housing stock as well as adding to it. During the 25 years following World War II, the United States had a tremendous spurt in residential building, as nearly half of the American population moved to the suburbs. Today there is continued building, particularly in the outlying areas of the suburbs (the exurbs) 50 to 100 miles from the nearest city, but the postwar housing boom has been over for more than 35 years.

Residential home building fluctuates considerably from year to year. Mortgage interest rates play a dominant role. For example, from 1979 to 1982, when mortgage rates reached 15 and 16 percent in most parts of the country, new housing starts plunged by nearly 40 percent. Another factor that causes steep declines in home construction is periodic overbuilding. Once the surplus of new homes on the market is worked off, residential construction goes into another boom period.

Since the new millennium there was a widespread and growing perception that tens of millions of Americans were using their home equities as ATMs to finance a huge buying spree. As long as residential real estate prices were increasing—often at annual rates of over 10 percent—homeowners could take out larger and larger home equity loans.

But would home prices keep rising at such a fast pace? By mid-2005 there were signs that prices were leveling off, and that the so-called housing bubble was about to burst. In the face of rising mortgage interest rates, millions of homeowners would be unable to meet their monthly payments, and some would even lose their homes. When the bubble did burst in 2006, housing prices began falling throughout most of the country. Millions of homeowners found that the amount of money they owed on their home mortgages was greater than the value of their homes. Many actually walked away from their homes, mailing their keys to their mortgage brokers—a phenomenon called "jingle mail."

Residential home building, which went into decline in early 2006, and continued to fall well into 2008, pulled down total investment during those years. We'll talk more extensively about the mortgage crisis near the end of Chapter 14.

Investment is very unstable.

What this all comes down to is that investment is the most volatile sector in the economy. Fluctuations in GDP are largely fluctuations in investment. More often than not, the country's recessions are touched off by declines in investment, and recoveries are brought about by rising investment.

Why Isn't Education Spending Classified as Investment?

We have defined investment as spending on plant, equipment, additional inventory, computer software, and residential housing. The rationale for this classification is that these goods all contribute to our future standard of living. None is a currently consumed good or service.

When you eat a restaurant meal, get a manicure, buy a dress, a camera, or a magazine, you are clearly consuming. But what about all the money you pay out each semester to attend college? Is that *also* consumer spending? Or would you consider that money an investment in your future earning power? Even if you love all your classes and consider these the best years of your life—at least so far—don't you think that the time and money you're spending now will begin paying off sometime after graduation? And isn't it true that college graduates earn a lot more than high school graduates?

Economists consider any spending on a person's education and training an investment in her or his *human capital. Human capital is the accumulation of knowledge and skills that make a worker productive.* Your college education is certainly adding to your stock of human capital.

Surely, then, we have a pretty strong case that education spending should really be considered as a form of investment. But it isn't. Because of our extensive public education system, the bulk of education spending is classified as government spending, a topic we'll take up in the next chapter. Our national income accounting, which is done mainly by the U.S. Department of Commerce, has classified private spending on education as consumption spending. Every economics textbook—including this one—conforms to the official

Foreign Investment in the United States

Why have foreigners been so happy to invest in America? Mainly because of our relatively high interest rates. Other important factors are proximity to the huge American consumer market and our safe and stable business environment.* As our trade deficit topped $300 billion in 2000 and continued rising, foreigners have found themselves awash in U.S. dollars. Many of those dollars were recycled through the purchase of U.S. government securities, corporate stocks and bonds, real estate, and an increasing amount of direct investment, which entailed setting up shop in the United States. A prime example of foreign direct investment is the Japanese automobile transplants, most significantly Honda, Toyota, and Nissan.

Given our shortage of savings, this inflow of foreign investment has been a tremendous help. Not only has it provided needed funds to corporate borrowers and helped finance most of the federal deficit, but it has kept interest rates from going sky-high. However, a significant side effect, which we'll examine closely in the chapter on international finance, is the implication of foreign ownership on our national economic sovereignty.

---

*Still another motivating factor, especially for foreign automobile firms, was the fear that, in response to mounting imports, Congress might put high import barriers in place. By setting up auto plants inside the U.S., they avoided this potential difficulty. In addition, of course, this also cut down greatly on shipping costs.

National Income Accounts definitions. But if you truly believe, as I do, that education spending should be considered an investment, then please write to your congressperson.

How Does Savings Get Invested?

How *does* savings get invested? A good question. Well, for starters, what do *you* do with the money you save? Put it in the bank? Buy stocks? Buy corporate bonds?

Nearly all the money that flows into the stock market buys stock that has already been issued. So you might buy 500 shares of Cisco, but someone else has sold those 500 shares. However, initial public offerings (IPOs) and new issues of stock raise more than $200 billion a year, all of which goes directly to the corporations issuing stock. And most of that money finances capital spending.

If you deposit your money in a bank, much of it will end up being invested by large business borrowers. What the banks do is package a large number of deposits into a much smaller number of substantial business loans. When IBM, Dell, General Motors, and Verizon come calling on their bankers, they're going to borrow hundreds of millions or even billions of dollars—so much, in fact, that loan syndicates of dozens of banks are often formed to raise the total amount needed.

Corporations also raise a substantial portion of their investment funds internally through retained earnings and depreciation (or capital consumption) allowances. Retained earnings are the portion of profits not paid to the owners of the business. Depreciation allowances are the tax-deductible funds that have been set aside to replace worn-out or obsolete plant and equipment. Still another important source of investment funds comes from abroad (see the box, "Foreign Investment in the United States").

Let's make a clear distinction between "financial" investment and "real" investment. When you buy corporate stocks and bonds, a bank certificate of deposit (CD), or any other financial security, you may consider that an investment. But economists will tell you that while you made a personal financial investment, it was not a "real" investment. The only investment that is real to economists is the purchase of a new home or the purchase by a business firm of new plant, equipment, or inventory. Only "real" investment is counted in GDP. Suppose you bought 100 shares of Amazon.com, or you invested $10,000 in a U.S. Treasury bond, or you bought part of Rockefeller Center. These were all investments, right? Wrong!

Remember that in economics there are only two types of investment: the purchase of (1) new plant, new equipment, and new residential housing, and (2) additional inventory. What about all that money you "invested" in stocks, bonds, and real estate? If those aren't investments, what *are* they? They are financial transactions—mere exchanges of assets. Now, there's nothing wrong with these transactions, but they don't go into GDP. And if they don't, then they're not investments.

Gross Investment versus Net Investment

In Chapter 9 we will be distinguishing between gross domestic product (GDP) and net domestic product (NDP): GDP − Depreciation = NDP.

We can even do a little generalizing now. *Gross domestic product is the sum of consumption, gross investment, government purchases, and net exports.* And how about net national product? *Net domestic product is the sum of consumption, net investment, government purchases, and net exports.* This leaves us with two simple relationships:

1. GDP − Depreciation = NDP
2. Gross investment − Depreciation = Net investment

Gross investment −
Depreciation = Net investment

Most of us are painfully familiar with the distinction between gross income (what your boss says you are earning) and net income (what you actually take home after taxes and other deductions). Gross and net investment are parallel concepts. In fact, when you subtract depreciation from gross investment, you get net investment.

We've said that investment is our nation's expenditure on any new plant, equipment, additional inventory, or residential housing. That's *gross* investment. To get net investment we need to subtract depreciation on plant and equipment and residential housing. (There is no depreciation on inventory accumulation.)

Each year our stock of residential housing depreciates by a certain percentage, say 2 or 3 percent. This depreciation takes place every year even though the market value of that housing stock may be rising. What we're really doing is accounting for the physical deterioration of those buildings. Now we'll take a closer look at depreciation on plant and equipment.

Let's say you started the year with 10 machines and bought another 6 during the year. Your gross investment would be 6. If 4 machines (of your original 10) wore out or became obsolete during the year, your depreciation would be 4. Therefore, your gross investment (6) − depreciation (4) = net investment (2). In other words, you added 2 machines during the year, raising your total from 10 to 12.

In Chapter 8 we'll be using an equation for GDP: $GDP = C + I + G + X_n$, where C is consumption, I is investment, G is government spending, and X_n is net exports (exports minus imports). I represents gross investment. From now on, I'll often refer to gross investment with the letter I.

Building Capital

At the end of Chapter 3, I stressed that capital (plant, equipment, software, and inventory) is built up by producing more, consuming less, or some combination thereof. Suppose you want to open a factory with one machine. You have various alternatives.

You might be able to borrow the money to buy the machine. But the person from whom you borrow has saved this money by not consuming all of his or her income. And someone else, who built the machine, spent many hours working on it.

Investment involves sacrifice.

Investment, or the building up of capital, takes sacrifice. If you decide to save the money yourself, you may have to work overtime, take on a second job, or cut back on your lifestyle.

Finally, if you decide to build the machine yourself, think of all the hours this might take you. These are hours you could be working at a paid job, or maybe just lying around watching TV. So no matter how you go about building up capital, there's a great deal of sacrifice involved.

Essentially, then, to build up our plant, equipment, and inventory, we need to work more and consume less. On this all economists agree. But Karl Marx parted company with the classical economists of the 19th century when he wrote his landmark *Das Kapital*. Capital, according to Marx, is created by labor but expropriated by the capitalist, the factory owner. He wrote:

> The owner of the money has paid the value of a day's labour-power; his, therefore, is the use of it for a day; a day's labour belongs to him. . . . On the one hand the daily sustenance of labour-power costs only half a day's labour, while on the other hand the very same labour-power can work during a whole day, that consequently the value which its use during one day creates, is double what he pays for that use.[5]

In other words, if it costs three shillings to keep a person alive for 24 hours and this person produces three shillings' worth of cloth in six hours, pay him three shillings for 12 hours of work. And if he objects, just tell him to look out the window at the factory gate where hundreds of people stand waiting for a chance to have his job. Marx called them the reserve army of the unemployed.

To invest we must work more and consume less.

The Determinants of the Level of Investment

Many factors determine the level of investment. We'll confine ourselves to four.[6]

(1) The Sales Outlook

If you can't sell your goods or services, there's no point in investing, so the ultimate determinant of the level of investment is the business firm's sales outlook. If business is good and sales are expected to be strong for the next few months, then business firms will be willing to take on more inventory. And if sales look good for the next few years, additional plant and equipment will probably be purchased.

You won't invest if your sales outlook is bad.

(2) Capacity Utilization Rate

The capacity utilization rate is the percentage of plant and equipment that is actually being used at any given time. Since it would be virtually impossible to use every single factory, office, and piece of machinery day in and day out, we will always have *some* idle plant and equipment.

Generally, manufacturing firms use about 80 to 85 percent of their capacity. When business really gets good, the capacity utilization rate approaches 90 percent; during severe recessions, like those of 1974–75 and 1981–82, this rate dips close to 70 percent (see Figure 3). But during the Great Recession, our capacity utilization rate reached a low of just 68.3 percent in mid-2009.

For our purposes, we can count on the capacity utilization rate as an important influence on the level of investment in plant and equipment. At high rates, companies have considerable incentive to build more plant and equipment because sales are pressing against factory capacity. During really bad recessions, when demand is slack, one-third of our factories and equipment may be idle. Why build more?

We must temper this analysis by taking note of three additional factors. First, it is likely that we are understating the capacity utilization rate by counting much obsolete or unusable capacity.[7] For example, steel mill and auto plant closings in the early 1980s indicated that some of the plant and equipment in those industries had been counted for

You won't invest if you have a lot of unused capacity.

---

[5]Karl Marx, *Das Kapital*, Vol. 1 (New York: International Publishers, 1967), pp. 193–94.

[6]Additional factors are corporate income tax rates, depreciation allowances, the level of technology, and the cost of constructing new plant and equipment.

[7]Suppose our capacity utilization rate is 80 percent, but 10 percent of our plant and equipment is obsolete or unusable. Then our true capacity utilization would be 89 percent (80/90).

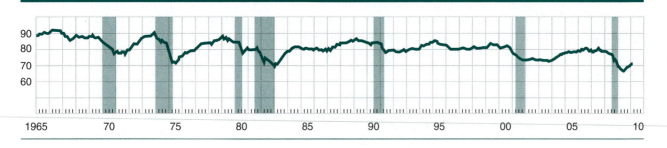

F*igure* **3**

Capacity Utilization Rate in Manufacturing, 1965–2010
Since the mid-1980s, our capacity utilization rate has been below 85. Note that it fell during each recession, which is indicated by a shaded area.
Source: Survey of Current Business, March 2010; *Business Cycle Indicators,* March 2010.

several years when their use was economically unfeasible. Second, manufacturing has been a shrinking part of our economy for at least four decades. It now accounts for just one out of every ten jobs in our economy.

Third, the growing importance of imports—along with increasing investment in overseas manufacturing facilities by U.S. multinational corporations—has reduced the significance of our capacity utilization rate. To illustrate, let's suppose that our economy is approaching full capacity. Although we may invest in new capacity, we may also increase our imports and our multinational corporations may build new manufacturing capacity abroad.

(3) The Interest Rate

The interest rate is the cost of borrowing money. There are actually many different interest rates, depending on a firm's creditworthiness and the size of the loan.

Suppose you want to borrow $1,000 for one year and the bank will charge you 12 percent interest. How much interest will you have to pay if you borrow the $1,000 for one year?

Go ahead. Work it out.

I hope your answer is $120. If it isn't, here's how to calculate the interest:

$$\text{Interest rate} = \frac{\text{Interest paid}}{\text{Amount borrowed}}$$

$$.12 = \frac{x}{\$1,000}$$

Now, multiply both sides by $1,000:

$$\$120 = x$$

You won't invest if interest rates are too high.

In general, the lower the interest rate, the more business firms will borrow. But to know how much they will borrow—or whether they will borrow at all in any particular instance—we need to compare the interest rate with the expected rate of profit on the investment.

(4) The Expected Rate of Profit

Economists are not happy unless they give virtually the same concept at least three different names. Therefore, the expected rate of profit is sometimes called the marginal efficiency of capital or the marginal efficiency of investment. We'll define it this way:

$$\text{Expected rate of profit} = \frac{\text{Expected profits}}{\text{Money invested}}$$

Now, of course, we have to work out a problem. Here's an easy one: How much is the expected profit rate on a $10,000 investment if you expect to make a profit of $1,650? You know how things work around here. Do it yourself, then check your result against mine. I'm always right. But you can't be right unless you try.

$$\begin{aligned}
\text{Expected rate of profit} &= \frac{\text{Expected profits}}{\text{Money invested}} \\
&= \frac{\$1,650}{\$10,000} \\
&= 16.5 \text{ percent}
\end{aligned}$$

The relationship between the interest rate and the expected profit rate was underscored by John Maynard Keynes in his landmark *The General Theory of Employment, Interest, and Money*. Keynes said that every profit opportunity would be exploited as long as the expected profit rate (which he called the "marginal efficiency of capital") exceeded the interest rate: "The rate of investment will be pushed to . . . where the marginal efficiency of capital in general is equal to the market rate of interest."[8]

> You won't invest unless the expected profit rate is high enough.

Suppose your business firm is interested in borrowing $100,000 at the going interest rate of 15 percent to buy inventory. If your expected profit rate is 18 percent, would it pay to borrow? In other words, after you paid off the interest, how much money would you have left? ($18,000 − $15,000 in interest = $3,000.) You would stand to make $3,000 profit. Of course you would borrow the money.

Now we're ready for an easy three-part problem. Suppose you could borrow money at 20 percent interest and someone offered to buy 100 pounds of a certain substance from you at $1,300 a pound. It costs you only $1,000 a pound to grow this substance. The only problem is that the money you borrow will be tied up for a year until you are able to pay it back.

Answer yes or no to each of these three questions:

1. Would you accept the deal as it stands?
2. Would the deal be acceptable if the interest rate were 10 percent?
3. Would the deal be acceptable if the interest rate were 30 percent?

You stand to make a profit of 30 percent using borrowed money. From those profits, you need to pay interest on your loan. If you borrowed the money at (*a*) 20 percent interest, you would still have money left over (net profit) after you paid the interest, so it would pay to accept the deal. If you borrowed money at (*b*) 10 percent interest, it would be even more profitable than at 20 percent interest. But if you accepted the deal at (*c*) 30 percent interest, after you paid the interest from your 30 percent profit, there would be no money left over from your sales.

Business firms do not always borrow the money that they use for investment projects. Actually, American businesses invest hundreds of billions of dollars a year that they have accumulated in depreciation allowances and retained earnings.

---

[8]John Maynard Keynes, *The General Theory of Employment, Interest, and Money* (New York: Harcourt Brace Jovanovich, 1958), pp. 136–37.

Why Do Firms Invest?

Firms tend to invest when (1) their sales outlook is good; (2) their capacity utilization rate is high; (3) interest rates are low; and (4) their expected profit rate is high. But *why* do they invest?

Some firms invest merely to replace worn-out equipment. A related purpose is to replace this equipment with equipment that is more technologically advanced. For example, an old photocopy machine that did 10 copies a minute may be replaced with a high-speed machine that can do more tricks than Houdini. In effect, then, we are replacing machinery and equipment that may not only be dilapidated but obsolete as well. A firm may have to do this just to keep up with the competition. So, in a large sense, just keeping up with current technology requires a substantial amount of investment.

A business may also invest to become larger. Of course, the incentive to invest is based on the sales outlook. No one will want to grow if it means operating at only 50 percent of capacity. In that case, you might be the biggest kid on the block, but you would certainly not be the richest—*or* the smartest.

Graphing the C + I Line

Do you remember the consumption function from Chapter 5? As income rises, consumption rises, but not as quickly. Do you remember induced consumption? As income rises, more consumption is induced.

Figure 4 here reproduces the consumption function graphed in Chapter 5. You'll note that, as income rises, the C line slopes upward. Higher income levels induce higher levels of consumption.

Would it be reasonable to assume that there is a parallel concept of induced investment? That as income rises, the level of investment rises as well? What do *you* think?

At very low levels of income, the country is in a depression. Nobody invests. At somewhat higher levels of income, more and more investment takes place, because

Figure 4
The Consumption Function

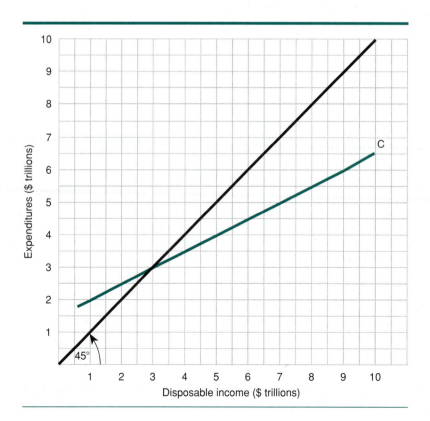

people are able to save *some* money and those funds are invested. So it would be reasonable to say that as income rises, higher levels of investment are induced.

That would be a reasonable assumption, but we need to keep things simple here, because we want to be able to read our graphs easily. So we're going to assume the level of investment stays the same for all levels of income. We know that in the real world, as income rises, I rises, but we're going to trade off some reality for some simplicity.

So far we've had a graph with just two lines—the 45-degree line and the C line, or consumption function. From this two-line graph, C and savings could be calculated. To calculate I (actually the C + I line), a third line is necessary. Figure 5 graphs a C + I line, which is drawn parallel to the C line. This is the same graph as in Figure 4, with the C + I line added.

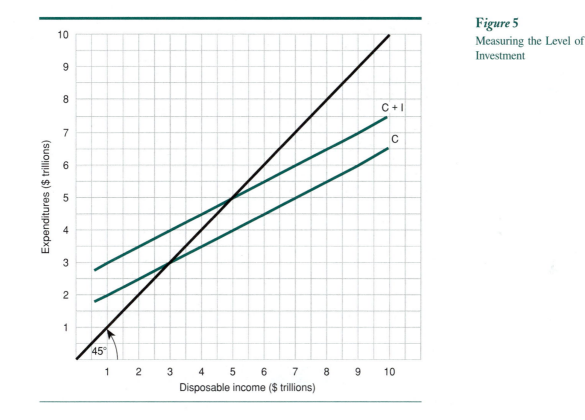

Figure 5
Measuring the Level of Investment

The question for you to solve has three parts: How much is I when disposable income is (*a*) $1 trillion, (*b*) $4 trillion, and (*c*) $8 trillion? Look at the graph and figure out the answers. Keep in mind that the C line and the C + I line are parallel.

Let's repeat the question: "How much is I when disposable income is (*a*) $1 trillion, (*b*) $4 trillion, and (*c*) $8 trillion? Since the C line and the C + I line are parallel, the vertical distance between them remains the same. So I is $1 trillion at every level of disposable income.

Before you go any further, you need to ask yourself this question: Self, do I really know how to measure I, or investment, in Figure 5? If the answer is a definite yes, then go directly to the next and final section of this chapter, The Summing Up of Investment. If you'd like a little extra help, you'll find it in the box, "Reading the C + I Graph."

The Summing Up of Investment

We're finally ready to include the last part of investment: residential construction spending. The data shown in Table 5 indicate the relative size of the components of investment.

HELP

Reading the C + I Graph

Do you remember how, in the last chapter, we found C, or consumption, at various levels of disposable income? All we did was take the vertical distance between the horizontal axis and the C line. For example, in the figure shown here, how much is C at a disposable income of $4 trillion? It's just a tad over $2.75 trillion—say $2.8 trillion.

How do we find I? Well, you tell *me*. How much is I, or investment, at a disposable income of $4 trillion? If you're not sure, just guess. Did you come up with about $500 billion, or $0.5 trillion? The way we measure I is to take the vertical distance between the C line and the C + I line. At a disposable income of $4 trillion, that vertical distance is about two boxes. Since each box counts for one-quarter of a trillion dollars (because there are four boxes between each trillion dollars), then two boxes equal half a trillion dollars, or $500 billion.

Now we'll do one more. How much is I when disposable income is $2.5 trillion? Did you get $500 billion, or $0.5 trillion? I certainly hope so. Just remember that we measure I by taking the vertical distance between the C line and the C + I line. It's as easy as counting the boxes.

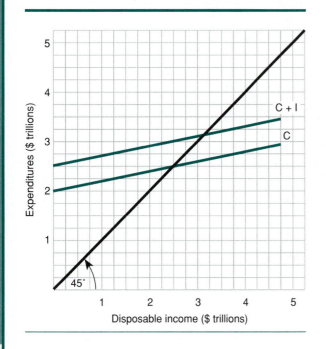

Figure A

TABLE 5 Gross Investment, 2009*

Equipment and software	909
Nonresidential structures	480
Inventory change	−121
Residential structures	361
Total	1629

*Numbers don't add up due to rounding.
Source: Survey of Current Business, March 2010, www.bea.gov.

We mentioned previously that investment is the most volatile sector of GDP. Between 1991 (a recession year) and early 2000 (about 12 months before 2001 began), real gross investment (removing the effects of inflation) rose every year. Over this 9-year period real gross investment more than doubled. But from mid-2000 to late 2001 gross private domestic investment fell by one-sixth (see top line of Figure 6).

But between mid-2006 and mid-2009, it fell by one-third. This was the steepest decline in investment since the Great Depression of the 1930s. And this decline was largely responsible for the severity of the Great Recession.

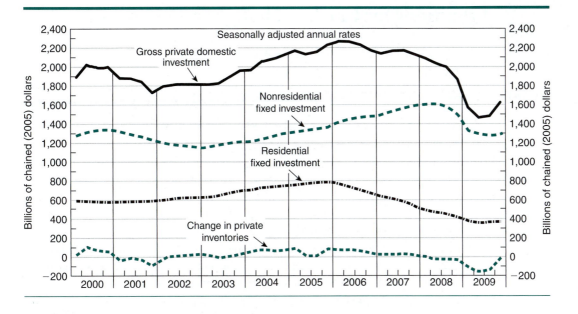

F*igure* **6**
Gross Investment and Its Components, 2000–2009, in 2005 Dollars
Investment fell during the 2001 recession and during the 2007–2009 recession.
Source: Economic Indicators, March 2010.

At the beginning of the chapter we said that the reason the United States is able to produce so much is that we have so much capital. But because we save very little, our rate of capital formation has been lagging. We have been able to make up for most of our savings shortfall by borrowing hundreds of billions of dollars a year from foreigners. Not only have they been providing much needed funding for investment, but they have also been financing most of our huge and growing federal budget deficits. In the next chapter, we'll be looking at government spending and taxation.

Current Issue: "Benedict Arnold Corporations"?

During the 2004 presidential campaign, Senator John Kerry castigated the many large companies that were shifting production and jobs abroad, calling them "Benedict Arnold corporations." As you'll recall, General Benedict Arnold betrayed his country by defecting to the British during the American Revolution. Where is the loyalty, Kerry asked, of companies that laid off longtime employees, often with little or no notice, so that they could cut costs by having their products made in Mexico, China, and other low-wage countries?

Clearly their loyalty was not to America. So it would be fair to ask: To whom *are* our corporate leaders loyal?

You can probably guess the answer. They're loyal to their bottom line. They're in business to not just make profits, but to maximize those profits. The chief executive officer of every large corporation serves at the pleasure of that company's board of directors, which, in turn, is elected by the common stockholders.

So what do these folks want above all else? I'll give you three choices: (1) to be fair to their employees; (2) to provide their customers with a great product or service; or (3) to maximize their profits.

Since we all know the answer is number three, it follows that if shifting production and jobs abroad is what it takes to maximize profits, then that's what nearly every firm will do.

So *are* these really Benedict Arnold corporations, betraying loyalties? That depends on where a corporation's loyalties lie. But one thing is perfectly clear: If a corporation does not maximize its profits, then it is disloyal to its owners.

Questions for Further Thought and Discussion

1. What are the advantages and disadvantages of the corporation as a form of business organization?

2. Explain how the capacity utilization rate and the interest rate affect the level of investment.

3. Explain why building up capital takes a great deal of sacrifice.

4. The Carolina Textile Corporation is capitalized at $200 million. If you wanted to buy control of this company, how much money would you have to spend? Since you don't have nearly enough information to make this decision, just make some reasonable assumption about its bonds, preferred stock, and common stock.

5. What has happened to our personal savings rate in recent years, and how has that affected our level of investment?

6. If you owned a business and were considering increasing your level of investment, what would be the most important factor you would consider in determining how much you planned to invest? Explain why you chose that factor.

7. Why are virtually all large business firms corporations?

8. The Swanson Company, a partnership, was formed in 1999 by Jill Swanson, Jenne Swanson, Duke Swanson, Gage Swanson, and Maggie Swanson. In 2000 Holly Swanson and Missy Swanson were taken into the partnership. In 2001 Duke Swanson left the partnership and Brenda Swanson and Jerry Swanson joined it. In 2002 Jill Swanson left the partnership and Buddie Swanson joined it. In 2003 Forrest Swanson joined the partnership. Explain why it would have been easier for this company to have begun as a corporation rather than as a partnership.

9. *Practical Application:* You and three friends have saved $100,000 and decided to form a computer repair business. Would you form a partnership or a corporation? Explain why you made this choice.

10. *Practical Application:* You own a furniture manufacturing company that employs 200 people, many of whom have worked for you for over 20 years. Although your company is profitable, you could raise your profits by 20 to 30 percent by shifting your production to Southeast Asia. Will you move your operations abroad? Explain why or why not.

11. *Web Activity:* Which is the most profitable company in the United States? How much were its profits? Go to **www.fortune.com,** click on Fortune 500, and then click on Full List.

Workbook for Chapter 6

Name _____

Date _____

Multiple-Choice Questions

Circle the letter that corresponds to the best answer.

1. In the United States, investment is done
   _____. (LO2)
   a) entirely by the government
   b) mostly by the government
   c) about half by the government and half by private enterprise
   d) mainly by private enterprise

2. Which of these is not investment? (LO2)
   a) additional inventory
   b) the building of a county courthouse
   c) the building of a shopping mall
   d) the building of an automobile assembly line

3. Which one of these statements is *false*? (LO2)
   a) Education spending is not officially classified as investment spending.
   b) Education spending is officially classified as investment spending.
   c) Education spending is classified as a form of consumption spending.
   d) A case could be made to consider education spending as an investment.

4. A business firm with one owner is _____. (LO1)
   a) a proprietorship   c) a corporation
   b) a partnership   d) none of these

5. A partnership _____. (LO1)
   a) must have exactly two owners
   b) must have more than two owners
   c) must have more than one owner
   d) may have more than one owner

6. A key advantage of a partnership over a
   proprietorship is _____. (LO1)
   a) limited liability
   b) division of responsibility
   c) perpetual life of the business firm
   d) none of these

7. A _____ is a legal person. (LO1)
   a) proprietorship   c) corporation
   b) partnership   d) business firm

8. Most corporations are _____. (LO1)
   a) publicly held   c) very small
   b) very large   d) none of these

9. Corporations collect about _____ percent of all business receipts. (LO1)
   a) 10   c) 61
   b) 32   d) 82

10. A key disadvantage of incorporating is that
    _____. (LO1)
    a) you will have to pay corporate income tax
    b) you will have to charge sales tax
    c) you will have to sell stock
    d) you will have to reorganize the corporation whenever an officer resigns or dies

11. Corporations are controlled by the
    _____. (LO1)
    a) employees   c) common stockholders
    b) bondholders   d) preferred stockholders

12. The last to be paid off, whether the corporation does well or goes bankrupt, are the _____. (LO1)
    a) employees   c) common stockholders
    b) bondholders   d) preferred stockholders

13. Ownership of a corporation is based
    on _____. (LO1)
    a) whether you work for the company
    b) whether you buy from the company
    c) whether you hold the bonds of the company
    d) whether you hold stock in the company

14. A corporation's capitalization is based on all of the
    following except _____. (LO1)
    a) preferred stock   c) bonds
    b) common stock   d) sales

15. Which is not investment? (LO3)
    a) the purchase of 100 shares of IBM
    b) the construction of a new factory
    c) the purchase of a new delivery truck
    d) the purchase of inventory

16. Inventory investment is _____. (LO2)
    a) always positive
    b) always negative
    c) can be either positive or negative
    d) can be neither positive nor negative

17. Inventory investment is _____. (LO2)
    a) very stable
    b) fairly stable
    c) fairly unstable
    d) very unstable

18. During severe recessions, inventory investment is _____. (LO2)
    a) negative
    b) stable
    c) fairly high
    d) very high

19. Gross investment _____. (LO4)
    a) plus depreciation equals net investment
    b) minus depreciation equals net investment
    c) plus net investment equals depreciation
    d) equals net investment minus depreciation

20. Each of the following might be used to acquire capital except _____. (LO5)
    a) working more
    b) consuming less
    c) borrowing
    d) consuming more

21. Karl Marx said that capital is produced by _____. (LO5)
    a) the worker
    b) the capitalist
    c) the government
    d) money

22. Which is the least stable? (LO6)
    a) investment in plant and equipment
    b) investment in residential housing
    c) investment in inventory
    d) overall investment

23. Business firms invest in plant and equipment during recession years for each of these reasons except (LO6)
    a) interest rates are lower.
    b) it has been planned years ahead.
    c) it replaces worn-out plant and equipment.
    d) it is needed because capacity may be fully utilized.

24. During bad recessions, investment in plant and equipment will _____. (LO6)
    a) be negative
    b) fall by around 15–20 percent
    c) fall somewhat
    d) rise

25. Each of the following is business investment except _____. (LO6)
    a) inventory investment
    b) investment in new plant
    c) investment in new equipment
    d) investment in new residential housing

26. Investment will be high when the capacity utilization rate is _____ and the interest rate is _____. (LO6)
    a) high, high
    b) low, low
    c) high, low
    d) low, high

27. Our capacity utilization rate is usually between _____. (LO6)
    a) 10 and 30
    b) 30 and 50
    c) 50 and 70
    d) 70 and 90

28. Firms will most likely borrow money for investment when _____. (LO6)
    a) interest rates are low
    b) interest rates are high
    c) the interest rate is higher than the expected profit rate
    d) the expected profit rate is higher than the interest rate

29. Which statement is the most accurate? (LO1)
    a) Almost all corporations are very large.
    b) If you want to be your own boss and don't want to share any of the decision making, the business form that would best suit you is a proprietorship.
    c) It is very expensive to form a corporation.
    d) Most business firms are partnerships.

30. Statement I. Inventory computerization has tended to reduce inventory levels.
    Statement II. Inventory investment tends to rise during recessions. (LO6)
    a) Statement I is true and statement II is false.
    b) Statement II is true and statement I is false.
    c) Both statements are true.
    d) Both statements are false.

31. Which is the most accurate statement? (LO1)
    a) In Middle-Eastern Islamic countries, the typical partnership consisted of just two members, who pooled their resources for perhaps a single trade mission.
    b) In virtually all countries, partnerships dissolve with the death of a member.
    c) Inheritance laws in Western Europe and in Islamic Middle-Eastern countries each have the effect of keeping large fortunes intact.
    d) The large partnership became the engine of economic growth in the second half of the 19th century throughout Western Europe.

Fill-In Questions

1. Of the big three spending sectors of GDP, the least stable is _____. (LO6)

2. There are about _____ million business firms in the United States. (LO1)

3. A partnership is owned by _____ people. (LO1)

4. The key advantage of incorporating is _____. (LO1)

5. The two main disadvantages of incorporating are (1) _____ and (2) _____. (LO1)

6. A corporation is owned by its _____ and its _____. (LO1)

7. A corporation is controlled by its _____. (LO1)

8. The creditors of a corporation are mainly its _____. (LO1)

9. Theoretically, you would need an investment of about $_____ to control a corporation that had $100 million in preferred stock, $50 million in common stock, and $350 million in bonds. (LO1)

10. The least stable form of investment is _____ investment. (LO6)

11. Gross investment − _____ = Net investment. (LO4)

12. According to Karl Marx, capital was created by the _____ and expropriated by the _____. (LO5)

13. In Marx's terms, the people who wait outside the factory gates for work are the _____. (LO5)

14. During severe recessions, our capacity utilization rate falls to around _____ percent. (LO6)

15. The expected profit rate is found by dividing _____ by _____. (LO6)

16. An investment will be undertaken if the expected profit rate is higher than the _____. (LO6)

17. Total investment is found by adding (1) _____; (2) _____; and (3) _____. (LO6)

Problems

1. If a corporation has $100 million in preferred stock, $150 million in common stock, and $250 million in bonds: (LO1)
    a) How much is its capitalization?
    b) Theoretically, how much would it take to control it?
    c) Practically speaking, it may take only about how much to control it?

2. If a corporation has gross investment of $150 million and depreciation of $40 million, how much is its net investment? (LO1)

3. Given the information in Table 1, find inventory investment in 2005. (LO1)

TABLE 1	
Date	Level of Inventory
January 1, 2005	$500 million
July 1, 2005	530 million
December 31, 2005	485 million

4. Use the information in Figure A to fill in Table 2: (LO7)

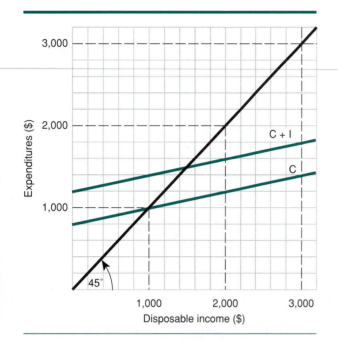

Expenditures ($) (y-axis)
Disposable income ($) (x-axis)

C + I

C

45°

Figure A

TABLE 2

Disposable Income	Consumption*	Savings*	Investment
(a) 1,000	_____	_____	_____
(b) 2,000	_____	_____	_____
(c) 3,000	_____	_____	_____

*If you don't remember how to find consumption and savings, you'll need to review parts of Chapter 5.

5. If a corporation has $2 billion in common stock, $1 billion in preferred stock, and $4 billion in bonds: a) How much is its capitalization? b) Theoretically, how much would it take to control it? c) Practically speaking, it may take only about how much to control it? (LO1)

6. If net investment is 400 and depreciation is 175, how much is gross investment? (LO5)

7. Given the information in Table 3, find inventory investment in 2018. (LO6)

TABLE 3 Colin Noel Manufacturing Corp.

Date	Level of Inventory
January 1, 2018	$2.0 billion
May 1, 2018	2.1 billion
Sept. 1, 2018	1.8 billion
Dec. 31, 2018	2.3 billion

8. Suppose Colin Noel could borrow $200,000 for one year at an interest rate of 10 percent. He is virtually certain that he can invest this money in inventory that he could sell over a year for $300,000. If his selling costs were $50,000 and he were to pay his interest out of his profits, how much would Colin Noel's expected profit rate be on his investment? (LO6)

9. Art Levine, Phyllis Levine, Leah Levine, and Suzannah Levine would like to gain control of the Sports Trading Card Corporation of America. If that corporation has $200 million in common stock, $300 million in preferred stock, and $500 million in bonds: a) Theoretically, how much would they need to invest to control it? b) Practically speaking, how much would they need to invest to control it? (LO6)

Chapter 7

The Government Sector

Are taxes too high? Do most government workers put in an honest day's work? Would we all be better off if we shrunk the size of our government down to the size it was a hundred years ago? When Ronald Reagan ran for president in 1980, he promised to "get the government off the backs of the American people." He won that election, presided over a massive tax cut, and went on to become one of the most popular presidents in history.

Shrinking the size of the federal government has long been a successful policy strategy among conservative politicians, but as our economy sank into recession in 2008, more and more voters demanded that the federal government do something. By late summer, when our financial system threatened to go into meltdown, the government finally began to act, passing a $700 billion financial bailout, and then in February 2009, a $787 billion economic stimulus bill.

LEARNING OBJECTIVES

After reading this chapter you should be able to:

1. Define and discuss federal, state, and local government spending.
2. Analyze the graph of the C + I + G line.
3. Define and compute the average and marginal tax rates.
4. Identify and discuss the types of taxes.
5. List and discuss the sources of federal government revenue.
6. Summarize recent federal tax legislation.
7. List and discuss the sources of state and local government revenue.
8. Explain and discuss the economic role of government.

Introduction: The Growing Economic Role of Government

The role of government has grown tremendously over the past seven decades. Actually, most of that growth took place between 1933 and 1945, during the administration of Franklin Delano Roosevelt. The two major crises of that period—the Great Depression and World War II—dwarfed anything our nation has faced since. In fact, we would have to go back to the Civil War to find an event as cataclysmic as either the Depression or what people over 70 still refer to as "the war."

Since 1945, the roles of government at the federal, state, and local levels have expanded, but the seeds of that expansion were sown during the Roosevelt administration. Americans seem determined never to experience again the traumatic events that overtook

Most of the growth was due to the Depression and World War II.

Government is not the solution to our problem. Government is the problem.

—Ronald Reagan

147

us during the 30s and 40s. *Never again* will we leave ourselves vulnerable to a depression or a military attack by another nation.

The government exerts four basic economic influences: It spends trillions of dollars, levies trillions of dollars in taxes, redistributes hundreds of billions of dollars, and regulates our economy. What does the government *do* with all our money? Some of it is spent on goods and services (that is, highways, police protection, defense), and some of it is redistributed to the poor, to retirees, and to the holders of government bonds.

The government also has an important regulatory role in our economy. We are subject to myriad local, state, and federal laws governing how business may be conducted. These will be examined toward the end of this chapter.

What does the government do with all our money?

Thank God we don't get all the government we pay for.
——Will Rogers

Government Spending

Federal Government Spending

While virtually all private businesses issue financial statements based on a normal calendar year—January 1 to December 31—the federal government's financial, or fiscal, year begins on October 1 and runs through September 30 of the following year. For example, fiscal year 2009 began on October 1, 2010.

In fiscal year 2011 the federal government plans to spend about $3.9 trillion. Who gets the biggest bite of the pie? As you can see from Figure 1, that goes to defense, followed by Social Security. In the accompanying box we spell out the chronology of the budget's preparation.

During the last 40 years, federal transfer payments—mainly Social Security, Medicare, and Medicaid—have gone through the roof. How come? There are several explanations for this huge increase in social spending. Much of it reflects continued expenditures on the Great Society programs of the 1960s, particularly Medicare, Medicaid, and food stamps. A second reason for the increase is that the prosperity our nation has enjoyed in recent years has not spread to tens of millions of poor Americans. Consequently, spending on public assistance, unemployment insurance benefits, and food stamps has shot up since

Figure 1

The Federal Government Dollar—Fiscal Year 2011 Estimate

Eighty cents of each dollar of federal revenue comes from individual income taxes and social insurance receipts, while slightly more than half of all federal expenditures goes for direct benefit payments for individuals.

Source: Economic Report of the President, 2010; www.whitehouse.gov/omb

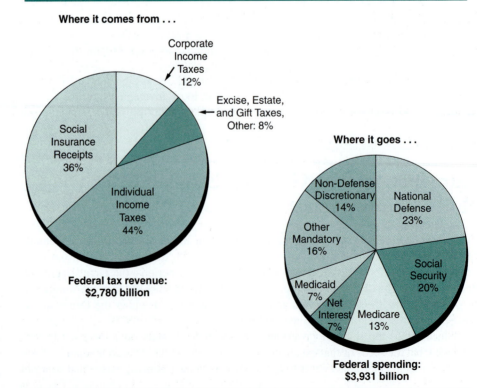

Where it comes from . . .

Corporate Income Taxes 12%

Excise, Estate, and Gift Taxes, Other: 8%

Social Insurance Receipts 36%

Individual Income Taxes 44%

Federal tax revenue: $2,780 billion

Where it goes . . .

Non-Defense Discretionary 14%

National Defense 23%

Other Mandatory 16%

Social Security 20%

Medicaid 7%

Net Interest 7%

Medicare 13%

Federal spending: $3,931 billion

The Chronology of Federal Budget Preparation

Preparation of the budget begins about two years before the beginning of the fiscal year. We'll be looking at the timetable for the preparation of the budget for fiscal year 2011, which began on October 1, 2010.

During early 2009, after months of internal studies, each department presented its budget for fiscal year 2009 to the Office of Management and Budget (OMB). That agency has the job of coordinating all budget requests to ensure that they are consistent with the president's economic program. The OMB then puts together a tentative budget for the president.

President Barack Obama was concerned not just with individual spending programs—foreign aid, defense, food stamps, Social Security—but with the bottom line, or total spending. The president and the director of the OMB then established spending ceilings for each department and the federal agencies, which were then asked to prepare a second round of expenditure plans over the summer.

During the fall of 2009 the OMB reviewed these revised programs, and in the late fall the budget was presented to President Obama for final approval. The final budget message was then drafted for submission to Congress in early February 2010.

Over the next eight months the ball was in Congress's court. Both houses of Congress have budget committees that prepare "concurrent resolutions" to be reported to their respective houses by April 15. These resolutions contain two key figures: overall expenditures and overall revenue. By May 15 Congress must pass a single concurrent resolution.

Between May 15 and October 1, Congress passed various appropriations bills—agricultural subsidies, veterans' benefits, aid to mass transit, public assistance—while trying to stay within the limits set by the concurrent resolution. Finally, a second budget resolution had to be passed by October 1, the first day of the fiscal year.

That's the chronology of federal budget preparation in theory. But in practice, the 13 required spending bills, which are the heart of the budget, are not passed until months after the fiscal year begins. It wasn't until February, 2003, that Congress got around to passing the last spending bill for the fiscal year 2003, which began on October 1, 2002. The start of fiscal year 2004 was just a bit better. Instead of passing none of the 13 appropriations bills by the deadline, as happened in 2002, Congress had passed a grand total of three.

the early 1970s. Finally, in 1955 relatively few people were collecting full Social Security benefits, because that program was then only 20 years old. Today, however, the number of retired people on the rolls is more than twice that of 1955, and benefits have gone up substantially because they are indexed for inflation.

The next big-ticket item is defense expenditures (including homeland security and our 15 or 16 different spy agencies), which will come to about $825 billion. This comes to nearly $2,700 for each person in the United States. Today we spend nearly as much on defense as the rest of the world combined. Are we spending too much? Before 9/11, many Americans saw no need to erect expensive defenses against nonexistent enemies. However, since the terrorist attacks, it has become a lot more difficult to argue against spending still more on defense. Some argue, of course, that the wars in Iraq and Afghanistan are another story.

One of the fastest-growing federal expenditures in the 1980s and early 1990s was interest on the national debt. The national debt is about ten times its 1980 size. When you owe ten times as much, you have to pay a lot more interest. As you can see in Figure 2, interest payments are expected to rise substantially in the coming decades.

The 800-pound budgetary gorilla is medical care, namely Medicare and Medicaid. Back in 1969, just 3 years after President Lyndon Johnson pushed these programs through Congress, they accounted for just 4 percent of all federal spending (see Figure 2). Forty-two years later, in 2011, they accounted for 20 percent. And according to the Congressional Budget Office's projection, the share of Medicare and Medicaid will reach 35 percent of the federal budget in 2049.

If you're like most taxpayers, you'd like to see the government trim some of the fat from its budget. So I'd like you to pick up your heaviest ax and start hacking away at Figure 1. But be careful—as soon as you lift your ax, a lot of people will start howling.

Begin with defense. You'll not only make the president unhappy, but you'll incur the wrath of the secretary of defense, the armed forces' top brass, and thousands of defense

Government is the great fiction, through which everybody endeavors to live at the expense of everybody else.

—Frédéric Bastiat, *Essays on Political Economy*, 1872

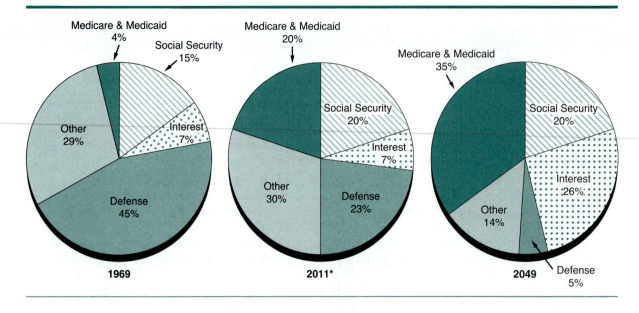

F*igure* 2

Federal Spending, 1969, 2011, and 2049

As a share of federal spending, Social Security, Medicare, and Medicaid have more than doubled in 40 years and will continue to grow, according to the Congressional Budget Office's "intermediate" projections.

*Figures are from President Barack Obama's 2011 budget. They are projected estimates of actual spending.

Source: Congressional Budget Office.

contractors—not to mention the millions of your fellow citizens who think any cut in the defense budget is the same as just handing the country over to our enemies.

OK, let's cut Social Security and Medicare. Just try it! There are over 50 million recipients of these benefits, and nearly all of them vote. What about federal pensions? First, we're legally obligated to pay pensions and other benefits to retired federal employees and veterans. Second, there's a political problem. Veterans' benefits have a powerful constituency. Just drop by your local American Legion hall and ask the people there how *they* would feel about the government cutting these benefits.

Many Americans feel we're giving away too much money to foreigners (see the box, "Are We Giving Away the Store?"). But this might be termed "chump change" compared to our big ticket budgetary items such as defense, Social Security, and Medicare.

State and Local Government Spending

Big state and local expenditures are education, health, and welfare.

State and local government spending has been rising rapidly since World War II, but it is still less than half the level of federal spending. Well over half of all state and local government expenditures goes toward education, health, and welfare. One of the problems faced by these governments is that they are expected to provide more and more services with limited tax bases. For example, more than 20 million teenagers are currently attending high school or college. Seventy years ago most people were working by the time they were 14, but now they are still in school. Supporting public education has traditionally been the role of the state and local governments, although in recent years Washington has provided supplementary funds covering about 6 percent of the costs of educating children through high school.

Another expenditure that has increased enormously is police protection. Although this is a function of local government, rising crime and the deterioration of neighborhoods have made it necessary to hire many more police officers. Until the 1950s, neighborhoods largely policed themselves informally, mainly because people spent a great deal of time on the street, most urban areas were more densely populated, and people tended

Are We Giving Away the Store?

For many Americans, "foreign aid" sounds suspiciously like "welfare for foreigners."

–James Traub, *The New York Times* columnist, 2/13/05–

Many taxpayers are asking whether it makes sense to be spending so much money to help foreigners when we have so many poor people in the United States. During fiscal year 2008, we provided our friends, our allies, and many of the poorer nations of the world with about $25 billion in economic and military aid. About half went to Israel, Egypt, Russia, and the other states of the former Soviet Union.

Recent polls found that two out of five Americans believe foreign aid is the largest single item in the federal budget.

Many Americans ask if we should be building schoolhouses in Baghdad and Kabul, rather than providing jobs for the 15 million Americans who were out of work in early 2010. Indeed, we are spending $12 billion a month in Iraq and Afghanistan, but just a small fraction could be considered foreign aid. The lion's share, of course, is being spent on fighting two wars.

Our foreign aid bill comes to less than 1 percent of the federal budget, or less than 0.2 percent of our GDP. Twenty-five billion dollars is a lot of money. The chart shows how U.S. foreign aid, as a percentage of GDP, compares with that of other leading international aid-givers. As you can see, the U.S. is at the bottom of the list.

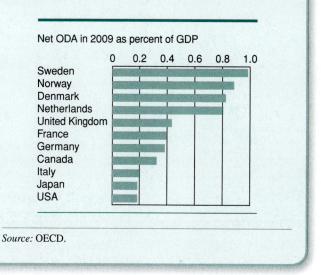

Net ODA in 2009 as percent of GDP

Source: OECD.

---

to know one another. All this has changed, and now the police are being called on to perform functions that neighborhoods used to handle themselves.

Sometimes local government and private businesses perform the same tasks. In New York and other major cities, the local sanitation department picks up residential garbage, while private carters pick up garbage from stores, restaurants, and other commercial establishments. While the police provide basic protection and apprehend criminals, private security guards are employed by stores and by more affluent neighborhoods. There are public and private hospitals, schools, and colleges.

Government Purchases versus Transfer Payments

The federal, state, and local governments spend over $5 trillion a year. Nearly half goes to individuals as transfer payments, and the rest is government purchases. We represent these purchases by the letter G, and they go into our GDP equation: $GDP = C + I + G + X_n$.

$$GDP = C + I + G + X_n$$

What do you think the biggest government purchase is? It's defense, which accounts for 16 cents out of every dollar that goes into G. Other biggies are education, police, health, and highway construction. A government purchase is the spending of government funds to purchase or provide the public with some good or service.

Transfer payments cannot be counted in G because they do not represent that kind of spending. What is the largest government transfer payment? I'm sure you know that it's Social Security. Of the $2.4 trillion that the federal, state, and local governments pay out in transfer payments, $730 billion goes to Social Security recipients.

You may want to ask why we bother to distinguish between government purchases and transfer payments. The reason is that we need to come up with a figure for GDP—the nation's expenditures on all final goods and services produced during the year at market prices. So we want to add in only what we produced and purchased that year. Don't people receiving transfer payments spend that money on consumer goods and

Figure 3
Measuring Government
Spending

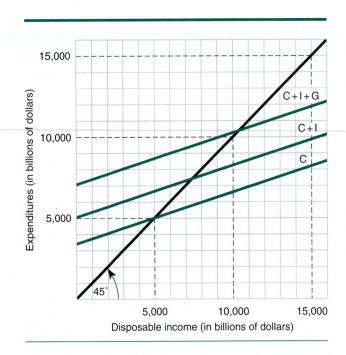

Figure 3
Measuring Government
Spending

services, or C in our GDP equation? Yes, they do. When they spend those Social Security, public assistance, or government employees' retirement and veterans' benefits, that money will go into GDP.

Federal and state and local transfer payments have grown from just 6 percent of GDP in 1960 to 16 percent today. Most of the impetus has come from two of President Lyndon Johnson's Great Society programs of the 1960s—Medicare and Medicaid—and from the rising proportion of retirees who are now collecting Social Security. It is conceivable that, in 25 years, when nearly all the baby boomers will have retired, total government transfer payments will be more than one-quarter of GDP.

Let's make sure we're clear on the difference between government spending and government purchases. Government spending is the total that the federal, state, and local governments spend on everything—transfer payments to individuals as well as purchases of goods and services. Which goes into GDP—transfer payments or government purchases? *Only government purchases are counted in GDP.* Now let's see how they're added in.

Graphing the C + I + G Line

In Chapter 5 we graphed the C line. In the last chapter we graphed the C + I line. Now we add another line to our graph: the C + I + G line. By now this should be old hat to you, so I'm going to ask you to figure out how much G is in Figure 3 (assuming the C + I + G line is parallel to the C + I line).

What did you get? You should have gotten 2,000 (or, $2,000 billion). You'll notice that the level of G remains at 2,000 no matter what the level of disposable income. The main reason for doing this is to keep our graph as simple as possible.

We're not quite finished with our graphs. We still need to draw the C + I + G + X_n line, but that won't happen until the beginning of the next chapter.

A fine is a tax for doing wrong.
A tax is a fine for doing right.
                    —Anonymous

The point to remember is that
what the government gives it
must first take away.
                    —John S. Coleman

Taxes

Presidents Ronald Reagan and George W. Bush will go down in history as two of our greatest tax cutters. Before we even begin to consider how high our taxes are and how much they've been cut, we'll need to understand something about tax rates and the types of taxes that exist. Once that's done, we'll see just how onerous the American tax system really is.

The Average Tax Rate and the Marginal Tax Rate

If someone asked you what your tax rate was, would you have a ready answer? Generations of attorneys have taught us that the best answer to any question (and especially those to which you don't know the answer) is another question. So the answer to the question "What's your tax rate?" is "Which tax rate are you referring to? My average tax rate or my marginal tax rate?"

But what if your questioner replies, "What is your average tax rate?" What do you do then? You tell her. And if she then happens to ask you your marginal tax rate, you tell her that as well.

The average rate is the overall rate you pay on your entire income, while the marginal rate is the rate you pay on your last few hundreds (or thousands) of dollars earned. Your marginal rate is often referred to as your tax bracket. In nearly all cases, I'm talking about the average and marginal rates that you're paying in personal income tax, but I'll apply the average tax rate to the Social Security tax as well.

The art of taxation consists in so plucking the goose as to obtain the largest possible amount of feathers with the smallest amount of hissing.

—Jean-Baptiste Colbert

The Average Tax Rate I kind of left you hanging there, didn't I? How do you answer the question "What is your average tax rate?"

Let's try a simple problem. The average tax rate is calculated by dividing taxes paid by taxable income:

$$\text{Average tax rate (ATR)} = \frac{\text{Taxes paid}}{\text{Taxable income}}$$

Suppose a person paid $3,000 on a taxable income of $20,000. How much is the average tax rate? Do your calculations right here:

$$\text{Average tax rate} = \frac{\text{Taxes paid}}{\text{Taxable income}} = \frac{\$3,000}{\$20,000} = 0.15 \text{ or } 15\%$$

$$\text{ATR} = \frac{\text{Taxes paid}}{\text{Taxable income}}$$

If you correctly calculated 15 percent, go on to the marginal tax rate in the next section. If not, let's go over all the steps in finding the average tax rate in the accompanying Extra Help box.

The Marginal Tax Rate The average tax rate is the overall rate you pay on your entire income, while the marginal tax rate is the rate you pay on the last few hundred dollars you earned. Suppose you made $100 in overtime and the government took $70. Would you work overtime? Chances are you wouldn't, and that supposition forms a cornerstone of supply-side economics. The supply-siders' basic belief is that our high marginal tax rates rob people of the incentive to work as hard and as long as they would with a lower tax burden.

The marginal tax rate is calculated by dividing additional taxes paid by additional taxable income:

$$\text{Marginal tax rate (MTR)} = \frac{\text{Additional taxes paid}}{\text{Additional taxable income}}$$

How Did We Get an Average Tax Rate of 15%?

How do we get from $^{\$3,000}/_{\$20,000}$ to 0.15? First, reduce the fraction to $^3/_{20}$. Whatever you do to the top of the fraction, you do to the bottom. Get rid of the three zeros on top and get rid of three zeros on the bottom. (While you're at it, you can get rid of the dollar signs as well.)

The next step is to divide 3 by 20. Remember, whenever you have a fraction, you may divide the bottom number into the top number. If you divide the top into the bottom, you will not only violate a basic law of arithmetic, but you will also get the wrong answer. $20\overline{)3}$ is the same as $20\overline{)3.00}$. We are allowed to put a decimal point after any whole number. And we are allowed to put zeros after the decimal point, because they don't change the number's value. These are more laws of arithmetic.

$$20\overline{)3.00} = 20\overline{)3.00}^{.15}$$

The average tax rate is 0.15, or 15 percent. Our final law of arithmetic is that, whenever you want to convert a decimal into a percentage, you move the decimal point two places to the right and write a percent sign after the number. Examples would be 0.235 = 23.5%; or, 0.71 = 71%; or, 0.406 = 40.6%. If a baseball player is hitting .406, he is getting a hit 40.6 percent of the times he bats. And if your average tax rate comes to .406, it means you are paying 40.6 percent of your taxable income to the Internal Revenue Service.

Let's try one more problem. Suppose you pay $12,000 on a taxable income of $50,000. How much is your average tax rate? To solve this problem: (1) write the formula, (2) substitute numbers into the formula, and (3) solve.

$$\text{Average tax rate} = \frac{\text{Taxes paid}}{\text{Taxable income}}$$

$$= \frac{\$12,000}{\$50,000} = \frac{12}{50} = \frac{6}{25}$$

$$25\overline{)6.00}^{.24} = 24\%$$

Suppose you had to pay an additional $420 on an additional taxable income of $1,000. How much is your marginal tax rate?

$$\text{MTR} = \frac{\text{Additional taxes paid}}{\text{Additional taxable income}}$$

$$= \frac{\$420}{\$1,000} = \frac{42}{100} = 0.42 = 42\%$$

Now we'll get a little fancier. Suppose your taxable income rose from $20,000 to $22,000 and the taxes you paid rose from $4,500 to $5,200. How much is your marginal tax rate?

$$\text{MTR} = \frac{\text{Additional taxes paid}}{\text{Additional taxable income}}$$

$$\text{Marginal tax rate} = \frac{\text{Additional taxes paid}}{\text{Additional taxable income}}$$

$$= \frac{\$700}{\$2,000} = \frac{7}{20} = 0.35 = 35\%$$

Again, if you need a little help with the math, see the accompanying Extra Help box.

Types of Taxes

There are two basic divisions of taxes. First we'll be looking at the difference between direct and indirect taxes. Then we'll take up progressive, proportional, and regressive taxes.

Direct Taxes   A direct tax is a tax with your name written on it. The personal income and Social Security taxes are examples. They are taxes on particular persons. If you earn a certain amount of money, you must pay these taxes.

  The corporate income tax is also a direct tax. You might not think so, but a corporation is considered a legal person. For example, in court, you would sue a corporation rather than its owners or officers. Thus, if a corporation makes a profit, it must pay a corporate income tax, and this is a direct tax.

Indirect Taxes   These are not taxes on people but on goods or services that we purchase. Taxes on things include sales and excise taxes. Examples are a state sales tax on most retail purchases and the excise taxes on tires, gasoline, movie tickets, cigarettes, and liquor.

  The distinction between direct and indirect taxes was made by John Stuart Mill more than a century ago:

> A direct tax is one which is demanded from the very persons who, it is intended or desired, should pay it. Indirect taxes are those which are demanded from one person in the expectation and intention that he shall indemnify himself at the expense of another.[1]

  Now we shall take up, in turn, progressive, proportional, and regressive taxes. The key variable we use to differentiate them is where the tax burden falls.

Progressive Taxes   A progressive tax places a greater burden on those best able to pay and little or no burden on the poor. The best example is, of course, the federal personal income tax. For the vast majority of American taxpayers today, the more they earn, the higher percentage they pay. In terms of the average tax rate, then, people in higher income brackets pay a substantially higher average tax rate than those in lower brackets.

Proportional Taxes   Proportional taxes place an equal burden on the rich, the middle class, and the poor. Sometimes a flat tax rate is advanced as a "fair" or proportional tax, but it is neither. For example, a flat income tax rate of, say, 15 percent with no deductions, would place a much greater burden on the poor and the working class than on the rich.[2] (See the box, "Nominally Progressive, Proportional, and Regressive Taxes.") It would be much harder for a family with an income of $10,000 to pay $1,500 in income tax (15 percent of $10,000) than it would be for a family with an income of $100,000 to pay $15,000 (15 percent of $100,000).

  Several Eastern European countries have adopted the flat tax, especially since the turn of the century. Russia (13 percent), Ukraine (13 percent), Serbia (14 percent), and Romania (16 percent) are the largest countries having flat taxes. These countries have greatly simplified their income taxes, but at the price of giving up nearly all their deductions. Many Americans want to have it both ways—a flat tax, while retaining most of the deductions. Which would leave us right where we started—a tax code in great need of simplification.

Regressive Taxes   A regressive tax falls more heavily on the poor than on the rich. An example is the Social Security tax. In 2010 the rate was 6.2 percent on all wages

In this world nothing can be said to be certain, except death and taxes.

—Benjamin Franklin

John Stuart Mill, English philosopher and economist

Where there is an income tax, the just man will pay more and the unjust less on the same income.

—Plato

People want just taxes more than they want lower taxes. They want to know that every man is paying his proportionate share according to his wealth.

—Will Rogers

A regressive tax falls mainly on the poor.

---

[1] John Stuart Mill, *Principles of Political Economy,* Book IV, ed. William J. Ashley (Philadelphia: Porcupine Press, 1979), p. 823.

[2] Steve Forbes, whose net worth is estimated to be about $400 million, made his flat tax proposal the major issue in his campaigns for the Republican presidential nomination in 1996 and 2000. He advocated a flat tax on wages and salaries, exempting profits, interest, and dividends. And for good measure, Forbes, who inherited his wealth, would abolish the federal tax on inheritances.

ADVANCED WORK

Nominally Progressive, Proportional, and Regressive Taxes

We have already defined these taxes in accordance with their effect, or burden, on taxpayers in different income groups. The burden of a progressive tax falls most heavily on the rich; the burden of a proportional tax falls equally on all income groups; and the burden of a regressive tax falls most heavily on the poor.

This three-part graph presents an alternative view of these types of taxes. I'll tell you up front that I strongly disagree with the implications of this view. Let's look at each part of this graph and see how *you* feel.

The graph in part (*a*) is nominally progressive because higher-income people pay a higher tax rate than lower-income people. For example, those earning $10,000 pay only 4 percent of their incomes, while those earning $100,000 pay 8 percent. But is this, in effect, a progressive tax? Is it as easy for a poor family to pay $400 as it is for a relatively rich family to pay $8,000? We could argue it either way. And, unfortunately, economic analysis cannot supply an answer. Now, I happen to feel that a $400 tax bill imposes a greater burden on a family earning $10,000 than an

$8,000 tax bill imposes on a family earning $100,000. What do *you* think?

Let's move on to the next part of the graph, (*b*), which shows a nominally proportional tax rate of 10 percent. Here's the question: Is it as easy for a poor family to hand over 10 percent of its income to the IRS as it is for a middle-class family, or a rich family? What do *you* think? My own view is that it isn't and that this nominally proportional tax is, in effect, a regressive tax.

The last part, (*c*), is easy. This is a nominally regressive tax because the tax rate declines as income rises. Obviously, by any measure, the burden falls most heavily on the poor.

Economists should avoid making value judgments, so perhaps I have gone a bit too far in claiming that nominally progressive taxes *could* be regressive in effect. And that nominally proportional taxes *are* regressive in effect (although this is somewhat less controversial). So if you disagree with my conclusions, that doesn't make one of us wrong and the other right. It means only that our values are different.

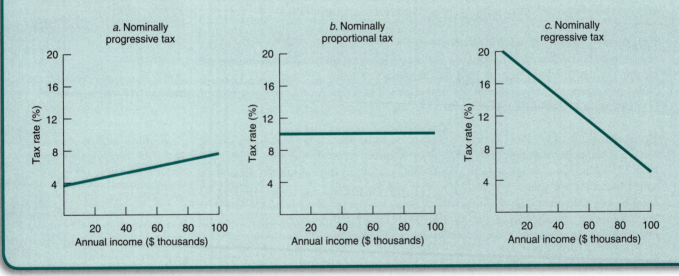

and salaries up to $106,800. The maximum you had to pay was $6,621.60. Where did this figure come from? I'll give you some space to come up with the answer:

That's right: multiply $106,800 by 6.2 percent, or 0.062. This comes to $6,621.60.

Now that I've had you do all these calculations, I have some bad news for you. The 6.2 percent of your wages deducted from your paycheck is not *all* the government takes. The Medicare tax of 1.45 percent is also taken out, but, unlike the Social Security tax, there's no wage-base limitation. If you earned $1 million, you'd pay a Medicare tax of $14,500.

So let's go back to the drawing board. The deduction from your pay is 7.65 percent (6.2 percent for Social Security and 1.45 percent for Medicare). How much, then, is deducted per year for these programs from the pay of a person earning $10,000? Work it out right here:

The answer is $765 ($10,000 × .0765). Of course, your employer also withholds money from your check for personal income taxes. But guess what! Seventy-five percent of all taxpayers pay more in payroll taxes (that is, Social Security and Medicare) than they do in personal income tax. Nearly everyone earning less than $75,000 pays more Social Security and Medicare tax than personal income tax.

Table 1 shows the Social Security taxes paid by people with various incomes. Only earned income (wages and salaries) is subject to this tax; rental income, interest, dividends, and profits are not. It might appear at first glance that the Social Security tax is proportional; but as you examine Table 1, you should observe that it is not only regressive in effect, but nominally regressive as well.

TABLE 1 The Incidence of the Social Security Tax at Various Income Levels in 2010*

Level of Earned Income	Taxes Paid	Average Tax Rate
$ 10,000	$ 620	6.20%
100,000	6,200	6.20
1,000,000	6,621.60	0.66

*The Social Security tax rate is set by law at 6.2 percent. Each year, however, the inflation rate of the previous year raises the wage base. In 2010, the wage base was set at $106,800.

Table 1 shows the Social Security taxes paid on earned income, which provides over 90 percent of the income of nearly everyone but the rich. The primary income sources of the rich are dividends, interest, and profit, none of which is subject to the Social Security tax. *Think* about it: Nearly all of the income of the non-rich is subject to the Social Security tax, but only a tiny fraction of the income of the rich is taxed. All the more reason to label the Social Security tax as regressive.

Sources of Federal Revenue

The Personal Income Tax As we indicated in Figure 1 near the beginning of the chapter, individual income taxes account for 44 percent of all federal tax revenue. It has long been the most important revenue source, although it may soon be outstripped by social insurance receipts, which pay for Social Security and Medicare. In general, the middle class and the rich pay nearly all federal income taxes. Indeed, 47 percent of all Americans owed no federal income tax in 2009—up from just 38 percent in 2007.

You don't pay tax on all of your income: You may subtract various deductions and exemptions, and, consequently, very few people with low incomes have to pay any federal income tax. In 2009 a single person paid a marginal tax rate of just 10 percent on her first $8,350 of taxable income, and 15 percent on the next $25,600. A married

The largest source of federal revenue is the personal income tax.

The Economic Recovery Tax Act of 1981

Figure 4

Federal Personal Income Tax:
The Top Marginal Tax Rate,
1993–2010

The top marginal rate of the federal
personal income tax has been
35 percent since 2003. The top
MTR was at its historic high in
1944 and 1945 when it reached
94 percent, and was as high as
91 percent as recently as 1963. In
the 1980s it fell from 70 percent to
28 percent, and has since ranged
from 31 percent to 39.6 percent.

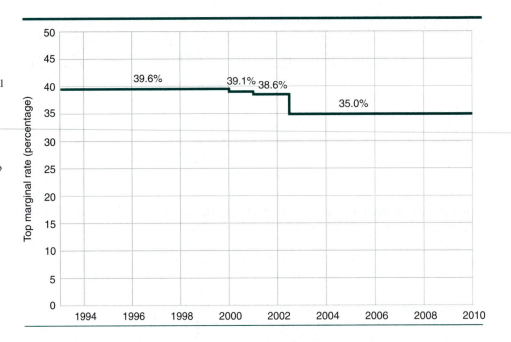

*The United States is the only
country where it takes more
brains to figure your tax than to
earn the money to pay for it.*

—Edward J. Gurney,
U.S. senator

*That which angers men most
is to be taxed above their
neighbors.*

—Sir William Petty, *A Treatise
of Taxes and Contributions,*
1662

couple filing jointly paid 10 percent on their first $16,700 of taxable income and 15 percent on the next $51,200.[3] In 2009 the marginal tax rates were 10, 15, 25, 28, 33, and 35 percent. Two-thirds of all taxpayers have MTRs of either 15 percent or 10 percent.

Anyone with a taxable income of over $372,950 paid a marginal tax rate of 35 percent. Figure 4 shows the maximum marginal tax rate since 1993. The federal personal income tax is considered progressive because the burden falls mostly on the rich. Some would disagree, saying that many rich people pay no taxes. We won't go there, except to mention that only an infinitesimal fraction of the rich pay no income tax. Others say that the rich are unfairly called upon to pay the lion's share of this tax. We'll come back to that argument toward the end of the chapter, when we discuss recent federal tax laws.

In 2011 the so-called "Bush tax cuts" expire and we'll revert to the somewhat higher marginal tax rates of 2001. These include a top rate of 39.6 percent. By the time you're reading these words, Congress may have passed legislation to avert a tax increase, at least for those in the lower tax brackets. But it is likely that those now in the 35 percent bracket will be subjected to a higher marginal tax rate.

We have mentioned that you don't have to pay tax on every dollar of your income. In fact, a married couple with one child earning less than $32,000 pays no federal income tax at all, because of a combination of deductions, exemptions, and child care tax credits. Randy Day is single and earns $10,000. If he is entitled to $9,000 in deductions and exemptions, how much federal personal income tax does he pay? Work it out right here:

Solution:
$10,000 − $9,000 = $1,000 taxable income. Since he is in the lowest income tax bracket, 10 percent, he would pay $100 in federal personal income tax ($1,000 × .10).

---

[3]Every year these tax brackets are adjusted upward for inflation. For example, in 2002 a single person paid 10 percent on her first $6,000 of taxable income, but by 2009 she had to pay 10 percent on her first $8,350 of taxable income.

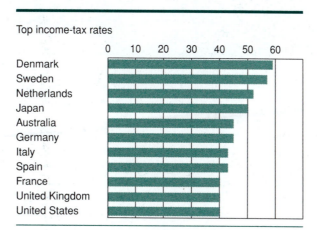

Top income-tax rates

Figure 5
Top Marginal Combined Income
Tax Rates in 11 Leading
Wealthy Nations, 2008*
Along with the United Kingdom and
France, the United States has the
lowest top personal income-tax rate
among these nine nations. While
our most affluent taxpayers pay a
marginal tax rate of just 35 percent,
those in Denmark, Sweden, and the
Netherlands all pay over 50 percent.
*Combined federal, state, and local
income taxes.
Source: OECD.

We know that the MTR for the rich is 35 percent, but there is a giant loophole in the tax code. Anyone selling a stock, bond, house or building, or any other investment which is held for at least a year pays a capital gains tax of just 15 percent. The richest 400 U.S. households earned an average income of $345 million in 2007. Almost three-quarters of that income was derived from long-term capital gains. Can you guess what their average tax rate was that year?

These folks paid, on average, an ATR of just 16.6 percent. Warren Buffett, the noted stock market investor, and the world's second richest person has noted, his average tax rate is lower than his secretary's.

How does our top marginal tax rate compare with those of other wealthy countries? Would you believe it's the lowest in the group shown in Figure 5?

In 2008 the honor of having the highest marginal income tax rate went to Denmark, which levies a tax of 59 percent on incomes above $70,000. Thousands of young Danes have been voting with their feet, by moving to neighboring nations with lower tax rates. Although not quite as easy as relocating from Michigan to Missouri, the citizens of the European Union are entitled to work in any of the 27 member countries.

The Payroll Tax   What's the payroll tax? Remember the Social Security and Medicare taxes that you pay? What you pay is matched by your employer. When you pay 7.65 percent of your wages (6.2 percent for Social Security and 1.45 percent for Medicare), your employer also pays 7.65 percent of your wages. The payroll tax is the federal government's fastest-growing source of revenue and now stands second in importance to the personal income tax.

Let's make sure we're clear on what the Social Security, Medicare, and payroll taxes are. Our employers deduct 6.2 percent of our pay (up to $106,800) in Social Security taxes and 1.45 percent of our pay in Medicare taxes. In other words, we pay 7.65 percent in payroll tax on wages of up to $106,800, and 1.45 percent on all wages. The employer matches the employee's payments dollar for dollar. So how much payroll tax would the government collect all together on wages of $20,000?

Solution: It would collect $3,060 ($20,000 × 0.153). Where did we get 0.153? We added the 0.0765 that the employee paid to the 0.0765 that the employer paid. The employee would pay $1,530 ($20,000 × .0765), and this would be matched by the employer.

The Corporate Income Tax   The corporate income tax is a tax on a corporation's profits. Those who believe profits provide our economy with its main incentive to produce goods and services are uneasy that they are so heavily taxed. However, corporate income taxes are now just 13 percent of all federal tax revenue and the maximum rate is 35 percent.[4] But according to a study of IRS data by University of Virginia law Professor George Ko Yin, the average large corporation paid less than 27 percent in 2006.

Giving money and power to the government is like giving whiskey and car keys to teenage boys.

—P. J. O'Rourke

The power to tax involves the power to destroy.

—Chief Justice John Marshall

---

[4]Corporations earning profits of less than $100,000 are taxed at lower rates.

Should Cigarettes Be Taxed?

Should cigarettes be taxed? Why not? If the tax is high enough, it will discourage smoking. Of course, we don't want to make it too high, or nobody will smoke, and the federal government will be out about $8 billion a year.

But there are two good reasons why a tax on cigarettes is inequitable. First, it's regressive. We can see that it's harder for a poor person to pay $8 dollars a pack (or $2,920 a year, if that person has a two-pack-a-day habit) than it is for a rich person to pay $8 dollars a pack. But if you're poor, you're much more likely to smoke than if you're rich.

In 2009 the federal excise tax on a pack of cigarettes shot up from 39 cents to $1.01. In New York City, where the combined state and local tax is $5.85, cigarettes are now selling for $11 a pack. There are people selling individual cigarettes on the street for 60 or 70 cents. It's poor people who can't afford to buy an entire pack who are buying cigarettes on the street, which shows quite vividly just how regressive cigarette taxes are.

According to the U.S. Centers for Disease Control in Atlanta (where I once worked as a management trainee), 16 percent of all college graduates smoke, while 36 percent of all high school dropouts continue to puff away. Your average college graduate is much more affluent than your average high school dropout, which means a cigarette tax is almost targeted at the poor.

We single out relatively poor people, we tax them on something they really like to do, and then, to add insult to injury, we make them stand outside the building.

Excise Taxes   An excise tax is a sales tax, but it is aimed at specific goods and services. The federal government taxes such things as tires, cigarettes, liquor, gasoline, and phone calls. Most excise taxes are levied by the federal government, although state and local governments often levy taxes on the same items. Cigarettes and gasoline, for example, are subject to a federal excise tax as well as to excise taxes in many states. In fact, the differential in state excise taxes encourages many people to "smuggle" cigarettes from North Carolina into New York.

Excise taxes, which account for about 4 percent of federal revenue, have another purpose beside serving as a source of revenue. They tend to reduce consumption of certain products of which the federal government takes a dim view. The surgeon general not only warns us about cigarettes but looks on approvingly as the government taxes them.

Excise taxes are usually regressive.

Excise taxes are generally regressive because they tend to fall more heavily on the poor and working class. The tax on a pack of cigarettes is the same whether you're rich or poor, but it's easier for the rich person to handle $3 or $4 a day than it is for a poor person. The same is true of liquor and gasoline. In fact, a tax on most consumer goods is regressive because the poor tend to spend a higher proportion of their incomes on consumption than the rich (who save 20 to 25 percent of their incomes). (See the nearby boxes regarding cigarette and gasoline excise taxes.)

Would a tax on jewelry be progressive or regressive? Clearly it would be progressive since the rich spend a much higher proportion of their income on jewelry than the poor.

It is generally allowed by all, that men should contribute to the publick charge but according to the share and interest they have in the public peace; that is, according to their estates or riches.

—Sir William Petty, *A Treatise of Taxes and Contributions,* 1662

The Estate Tax   A tax on estates of people who die has been termed by its opponents as the "death tax." In the past more than 90 percent of estates taxes were paid by the estates of people with incomes exceeding $200,000 a year at the time of death.

This tax expired on December 31, 2009. The estates of those who died in 2010 paid no federal taxes. But on January 1, 2011, under the snap-back tax plan, estates will once again be taxed at a rate of 55 percent of everything over $1 million. By the time you read this, it is likely that Congress will have modified the tax to enable inheritors of farms and other businesses to carry on without having to pay such a high tax.

Recent Tax Legislation

Kemp-Roth Tax Cut of 1981   This law, which lowered the average citizen's tax bill by 23 percent over a three-year period, was strongly supported by President Ronald Reagan. The top marginal income tax rate was cut from 70 percent to 50 percent.

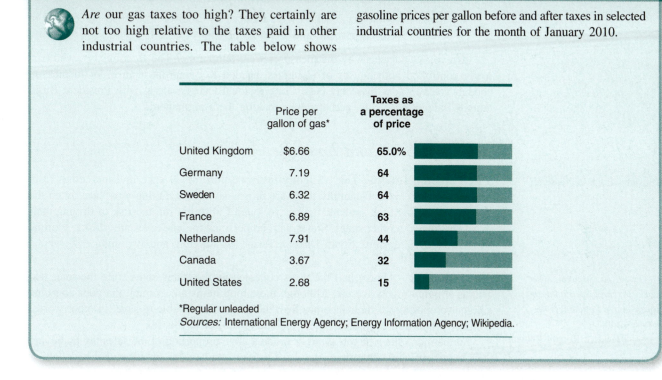

Should Our Gasoline Taxes Be Raised?

Are our gas taxes too high? They certainly are not too high relative to the taxes paid in other industrial countries. The table below shows gasoline prices per gallon before and after taxes in selected industrial countries for the month of January 2010.

	Price per gallon of gas*	Taxes as a percentage of price	
United Kingdom	$6.66	65.0%	
Germany	7.19	64	
Sweden	6.32	64	
France	6.89	63	
Netherlands	7.91	44	
Canada	3.67	32	
United States	2.68	15	

*Regular unleaded
Sources: International Energy Agency; Energy Information Agency; Wikipedia.

Tax Reform Act of 1986   This cut personal income taxes still further. The maximum rate was lowered to 28 percent, and millions of poorer families were taken off the income tax rolls entirely.

In 1990 the top marginal rate was raised to 31 percent, and in 1993 to 39.6 percent. There were no more changes until 2001.

The Tax Cut of 2001   This law, passed at the behest of President George W. Bush, immediately lowered the minimum marginal tax rate from 15 percent to just 10 percent, and gradually lowered the other marginal tax rates over the next 10 years. By the end of the decade the top marginal tax rate would fall to 33 percent. In addition, the inheritance tax would be phased out completely. Weirdly, however, unless Congress made this law permanent, it was set to expire on January 1, 2011, and we would revert to the tax rates that were in effect in 2001, unless Congress has enacted a new tax law.

The two main criticisms of this tax cut were that most of the benefits would go to the rich and that it would push up the federal budget deficit. President Bush countered that the rich paid most of the taxes, so it would be only fair that they should receive most of the benefits of a tax cut. The top 5 percent of all households pay 51 percent of the federal income tax, while the poorest 50 percent pay just 4 percent. Still, one must wonder why nearly *every* one of the president's tax proposals seems to be skewed toward helping the rich.

Only the little people pay taxes.
—attributed to Leona Helmsley, billionaire who went to jail for tax evasion

President Bush also maintained that a tax cut would give people more incentive to work, the economy would grow faster, and the budget deficit would subsequently shrink. Again, critics note that after we enacted massive tax cuts in 1981, the federal budget deficit almost tripled by the end of the decade.

The Tax Cut of 2003   This law, passed by Congress with strong support from President Bush, had three main provisions: The top federal personal income tax rate paid by stockholders on corporate dividends and on capital gains was lowered to 15 percent, but in 2011 the rate would revert back to the current higher rate.

- The child income tax credit was raised from $600 to $1,000.
- The highest income tax brackets were reduced as follows: 38.6 to 35 percent; 35 to 33 percent; 30 to 28 percent; and 27 to 25 percent.

Are you wondering why the measures were temporary? The Republicans, who narrowly controlled both houses of Congress, needed to compromise in order to pick up enough votes to pass these tax cuts. Congressional leaders, along with President Bush, hope to extend these cuts, perhaps even making them permanent.

Sources of State and Local Revenue

The sales tax is regressive.

The Personal Income Tax   Slightly over one third of all state revenue comes from personal income taxes. Generally these are progressive taxes, falling most heavily on the rich. However, high tax states like New York and California run the risk of driving their richest residents to other states. States with no personal income taxes are Alaska, Florida, Nevada, New Hampshire, South Dakota, Texas, Washington, and Wyoming.

The taxpayer: Someone who works for the government but doesn't have to take a civil service exam.

—President Ronald Reagan

The Sales Tax   Almost half the taxes collected by the states come from the sales tax. This is a highly regressive tax. Although most food items are exempt, the poor consume a higher proportion of their incomes than the rich, who are able to save. In other words, a higher proportion of poor people's income is subject to this tax.

Furthermore, the rich can avoid or evade a large proportion of the sales tax by buying their big-ticket items—furniture, stereos, TVs, cars, and so on—in states that have low or no sales tax. They can also evade the sales tax by buying expensive items with cash (an option not feasible for the poor) from merchants who don't declare their cash incomes.

Still another problem with the sales tax is that it can distort business decisions about where to locate. Why did Amazon.com buy warehouses in Nevada near the California border to serve its West Coast market, when warehouses in California's Central Valley would probably have been more cost-effective? Because a physical presence in California would make Amazon responsible for collecting sales taxes on items sold to Californians, something which Amazon wants to avoid. According to the U.S. Constitution, one state cannot require businesses in another state to collect taxes for it.

You probably never heard of the Internet Tax Freedom Act, which declared a tax moratorium for online sales, exempting buyers from paying state and local sales taxes. As these sales multiply, the states stand to lose an increasing proportion of their most important source of revenue. This loss was estimated at $20 billion in 2006. The Internet Freedom Act was extended for another 7 years in 2007.

The Property Tax   Nearly 80 percent of all local tax revenue is derived from the property tax. There is some disagreement about whether this is a regressive tax, but it is a deduction that you may take on your federal income tax. For example, if you paid $3,000 in property tax, you are entitled to a $3,000 deduction on your federal income tax return.

Are State and Local Taxes Regressive?   Yes! The people with the lowest 20 percent of household incomes—below $18,000—pay 11.4 percent of their income for state and local taxes. Those in the top 1 percent—earning over $350,000—pay just 5.2 percent. The prize for most regressive taxes goes to the state of Florida, where the lowest-income families pay 14.4 percent of their income for state and local taxes, while the top 1 percent pay just 2.7 percent. But Washington state can certainly make a valid claim that *it* has the most regressive state and local taxes. These taxes cost the poor 17.6 percent of their income, while the families in the top 1 percent income bracket pay just 3.1 percent.

on the web

Some states have a sales tax, some have an income tax, some have both, and a very few have neither. See how heavily the citizens of *your* state are taxed. Go to www.taxadmin.org and click on "State Comparisons" at the top of the left column.

The State and Local Fiscal Dilemma

Since World War II, state and local governments have been expected to provide an increasing number of services, most notably health, welfare, education, and police protection. According to the 1940 census, just one-third of all Americans who were 25 or older had gone beyond the eighth grade. Today more than 85 percent of those 25 or older are at least high school graduates. Education is perhaps the main job of local government, but it is paid for not just by local taxes, but by state and federal taxes as well. In 1945 state and local taxes were about 5 percent of GDP; now they are almost 14 percent (see Figure 6).

Furthermore, under our federal system, neighboring states and local governments are in direct competition with one another for tax dollars. If one government's tax rates— particularly the sales and property taxes—rise too far above the levels of its neighbors, its citizens will vote with their feet. They will shop or even move to the areas that have lower tax rates. Were there a uniform national sales or property tax, it could be more easily raised when necessary. As long as neighboring government units are in direct competition, raising the necessary tax revenues will be difficult.

The federal government has piled new obligations on state and local government, without providing nearly enough money to pay for them. The largest unfunded mandate is the No Child Left Behind Act of 2001, which requires all public schools to test students, in order to improve their education. In theory, the act fully finances the new tests, but in practice, say local officials, implementing the act requires changes in the whole educational system, not just adding a few extra tests. The cost, they say, is $35 billion a year more than the act provides.

The Department of Homeland Security requires states and localities to hire new police officers, but provides no money to pay their salaries. Another huge drain on state budgets is Medicaid spending, to provide health care for the poor. The states must fund about 40 percent of Medicaid. In 2008 this came to $130 billion; it now accounts for 22 percent of all state spending.

Through the 1970s, the 1980s, and the 1990s, the states ran substantial surpluses. But the 2001 recession, the events of 9/11, and the recent federal government spending mandates

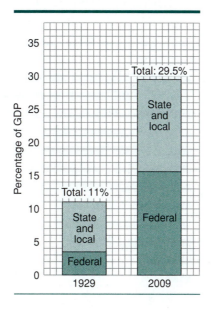

Figure 6

Government Tax Receipts as Percentage of GDP, 1929 and 2009

Since 1929 Federal taxes have risen much more quickly than state and local taxes as a percentage of GDP.

Source: Economic Report of the President, 2010; *Survey of Current Business,* March 2010, www.bea.gov.

have driven many state governments—and with them thousands of local governments—into very serious financial difficulty. Faced with sharply rising projected budget deficits, every state but Vermont was legally obligated to balance its budget. In 2002 and 2003, state after state slashed services and raised taxes. College tuitions were raised in some states by over 20 percent, tens of thousands of state employees were laid off, prisoners were released early, and sales, personal income, and property taxes were increased across the nation.

The onset of the 2007–2009 recession created a fiscal crisis for state budgets not seen since the Great Depression. As tax revenues fell, many states and localities were forced to cut services to the bone. Despite large infusions of federal aid under the 2009 economic stimulus plan, the states faced a combined deficit of over $400 billion during the period from 2009 through 2011. Hardest hit were California, Oklahoma, Arizona, Illinois, Hawaii, New Jersey, New York, Nevada, Colorado, and Michigan.

Comparison of Taxes in the United States and Other Countries

Contrary to popular opinion, Americans are not heavily taxed in comparison with the citizens of other industrial countries. As we see in Figure 7, our taxes were at the low end of the world's leading rich countries. Keep in mind that these taxes include federal, state, and local taxes, and that almost half of that total is redistributed in the form of transfer payments, such as Social Security, public assistance, food stamps, and unemployment insurance payments.

Who pays the highest taxes in North America? OK, I'll give you a hint: In which *province* do they pay the highest taxes? In case you didn't know, it's Quebec, which boasts a 51.7 percent tax bite, which includes a sales tax of about 15 percent. So the next time you hear someone complaining about high taxes, just tell them to move to Quebec.

So what's our problem? Why all this whining and carrying on about our high taxes when people in other countries pay so much more? Much of the dissatisfaction has to do with the lack of tangible benefits we get in return for our taxes. In many European countries medical care is free, college is free, and day care is heavily subsidized. Indeed, parents of young children receive $1,000 or more every year in child care allowances from their governments. So the United States would definitely have many more happy campers if its citizens got to see more of what they've been paying for.

Do you remember the concept of *opportunity cost,* which we covered in Chapter 2? Because we're always having to make choices, *the opportunity cost of any choice is the foregone value of the next best alternative.* The tax cut debate is really over opportunity cost: What do we need to *give up* in exchange for lower taxes? How about a cut in Social

A tax is a compulsory payment for which no specific benefit is received in return.

—U.S. Treasury

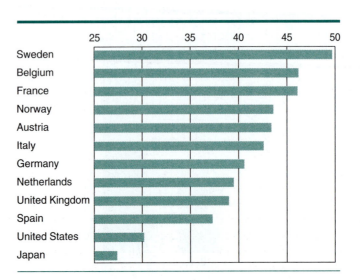

Figure 7

Tax Receipts as a Percentage of GDP in United States and Selected Countries, 2008
American taxpayers have a relatively low burden in comparison to taxpayers in other rich nations.
Source: Organization for Economic Cooperation and Development.

Security benefits? A smaller armed forces? Lower pay for teachers, firefighters, and the police? Just as you can't have your cake and eat it too, the concept of opportunity cost shows us that we can't cut taxes *and* maintain the level of government spending that we would like.

The Economic Role of Government

This chapter has talked a lot about taxes and government spending. In short, the government giveth and the government taketh away.

One fact that should be readily apparent is that the federal government and, to a lesser degree, state and local governments have a tremendous impact on the economy. This analysis, however, will be confined to the federal government. Although there is a great deal of overlap, we are going to consider, sequentially, four specific economic functions of government: provision of public goods and services, redistribution of income, stabilization, and economic regulation.

(1) Provision of Public Goods and Services

Government provides a wide range of goods and services. Private enterprise would supply few of these because they are not profitable. Back in the 1950s, most of the country was served by private intercity bus lines. In New Jersey, when these companies began losing money, the state had to subsidize them just to keep the buses running. Finally, more than 25 years ago the state was forced to take over all the remaining private bus lines. Other states and regions were also forced to form public transportation authorities, while the federal government formed Amtrak to take over the national rail lines. Add to these all the other government operations and you're talking about some $3 trillion of public goods and services.

Some of the main services our government provides include defense of the country, maintenance of internal order and a nationwide highway network, and provision of a money supply to facilitate exchanges of goods and services. While certain services, such as public education and the running of the criminal justice system, are very obvious, others, such as bank inspections, environmental protection, and the carrying out of scientific research are less visible to most citizens.

Our interstate highway network is an excellent example of the social infrastructure that our government provides. Imagine how much lower our standard of living would be without it. Compare our infrastructure with that of a poor country and you'll have a much better appreciation of the economic role of the government.

(2) Redistribution of Income

The government is sometimes seen as a modern-day Robin Hood, redistributing money from rich taxpayers to poor welfare recipients, or from huge corporations to unemployment benefit recipients. Food stamps, Medicaid, and disability payments are all programs aimed mainly at the needy, while the relatively well-to-do taxpayer foots the bill.

Some would argue that there is also welfare for the rich, whether in the form of subsidies to corporate farmers and shipbuilders; tax breaks for defense contractors, oil companies, and other large corporations; or huge government contracts for missile systems, aircraft, and highway construction.

The top 1 percent of income earners paid about 38 percent of federal income taxes in 2009. By contrast, families in the bottom 50 percent of income earners paid little or no federal income tax, and millions of them received money back from the government, mainly in the form of the Earned Income Tax Credit, which is discussed in the chapter on income distribution and poverty near the end of the book.

Does the government take from the rich and give to the poor—or is it the other way around?

A government which robs Peter to pay Paul can always depend on the support of Paul.
—George Bernard Shaw

Regardless of whether the rich or the poor are on the receiving end, one thing is perfectly clear: The government does redistribute a lot of money. The federal, state, and local governments combined provide Americans with $2.4 trillion a year in the form of transfer payments such as Social Security, veterans' pensions, public assistance, and unemployment insurance benefits.

(3) Stabilization

It is the aim of good government to stimulate production, of bad government to encourage consumption.

—Jean-Baptiste Say

Two basic goals of the federal government are stable prices and low unemployment. Stated somewhat differently, the goals may be seen as a fairly high rate of economic growth (which would hold the rate of unemployment to a minimum) with no inflation.

How the government might go about attaining these goals is the subject of Chapters 10 through 16. But at this time we can already gauge some of the economic impact of the federal budget and how that budget might affect the stability of our economy.

The $3.9 trillion that the federal government now dispenses annually puts a floor under our economy's purchasing power. During the early stages of the Great Depression, the federal government was only a minor economic player. The total federal budget was less than 5 percent of GDP. Now it's 25 percent. Thus, no matter how bad things get, at least the government will provide a floor under total spending.

From the day it took office, the Obama administration needed to deal with the effects of the worst economic downturn since the 1930s. Between fiscal year 2009 and fiscal year 2011 federal spending leapt from $3.2 trillion to $3.9 trillion. In addition, taxes were cut, while the U.S. Treasury and the Federal Reserve provided over $2 trillion in loans and loan guarantees to the nation's major financial institutions and to other large corporations. All of this gave rise to federal budget deficits in excess of $1 trillion and a soaring national debt—topics that we shall cover in Chapter 12. This massive government intervention did help end the Great Recession, but it so alarmed millions of citizens that they joined "Tea Parties" to combat what they believed was the unwarranted increase in the economic role of the federal government. And then too, the health care reform act that was passed in March 2010—which many viewed as a major step toward "socialized medicine"—fueled their anger still more.

(4) Economic Regulation

Another important function of government is to provide the economic rules of the game and, somewhat more broadly, the social and political context in which the economy operates. Some of these rules are easily understood: the fostering of competition among business firms, environmental protection laws, child labor laws, the setting of a minimum hourly wage rate, consumer protection laws, and a court system to adjudicate disputes and punish offenders. Beyond these, the government helps provide the social and political framework within which individuals and business firms are able to function smoothly.

In Chapter 3 we talked about the role of competition and the price mechanism in our economic system. A competitive system will function only as long as there is competition. If there are only a handful of firms in several industries, there is no competition. The government's job is to make sure this doesn't happen.

Government provides the legal framework that enables private ownership and the enforcement of contracts. These protections are generally absent in primitive economies which lack entrepreneurs willing to create business firms. The government also provides a reliable money supply, which facilitates specialization and exchange, the development of financial markets, and a smoothly functioning banking system.

Within our political and social framework, the government must also allow individuals and business firms to operate with the maximum degree of freedom. There are those who consider the current level of government regulation blatant interference with their economic freedom.

Does that freedom imply the right to pollute the environment or to monopolize an industry by driving competitors out of business? Perhaps Justice Oliver Wendell Holmes put it best when he noted that a person's freedom to swing his fist extended only as far as his neighbor's nose. Unfortunately, in the economic environment, there is little agreement as to how far economic freedom may be extended without interfering with society as a whole or the economic rights of specific individuals or business firms.[5]

Conclusion

Adam Smith, in his monumental *The Wealth of Nations,* published in 1776, summed up the dos and don'ts of economic endeavor: "Every man, as long as he does not violate the laws of justice, is left perfectly free to pursue his own interest his own way, and to bring both his industry and capital into competition with those of any other man, or order of men."[6]

Adam Smith's dos and don'ts

Smith went on to define the economic role of government:

> According to the system of natural liberty, the sovereign has only three duties to attend to; three duties of great importance, indeed, but plain and intelligible to common understandings: first, the duty of protecting the society from the violence and invasion of other independent societies; secondly, the duty of protecting, as far as possible, every member of the society from the injustice or oppression of every other member of it, or the duty of establishing an exact administration of justice; and, thirdly, the duty of erecting and maintaining certain public works and certain public institutions, which it can never be for the interest of any individual, or small number of individuals, to erect and maintain; because the profit could never repay the expense to any individual or small number of individuals, though it may frequently do much more than repay it to a great society.[7]

If we were to take Adam Smith's description of the government's economic role as our starting point, let's see how far it might be expanded. Should the government try to curb air and water pollution? What about prohibiting the dumping of toxic waste or regulating the disposal of nuclear waste? One can only wonder what Smith would have said about Medicare's drug prescription program.

How much should the government be involved in helping the homeless and the 37 million Americans officially classified as poor?[8] Or the 49 million people without medical insurance? And what more should be done about crime and drugs? The government's economic role has grown tremendously these last seven decades, and it will continue to grow in coming years. Indeed, when your children take macroeconomics, the author of their textbook may look back at the first decade of the 21st century as a period when the economic role of government was still relatively small.

Current Issue: Will Social Security Be There for You?

Please answer these two questions:

1. Do you believe in flying saucers?
2. Do you believe you will be able to collect Social Security benefits when you're 65?

Surveys conducted over the last dozen years found that more people in their 20s believe that there are flying saucers than that they will be able to collect Social Security benefits. According to a July 2010 USA Today/Gallup Poll, three-fourths of those 18 to 34 don't expect to get a Social Security check when they retire.

---

[5]We discuss these issues in the chapter on corporate mergers and antitrust in *Economics* and in *Microeconomics.*

[6]Adam Smith, *The Wealth of Nations* (London: Methuen, 1950), p. 208.

[7]Ibid., pp. 208–9.

[8]Poverty is the subject of a later chapter.

When you reach the age of 65, will you be able to collect Social Security benefits? After all, you will pay Social Security taxes your entire working life. And ditto for Medicare. There's no question that you're entitled. But will you be able to *collect*?

My own guess is that before mid-century there will be a watered down version of both programs. You'll receive *some* benefits, but not at nearly the level that your grandparents received.

For decades we have been paying more in Social Security taxes than we're spending on Social Security benefits. That surplus is deposited in the Social Security trust fund, which consists of trillions of dollars of U.S. government securities. But what's also happening is that the government, which has been running humongous budget deficits, is using the Social Security surpluses each year to offset the deficits. Each year, then, the U.S. Treasury spends the surplus and places its i.o.u.'s into the Social Security trust fund.

In 2010 benefits paid were expected to exceed taxes paid because of the effects of the recession. Tax receipts lagged, since over 15 million people were unemployed. In addition, countless millions in their early and mid-sixties, many of whom were out of work, applied for their benefits sooner than they had planned. As the economic recovery continues, Social Security tax payments are expected to once again exceed benefits.

In this decade most of the baby boomers (born between 1946 and 1964) will retire, and by 2017, the annual Social Security surplus will disappear. But don't worry, because we can just draw down the trust fund until it runs out of money around 2037. The only problem is that the trust fund consists of U.S. treasury bills, bonds, notes, and certificates. The trust fund administrators aren't going to send people these U.S. government securities every month instead of checks. No problem, the administrators can just go out and sell the securities to the public. But they'd soon be selling hundreds of billions of U.S. government securities on top of financing our huge—and probably growing—federal budget deficit.

Long before the trust fund runs out of money around 2037, this massive government borrowing will very likely push up interest rates to record levels and possibly precipitate a financial crisis. That's if no strong measures are taken to raise Social Security taxes and lower benefits.

OK, that's the good news. The bad news is Medicare, which is even more seriously underfunded than Social Security. By 2028, Medicare spending will surpass Social Security spending. Remember all those retiring baby boomers? Medicare is a lot more complex than Social Security, so I promise that you'll soon be hearing more about an impending Medicare crisis.

In 2008 the first of the 77-million-strong baby boom generation began to collect Social Security retirement benefits, and in 2011, as they begin reaching the age of 65, they will enroll in Medicare. Health care costs, which have been rising much faster than the rate of inflation, may begin rising even faster. Already health care spending accounts for one of every six dollars of GDP. And so, as your grandparents, and then your parents reach retirement age, your generation will be called upon to pay an increasing share of your income—most likely in the form of higher taxes—to ensure that they receive everything their government has promised them.

Questions for Further Thought and Discussion

1. If a political candidate said that if she were elected to Congress, she would work toward cutting federal government spending by one-third over the next four years, would she stand much chance of fulfilling her promise? Why or why not?

2. When you retire, will you be able to collect Social Security benefits? Give the reasons why you might not be able to collect.

3. Discuss the pros and cons of having a high cigarette excise tax.

4. Make up a numerical example to show why the Social Security tax is regressive.

5. If Adam Smith were alive today, to what degree would he approve of the present economic role of the American government?

6. What additional goods and services do we expect from government today as opposed to 60 years ago?

7. Some politicians say that Americans pay too much in taxes. Explain why you agree or disagree with them.

8. Describe the growth of the economic role of the federal government since the 1930s.

9. Explain the difference between government spending and government purchases of goods and services.

10. Give two examples of public goods or services that you use.

11. *Practical Application:* If you could order a cut of $100 billion in federal spending, which programs would you cut and why would you cut them?

12. *Practical Application:* In what ways is our tax system—federal, state, and local—too regressive? How would you make it less regressive without reducing tax revenue?

13. *Practical Application:* About how much personal income tax would you have to pay on a job that paid $100 million? See if you can come up with the correct answer in less than 10 seconds.

14. *Web Activity:* On January 1 of each year, the Social Security wage base rises. To find the wage base for the current year, go to google.com, type in "Social Security Wage Base," and click on the first listing.

15. *Web Activity:* Which states have no sales tax? Go to www.taxadmin.org and click on "State Comparisons" at the top of the left column.

Name _____   Date _____

Multiple-Choice Questions

Circle the letter that corresponds to the best answer.

1. The role of government grew most rapidly during the period _____. (LO1)
   a) 1920–1933
   b) 1933–1945
   c) 1945–1960
   d) 1960–1975

2. The seeds of the expansion of the federal government's economic role were sown during the administration of _____. (LO1)
   a) Franklin Roosevelt
   b) Dwight Eisenhower
   c) Richard Nixon
   d) Ronald Reagan

3. Which couple pays the most in federal taxes? (LO5)
   a) Todd Lhuillier and Stacey Lhuillier derive their entire $100,000 income from dividends and have two young children, Chloe Lhuillier and Taylor Lhuillier.
   b) Eric Church and Kim Swanson Church each have jobs that pay $50,000; they have no children.
   c) Teodor Barnett and Miriam Barnett each have jobs that pay $51,000 and have two dependent grandchildren living with them—Sarah Jones and Emma Jones.
   d) Patricia Judge has a job paying $55,000 and her husband, John Judge, has one that pays $52,000. They have five dependent grandchildren living with them—Jack Alaska Watt, William Watt, Matthew Watt, Blake Armstrong, and Susan Armstrong.

4. Which is the most accurate statement? (LO5)
   a) The rich pay most of the federal personal income tax.
   b) President George W. Bush raised taxes that the poor must pay.
   c) As a result of the events of 9/11, Americans are very supportive of tax cuts.
   d) Government spending on defense declined between 2001 and 2006.

5. The federal government's fiscal year begins on _____. (LO1)
   a) January 1
   b) July 1
   c) October 1
   d) November 1

6. Transfer payments to individuals are _____ percent of the federal budget. (LO1)
   a) 25
   b) 50
   c) 65
   d) 85

7. Which statement is true? (LO5)
   a) Bill Gates pays more Social Security tax than most American workers.
   b) The rich pay a higher proportion of their income in Social Security tax than in federal personal income tax.
   c) Most wage earners pay more in federal personal income tax than in Social Security tax.
   d) The rich pay Social Security tax on nearly their entire income.

8. Compared to federal spending, state and local spending is _____. (LO1)
   a) almost twice as large
   b) about the same
   c) less than half as large
   d) one-quarter as large

9. The largest federal government purchase of final goods and services is _____. (LO1)
   a) Social Security
   b) defense
   c) interest on the national debt
   d) foreign aid

10. If Kathie Barnes earns $50,000 and Katie Harvey earns $500,000 a year, they both will pay Social Security tax _____. (LO5)
   a) at the same average tax rate
   b) but Kathie Barnes will pay at a higher average tax rate
   c) but Katie Harvey will pay at a higher average tax rate
   d) but it is impossible to tell what their average tax rates are

11. The most progressive tax listed here is the _____. (LO4)
   a) Social Security tax
   b) federal personal income tax
   c) federal excise tax
   d) state sales tax

12. Each of the following is a direct tax except the _____ tax. (LO4)
   a) Social Security
   b) federal personal income
   c) corporate income
   d) federal excise

13. Which is true? (LO4)
   a) The rich are hurt more than the poor by regressive taxes.
   b) The poor are hurt more than the rich by progressive taxes.
   c) The federal personal income tax is a regressive tax.
   d) None of these statements is true.

14. A tax with an average rate of 20 percent for the rich and 2 percent for the middle class is _____. (LO3, 4)
   a) progressive
   b) regressive
   c) proportional
   d) none of these

15. In 2010 Brian Murray earned $300,000; he paid Social Security tax on _____. (LO5)
   a) none of his income
   b) all of his income
   c) nearly all of his income
   d) less than half of his income

16. Which statement is true? (LO1, 5)
   a) There is no overlap between the duties of local government and private businesses.
   b) Medicare and Medicaid spending account for over 20 percent of the federal budget.
   c) We spend as much on defense than do the rest of the world's nations combined.
   d) Although President George W. Bush cut the tax rates of the rich, they generally ended up paying more taxes because they were willing to work more hours.

17. Which would be the most accurate description of the top marginal tax rate of the federal income tax? (LO3)
   a) It is higher than it has ever been.
   b) It is lower than it has ever been.
   c) It is much lower than it was in 1980.
   d) It is much higher than it was in 1980.

18. The most important source of federal tax revenue is the _____. (LO5)
   a) personal income tax
   b) corporate income tax
   c) federal excise tax
   d) payroll tax

19. Until 1981 the maximum marginal tax rate on the federal income tax was _____ percent. (LO5)
   a) 70
   b) 50
   c) 40
   d) 33

20. Taxes (including federal, state, and local) are about _____ of our GDP. (LO5, 7)
   a) 10 percent
   b) 20 percent
   c) 30 percent
   d) 40 percent

21. The most important source of local tax revenue is the _____ tax. (LO7)
   a) property
   b) income
   c) excise
   d) sales

22. Compared with the citizens of other rich countries, Americans are _____. (LO5)
   a) much more heavily taxed
   b) somewhat more heavily taxed
   c) taxed at about the same rate
   d) not as heavily taxed

23. Adam Smith endorsed each of the following roles of government except _____. (LO8)
    a) providing for defense
    b) establishing a system of justice
    c) erecting a limited number of public works
    d) guaranteeing a job to every person ready, willing, and able to work

24. An example of a public good is _____. (LO1, 8)
    a) a Honda Accord
    c) a Boeing 747
    b) a movie theater
    d) a lighthouse

25. Which statement is true? (LO6)
    a) Americans pay the highest taxes in the world.
    b) Public goods are provided by private enterprise.
    c) The economic role of the federal government has shrunk over the last 30 years.
    d) In 1990 and in 1993 tax rates for the rich were increased substantially.

26. Major league baseball stars like Derek Jeter, Alex Rodriguez, and Prince Fielder all pay _____. (LO5)
    a) more Social Security tax than Medicare tax
    b) more Medicare tax than Social Security tax
    c) neither Medicare tax nor Social Security tax

27. Gasoline taxes in the United States are _____ than they are in other leading industrial nations. (LO5)
    a) much higher
    b) a little higher
    c) a little lower
    d) much lower

28. State and local taxes are basically (LO5, 7)
    a) progressive.
    b) proportional.
    c) regressive.

29. Which is the most accurate statement about the federal personal income tax top MTR? (LO5)
    a) It has been higher than 90 percent.
    b) It is now the lowest it has ever been.
    c) It is nearly the highest it has ever been.
    d) It was at its highest in the 1980s.
    e) It was at its lowest in the 1950s.

Fill-In Questions

1. The economic role of the federal government began to get very large in the year _____. (LO1)

2. Name basic economic influences of the federal government: (1) _____; (2) _____; and (3) _____. (LO8)

3. Fiscal year 2007 began on _____ (fill in month, day, and year). (LO1)

4. The largest federal government transfer payment is _____. (LO5)

5. The average tax rate is found by dividing _____ by _____. (LO3)

6. Progressive taxes place the greatest burden on the _____. (LO4)

7. Examples of regressive taxes include _____ and _____. (LO4)

8. In 2010 the Social Security tax rate was _____ percent. (LO5)

9. The most important source of federal tax revenue is the _____ tax. (LO5)

10. The maximum marginal tax rate of the federal personal income tax today is _____ percent. (LO5)

11. If you earned $10,000 in 2010, how much did the federal government collect in payroll tax? $_____. (LO5)

    (Hint: both you and your employer pay this tax.)

12. If Adam Smith were alive today, he would say that our government is too _____. (LO8)

13. As disposable income rises, C + I + G _____. (LO2)

Problems

1. If Cayden Noel earned $80,000 in 2010, how much Social Security tax did he pay? (LO5)

2. If Haley My Hang Althaus earned $10,000 in 2010, how much Social Security tax did she pay? (LO5)

3. If Taryn Goulding had earned a taxable income of $20,000 and paid $1,000 in federal income tax, how much was her average tax rate? (LO3)

4. If Mike DelMastro had a marginal tax rate of 28 percent and earned an extra $10,000, how much tax would he pay? (LO5)

5. If Alex Lawson Ballard earned an extra $1,000 and paid $150 in taxes on that income, how much would his marginal tax rate be? (LO3)

6. If Kyle Rollings Cavedo were in the lowest personal income tax bracket, how much personal income tax would he have to pay on $5,000 of taxable income? (LO5)

7. Suppose that Warren Buffett's income were to increase by $100 million. How much more personal income tax would he have to pay? (LO5)

8. If Christian Collins' taxable income rose from $30,000 to $40,000 and his tax bill rose from $4,500 to $7,000, how much is his marginal tax rate? (LO3)

9. If Terry Horn pays $5,000 on a taxable income of $40,000, how much is her average tax rate? (LO3)

10. The Speedy Delivery Service paid its 10 drivers $30,000 each. How much did the company owe in payroll tax? (LO5)

11. If Tanner Church earned $100,000, how much would he pay in Social Security tax and in Medicare tax? (LO5)

12. Prove that a married person with three dependents (including himself) and an income of $12,000 pays more in Social Security tax than in federal income tax. (LO5)

13. If Cynthia Moore were the only working member of a family of a husband, wife, and their two children and earned $15,000, (a) approximately how much federal personal income tax would she pay? (b) How much Social Security and Medicare tax would she pay? (LO5)

14. If Jack Swanson paid $1,000 in federal income tax, how much is his marginal tax rate and his total tax rate? (There is enough information for you to figure out the answer.) (LO3)

15. Caroline Krause earned a salary of $1,000,000. (a) How much Social Security tax did she pay? (b) How much Medicare tax did she pay? (c) What is her marginal tax rate on her federal personal income tax? (LO3, 5)

16. How large a salary would you need to earn in order to be paying more in Medicare tax than in Social Security tax? (LO5)

Chapter 8

The Export-Import Sector

The American economy is, by far, the largest and most productive in the world. Consequently, we are by far, the world's largest importer of goods and services. Until 2004, when Germany overtook the U.S., we were also the largest exporter.[1] And then, in 2009, China overtook Germany so the best we could do in the world export olympics is a bronze medal for our third-place finish. Yet foreign trade is less important to the U.S. economy than it is to those of nearly all other industrial nations. But in spite of the relatively small percentage of U.S. GDP accounted for through foreign trade, we have become thoroughly integrated into the global economy.

So far we've looked at the three main sectors of GDP—C (consumption), I (investment), and G (government spending). Now let's consider X_n (net exports). X_n = exports − imports.

LEARNING OBJECTIVES

After reading this chapter you should be able to:

1. Explain and discuss the basis for international trade.
2. Demonstrate the relationship between specialization and exchange.
3. Summarize post–World War II trends in our imports and exports.
4. Distinguish between outsourcing and offshoring.
5. Analyze the graphing of the C + I + G + X_n line.
6. Discuss the imports and exports of the world's leading trading nations.
7. Summarize the world trade agreements and discuss the free trade zones.

The Basis for International Trade

Let's look at trading, first between individuals, and then between nations. There are a lot of people who like to putter around the house, doing their own repairs. So how would you feel about doing a really *big* job, like building a 12′ × 20′ deck in your backyard? If you're really good with tools, it might take you 60 hours from start to finish.

Let's say you're a very successful attorney, who earns $300 an hour. Now you could hire a carpenter to do the deck for you at $20 an hour. And to make things interesting, let's say that this person will also need 60 hours to complete the deck. Question: Should you hire him or her or build the deck yourself?

---

[1]China, in turn, overtook Germany in 2009, so the United States is now the world's third largest exporter.

I'm sure that, unless you would rather do carpentry than anything else in the world, you would hire this person to build your deck. The labor will cost you $1,200. You could make $1,200 in just four hours by practicing law.

By the way, can you figure out the opportunity cost of building the deck yourself? It would be $18,000 (60 hours × $300). So you would save yourself $16,800 (the $18,000 that you earned − the $1,200 you paid the deckbuilder). If this sounds at all familiar, it may be because we talked about this in the section on specialization and exchange in Chapter 3.

Back in 1776 Adam Smith made *this* observation:

It is the maxim of every prudent master of a family, never to attempt to make at home what it will cost him more to make than to buy. The taylor does not attempt to make his own shoes, but buys them of the shoemaker. The shoemaker does not attempt to make his own clothes, but employs a taylor. The farmer attempts to make neither the one nor the other, but employs those different artificers. . . .

What is prudence in the conduct of every private family, can scarce be folly in that of a great kingdom. If a foreign country can supply us with a commodity cheaper than we can make it, better buy it of them with some part of the produce of our own industry, employed in a way in which we have some advantage.[2]

Specialization and Exchange

We could not have a modern, highly productive economy without specialization and exchange. Imagine if we all had to be self-sufficient. Each of us would live on a farm where we would grow our own food, weave our own cloth, build our own homes, make our own tools and clothes—even our own pins and needles and nails.

In modern economies, virtually everyone specializes. We can sell whatever good or service we produce. By specializing, we get good at producing something, and we are able to sell it for a relatively low price. So instead of spending hours trying to make your own nails, you can buy all the nails you need at the hardware store for less than a dollar.

When people specialize, they are usually far more productive than if they attempt to be generalists. Doctors, lawyers, accountants, engineers, and, of course, college professors, all specialize.

People specialize in every field of learning. Your economics professor, for example, may have specialized in banking, and not only can tell you all the dirt on the 1980s savings and loan scandal, but can explain exactly how banks operate, how they determine the creditworthiness of borrowers, and even how you can wire money to other countries.

We've seen that, when you specialize in a certain type of work, you can get very good at it and have a much higher standard of living than you would as a jack-of-all-trades. In this case, what makes sense for individuals also makes sense for nations. Nations generally export the goods and services they can produce efficiently (that is, cheaply), and they import the goods and services that other nations produce more efficiently.

Because of our abundant fertile farmland and eventually our tremendous stock of farm equipment, we have been a major exporter of wheat, corn, cotton, and soybeans since colonial times. Today we are the world's leading exporter of computer software and entertainment goods and services. We were a major exporter of steel and textiles, but now that other nations can produce these more cheaply, we are a major importer of these products. Similarly, immediately after World War II we produced more than 60 percent of the world's oil, much of which we exported. Now that we have exhausted most of our easily extractable reserves, we import over 60 percent of our oil.

Tables 1, 2, and 3 provide a hypothetical example of two countries that can benefit from specialization and trade. Assume that both Algeria and Zaire produce just two goods—planes and trains. Table 1 shows how many trains and planes both countries currently produce.

The citizens of Algeria and Zaire spend all of their income taking train trips and plane trips. Now suppose that Algeria decided to devote all its resources to building

---

[2]Adam Smith, *The Wealth of Nations* (New York: Modern Library, 1937), p. 424. (Originally published in 1776.)

TABLE 1	Production of Trains and Planes before Specialization	
	Trains	Planes
Algeria	5	10
Zaire	10	5

planes, while Zaire used all its resources to build trains. Their new production totals are shown in Table 2.

TABLE 2	Production of Trains and Planes with Specialization	
	Trains	Planes
Algeria	0	20
Zaire	20	0

Algeria specializes in building planes because it is especially good at it. Similarly Zaire specializes in building trains at which it excels.

What if in the world market trains and planes were sold for an identical price? Then Zaire could trade one train for each plane it received from Algeria. Suppose, then, that

TABLE 3	Consumption of Planes and Trains after Trade	
	Trains	Planes
Algeria	10	10
Zaire	10	10

Zaire traded 10 trains for 10 of Algeria's planes. Table 3 shows how the two countries would end up.

Compare the numbers in Tables 1 and 3. Did both nations gain from specialization and trade? They certainly did.

This extremely simplified model makes the case for free trade. In the next-to-last chapter of this book you'll find a more detailed presentation of the argument for free trade.

U.S. Exports and Imports

From the earliest days of our nation's history, we engaged in trade. As colonies of England in the 17th and 18th centuries, Americans were expected to provide her with raw materials and to buy England's manufactured goods. Indeed, we were largely prohibited from competing with her own manufacturers.

However, after independence, we became increasingly self-sufficient. As we noted back in Chapter 1, we were not only self-sufficient agriculturally, but by the time of the Civil War we had built a powerful manufacturing base in the North.

Our self-sufficiency in food production and our huge manufacturing base were important factors in helping us win World Wars I and II. America was called "the arsenal of democracy" because of the vast quantity of armaments we sent our allies, especially Great Britain and the Soviet Union during World War II. This self-sufficiency continued until well into the 1970s, when our relatively small export-import sector began to grow significantly.

Figure 1 provides a summary of our changing relationship to the global economy. For the first three-quarters of the 20th century we exported more than we imported virtually

Figure 1

U.S. Imports and Exports as
Percentage of GDP, 1970–2009
Note the growing gap between
imports and exports through 2005.
Source: U.S. Bureau of Economic
Analysis, www.bea.gov

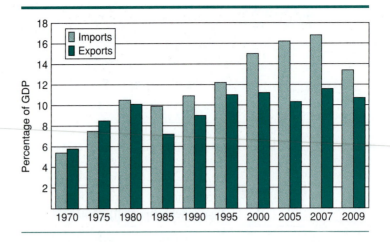

every year. But then we began importing more than we exported. You'll notice also that trade has become much more important to our economy than it was in 1970. In that year, our imports and exports together were just over one-tenth of our GDP; now they are about one-quarter of our GDP.

We're going to be using a couple of new terms: positive balance of trade and negative balance of trade. *We run a positive balance of trade when we export more than we import.* You can easily figure out, then, what a negative balance of trade is. *We run a negative balance of trade when we import more than we export.* In recent years the United States has been running huge and growing negative trade balances. We have been buying a lot more goods and services from foreigners than they have been buying from us. Sometimes we refer to a negative trade balance as a trade deficit.

What do we import and what do we export? We import and export both goods and services. The goods we import include cars, DVD players, TVs, microwave ovens, computer chips, cameras, wine, oil, toys, clothing, and steel. Among the goods we export are cotton, wood, wheat, cars, chemicals, computer software, cigarettes, pharmaceuticals, tractors, and airplanes. In 2009 we imported $392 billion more in goods from foreigners than we exported to them.

We import and export services such as hotel stays, restaurant meals, and car rentals for tourists, plane trips, movies, TV programming, compact discs, banking, insurance, legal, and accounting services. In recent years we have been running a large positive balance of trade in services. In 2009 we exported $145 billion more in services to foreigners than we imported from them. The biggest contributor to our positive service balance was royalties and license fees: our export earnings were $65 billion greater than our payments to foreigners.

As noted in the 2007 Annual Report of the Federal Reserve Bank of Dallas:

> We're world class providers of financial, legal, medical, construction and industrial engineering services. We excel in supplying entertainment, education and information management. We lead in telecommunications, management and consulting, travel services and tourism.[3]

When foreign tourists fly to the United States on U.S.-owned airlines and spend billions of dollars on hotels, meals, and local transportation, they are contributing to our positive balance of trade in services. That spending is added to our export of services. So the next time you see Japanese tourists snapping pictures of one of our national monuments, please thank them. They might even ask you to pose with them.

In the final chapter of this book we'll talk quite extensively about foreign exchange rates, but for now, let's consider how they might affect you. If you happen to be planning a trip to Europe, you'll certainly be very concerned about the exchange rate between dollars and euros. Let's say that on your first night in Paris, your restaurant bill comes to 40 euros. In recent years the exchange rate between dollars and euros has fluctuated

---

[3]"Opportunity Knocks: Selling Our Services to the World," Federal Reserve Bank of Dallas, 2007 Annual Report.

TABLE 4 U.S. Balance of Trade, 2009 *(in billions of dollars)**			
Exports of goods	$1038	Imports of goods	$1575
Exports of services	$526	Imports of services	$381
Exports of goods and services	$1564	Imports of goods and services	$1957
	$X_n = -\$392$		

*Numbers may not add up due to rounding.
Source: U.S. Bureau of Economic Analysis, www.bea.gov.

between about $0.85 to about $1.60 for 1 euro. So do the math and figure out how much that meal would have cost at each of these exchange rates.

Solution:
If you could get 1 euro for $0.85, then your meal would have cost you just $34 (0.85 × 40). But if the euro were exchanged for $1.60, that same meal would have set you back $64 (1.60 × 40).

The cost of all the foreign goods and services will vary with the dollar's exchange rate with euros, Japanese yen, British pounds, Canadian dollars, Mexican pesos, Chinese yuan, and a variety of other currencies. The financial section of most daily newspapers lists these exchange rates.

One of the services we provide to foreigners is education. There are more than 500,000 foreign college students in the United States spending over $13 billion, 75 percent of which is funded by overseas sources. Over half of these foreign students are studying management, mathematics, the sciences, or computer science. At some of our leading engineering schools, such as New Jersey Institute of Technology and Stevens Institute of Technology, over 70 percent of the doctoral degrees are awarded to foreigners. At the Polytechnic University of New York, one of the nation's leading engineering schools, the Russian students often complain that they cannot understand the English spoken by their Chinese professors.

Our balance of trade in goods is a completely different story. From the outbreak of World War I until 1970 we maintained a positive trade balance in merchandise. By the late 1970s we were beginning to run substantial deficits.

Table 4 summarizes our balance of trade in 2009. As you'll notice, we imported more goods than we exported. And we exported more services than we imported. But our positive balance of trade in services (+$145 billion) was far outweighed by our negative balance of trade in goods (−$537 billion). That left us with a balance of trade in goods and services, X_n, of −$392 billion (after rounding to the nearest billion).

Outsourcing and Offshoring

Many companies contract out some of their jobs to other firms. For example, Walmart hires local janitorial firms to clean their stores at night. Magazine and newspaper subscriptions are sold by telemarketers who are employed by companies that specialize in telephone soliciting. Briefs for law firms may be typed by people in the West Indies.

All of these jobs are outsourced. But if they are performed abroad, then they are also offshored. When a company shuts down a textile mill in South Carolina and replaces it with one in China, those jobs were not just outsourced but offshored as well.

As long as outsourced jobs remain in the United States, one American's job loss is another American's job gain. But when a job is offshored, our employment goes down by one. While most of those whose jobs are offshored do eventually find other jobs, it may take them months or even years to do so, and then the new job will generally pay less than the job that was lost.

Since 1970 at least five million relatively high-paying factory jobs—in autos, steel, textile, apparel, and consumer electronics—have been offshored. Today over 80 percent of our labor force is employed in the service sector, and now these jobs, too, are being sent abroad. Huge call centers are springing up in India to provide American customers with technical support. When you need help with your computer, you may get to talk with "Randy" in Bangalore, or perhaps "Samantha" in New Delhi.

A survey by McKinsey and Robbins indicates only about 10 percent of all service jobs are vulnerable to offshoring, and only a small fraction of these will actually be offshored in the foreseeable future. Still, who would have ever imagined that physicians in India would be reading MRIs sent over the Internet, and doing so at just one-tenth the price charged by American physicians.

And yet, in the whole scheme of things, how much do we really have to fear off-shoring? Every year about 40 percent of all the jobs in our economy change hands. Since only a fraction of one percent is sent offshore every year, it is certainly something that we can live with. But if *your* job is offshored, then that's another story.

A Summing Up: $C + I + G + X_n$

Subtract imports from exports to get net exports.

X_n = Exports − Imports

The last three chapters examined the three main components of GDP: C, or consumption; I, or investment; and G, or government spending. One more variable goes into GDP—net exports, or X_n. *Net exports = Exports − Imports.* If we subtract all the money the United States spends on foreign goods and services from what foreigners spend on U.S. goods and services, we get net exports. This number represents the difference between what we sell to foreigners and what they sell to us.

Until recently many economists more or less ignored this last item in the GDP equation. The figure for net exports, while positive, was usually less than 1 percent of GDP. For the first seven decades of the 20th century, we sold more to foreigners every single year than they sold to us. But in the early 1970s our balance of trade turned negative, with net exports averaging well over $700 billion from 2005–2008. Why did net exports turn negative in the early 1970s, and what accounts for our growing negative trade balance since then? You'll find out when you reach the next-to-last chapter, "International Trade."

Why is the $C + I + G + X_n$ line drawn below the $C + I + G$ line?

Now we're going to graph the $C + I + G + X_n$ line. Keep in mind that X_n has been negative since the early 1970s and will probably continue to be negative for decades. In Figure 2, why did we draw the $C + I + G + X_n$ line *below* the $C + I + G$ line? Because X_n is a negative number, so the sum of $C + I + G + X_n$ is *less* than the sum of $C + I + G$.

Figure 2
Hypothetical $C + I + G + X_n$ Line

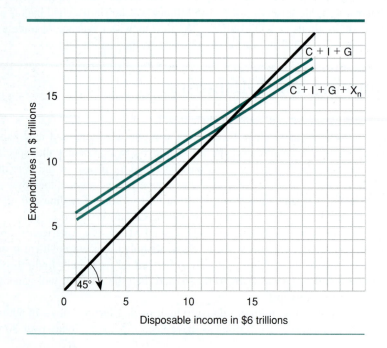

World Trade Agreements and Free Trade Zones

Since the end of World War II in 1945 there has been an accelerating movement toward free trade. The formation of the European Common Market, renamed the European Union, and of NAFTA (the North American Free Trade Agreement) has placed most of the industrial world within two virtual free trade zones. In addition, the General Agreement on Trade and Tariffs (GATT), now the World Trade Organization, has reduced trade barriers worldwide.

Free Trade Zones

NAFTA   The North American Free Trade Agreement, which was ratified by Congress in 1993, created a free trade area including Canada, the United States, and Mexico, a market of some 450 million consumers. Here is how the agreement is described in the 1994 *Economic Report of the President:*

> In addition to dismantling trade barriers in industrial goods, NAFTA includes agreements on services, investment, intellectual property rights, agriculture, and strengthening of trade rules. There are also side agreements on labor adjustment provisions, protection of the environment, and import surges.[4]

How well has the agreement worked so far? Has a flood of cheap Mexican goods resulted in "the sound of jobs being sucked out of the United States"? Hardly. But the threat of moving operations to Mexico, where hourly wages and fringe benefits average about $1.50 an hour, has had a depressing effect on American factory wages. Furthermore, our trade deficits with both Mexico and Canada have gone up substantially since the passage of NAFTA.

Mexico is becoming a manufacturing export platform. Over 60 percent of all U.S. exports to Mexico are eventually re-exported back to the United States—up from 40 percent before NAFTA. Mexican autoworkers performing sophisticated, highly productive manufacturing work that used to be done in America do it at one-eighth the U.S. wage.

Currently the United States absorbs over 80 percent of Mexico's exports. This figure should fall substantially during the next decade, especially after the trade deal negotiated between Mexico and the European Union, which will abolish most tariffs between them by 2007. Volkswagen, which makes the New Beetle solely in Mexico, currently pays a 7 percent duty when it ships to Europe, but under the new pact, these cars will be shipped to Europe duty-free.

NAFTA was an extension of an earlier trade agreement with Canada. We import more from Canada than any other country, and we export more to Canada than any other country. Because of our mutual interdependence—and because of the integration of our economies—it would be unthinkable for either country to erect trade barriers to keep out imports from the other. Under the agreement, duties on most goods will be phased out within the next few years.

Canada is our most important trading partner.

Table 5 summarizes the change in our trade position with Mexico and Canada between 1993 (the year before NAFTA went into effect) and 2009. While our trade with both nations expanded sharply, our trade deficit with both nations went up still faster. During this same period, however, our trade deficit with the rest of the world also rose very rapidly.

Our trade deficit with China was $227 billion in 2009, more than double our recent deficits with Japan. Just as many Americans engaged in Japan-bashing in earlier years, now Chinese trade practices have been targeted. One wonders if our trade deficits with Mexico and Canada continue to mount, whether there will be more demands that we disband NAFTA.

---

[4]See page 225 of the *Report.*

TABLE 5   U.S. Trade with Mexico and Canada, 1993 and 2009
(in billions of U.S. dollars)

Year	Exports to Mexico	Imports from Mexico	U.S. Trade Balance with Mexico
1993	42	40	2
2009	129	177	−46

Year	Exports to Canada	Imports from Canada	U.S. Trade Balance with Canada
1993	100	111	−11
2009	205	225	−20

Source: www.census.gov

CAFTA   The Central American–Dominican Republic Free Trade Agreement is a trade agreement between the U.S. and the Dominican Republic as well as five small Central American nations—Costa Rica, El Salvador, Guatemala, Honduras, and Nicaragua. Pushed through Congress by President George W. Bush, this agreement will eventually eliminate all tariffs among the seven nations. But its immediate impact will be very small, since 80 percent of Central American products were already entering the U.S. duty-free.

The European Union (EU)   Although this free trade association of 27 nations (see Figure 3) can trace its origins back to the 1950s, it wasn't until 1992 that a truly common market was formed. Freight was now able to move anywhere within the EU without checkpoint delays and paperwork. So-called "quality" codes such as German beer-purity regulations and Belgian chocolate-content restrictions were ended. Workers from any EU country could work in any other member country.

With a larger population and GDP than the United States, the EU is an economic powerhouse. In 1999, 11 EU countries formed the European Monetary Union, which established the euro as a common currency,[5] making trade among participating member nations much easier to conduct. A German tourist buying a meal in a Parisian restaurant no longer has to convert her marks into francs, and a Dutch businessman buying Italian wine no longer has to convert his guilders into lira.

China-Asean Free Trade Area   On New Year's Day, 2010, the world's third largest free trade area was formed by China and 10 other Asian nations (Brunei, Cambodia, Indonesia, Laos, Malaysia, Myanmar, the Philippines, Singapore, Thailand, and Vietnam). Tariffs will be gradually reduced between 2010 and 2015. Trade has more than tripled among the members between 2003 and 2008, and it is hoped that the formation of the new free trade area will bolster this trend. It is expected to help the Asean nations to increase exports, particularly those with commodities that resource-hungry China sorely needs, while providing China with a wider market for its manufactured goods.

Mercosur   Much less well known than NAFTA and the EU, this free trade zone includes Argentina, Brazil, Paraguay, Uruguay, and Venezuela, and associate members Bolivia, Chile, Columbia, Ecuador, and Peru. It is the fourth largest integrated market after NAFTA, the EU, and China-Asean. Mercosur is an acronym for Mercado Común del Sur, or Common Market of the South. Formed in 1991, it has succeeded in eliminating all internal tariffs while imposing a common external tariff on goods imported from countries outside the union. However, some trade restrictions—especially between Brazil and Argentina—still persist.

---

[5]Twelve countries are now members.

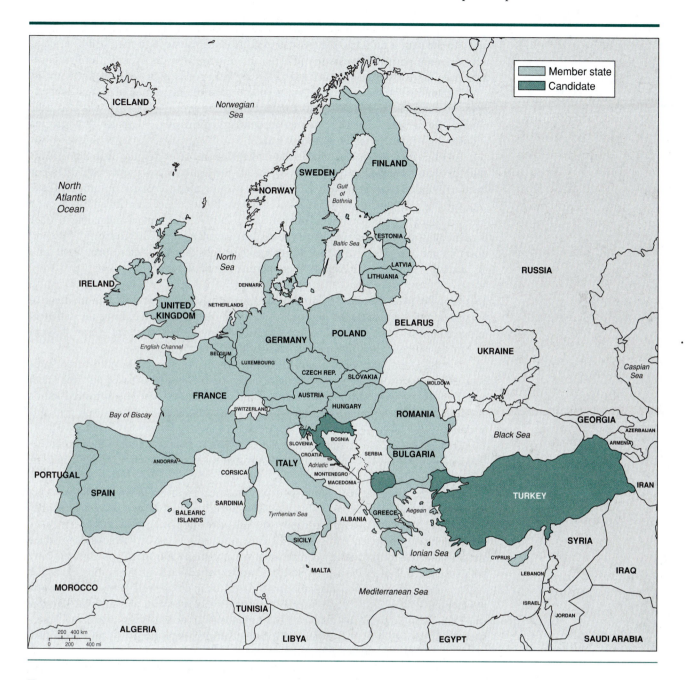

Figure 3

European Union: Member Countries and Candidates for Membership, 8/1/10

Members: Austria, Belgium, Bulgaria, Cyprus, Czech Republic, Denmark, Estonia, Finland, France, Germany, Greece, Hungary, Ireland, Italy, Latvia, Lithuania, Luxembourg, Malta, Netherlands, Poland, Portugal, Romania, Slovakia, Slovenia, Spain, Sweden, and United Kingdom. Croatia, Macedonia, and Turkey are membership candidates.

World Trade Agreements

GATT   The General Agreement on Trade and Tariffs was drafted in 1947 and has since been signed by more than 150 nations. GATT is a uniform system of rules for the conduct of international trade. Its latest version, which was ratified by Congress in 1994, was the culmination of years of negotiations. It will reduce tariffs worldwide by an average of 40 percent, lower other barriers to trade such as quotas on certain products, and provide patent protection for American software, pharmaceuticals, and other industries.

Will GATT hurt our trade balance, unleash a flood of cheap foreign imports, and result in the loss of millions of American jobs? Although some industries will be affected adversely, the positive appears to outweigh the negative. On the average, foreign countries have more trade restrictions and tariffs on U.S. goods than we have on theirs, so GATT should help us much more than it hurts us. For the first time intellectual property rights like patents, trademarks, and copyrights will be protected. GATT will also open markets for service industries such as accounting, advertising, computer services, and engineering—fields in which Americans excel.

GATT brings agriculture under international trade rules for the first time. Many countries heavily subsidize their farmers (in 2005 the United States spent over $20 billion in crop subsidies), but European subsidies dwarf those paid to American farmers. President Clinton's Council of Economic Advisors noted that, "Since the United States has a strong underlying comparative advantage in agriculture, the mutual reduction in trade barriers and subsidization will be to the distinct advantage of U.S. producers."[6] Proportionately, the Europeans will have to reduce their subsidies a lot more than we'll have to, making American crop exports even more competitive.

WTO   The World Trade Organization has sometimes been confused with the International Monetary Fund (IMF) and with the World Bank. Each has been the target of massive protests against globalization. The accompanying box provides a brief description of the purposes and functions of each of these organizations.

The basic purpose of the World Trade Organization is to promote free trade between nations. It was set up in 1995 as a successor to GATT. It is based on three major principles: (1) liberalization of trade; (2) nondiscrimination—the most-favored-nation principle; and (3) no unfair encouragement of exports. Let's consider each principle in detail.

Trade barriers, which were reduced under GATT, should continue to be reduced. Incidentally, barriers have been falling *within* free trade zones such as NAFTA and the European Union.

Under the most-favored-nation principle, members of the WTO must offer all other members the same trade concessions as any member country. Which is a lot like when the teacher says that if you bring candy to class, you must bring some for *everyone*.

Finally, no unfair encouragement of exports encompasses export subsidies, which are considered a form of unfair competition. American and European governments have long subsidized their farmers, who, in turn, have exported much of their crops. Subsidies enable American and European producers to sell their crops well below their cost of production. This sets the world price of corn and other agricultural staples so low that small farmers in developing countries can't compete. How bad *is* this problem? Three-quarters of the world's poor scratch out a living working small farms. As they are forced off their land by subsidized grain imports, they have no means to survive.

At the WTO meeting in Cancun, Mexico, in September 2003, the world's poor nations demanded that the richer nations cut their agricultural subsidies to create a more level playing field. But the United States, the European Union, Japan, and the other rich nations refused to lower their subsidies and the meeting ended abruptly. Since then there have been a few more unsuccessful attempts to lower subsidies.

The WTO has a Dispute Settlement Body to handle trade disagreements among member nations. Many of the disputes involve the charge of the dumping of products below cost. Although many politicians in the United States have very reluctantly accepted the jurisdiction of the WTO, we have won almost all the more than two dozen cases in which we have been the complaining party.

If you've ever been to a major protest demonstration, it's usually pretty clear what all the demonstrators are *against*. Beginning with the Seattle protest in late 1999 during the WTO meeting, there have been major protests in Washington, Prague, Quebec City,

---

[6]*Economic Report of the President,* 1995, p. 208.

The WTO, the IMF, and the World Bank

What do the WTO and the IMF stand for, and what do they do? And what is the World Bank? You don't have a clue? Don't worry—you are not alone.

The WTO stands for the World Trade Organization, which was set up to encourage world trade by bringing down existing trade barriers.

The International Monetary Fund (IMF), an organization of more than 150 nations, was set up in 1944 as a lender of last resort to discourage member nations from devaluating their currency. For example, the IMF would lend dollars to Japan if the Japanese yen were falling relative to the dollar. Let's say that 100 yen were trading for one dollar and the yen fell to 105 for one dollar, and then to 110 for one dollar. The IMF would lend reserves to Japan to stabilize the yen.

The IMF has played an increasing role in providing loans to countries in financial crisis. For example, in 1997, when it became clear to international lenders that Korean banks and corporations were unable to repay the loans they had taken on, the IMF arranged for $55 billion in loans. But IMF loans do come with certain strings attached, such as a balanced budget and a tight monetary policy.* Some critics feel that by standing by as an international lender of last resort, the IMF actually encourages irresponsible behavior. Borrowers may take risks they would have otherwise not taken, knowing that the IMF stood ready to bail them out.

The World Bank, also created in 1944, makes long-term, low-interest loans to developing countries, mainly to build highways, bridges, dams, power generators, and water supply systems. In addition, it acts as a guarantor of repayment to encourage some private lending.

Joseph Stiglitz, a Nobel Prize–winning economist and former chief economist for the World Bank, wrote a highly critical book about the practices of the IMF, and, to a lesser degree, the World Bank and the WTO.

Over the years since its inception, the IMF has changed markedly. Founded on the belief that markets often worked badly, it now champions market supremacy with ideological fervor. Founded on the belief that there is a need for international pressure on countries to have more expansionary economic policies—such as increasing expenditures, reducing taxes, or lowering interest rates to stimulate the economy—today the IMF typically provides funds only if countries engage in policies like cutting deficits, raising taxes, or raising interest rates that lead to a contraction of the economy.[†]

Since countries approach the IMF only when they are desperate for money, the fund has a good deal of leverage, which it uses to force governments to cut their budget deficits and shut down or sell off government enterprises. While these reforms are sometimes necessary, Stiglitz maintains that the IMF's representatives are often oblivious to the human suffering they cause.

on the web

If you would like to learn more about what these three organizations do, go to www.imf.org, www.wto.org, and www.worldbank.org.

---

*Tight monetary policy and a balanced budget will be discussed in Chapters 12 and 14, respectively.

[†]Joseph Stiglitz, *Globalization and Its Discontents* (New York: W. W. Norton, 2002), pp. 12–13.

Genoa, and elsewhere targeting the WTO, the IMF, the summit of the Americas, and the World Bank.

BusinessWeek outlined the reasons for the protests:

> Environmentalists argue that elitist trade and economic bodies make undemocratic decisions that undermine national sovereignty on environmental regulation. Unions charge that unfettered trade allows unfair competition from countries that lack labor standards. Human rights and student groups say the IMF and the World Bank prop up regimes that condone sweatshops and pursue policies that bail out foreign lenders at the expense of local economies.[7]

The most potent argument against globalization is that workers in poorer countries are exploited to produce goods that are shipped to the United States and other relatively rich countries. This view was summarized by Tina Rosenberg.

---

[7]*BusinessWeek*, April 24, 2000, p. 40.

In many of the factories in Mexico, Central America and Asia producing American-brand toys, clothes, sneakers and other goods, exploitation is the norm. The young women who work in them—almost all sweatshop workers are young women—endure starvation wages, forced overtime and dangerous working conditions.[8]

Many Americans, as well as citizens of other leading industrial nations, have strong reservations about ceding their national sovereignty to international organizations, especially the WTO. Much of their concern centers on the possible loss of jobs and the reduction of wages in their countries if their workers were forced to compete with low-wage workers in the world's poorer countries, most of whom earn just one or two dollars a day. Is it fair to make American factories, which uphold relatively high environmental standards, compete with Third World factories that are not similarly burdened? If the United States and other industrial countries were subject to the rules and regulations of the WTO, their own governments would be unable to prevent a flood of cheap imports.

Most economists as well as most business leaders supported the establishment of NAFTA as well as of GATT. Like rock 'n' roll back in the 1950s, globalization is here to stay. Still, there are growing reservations about some of its outcomes, even among those who call themselves "free traders."

Tim Harford, in *The Undercover Economist,* agrees that sweatshop employees endure terrible working conditions, long hours, and pitiful wages. *But* sweatshops are the symptom, not the cause, of shocking global poverty. Workers go there voluntarily, which means—hard as it is to believe—that their alternatives are even worse. Turnover rates of multinational-owned factories are low, because conditions and pay, while bad, are better than those in factories run by local firms.[9]

Current Issue: Is Your School Sweatshirt Sewn in a Sweatshop?

I felt it was a fairly small thing, just hitting and swearing at the workers and not giving them wages.

—Heng Tinghan, who was accused of virtually enslaving workers in Shanxi Province, China

Your school does not manufacture any of the products bearing its name. College names are licensed to apparel makers and other companies for a royalty of about 7 percent of the retail price of each T-shirt, sweatshirt, or key chain. Indeed, no one at your school has any idea of just who makes the products that bear the school's name. A global supply chain stretches from the licensee companies to large-scale factories in China, Mexico, Thailand, Indonesia, and dozens of other low-wage countries, to small-scale subcontractor factories everywhere in between, and in some cases, all the way to women stitching garments in their living rooms.

There are two questions that colleges have only begun to ask. How well are these workers paid and how decent are their working conditions? If well under a dollar an hour is satisfactory—the prevailing wage rate in these countries—then few college administrators are losing much sleep over this issue. Even the fact that many workers are forced to work over 300 hours a month—in violation of local law—does not seem to be too much cause for concern.

Various colleges as well as other organizations have banded together to inspect the actual factories. In addition, Nike, Adidas, Levi-Straus, Liz Claiborne, and Philips Van Heusen use monitors to check up on the factories producing their goods. But the inspectors rarely witness

---

[8]Tina Rosenberg, "Globalization, the Free-Trade Fix," *New York Times Magazine,* August 18, 2002, p. 32.

[9]Tim Harford, *The Undercover Economist* (New York: Oxford University Press, 2006), p. 222.

day-to-day conditions in these factories. Often the managers are tipped off about impending inspections and sometimes the contractors themselves choose the factories to be visited. Nevertheless here are some of the common working conditions inspectors have found:

- Lack of guards on sewing and cutting machines.
- High levels of cotton dust.
- Blocked aisles and fire exits.
- No running water in toilets.
- No information about hazardous chemicals workers are using.
- Restricted bathroom break times.

College administrators and the students themselves are indirectly responsible for these abysmal working conditions—not to mention the measly pay—of the workers making their college paraphernalia. In the words of Bob Dylan's 1962 classic folk song, *Blowin' in the Wind:*

> An' how many times can a man turn his head,
> An' pretend that he just doesn't see?

Still, there's actually another side to this issue. As *New York Times* reporters Nicholas D. Kristof and Sheryl WuDunn observed, ". . . it's sometimes said in poor countries that the only thing worse than being exploited in a sweatshop is not being exploited in a sweatshop."

As terribly as these workers are treated, and as much as they are exploited, for them, a job in a sweatshop is still a lot better than any other available means to earn a livelihood. Which makes these jobs much sought after. And so, in accordance with the law of unintended consequences, if we all stopped buying the products made in sweatshops, we would end up hurting the very people we wished to help.[10]

Questions for Further Thought and Discussion

1. Explain how and why trade barriers have come down in recent decades.
2. Do you think we should have joined NAFTA? Try to argue this question from both sides.
3. List the reasons why our trade deficit has grown so quickly since the mid-1990s. What can we do to help bring it down?
4. Identify the goods and services that you purchase that are imported. How would your lifestyle change if these imports were unavailable?
5. How would your life change if the United States were no longer the world's leading exporter?
6. Explain how international trade (exports and imports) affects a nation's output, employment, and income.
7. *Practical Application:* Should the United States pull out of NAFTA? Explain why we should or why we should not.
8. *Practical Application:* A group at your school has called a meeting to discuss a boycott of the college bookstore if it continues selling clothing made with sweatshop labor. Would you support such a boycott? Explain why you would or why you would not.

---

[10]Nicholas D. Kristof and Sheryl WuDunn, "The Oppression of Women Worldwide Is the Human Rights Cause of Our Time," *The New York Times Magazine,* August 23, 2009, p. 34.

Workbook for Chapter 8

Name _____   Date _____

Multiple-Choice Questions

Circle the letter that corresponds to the best answer.

1. Today world trade is regulated by
   _____. (LO7)
   a) NAFTA   c) WTO
   b) GATT   d) EU

2. Which statement is true? (LO4)
   a) Offshoring is a type of outsourcing.
   b) Outsourcing is type of offshoring.
   c) Outsourcing and offshoring are identical concepts.
   d) Outsourcing is the opposite of offshoring.

3. Which is the most accurate statement? (LO3)
   a) Our trade deficit has narrowed since 1995.
   b) We export more merchandise than services (in terms of dollars).
   c) The largest service purchase that foreigners make from the United States is educational services.
   d) In recent years foreigners have generally refused to accept U.S. dollars in payment for their goods and services.

4. Since the early 1990s our trade deficit has
   _____. (LO3)
   a) fallen substantially   c) risen slightly
   b) fallen slightly   d) risen substantially

5. In the 20th century our balance of trade was positive
   until the _____. (LO3)
   a) 1950s   d) 1980s
   b) 1960s   e) 1990s
   c) 1970s

6. Statement I: The European Union was formed as a trading counterweight to NAFTA.
   Statement II: Since the formation of NAFTA, the United States has lost millions of jobs to Mexico. (LO7)
   a) Statement I is true, and statement II is false.
   b) Statement II is true, and statement I is false.
   c) Both statements are true.
   d) Both statements are false.

7. The basis for international trade is that
   _____. (LO1)
   a) a nation can import a particular good or service at a lower cost than if it were produced domestically
   b) we stand to gain if we can sell more to other nations than they buy from us
   c) there are winners and losers
   d) it pays to trade, provided we remain independent by producing all our necessities

8. Adam Smith believed that _____. (LO1)
   a) people should never buy anything if they can make it themselves
   b) what makes sense in the conduct of a private family's economic endeavors also makes sense in those of a nation
   c) trading with other nations promotes full employment
   d) a nation will gain if its citizens trade among themselves, but it will probably lose if it trades with other nations

9. $GDP = C + I + G + X_n$. If X_n were not included, our GDP would be _____. (LO5)
   a) higher
   b) about the same
   c) lower

10. The most-favored-nation clause of the WTO agreement stipulates that _____. (LO7)
    a) no member nation may impose a tariff on the goods of any other member nation
    b) all member nations must offer all other member countries the same trade concessions as any member country
    c) each member may designate another member as a favored nation, providing that nation with trade concessions
    d) all member nations must sell their goods to other member nations at cost

11. Statement I: The United States has a much larger population and GDP than the European Union.
Statement II: The European Union has attained a higher degree of economic integration than NAFTA. (LO7)

a) Statement I is true, and statement II is false.

b) Statement II is true, and statement I is false.

c) Both statements are true.

d) Both statements are false.

12. Statement I: Our trade deficit, although still high, is lower than it was five years ago.
Statement II: Taken together, our imports and exports are over one-quarter of our GDP. (LO3)

a) Statement I is true, and statement II is false.

b) Statement II is true, and statement I is false.

c) Both statements are true.

d) Both statements are false.

13. Most economists and people in the business community supported the establishment

of _____. (LO7)

a) both NAFTA and GATT

b) neither NAFTA nor GATT

c) NAFTA but not GATT

d) GATT but not NAFTA

14. Which statement is true? (LO5)

a) X_n has always been positive.

b) X_n has always been negative.

c) X_n had been positive from the turn of the century until the 1970s.

d) X_n had been negative from the turn of the century until the 1970s.

e) None of these statements is true.

15. Statement I: Since the late 1990s, our negative balance of trade has become much larger.
Statement II: The United States has the world's largest negative balance of trade. (LO3)

a) Statement I is true, and statement II is false.

b) Statement II is true, and statement I is false.

c) Both statements are true.

d) Both statements are false.

16. In 2009 which number is closest to our balance of trade? (LO2)

a) $700 billion

b) $400 billion

c) 0

d) −$400 billion

e) −$700 billion

17. Since the passage of NAFTA our trade deficit with Mexico has gone _____ and our trade deficit with Canada has gone _____. (LO7)

a) up, up

c) up, down

b) down, down

d) down, up

18. Statement I: The United States has a much less self-sufficient economy than those of countries in Western Europe.
Statement II: Mexico sends the United States more than 80 percent of its exports. (LO2, 7)

a) Statement I is true, and statement II is false.

b) Statement II is true, and statement I is false.

c) Both statements are true.

d) Both statements are false.

19. Which one of these statements is true? (LO4)

a) To save money, most colleges manufacture their own sweatshirts.

b) Most college administrators are well informed about the pay and working conditions of the people who sew their college's sweatshirts.

c) Most of the people who sew college sweatshirts work in what may be termed sweatshops.

d) Manufacturers of college sweatshirts in poor countries are usually under strict supervision to ensure that they don't violate local laws regulating pay, overtime hours, and working conditions.

20. Each of the following is a characteristic of the European Union EXCEPT that _____. (LO7)

a) workers from any EU country can seek work in any other member country

b) the euro replaced the domestic currencies (for example, francs, marks, lira) in 1999

c) its population and GDP are comparable to those of the United States

d) freight is able to move anywhere within the EU without checkpoint delays and paperwork

21. The trading bloc that has eliminated all internal tariffs is _____. (LO7)

a) the European Union

b) NAFTA

c) Mercosur

d) the World Trade Organization

22. Which one of these statements best describes the complaints of the protesters at meetings of the WTO, IMF, and World Bank? (LO7)

a) They opposed military aid to Third World dictatorships.

b) They opposed trade with poor countries because of the exploitative nature of that trade.

c) They opposed free trade with nations whose people worked under sweatshop conditions and opposed ceding national sovereignty to an international group.

d) They opposed strict environmental standards, which they felt would increase our cost of living.

23. Which was NOT an argument of the protesters against the IMF, WTO, and World Bank? (LO7)

a) We are exploiting factory workers in poor countries.

b) Our subsidized grain exports are sold below cost in poor countries, driving local farmers out of business.

c) Globalization is hurting the American standard of living.

d) Globalization is lowering American wages and exporting high-paying jobs.

24. Which statement would best describe the situation of the American economy? (LO1, 3)

a) We are more dependent on foreign trade than most other nations.

b) We are much more dependent on foreign trade than we were 30 years ago.

c) We are much less dependent on foreign trade than we were 30 years ago.

d) We are virtually self-sufficient.

25. Which statement is false? (LO3)

a) During World War I and World War II, the sum of our imports and exports as a percent of GDP rose sharply.

b) Foreign trade in goods is much more important to the American economy than foreign trade in services.

c) Because the American economy is much larger than any other economy, we can continue running larger and larger trade deficits for as long as we like.

d) We pay for a large chunk of our trade deficit with U.S. dollars.

26. The main criticism Joseph Stiglitz levels at the IMF is that _____. (LO7)

a) it provides too many loans that are not repaid

b) it no longer promotes economic growth, but rather contraction

c) it does not provide enough loans

d) it does not sufficiently promote the market system

27. Of the policy actions by richer countries shown below, which one would be most favored by poor countries? (LO7)

a) The elimination of agricultural subsidies

b) The elimination of tariffs on industrial goods

c) More vigorous enforcement of environmental laws

d) Government promotion of labor union membership

28. Which would be the most accurate statement? (LO1, 7)

a) Globalization has helped almost everyone and hurt almost no one.

b) Aside from a few malcontents who turn up at demonstrations, there is almost no opposition to globalization in the United States.

c) It can be argued that globalization has hurt many poorer countries.

d) Globalization is an unmitigated economic disaster and should be reversed.

29. A characteristic of a modern economy is _____. (LO2)

a) self-sufficiency

b) specialization and exchange

c) a high percentage of people who make their living as jacks-of-all-trades

d) a high proportion of people employed in agriculture

30. Which statement is true about the European Union? (LO7)

a) It has not taken in any new member nations since its formation.

b) All of its members must use the euro as its official currency.

c) It is essentially a free trade area.

d) It has been basically a failure.

31. Which is the most accurate statement? (LO4)

   a) The agricultural subsidies paid to American and European farmers have benefited farmers in poorer countries as well.

   b) Agricultural subsidies have been largely phased out since the turn of the century.

   c) Agricultural subsidies are a matter of great contention between rich and poor nations.

   d) Agricultural subsidies are paid by rich nations to poor nations.

32. Specialization and exchange can result in each of the following except _____. (LO2)

   a) a higher standard of living

   b) free trade

   c) more output

   d) more national self-sufficiency

33. Which statement would you agree with? (LO2)

   a) The exchange rate between the dollar and foreign currencies has no effect on our standard of living.

   b) The exchange rate between the dollar and foreign currencies affects our standard of living only when we travel abroad.

   c) Our standard of living is raised when we can get more yen, yuan, pounds, and euros for our dollars.

   d) Most Americans closely follow changes in the exchange rate between the dollar and foreign currencies.

34. Suppose that in the year 2018 C = $12 trillion, I = $2 trillion, and G = $3 trillion. Which would be your estimate of GDP? (LO5)

   a) $16 trillion   c) $18 trillion

   b) $17 trillion   d) $19 trillion

35. Compared to our trade deficits in 2006 through 2008, our trade deficit in 2009 was_____. (LO3, 5)

   a) much lower

   b) a little lower

   c) about the same

   d) a little higher

   e) much higher

36. Which one of these is the most accurate statement that can be made about the issue of buying a product that is made with sweatshop labor? (LO7)

   a) All products made with sweatshop labor should be boycotted.

   b) Everyone should be encouraged to buy products made with sweatshop labor.

   c) Virtually all the goods we import are made with sweatshop labor.

   d) Although wages in sweatshops are very low, they are generally higher than workers could earn in other jobs.

37. Which of the following statements is the most accurate? (LO7)

   a) Free trade zones rarely lower tariff barriers.

   b) Most large industrial nations are members of a free trade zone.

   c) NAFTA is, by far, the largest free trade zone in terms of imports and exports.

   d) Over the last 10 years, more nations have been leaving free trade zones than joining them.

Fill-In Questions

1. $X_n = $ _____ − _____. (LO5)

2. The three members of NAFTA are _____, _____, and _____. (LO7)

3. In the year 2009 we ran a trade deficit of $ _____ billion. (LO3)

4. Farmers in poor countries with foreign grain imports have been most hurt by American and European _____. (LO4)

5. Our exports of goods and services are about _____ percent of our GDP. (LO3)

6. The only trading bloc that has eliminated all its internal tariffs is _____. (LO7)

7. The main concern of the labor union members who were protesting against the WTO, the IMF, and the World Bank was _____. (LO7)

8. The world's biggest exporting nation is _____. (LO6)

Chapter 9

Gross Domestic Product

Imagine that you're at a college football game and your school has just won the national championship. Tens of thousands of fans are jabbing their index fingers in the air and chanting, "We're number *one*! We're number *one*!"

Well, it just so happens that the United States has had the largest GDP in the world for probably 100 years. We're so used to being number one that we kind of take it for granted. But we may not be number one for too much longer. China, with more than four times our population, has been rapidly gaining on us, and is already the world's top manufacturer. Robert Fogel, a Nobel Prize–winning economist, predicts that by 2040 China will produce 40 percent of the world's GDP.

LEARNING OBJECTIVES

After reading this chapter you should be able to:

1. Define and discuss GDP.
2. Explain how GDP is measured.
3. List and illustrate the two things to avoid when compiling GDP.
4. Distinguish among Gross Domestic Product, Net Domestic Product, and National Income.
5. Compare and contrast nominal GDP and real GDP and compute real GDP.
6. Discuss how our GDP compares to those of other nations.
7. Calculate per capita GDP.
8. List and explain the shortcomings of GDP as a measure of national economic well-being.
9. Explain and analyze the Genuine Progress Index and compare it to GDP.

What Is Gross Domestic Product?

What is GDP? *It is the nation's expenditure on all the final goods and services produced during the year at market prices.* For example, if we spent $18,000 per car on 10 million American cars, that $180 billion would go into GDP. We'd add in the 15 billion Big Macs at $3 for another $45 billion, and the 1.8 million new homes at $175,000 each for $315 billion. Then, for good measure, we'd add the 5 billion visits to doctors' offices at $90 apiece for $450 billion and the 20 billion nightclub admissions at $15 each for $300 billion. Add everything up and we'd get $14,256,300,000,000 in the year 2009.

An alternate definition of GDP is *GDP is the value of all the final goods and services produced within a nation's boundaries during the year.* This would include the wages, rent, interest, and profits earned by the few million foreigners who work in the United States. For example, there are a lot of Japanese in Tennessee and a lot of Germans in

Definition of GDP

Figure 1
Hypothetical $C + I + G + X_n$
Line

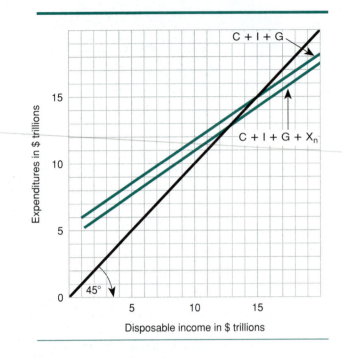

South Carolina who make cars. But our GDP would not include the wages, rent, interest, and profits earned by Americans living abroad.

Did you notice the word *final* in the definition of GDP? We include only those goods and services that consumers, businesses, and governments buy for their own use. So when you buy a telephone answering machine or you get your hair cut, or if the government repaves a highway, we count those goods and services in GDP. But if Liz Claiborne buys 10,000 yards of fabric to make dresses, that purchase is not recorded in GDP. When the dresses are sold, *then* they're counted in GDP.

Why is the $C + I + G + X_n$ line *below* the $C + I + G$ line? It's because X_n is negative, so when it's added to $C + I + G$, it reduces its value.

Over the last four chapters we worked our way toward the graph in Figure 1 that depicts GDP. We began with the consumption function in Chapter 5, added investment in Chapter 6, government spending in Chapter 7, and finally, net exports in Chapter 8.

GDP = C + I + G + X_n

Let's get back to our GDP equation:

$$GDP = C + I + G + X_n$$

Substituting the year 2009 data into this equation, we get:

$$GDP^1 = 10,089 + 1,629 + 2,931 - 392$$

$$GDP = 14,256$$

In 2009 we produced over \$14 trillion worth of final goods and services. Nearly seventy-one percent were consumer goods and services, followed in size by government purchases, investment spending, and, finally, net exports, which were negative. Now we'll draw a few graphs and then move on to how GDP is measured.

About seven out of every ten dollars of our GDP is spent on consumer goods. Figure 2 shows the percentage share of each of the four components of GDP. You'll notice that X_n is negative.

---

[1]The numbers don't add up exactly because of rounding.

TABLE 1	The Components of GDP, 2009 *(in $ billions)**	
Consumption:		
Durable goods	1,035	
Nondurable goods	2,220	
Services	6,834	
C		10,089
Investment:		
Plant, equipment, and software	1,389	
Residential housing	361	
Inventory change	−121	
I		1,629
Government purchases:		
Federal	1,145	
State and local	1,786	
G		2,931
Net exports:		
Exports	1,564	
−Imports	1,957	
X_n		−392
GDP		14,256

*Figures may not add up due to rounding.
Source: Economic Report of the President, 2010; www.bea.gov.

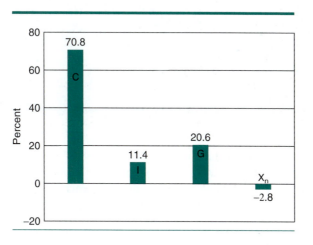

Figure 2

The Components of GDP as a Percentage of GDP, 2009
Source: See Table 1.

How GDP Is Measured

From time to time we will go back to the definition of GDP: *the nation's expenditure on all the final goods and services produced during the year at market prices.* Only "final" goods and services are counted. These include those goods and services purchased by their ultimate consumers. They are represented by the variables in our equation:

$$GDP = C + I + G + X_n$$

Substituting the year 2009 data for these variables, we get:

$$14,256 = 10,089 + 1,629 + 2,931 − 392$$

Two ways to measure GDP are the flow-of-income approach and the expenditures approach.

GDP is the nation's expenditure on all the final goods and services produced during the year at market prices.

ADVANCED WORK

Why NDP Is Better than GDP

Although people commonly use GDP when they talk about national output, most economists prefer NDP. Why? Because it allows for depreciation of plant and equipment. Let's illustrate this with two hypothetical countries in the table below:

North Atlantis		South Atlantis	
GDP	500	GDP	500
−Depreciation	50	−Depreciation	100
NDP	450	NDP	400

We see that North Atlantis and South Atlantis had identical GDPs, but that North Atlantis had depreciation of $50 billion while South Atlantis's depreciation was $100 billion.* Consequently, North Atlantis ended up with an NDP of $450 billion, while South Atlantis had an NDP of just $400 billion.

This distinction is important. North and South Atlantis had the same GDP, but North Atlantis's NDP was $50 billion greater than that of South Atlantis. Why? Because South Atlantis had to replace $100 billion of worn-out or obsolete plant and equipment that year, while North Atlantis had to replace just $50 billion of plant and equipment.

In 1930 Babe Ruth held out for a salary of $80,000. A reporter asked him if it would be fair for a baseball player to earn more than Herbert Hoover, the president of the United States. "Why not? I had a better year than he did," the Babe replied. And so, we too may ask, who had a better year, North or South Atlantis? Based on GDP, they did equally well; based on NDP, North Atlantis did better.

South Atlantis had a lower NDP because it had to devote twice as much production to replacing worn-out and obsolete plant and equipment as did North Atlantis. When you are devoting such a large portion of your resources to replacing plant and equipment, these resources can't go toward adding to your stock of plant and equipment or, for that matter, to producing consumer goods and services.

Suppose North Atlantis devoted that extra $50 billion to production of more plant and equipment. It would now have $50 billion worth of additional plant and equipment. Or if it had produced $50 billion worth of consumer goods and services, its citizens would have enjoyed a much higher standard of living.

So who enjoyed a better year? Virtually every economist would tell you that North Atlantis did because it had a higher NDP. Stated differently, it's not as significant to know how much a country grossed as to know how much it netted.

---

*Economists use this shorthand way of writing billions (for example, 50 = $50 billion; 100 = $100 billion).

GDP − Depreciation = NDP

Many economists are unhappy with the concept of gross domestic product. It's simply too gross. They much prefer net domestic product (NDP) (see the box, "Why NDP Is Better than GDP"). What's the difference? The main difference is depreciation.

$$\text{Gross domestic product} - \text{Depreciation} = \text{Net domestic product}$$

Using 2009 data and applying this formula, we can find our Net Domestic Product:

$$\begin{array}{ccccc} \text{GDP} & - & \text{Depreciation} & = & \text{NDP} \\ 14{,}256 & - & 1{,}864 & = & 12{,}392 \end{array}$$

GDP includes, among other things, $1,389 billion worth of spending on plant, equipment, and computer software. This is money spent on new office buildings, shopping malls, factories, stores, assembly lines, office machines, computers, computer software, and a host of other machinery and equipment.

Why are we so anxious to get rid of depreciation? Depreciation represents the buildings and machinery (plant and equipment) that have worn out or become obsolete over the course of the year. Usually these are replaced with new plant and equipment, but this doesn't represent a net gain because the company ends up right where it started. For example, if a firm begins the year with eight machines and replaces three that wore out during the year, it still has eight machines at the end of the year.

Similarly, when we measure a nation's GDP, one of the things we are counting is the replacement of plant and equipment, which can lead to some dubious conclusions about a nation's economic well-being. For example, suppose Sweden and Canada each have a GDP of 200, but depreciation in Sweden is 50, while in Canada it is only 30. The NDP of Sweden would be 150 (GDP of 200 − Depreciation of 50); Canada's NDP would be 170 (GDP of 200 − Depreciation of 30). A more elaborate example appears in the box, "Why NDP Is Better than GDP."

Are you ready for a big question? All right then, here it comes. What's the difference between gross investment and net investment? *Gross* investment is the total amount we invest in new plant and equipment (as well as new residential housing and additional inventory). *Net* investment is the additional plant and equipment with which we end up by the end of the year. So we have this equation:

$$\text{Gross investment} - \text{Depreciation} = \text{Net investment}$$

The I in the equation GDP = C + I + G + X_n is *gross* investment. We distinguished between *gross* investment and *net* investment back in Chapter 6.

Now we need to subtract indirect business taxes (mainly general sales taxes and taxes on specific items such as gasoline, liquor, and cigarettes) and add subsidies (such as government payments to farmers).

$$\text{NDP} - \text{Indirect business taxes and subsidies} = \text{National Income}$$

12,392 −	104	=	12,288

About seven-tenths of national income is compensation of employees, which includes wages, salaries, and fringe benefits (such as medical insurance and pension contributions). Other components are corporate profits, interest income, rental income, and business proprietors' income.

Two Things to Avoid When Compiling GDP

Two mistakes are commonly made when GDP is compiled. First we'll talk about multiple counting, that is, counting a particular good at each stage of production. Then we'll look at the inclusion of transfer payments. To compile GDP correctly, we count each good or service only once, and we don't count transfer payments as part of GDP.

Multiple Counting

We need to avoid multiple counting when we compile GDP. Only expenditures on final products—what consumers, businesses, and government units buy for their own use—belong in GDP. This is clearly illustrated by the journey wheat makes from the farm to the supermarket.

The farmer gets about 2 cents for the wheat that goes into a loaf of bread. This wheat is ground into flour at a mill and is now worth, say, 4 cents. When it is placed in 100-pound packages, it is worth 5 cents, and when it is shipped to a bakery, it is worth 10 cents. Baked bread is worth 20 cents, packaged baked bread is worth 23 cents, and bread delivered to the supermarket is worth 35 cents. The supermarket sells it for 89 cents.

How much of this goes into GDP? Do we add up the 2 cents, 4 cents, 5 cents, 10 cents, 20 cents, 23 cents, 35 cents, and 89 cents? No! That would be multiple counting. We count only what is spent on a final good, 89 cents, which is paid by the consumer. Of this entire process, only 89 cents goes into GDP.

We could also avoid multiple counting be taking the *value-added* approach. *Value added is the market value of a firm's output less the value of the inputs the firm has*

TABLE 2	Value Added in the Process of Producing and Selling Bread	
	Sales Value of Materials or Product $0.00	Value Added
Farmer produces wheat	0.02	$0.02
Flour mill grinds wheat into flour	0.04	0.02
Flour mill packages flour	0.05	0.01
Flour shipped to bakery	0.10	0.05
Flour baked into bread	0.20	0.10
Bread is packaged	0.23	0.03
Bread delivered to supermarket	0.35	0.12
Bread is sold	0.89	0.54

bought from the previous seller. Using our bread example, we've illustrated the value-added approach in Table 2.

GDP counts only what we spend on final goods and services.

GDP, then, counts only what we spend on final goods and services—not those of an intermediate nature. We are not interested in the money spent on wheat or flour, but only that which the buyer of the final product, bread, spends at the supermarket. If we count intermediate goods, we will greatly inflate GDP by counting the same goods and services over and over again.

Just as we don't include intermediate goods in GDP, we don't count used goods either. If you buy a used car, a 10-year-old house, or almost anything at a flea market or on eBay, your purchase does not go into GDP. Remember, we count only final goods and services that were purchased in the current year.

However, anything done this year to make a used product salable is counted (for example, a paint job for a used car). What if you add a room to your house? If you do it yourself, then the cost of materials will be included in GDP. If you pay someone to build the addition, then we'll include the full cost of the job.

Treatment of Transfer Payments and Financial Transactions

At first glance, transfer payments appear to belong in GDP. When the government issues a Social Security or unemployment insurance check, isn't this a form of government spending? Shouldn't it be part of G, like defense spending or the salaries paid to government employees?

GDP includes only payments for goods and services produced this year. A person receiving a Social Security check is not being reimbursed for producing a good or service this year. But a government clerk or the employee of a defense contractor *is* providing a good or service this year so their pay would therefore be included under government purchases, designated by the letter G.

Transfer payments don't go directly into GDP.

Because Social Security, public assistance, Medicare, Medicaid, and other government transfer payments—which now make up more than half of the federal budget—are not payments for currently produced goods and services, they are not included in GDP. However, those who receive these payments will spend nearly all of that money, so, ultimately, the payments will go toward GDP in the form of consumer spending for the purchase of final goods and services produced in the current year.

Financial transactions don't go into GDP.

Something else not counted in GDP is financial transactions. The purchase of corporate stocks and bonds does not add anything to GDP. Isn't it an investment? It certainly is from an individual's point of view; but in strictly economic terms, the purchase of corporate stocks and bonds, government securities, real estate, and other financial assets does not constitute investment because it does not represent the purchase of new plant and equipment. But aren't these funds used to buy new plant and equipment? Perhaps. If and when they are, those purchases qualify as investment and therefore as part of GDP.

Nominal GDP versus Real GDP

Every July 4 we order a large pizza. After all, what could be more American? In 2002 the pie cost $8. Each year it went up a dollar, so by 2006 we were paying $12 for the same size pizza. Question: If the price of pizza went from $8 to $12, by what percentage did it go up?

Solution:

$$\text{Percentage change} = \frac{\text{Current price} - \text{Original price}}{\text{Original price}}$$

$$= \frac{\$12 - \$8}{\$8} = \frac{\$4}{\$8} = \frac{1}{2} = 0.50 = 50\%$$

You're going to have to calculate percentage changes in this chapter and the next, so please work your way through the accompanying box, "Calculating Percentage Changes," if you need some extra help.

Think of our GDP as a pizza. In this example our GDP went up a dollar a year from 2002 through 2006. We'll call that our nominal GDP. Our real GDP would be the actual pizza we produce each year. Between 2002 and 2006 we produced the same size pizza each year. So real GDP stayed the same.

Nominal GDP has gone up virtually every year since the late 1940s and real GDP has gone up every year, except during recessions. You can find annual GDP figures and real GDP figures on the inner front cover of this book. Suppose nominal GDP grew by 8 percent in 2019 and there was a 3 percent rate of inflation. Can you guess by how much real GDP grew that year?

It grew by 5 percent. All we did was subtract the inflation rate (3%) from the GDP growth rate (8%). We can say, then, that nominal GDP rose by 8 percent but real GDP rose by just 5 percent.

GDP is the basic measure of how much the country produced in a given year. However, comparisons of GDP from one year to the next can be misleading. We need to be able to correct GDP for price increases so we can measure how much actual production rose. To do this we use the GDP deflator, which is calculated quarterly by the Department of Commerce.

The GDP deflator

In the base year the GDP deflator is 100. If the GDP deflator is 120 in the current year, prices have risen 20 percent since the base year.

Calculating Percentage Changes

When we go from 100 to 120, that's an increase of 20 percent. From 150 to 200 is an increase of 33⅓ percent. When we go from 50 to 25, that's a percentage decline of 50 percent. How do we know? We use this formula:

$$\% \text{ change} = \frac{\text{Change}}{\text{Original number}}$$

Using the first example, from 100 to 120 is a change of 20, and as our original number is 100, we have 20/100. Any number divided by 100 may be read as a percentage—in this case, 20 percent.

Another way of figuring this out—and we'll need this method most of the time because 100 will rarely be the original number—is to divide the bottom number into the top number. Remember, whenever you have a fraction, you may divide the bottom number into the top:

$$\frac{\text{Change}}{\text{Original number}} = \frac{12}{50} = 0.24$$

0.24 = 24 percent. Any decimal may be read as a percent if you move the decimal point two places to the right and add the percent sign (%).

Now let's do the other two. First, the percentage change when we go from 150 to 200. Work it out yourself in the space provided here, and then go on to the last one—when we go from 50 to 25.

$$\frac{\text{Change}}{\text{Original number}} = \frac{50}{150} = \frac{5}{15} = \frac{1}{3} = 33\frac{1}{3}\%$$

Finally, find the percentage change when we go from 50 to 25.

$$\frac{\text{Change}}{\text{Original number}} = -\frac{25}{50} = -\frac{1}{2} = -0.50 = -50\%$$

Problem: GDP rises from $10 trillion in 2004, the base year, to $15 trillion in 2009, the current year. If the GDP deflator is 125 in 2009, find real GDP in 2009.

Solution:

$$\text{Real GDP} = \frac{\text{Nominal GDP}}{\text{GDP deflator}} \times 100$$

$$= \frac{15,000}{125} \times 100 = \frac{120}{1} \times 100 = 12,000$$

Next question: Find the percentage increase in real GDP between 2004 and 2009.

Solution:

$$\text{Percentage change} = \frac{\text{Current real GDP} - \text{Original real GDP}}{\text{Original real GDP}}$$

$$= \frac{(12{,}000 - 10{,}000)}{10{,}000} = \frac{2{,}000}{10{,}000} = 0.20 = 20\%$$

Here's one more problem: GDP rises from \$3 trillion in 1982 to \$6 trillion in 1988. The GDP deflator in 1988 is 150. Find the real GDP in 1988. Find the percentage increase in real GDP between 1982 and 1988.

Solution:

$$\text{Real GDP} = \frac{\text{Nominal GDP}}{\text{GDP deflator}} \times 100$$

$$= \frac{6{,}000}{150} \times 100 = \frac{40}{1} \times 100 = 4{,}000$$

$$\text{Percentage change} = \frac{\text{Current real GDP} - \text{Original real GDP}}{\text{Original real GDP}}$$

$$= \frac{4{,}000 - 3{,}000}{3{,}000} = \frac{1{,}000}{3{,}000} = \frac{1}{3} = 33\frac{1}{3}\%$$

Figure 3 provides an eight-decade record of real GDP. According to U.S. government measurements, we produce about 14 times as much as we did in 1930 and about 5 times as much as we did in 1955. Although real GDP comparisons over 65- and 80-year periods cannot be made with precision, they certainly give us a fair approximation of the growth of our national output.

Real GDP measures our output, or production. Output, or real GDP, falls during recession years. But GDP, by definition, is *the nation's expenditure on all final goods and services produced during the year at market prices*. If prices rise by a larger percentage than output falls, then GDP will increase. For example, if output goes down by 4 percent and prices go up by 7 percent, by what percentage does GDP go up?

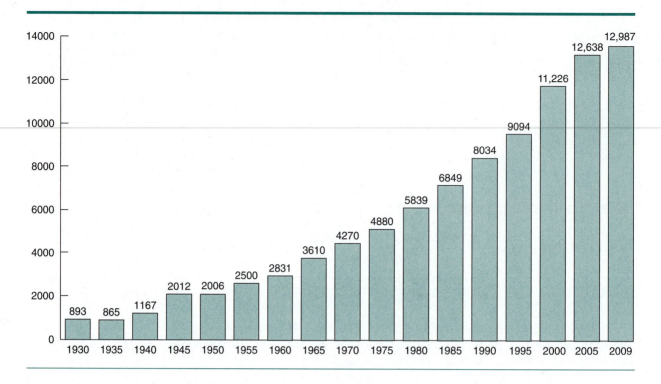

Figure 3

GDP, 1930–2009, in billions of 2005 dollars

Real GDP fell during the Great Depression and again after World War II. Since the late 1940s there has been a steady upward climb of real GDP.

Source: www.bea.gov

It goes up by 3 percent. GDP measures changes in output *and* prices. Real GDP measures just changes in output.

Now let's see if you can work out some verbal GDP problems. If GDP rose and real GDP fell, explain what happened.

Answer: The GDP deflator (or, rate of inflation) rose more than real GDP fell. For instance, if GDP rose by 3 percent, while real GDP fell by 2 percent, then the GDP deflator must have risen by 5 percent.

Next problem: Real GDP remains unchanged, while GDP falls. What happened?

Answer: What happened was deflation, or a decline in the price level (that is, the GDP deflator dropped below 100). While those of us born after the administration of Herbert Hoover never experienced deflation, it *does* happen. In the next chapter we'll consider whether we might soon be seeing some deflation.

One more problem: GDP doubles and the price level doubles. What happened to real GDP?

Answer: Real GDP stayed the same. Let's make up a problem with real numbers: GDP rises from 1000 to 2000, and the GDP deflator is 200 in the current year. What happened to real GDP?

$$\text{Real GDP} = \frac{\text{Nominal GDP}}{\text{GDP deflator}} \times 100$$

$$= \frac{2{,}000}{200} \times 100 = 10 \times 100 = 1{,}000$$

Real GDP remained at a level of 1000. If you're still confused about the difference between a change in GDP and a change in real GDP, please see the Extra Help box, "Read Only if You're Still Confused."

Read Only if You're Still Confused about the Difference between a Change in GDP and Real GDP

From August 1981 through November 1982 we suffered our worst recession since the Great Depression of the 1930s. But GDP actually rose in 1981 and 1982. And what happened to real GDP?

Real GDP went down in 1982. How can you explain a rise in GDP accompanied by a decline in real GDP, or actual output?

Prices, measured by the GDP deflator, must have gone up at a higher rate than output declined. In the accompanying chart you'll see that GDP rose by 4.1 percent and that real GDP declined by 2.1 percent.

By how much did the price level rise from 1981 to 1982? This rise, measured by the GDP deflator, was 6.2 percent.

There's a very simple relationship among percentage changes in GDP, real GDP, and the GDP deflator from one year to the next:

Percentage change in GDP = Percentage change in real GDP + Percentage change in GDP deflator

Question: If real GDP rose by 3 percent and the GDP deflator fell by 1.2 percent, what was the percentage change in GDP?

Solution: Percentage change in GDP = Percentage change in real GDP (3%) + Percentage change in GDP deflator (−1.2%).

Percentage change in GDP = 3% + (−1.2%)
= 3% − 1.2% = 1.8%

One more question: If GDP rose by 3.8 percent and the GDP deflator rose by 2.5 percent, find the percentage change in real GDP.

Solution: Percentage change in GDP = Percentage change in real GDP + Percentage change in GDP deflator.

3.8% = Percentage change in real GDP + 2.5%
1.3% = Percentage change in real GDP

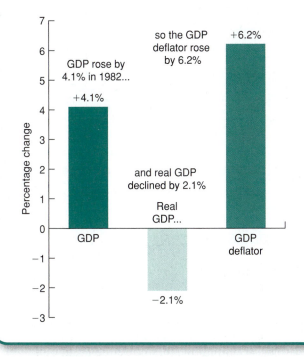

In recent years which grew faster—GDP or real GDP? *Think* about it. OK, what's your answer?

I hope you said, "GDP." That's because GDP was pushed up not just by rising output but by rising prices as well. Figure 4 illustrates that point. Because real GDP is measured in dollars of the year 2000, GDP and real GDP are equal in that year. You'll notice that in the years preceding 2000, real GDP was higher than GDP, and that after 2000, GDP was higher.

Here's a trick question. Suppose way in the future, the base year is 2050. In 2051 GDP rises more slowly than real GDP. What must have happened?

If GDP measures changes in output and prices, and real GDP measures changes in output, what *must* have happened to prices in 2051? They must have fallen. When there's a widespread decline in prices (which is called deflation), then GDP rises more slowly than real GDP.

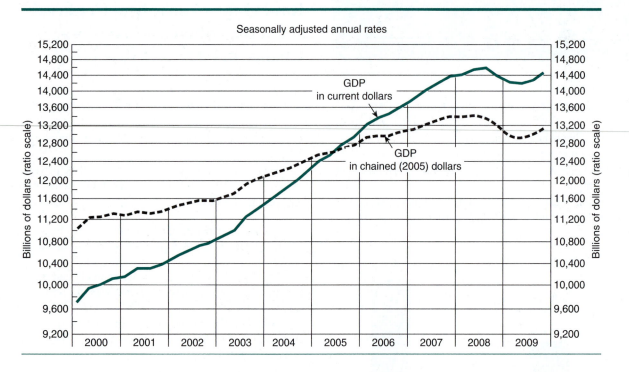

Figure 4
Nominal GDP and Real GDP, 2000–2009
Source: www.bea.gov.

International GDP Comparisons

Which country has the world's largest GDP? I hope you didn't forget that the United States does. Figure 5 shows the 2008 GDPs of the world's fourteen trillion-dollar economies.

Different countries use different national income accounting systems, and international exchange rates fluctuate (we'll take up international exchange rates in the last chapter of this book). Hence GDP comparisons among countries cannot be made with great precision. Yet it's reasonable to say that such comparisons do give us fairly close approximations.

Per Capita Real GDP

You may still be wondering, how are we doing in comparison to other countries? And how are we doing right now, compared to how we were doing 15 years ago—or 50 years ago?

GDP may be used to compare living standards among various countries or living standards during different time periods within one country. Such comparisons would usually be on a per capita (or per person) basis. Per capita GDP = GDP/Population. In the United States, per capita GDP in 2009 was:

$$\text{Per capita GDP} = \frac{\text{GDP}}{\text{Population}} = \frac{\$14,256,300,000,000}{307,000,000} = \$46,437$$

This means that in 2009 we produced $46,437 worth of final goods and services for every man, woman, and child in this country.

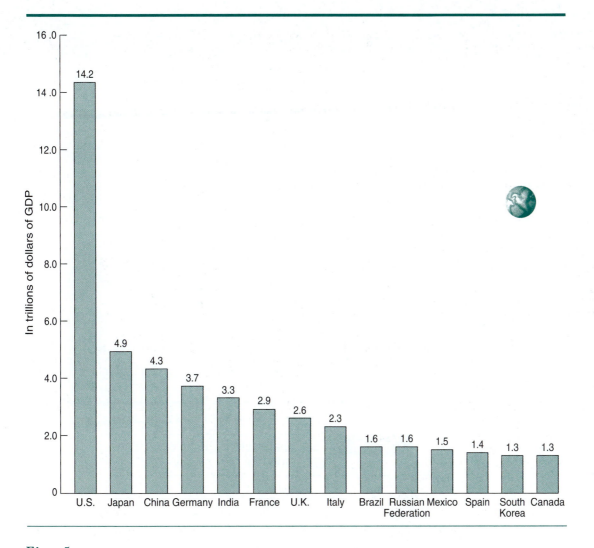

Figure 5

Trillion Dollar Economies, 2008

China, which has the most secretive national income accounting system of these trillion dollar economies, may well have a much larger GDP than shown here. By some measures it is even larger than Japan's.
Source: World Development Indicators database, World Bank, 1 July 2009.

To compare 2009 per capita GDP with that of another year, we would have to correct for inflation. In other words, we really need to revise our formula:

$$\text{Per capita real GDP} = \frac{\text{Real GDP}}{\text{Population}}$$

Per capita real GDP = Real GDP/Population

How does our per capita real GDP compare with earlier years? Just take a look at Table 3. Since World War II per capita real GDP has tripled. The calculation of per capita real GDP is shown in the accompanying Advanced Work box.

How valid are per capita real GDP comparisons over time? Over the short run, say, up to 10 years, they are quite valid. But comparisons over 20, 30, or 40 years become more and more like comparing apples and oranges, or, more to the point, like comparing video games and pocket calculators with nine-inch RCA TVs and those big old office adding machines whose lever you pulled every time you entered a number. Or like comparing Ford T-birds with Model-T Fords. Yale economists have calculated that under 30 percent of the goods and services consumed at the end of the 20th century were variants of the goods and services produced 100 years earlier.

Per capita real GDP comparisons over time

ADVANCED WORK

Calculating Per Capita Real GDP

Earlier in the chapter we worked out several problems in which we converted GDP into real GDP. And we've just done some per capita GDP problems. So what's left to do? Calculating per capita real GDP.

Suppose our GDP were to rise from $12 trillion in 2006 to $18 trillion in 2016, when the GDP deflator is 120. And suppose that our population rose from 280 million in 2006 to 300 million in 2016. What we want to find is (1) How much is per capita real GDP in 2016, and (2) By what percentage did per capita real GDP rise between 2006 and 2016?

See if you can work this out. I would suggest doing this problem in four steps: (1) Find real GDP in 2016; (2) find per capita real GDP in 2016; (3) find per capita real GDP for 2006; and (4) find the percentage rise in per capita real GDP between 2006 and 2016.

Solution:

$$(1) \quad \text{Real GDP}_{2016} = \frac{\text{Nominal GDP}}{\text{GDP deflator}} \times 100$$

$$= \frac{\overset{150}{\cancel{18,000}}}{\underset{1}{\cancel{120}}} \times 100$$

$$= 15,000$$

$$(2) \quad \begin{array}{l}\text{Per capita} \\ \text{real GDP}_{2016}\end{array} = \frac{\text{Real GDP}_{2016}}{\text{Population}_{2016}} = \frac{15,000}{.3} = \$50,000$$

$$(3) \quad \begin{array}{l}\text{Per capita} \\ \text{real GDP}_{2006}\end{array} = \frac{\text{Real GDP}_{2006}}{\text{Population}_{2006}} = \frac{12,00\cancel{0}}{.28\cancel{0}}$$

$$= \frac{6000}{.14} = \frac{3000}{.07} = \$42,857$$

$$(4) \quad \begin{array}{l}\text{Percentage} \\ \text{change}\end{array} = \frac{\text{Change}}{\text{Original number}} = \frac{\$7,143}{42,857} = 16.7\%$$

TABLE 3	Per Capita Real GDP, Selected Years, 1776–2009 (*in 2009 dollars*)	
Year	Period	
1776	Revolutionary War	$ 1,783
1917–19	World War I	7,761
1941–45	World War II	14,422
1969	Vietnam War	23,126
1989	Pre-1990s boom	31,035
2009	Latest year available	46,437

Sources: Economic Report of the President, 2010; Survey of Current Business, March 2010; Federal Reserve Bank of Dallas Annual Report, 2001.

International per capita real GDP comparisons

Per capita real GDP is not an accurate measure of international differences in production levels, but it does provide a rough measure. Comparisons of countries at similar stages of economic development are much more accurate, however, than comparisons of countries at different stages.

How does our per capita GDP compare with those of other leading industrial nations? Thirty years ago, we were clearly number one. By the late 1980s, however, we had probably lost our lead. As you can see in Figure 6, Luxembourg, Norway, Switzerland, Denmark, and Ireland have surpassed us. Still, because of differences in how these nations compute their per capita GDP, this measure provides, at best, a fairly good appproximation of relative living standards of different nations.

on the web

If you'd like to find the GDP and GDP per capita of any country in the world, go to www.worldbank.org/data

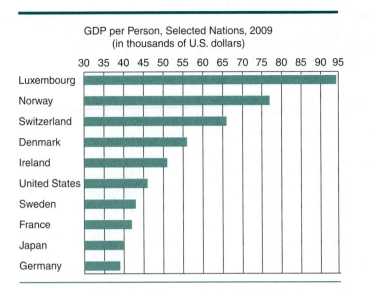

GDP per Person, Selected Nations, 2009
(in thousands of U.S. dollars)

Figure 6
Per Capita GDP of the Selected
Rich Countries, 2009
Although the United States is not
number one, we clearly have one of
the highest living standards in the
world. International comparisons
for per capita GDP are at least
somewhat suspect because of
varying national income accounting
systems as well as fluctuations
of foreign exchange rates.
Source: World Bank, www.worldbank.org.

Shortcomings of GDP as a Measure of National Economic Well-Being

Production That Is Excluded

Household Production　　Household production consists mainly of the work done by homemakers—care of children, cleaning, shopping, and cooking. Were a housekeeper hired to do these tasks, this would be counted in GDP. Were two homemakers to work for each other as housekeepers (why, I don't know), their work would be counted in GDP. So why not count homemakers' work in their own homes? Because no money changes hands. No payments are recorded.

If a man marries his housekeeper or his cook, the national dividend is diminished.

—A. C. Pigou,
Economics of Welfare

Food grown in backyard plots, home repairs, clothes made at home, and any other do-it-yourself goods and services that people make or do for themselves, their families, or their friends are not counted in GDP. (The National Gardening Association reports that about 35 million households have garden plots that produce over $1 billion worth of food. The most popular crop is tomatoes, which are grown on 85 percent of the plots.) When you buy these goods and services from other people, the goods and services are counted (assuming they are reported by the sellers as income).

For decades, market production has been replacing household production because of two trends. As more and more women with children have been joining the labor force, some household production has shifted to the marketplace. Mothers' child care has been replaced by daycare and preschool. Five decades ago the large majority of children and adults brought their lunch to school or work. Now, of course, when away from home, the overwhelming majority of Americans eat out, mainly at fast food restaurants. So what had been two mainstays of household production (and not counted in GDP)—child care and home-cooked meals—have been largely replaced by paid child care and restaurant meals (which *are* counted in GDP).

Closely related to household production is bartering, or exchange of services. I'll tutor your children in math if you fix my car. Or you'll paint your friend's house in exchange for her free legal advice. We're performing useful services, but no money is exchanged. While there's no way of quantifying how much all these services are worth, they surely must be worth tens of billions of dollars. But none of this is counted in our GDP.

Illegal Production　　Illegal goods and services are not counted in GDP. The big three—dope, prostitution, and gambling—are ignored even though people spend hundreds of billions on these goods and services. Of course, if you place a bet at a racetrack or an offtrack betting parlor, it is legal and counts in GDP. But a bet placed with a bookie is illegal. If you play the state lottery, your bet is counted toward GDP, but not if you play the numbers.

California is our leading agricultural state. Do you know its number one crop? Lettuce? Grapes? Citrus fruit? Sorry, it's none of the above. California's number one crop is grass—that's right, grass, as in marijuana. It is also the number one cash crop in Kentucky, Tennessee, and West Virginia. How much do Americans spend on illegal drugs? Estimates vary widely, but it is likely that more than $100 billion a year is spent on heroin and cocaine alone.

The Underground Economy   In every large city, on country roads, in flea markets, and even in suburban malls, there are people selling everything from watches to watermelons, and from corn to collectibles. Chances are, the proceeds of these sales are not reported to the government. Not only are no taxes paid, but the sales are not reflected in GDP.

Some of the items sold were stolen, but most are simply goods produced without the government's knowledge. Together with illegal goods and services, these markets form a vast underground economy. How vast? Maybe 10 or 15 percent of GDP. Who knows? How much of *your* income is spent in the underground economy? Or perhaps I should be asking, how much of your income *comes* from the underground economy? (See the box, "Pirated CDs and Videos.")

Our underground economy is not composed of only the street peddlers, cabdrivers, and low-life entrepreneurs who underreport their incomes. Oh no. The underground economy gets a very nice class of people—doctors, dentists, lawyers, and even, heaven forbid, accountants. In fact, there is a whole branch of accounting dedicated to the underground economy. It's called creative accounting. Often it involves keeping three separate sets of books—one for your creditors (showing an inflated profit), one for the government, and one for yourself, so you know how you're doing.

The underground economy adds hundreds of billions of dollars of goods and services to our national output. In addition, it is a safety valve, a generator of jobs and business opportunities that provide a great deal of economic support to the poor and near-poor. Go into any low-income housing project and you'll discover that many people are engaged in some underground economic activity—whether doing hairstyling, fixing cars, or providing child care.

A large proportion of illegal immigrants are heavily employed in activities that can easily be conducted off the books. Tens of thousands of women work in garment sweatshops,

Pirated CDs and Videos

Not everything sold on the street "fell off the truck."* A lot of those "designer" clothing items are illegal "knockoffs" of the real thing. What about those $5 CDs and $10 videos? Where do *they* come from?

Hollywood producers were amazed to find videos of their films being sold in the street just days after they opened and months before their own videos were released. The mystery was easily solved. When the films opened, people with camcorders would seat themselves just off the center aisles of the theaters and tape the films. These tapes would then be reproduced in quantity, put in authentic-looking jackets, and sold on the street.

Pirating CDs is even easier. Using a home computer anyone can copy CDs onto blank disks called CD-recordables, or CD-Rs, through a digital process that maintains the quality of the recording. Since CD-Rs cost just a dollar, there's a nice $4 markup when the CDs are sold by street peddlers. Meanwhile the customer gets a $15 CD of Britney Spears, TLC, the Backstreet Boys, or Puff Daddy for just five bucks. The only ones who lose are the record companies, the recording artists, and the government (assuming that no income is declared and no sales taxes are paid).

Ninety-five percent of all downloaded music is stolen. If you download music on your computer for free using any popular file-sharing program, you may be guilty of copyright infringement. And if you share these files with your friends then welcome to the underground economy. It would be a fair assumption that millions of American families have at least one member employed in the underground economy.

---

*A euphemism for goods that are stolen.

often for substantially less than the legal minimum wage of $7.25 an hour. In New York you'll often find illegal immigrants peddling T-shirts and mood rings on the sidewalk in front of the Immigration and Naturalization Service office.

How much of *your* family's income is spent on services provided by the underground economy? According to estimates by the U.S. Department of Labor and the University of Michigan Institute for Social Research, the underground economy provides 90 percent of our lawn maintenance, 83 percent of our domestic help, 49 percent of our child care, and 34 percent of our home repair and improvements.

If our underground economy is, say, 10 or 15 percent of our GDP, we are underestimating our GDP by as much as 15 percent. But that's tiny compared to the underground economies of such countries as Egypt, Bolivia, Zimbabwe, Nigeria, and Thailand, which are about two-thirds the size of the official GDP. In other countries, such as Mexico, the Philippines, Peru, and Russia, the underground economy is about half the size of the official economy. So when we make international comparisons, we are seriously underestimating the GDP of these countries.

Let's step back for a minute and look once again at our definition of GDP: *the nation's expenditure on all the final goods and services produced during the year at market prices.*

What exactly is production? What we produce? For once economists are in agreement and quite clear about what something means. *Production is any good or service that people are willing to pay for.* And that means anything!

You go to a concert and fall asleep. How much was your ticket? $20? That was $20 worth of production.

You went to a brilliant lecture on the future of the universe. It was free. The speaker wasn't paid. No production.

You grow tomatoes in your backyard for your family's consumption. No production.

You take a course in philosophy. The professor walks into the room and lies down on the floor in the front of the class. This happens all term. How much tuition did you pay to take this course? That's how much production took place.

Let's put a number on the production of the underground economy. Edgar L. Feige, a retired economics professor at the University of Wisconsin, is an authority on the underground economy. He estimates that unreported income in the U.S. more than doubled during the 1990s, reaching $1.25 trillion in 2000, more than one-seventh of our national income.

The problem we have, then, is an inconsistency between the definition of GDP and the way it is compiled by the U.S. Department of Commerce. There's a lot of stuff going on out there that the department misses. The government not only refuses to count the underground economy—legal *or* illegal—but it will not even admit its existence. The bottom line is that it does not go into GDP, even as an estimate. So we are grossly (no pun intended) undercounting GDP.

> Production is any good or service that people are willing to pay for.

Volunteer Work

A woman in my neighborhood named Janet spends countless hours picking up trash and depositing it in garbage cans. OK, maybe she *is* a little compulsive, but she does a great job. If a Sanitation Department employee did what Janet does, his work would be counted in our GDP. But since Janet is an unpaid volunteer, her work is not added into this measure of national output.

Tens of millions of Americans help out in soup kitchens, museums, libraries, schools, and hospitals. They read to the blind, deliver meals to the homebound, tutor children, and teach English to recent immigrants. Although their labor contributes greatly to our national well-being, it is not counted in our GDP.

Treatment of Leisure Time

GDP does not take leisure time into account. We have no way of telling if the people of a country enjoy a 30-hour week or have to work 60 hours a week. In the United States recent immigrant groups, whether the Mexicans or Pakistanis in the 1990s, the Vietnamese and Koreans in the 1970s and 1980s, the Cubans in the 1960s, the eastern and southern Europeans from the 1880s to the 1920s, or the Irish in the 1840s, have been resented for putting in longer hours than native-born Americans. For these immigrants long hours were necessary for survival, not only in America, but in their native lands.

The rice farmer in Egypt, the factory worker in Mexico, and the manual laborer in India do not have seven-hour workdays, paid sick leave, long vacations, 10 paid holidays, and a couple of days off for Christmas shopping.

The decline in the average workweek

Until the close of World War II, most workers still put in five and a half or six days a week. In 1900 the 10-hour day was common, and when you wanted to take a vacation, if your boss liked you, he reached into his pocket and gave you $5 spending money. The average workweek in the United States, as in the rest of the industrial world, has gradually declined.

In his novel, *The Plot Against America,* Philip Roth described the daily lives of people in the years before World War II. For most adults in those times, there *was* no such thing as leisure time.

> The men worked fifty, sixty, even seventy or more hours a week; the women worked all the time, with little assistance from labor-saving devices, washing laundry, ironing shirts, mending socks, turning collars, sewing on buttons, mothproofing woolens, polishing furniture, sweeping and washing floors, washing windows, cleaning sinks, tubs, toilets, and stoves, vacuuming rugs, nursing the sick, shopping for food, cooking meals, feeding relatives, tidying closets and drawers, overseeing paint jobs and household repairs, arranging for religious observances, paying bills and keeping the family's books while simultaneously attending to their children's health, clothing, cleanliness, schooling, nutrition, conduct, birthdays, discipline, and morale. A few women labored alongside their husbands in the family-owned stores on the nearby shopping streets, assisted after school and on Saturdays by their older children, who delivered orders and tended stock and did the cleaning up.[2]

While the average workweek has declined, many more mothers with young children have gone to work. Back in 1960, 79 percent of all families with children had at least one stay-at-home parent. Forty-eight years later, this percentage has fallen to just 25.

Human Costs and Benefits

Another problem with comparing our GDP with those of other countries, or with our own GDP in previous years, is that the physical and psychological costs of producing that GDP and any human benefits associated with producing it are ignored.

First the costs. The strain of commuting long distances along congested routes, the tedium, the dangers, the low status, and other unpleasant factors associated with certain jobs are some of the costs. Other jobs cause anxiety because the worker is always worrying about getting ahead or just getting along. Advertising account executives, air traffic controllers, and bomb squad members are all under the gun, so to speak, during most of their working hours. Economists call the psychological strain associated with work *psychic cost.* Psychic costs detract from one's enjoyment of a job, while *psychic income* adds to that enjoyment.

Psychic cost

There are also physical strains and benefits associated with work. Not only have we shifted nearly completely from human power to mechanical power, but the nature of work has also changed from farming and manufacturing to service jobs, most of which require no physical labor. This is not to say that there are no longer any jobs requiring physical labor or being performed under unpleasant circumstances. Just ask the people who work in toy, handbag, textile, or automobile factories. Or talk to coal miners, sandhogs, day laborers, printing plant employees, migrant farm workers, slaughterhouse workers, and police officers. Or watch the mail sorters who work the graveyard shift in a large post office.

---

[2]Philip Roth, *The Plot Against America* (New York: Vintage Books, 2004), p. 3.

Some people, on the other hand, really enjoy their jobs. Take actors. They are willing to hold all kinds of stopgap jobs—waitress, hotel clerk, theater doorman, short-order cook, office temporary—while waiting for that big chance. For most, of course, it never comes. In New York, where there are no more than 2,000 people who earn their entire livelihood from acting, there are tens of thousands of aspiring actors. Why are they willing to buck such outrageous odds? Because they love acting. The *psychic income* from working in the theater—the smell of the grease paint, the roar of the crowd, the adulation, the applause—is the compensation they seek.

Psychic income

Finally, let's consider the physical benefits from work. Literally. My friend Marty, the gym teacher, is always in great shape. What do you expect? But I really want to talk about Mr. Spalter, a little bald-headed man who taught gym (how can you *teach* gym?) at Brooklyn's James Madison High School in the 1950s. The guy had to be at least 80. Anyway, Mr. Spalter could go up a 30-foot rope in less than 15 seconds—and do it in perfect form, with his legs exactly perpendicular to his body. The physical benefits of being a gym teacher, farmer, or a health club employee are obvious.[3]

Let's put psychic costs and benefits of work on an even more personal level. The Banana Republic and the Duchy of Fenwick have identical per capita GDPs. In the Banana Republic every single worker loves her job so much, she would be willing to work for half her salary. But in the Duchy of Fenwick, all the workers hate their jobs so much that each needs to spend several hours a week getting psychiatric help to deal with his or her unhappiness. By just looking at the per capita income figures of these two countries, you wouldn't have a clue that the people in the Banana Republic were much happier than those of the Duchy of Fenwick. Happiness and sadness are things that GDP just doesn't measure.

Today's GDP is produced by an entirely different type of labor force doing different work from that of 50 or 100 years ago. And our labor force works very differently from those of developing countries. This makes GDP comparisons that much less valid.

What Goes into GDP?

Other problems with GDP as a measure of national economic well-being have to do with what goes into GDP. When a large part of our production goes toward national defense, police protection, pollution control devices, repair and replacement of poorly made cars and appliances, and cleanups of oil spills, a large GDP is not a good indicator of how we're doing. And if a large part of our labor force staffs the myriad bureaucracies of state, local, and federal governments, as well as those of the corporate world, we're not all that well off. GDP tells us how much we produce. We need to ask: How much of *what?*

We also need to ask about the production of new goods and services and about the improvement of product quality. Let's use television sets as an example. Very few American families had TV sets before the late 1940s, and those who did had 9″, 13″, or the "big screen" 17″ black-and-white sets. We counted the $600 17″ black-and-white Philco, RCA, or Dumont (American TV-makers back in prehistoric times) at its selling price in the 1948 GDP. But the $600 Samsung 28″ ultra-flat-screen stereo color TV also counts for just $600 in this year's GDP, even though television sets today are vastly superior to those of the late 1940s. Of course the entire mix of goods and services that go into GDP is very different from what was available just 20 or 30 years ago. Personal computers, cell phones, DVD players, MRIs, laser surgery, CDs, disposable contact lenses, and faxes were not yet even part of our vocabulary, let alone available to the American consumer.

GDP measures how *much* we produce, but not *what* we produce. For example, we spend almost twice as much per capita on health care as nearly every other economically

---

[3]Mr. Spalter must have been doing *something* right. Two Madison graduates have won the Nobel Prize in economics. Robert Solow, who graduated in 1940, won it in 1987, and Gary Becker, class of 1948, won it in 1992. Thus the high school I attended has had more economics Nobel Prize winners than any other high school in the country. And who knows, maybe lightning will strike a third time. If you're curious, I graduated in 1957.

advanced country. One out of every six dollars of our GDP is spent on health care. And yet, the health of the average American is no better than that of the average German, Italian, Japanese, Canadian, or Britisher. As much as one-third of our health care bill goes toward administrative costs, which are, by far, the highest in the developed world. Furthermore, a relatively high proportion of the treatments we receive are medically unnecessary. But if you were to look at the part of our GDP accounted for by health care spending, it would appear that Americans receive almost twice as much actual health care as the citizens of Western Europe, Japan, and Canada.

In general, the problem with using GDP as a measure of national economic well-being is that GDP is just one number, and no single number can possibly provide us with all the information we need. Just as a single number—whether it's your pulse, your weight, your cholesterol, or your blood sugar level—cannot provide a comprehensive measure of your health, neither can a single number such as GDP, accurately measure our economic well-being. So the next time you hear economists chanting "We're number *one*," with respect to our GDP, just remind them that GDP is only a partial and imperfect measure of our economic performance.

Current Issue: GDP or GPI?

As you remember, Hurricane Katrina not only caused a huge loss of life, property, and jobs on the Gulf Coast, but it disrupted our oil supply and wreaked havoc with shipping. So you would think it slowed the growth of real GDP. But the massive federal spending on hurricane relief and recovery far outweighed the negative economic effects of the storm. So if we went strictly by our real GDP figures, we might conclude that the worst natural disaster in U.S. history was actually good for our economy.

There is something wrong with our national income accounting system if a natural disaster like Hurricane Katrina ends up being recorded as a positive, despite the suffering and material loss left in its wake. Similarly, the $10 billion a month we spend on the Iraq War is simply added into our GDP, although it certainly builds no schools or highways. What GDP measures as growth is merely increased spending, but it doesn't indicate whether the spending is good or bad. GDP rises with every oil spill, increase in air pollution, and nearly every other environmental disaster.

In an article that differentiates GPI from GDP, John Talberth, Clifford Cobb, and Noah Slattery sum up the shortcomings of GDP.[4]

> It is merely a gross tally of products and services bought and sold, with no distinctions between transactions that enhance well-being and those that diminish it. Instead of distinguishing costs from benefits, productive activities from destructive ones, or sustainable ones from unsustainable ones the GDP simply assumes that every monetary transaction adds to social well-being by definition. In this way, needless expenditures triggered by crime, accidents, toxic waste contamination, preventable natural disasters, prisons and corporate fraud count the same as socially productive investments in housing, education, healthcare, sanitation, or mass transportation.

The Genuine Progress Index (sometimes called the Genuine Progress Indicator) is an alternate measure of our national well-being. Using GDP as its starting point, the GPI adds in sectors usually excluded from the market economy such as housework and volunteer work, and subtracts crime, natural resource depletion, and the loss of leisure time. It also adds in crucial contributions of the environment, such as clean air and water, moderate climate, and protection from the sun's burning rays. Agricultural activity that uses replenishing water resources, such as river runoff, will score a higher GPI than the same level of agricultural activity that drastically lowers the water table by pumping irrigation water from wells.

---

[4]Dr. John Talberth, Clifford Cobb, and Noah Slattery, *The Genuine Progress Indicator 2006,* p. 2. (www.rprocess. org/index.htm).

One of the developers of the GPI, Philip Lawn, came up with this list of the "costs" of economic activity, which need to be subtracted from GDP:

- Cost of resource depletion.
- Cost of crime.
- Cost of ozone depletion.
- Cost of family breakdown.
- Cost of air, water, and noise pollution.
- Loss of farmland.
- Loss of wetlands.

The next step in the calculation of the GPI is to come up with dollar figures for all the costs and benefits of economic activity. Reasonably accurate estimates may be made for housework, child- and elder-care, home repairs, and volunteer work by determining how much people are paid to do this work in the private sector. But how do you quantify the cost of ozone depletion or of family breakdown?

According to GPI calculations, our per capita GPI was less than one-quarter of the official 2009 per capita GDP of $46,437. And real per capita GPI has fallen by about 40 percent since the early 1970s. What do *you* think about these conclusions?

on the web

If you'd like to learn more about the GPI, please go to www.rprocess.org/index.htm

Questions for Further Thought and Discussion

1. Suppose we want to compare this year's GDP with those of previous years. As we go back in time—to 1980, to 1970, to 1960, and to still earlier years—what happens to the validity of these comparisons? Why does this happen?

2. If our GDP rose from 11,000 to 11,500, there could be a few different explanations. List each of these possibilities.

3. Which has been increasing faster, GDP or real GDP? Explain your answer.

4. GDP is not an ideal measure of national economic well-being. Make a list of all the things you would do to improve this concept. Include in your list the goods and services that GDP does not count.

5. "Americans enjoy the highest standard of living in the world." Discuss why this statement is not perfectly accurate.

6. Under what circumstances could real GDP for a given year be greater than GDP for that same year? For example, if 2015 were the base year and 2016 were the current year, how could real GDP in 2016 exceed GDP for 2016?

7. Explain how GDP is affected by the sale of
   a. a new house.
   b. an hour session with a physical trainer.
   c. 1,000 shares of AT&T.
   d. an antique rolltop desk.

8. If you were comparing the economic well-being of two countries and had a choice of using one of the following four measures, which one would you choose and why would you choose it?
   a. GDP
   b. Real GDP
   c. Per capita GDP
   d. Per capita real GDP

9. Do you think we should switch from using GDP to GPI as our basic measure of national well-being?

10. *Practical Application:* Make a list of the dollar value of everything you consume during the next seven days. Then figure out the percentage that isn't counted in our GDP. Don't forget home-cooked meals, pirated music, and other goods and services are not counted.

11. *Practical Application:* You have just been hired by the Bureau of Economic Analysis of the U.S. Department of Commerce to come up with an improved measure of national output. Use GDP as your starting point.

12. *Web Activity:* Which country has the highest per capita GDP and which country has the lowest? Go to google.com and type in CIA GDP per capita, and then click on "The World Factbook—Country Comparison GDP—per capita."

Workbook for Chapter 9 **connect** |ECONOMICS

Name _____   Date _____

Multiple-Choice Questions

Circle the letter that corresponds to the best answer.

1. Nearly all of our output is produced by
   _____. (LO1)
   a) the government
   b) private business firms
   c) individual consumers

2. GDP may be found by _____. (LO2, 3)
   a) adding together money spent on goods and services and incomes received by the factors of production
   b) subtracting incomes received by the factors of production from the money spent on goods and services
   c) subtracting the money spent on goods and services from the incomes received by the factors of production
   d) adding the money spent on final goods and services

3. Which equation is correct? (LO2)
   a) GDP − Depreciation = NDP
   b) NDP − Depreciation = GDP
   c) GDP + NDP = Depreciation

4. Which would be the most accurate statement? (LO8)
   a) There is almost no underground economy in the United States.
   b) Nearly half the goods and services that Americans consume are produced by the underground economy.
   c) Most of our lawn maintenance and domestic help is supplied by the underground economy.
   d) The production of the underground economy is included in our GDP.

5. In 2030 Nigeria had a GDP of $700 billion and depreciation of $100 billion. The price level did not rise in 2031, but its GDP rose to $710 billion and its depreciation rose to $180 billion. Most economists would say that _____. (LO2)
   a) the Nigerian economy did better in 2030
   b) the Nigerian economy did better in 2031
   c) there is no way of determining which year was better

6. Pirated CDs and videos are _____. (LO8)
   a) part of the underground economy
   b) sold only in other countries
   c) sold by recording studios and Hollywood movie producers
   d) encouraged by the federal government because their manufacture and sale provides tens of thousands of jobs to marginal workers

7. In declining order of size, which of these is the proper ranking? (LO2, 4)
   a) GDP, NDP, national income
   b) NDP, GDP, national income
   c) National income, GDP, NDP
   d) National income, NDP, GDP
   e) GDP, national income, NDP
   f) NDP, national income, GDP

8. Which of the following statements is true? (LO6, 7)
   a) The United States has the world's largest GDP and per capita GDP.
   b) The United States has the world's largest GDP, but not the world's largest per capita GDP.
   c) The United States has the world largest per capita GDP, but not the world's largest GDP.
   d) The United States has neither the world's largest GDP nor the world's largest per capita GDP.

9. The largest sector of GDP is _____. (LO1, 2)
   a) investment   c) net exports
   b) government spending   d) consumer spending

10. Which is not counted in GDP? (LO2)
    a) A Social Security check sent to a retiree.
    b) Government spending on highway building.
    c) Money spent on an airline ticket.
    d) Money spent by a company to build a new office park.

11. Which one of these goes into the investment sector of GDP? (LO2)
    a) The purchase of a new factory
    b) The purchase of 100 shares of Intel stock
    c) The purchase of a 10-year-old office building
    d) The purchase of a U.S. savings bond

12. When there is inflation _____. (LO5)

    a) real GDP increases faster than GDP

    b) GDP increases faster than real GDP

    c) GDP and real GDP increase at the same rate

    d) there is no way of telling whether GDP or real GDP increases faster

13. If GDP rose from $6 trillion to $9 trillion and prices rose by 50 percent over this period, _____. (LO5)

    a) real GDP fell by 100 percent

    b) real GDP fell by 50 percent

    c) real GDP stayed the same

    d) real GDP rose by 50 percent

    e) real GDP rose by 100 percent

14. Which of the following is counted in GDP? (LO8)

    a) Household production

    b) Illegal production

    c) Leisure time

    d) Government spending

    e) Voluntary work

15. Which statement is true? (LO8)

    a) There is an inconsistency between the definition of GDP and the way it is compiled by the U.S. Department of Commerce.

    b) GDP is an accurate measure of production in the United States.

    c) U.S. GDP figures include estimates for production in the underground economy.

    d) Our GDP would grow faster if we had less inflation.

16. Suppose the GDP of Argentina were 10 times that of Uruguay. Which statement would be most accurate? (LO6)

    a) There is no way of comparing the output of Argentina and Uruguay.

    b) Argentina's output is greater than that of Uruguay.

    c) Argentina's output is probably around 10 times that of Uruguay.

    d) Argentina's output is 10 times that of Uruguay.

17. Which statement is true? (LO2, 8)

    a) GDP tells us how much we produce as well as what we produce.

    b) GDP tells us neither how much we produce nor what we produce.

    c) GDP tells us what we produce.

    d) GDP tells us how much we produce.

18. We would like to compare real per capita GDP. Which would be the most valid comparison? (LO6, 7)

    a) China in 2004 and Thailand in 2004

    b) Germany in 2002 and 2004

    c) The United States in 1980 and 2004

    d) Nigeria in 1960 and the United Kingdom in 1990

19. Per capita real GDP is found by _____. (LO7)

    a) dividing population by real GDP

    b) dividing real GDP by population

    c) adding population to real GDP

    d) multiplying real GDP by population

20. Which statement is true? (LO7)

    a) Over longer and longer periods of time, comparisons of real per capita GDP become increasingly valid.

    b) Over the short run, say, up to 10 years, comparisons of per capita real GDP are quite valid.

    c) International comparisons of per capita real GDP may be made with less caution than comparisons over time within a given country.

    d) None of these statements is true.

21. Since World War II our per capita real GDP has _____. (LO7)

    a) stayed about the same

    b) risen by 50 percent

    c) more than tripled

    d) risen by almost 700 percent

22. Which statement is true? (LO6, 7)

    a) The Japanese have a higher standard of living than we do.

    b) The Japanese have a larger GDP than we do.

    c) The typical Japanese family has more living space than the typical American family.

    d) None of these statements is true.

23. $C + I + G + X_n$ is _____ approach(es) to GDP. (LO1, 2)

    a) the flow-of-income

    b) the expenditures

    c) both the expenditures and the flow-of-income

    d) neither the expenditures nor the flow-of-income

24. Which statement is true? (LO1)
    a) Consumption as a percentage of GDP is higher today than it was in 1979.
    b) Government purchases are about 30 percent of GDP.
    c) Real GDP has risen faster than GDP since 1999.
    d) Consumption is a little over half of GDP.

25. Which is the most accurate statement about the underground economy? (LO8)
    a) It adds hundreds of billions of dollars to our GDP.
    b) It provides employment to hundreds of thousands of illegal immigrants.
    c) It is run almost entirely by organized crime.
    d) It makes the rich richer and the poor poorer.

26. Which would be the most valid statement? (LO7, 8)
    a) The American standard of living is, by far, the highest in the world.
    b) The standard of living of the average American is about twice that of the average Russian.
    c) The standard of living of the average American is comparable to that of the average person in Switzerland, Germany, and Japan.
    d) If the underground economy, illegal production, and household production were accurately measured and added to GDP, our GDP would probably rise by less than 1 percent.

27. Which is the most accurate statement? (LO6, 8)
    a) We may be underestimating our GDP by as much as 50 percent by not taking into account the underground economy.
    b) Bartered goods and services are generally counted in GDP.
    c) Within the next five years, China will have a larger GDP than the United States.
    d) Although GDP has many shortcomings, it is still a very useful economic concept.

28. GDP is _____ GPI. (LO9)
    a) much higher than
    b) about the same size as
    c) much lower than

29. Which of the following is the most accurate statement? (LO7, 9)
    a) On a per capita basis, GPI is greater than GDP.
    b) GPI has more than doubled over the last 40 years.
    c) The difference between GDP and GPI is the annual rate of inflation.
    d) GPI is about one-quarter of GDP on a per capita basis.

30. Which one of the following statements would you agree with? (LO8)
    a) GDP includes only market transactions, while GPI includes both market transactions and other factors affecting our national well-being.
    b) GPI is a very accurate measure of national well-being.
    c) As a measure of national well-being, GDP has no major shortcomings.
    d) GDP takes into account many more economic, social, and environmental activities than GPI.

Fill-In Questions

1. The nation's expenditure on all the final goods and services produced during the year at market prices is _____. (LO1)

2. Nearly all our goods and services are produced by _____. (LO1, 2)

3. GDP − _____ = NDP. (LO2)

4. NDP − _____ = national income. (LO2, 4)

5. If Diane Hilgers had been alive during the American Revolution, her standard of living would have been about _____ percent of what it would be today. (LO7)

6. Had Anne Gindorff Heinz been alive during World War I, her standard of living would have been about _____ percent of what it would be today. (LO7)

7. GDP includes only payments for _____ _____. (LO3)

8. _____ measures total production in one year. (LO1)

9. Goods and services produced without the government's knowledge are part of the _____ economy. (LO8)

10. Economists call any good or service that people are willing to pay for _____. (LO8)

11. Economists call the psychological strain associated with work _____. (LO8)

12. Per capita real GDP is found by dividing _____ by _____. (LO7)

13. Over time, per capita real GDP comparisons become _____ valid. (LO7)

Problems

1. Given the following information, calculate NDP and national income: GDP = $5 trillion, Indirect business taxes = $300 billion, and Depreciation = $500 billion. (LO2, 4)

2. If national income is $3 trillion, depreciation is $400 billion, and indirect business taxes are $300 billion, how much are NDP and GDP? (LO2, 4)

3. Given: C = 65 percent of GDP; I = 15 percent of GDP; G = 25 percent of GDP. What percent of GDP is X_n? (LO2)

4. If GDP doubles from 2023 to 2028, the GDP deflator doubles, and the population remains the same, by what percentage does real GDP per capita change? (LO7)

5. If consumption spending is $3 trillion, investment is $800 billion, government spending is $1 trillion, imports are $1.2 trillion, and exports are $900 billion, how much is GDP? (LO4)

6. If consumption is $3.8 trillion, investment is $1.1 trillion, government spending is $1.1 trillion, imports are $1.6 trillion, and exports are $1.4 trillion, how much is GDP? (LO1, 4)

7. GDP rises from $4 trillion in 1986, the base year, to $5 trillion in 1989. The GDP deflator in 1989 is 120. Find real GDP in 1989. Find the percentage increase in real GDP between 1986 and 1989. (LO5)

8. GDP rises from $5 trillion in 1990, the base year, to $7 trillion in 1994. The GDP deflator in 1994 is 140. Find real GDP in 1994. Find the percentage increase in real GDP between 1990 and 1994. (LO5)

9. GDP rises from $20 trillion in 2017 to $21 trillion in 2018, but the price level remains the same. (a) How much is real GDP in 2018? (b) By what percentage did real GDP rise between 2017 and 2018? (LO5)

10. Find per capita GDP when population is 100 million and GDP is $2 trillion. (LO7)

11. Find per capita GDP when GDP is $1.5 trillion and population is 300 million. (LO7)

12. Suppose our GDP were to rise from $10 trillion in 2007 to $20 trillion in 2027, when the GDP deflator is 125. And suppose that our population rose from 300 million in 2007 to 330 million in 2027. (a) How much is per capita real GDP in 2027? (b) By what percentage did per capita real GDP rise between 2007 and 2027? [Hint: Do the problem in four steps: (1) Find real GDP in 2027; (2) find per capita real GDP in 2027; (3) find per capita real GDP for 2007; and (4) find the percentage rise in per capita real GDP between 2007 and 2027.] (LO7)

13. Suppose the GDP of South Korea were to rise from $600 billion in 2005 to $1.5 trillion in 2015, when the GDP deflator is 150. And suppose that Korea's population rose from 40 million in 2005 to 50 million in 2015. (a) How much is per capita real GDP in 2015? (b) By what percentage did per capita real GDP rise between 2005 and 2015? (LO5, 7)

14. If GDP rises from $10 trillion to $10.4 trillion and real GDP rises from $10 trillion to $10.3 trillion, find the percentage change in the GDP deflator. (LO5)

15. If real GDP goes up by 3.7 percent and the GDP deflator goes up by 1.6 percent, find the percentage change in GDP. (LO5)

16. Suppose that in 2015 we were to have a deflationary recession. If GDP in 2013 were $17 trillion predict GDP and real GDP in 2015. (LO5)

Chapter 10

Economic Fluctuations, Unemployment, and Inflation

Economics is not called the dismal science for nothing. Right now we'll be examining some of the problems that have contributed to this reputation—recessions, inflation, and unemployment. It would be wonderful if our economy could grow steadily at, say, 3 percent a year, with no recessions, no inflation, and no unemployment. But as you know, the real world is a lot more dismal.

Still, for every problem, there may be a solution. For much of the following six chapters, we'll consider how to ameliorate, if not solve, the problems of recession, inflation, and unemployment.

LEARNING OBJECTIVES

After reading this chapter you should be able to:

1. Analyze the business cycle.
2. List and discuss various business cycle theories.
3. Understand how economic forecasting is done.
4. Calculate the unemployment rate.
5. List and identify the types of unemployment.
6. Construct a consumer price index.
7. Name and explain the theories of inflation.
8. Compute the misery index.

Economic Fluctuations

Figure 1 shows the country's economic record since 1960, but before we are in a position to analyze that record, we need a little background information on the business cycle.

Is There a Business Cycle?

Economists and noneconomists have long debated whether there is a business cycle. It all depends on what is meant by the term. If *business cycle* is defined as increases and decreases in business activity of fixed amplitude that occur regularly at fixed intervals, then there is no business cycle. In other words, business activity does have its ups and downs, but some ups are higher than other ups and some downs are lower than others. Furthermore, there is no fixed length to the cycle. For example, as Figure 1 shows, the United States went for nearly the entire decade of the 1960s without a recession but had back-to-back recessions in 1980 and 1981.

Q: Why did God create economists?
A: In order to make weather forecasters look good.

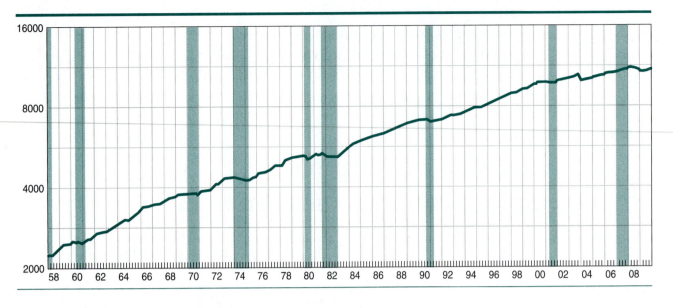

Figure 1
Real GDP 1958–2009, in 2000 dollars
Source: U.S. Dept. of Commerce, in *Business Cycle Indicators,* March 2010.

Upswings don't die of old age.
    —Economics saying

Over a 25-year period—from November 1982 through the end of 2007—we had just two recessions. The economic expansion that began in March 1991 was the longest in history. Then came the Great Recession of 2007–2009.

If we define the business cycle as alternating increases and decreases in the level of business activity of varying amplitude and length, then there is definitely a business cycle. What goes up will eventually come down, and what goes down will rise again.

Cycle Turning Points: Peaks and Troughs

Peaks

Troughs

At the end of economic expansion, business activity reaches a peak. At the peak real GDP, or output, reaches a maximum and then begins to fall. When the economy bottoms out, a trough occurs. From this low point, economic recovery sets in, and eventually most sectors share in the expansion.

Business cycles may be measured from peak to peak, or trough to trough. As we have noted, these cycles vary greatly in amplitude and length. Since the end of World War II, the economy's expansions have been as brief as 16 months or as long as 10 years. The contractions fall into a much narrower range—from 6 to 19 months (see Table 1). And so we may conclude that, like snowflakes, no two business cycles are exactly alike. Most of the 11 post–World War II recessions have been mild and brief. But three of them— 1973–1975, 1981–1982, and 2007–2009—were relatively severe and lengthy.

A recession is when you get socks and underwear for Christmas.

    —Bob Rogers, cartoonist

When does an economic downturn qualify as a recession? In general if real GDP declines for two consecutive quarters, that's a recession. But it's not officially a recession until the Business Cycle Dating Committee of the National Bureau of Economic Research (a private research organization whose members include many prominent economists) says it is. These seven gentlemen take a much more nuanced approach than just waiting for two quarterly declines in real GDP.

The committee uses four crucial barometers to determine if the economy has reached a peak, and will look at other data. The main measure is employment, based on nonfarm payrolls. The second is industrial production. The third is personal income minus government transfer payments, and the fourth is manufacturing and trade revenue. A recession is defined by the National Bureau of Economic Research as "a significant decline in economic activity spread across the economy, lasting more than a few months."

TABLE 1	Post-World War II Recessions*		
Recession dates	Duration (months)	Percentage decline in real GDP	Peak unemployment rate
Nov. 1948–Oct. 1949	11	−1.7%	7.9%
July 1953–May 1954	10	−2.7	5.9
Aug. 1957–Apr. 1958	8	−1.2	7.4
Apr. 1960–Feb. 1961	10	−1.6	6.9
Dec. 1969–Nov. 1970	11	−0.6	5.9
Nov. 1973–Mar. 1975	16	−3.1	8.6
Jan. 1980–July 1980	6	−2.2	7.8
July 1981–Nov. 1982	16	−2.9	10.8
July 1990–Mar. 1991	8	−1.3	6.8
Mar. 2001–Nov. 2001	8	−0.5	6.0
Dec. 2007–June 2009**	19	−3.6	10.1

*The February 1945–October 1945 recession began before the war ended in August 1945.

**As of early June 2010, the Business Cycle Dating committee had not yet determined when the 2007–2009 recession had ended. The author, however, had run out of time because this book would soon be going to press. June 2009 is the author's guess as to when the recession ended.

Since October 2003 the committee began using estimates of monthly GDP. Figure 2 provides another look at the 11 recessions since World War II. As you can see, they vary in length from just 6 months up to 19 months. In fact, except for the 1973–75 and 1981–82 recessions, each lasted less than a year. And since 1982 we've had just three recessions.

The Conventional Three-Phase Business Cycle

We'll begin our analysis with the first peak in Figure 3. The decline that sets in after the peak is called a recession, which ends at the trough. Occasionally there is a false recovery when business activity turns upward for a few months but then turns down again. If the next low point is the lowest since the previous peak, then *that* is the trough.

Recovery begins at the trough, but the expansion must eventually reach the level of the previous peak. Occasionally business activity rises without reaching the previous peak; unless it does, it does not qualify as a recovery.

Once recovery definitely *has* set in, real GDP moves upward until it passes the level of the previous peak, when it enters the third phase of the cycle: prosperity. This phase does not necessarily mean there is full employment, or even that we are approaching full employment. As long as production (real GDP) is higher than it was during the previous peak, we are in the prosperity phase.

Prosperity is the second part of the economic expansion and is accompanied by rising production, falling unemployment, and often accelerating inflation. Sooner or later we reach a peak and the process starts all over—recession, recovery, and prosperity.

Some people say prosperity is when the prices of the things that you are selling are rising, and inflation is when the prices of things that you are buying are rising.

—Anonymous

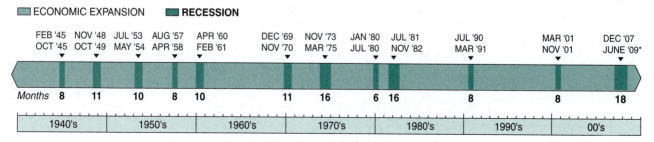

Figure 2
Recessions since 1945

*The Business Cycle Dating Committee had not declared the month in which the 2007–2009 recession ended before this book went to press. The author has gone out on a limb by stating here the recession ended in June 2009.

Source: National Bureau of Economic Research.

Figure 3

Hypothetical Business Cycles

The three-phase business cycle runs from peak to peak, beginning with a recession, which ends at a trough, followed by a recovery. When the level of the previous peak is attained, prosperity sets in, continuing until a new peak is reached.

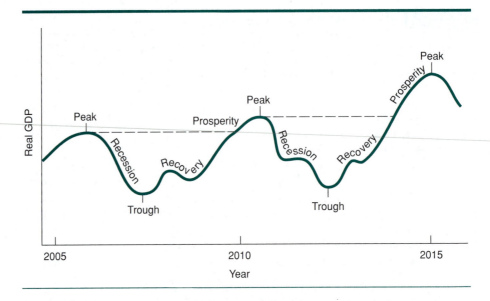

This is the conventional three-phase cycle. Some people talk of a fourth phase: depression. Although depressions are relatively rare—we have not had one since the 1930s—there is always talk about the possibility that a recession could turn into a depression.

What is the dividing line between a recession and a depression? There is no agreed-on or official definition. Obviously, an unemployment rate of 20 percent would be a depression. But would 15 percent qualify?

What is the dividing line between recession and depression?

Perhaps the best definition was proposed by, among others, the late George Meany, longtime president of the AFL-CIO. He said that if his neighbor were unemployed, it would be a recession. If *he* were unemployed, it would be a depression!

Are Economic Fluctuations Becoming Less Extreme?

Are recessions becoming milder and expansions less exuberant? Just a glance at Figure 4 will provide the answer. The answer is "Yes!" After the very brief period of conversion from wartime to peacetime production immediately after World War II, our economy has experienced six decades of relative stability. Compared to the eight decades preceding the war, the recessions have been milder, shorter, and less frequent. While the booms have also been less pronounced, it would be fair to say that our economy has been on a relatively even keel since the late 1940s.

Figure 4

Fluctuations in Real GDP, 1860–2009

Source: Historical Statistics of the United States, Colonial Times to 1970, and U.S. Department of Commerce (www.commerce.gov).

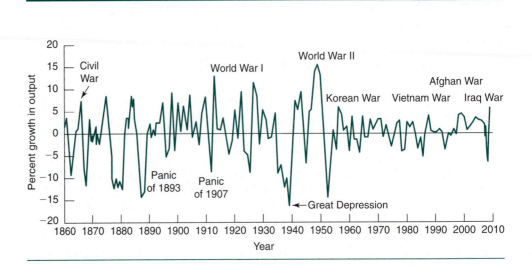

Business Cycle Theories

I have stated that business cycles are inevitable; what goes up must come down, and what goes down must come back up. Although economists generally agree that business cycles exist, they have many competing theories explaining their causes. We'll briefly consider two types of theories: endogenous (internal) and exogenous (external).

Endogenous Theories   These theories place the cause of business cycles within rather than outside the economy. We'll consider first the theory of innovations, which was advanced primarily by Joseph Schumpeter.

    Innovation theory

When a businessman attempts to market a new product such as a car or a television set, at first he will encounter resistance ("Get that contraption off the road—it's frightening my horses!"). But when others perceive the profits being made by the innovator, they will imitate his new product with their own versions, and production will soar. Eventually the market will be saturated—as it was by cars in 1929 and televisions in 1953—and an economic downturn will occur. The downturn continues until a new innovation takes hold and the process begins anew.

A second endogenous theory is the psychological theory of alternating optimism and pessimism, which is really an example of a more general theory of the self-fulfilling prophecy. If businessowners are optimistic, they will invest in plant, equipment, and inventory. This will provide more jobs and result in more consumer spending, justifying still more investment, more jobs, and more spending. But eventually businessowners will turn pessimistic, perhaps because they figure this prosperity can't continue. As pessimism sets in, investment, jobs, and consumer spending all decline, and a recession begins. The contraction continues until businessowners figure that things have gone down so far, there's no place to go but back up again.

    Psychological theory

Still another endogenous theory is that of the inventory cycle. During economic recovery, as sales begin to rise, businessowners are caught short of inventory, so they raise their orders to factories, thus increasing factory employment. As factory workers are called back to work, they begin to spend more money, causing businessowners to order still more from factories. Eventually the owners are able to restock their inventories, so they cut back on factory orders. This causes layoffs, declining retail sales, further cutbacks in factory orders, and a general economic decline. The decline persists until inventory levels are depleted low enough for factory orders to increase once again. While this theory explains most of the recessions from the late 1940s through the late 1960s, the declining role of manufacturing over the last four decades has made our economy less vulnerable to inventory cycles.

    Inventory cycle theory

Yet another endogenous theory of the business cycle is the monetary theory. When inflation threatens, the monetary authorities slow or stop the growth of the money supply. This causes a recession. When they are satisfied that inflation is no longer a problem—or if the recession they have caused has become even more of a concern than inflation—the monetary authorities allow the money supply to grow at a faster rate, which brings about economic recovery. The monetary theory may well explain the 1980 and 1981–82 recessions, when the Federal Reserve stepped heavily on the monetary brakes, as well as our subsequent recoveries, when monetary growth was increased. And then, too, the extreme tightening of credit in the summer of 2008—a by-product of the financial meltdown—contributed substantially to the severity of the 2007–2009 recession. We'll have a lot more to say about monetary policy in Chapter 14.

    Monetary theory

One last theory and we're out of here. The underconsumption or overproduction theory stipulates that our economy periodically produces more goods and services than people want or can afford. A variant is the overinvestment theory, which says that business firms periodically overinvest in plant and equipment.

    Underconsumption theory

Exogenous Theories   Just as endogenous theories place the causes of the business cycle within the economy, exogenous theories place the causes of the business cycle outside the economy.

It has long been said that if the American economy catches a cold, many other economies catch pneumonia. The Chinese, Mexican, and Canadian economies are very dependent on American imports of their goods. If an American recession caused us to

The war theory

cut back sharply on imports, this could cause their own economies to go into recession. Let's call this the external demand shock theory.

Another external theory is the war theory. The production surge caused by preparation for war and war itself causes prosperity, and the letdown after war causes a recession. Our experiences before, during, and after World War II, the Korean War, and the Vietnam War seem to validate this theory.

Although nearly all recessions have endogenous causes, the quadrupling of oil prices by the OPEC cartel in 1973 was the prime cause of the 1973–75 recession. We can call this the price shock theory. In this particular case, the price shock was exogenous.

Perhaps no single explanation, whether exogenous or endogenous, can explain each of the cycles we have experienced. The best we can do, then, is to treat each cycle separately, seeking causes that apply.

Business Cycle Forecasting

Who was the first person to forecast a business cycle? Here are a couple of hints. You can find him in the Book of Genesis and he made his forecast by interpreting the Pharaoh's dreams.

In those dreams the Pharaoh saw seven fat cows and then seven lean cows. Joseph told the king that there would be seven fat years—years of good harvests—followed by seven lean years—years of very poor harvests. And sure enough, there were seven straight good harvests. During this period, some of the grain was set aside. When seven years of poor harvests followed, the Egyptians survived by consuming the grain they had stored.

Business cycle forecasting has come a long way over the intervening millennia, but its objective remains the same—forecasting the turning points of the business cycle.

The most widely used forecasting device is the index of leading economic indicators, which is compiled monthly by the Conference Board, a private business group. This series, which is a weighted average of 10 variables, is a valuable forecasting tool, particularly when used with caution.

The 10 leading indicators consist of variables that "lead" general economic activity by several months. (See the box, "The Ten Leading Economic Indicators.") When the index turns downward, particularly for two or three months in a row, there is a good chance the economy may be heading into a recession. However, as some pundits have put it, the index has predicted 13 of the last 5 recessions. In other words, the index may have turned downward for three or four months a total of 13 times, but in only 5 instances did a recession follow.

If the index moves steadily upward, there is virtually no chance of a recession in the next few months. But when it begins to move downward, watch out! A downturn *may* be at hand.

Similarly, when the index of leading economic indicators moves down steadily for 11 months in a row, as it did from April 1981 through March 1982, we were in a recession, but there was virtually no chance of an upturn until later in the year. And that's exactly what happened.

How well did the index of leading economic indicators predict the 2007–2009 recession? Very well, as it turns out. The index began falling in August 2007, and except for a small increase of 0.2 percent in September, it fell in each of the next 5 months—a very strong prediction of a recession.

If economists could accurately forecast business cycle turning points—the peaks and troughs—then they're doing their job. But in a March 2001 survey, 95 percent of American economists said there would not be a recession—although in fairness, that recession was very mild. Then, in late 2001, that same gang predicted that real GDP would grow by just 0.1 percent in the first quarter of 2002, but it actually grew at an annual rate of 5 percent. It would be fair to say that economic forecasters aren't always right on the money.

Here's a very reliable way to forecast recessions. Just monitor the number of people who are unemployed, which is reported by the U.S. Department of Labor on the first Friday of each month. If that number is rising—*watch out!* And if the number of people who are unemployed rises by at least 13 percent, then a recession has already started, or is about to.

An economist is an expert who will know tomorrow why the things he predicted yesterday didn't happen today.

—Laurence J. Peter,
Peter's Quotations

To err is human; to get paid for it is divine.

—William Freund,
economic consultant

We have two kinds of forecasters: Those who don't know . . . and those who don't know they don't know.

—John Kenneth Galbraith

The Ten Leading Economic Indicators

1. **Average workweek of production workers in manufacturing**   When workers get less overtime, output may be declining.

2. **Average initial weekly claims for state unemployment insurance**   When first-time claims for unemployment insurance benefits rise, employment may be falling.

3. **New orders for consumer goods and materials**   When manufacturers receive smaller orders, they may cut back on output.

4. **Vendor performance (companies receiving slower deliveries from suppliers)**   Better on-time delivery by suppliers means they have a smaller backlog of orders.

5. **New orders for capital goods**   If these orders drop, then businesses are planning less output.

6. **New building permits issued**   This provides a good indication of how much construction activity there will be three or four months from now.

7. **Index of stock prices**   Declining stock prices may reflect declining prospects for corporate sales and profits.

8. **Money supply**   If the Federal Reserve slows the growth of the money supply, interest rates will rise, and it will be harder for businesses and individuals to borrow money.

9. **Spread between rates on 10-year Treasury bonds and Federal funds**   Long-term interest rates are usually much higher than short-term interest rates. Federal reserve policies designed to slow the economy raise short-term interest rates with little effect on long-term rates. So a smaller spread between short-term and long-term interest rates implies a restrictive monetary policy and a decline in output.

10. **Index of consumer expectations**   As consumers grow less confident about the future, they plan to make fewer major purchases.

Suppose that there were 10 million people unemployed one year ago, and now there are at least 11.3 million people out of work. It's almost certain, then, that our economy has already gone into, or is about to go into, a recession. There have been 10 recessions since 1950 in which the annual rise in unemployment was 13 percent or higher. So a 13 percent annual rise is the magic number; it has been the sign of a recession every time.

Let's see how this forecasting tool was used from early 2007 through early 2008, when an economic slowdown was developing, as increasing numbers of economists believed that a recession was imminent, or that one had already begun. Take a look at the numbers in Table 2. Unemployment was trending upward since March 2007.

TABLE 2	Unemployed Persons (in thousands), February 2007–March 2008
Month and Year	**Unemployed**
February 2007	6,837
March 2007	6,738
April 2007	6,829
May 2007	6,863
June 2007	6,997
July 2007	7,137
August 2007	7,133
September 2007	7,246
October 2007	7,291
November 2007	7,181
December 2007	7,655
January 2008	7,576
February 2008	7,381
March 2008	7,815

Source: www.bls.gov
As you'll notice, the number of unemployed began to rise from 6,738,000 in March 2007 to 7,815,000 in March 2008—an increase of 16 percent.

Back in March 2007 our unemployment stood at 6,738,000; by March 2008 it had risen to 7,815,000. In all the recessions since 1950, there was an annual rise in the number of unemployed of at least 13 percent. From March 2007 through March 2008 unemployment rose by 16 percent.

The unemployment rate usually peaks well after a recession ends. The 1990–91 recession ended in March 1991, but the unemployment rate did not peak until June 1992. The 2001 recession ended in November of that year, but the unemployment rate kept climbing for more than a year, finally reaching a peak in June 2003. Although the Great Recession ended in June 2009, unemployment peaked at 15,612,000 in October of that year. However, total employment did not begin to rise until January 2010, so evidently hundreds of thousands of people were either dropping out of the labor force or choosing not to enter it because of their poor employment prospects.

Why doesn't the unemployment rate go down as soon as the recession ends? There are two main reasons. First, it takes many employers at least a few months to become convinced that the economy is actually in recovery. Indeed, unless the sales outlook improves, few employers will want to take on more workers. A second reason for holding off on hiring new workers—or recalling laid-off workers—is that many employers have reduced the hours of their current employees during the recession. Before they add more workers, they may want to increase the hours of their current workers.

Unemployment

The Problem

How can you expect somebody who's warm to understand somebody who's cold?
—Aleksandr Solzhenitsyn,
One Day in the Life of Ivan Denisovich

One of the most devastating experiences a person can have is to be out of work for a prolonged period. Most of us have been unemployed once or twice, but only those who have been unable to find work after looking for six to eight months, or even longer, really know that feeling of hopelessness and self-doubt, not to mention a depressed standard of living.

The Bureau of Labor Statistics (BLS) defines "discouraged workers" as those who have given up looking for work and have simply dropped out of the labor force. Where have all the discouraged workers gone?

Walk around the slums of our great cities. Walk through East St. Louis, Camden (New Jersey), Watts, Bedford-Stuyvesant, and the Hough district of Cleveland. Walk through Flint, Michigan, Gary, Indiana, or central Newark, or through most of our nation's capital. Walk through any of these places in midafternoon and you'll see block after block of teenagers and adults hanging around with nothing to do.

Wanted: a *real* job

Ask them what they want more than anything else. A bigger welfare check? More food stamps? A big-screen TV? Most of them would tell you that all they want is a decent job. Not a dead-end, minimum-wage, low-status, menial job, but a *real* job.

Are these people unemployed? No, these people have given up, dropped out, and are, for all intents and purposes, no longer living in the United States. They may reside here physically, but they are not part of our society.

How the Unemployment Rate Is Computed

The unemployment rate is the percentage of people in the labor force who are willing and able to work, but who are not working.

Where unemployment data comes from

The Bureau of Labor Statistics (BLS) is in charge of compiling statistics on the number of Americans who are employed and unemployed. Where does it get its data? Most people believe it gets statistics from unemployment insurance offices, but if you stop and think about it, just 32 percent of all unemployed Americans were collecting unemployment insurance benefits in October 2008. The BLS gets its unemployment statistics by conducting a random telephone survey of more than 60,000 households.

Read Only if You're Not Sure How to Calculate the Unemployment Rate

In January 2008, 7,576,000 Americans were unemployed and 146,248,000 held jobs. Go ahead and calculate the unemployment rate:

$$\text{Unemployment rate} = \frac{\text{Number of unemployed}}{\text{Labor force}}$$

$$= \frac{7,576,000}{153,824,000}$$

OK, where did we get the 153,824,000? That's the labor force—the number of unemployed (7,576,000) plus the number of employed (146,248,000).

The next step is simple division: 153,824,000 into 7,576,000, which gives us an unemployment rate of 4.9 percent.

Incidentally, a common mistake in this type of problem is to divide 7,576,000 into 153,824,000. Some people insist on dividing the smaller number into the larger number. But the rule we must always follow is to divide the bottom number into the top number.

Essentially, the bureau asks a series of questions: (1) Are you working? If the answer is no, (2) Did you work at all this week—even one day? Anyone who has answered yes to questions 1 or 2 is counted as employed. For those who have not been working the BLS has one more question: (3) Did you look for work during the last month (that is, did you go to an employment agency or union hall, send out a résumé, or go on an interview)? If your answer is yes, you're counted as unemployed. If your answer is no, you're just not counted; you're not part of the labor force. If you want to work but have given up looking for a job, you're a "discouraged worker," but you are not in the labor force and you are not considered "unemployed."

Are people collecting unemployment insurance counted among the unemployed? Yes! To be able to collect unemployment insurance benefits, you must be ready, willing, and able to work. In addition, you are expected to be actively seeking work. As someone who collected unemployment insurance twice for the full 26 weeks, I kept a list of companies where I had looked for a job to prove that I was making an effort to find work.

The labor force consists of the employed and the unemployed. For example, in May 2003, 137,487,000 Americans were employed and 8,998,000 were unemployed. We can compute the unemployment rate by using this formula:

$$\text{Unemployment rate} = \frac{\text{Number of unemployed}}{\text{Labor force}}$$

$$\text{Unemployment rate} = \frac{\text{Number of unemployed}}{\text{Labor force}}$$

How much was the unemployment rate in May 2003? Work it out right here.

Did you get 6.1 percent? The key here is to figure out how many people are in the labor force. Add the employed (137,487,000) and the unemployed (8,998,000), and you'll get a labor force of 146,485,000. So in May 2003 the official unemployment rate was 6.1 percent. (If you need more practice, see the accompanying Extra Help box.)

As you can see from the unemployment rates in Table 3, teenagers had, by far, the highest unemployment rate. The overall unemployment rate was 9.5 for whites and 15.7 for blacks. It's been said that when there's a recession for whites, it's a depression for blacks. If you traced the unemployment rates for blacks and whites over the last six decades, you would find that the rate for blacks was consistently double the rate for whites.

Remember how you were always being urged to stay in school? As you'll notice, high school drop-outs were more than three times as likely to be unemployed as college graduates. It really does pay to stay in school.

When you lose your job, the unemployment rate is not 5.2 percent; it's 100 percent.
—Thomas Friedman

TABLE 3	Unemployment Rate for Selected Groups of American Workers, October 2009

	Unemployment rates
All workers	10.1
Teenagers	27.6
White	9.5
Black or African American	15.7
Hispanic or Latino ethnicity	13.1
Asian	7.5
Education level	
Less than high school	15.5
High school	11.2
Some college	9.0
Bachelor's or higher	4.7

*Teenagers and African Americans have much higher unemployment rates than the average for all workers.

Source: Bureau of Labor Statistics: http://www.bls.gov/ces/.

Teenagers, and young workers in general, tend to have relatively high unemployment rates. The "Comparative Unemployment Rates" box shows how the unemployment rates of young workers varied in major industrial nations around the world.

on the web

On the first Friday morning of each month the U.S. Department of Labor reports the previous month's unemployment rate, and the change in the number of people employed and unemployed from the previous month. Go to www.bls.gov.

How Accurate Is the Unemployment Rate?

When the Bureau of Labor Statistics announced that the unemployment rate dipped from 9.5 percent in June of 2009 to 9.4 percent in July, one might have thought that the BLS was so accurate that it can calculate our unemployment rate to within one-tenth of a percent of its actual rate. But many liberal economists believe the actual unemployment rate is substantially *higher* than the official rate, while many conservative economists believe the actual rate is substantially *lower*. Obviously they can't *both* be right.

The liberal economists (does anyone still call herself a "liberal"?) would say that the true rate of unemployment is 2 or 3 percent higher because we should count all the jobless people who are ready, willing, and able to work. Let's ask about the 3 or 4 million people who are not working but are not officially unemployed. If we asked the BLS, it would tell us that they are discouraged workers.

The liberals have a couple of additional bones to pick with the BLS definition. A person who worked one day in the last month is counted as employed. Also, someone who works part-time but wants to work full-time is counted as employed. The liberals ask, "Doesn't this sort of measurement overstate the number of employed?" When you put it all together, they maintain, the BLS is overstating employment and understating unemployment. The result is an unemployment rate that is perhaps a couple of points too low.

That's the liberal view. As you would expect, the conservatives say the official unemployment rate *over*estimates the true rate of unemployment. Using the BLS definition of an unemployed person—someone who has not worked this month and who has actively sought work—the conservative focuses on those who are required to report to state employment or other government employment offices to remain eligible for unemployment insurance, welfare, or food stamps. Is this, asks the conservative, really an effort to look for work, or are these guys just going through the motions?

The liberals say the true unemployment rate is higher than the official rate.

Who are the discouraged workers?

The conservatives say the true unemployment rate is lower than the official rate.

Comparative Unemployment Rates

Among the hardest hit by the worldwide recession of 2007–2009 have been workers under 25 years of age. Throughout the industrialized world—in Asia, in Europe, and in North America—tens of millions of these workers have been unable to find jobs. In Figure A we see that as high as our unemployment rate has been for those under 25—it was much higher in Spain, Italy, and France.

Between 2007 and 2009 the unemployment rate for under-25-year-olds nearly doubled in Spain and the United States, two nations whose economies were especially hard hit by the Great Recession.

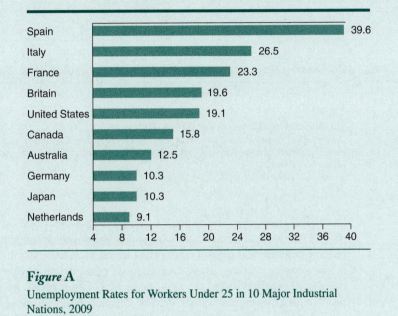

Figure A
Unemployment Rates for Workers Under 25 in 10 Major Industrial Nations, 2009
Sources: OECD; *The New York Times,* April 17, 2010 p. B3.

Some conservatives also cite the huge numbers of Americans—as well as illegal immigrants—working in the underground economy (see the section on this near the end of the previous chapter). There are a few million people out there working as hair dressers, livery cab operators, unlicensed plumbers, carpenters, electricians, and auto mechanics, as well as street peddlers, day laborers, and sewing machine operators in illegal garment sweat shops. All these people are employed off the books, do not report their income, and are not counted as employed by the Bureau of Labor Statistics.

The bottom line, according to the conservatives, is that perhaps a couple of million of the "officially" unemployed are not really looking for work. The liberal bottom line is that at least a couple of million people out there want to work but aren't being counted.

For decades the unemployment rate for blacks has been double that of whites. During recessions, the black unemployment rate is rarely below 10 percent. They also make up a disproportionate share of discouraged workers.

Two major changes have pushed down the unemployment rate—the work requirements under the 1996 Welfare Reform Act and the more than quadrupling of the U.S. prison population since 1980.

Over 2 million Americans are currently occupying cells in federal, state, or local prisons. The average convict has a much lower IQ and is considerably less educated than the average American. If these folks were not imprisoned, would they be legitimately employed? Most would not be. So keeping these people incarcerated has probably lowered our unemployment rate by about one percent.

The welfare work requirements have moved perhaps two million single mothers into low-wage jobs. Although few of these women previously had been in the labor force, they have been added to the ranks of the officially employed.

Figure 5

The Annual Unemployment Rate, 1948–2009

Unemployment trended upward between 1969 and 1982 and trended downward after that. After going above 10 percent in late 2009, it is very unlikely that our unemployment will get down again to 5 percent before mid-decade.

Source: Economic Report of the President, 2010.

Illegal immigrants are about 5 percent of our labor force, most of whom are working off the books for employers who appreciate cheap, compliant labor free of employment regulations and payroll taxes. They make up at least one in four farm workers, one in six cleaning workers, about one in seven construction workers, and perhaps nine of every ten landscapers. And then too, many illegal immigrants are self-employed as street peddlers, handymen, car service drivers, or small business owners, all part of the underground economy. Were all these people counted as employed, the unemployment rate would be much lower.

In recent years the children of the baby boomers have been entering the labor force. Young adults tend to have a relatively high unemployment rate because, like homemakers returning to work, they need time to find a job. Because so many live at home or receive help from their parents, there is less pressure to take the first job that comes along. Then, they tend to drift from job to job, until, like Goldilocks, they find a position that is "just right."

Clearly it would go down. The number of unemployed would remain the same, the number of employed would go up, the labor force would go up, so the unemployment rate would go down.

The next time someone asks you if the official unemployment rate is an accurate measure of unemployment, just tell them that even economists can't agree on whether it's too high, too low, or just right.

Figure 5 is a record of the official unemployment rate from 1948 through 2009. You'll notice a marked upward trend from the late 1960s through the early 1980s. But the trend seems to have reversed since then, heading back down again. It's too soon to tell whether we are witnessing the beginning of an upward trend in the unemployment rate. Is it just a by-product of the Great Recession, or will we see years of relatively high unemployment? We may not know for sure until the middle of this decade.

The rate of unemployment is 100 percent if it's you who is unemployed.

—David L. Kurtz

Types of Unemployment

Frictional Unemployment   Our economy is far from a well-tuned, efficient, smoothly functioning machine. When a job opening occurs somewhere, it is rarely filled instantaneously, even when there is someone ready, willing, and able to fill it. In a word, our economy has a certain degree of friction.

The frictionally unemployed are people who are between jobs or just entering or reentering the labor market. Because our system of filling jobs—newspaper classified ads, employment agencies, corporate recruiters, executive headhunters, help-wanted signs, Internet postings, and word of mouth—is imperfect, usually weeks or months pass before positions are filled.

At any given time, about 2 or 3 percent of the labor force is frictionally unemployed. Students who are looking for their first full-time jobs, homemakers reentering the labor market after 5, 10, or 20 years, and servicemen and -women who have recently been discharged by the armed forces are frictionally unemployed until they find jobs. In addition, there are those who leave their jobs voluntarily, perhaps so they can spend all their time looking for better jobs. Maybe they're looking in another part of the country. Add to these the people who get fired or quit. These people, too, are between jobs, or frictionally unemployed.

About 2 to 3 percent of our labor force is always frictionally unemployed.

When people change jobs, they may have time between jobs, or they may leave one job on a Friday and start a new one on Monday. Officials at the Labor Department estimate that 40 percent of the labor force, or roughly 60 million workers, change jobs within a year. But even during 2008, some 57 million people found new jobs. Most had left a job recently—by choice or not—but successfully found a new one in the same industry.

Structural Unemployment   Former U.S. Attorney General Robert F. Kennedy[1] once asked, "Have you ever told a coal miner in West Virginia or Kentucky that what he needs is individual initiative to go out and get a job where there isn't any?" A person who is out of work for a relatively long period of time, say, a couple of years, is structurally unemployed. The economy does not have any use for this person. The steelworker in Youngstown, Ohio, the autoworker from Flint, Michigan, and the coal miner from Kentucky are no longer needed because the local steel mills, auto plants, and coal mines have closed. And the skills of clerical workers, typists, and inventory control clerks who once staffed corporate offices have been made obsolete by computer systems. Add to these the people whose companies have gone out of business or whose jobs have been exported to low-wage countries and you've got another 2 to 3 percent of the labor force structurally unemployed.

About 2 to 3 percent of our labor force is always structurally unemployed.

Ours is a dynamic economy, and the opportunities for retraining and subsequent employment *do* exist. But the prospects for a 50- or 60-year-old worker embarking on a second career are not auspicious. To compound the problem, most of the structurally unemployed reside in the Rust Belt of the East and Midwest, while most of the new career opportunities are in the Sun Belt and in several states on the East and West coasts.

One out of five adult Americans is functionally illiterate. These people cannot read, write, or do simple numerical computations. In a workplace that increasingly demands these minimal skills, more and more of these people are finding themselves virtually shut out of the labor force. Each year our educational system turns out 1 million more functional illiterates, most of whom will face long periods of structural unemployment. Many of these young adults come from very poor families where no one has held a job. They have no idea of how to dress for a job interview, what to say, or even the need to show up on time. Unless these people are given some kind of vocational training and provided with entry-level jobs, they will be out of work for most of their lives.

The "unemployables"

What if someone were "between jobs" for six months, or a year, or even two years? When someone is out of work for a long period of time, he or she is classified as "structurally unemployed." But where do we draw the line between frictional and structural unemployment? The answer is that we don't. There *is* no clear dividing line.

Cyclical Unemployment   As you know, our economy certainly has its ups and downs, a set of fluctuations known as business cycles. During a recession, the unemployment rate sometimes rises to 8, 9, or even 10 percent. During the Great Depression, the "official" unemployment rate hit 25 percent, which definitely understated the true unemployment picture.

Fluctuations in our unemployment rate are due to cyclical unemployment.

---

[1]Robert Kennedy also served as a U.S. senator from 1965 to 1968 and was the brother of President John F. Kennedy.

If we allow for a certain amount of frictional and structural unemployment, anything above the sum of these two would be cyclical unemployment. Let's say that the sum of frictional and structural unemployment is 5 percent. If the actual rate of unemployment is 7.7 percent, then the cyclical rate is 2.7 percent.

If we take a 5 percent unemployment rate as our working definition of full employment, anything above 5 percent would be cyclical unemployment. You may wonder whether 5 percent is a reasonable level for full employment. Surely we can never expect our unemployment rate to reach zero, since we'll always have some frictionally and structurally unemployed people. Our unemployment rate did get down to 1.2 percent in 1944, but as they said back then, "There's a war going on." With 12 million men in the armed forces and the economy going full-steam ahead, employers were desperate for help, and anyone who could walk and spell his or her name had no trouble finding a job.

There are liberal economists who insist that we could realistically get the unemployment rate down to 4 percent, while there are conservative economists who consider 6 percent the lowest attainable rate. As I've said before, we'll split the difference and call 5 percent full employment.

Seasonal Unemployment   At any given time a couple of hundred thousand people may be out of work because this is their "slow season." The slack seasons in the ladies' garment industry are in the spring and fall after those seasons' new fashions have been shipped to the stores. The tourist season is slow all summer in Florida, and elsewhere some employees at Carvels and Dairy Queen are laid off in the winter. My aunt Betty, who worked in the garment industry for nearly 60 years, turned her seasonal unemployment to her advantage by arranging to get laid off each year in early November, registering for unemployment insurance benefits, and then taking off for Florida.

Seasonal unemployment is not nearly as large as frictional, structural, or cyclical unemployment, so it hasn't figured in our discussion of total unemployment. But if it weren't mentioned here, someone would be sure to ask why it wasn't included.

Natural Unemployment Rate

As the unemployment rate falls, and it becomes increasingly difficult to find employees, employers will bid up wage rates, pushing up the rate of inflation. Once the unemployment rate falls below its natural rate, which most economists estimate to be 5 or 6 percent, then inflationary wage pressure emerges.

Our unemployment rate fell below 6 percent in 1994, below 5 percent in 1997, and averaged just 4 percent in 2000 while the rate of inflation stayed below 4 percent. Could it be that the natural rate of unemployment was falling? There are at least five reasons to support this view.

First, the natural unemployment rate tends to fall when the proportion of youths in the labor force is shrinking. The baby boom generation—born between 1946 and 1964—had all entered the labor force by the mid-1980s, at which point the youth contingent began to shrink. However, now that *their* children have now been entering the labor force, this may have tended to push up the natural rate of unemployment.

A second factor is the quadrupling of the adult population in prison since 1980—with 2.3 percent of the male labor force behind bars at last count. Assuming a fair number of these inmates would be counted as unemployed if they weren't locked up, this too has pushed down our natural unemployment rate.

Worker insecurity, based on massive corporate downsizing and plant closings, as well as the offshoring of millions of manufacturing jobs, has also tended to reduce the natural unemployment rate. Rather than risk the ire of their employers, many workers have been willing to accept small pay increases—and sometimes pay reductions.

Next, there is the rapid growth of the temporary-help industry, whose share of employment has jumped from 0.5 percent in the early 1980s, to 2.2 percent today. Not only do many people who would otherwise be unemployed now work as temps as they look for permanent jobs, but the availability of temp agencies allows employers to fill vacancies more easily and, in some cases, to minimize wage pressures by keeping the new hires on temp payrolls.

Austan Goolsbee, who served as Barack Obama's economic advisor during his presidential campaign, believes that the unemployment rate has declined over the last two decades as millions of people who might have otherwise been classified as unemployed were able to collect Social Security disability payments. As Congress began loosening the standards to qualify for these payments in the late 1980s, these millions of Americans, rather than being "unemployed," were now considered "not in the labor force."

Finally, the labor force has been expanding rapidly. The Census Bureau estimates more than 6 million illegal immigrants are working here today. In addition, many new workers are unmarried mothers with at least one child younger than three years old. The percentage of these women now in the labor force rose to 67 percent in 2008 from only 54 percent in 1995. Most astonishing is that in 2009, for the first time in our nation's history, the number of women in the labor force surpassed the number of men.

Whether or not you're currently looking for work, it makes sense to keep your résumé updated. Increasingly the Internet is becoming a prime meeting place for job seekers and prospective employers.

Here are three job sites you can find on the Web:
America's Job Bank—www.jobbanking.org
The Monster Board—www.monster.com
Yahoo! Classifieds—www.hotjobs.yahoo.com

Inflation

> Inflation is like toothpaste. Once it is out of the tube, it is hard to get it back in again.
>
> –Karl Otto Pohl,
> former president of the German Bundesbank–

Defining Inflation

Inflation is not all that bad. After all, it enables us to live in a more expensive neighborhood without having to move.

—Anonymous

What exactly *is* inflation? It is a broadly based rise in the price level. *Generally, we consider inflation a sustained rise in the average price level over a period of years.* In our own lifetimes, we have known little *but* inflation.

If the rate of inflation had been 4 percent, would that mean the price of every good and service went up by 4 percent? Of course not! The prices of some things went up by much more than 4 percent, and the prices of others rose by less than 4 percent. The prices of some things may not have changed. And when the overall price level is rising, the prices of some goods and services are actually going down. Can you think of any examples? In the 1970s and 1980s color TV prices came way down. Average prices of 30-inch LCD TVs tumbled from more than $5,000 in 2000 to under $800 today. The prices of cell phones, fax machines, laser printers, DVD players, iPods, contact lenses, microwave ovens, digital cameras, and graphing calculators have also fallen substantially.

U.S. inflation has been persistent since World War II, particularly in the 1970s when, for some of the decade, it was at double-digit proportions. But since 1990, our rate of inflation has remained below 4 percent.

Ask the man on the street what inflation is and he'll tell you that everything costs more. To be more precise, the U.S. Department of Labor's Bureau of Labor Statistics compiles an average of all items that consumers buy—the prices of cars, gasoline, appliances, haircuts, TVs, contact lenses, dresses, steaks, medical services, plane tickets, motel rooms, and Big Macs—and figures out how much it costs the average family to live. Every month several hundred BLS employees around the country check the cost of 80,000 items—ranging from

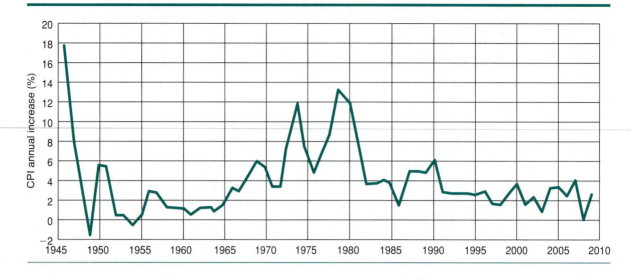

Figure 6

Annual Percentage Change in Consumer Price Index, 1946–2009
Since World War II we have had two periods of price stability—from 1952 through 1965, and from 1991 to the present.
Source: Economic Report of the President, 2010.

airline tickets to cat food. Let's say that in January 2008 it cost the Jones family $20,000 to maintain a certain standard of living. If it cost the Joneses $22,000 to buy the same items in January 2011, we would say that the cost of living went up 10 percent.

The consumer price index (CPI), which measures changes in our cost of living, is reported near the middle of every month by the Bureau of Labor Statistics. For example, you'll hear on the radio, "There was some good news today on the inflation front. Consumer prices rose just two-tenths of 1 percent last month, and the consumer price index now stands at 136.4." Before you have a chance to digest this information, the announcer is doing sports and weather.

The consumer price index is based on what it costs an average family to live.

Figure 6 provides a record of our year-to-year changes in the Consumer Price Index since the end of World War II. Although we suffered serious bouts of inflation, most recently from the late 1960s through the early 1980s, since the early 1990s, the inflation rate has generally stayed below 4 percent.

If our consumer price index is 136.4, what does that tell us? Unless you're familiar with the consumer price index, how it's constructed, and what it measures, you won't be able to fully appreciate the significance of that number. So let's see exactly what this index is all about.

The number 100 is a magic number. It lends itself well to calculating percentage changes. Suppose, for example, that we want to find out by what percentage prices rose since the base year for the consumer price index. The base year is set at 100. If the CPI were 136.4 today, by what percentage did prices rise since the base year?

They rose by 36.4 percent. What I did was subtract 100 from 136.4. Try this one: If the CPI is now 201.6, by what percentage did prices rise since the base year? Work it out right here:

They rose by 101.6 percent (201.6 − 100). Now you're getting it—I hope. You'll notice that we take the CPI in the current year and subtract the CPI in the base year, which is always 100.

Finding Percentage Changes in the Price Level

Here's a chance to work out a few problems: Find the percentage change in price since the base year if the CPI is now 94.7.

Now try *this* one: If the CPI rises from 129.6 in 2029 to 158.3 in 2045, find the percentage increase in the CPI.

The answer is −5.3 percent. The price level declined (94.7 − 100 = −5.3). By what percentage did prices rise since the base year if the CPI is now 485.2?

Solution:

Percent increase in CPI

$$= \frac{(\text{CPI in current year} - \text{CPI in previous year})}{\text{CPI in previous year}} \times 100$$

$$= \frac{(158.3 - 129.6)}{129.6} \times 100 = \frac{28.7}{129.6} \times 100 = 22.1\%$$

They rose by 385.2 percent (485.2 − 100 = 385.2). So when you're figuring out the percentage change in prices since the base year, all you have to do is subtract 100 from the current CPI.

No one would complain if the cost of living rose 2 or 3 percent a year, but during the 10-year period from 1972 to 1982 the consumer price index rose from 125.3 to 289.1. By what percentage did the cost of living rise? Figure it out here:

Solution:

$$\text{Percent increase in CPI} = \frac{(\text{CPI in current year} - \text{CPI in previous year})}{\text{CPI in previous year}} \times 100$$

$$= \frac{(289.1 - 125.3)}{125.3} \times 100 = \frac{163.8}{125.3} \times 100 = 130.7\%$$

The cost of living rose by 130.7 percent, so it cost the typical American family more than twice as much to live in 1982 as it did just 10 years earlier.

That problem was so much fun, let's try one more. If the CPI rose from 114.3 in 2013 to 126.1 in 2020, by what percent did the CPI rise?

Solution:

$$\text{Percent increase in CPI} = \frac{(\text{CPI in current year} - \text{CPI in previous year})}{\text{CPI in previous year}} \times 100$$

$$= \frac{(126.1 - 114.3)}{114.3} \times 100 = \frac{11.8}{114.3} \times 100 = 10.3\%$$

If you had any trouble with these problems, then you can use some help calculating percentage changes. You'll find that help in the box, "Finding Percentage Changes in the Price Level."

Deflation and Disinflation

Deflation   *Deflation is a broadly based decline in the price level, not for just a month or two but for a period of years.* The last deflation the United States had was from 1929 to 1933, when prices fell 50 percent. Significantly, that deflation was accompanied by the Great Depression.

Until the inflationary recessions of the 1970s, business downturns were called deflations, for they were invariably accompanied by price declines. As much as business owners dislike inflation, particularly that of double-digit proportions, they hate deflation a lot more.

Suppose your store sells air conditioners, refrigerators, and other appliances. You place orders with manufacturers a few months before delivery and generally hold two months' worth of inventory in your warehouse. If there is a 2 or 3 percent rate of deflation, instead of the 2 or 3 percent rate of inflation you had been counting on, you'll probably have to charge 2 or 3 percent less than you had been planning to charge. You paid your suppliers more than you should have, and you'll collect less from your customers than you had expected to. So even a little deflation can be very bad news to business firms, especially retailers.

But deflation is great news to consumers, because it means that they'll be paying lower prices. If you happen to have a lot of money—in the form of currency or bank deposits—you will be sitting pretty, because each dollar that you hold will be going up in value. And if you're living on a fixed income, you'll be able to buy more for your money.

Deflation may sound like a very appealing state of affairs. Every time we visit supermarkets, department stores, and clothing shops, we find that prices have been reduced again and again. Doctors, lawyers, personal trainers, and beauticians charge us less and less. The only ones hurting are the business owners. But that's exactly why deflation is not such a wonderful thing.

Business owners would be losing money, cutting the wages of their employees, eventually laying them off, and even going out of business. Each wave of price and wage decreases would set off another wave of decreases, and soon we would be caught in a deflationary spiral. As prices drop, customers would delay their purchases, expecting further price cuts. As more and more businesses shut their doors and the unemployment rolls grow larger, we would end up with a depression like the one we suffered in the 1930s. In fact, well into the 1950s, many people still referred to the Great Depression as "the deflation."

Deflation has not been a concern in the United States since the 1930s, but it has been a problem in Japan where consumer prices fell virtually every month between April 1998 and the end of 2005. Deflation chipped away at asset values, increasing credit risks, pinching wages and salaries, and preventing the economy from generating any sustained growth after a decade of stagnation. Stocks were trading at the same prices in 2005 as they had been in the mid-1980s, and real estate prices had fallen for 10 consecutive years. Consumer prices were dropping at an annual rate of about 3 percent in 2003, and the Japanese economy was running the risk of getting caught in a deflationary spiral similar to the Great Depression when prices and wages fell sharply throughout the world. But by 2005, at long last, Japan finally had recovered.

Can deflation happen again in the United States? Remember, deflation is a *broad* decline in the price level. So while the prices of some goods and services are going up—gasoline, health care, and college tuition are prime examples—keep in mind that the prices of many other goods and services have been falling—personal computers, TVs, toys, long-distance phone calls, and audio equipment. *Will* there be deflation in our immediate future? It seems very unlikely. But it *can* happen here.

Disinflation   Immediately after World War II we had a great deal of inflation. But when recessions occurred, inflation would disappear and prices actually declined slightly. By the late 1950s, even though the rate of inflation was quite moderate, recessions no longer eliminated rising prices. They continued to rise, albeit at a slower rate. This gave us our definition of disinflation: *Disinflation occurs when the rate of inflation declines.*

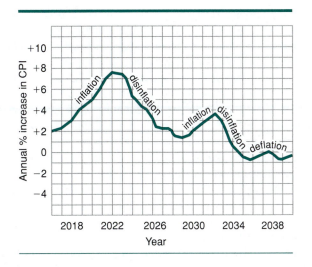

Figure 7
Hypothetical Annual Rate of
Increase of CPI, 2016–2040
Notice that after 2034 there was
deflation because the annual
percentage increase in the
CPI was 0.

For example, during the recession of 1981–82, the rate of inflation fell from about 12 percent to about 4 percent. And again, the rate of inflation fell from 4.1 percent in 2007 to just 0.1 percent in 2008. In fact, disinflation occurred during virtually every recession since World War II (see Figure 6).

In Figure 7 we've constructed a hypothetical graph illustrating inflations, disinflation, and deflation. Please observe that disinflation is a decline in the rate of inflation. But when there is a *decline* in the price level, as there is after 2034, that's *deflation*.

The Post–World War II History of Inflation

During every major war in U.S. history, prices rose sharply. Each war was accompanied by a combination of money supply increases and large budget deficits.

In 1945, as World War II ended, a tremendous pent-up demand for consumer goods was unleashed as price and wage controls were abolished. Consumer prices rose sharply. Too many dollars were chasing too few goods. Just as the inflation was being brought under control, the Korean War broke out. This brought on another wave of consumer spending and price increases.

President Dwight David Eisenhower took office in 1953, pledging to end the war in Korea and the inflation at home. It took him only a couple of months to end the war, but it wasn't until 1960, three recessions later, that inflation was finally brought under control. Until 1965, consumer prices rose at an annual rate of only 1 percent (see again Figure 6). Then the Vietnam War, accompanied by huge federal budget deficits, rekindled another inflationary fire.

By this time most Americans had become conditioned to rising prices; they seemed inevitable. When prices have been rising for some time, it is reasonable to assume they will keep rising. So what did we do? We ran out to buy still more goods and services before prices rose still further. And when businessowners saw that demand for their products was high, they were encouraged to raise *their* prices.

In 1971, in an effort to combat an escalating rate of inflation, President Richard Nixon imposed wage and price controls. But Nixon's wage and price freeze didn't really take, perhaps because it was applied only halfheartedly. When OPEC quadrupled oil prices in the fall of 1973, inflation accelerated (see Figure 6). The deep recession that followed did damp down the inflation, but in the late 1970s it returned with renewed vigor. Not until the back-to-back recessions of 1980 and 1981–82 was the rate of inflation finally brought down to acceptable levels.

In the 1970s we did get to add a new word to our vocabulary—*stagflation*—which is a contraction of the words *stagnation* and *inflation*. The new word got a great deal of use during the recessions of 1973–75, 1980, and 1981–82, when we experienced the worst of both worlds: declining output *and* inflation.

At its present cost, life is worth about 30 cents on the dollar.
—Don Herold

Hobson's choice: You lose either way—more inflation or a possible recession.

So far I haven't heard of anybody who wants to stop buying on account of the cost.
—Frank McKinney Hubbard

Since 1992, the inflation rate has stayed at or below 3 percent nearly every year. What accounts for this? Five factors come to mind. First is the rising tide of imported goods. When these imports compete with goods made in America, the competition drives down prices. Imported goods reduce our inflation rate by 1 or 2 percent.

A second factor is the rise of huge discounters, like Walmart, Toys 'R' Us, Staples, and Price-Costco. In 2009, discount stores sold 50 percent of all general merchandise, up from 37 percent just 19 years earlier. Discounters work closely with suppliers to minimize distribution costs, and these savings are largely passed on to consumers as lower prices.

A third cause of our low rate of inflation is the advent of e-commerce, which has added a new layer of competition. Nearly every item that can be purchased at a traditional retail store is available on the Web, and for cost-conscious consumers, this provides unparalleled leverage, because buyers can comparison-shop across dozens of stores at the click of a mouse. Books, for example, cost about 20 percent less online than in bookstores. And when content can be delivered digitally—for example, songs, e-books and movies—prices can be reduced still further. Did someone mention Amazon Kindle and Apple iPad? For sellers, savings come via lower real estate and rental costs, as well as reduced outlays for advertising, inventory, and transportation—items that ordinarily account for some 40 percent of the consumer price of goods.

A fourth cause is the accelerating pace of technological advance. When color TV appeared in 1956, it took two decades before the price dropped in half. It took a decade for VCR prices to halve. In contrast, prices for DVD players, launched in 1997 for $700, halved in about two years, and now they sell for under $50.

Finally, the efforts of business firms to become leaner and meaner have been paying off in rising efficiency and productivity. Wage increases have been held down, millions of workers have been discharged, and, again, savings have been passed on to consumers. Are the bad old inflationary days of the 1970s and early 1980s behind us, or will inflation come roaring back again? My own guess is that another round of inflation is highly unlikely until at least mid-decade.

The Construction of the Consumer Price Index

To find the CPI in the current year, divide the cost of living in the current year by the cost of living in the base year and multiply by 100.

The most important measure of inflation is the consumer price index. Now we'll see how the Bureau of Labor Statistics goes about constructing this index.

First a base year is picked. In early 1998 we used the period 1982–84 as our base, setting the average price level of those years equal to 100. By January 2010 the CPI stood at 217.6, which meant, of course, that the price level had risen 117.6 percent since 1982–84. So the CPI measured the rise in the cost of living from the base years to January 2010.[2]

If you're *really* curious about the mechanics of how the CPI is constructed, it's worked out in the box, "Construction of the Consumer Price Index." Of course, this is a very simplified version containing just six items. The Bureau of Labor Statistics compiles a market basket of 80,000 goods and services that the typical urban family buys in 1987. Assuming they buy that same market basket of goods and services in 1995, the BLS figures out how much that family would have had to spend. It then comes up with an index number for 1995. In fact, it does this every month.

The consumer price index tends to overstate the actual rate of inflation by failing to account completely for gains in the quality of the goods and services that people buy as well as improvements in technology. Back in 1987, when there were personal computers in just 18 percent of all American households, you would have paid a lot more and gotten a lot less computing power than you would today. But the CPI utterly fails to take into account such improvements in product quality. In the accompanying

---

[2]The Bureau of Labor Statistics overhauls the CPI periodically, doing a survey of some 10,000 families to find out what they're buying and how much they're paying.

Construction of the Consumer Price Index

We're going to calculate how much it cost a family to live in March 1987 and in March 1995. In the tables below showing hypothetical costs of living for these months, Table A has a month's expenditures for 1987, the base year. To find these expenditures, we multiply quantity purchased by price. Then, adding up the money spent on each item, we find the total amount of money spent in March 1987.

Now we'll compare that amount with the amount spent in March 1995, which is shown in Table B.* What happened, then, was that the family spent $848 for these six items in 1987 and $994 for these same items in 1995. Obviously, their cost of living went up. But by how much?

To find out, we'll construct a consumer price index. To do this, divide the cost of living in the base year, 1987, into the cost of living in the current year, 1995. After you've done that multiply your answer by 100 to convert it into an index number.

Do your work in the space provided and then check it with the calculations shown.

$$994/848 = 1.172$$
$$1.172 \times 100 = 117.2$$

That's our consumer price index for 1995. You'll notice that we've carried it to one decimal place, which is exactly how the Bureau of Labor Statistics does it and how you'll find it listed in the newspaper.

One last question. By what percentage did prices rise between 1987 and 1995? The envelope please. Prices rose by 17.2 percent (117.2 − 100).

If you're still having trouble figuring out percentage changes, reread the box titled, "Finding Percentage Changes in the Price Level," a little earlier in this chapter.

Table A   March 1987

Item	Quantity	Price	Quantity × Price
Loaf of bread	10	.70	7.00
Quart of milk	15	.60	9.00
Pair of jeans	2	28.00	46.00
New car	0.02	7800.00	156.00
Mortgage payment	1	590.00	590.00
Movie admission	8	5.00	40.00
Total			848.00

Table B   March 1995

Item	Quantity	Price	Quantity × Price
Loaf of bread	10	.90	9.00
Quart of milk	15	.80	12.00
Pair of jeans	2	31.00	62.00
New car	0.02	9000.00	180.00
Mortgage payment	1	675.00	675.00
Movie admission	8	7.00	56.00
Total			994.00

*We're assuming family has not altered its consumption pattern.

box, we consider an alternate cost of living measure. (See "The Declining *Real* Cost of Living.")

Suppose that in 2012 the CPI is recalculated so that the rate of inflation is adjusted downward by 1 percent. Because Social Security benefits are raised by the same percent that the CPI rises, the average Social Security recipient would get about $120 less that year. In Chapter 12 we'll look at the effects of an adjustment in the CPI on government spending and tax receipts.

Anticipated and Unanticipated Inflation: Who Is Hurt by Inflation and Who Is Helped?

Traditionally, inflation has hurt creditors and helped debtors. Throughout our history, the farmers have been debtors. During times of deflation or stable prices, the farmers' anguished cries were heard loud and clear all the way to Washington; but during times of inflation, there was scarcely a peep out of them.

Why farmers like inflation

The Declining Real Cost of Living

The CPI measures the cost of living in money terms. "The real cost of living," say W. Michael Cox and Richard Alm, "isn't measured in dollars and cents, but in the hours and minutes we must work to live."* For example, back in 1916, you would have needed to work 3,162 hours to buy a refrigerator, 333 hours in 1958, and just 68 hours in 1997. And the 1997 model could do a lot more tricks. In 1919 you would have worked 80 minutes to buy a dozen eggs, but by 1997 you would have worked just 5 minutes.

Of course not everything is cheaper, when measured in hours worked. Take private college tuition. Today it costs about 1500 hours of work; in the mid-1960s, it cost just 500 hours of work. But if you're a Texan who happens to attend the University of Texas, the cost today of just over 200 hours' work is only a bit higher than it was in the mid-1930s.

*W. Michael Cox and Richard Alm, "Time Well Spent," *1997 Annual Report of the Federal Reserve Bank of Dallas.*

Creditors have better memories than debtors.

—James Howell, 1659

It is easy to see why. Suppose a farmer borrows $100, which he agrees to repay in one year along with 4 percent interest ($4). In one year he pays back $104. But what if, during the year, prices double? The money he pays back is worth half as much as the money he borrowed.

Let's say that when the farmer borrowed the money, wheat was selling at $2 a bushel. He would have been able to buy 50 bushels of wheat ($100/$2). But farmers don't buy wheat; they sell it. So one year later, this farmer harvests his wheat and pays back the loan. If the price level doubles, assume the price of wheat doubles. How much wheat would the farmer need to sell at $4 a bushel to pay off the $104 he owes? He would need to sell only 26 bushels ($104/$4).

This farmer, who is a debtor, benefits magnificently from unanticipated inflation because he has borrowed money worth some 50 bushels of wheat and pays back his loan—with interest—in money worth only 26 bushels of wheat. Debtors, in general, gain from unanticipated inflation because they repay their loans in inflated dollars.

The issuers may have, and in the case of government paper, always have, a direct interest in lowering the value of the currency, because it is the medium in which their own debts are computed.

—John Stuart Mill

Just as obviously, those hurt by unanticipated inflation are people who lend out the money—the creditors. We generally think of creditors as banks, but banks are really financial middlemen. The ultimate creditors, or lenders, are the people who put their money in banks, life insurance, or any other financial instrument paying a fixed rate of interest. And the biggest debtor and gainer from unanticipated inflation has been the U.S. government. The national debt, which topped $13 trillion in June 2010, would be a lot easier to pay off if there were a great deal of inflation.

Another group helped by unanticipated inflation is businessowners. Just as businesses suffer losses on their inventory during periods of deflation, during inflations they obtain inventory price windfalls. Between the time inventory is ordered and the time it is sold, prices have crept upward, swelling profits.

Who is hurt by inflation?

Among those who are hurt by unanticipated inflation are people who live on fixed incomes, particularly retired people who depend on pensions (except Social Security) and those who hold long-term bonds, whether corporate or U.S. government bonds. Finally, people whose wages are fixed under long-term contracts and landlords who have granted long-term leases at fixed rent are hurt by unanticipated inflation. In other words, under unanticipated inflation, some people gain and others lose. In fact, the gains and losses are exactly equal.

If all prices and incomes rose equally, no harm would be done to anyone. But the rise is not equal. Many lose and some gain.

—Irving Fisher, 1920

When inflation is fully anticipated, there are no winners or losers. The interest rate takes into account the expected rate of inflation. Normally, without anticipated inflation, the interest rate would be around 3 or 4 percent. In 1980, and again in 1981, when the rate of inflation ran at close to 15 percent, the prime rate of interest (paid by top credit-rated corporations) soared over 20 percent.

For inflation to be fully anticipated and built into interest rates, people need to live with it for several years. Although the country had relatively high inflation for most of the 1970s, it was only in 1979 that the prime interest rate (which top credit-rated corporate borrowers pay) finally broke the 12 percent barrier. Today, however, unanticipated inflation is largely a thing of the past.

Creditors have learned to charge enough interest to take into account, or anticipate, the rate of inflation over the course of the loan. This is tacked onto the regular interest rate that the lender would charge had no inflation been expected. In addition borrowers have been issuing inflation-indexed bonds.

We'll work out a few examples. If the real rate of interest (the rate that would be charged without inflation) were 5 percent, and there was an expected rate of inflation of 3 percent, then obviously the creditors would charge 8 percent.

Real rate of interest

If the real rate of interest were 4 percent and the expected inflation rate were 6 percent, how much would the nominal rate (the rate actually charged) be? Good! I know you said 10 percent. Thus, the real rate of interest plus the expected rate of inflation equals the nominal rate of interest.

Are you ready for a tricky one? If the nominal interest rate is 6 percent and the expected rate of inflation is 8 percent, how much is the real rate of interest? Have you found it yet? The real rate of interest is −2 percent. How can a real rate of interest be negative? It can be negative if the rate of inflation is greater than the rate of interest that you pay or receive (that is, the nominal rate of interest).

If the nominal interest rate accurately reflects the inflation rate, then the inflation has been fully anticipated and no one wins or loses. This is a good thing for the economy because it means no one is hurt and no one is forced out of business because of inflation.

But if the rate of inflation keeps growing—even if it is correctly anticipated— our economy will be in big trouble. In a hyperinflation there are ultimately only losers.

Social Security benefits are indexed for inflation, protecting those who collect Social Security from inflation. Many wage-earners, too, are protected against inflation by cost-of-living adjustment clauses (called COLA agreements) in their contracts.[3] One way or another, many sectors of our society have learned to protect themselves from at least the short-term ravages of inflation.

What's a Dollar Worth Today?

> What this country needs is a good five-cent cigar.
>
> –Franklin Pierce Adams–

Some people say that today a dollar is worth only fifty cents. Others say a dollar today is worth only a quarter. And real old-timers claim that a dollar isn't worth more than a nickel.

When you lament the decline of the dollar's purchasing power, you need to specify which year's dollar you're comparing with today's dollar. Figure 8 shows us the five-year changes in the CPI since 1915. Let's compare prices in 1945 with those in 2009. How much higher was the cost of living in 2009? Since the CPI rose from 53.9 in 1945 to 642.6, the cost of living was about 12 times as high in 2009. So we could say that a dollar today could buy less than what a dime could buy in 1945.

Theories of the Causes of Inflation

Demand-Pull Inflation   When there is excessive demand for goods and services, we have demand-pull inflation. What is excessive? When people are willing and able to buy more output than our economy can produce. Something's gotta give. And what gives are prices.

Excessive demand causes demand-pull inflation.

Demand-pull inflation is often summed up as "too many dollars chasing too few goods." The problem is that we can't produce any more goods because our economy is already operating at full capacity.

---

[3]About one worker in four is covered by a COLA. See Chapter 29 of *Economics* or Chapter 17 of *Macroeconomics*.

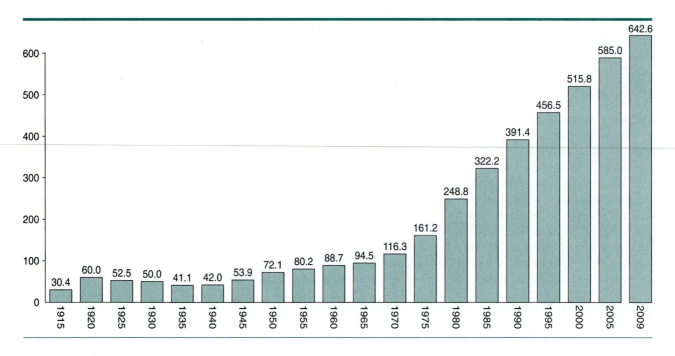

F*igure* 8

Consumer Price Index, 1915–2009 (1967 = 100)

Source: U.S. Bureau of Labor Statistics, http://stats.bls.gov.

Inflation is a form of taxation that can be imposed without legislation.

—Milton Friedman

What happens next if demand keeps rising? What if people have money in their pockets and the desire to spend it? Again, something's gotta give. Output can't rise any more. There's only one thing that can go up: prices.

This usually happens during wars. The government spends a lot of money on uniforms, tanks, planes, rifles, bullets, bombs, and missile systems. Private citizens want more consumer goods and services. Business firms are also bidding for resources to build more plant and equipment, expand their inventories, buy more raw materials, and hire more employees. So everyone's out there spending a lot of money to buy what they want.

At very low levels of output—depression levels—it is easy to increase output without raising prices. After all, with high unemployment and idle plant and equipment those resources can be put back to work without raising costs much. For example, if a person who has been out of work for several months is offered a job at the going wage rate, she will jump at the chance to get back to work.

As output expands, most of the idle resources will be back in production. Firms that need more plant and equipment will have to buy them. Employers will have to raise wages to induce new employees to work for them. In effect, then, businesses will have to bid for resources, and in doing so, they will bid up the prices of land, labor, and capital.

As their costs go up, business firms will be forced to raise their prices. We're moving closer and closer to full employment. It becomes increasingly difficult to get good help. New workers have to be lured away from other employers. There's only one way to do this—pay them more.

This pushes costs up still further until finally we've reached the full-employment level of output. Any further spending on goods and services will simply bid up prices without any corresponding increase in output.

Both depressions and runaway inflations are relatively rare occurrences, though they *do* happen. The twin goals of macroeconomic policy are to avoid these extremes, or anything approaching them. But runaway inflations in particular are sometimes unavoidable. This happens when macroeconomic policy must subordinate itself because of military necessity. During World War II, for example, the federal government bought up almost half the national output for military use. The only problem was that private citizens had plenty of money to spend and not enough output to spend it on. So civilians and the government had a bidding war for the country's limited resources. It was a classic case of too much money chasing too few goods.

It would not be unreasonable to ask, Just *where* did all this money come from? The late Milton Friedman, a Nobel laureate in economics, who was the world's leading exponent of monetary economics, rounded up the usual suspects: the seven governors of the Federal Reserve System, which controls the money supply's rate of growth. Chapter 14 provides a detailed account of how the Board of Governors exercises that control.

Cost-Push Inflation   There are three variants of cost-push inflation. Most prominent is the wage-price spiral. Because wages constitute nearly two-thirds of the cost of doing business, whenever workers receive a significant wage increase, this increase is passed along to consumers in the form of higher prices. Higher prices raise everyone's cost of living, engendering further wage increases.

The wage-price spiral

Imagine a 3 percent rise in the cost of living. Labor unions will negotiate for a 3 percent catch-up increase and a 3 percent increase on top of that for an anticipated cost-of-living increase *next* year. That's 6 percent. If every labor union gets a 6 percent increase, prices will undoubtedly rise not 3 percent but you guessed it—6 percent! In the next round of labor negotiations, the unions might want not just a 6 percent catch-up but 12 percent, to take care of next year as well.[4]

All of this can be described as the wage-price spiral. Regardless of who is to blame for its origin, once it gets started the wage-price spiral spawns larger and larger wage and price increases. Round and round it goes, and where it stops, nobody knows.

One man's wage rise is another man's price increase.
—Sir Harold Wilson, 1970

This variant of cost-push inflation may well explain a great deal of the inflation the country experienced through the early 1970s. However, in recent decades the membership and bargaining power of U.S. labor unions have been sharply declining, so the wage-price spiral would serve today, at best, as a partial explanation for inflation.

The second variant of cost-push inflation is profit-push inflation. Because just a handful of huge firms dominate many industries (for example, computer software, publishing, cigarettes, detergents, breakfast cereals, cars, and oil), these firms have the power to administer prices in those industries rather than accept the dictates of the market forces of supply and demand. To the degree that they are able to protect their profit margins by raising prices, these firms will respond to any rise in costs by passing them on to their customers.

Profit-push inflation

Finally, we have supply-side cost shocks, most prominently the oil price shocks of 1973–74 and 1979. When the OPEC nations quadrupled the price of oil in the fall of 1973, they touched off not just a major recession but also a severe inflation. When the price of oil rises, the cost of making many other things rises as well, for example, electricity, fertilizer, gasoline, heating oil, and long-distance freight carriage. And as we've seen again and again, cost increases are quickly translated into price increases. Cost-push inflation is shown graphically in the Advanced Work box, "Graphing Demand-Pull and Cost-Push Inflation."

Supply-side cost shocks

Inflation as a Psychological Process

Once inflation gets under way, the initial cause is of little consequence because the process takes on a life of its own. If people believe prices will rise, they will act in a way that keeps them rising. The only way to curb inflation is to counter inflationary psychology. Various things can set off an inflationary spiral—wars, huge federal budget deficits, large increases in the money supply, sudden increases in the price of oil—but once the spiral begins, inflationary psychology takes over.

Inflation takes on a life of its own.

When prices have been jolted upward, the original cause no longer matters; other forces are activated. Labor unions seek catch-up wage increases. Businesspeople raise

---

[4]Labor unions are covered in Chapter 27 of *Economics* and Chapter 15 of *Microeconomics*.

Graphing Demand-Pull and Cost-Push Inflation

Demand-pull inflation is set off by an increase in demand for goods and services without any increase in supply. The left graph shows how prices rise.

Cost-push inflation happens when production costs rise. Sellers can no longer supply the same output at current prices. This results in a decrease in supply. We see how prices go up in the right graph.

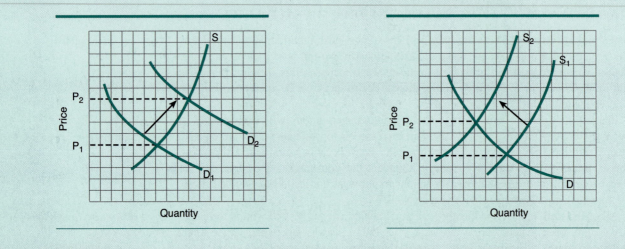

their prices to keep up with costs—primarily wage increases. Consumers with money in their pockets spend it before prices rise further. To stop inflation, then, we need to convince workers, businesspeople, and consumers that prices will stop rising. If we can do that, prices *will* stop rising.

Once we attain a period of price stability, the psychology of inflation will be destroyed. We will enjoy that stability as long as we can avoid triggering another round of inflation. In the early 1960s we attained such a period of stability, but then came the Vietnam War and its attendant federal budget deficits.

Breaking the back of the inflationary psychology

To break the back of the inflationary psychology is to bring down the rate of inflation for a sufficiently long period of time for people actually to expect price stability to continue. It took four recessions over a 13-year period (1969–1982) to wring inflation out of the economy. To date, this has been the only cure we've come up with, and obviously it's a cure with some unpleasant side effects, particularly for those who lose their jobs during these recessions. After we examine creeping inflation and hyperinflation, we'll return to the problem of unemployment.

Creeping Inflation and Hyperinflation

Creeping inflation in one country would be hyperinflation in another.

An annual rate of increase in the consumer price index of 1 or 2 percent is something that virtually everyone would agree is creeping inflation. Very few people would be alarmed by this price-level increase. Businesspeople would generally like it because it would swell profits and be good for business. And as we have seen, many wage-earners and all Social Security recipients are protected from inflation by cost-of-living increases.

Having a little inflation is like being a little pregnant.
—Leon Henderson

While there is no clear dividing line between creeping inflation and hyperinflation, why don't we say that once the annual rate of inflation reaches double digits, say 10 or 12 percent, *that's* hyperinflation. Once hyperinflation sets in, it becomes increasingly difficult to conduct normal economic affairs. Prices are raised constantly. It becomes impossible to enter into long-term contracts. No one is sure what the government might do.

Prices serve as a signal system for business firms. If prices are rising, business firms will produce more goods and services. But what if costs are rising faster?

Suppose Nucor Steel agrees to supply General Motors with 50,000 tons of steel at $300 a ton. Suddenly Nucor's costs rise by 50 percent. Would GM go along with a $150 increase, raising the price from $300 to $450 a ton? Would *you?* Not if you had signed a contract calling for only $300 a ton.

Meanwhile, the government—meaning Congress, the president, and the Federal Reserve Board[5]—may decide to act precipitously. On August 15, 1971, President Nixon suddenly announced the imposition of wage and price controls—based on a law he said he would never use. In October 1979 the Federal Reserve Board suddenly stopped monetary growth, sending interest rates through the roof and touching off a sharp recession.

The classic hyperinflation took place in Germany after World War I. You may think that double-digit inflation (10 percent or more per year) is hyperinflation, but in Germany prices rose 10 percent an hour! The German government had to print larger and larger denominations—100-mark notes, then 1,000-mark notes, and, eventually, 1 million-mark notes. The smaller denominations became worthless; parents gave them to children as play money.

The German inflation

The German inflation eventually led to a complete economic breakdown, helped touch off a worldwide depression, and paved the way for a new chancellor named Adolf Hitler. No wonder the Germans get nervous whenever their inflation rate begins to inch up.

Another classic example is what happened in Hungary during and after World War II. Before the war, if you went into a store with a pengö, you had some money in your pocket. In those days a pengö was a pengö. But by August 1946, you needed 828 octillion pengös—that's 828 followed by 27 zeros—to buy what one pengö bought before the war.

More recently, there have been runaway inflations in Nicaragua (a 12 billion percent rise in prices between June 1986 and March 1991), in Zimbabwe, which currently has a 150,000 percent inflation rate, and in Bolivia, which attained an annual inflation rate of 116,000 percent in 1985. Here is how the Bolivian inflation was described by a *Wall Street Journal* article:[6]

Hungary's pengö provides an example of inflation.

> A courier stumbles into Banco Boliviano Americano, struggling under the weight of a huge bag of money he is carrying on his back. He announces that the sack contains 32 million pesos, and a teller slaps on a notation to that effect. The courier pitches the bag into a corner. "We don't bother counting the money anymore," explains Max Lowes Stah, a loan officer standing nearby. "We take the client's word for what's in the bag." Pointing to the courier's load, he says, "That's a small deposit."

When inflation really gets out of hand, people begin to refuse to accept money as a means of payment. Society is reduced to a state of barter, making it extremely difficult for the economy to function. If you don't have what I want or I don't have what you want, we can't do business.

Those of us old enough to remember the relatively high rates of inflation in the 1970s and early 1980s tend to worry that such inflationary times may return. Is there any reason to worry? During wartime and during times of very heavy government borrowing, we have tended to have inflation. But not during the current war and the current record-setting government deficits. Maybe history is not repeating itself—at least not yet—because the massive influx of low-priced imported goods has held down inflation. And then, too, the hundreds of billions of dollars that foreigners lend us each year have held down interest rates, and indirectly, the cost of buying a home, a car, and the cost of other interest-sensitive goods and services.

---

[5]Technically, the Federal Reserve Board is not part of the government. We'll consider its role in regulating the rate of growth of our money supply in Chapter 14.

[6]Sonia L. Nazario, "When Inflation Rate is 116,000 Percent, Prices Change by the Hour," *The Wall Street Journal*, February 7, 1985, p. 1.

So the big question is this: Will our luck continue to hold—or will we soon be seeing another bout of inflation? What do *you* think? And what does your professor think?

The Misery Index

One thing the economy has rarely been able to attain simultaneously is a low unemployment rate and stable prices. A British economist, A. W. Phillips, even had a curve named after him illustrating that there is a trade-off between price stability and low unemployment.

As Phillips showed, in the 1950s and 1960s we attained price stability at the cost of higher unemployment and vice versa. In the 1970s, though, we had high unemployment *and* rapidly rising prices. During the presidential campaign of 1976, Jimmy Carter castigated President Gerald Ford with his "misery index," which was the inflation rate and the unemployment rate combined.[7] Anything over 10 was unacceptable, according to Carter.

During the 1980 presidential debates, Ronald Reagan resurrected the misery index for the voters, reminding them that it had risen by more than 50 percent since President Carter took office.

Although the misery index has obvious political uses, it also provides us with a snapshot view of our economic performance over the last four decades. From Figure 9 we can gauge just how stable our economy has been during this period. Which were the best two extended periods? I would say from the late 1950s through the late 1960s and since 1993. During both stretches our misery index stayed well below 10.

Whatever else might be said about Bill Clinton's two terms as president (January 1993–January 2001), he enjoyed great popularity and was overwhelmingly reelected in 1996. Why was he so popular? We need look no further than Figure 9. Both inflation and unemployment were not only quite low during his presidency, but the misery index declined almost steadily during both his terms. As his campaign slogan put it, "It's the economy, stupid!"

The misery index

Figure 9

The Misery Index, 1948–2009

You'll note that this combined rate of unemployment and inflation rose to a peak in 1979 and has declined substantially since then.

Source: Economic Report of the President, 2010.

---

[7]During the 1960s Arthur Okun, while he was President Lyndon Johnson's chairman of the Council of Economic Advisors, coined the term *economic discomfort index,* which Jimmy Carter renamed the *misery index.*

In other words, no matter how else a president might sin, if our economy prospers, then all may be forgiven.

Whatever else might be said about President George W. Bush's economic steward-ship, he would receive an "A" for helping to keep the misery index under 10—even though we went into our worst recession since the 1930s during the last year of what he was fond of calling his "watch."

What drove up the misery index in 2009? If you're not sure, glance back at Figures 5 and 6. You'll see that the unemployment rate shot up in 2009. That's what drove up the misery index.

Current Issue: Where Are All the Jobs?

Every month about 150,000 people enter or reenter the labor force, so we need to create that many new jobs. During the presidential administration of George W. Bush, we averaged a monthly gain of less than 70,000 jobs. So we need to ask: Where are all the jobs?

A large part of the explanation is that during this period, we lost nearly 5 million manufacturing jobs. For decades, these jobs have been sent abroad to low-wage coun-tries or eliminated through automation. The problem is that, at least since the new millennium, factory jobs have not been replaced by service sector jobs paying compa-rable wages.

Many Americans believe that there has been a great offshoring of jobs in recent years, but this is a case of perception leading reality. While the loss of manufacturing jobs has been very real, to date relatively few service jobs have been sent abroad. Though we hear about all those calling centers in India, in fact we are losing just a few hundred thousand jobs a year to offshoring. But these numbers will very likely increase over the next few years as employers scramble to cut labor costs.

High productivity rates and soaring health costs may also have contributed to the slow pace of hiring new workers. Employers, especially during the jobless recovery, managed to squeeze more production from their current workers, rather than hire new ones. And they were also reluctant to take on the expensive health care insurance pay-ments for new employees. But high productivity growth and rapidly rising health costs are nothing new. Still, during the administration of Bush's predecessor, Bill Clinton, we added an average of 230,000 jobs per month.

Questions for Further Thought and Discussion

1. Why is a high rate of inflation bad for the economy?

2. Right now, our economy is going through what phase of the business cycle? How do you know this?

3. Explain the difference between deflation and disinflation.

4. Being unemployed means different things to different people. Illustrate this by making up examples of three different unemployed people.

5. How would you improve upon the way the Bureau of Labor Statistics computes the unemployment rate?

6. Leo Krause is laid off. How does he make ends meet until he finds another job?

7. If we succeeded in setting up a computer-based national job bank with listings of virtually every job opening, what type of unemployment would this nearly eliminate? Explain how this would happen.

8. *Practical Application:* How were you and your family affected by the recession of 2007–2009?

9. *Practical Application:* On February 5, 2010, the BLS announced that employment fell by 20,000 in January, while the unemployment rate fell from 10.0 to 9.7. How do you explain that seeming contradiction?

10. *Web Activity:* On the first Friday of each month the Bureau of Labor Statistics announces the previous month's unemployment rate. Go to www.bls.gov to find last month's unemployment rate.

11. *Web Activity:* The Great Recession began in December 2007 and ended in June 2009. In what month and year did the unemployment rate peak? What was its peak rate? Go to www.bls.gov.

Workbook for Chapter 10 MG connect |ECONOMICS

Name _____   Date _____

Multiple-Choice Questions

Circle the letter that corresponds to the best answer.

1. If the CPI rose from 160.5 in 1998 to 168.7 in 1999 to 173.4 in 2000, this would be an example of

   _____. (LO6)

   a) deflation

   b) disinflation

   c) inflation

2. Disinflation generally occurs during

   _____. (LO6, 7)

   a) recessions

   b) economic booms

   c) periods of hyperinflation

   d) times of deflation

3. In the three-phase business cycle, the prosperity phase is always followed immediately by

   _____. (LO1)

   a) recovery   c) depression

   b) the trough   d) recession

4. If our economy is at full employment, the cyclical rate of unemployment would be _____. (LO4, 5)

   a) 0   c) 5 percent

   b) 2 percent   d) impossible to find

5. During the Great Depression most unemployment

   was _____. (LO5)

   a) frictional   c) cyclical

   b) structural   d) seasonal

6. If the CPI rose from 100 to 500, the price level rose

   by _____. (LO6)

   a) 100 percent   d) 400 percent

   b) 200 percent   e) 500 percent

   c) 300 percent

7. Which would be the most accurate statement? (LO7)

   a) Most business owners prefer deflation to inflation.

   b) In recent years Japan has suffered from deflation.

   c) Deflation is very likely in the United States over the next few years.

   d) Deflation is a form of disinflation.

8. If there are 90 million people employed, 10 million unemployed, 5 million collecting unemployment insurance, and 5 million discouraged workers, there

   are _____ in the labor force. (LO4)

   a) 90 million   d) 105 million

   b) 95 million   e) 110 million

   c) 100 million

9. During the 1970s, we experienced

   _____. (LO8)

   a) high inflation and high unemployment

   b) low inflation and low unemployment

   c) high inflation and low unemployment

   d) low inflation and high unemployment

10. The misery index was highest in which of these years? (LO8)

    a) 1960   d) 1990

    b) 1970   e) 2000

    c) 1980

11. The last entire year we had full employment was

    _____. (LO4, 8)

    a) 1945   c) 1969

    b) 1957   d) 2007

12. We have business cycles of _____. (LO1)

    a) the same length and amplitude

    b) the same length but different amplitudes

    c) the same amplitude but different lengths

    d) different lengths and amplitudes

13. During business cycles _____. (LO1)
    a) troughs are followed by recessions
    b) troughs are followed by peaks
    c) peaks are followed by troughs
    d) peaks are followed by recessions

14. The second part of the expansion phase of the cycle is _____. (LO1)
    a) recovery   c) recession
    b) prosperity   d) depression

15. An example of an exogenous business cycle theory would be _____. (LO2)
    a) overinvestment   c) money
    b) inventory   d) war

16. In 2025 the CPI rose 10 percent; in 2026 it rose 6 percent; and in 2027 it rose 2 percent. We could describe 2027 as a year of _____. (LO6)
    a) inflation
    b) disinflation
    c) deflation

17. The Business Cycle Dating Committee of the National Bureau of Economic Research would most likely classify which one of the following as a recession? (LO3)
    a) A one-tenth of 1 percent decline in real GDP for two consecutive quarters
    b) An increase in the unemployment rate for two consecutive months
    c) A decline in nonfarm payrolls, industrial production, and personal income over six months
    d) A 1 percent rate of deflation over at least three months accompanied by rising interest rates

18. Which one of the following best describes a recession? (LO1, 2)
    a) A slowing of real GDP growth
    b) A rise in unemployment accompanied by a decline in total employment
    c) A decline in real GDP for two consecutive quarters
    d) A decline in GDP for two consecutive quarters

19. The unemployment rate is computed by the _____. (LO4)
    a) nation's unemployment insurance offices
    b) Bureau of Labor Statistics
    c) Department of Commerce
    d) Office of Management and Budget

20. If the number of unemployed stays the same and the number of people in the labor force rises, _____. (LO4)
    a) the unemployment rate will rise
    b) the unemployment rate will fall
    c) the unemployment rate will stay the same
    d) there is not enough information to determine what will happen to the unemployment rate

21. Which statement is true? (LO4, 5)
    a) Both liberals and conservatives feel that the official unemployment rate is too high.
    b) Both liberals and conservatives feel that the official unemployment rate is too low.
    c) The liberals believe that the official unemployment rate is too high, and the conservatives feel that it is too low.
    d) The conservatives feel that the official unemployment rate is too high, and the liberals feel that it is too low.

22. Which is the most accurate statement? (LO3)
    a) Business cycle forecasting dates back to biblical times.
    b) Business cycle forecasts are nearly always inaccurate.
    c) Business cycle forecasts are almost always accurate.
    d) It is virtually impossible to forecast business cycle turning points.

23. Which statement is false? (LO5)
    a) Over the last two decades there has been an upward drift in the unemployment rate.
    b) The unemployment rate for blacks is about twice that for whites.
    c) The official unemployment rate includes "discouraged" workers.
    d) None of the above is false.

Answer questions 24 through 29 by using one of these three choices:

    a) frictionally unemployed

    b) structurally unemployed

    c) cyclically unemployed

24. Ella Jillian Fosnough, an autoworker who is still out of work two years after her plant closed, is _____. (LO5)

25. Sophia King, a homemaker returning to the labor market after an absence of 10 years and looking for work, is _____. (LO5)

26. Brian Horn, a factory worker who is laid off until business picks up again, is _____. (LO5)

27. Austin Noorda, Mark Noorda, and Debbie Noorda are "between jobs." They are _____. (LO5)

28. Brad Peterson, a man in his mid-50s whose skills have become obsolete, would be _____. (LO5)

29. When the unemployment rate goes above 5 percent, anything above that 5 percent level is _____. (LO5)

30. An example of deflation since the base year would be a CPI in the current year of _____. (LO7)

    a) 90   c) 110

    b) 100   d) 200

31. Inflation generally occurs _____. (LO7)

    a) during wartime   c) during recessions

    b) before wars   d) during peacetime

32. The period of greatest price stability was _____. (LO6)

    a) 1950–56   c) 1968–76

    b) 1958–64   d) 1976–82

33. Traditionally, those hurt by inflation have been _____. (LO7)

    a) creditors and people on fixed incomes

    b) debtors and people on fixed incomes

    c) debtors and creditors

34. Farmers have generally been _____ by inflation. (LO7)

    a) hurt

    b) helped

    c) neither helped nor hurt

35. Creditors generally do better when inflation is _____. (LO7)

    a) anticipated

    b) unanticipated

    c) neither anticipated nor unanticipated

36. Businesspeople generally like a little _____ but dislike a little _____. (LO7)

    a) inflation, deflation

    b) deflation, inflation

37. Inflationary recessions first occurred in the _____. (LO6)

    a) 1950s   c) 1970s

    b) 1960s   d) 1980s

38. Most post-World War II recessions lasted less than _____. (LO1)

    a) three years   c) one year

    b) two years   d) six months

39. According to the Book of Genesis, Joseph may have been the first person to _____. (LO3)

    a) forecast a business cycle

    b) collect unemployment insurance benefits

    c) formulate the misery index

    d) differentiate between demand-pull inflation and cost-push inflation

40. The 1996 Welfare Reform Act has pushed _____ our unemployment rate; our high prison population has pushed _____ our unemployment rate. (LO4, 5)

    a) up, up   c) down, up

    b) down, down   d) up, down

41. During the mid-1980s, both Bolivia and Nicaragua experienced _____. (LO7)

    a) creeping inflation   c) disinflation

    b) hyperinflation   d) deflation

42. The rate of job creation during the administration of George W. Bush has been _____. (LO5)
    a) relatively low
    b) relatively high
    c) about average

43. There are over 2 million Americans in prison. This tends to _____ the official unemployment rate. (LO5)
    a) raise
    b) lower
    c) have no effect on

44. Which is the most accurate statement? (LO4)
    a) The monthly rate of job creation during the administration of George W. Bush was faster than that during Bill Clinton's administration.
    b) We need to create about 150,000 new jobs every month to accommodate the people entering or reentering the labor force.
    c) Every year millions of American jobs are offshored.
    d) There are as many manufacturing jobs in the United States today as there were when George W. Bush became president.

45. Which would be the most accurate description of the six decades since the late 1940s compared to the eight decades preceding the 1940s? (LO1)
    a) The recessions were milder and the booms less pronounced.
    b) The recessions were more severe and the booms more pronounced.
    c) The recessions were more severe and the booms less pronounced.
    d) The recessions were milder and the booms more pronounced.

46. In recent years, which one of the following has tended to push up our natural unemployment rate? (LO5)
    a) Our increasing disability roles
    b) The quadrupling of our prison population
    c) The rapid growth of the temporary-help industry
    d) Growing worker insecurity
    e) The entry of millions of teenagers into the labor force

Fill-In Questions

1. The three worst recessions since World War II began in the years _____, _____, and _____. (LO1)

2. Stagflation is a contraction of the words _____ and _____. (LO7)

3. To find the number of people in the labor force we need to add the _____ and the _____. (LO4)

4. To find the unemployment rate we need to divide the _____ by the _____. (LO4)

5. A person who is functionally illiterate faces long periods of _____ unemployment. (LO5)

6. When the overall unemployment rate is 6.5 percent, the cyclical unemployment rate is _____. (LO5)

7. The upper turning point of a business cycle just before the onset of a recession is called the _____. (LO1)

8. In the year _____ the OPEC nations quadrupled the price of oil. (LO7)

9. The low point of a business cycle is the _____; the high point is the _____. (LO1)

10. Theories that place the cause of business cycles within the economy rather than outside are known as _____ theories. (LO2)

11. According to the inventory theory of the business cycle, a recession is set off when retailers _____. (LO2)

12. The monetary theory of the business cycle hypothesizes that recessions are set off when _____ and recoveries begin when the monetary authorities _____. (LO2)

13. Liberals say the unemployment rate is actually _____ than the BLS says it is; conservatives say it is really _____. (LO4)

14. Between the mid-1970s and the mid-1980s, our unemployment rate never dipped below _____ percent. (LO4)

15. The unemployment rate for blacks is about _____ times the white unemployment rate. (LO4)

16. The misery index is found by adding the _____ and the _____. (LO8)

17. The monthly unemployment rate reached a high of about _____ percent in 2009. (LO4)

18. During a very severe recession when more than 11 percent of the labor force is out of work, most of the unemployment is _____ unemployment. (LO4)

19. Two exogenous business cycle theories are the _____ theory and the _____ theory. (LO2)

20. According to A. W. Phillips, there is a trade-off between _____ and _____. (LO8)

21. If the consumer price index rises from 150 to 180, the cost of living rose by _____ percent. (LO6)

22. Once inflation is under way, a(n) _____ takes over. (LO7)

23. To stop inflation, we need to convince people that _____. (LO7)

24. In 2009 the rate of inflation was _____ percent. (LO6, 7)

Problems

1. If the unemployment rate is 7 percent, how much is cyclical unemployment? (LO5)

2. Compute the unemployment rate given the following information: 8 million unemployed, 117 million employed. (LO4)

3. Given the following information, how many people are in the labor force? 3 million people are collecting unemployment insurance; 7 million people are officially unemployed; 2 million people are discouraged workers; and 110 million people are employed. (LO4)

4. How much would the nominal interest rate be if the real rate of interest were 6 percent and the expected rate of inflation were 7 percent? (LO7)

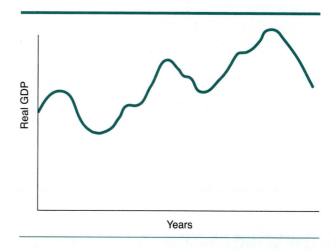

Figure 1

Real GDP

Years

5. How much would the real rate of interest be if the nominal interest rate was 12 percent and the expected rate of inflation was 4 percent? (LO7)

6. If the CPI is currently 178.9, by what percentage did prices rise since the base year? (LO6)

7. If the CPI rose from 200 in 1991 to 240 in 1997, by what percentage did prices increase? (LO6)

8. If the rate of inflation is 5 percent, the prime rate of interest is 6 percent, and the unemployment rate is 7 percent, how much is the misery index? (LO7)

9. If the overall rate of unemployment is 8.3 percent, what is the rate of cyclical unemployment? (LO5)

10. Label the graph in Figure 1 with respect to the three phases of the business cycle and the cycle turning points. (LO1)

11. Answer these questions, given the information that follows: (a) How many people are in the labor force? (b) What is the unemployment rate? Employed: 90 million; discouraged workers: 4 million; unemployed: 10 million; people collecting unemployment insurance: 8 million. (LO4)

12. (a) If the CPI fell from 180 to 150, by what percentage did the price level fall? (b) If the CPI rose from 150 to 180, by what percentage did the price level rise? (LO6)

13. In which year was the misery index (a) the highest? (b) the lowest? (LO8)

Year	Unemployment Rate (percent)	Inflation Rate (percent)
1948	8.0	3.0
1949	5.9	−2.1
1950	5.3	5.9
1951	3.3	6.0
1952	3.0	0.8
1953	2.9	0.7
1954	5.5	−0.7
1955	4.4	0.4
1956	4.1	3.0
1957	4.3	2.9
1958	6.8	1.8
1959	5.5	1.7
1960	5.5	1.4
1961	6.7	0.7

14. If the unemployment rate is 10 percent, there are 150 million people in the labor force, and there are 5 million discouraged workers, how many people are unemployed? (LO4)

15. (a) In which year did disinflation set in? (b) In which year did deflation set in? (LO7)

Year	CPI
2010	100.0
2011	104.0
2012	110.2
2013	121.7
2014	129.4
2015	132.0
2016	133.5
2017	134.0
2018	133.8
2019	133.0
2020	131.6

16. If cyclical unemployment is 6 percent, how much is the unemployment rate? (LO5)

17. If the unemployment rate is 10 percent and 90 million people are working, how many people are unemployed? (LO4)

18. Cameron Amundson and Carter Amundson reside in Eagle's Nest, Iowa, which has an unemployment rate of 6 percent and a labor force of 100. Cameron is a senior at the University of Dubuque and Carter is unemployed. Cameron graduates and finds a job; Carter gives up looking for work and enrolls in Loris College. Compute the new unemployment rate of Eagle's Nest. (LO4)

19. In which year and quarter did the prosperity phase of the business cycle begin? (LO1)

Year	Quarter	Real GDP
2020	I	18,215
2020	II	18,703
2020	III	19,496
2020	IV	19,002
2021	I	18,771
2021	II	18,563
2021	III	18,428
2021	IV	18,737
2022	I	19,114
2022	II	19,385
2022	III	19,739
2022	IV	20,058

Chapter 11

Classical and Keynesian Economics

The first commandment of medicine is, "Do no harm." Until the Great Depression, the even stricter first commandment of economics was, "Do nothing." The workings of the price system would ensure that our economy be at, or moving toward, full employment. In the immortal words of Thomas Jefferson, "The government that governs least, governs best." But as the depression got worse, it became clear that the government needed to take very decisive measures to get the economy moving again. John Maynard Keynes outlined just what measures were needed.

This chapter is divided into three parts: (1) the classical economic system, (2) the Keynesian critique of the classical system, and (3) the Keynesian system. The basic difference between Keynes and the classicals is whether our economy tends toward full employment.

LEARNING OBJECTIVES

After reading this chapter you should be able to:

1. Discuss Say's law.
2. Analyze classical equilibrium.
3. Explain and discuss the real balance, interest rate, and foreign purchases effects.
4. Demonstrate the interaction between aggregate demand and aggregate supply.
5. Summarize the Keynesian critique of the classical system.
6. Describe equilibrium and disequilibrium and distinguish between them.
7. Summarize and discuss the Keynesian policy prescriptions.

Jean Baptiste Say, French economist and entrepreneur

Part I: The Classical Economic System

Say's Law

The centerpiece of classical economics is Say's law. Named for Jean Baptiste Say, a late-18th-century (the late 1700s) French economist, the law stated, *"Supply creates its own demand."* Think about it. Somehow what we produce—supply—all gets sold.

A few years later the great English economist David Ricardo elaborated on Say's law:

No man produces but with a view to consume or sell, and he never sells but with an intention to purchase some other commodity which may be immediately useful to him or which may contribute to future production. By producing, then, he necessarily becomes

Say's law

Man produces in order to consume.

—Claude-Frédéric Bastiat, French economist

either the consumer of his own goods, or the purchaser and consumer of the goods of some other person.[1]

People who produce things are paid. What do they do with this money? They spend it. On what? On what *other* people produce.

We can illustrate Say's law using the production figures in Table 1. Let's look at Table 1. Everyone eats tomatoes, bread, and butter, and wears tee shirts and wooden shoes. Joe sells eight bushels of tomatoes, keeping two for his own use. Sally wears one of her tee shirts and sells the other four. And so forth.

What do they do with the proceeds from their sales? They use them to buy what they need from each of the others. Joe, for example, buys a tee shirt from Sally, four loaves of bread from Mike, two pounds of butter from Bill (they all like to put a lot of butter on their bread), and a pair of wooden shoes from Alice.

"Why does anybody work?" asked Say. People work to make money with which to buy things. Why do *you* work?

As long as everyone spends everything that he or she earns, we're OK. But we begin having problems when people start saving part of their incomes.

TABLE 1	Production in a Five-Person Economy
Joe	10 bushels of tomatoes
Sally	5 tee shirts
Mike	20 loaves of bread
Bill	10 pounds of butter
Alice	5 pairs of wooden shoes

Basically, producers need to sell everything they produce. If some people save, then not everything produced will be sold. In a world with large companies instead of self-employed producers, some workers must be laid off when demand for production falls. In fact, as unemployment mounts, demand falls still further, necessitating further cutbacks in production and employment.

The villain of the piece is clearly saving. If only people would spend their entire incomes, we'd never have unemployment. But people do save, and saving is crucial to economic growth. Without saving we could not have investment.

Think of production as consisting of two products: consumer goods and investment goods (for now, we are drastically simplifying).[2] People will buy consumer goods; the money spent on such goods is designated by the letter C. Money spent by businesses on investment goods is designated by the letter I.

If we think of GDP as total spending, then GDP would be C + I. Once this money is spent, other people receive it as income. And what do they do with their income? They spend some of it and save the rest.

If we think of GDP as income received, that money will either be spent on consumer goods, C, or saved, which we'll designate by the letter S. If we put all this together, we have two equations:

$$GDP = C + I$$
$$GDP = C + S$$

---

[1]David Ricardo, *The Principles of Political Economy and Taxation* (Burr Ridge, IL: Richard D. Irwin, 1963), p. 166.

[2]GDP = C + I + G + X$_n$. Leaving out government spending and net exports allows us to concentrate on C and I.

These two equations can be simplified to one short equation. First, because things equal to the same thing are equal to each other:

$$C + I = C + S$$

This step is justified because $C + I$ and $C + S$ are both equal to GDP. Therefore, they are equal to each other.

Next, we can subtract the same thing from both sides of an equation. In this case we are subtracting C:

$$C + I = C + S$$
$$I = S$$

$$C + I = C + S$$
$$I = S$$

Going back to Say's law, we can see that it holds up, at least in accordance with classical analysis. Supply *does* create its own demand. The economy produces a supply of consumer goods and investment goods. The people who produce these goods spend part of their incomes on consumer goods and save the rest. Their savings are borrowed by investors who spend this money on investment goods. The bottom line is that everything the economy produces is purchased.

This is a perfect economic system. Everything produced is sold. Everyone who wants to work can find a job. There will never be any serious economic downturns, so there is no need for government intervention to set things right.

Supply and Demand Revisited

Say's law provides one of the basic building blocks of classical economics. The law of supply and demand, the subject of Chapter 4, was another.

How much is the equilibrium price in Figure 1? I'm sure you got both of these right. And the equilibrium quantity? You followed the horizontal dotted line to a price of about $7.20 and the vertical dotted line to a quantity of 6.

Incidentally, we call the price that clears the market *equilibrium price* and the quantity purchased and sold *equilibrium quantity*. At the equilibrium price the quantity that buyers wish to purchase is equal to the quantity that sellers wish to sell.

Equilibrium price and quantity

Now let's see how the classical economists applied the law of supply and demand to help prove Say's law and, more specifically, to prove that $I = S$ (Investment = Saving). This is done in Figure 2, which graphs the demand for investment funds and the supply of savings.

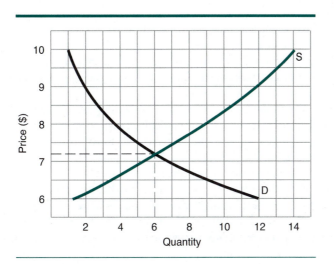

Figure 1
Demand and Supply Curves
The curves cross at a price of $7.20 and a quantity of 6.

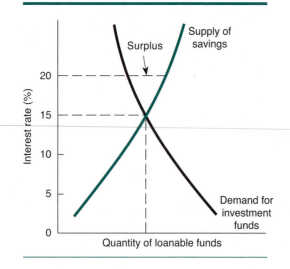

Figure 2

The Loanable Funds Market
The demand and supply curves cross at an interest rate of 15 percent.

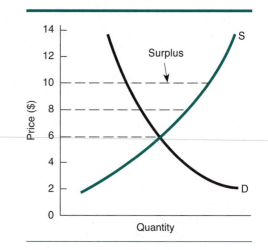

Figure 3

Market for Hypothetical Product
If the quantity supplied is greater than the quantity demanded at a certain price (in this case, $8), the price will fall to the equilibrium level ($6), at which quantity demanded is equal to quantity supplied.

What if savings and investment were not equal? For instance, if savings were greater than investment, there would be unemployment. Not everything being produced would be purchased.

Savings and investment will be equal.

There's nothing to worry about, according to the classical economists. And they proved this by means of the two curves in Figure 2. If savings were greater than investment, the interest rate would fall. Why? Because some savers would be willing to lend at lower interest rates and some additional investors would be induced to borrow at lower interest rates.

For example, if the interest rate was 20 percent, the supply of savings would be greater than the demand for loanable funds. There would be a surplus of savings. The interest rate would fall to 15 percent, the surplus of savings would disappear and savings would equal investment.

Prices and wages will fall to bring about equilibrium between saving and investing.

The classical economists had a fallback position. Even if lower interest rates did not eliminate the surplus of savings relative to investment, price flexibility would bring about equilibrium between saving and investing. Business firms, unable to sell their entire output, would simply lower prices. And then people would buy everything produced.

One might ask whether business firms could make a profit if prices were reduced. Yes, answered the classical economists, if resource prices—especially wages—were also reduced. Although output and employment might decline initially, they would move back up again once prices and wages fell. At lower prices people would buy more, and at lower wages employers would hire more.

Falling prices and falling wage rates can also be illustrated by a supply and demand graph. Look at Figure 3. If sellers of a particular good are not selling all they wish to sell *at the current market price,* some of them will lower their price. In Figure 3 the price falls from $8 to $6, which happens to be the equilibrium price. At the equilibrium price of $6, the surplus inventory has been eliminated.

Exactly the same thing happens in the labor market (see Figure 4). At a wage rate of $9 an hour, there are many unemployed workers. Some are willing to accept a lower wage rate. When the wage rate falls to $7 an hour, everyone who wants to work at that rate can find a job, and every employer willing to hire workers at that rate can find as many workers as she wants to hire.

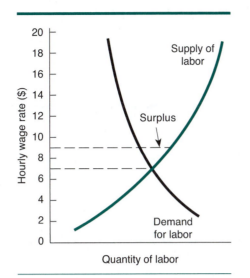

Figure 4
Hypothetical Labor Market
If the wage rate is set too high ($9 an hour), the quantity of labor supplied exceeds the quantity of labor demanded. The wage rate falls to the equilibrium level of $7; at that wage rate the quantity of labor demanded equals the quantity supplied.

The Classical Equilibrium: Aggregate Demand Equals Aggregate Supply

What exactly *is* equilibrium GDP? We've seen back in Chapter 4, on a microeconomic level, that when quantity demanded equals quantity supplied, we're at equilibrium. Similarly, on a macroeconomic level, when aggregate demand equals aggregate supply, we're at equilibrium. At equilibrium there is a state of balance between opposing forces such that there is no tendency for change.

The classical economists believed our economy was either at, or tending toward, full employment. So at the classical equilibrium—the GDP at which aggregate demand was equal to aggregate supply—we were at full employment. And as long as aggregate demand and aggregate supply did not change, our economy would continue operating at full employment.

We've been weaving back and forth between macro and micro analysis. From here on it's going to be macro. We'll begin with the economy's aggregate demand curve, go on to the economy's aggregate long-run and short-run supply curves, and finally put these curves together to derive the economy's equilibrium GDP.

Our economy is either at or tending toward full employment.

The Aggregate Demand Curve

At the beginning of Chapter 9 we defined GDP as *the nation's expenditure on all the final goods and services produced during the year at market prices*. Stated mathematically, GDP = C + I + G + X_n.

The aggregate demand curve of Figure 5 depicts an inverse relationship between the price level and the quantity of goods and services demanded: As the price level declines, the quantity of goods and services demanded rises. Similarly, as the price level rises, the quantity of goods and services demanded declines. This relationship is illustrated by an aggregate demand curve that slopes downward to the right.

What does this curve tell us? We'll begin by defining aggregate demand as *the total value of real GDP that all sectors of the economy are willing to purchase at various price levels*. You'll notice that as the price level declines, people are willing to purchase more and more output. Alternatively, as the price level rises, the quantity of output purchased goes down.

The aggregate demand curve shows that as the price level declines, the quantity of goods and services demanded rises.

Definition of aggregate demand

Figure 5

Aggregate Demand Curve
(in trillions of dollars)
The level of aggregate demand
varies inversely with the price level:
As the price level declines, people
are willing to purchase more and
more output. Alternatively, as the
price level rises, the quantity of
output purchased goes down.

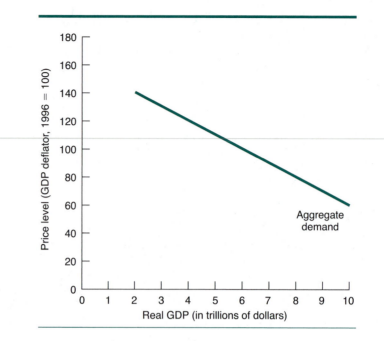

There are three reasons why the
quantity of goods and services
purchased declines as the price
level increases.

There are three reasons why the quantity of goods and services purchased declines
as the price level increases: (1) An increase in the price level reduces the wealth of
people holding money, making them feel poorer and reducing their purchases; (2) the
higher price level pushes up the interest rate, which leads to a reduction in the purchase
of interest-sensitive goods, such as cars and houses; and (3) net exports decline as foreigners buy less from us and we buy more from them at the higher price level.

(1) The Real Balance Effect   When the price level goes up, your purchasing power
goes down. The money you have in the bank, your stocks and bonds, and all your other
liquid assets shrink in terms of what they can buy. You *feel* poorer, so you'll tend to
spend less.

The *real balance effect* is the influence of a change in your purchasing power on
the quantity of real GDP that you are willing to buy. Here's how it works. Suppose you
are holding $800 in money and your only other asset is $200 worth of CDs (compact
discs). Now, what if the prices of most goods and services fell, among them those of
CDs. The $800 that you're holding now buys more CDs than before. You've got a larger
real balance.

Before prices fell, you were very happy holding 80 percent of your assets in the
form of money ($800 of $1,000) and 20 percent in the form of CDs ($200 of $1,000).
But now those CDs you're holding are worth less than $200 because their price has
fallen, while your money is worth more. Let's say there was so much deflation that the
purchasing power of your money doubled, to $1,600, while the value of your CDs fell
to $100. Question: Wouldn't you like to take advantage of the price decrease to buy more
CDs? Of course you would. And how many more dollars' worth of CDs would you buy
if you wanted to keep 20 percent of your assets in the form of CDs (and 80 percent in
the form of money)? Answer: Your total assets are now $1,700 ($1,600 in money and
$100 in CDs), so you'd want to hold 20 percent of the $1,700, or $340, in CDs. In other
words, you'd buy $240 worth of CDs.

Let's sum up. A decrease in the price level increases the quantity of real money.
The larger the quantity of real money, the larger the quantity of goods and services
demanded. Similarly, an increase in the price level decreases the quantity of real money.
The smaller the quantity of real money, the smaller the quantity of goods and services
demanded.

(2) The Interest Rate Effect   A rising price level pushes up interest rates, which in turn lower the consumption of certain goods and services and also lowers investment in new plant and equipment. Let's look more closely at this two-step sequence.

First, during times of inflation, interest rates rise, because lenders need to protect themselves against the declining purchasing power of the dollar. If you lent someone $100 for one year and there was a 10 percent rate of inflation, you would need to be paid back $110 just to be able to buy what your original $100 would have purchased.

Second, certain goods and services are more sensitive to interest rate changes than others. Can you name some especially sensitive ones? Try auto purchases and home mortgages. Clearly, then, when interest rates rise, the consumption of certain goods and services falls, and when interest rates fall, their consumption rises.

Now let's see how a rising price level (which pushes up interest rates) affects investment spending. We saw in Chapter 6 that rising interest rates choke off investment projects that would have been carried out at lower rates. Some projects, especially in building construction, where interest is a major cost, are particularly sensitive to interest rate changes. So we know that a rising price level pushes up interest rates and lowers both consumption and investment. Similarly, a declining price level, which pushes down interest rates, encourages consumption and investment. Clearly the interest rate effect can be very powerful.

(3) The Foreign Purchases Effect   When the price level in the United States rises relative to the price levels in other countries, what effect does this have on U.S. imports and exports? Because American goods become more expensive relative to foreign goods, our imports rise (foreign goods are cheaper) and our exports decline (American goods are more expensive).

In sum, when our relative price level increases, this tends to increase our imports and lower our exports. Thus, our net exports (exports minus imports) component of GDP declines. When our relative price level declines, the net exports component (and GDP) rises.

The Long-Run Aggregate Supply Curve

First we'll define aggregate supply as *the amount of real output, or real GDP, that will be made available by sellers at various price levels.* Next let's see what the long-run aggregate supply curve looks like. It looks like the vertical line in Figure 6.

Definition of aggregate supply

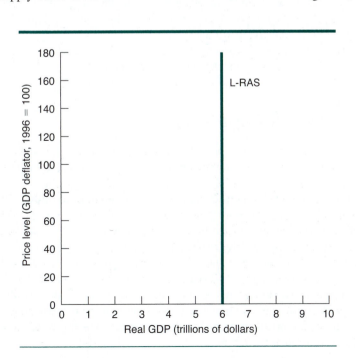

Figure 6

Long-Run Aggregate Supply Curve (in trillions of dollars)
Why is this curve a vertical line? The classical economists made two assumptions: (1) In the long run, the economy operates at full employment; (2) in the long run, output is independent of prices.

Figure 7

Figure 7

Aggregate Demand and Long-Run Aggregate Supply (in trillions of dollars)

The long-run equilibrium of real GDP is $6 trillion at a price level of 100.

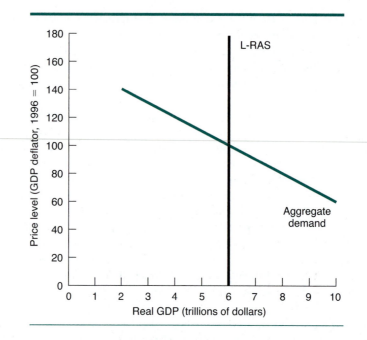

This curve is based on two assumptions of the classical economists. First, in the long run, the economy operates at full employment. (In Chapter 10 we decided that, because there would always be frictional and structural unemployment totaling about 5 percent of the labor force, a 5 percent unemployment rate meant the economy was operating at full employment.) Second, in the long run, output is independent of prices.

Ready for a little action? We're going to put the aggregate demand curve and the long-run aggregate supply curve together on one graph and see what happens. Figure 7 does this.

The equilibrium full-employment level of real GDP

What happens is that we find two things: (1) the equilibrium full-employment level of real GDP and (2) the corresponding price level, which happens to be 100.

What does this _mean?_ It means that in the long run our economy will produce the level of output that will provide jobs for everyone who wants to work (that is, the unemployment rate will be 5 percent). In other words, in the long run our economy will produce at full-employment GDP. And how much _is_ full-employment GDP, according to Figure 7? It comes to exactly $6 trillion.

This is what the classical economists predicted, and it's completely consistent with Say's law: Supply creates its own demand. Our economy, then, will always be at full employment in the long run. But what about in the short run?

The Short-Run Aggregate Supply Curve

The economy may operate below full-employment GDP in the short run.

In the short run, according to the classical economists, some unemployment _is_ possible. Some output _may_ go unsold. And the economy _may_ operate below full-employment GDP. Figure 8 shows all of this.

Why does the short-run aggregate supply curve sweep upward to the right? Because business firms will supply increasing amounts of output as prices rise. Why? Because wages, rent, and other production costs are set by contracts in the short run and don't increase immediately in response to rising prices. Your landlord can't come to you while your lease still has two years to go and tell you that he must raise your rent because _his_ costs are going up. Your employees who are working under two- and three-year contracts can't ask you to renegotiate. (They can _ask_ you to, but you probably won't.) And your suppliers may also have agreed contractually to send you their goods at set prices. So, in the short run, higher prices mean higher profit margins, which give business firms like yours an incentive to increase output.

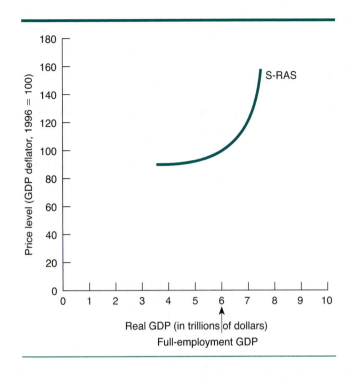

Figure 8
Short-Run Aggregate Supply
Curve (in trillions of dollars)
Why does the short-run aggregate
supply curve sweep upward to the
right? Because business firms will
supply increasing amounts of output
as prices rise.

As output continues to rise, land, labor, and capital become more expensive and
less-efficient resources are pressed into service. To get homemakers to work, employers
need to make wage rates attractive enough (and some even go to the expense of setting
up child care facilities) to entice them back into the labor force. As output approaches
full employment, antiquated machinery and less-productive facilities must be used. And
so, as the full-employment level of GDP is approached, the short-run aggregate supply
curve is becoming steeper and steeper. You'll notice that full-employment GDP is still
$6 trillion, as in Figure 7.

As output rises, costs rise.

You'll also notice in Figure 8 that output continues to rise even after we've exceeded
full-employment GDP. Is this *possible*? Can our real GDP ever exceed our full-employment
GDP? Yes, it can. But only in the short run.

Beyond full employment

Let's extend the example of luring homemakers into the labor force with better pay.
How about enticing full-time college students who are working part-time to give up their
education (or perhaps switch to night school) and work full-time? Or how about persuad-
ing retired people, or those about to retire, to take full-time jobs? How would we do
this? By paying attractive wage rates and providing whatever other incentives are necessary. We can also keep putting back into service aging or obsolete plant and equipment,
and make use of marginal land as well.

Why, then, does the short-run aggregate supply curve eventually become vertical?
Because there is a physical limit to the output capacity of the economy. There is just so
much land, labor, and capital that can be put to work, and when that limit is reached,
there is no way to increase production appreciably. During World War II, U.S. factories
ran 24 hours a day, and millions of people worked 50 or 60 hours a week. But everyone
simply could not have kept up this effort year after year. As Americans said at the time,
"There's a war going on." Just in case someone hadn't noticed.

*Why does the short-run
aggregate supply curve
eventually become vertical?*

So, in the short run, we can push our output beyond the level of full-employment
GDP and get our economy to operate beyond full employment. But this is possible only
in the short run. In the long run, we're back at the long-run aggregate supply curve.

Figure 9 puts this all together for you. You see the point at which the short- and
long-run aggregate supply curves intersect the aggregate demand curve? That's the long-
run equilibrium level of GDP. At that point, the price level happens to be 100 and GDP
is $6 trillion.

Figure 9

Aggregate Demand, Long-Run
and Short-Run Aggregate Supply
(in trillions of dollars)
The long-run aggregate supply
curve, the short-run aggregate
supply curve, and the aggregate
demand come together at full
employment.

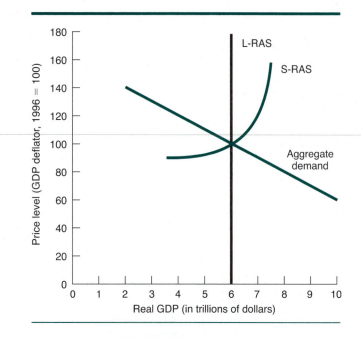

In the classical system, all the parts fit together neatly. The long-run aggregate supply curve, the short-run aggregate supply cost curve, and the aggregate demand curve come together at full employment. If there *is* some unemployment in the short run, it will automatically be eliminated as the economy returns to its long-run, full-employment equilibrium. And if there is more than full employment, this is again only a temporary phenomenon that will end as the level of economic activity returns to its full-employment level. In short, the economy can temporarily slide up and down its short-run aggregate supply curve, but it inevitably returns to its long-run equilibrium at full employment.

Now let's see how, according to classical economic analysis, our economy would react to a recession. We'll begin at equilibrium point E_1 in Figure 10, with AD_1 = L-RAS. Our real GDP of $6 trillion represents a state of full employment. Suppose that aggregate demand falls from AD_1 to AD_2. That would create a surplus inventory of $2 trillion in unsold goods. And at a real GDP of just $4 trillion, our economy is now in a serious recession with substantial unemployment. But, as President Herbert Hoover used to say, "Prosperity is just around the corner." In this instance he was right. When our GDP deflator (which is our price

Figure 10

The Classical View of How Our
Economy Responds to a
Recession

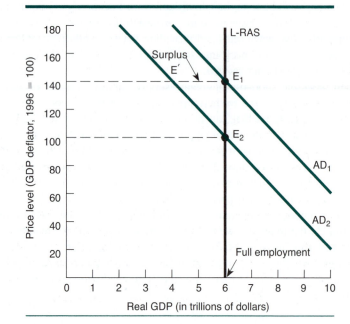

level) drops from 140 to 100, our economy reaches a new equilibrium level at E_2. At E_2 our real GDP has shot back up to $6 trillion and we are once more at full employment.

Using classical economic analysis, what would you suggest that the government do when there's a recession? The correction answer would be, "Nothing." And that's largely what our government did back in the early 1930s when our economy was decimated by the Great Depression. That brings us to John Maynard Keynes and his analysis of that situation.

AD falls from AD_1 to AD_2, as the economy moves from E_1 to E'. At E' there is substantial unemployment and a large surplus of unsold goods and services. Prices and wages fall and the economy moves from E' to E_2, at which we are again at full employment.

Part II: The Keynesian Critique of the Classical System

> Our free enterprise system has rightly been compared to a gigantic computing machine capable of solving its own problems automatically. But anyone who has had some practical experience with large computers knows that they do break down and can't operate unattended.
>
> –Wassily Leontief, March 1971–

Until the Great Depression, classical economics was the dominant school of economic thought. Adam Smith, credited by many as the founder of classical economics, believed the government should intervene in economic affairs as little as possible. Indeed, laissez-faire economics was practiced down through the years until the time of President Herbert Hoover, who kept predicting that prosperity was just around the corner. John Maynard Keynes finally proclaimed the end of the classical era when he advocated massive government intervention to bring an end to the Great Depression.

John Maynard Keynes, a prominent classically trained economist, spent the first half of the 1930s writing a monumental critique of the classical system.[3] If supply creates its own demand, he asked, why are we having a worldwide depression? Keynes set out to learn what went wrong and how to fix it.

Keynes posed this problem for the classical economists: What if saving and investment were not equal? For instance, if saving were greater than investment, there would be unemployment. Not everything being produced would be purchased.

Keynes asked, "What if saving and investment were not equal?"

No problem, said the classicals, pointing back to Figure 2, which showed that the interest rate would equilibrate savings and investment. If the quantity of savings exceeded the quantity of loanable funds demanded for investment purposes, the interest rate would simply fall. And it would keep falling until the quantity of savings and the demand for investment funds were equal.

Keynes disputed this view. Saving and investing are done by different people for different reasons. Most saving is done by individuals for big-ticket items, such as cars, stereo systems, and major appliances, as well as for houses or retirement. Investing is done by those who run business firms basically because they are trying to make a profit. They will borrow to invest only when there is a reasonably good profit outlook. Why sink a lot of money into plant and equipment when your factory and machines are half idle? Even when interest rates are low, business firms won't invest unless it is profitable for them to do so.

Keynes: Saving and investing are done by different people for different reasons.

Even *this* posed no major problem to the classical economists, because they assumed wages and prices were downwardly flexible. If there were unemployment, the unemployed would find jobs as wage rates fell. And, similarly, if sellers were stuck with unwanted inventory, they would simply lower their prices.

Keynes questioned whether wages and prices *were* downwardly flexible, even during a severe recession. In the worst recession since the Great Depression, the downturn of 1981–82, there were very few instances of price or wage declines even in the face of falling output and widespread unemployment. Studies of the behavior of highly concentrated

---

[3]*The General Theory of Employment, Interest, and Money* is considered one of the most influential books of the 20th century.

industries indicate that prices are seldom lowered, while similar studies of large labor unions indicate that wage cuts (even as the only alternative to massive layoffs) are seldom accepted. Even if wages *were* lowered, added Keynes, this would lower workers' incomes, consequently lowering their spending on consumer goods.

We are not always at, or tending toward, full employment.

All of this led Keynes to conclude that the economy was not always at, or tending toward, a full-employment equilibrium. Keynes believed three possible equilibriums existed—*below* full employment, *at* full employment, and *above* full employment. Using the same demand and supply analysis as the classicals, Keynes showed that full employment was hardly inevitable.

The Keynesian long-run aggregate supply curve was really a hybrid of the classical short-run and long-run aggregate supply curves. It is drawn in Figure 11.[4] At extremely low levels of real GDP, when output is at, say, $3 trillion, our economy is in a catastrophic depression. As the economy begins to recover, output can be raised to about $4.7 trillion without any increase in prices. Why? Because millions of unemployed workers would be happy to work for the prevailing wage, so wage rates would certainly not have to be raised to entice people back to work. Furthermore, businessowners would also be happy to sell additional output at existing prices. But as real GDP continues to rise above $4.7 trillion, costs begin to rise, and bottlenecks eventually develop in certain industries, making greater and greater price increases necessary. Eventually, of course, at a real GDP of $6 trillion, we are at full employment and cannot, in the long run, raise output above that level. (See the box, "The Ranges of the Aggregate Supply Curve.")

The Keynesian and classical aggregate supply analyses are virtually identical.

Figure 12 shows three aggregate demand curves. AD₁ represents a very low level of aggregate demand, which, Keynes believed, was the basic problem during recessions

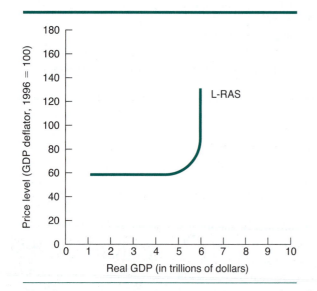

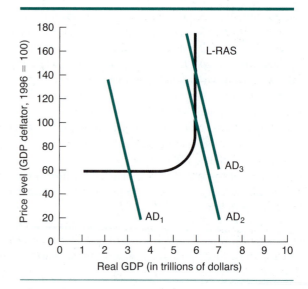

Figure 11

Modified Keynesian Aggregate Supply Curve

As an economy works its way out of a depression, output can be raised without raising prices, so the aggregate supply curve is flat. However, as resources become more fully employed and bottlenecks develop, costs and prices begin to rise. When this happens the aggregate supply curve begins to curve upward. When we reach full employment (at a real GDP of $6 trillion), output cannot be raised any further.

Figure 12

Three Aggregate Demand Curves

AD₁ represents aggregate demand during a recession or depression; AD₂ crosses the long-run aggregate supply curve at full employment; and AD₃ represents excessive demand.

---

[4]The curve shown in Figure 11 is actually a slightly modified Keynesian aggregate supply curve. Keynes originally assumed prices would not rise at all until full employment was attained (when real GDP was $6 trillion), but we've allowed here for an accelerating rise in prices from a real GDP of about $4.7 trillion to one of $6 trillion.

The Ranges of the Aggregate Supply Curve

The curve shown in the figure to the right is just slightly more elaborate than that in Figure 11. Here we have the three ranges: Keynesian, intermediate, and classical. The Keynesian range is thus named because John Maynard Keynes was writing during the Great Depression. People were so anxious to find work that they were happy to take a job—virtually any job—at the going wage rate. Thus, business firms could easily expand output without encountering rising wages.

Would they raise prices? Not for quite a while. After suffering through a few years of extremely low sales, they would be grateful for more business, albeit at the same price.

As the economy expanded, bottlenecks would begin to develop, shortages of resources (especially labor) would occur here and there, and costs would begin to rise in some sectors and eventually spread throughout the economy. And then business firms would begin raising their prices as well.

Eventually the economy would reach the maximum output level, at which point the only give would be in the form of higher prices. This would be the classical range of the aggregate supply curve. Remember that the classical economists believed that full employment was our normal state of affairs.

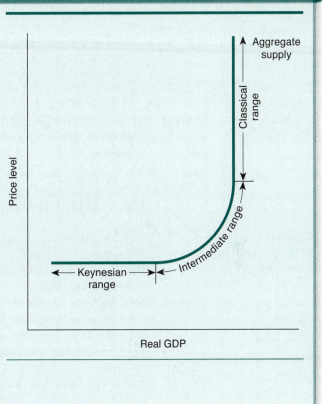

and depressions. The AD$_2$ curve shows the same full-employment equilibrium shown in Figures 9 and 10. And finally, AD$_3$ represents excessive demand, which would cause inflation.

In the last chapter we talked about demand-pull inflation, which was described as "too much money chasing too few goods." Demand-pull inflation occurs in the intermediate range of the aggregate supply curve in the figure in the box, "The Ranges of the Aggregate Supply Curve." Or, looking at Figure 12, start with an aggregate demand of AD$_1$ and imagine a series of higher and higher aggregate demand curves. At first we would have increases in real GDP without any price increases, but as aggregate demand moved closer to AD$_2$, we would eventually be able to keep pushing up real GDP only at the cost of some inflation. And as aggregate demand approached AD$_2$, we would be obtaining smaller and smaller increments of added output at the cost of larger and larger rises in the price level.

So we see that increases in aggregate demand will eventually lead to inflation. Applying this same analysis but moving in the opposite direction, we'll observe that decreasing aggregate demand leads to declining output and a decline in the rate of inflation. Starting at AD$_2$ and moving toward AD$_1$ in Figure 12, we see that real GDP is declining. As we noted toward the beginning of the last chapter, a decline in real GDP for two consecutive quarters is, by definition, a recession. And if continued decreases in aggregate demand pushed real GDP down still further, the recession would deepen and we might even sink into a depression.

Under this Keynesian analysis, we have three distinct possible equilibriums—below full employment, at full employment, and above full employment (with respect to prices,

John Maynard Keynes, British economist

not output). Our economy, according to Keynes, does not necessarily tend toward full employment, as the classicals maintained.

Our economy, said Keynes, can get stuck at an equilibrium that is well below full employment:

> Indeed it seems capable of remaining in a chronic condition of subnormal activity for a considerable period without any marked tendency either toward recovery or toward complete collapse. Moreover, the evidence indicates that full, or even approximately full, employment is a rare and short-lived occurrence.[5]

Let's examine the Keynesian system in more detail. Then we'll be ready to consider what the government should (or should not) do to prevent or to moderate recessions and inflations.

Part III: The Keynesian System

The classical equilibrium could not explain the Great Depression.

The classical theory of equilibrium was great at explaining why we would be either at full employment or tending toward it. But it wasn't much good at explaining why, in the 1930s, the entire world was in a depression. We needed a new theory to explain what was happening, and we needed a policy prescription to bring us out of this depression. John Maynard Keynes provided both.

Keynes used the same aggregate demand and supply apparatus as the classicals had, but he came up with very different conclusions. The key to his analysis was the role of aggregate demand. According to Keynes, the equilibrium level of GDP was determined primarily by the volume of expenditures planned by consumers, business firms, governments, and foreigners. Keynes concentrated on aggregate demand because he viewed rapid declines in this variable as the cause of recessions and depressions. Changes in aggregate supply—changes brought about by new technology, more capital and labor, and greater productivity—came about slowly and could therefore be neglected in the short run.

What about Say's law that "Supply creates its own demand"? Keynes stood Say's law on its head. In fact, we can summarize Keynesian theory with the statement, "Demand creates its own supply."

Keynes: Aggregate demand is our economy's prime mover.

Aggregate demand, said Keynes, is our economy's prime mover. Aggregate demand determines the level of output and employment. In other words, business firms produce only the quantity of goods and services they believe consumers, investors, governments, and foreigners plan to buy.

The centerpiece of his model was the behavior of the consumer. If consumers decide to spend more of their incomes on goods and services—or less, for that matter—then the effect on output and employment can be substantial.

The Keynesian Aggregate Expenditure Model

Since the Keynesian model assumes a constant price level, we'll return to our original graphic presentation, which we began in Chapter 5. We'll be on familiar ground because we'll be using some of the concepts covered in Chapters 5 through 9. You already have quite a bit of Keynesian analysis under your belt without knowing it.

In a nutshell, here's what we're going to be working with: (1) the consumption function; (2) the saving function; and (3) investment, which will be held constant. To

---

[5]John Maynard Keynes, *The General Theory of Employment, Interest, and Money* (New York: Harcourt Brace Jovanovich, 1958), pp. 249–50.

keep things as simple as possible, we are including only the private sector, so government purchases (and net exports, as well) are excluded from our model. This means changes in aggregate demand are brought about only by changes in C. So the centerpiece of the Keynesian model is the behavior of the consumer.

The Consumption and Saving Functions   Here's the consumption function: *As income rises, consumption rises, but not as quickly.* It is a "fundamental psychological law," said Keynes "that men are disposed, as a rule and on the average, to increase their consumption as their income increases, but not by as much as the increase in their income."[6]

So what people do, then, as incomes rise, is spend some of this additional income and save the rest—which brings us to the saving function: *As income rises, saving rises, but not as quickly.* No surprises here.

Hypothetical consumption and savings functions appear in Figure 13. As disposable income rises, consumption and saving rise as well. Because disposable income rises as output, or real GDP rises, we can say that as real GDP rises, consumption and saving rise. What about investment?

The Investment Sector   We learned in Chapter 6 that investment is the loose cannon on our economic deck. Keynes was well aware of this. What causes recessions in the Keynesian model? A decline in profit expectations causes recessions, or as Keynes puts it, the marginal efficiency of capital. Although rising interest rates may play an important role in setting off recessions, Keynes stressed profit expectations:

> But I suggest that a more typical, and often the predominant, explanation of the crisis is, not primarily a rise in the rate of interest, but a sudden collapse in the marginal efficiency of capital.[7]

How do we allow for planned investment in the Keynesian model? We've seen that planned consumption rises with disposable income and real GDP. What about

Investment is unstable.

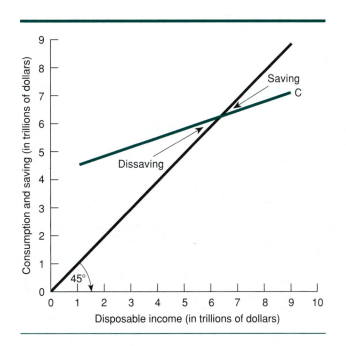

Figure 13
Disposable Income (in trillions of dollars)
When consumption is greater than disposable income, savings is negative; when disposable income is greater than consumption, savings is positive.

---

[6]Ibid., p. 96.

[7]Ibid., p. 315.

Finding Equilibrium GDP

inding equilibrium GDP is as easy as finding the level of spending at which saving and investment are equal. Try to find that level of spending in Figure A.

What did you get? Equilibrium GDP is $5.5 trillion. Now, how much is saving? At equilibrium GDP, saving—the vertical distance between the C line and the 45-degree line—is about $1.7 trillion. And how much is I? It's the vertical distance between the C line and the C + I line—also about $1.7 trillion. And so, at an equilibrium

GDP of $5.5 trillion, saving and investment are equal at $1.7 trillion.

In Figure B we come back to the $C + I + G + X_n$ graph from Chapter 8. $C + I + G + X_n$ is aggregate demand, or GDP. We've simply added the government and foreign sectors to the consumption and investment sectors.

How much is equilibrium GDP in Figure B? It's $5 trillion. We'll be making good use of this type of graph at the beginning of the next chapter.

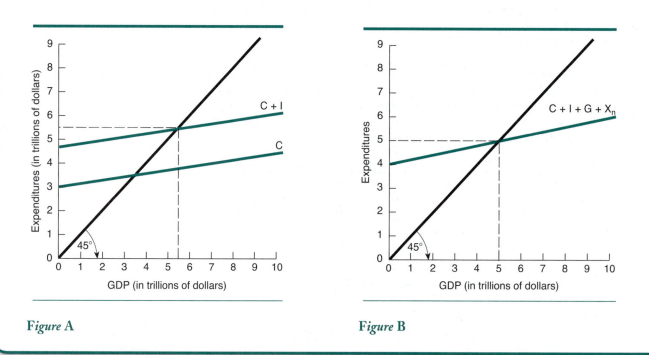

Figure A

Figure B

planned investment? It, too, probably varies directly with disposable income and real GDP. But we need to keep things simple. So we're going to come up with an arbitrary figure for planned investment—$500 billion—and keep it constant for all levels of real GDP.

We'll add just one line to our graph, the C + I line, and then we'll be able to wind up our analysis. We've done that in Figure 14. Assuming C + I constitutes aggregate demand, how much is equilibrium GDP? It comes out to $7 trillion.

And how much is investment? It's a constant of $500 billion.

So, at equilibrium GDP, all our ducks are in a line, so to speak. Aggregate demand, C + I (measured vertically), is equal to aggregate supply, or real GDP (measured on the horizontal scale). The level of output produced is exactly equal to the amount that buyers wish to purchase.

Also, saving and investment are equal. Saving is the vertical distance between the C line and the 45-degree line. The vertical distance between the C line and the C + I line is I. Therefore, the vertical distance between the C line and the 45-degree line must be equal to (actually, identical to) the vertical distance between the C line and the C + I line. (For extra help with finding equilibrium GDP, see the box, "Finding Equilibrium GDP.")

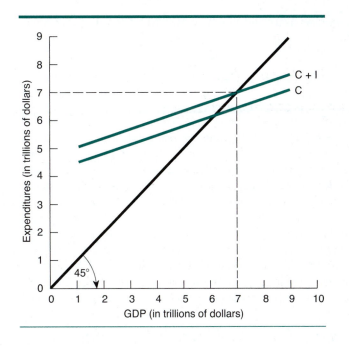

Figure 14

GDP (in trillions of dollars)
When C + I represents aggregate demand, how much is equilibrium GDP? It's $7 trillion.

Disequilibrium and Equilibrium

In both Keynesian and classical economic systems, the economy is always tending toward equilibrium, where aggregate demand and aggregate supply are equal. Let's look at this process from two perspectives: first, when aggregate demand is larger than aggregate supply and second, when aggregate supply is larger than aggregate demand.

(1) Aggregate Demand Exceeds Aggregate Supply

When aggregate demand exceeds aggregate supply, a chain reaction is set off and continues until the economy is back in equilibrium. The first thing that happens is that inventories start declining. What do business firms do? They order more inventory. Consequently, orders to manufacturers rise, and, of course, production rises. Manufacturers will hire more labor, and eventually, as plant utilization approaches capacity, more plant and equipment are ordered.

> When aggregate demand exceeds aggregate supply, inventories decline.

Suppose you own an appliance store. You have been ordering 50 blenders a month because that's about how many you sell. But during the last month your blender sales doubled, so you decide to order 100 blenders instead of your usual 50. Think of what this does to the production of blenders, assuming the other appliance stores double their orders as well.

As more people find employment, they will consume more, raising aggregate demand. Business firms may also begin raising their prices. Retailers may perceive that their customers are willing to pay more. Eventually, the manufacturers may have trouble increasing output much farther because of shortages in labor, raw materials, plant and equipment, or the funds to finance expansion. These shortages will occur at some point—and consequently, most prices will rise—because what is happening in the appliance industry is probably happening in the rest of the economy. As the economy approaches full capacity (and full employment), prices will have begun to rise.

We started with aggregate demand exceeding aggregate supply, but this disparity told manufacturers to increase aggregate supply. First, output was increased; eventually, so were prices. As GDP (which is identical to aggregate supply) is defined as the nation's output of goods and services at market prices, it appears that there are two ways to raise aggregate supply—by increasing output and by increasing prices. By doing this, we raise aggregate supply relative to aggregate demand and quickly restore equilibrium.

(2) Aggregate Supply Exceeds Aggregate Demand

When aggregate supply exceeds aggregate demand, inventories rise.

When aggregate supply is greater than aggregate demand, the economy is in disequilibrium. Aggregate supply must fall. Because aggregate supply is greater than aggregate demand, production exceeds sales, and inventories are rising. When retailers realize this, what do they do? They cut back on orders to manufacturers. After all, if you found you were accumulating more and more stock on your shelves, wouldn't you cut back on your orders? Remember, not only does it cost money to carry large inventories—shelf space as well as money is tied up—but also there is always the risk that you may not be able to sell your stock.

When manufacturers receive fewer orders, they reduce output and consequently lay off some workers, further depressing aggregate demand as these workers cut back on their consumption. Retail firms, facing declining sales as well as growing inventories, may reduce prices, although during recent recessions price reductions have been relatively uncommon. Eventually, inventories are sufficiently depleted. In the meantime, aggregate supply has fallen back into equilibrium with aggregate demand.

(3) Summary: How Equilibrium Is Attained

When the economy is in disequilibrium, it automatically moves back into equilibrium.

We can make an interesting observation about the entire process. When the economy is in disequilibrium, it automatically moves back into equilibrium. It is always aggregate supply that adjusts. When aggregate demand is greater than aggregate supply, the latter rises, and when aggregate supply exceeds aggregate demand, aggregate supply declines.

Please keep in mind that aggregate demand (C + I) must equal the level of production (aggregate supply) for the economy to be in equilibrium. When the two are not equal, aggregate supply must adjust to bring the economy back into equilibrium.

Keynesian Policy Prescriptions

The classicals believed recessions were temporary because the economy is self-correcting.

Let's summarize the classical position. Recessions are temporary because the economy is self-correcting. Declining investment will be pushed up again by falling interest rates, while, if consumption falls, it will be raised by falling prices and wages. And because recessions are self-correcting, the role of government is to stand back and do nothing.

Keynes's position was that recessions were not necessarily temporary, because the self-correcting mechanisms of falling interest rates and falling prices and wages might be insufficient to push investment and consumption back up again. The private economy does not automatically move toward full employment. Therefore, it would be necessary for the government to intervene.

What should the government do? Spend money! How *much* money?[8] If the economy is in a bad recession, it will be necessary to spend a lot of money. And if it's in a depression, then it must spend even more.

Aggregate demand is insufficient to provide jobs for everyone who wants to work; thus it is necessary for the government to provide the spending that will push the economy toward full employment. Just spend money; it doesn't matter on what. Keynes made this point quite vividly:

> If the Treasury were to fill old bottles with banknotes, bury them at suitable depths in disused coal mines which are then filled up to the surface with town rubbish, and leave it to private enterprise on well-tried principles of laissez-faire to dig the notes up again . . . ,

---

[8]We'll be much more specific in the next chapter. But let's be clear now that, when the government *spends* more money, that's not the same thing as *printing* more money. Generally it borrows more money and then spends it.

there need be no more unemployment. . . . It would, indeed, be more sensible to build houses and the like; but if there are political and practical difficulties in the way of this, the above would be better than nothing.[9]

If all it takes is government spending to get us out of a depression, then why didn't President Franklin Roosevelt's massive New Deal spending get us out of the Great Depression? First of all, it *did* succeed in bringing about rapid economic growth between 1933 and 1937. But then, just when the economy seemed to be coming out of its depression, Roosevelt suddenly tried to balance the federal budget; he got Congress to raise taxes and cut government spending. On top of this, the Federal Reserve sharply cut the rate of growth of the money supply. So back down we went, with output plunging sharply and the unemployment rate soaring once again.

Why didn't New Deal spending get us out of the economic crisis of the 1930s?

Not until the huge World War II armaments expenditures in the early 1940s did the United States finally emerge from the Depression. So what, then, did we learn from all of this? One possibility is that the only way to end a depression is to go to war. But what I hope you learned is that massive government spending of *any* kind—whether on highways, school construction, AIDS research, crime prevention, space exploration, *or* on soldiers' salaries—will pull us out of a depression.

In recent times, the most expensive application of Keynes's policy prescription for recessions has been carried out by Japan. For nearly the entire decade of the 1990s, the Japanese economy was mired in recession. During this period Japan spent more than $1 trillion, much of it on bridges, tunnels, airports, concert halls, and highways. Although none of these projects was as unproductive as burying bottles of banknotes, the new $10 billion Tokyo subway line, which was supposed to provide a direct route from the northern part of the city to the southwest, does not do so. It was just one of many Japanese public works projects that seem extravagant, wasteful, or even pointless.

But the million-dollar question—or, in this case, the trillion-dollar question—is how this giant public works program benefited the Japanese economy. Clearly it has kept a lingering recession from slipping into a more severe one, or even into a depression. Maybe the Japanese government, like the American New Deal of the 1930s, just did not spend enough for long enough. Or just maybe, what really counts is not just how *much* you spend, but *how* you spend it.

Over the last eight decades, our economy has been racked by repeated bouts of inflation, recession, and, of course, the decade-long Great Depression. According to John Maynard Keynes, our problem during periods of recession and depression has been insufficient aggregate demand. And though he died in 1946, before we encountered periods of sustained inflation, he would have prescribed lowering aggregate demand to bring down the inflation rate.

In the next chapter we shall deal specifically with this Keynesian manipulation of the level of aggregate demand to deal with inflation and recession. Fiscal policy, which is the name that has been assigned to Keynesian taxation and government spending prescriptions, became the basic government policy tool to ensure price stability and high employment from the 1930s through the 1960s. Keynesian fiscal policy is once again in the ascendency, and we'll see how it has been employed to fight the Great Recession of 2007–2009.

Current Issue: Keynes and Say in the 21st Century

Until the 1970s the American economy was essentially a closed system. Mass production and mass consumption fed off each other. We made it and then we bought it. Our system was best described by Say's law: Supply creates its own demand.

There was no problem as long as American workers used their wages to buy up the goods and services they produced. Henry Ford recognized this truth back in 1914 when he doubled the wages of his semiskilled assembly line workers to the unheard sum of $5 a day. He recognized that every worker was a potential customer.

---

[9]Keynes, *The General Theory of Employment, Interest, and Money*, p. 129.

When our economy collapsed in the 1930s, John Maynard Keynes declared that our problem was inadequate aggregate demand for goods and services. Standing Say's law on its head, Keynes believed that demand creates its own supply. If individual consumers, business firms, and the government spent a lot more money, then a lot more goods and services would be produced.

The next three decades were quite prosperous as consumers, businesses, and the government spent enough money to buy up a steadily growing supply of goods and services. Almost every year we spent more and we produced more. We churned out suburban homes, station wagons, highways, TVs, furniture, clothing, school buildings, shopping malls, and foodstuffs, not to mention a vast array of weaponry.

During those decades we were nearly self-sufficient. But after Japan, Germany, and the rest of the industrial world rebuilt their war-devastated economies, American manufacturers began to face competition. In foreign markets, and even on our home turf, foreign manufacturers of TVs, cars, clothing, and other consumer goods began eating our lunch.

Things went from bad to worse as manufacturing employment fell from 22 percent of total employment in 1979 to just 10 percent today. We no longer were operating a closed system in which we bought up our own output.

Neither Say nor Keynes are giving us the answers we need. Supply is certainly *not* creating its own demand. Nor is a robust aggregate demand preventing our manufacturing base from eroding. To sum up: Because we consume much more than we produce, our aggregate demand is much greater than our aggregate supply. As a result, we are running huge trade deficits. These deficits will be a major topic of the next to last chapter of this book.

Questions for Further Thought and Discussion

1. The classical economists believed that our economy was always at full employment or tending toward full employment. If our economy were operating below full employment, what would happen, according to the classicals, to move the economy back toward full employment?

2. When the price level increases, the quantity of goods and services purchased declines. Why does this happen?

3. Explain the difference between the long-run aggregate supply curve and the short-run aggregate supply curve.

4. What were the major areas of disagreement between John Maynard Keynes and the classical economists?

5. Describe the chain reaction that is set off when (a) aggregate demand exceeds aggregate supply; (b) aggregate supply exceeds aggregate demand.

6. *Practical Application:* If you lived in a village cut off from the rest of the world, show how Say's law would apply to your village's economy.

Workbook for Chapter 11

Name _____   Date _____

Multiple-Choice Questions

Circle the letter that corresponds to the best answer.

1. Until the Great Depression, the dominant school of economic thought was _____. (LO4, 5)
   a) classical economics
   b) Keynesian economics
   c) supply-side economics
   d) monetarism

2. The classical economists believed in _____. (LO2)
   a) strong government intervention
   b) laissez-faire
   c) a rapid growth in the money supply
   d) none of these

3. Say's law states that _____. (LO1)
   a) we can have an inflation or a recession, but never both at the same time
   b) the normal state of economic affairs is recession
   c) demand creates its own supply
   d) supply creates its own demand

4. People work, according to Jean Baptiste Say, so that they can _____. (LO1)
   a) consume   c) stay busy
   b) save   d) none of these

5. According to the classical economists, _____. (LO2)
   a) people will always spend all their money
   b) any money that is saved will be invested
   c) saving will always be greater than investment
   d) saving will always be smaller than investment

6. Keynes believed _____. (LO5)
   a) recessions were temporary
   b) once a recession began, it would always turn into a depression

   c) the real problem that modern economies faced was inflation
   d) none of these

7. "Our economy is always at full employment" was a claim made by _____. (LO2, 4)
   a) both Keynes and the classicals
   b) neither Keynes nor the classicals
   c) Keynes but not the classicals
   d) the classicals but not Keynes

8. According to the classical economists, if the amount of money people are planning to invest is greater than the amount that people want to save, _____. (LO3)
   a) interest rates will rise and saving will rise
   b) interest rates will fall and saving will fall
   c) interest rates will fall and saving will rise
   d) interest rates will rise and saving will fall

9. Each of the following supports the classical theory of employment except _____. (LO3, 4)
   a) Say's law
   b) wage-price flexibility
   c) the interest mechanism
   d) government spending programs

10. Our economy is definitely at equilibrium in each case except when _____. (LO4)
    a) saving equals investment
    b) aggregate demand equals aggregate supply
    c) the amount people are willing to spend equals the amount that producers are producing
    d) equilibrium GDP equals full-employment GDP

11. That we are always tending toward full employment is a belief of _____. (LO6)
    a) Keynes
    b) the classicals
    c) both Keynes and the classicals
    d) neither Keynes nor the classicals

12. Keynes said _____. (LO5)
    a) the expected profit rate was more important than the interest rate
    b) the interest rate was more important than the expected profit rate
    c) the expected profit rate and the interest rate were equally important
    d) neither the expected profit rate nor the interest rate was important

13. John Maynard Keynes is most closely associated with the _____. (LO5)
    a) American Revolution
    b) French Revolution
    c) Great Depression
    d) Russian Revolution

14. The classical economists' aggregate supply curve is vertical _____. (LO4)
    a) both in the short run and in the long run
    b) in neither the short run nor the long run
    c) in the short run, but not in the long run
    d) in the long run, but not in the short run

15. To end a bad recession, we need to _____. (LO7)
    a) go to war
    b) spend a lot of money
    c) balance the federal budget

16. Which statement best describes the classical theory of employment? (LO2)
    a) We will always have a great deal of unemployment.
    b) We will usually have a great deal of unemployment.
    c) We will occasionally have some unemployment, but our economy will automatically move back toward full employment.
    d) We never have any unemployment.

17. According to Keynes, our economy always tends toward _____. (LO5, 6)
    a) equilibrium GDP
    b) full-employment GDP
    c) recessions
    d) inflations

18. When saving is greater than investment, we are _____. (LO2, 6)
    a) at equilibrium GDP
    b) at full-employment GDP
    c) below equilibrium GDP
    d) above equilibrium GDP

19. Keynes considered full-employment GDP to be _____. (LO5, 6)
    a) the normal state of economic affairs
    b) a rare occurrence
    c) an impossibility
    d) none of these

20. Keynes was concerned mainly with _____. (LO4, 5)
    a) aggregate supply
    b) aggregate demand
    c) the interest rate
    d) inflation

21. When aggregate demand is greater than aggregate supply, _____. (LO4)
    a) inventories get depleted and output rises
    b) inventories get depleted and output falls
    c) inventories rise and output rises
    d) inventories rise and output falls

22. When the economy is in disequilibrium, _____. (LO4)
    a) production automatically rises
    b) production automatically falls
    c) it automatically moves back into equilibrium
    d) it stays in disequilibrium permanently

23. As the price level rises, _____. (LO4)
    a) the quantity of goods and services demanded falls
    b) the quantity of goods and services demanded rises
    c) the quantity of goods and services demanded stays the same
    d) none of the above is correct

24. The slope of the aggregate demand curve is explained by each of the following except _____. (LO3, 4)
    a) the real balance effect
    b) the interest rate effect
    c) the foreign purchases effect
    d) the profit effect

25. Which of the following antirecession (or antidepression) programs would not be one that John Maynard Keynes would have prescribed? (LO7)
    a) The New Deal under President Franklin Roosevelt
    b) The one-trillion-dollar Japanese public works program of the 1990s
    c) Letting the forces of supply and demand allow the economy to reattain full employment
    d) Burying bottles containing banknotes

26. Which of the following is the most accurate statement about meeting our current economic needs? (LO2, 7)
    a) John Maynard Keynes, rather than Jean Baptiste Say, is providing the economic answers we need.
    b) Say, rather than Keynes, is providing the economic answers we need.
    c) Neither Keynes nor Say is providing the economic answers we need.
    d) Together, Keynes and Say are providing the economic answers we need.

27. If we are operating in the classical range of the aggregate supply curve and aggregate demand rose, then _____. (LO 4)
    a) output would rise and the price level would remain the same
    b) output would remain the same and the price level would rise
    c) output would rise and the price level would rise
    d) output would remain the same and the price level would remain the same

28. Keynes and the classical economics would agree that _____. (LO 6)
    a) our economy is always at equilibrium or tending toward equilibrium
    b) our economy is never at or tending toward equilibrium
    c) the prime mover of our economy is aggregate supply
    d) the prime mover of our economy is aggregate demand

Fill-In Questions

1. Laissez-faire was advocated by the _____ school of economics. (LO1, 2)

2. The two reasons why the aggregate supply curve moves upward to the right are: (1) _____ and (2) _____. (LO4)

3. According to Say's law, people work so that they can _____. (LO1)

4. According to Say's law, people spend _____ _____. (LO1)

5. The classical economists believed savings would equal _____. (LO2, 3)

6. If supply creates its own demand, asked Keynes, why are we having a _____? (LO5)

7. If saving were greater than investment, said the classical economists, they would be set equal by the _____. (LO2)

8. The classical economists believed that wages and prices were _____ flexible. (LO2)

9. The classical economists believed recessions were _____. (LO2)

10. During recessions, said the classical economists, the government should _____. (LO2)

11. When aggregate demand is greater than aggregate supply, inventories will _____ and output will _____. (LO4, 6)

12. When individuals, business firms, and the government are spending just enough money to provide jobs for everyone willing and able to work, we are at _____ GDP. (LO6)

13. At equilibrium GDP, _____ will be equal to _____. (LO4, 6)

14. Our economy always tends toward _____ GDP. (LO6)

15. When investment is greater than savings, we are _____ equilibrium GDP. (LO6)

16. Full-employment GDP and equilibrium GDP are _____ equal. (LO6)

17. Keynes was most concerned with one main variable, _____. (LO5)

18. According to John Maynard Keynes, the level of aggregate supply is determined by the _____ _____. (LO6)

19. When we are far below the full-employment level of GDP, Keynes policy prescription was _____ _____. (LO6)

20. When aggregate supply is greater than aggregate demand, the economy is in _____. (LO4, 6)

Problems

1. If GDP = C + I and if GDP = C + S, then

   _____ = _____. (LO1)

2. Given the information in Figure 1, and assuming an interest rate of 15 percent: (a) Will the economy be at equilibrium? (b) Will savings equal investment? (c) What will happen, according to the classical economists? (LO3, 6)

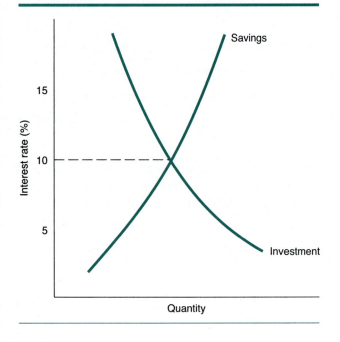

Figure 1

3. Given the information in Figure 2: (a) If aggregate demand shifts from AD_1 to AD_2, what happens to the level of prices and to output? (b) If aggregate demand shifts from AD_2 to AD_3, what happens to the level of prices and to output? (c) If aggregate demand shifts from AD_3 to AD_4, what happens to the level of prices and to output? (LO4)

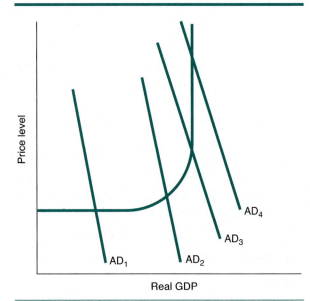

Figure 2

4. Given the information in Figure 2: (a) Which aggregate demand curve represents our economy during the Great Depression? (b) Which aggregate demand curve represents our economy during nearly all the years since World War II? (c) Which aggregate demand curve represents our economy during a period of full employment with a great deal of inflation? (LO6)

Chapter 12

Fiscal Policy and the National Debt

These are exciting times—at least for economists. In 2000 we had the largest federal government budget surplus in our history; in 2009 and 2010 we ran—by far—the largest deficits. Fiscal policy is *the manipulation of the federal budget to attain price stability, relatively full employment, and a satisfactory rate of economic growth.* To attain these goals, the president and Congress must manipulate its spending and taxes. Later, in Chapter 14, we'll look at monetary policy, which uses very different means to promote the same ends.

LEARNING OBJECTIVES

After reading this chapter you should be able to:

1. Analyze the recessionary and inflationary gaps.
2. Calculate and apply the multiplier.
3. List and discuss the automatic stabilizers.
4. Assess discretionary fiscal policy.
5. Distinguish between budget deficits and surpluses.
6. Discuss fiscal policy lags.
7. Define and differentiate between the crowding-out and crowding-in effects.
8. Assess the success of fiscal policy measures in ending the Great Recession.
9. Discuss and analyze the national debt.
10. Explain why the recovery from the Great Recession will be "jobless."
11. Explain predictions for federal budget deficits in the future.

Putting Fiscal Policy into Perspective

Until the time of the Great Depression, the only advice economists gave the government was to try to balance its budget every year and to not interfere with the workings of the private economy. Just balance the books and then stay out of the way. There was no such thing as fiscal policy until John Maynard Keynes invented it in the 1930s.

He pointed out that there was a depression going on and that the problem was anemic aggregate demand. Consumption was lagging because so many people were out of work. Investment was extremely low because businessowners had no reason to add to their inventories or build more plant and equipment. After all, sales were very low and much of their plant and equipment was sitting idle. So the only thing left to boost aggregate demand was government spending.

What about taxes? Well, certainly, we would not want to *raise* them. That would push aggregate demand even lower. We might even want to *cut* taxes to give consumers and businesses more money to spend. OK, now if we were to follow this advice, would the government be able to balance its budget? No way! But if we ran a big enough budget deficit, we could jump-start the economy and, in effect, spend our way out of this depression.

You don't have to be a great economist to see that we haven't been too successful at attaining our fiscal policy goals, particularly since the mid-1960s. It's important that the aggregate supply of goods and services equal the aggregate demand for goods and services at just the level of spending that will bring about full employment at stable prices.

Equilibrium GDP tells us the level of spending in the economy. Full-employment GDP tells us the level of spending necessary to get the unemployment rate down to 5 percent (which we have been calling full employment). We'll see how fiscal policy is used to push equilibrium GDP toward full-employment GDP.

In terms of equilibrium GDP, sometimes we are spending too much, and at other times we are spending too little. When equilibrium GDP is too big, we have an inflationary gap, and when it's too small, a recessionary gap. Remember Goldilocks and the Three Bears? Remember the porridge that was too hot and the porridge that was too cold? Like Goldilocks seeking the perfect porridge, our policy objective is to find a level of GDP that is just right. We will deal with recessionary and inflationary gaps and GDPs that are just right in the next few pages.

Part I: The Recessionary Gap and the Inflationary Gap

Equilibrium GDP is the level of output at which aggregate demand equals aggregate supply.

Before we go to the gaps, we need to review some terms from Chapter 11. First: *equilibrium GDP*. Our economy is always at equilibrium GDP or tending toward it. *Equilibrium GDP is the level of output at which aggregate demand equals aggregate supply.* What is *aggregate demand*? It's *the sum of all expenditures for goods and services* (that is, C + I + G + X_n). And what is *aggregate supply*? Aggregate supply is *the nation's total output of final goods and services.* So at equilibrium GDP, everything produced is sold.

Full employment GDP is the level of spending necessary to provide full employment of our resources.

We need to review one more term: *full-employment GDP*. Full employment means nearly all our resources are being used. For example, if our plant and equipment is operating at between 85 and 90 percent of capacity, *that's* full employment. Or if only 5 percent of our labor force is unemployed, then *that's* full employment. So, what's full-employment GDP? Full-employment GDP is *the level of spending necessary to provide full employment of our resources.* Alternatively, it is the level of spending necessary to purchase the output, or aggregate supply, of a fully employed economy.

The Recessionary Gap

A recessionary gap occurs when equilibrium GDP is less than full-employment GDP. Equilibrium GDP is the level of spending that the economy is at or is tending toward. Full-employment GDP is the level of spending needed to provide enough jobs to reduce the unemployment rate to 5 percent. When too little is being spent to provide enough jobs, we have a deflationary gap, which is shown in Figure 1.

How much is equilibrium GDP in Figure 1? Write down the number. What did you get? Did you get $5 trillion? That's the GDP at which the C + I + G + X_n line crosses the 45-degree line.

How can we close the recessionary gap?

How do we close this gap? We need to raise spending—consumption (C) or investment (I) or government expenditures (G)—or perhaps some combination of these. John Maynard Keynes tells us to raise G. Or we may want to lower taxes. Lowering business taxes might raise I; lowering personal income taxes would increase C.

How much would we have to raise spending to close the recessionary gap shown in Figure 1? Would you believe $1 trillion? That's right! This is *some* recessionary gap. There would have to be a depression going on, so we would need to raise spending by $1 trillion. Anything less would reduce, but not eliminate, the gap.

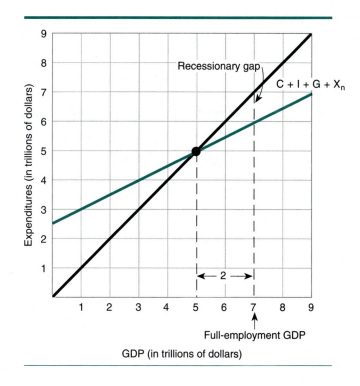

Figure 1
The Recessionary Gap
When full-employment GDP is
greater than equilibrium GDP, there
is a recessionary gap. How much is
it in this graph? The recessionary
gap is $1 trillion.

Note that equilibrium GDP is $2 trillion less than the full-employment GDP of $7 trillion. In a few pages we'll do some multiplier analysis. This analysis will show us that raising G by $1 trillion will raise equilibrium GDP by $2 trillion and eliminate the recessionary gap. But let's not get ahead of ourselves.

Note how the points in Figure 1 line up. Equilibrium GDP is to the left of full-employment GDP. The recessionary gap is directly above the full-employment GDP. It is the vertical distance between the 45-degree line and the $C + I + G + X_n$ line.

The Inflationary Gap

Figure 2 shows the inflationary gap. The key difference between this graph and that of the recessionary gap is the position of equilibrium GDP. When there is an inflationary gap, equilibrium GDP is to the right of full-employment GDP. It is to the left when there's a recessionary gap. *Equilibrium GDP is greater than full-employment GDP when there's an inflationary gap.* When there's a recessionary gap, full-employment GDP is greater than equilibrium GDP.

In both graphs the gap is the vertical distance between the $C + I + G + X_n$ line and the 45-degree line, and in both graphs the gap is directly above full-employment GDP. In short, when there's a recessionary gap, equilibrium GDP is too small; when there's an inflationary gap, it's too big. To eliminate an inflationary gap, Keynes would suggest cutting G and raising taxes. Both actions are aimed at reducing spending and, therefore, equilibrium GDP.

Recessionary gap: Equilibrium GDP is too small.

In Figure 2 the inflationary gap is $200 billion ($1,200 billion − $1,000 billion). If we cut spending by $200 billion, it would have a multiplied effect on GDP. Equilibrium GDP would decline by $500 billion ($1,500 billion − $1,000 billion) to the full-employment level.

Inflationary gap: Equilibrium GDP is too large.

I'm tossing around billions and trillions as if they were pocket change. Remember that 1,000 billion equals 1 trillion.

To summarize, if spending is too high, equilibrium GDP is above the full-employment level. To eliminate the inflationary gap, we cut G and/or raise taxes. If equilibrium GDP is less than full-employment GDP, we eliminate the recessionary gap by raising G and/or cutting taxes.

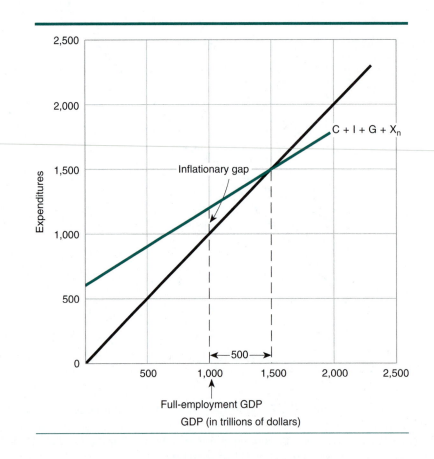

Figure 2

The Inflationary Gap

When equilibrium GDP is greater than full-employment GDP, there is an inflationary gap. How large is the inflationary gap in this graph? The inflationary gap is $200 billion.

For the last three decades Republicans have labeled every Democratic presidential candidate a "tax and spend liberal." And by inference these Republicans wanted to be called "low-tax and low-spend conservatives." To generalize, liberals would seem to favor a high-spending, high-taxing, big government, and conservatives a low-spending, low-taxing, relatively small government. How would these philosophies lend themselves to fiscal policy?

If there were a recession, conventional fiscal policy calls for tax cuts and more government spending. If the liberal could choose just one of these measures, which would she favor? And which one would the conservative favor? The liberal would choose higher government spending (which would increase the role of government), while the conservative would cut taxes, thereby reducing the government's role.

Now figure out the liberal's and conservative's respective policy prescriptions for dealing with inflation. Write them down right here:

The liberal would raise taxes, and the conservative would cut government spending. To generalize—or perhaps overgeneralize—the liberal tends to favor bigger government, and the conservative, smaller government.

Part II: The Multiplier and Its Applications

We're going to put together some concepts introduced in earlier chapters: aggregate demand (Chapters 9 and 11), the marginal propensity to consume (Chapter 5), and equilibrium GDP (Chapter 11). We know that an increase in G will raise aggregate demand, but by how much? We also know that a tax increase will lower aggregate demand, but, again, by how much? The multiplier will tell us by just how much.

The Multiplier

The multiplier is based on two concepts covered in Chapter 9: (1) GDP is the nation's expenditure on all the final goods and services produced during the year at market prices. (2) GDP $= C + I + G + X_n$.

It is obvious that if C goes up, GDP will go up. Or if I goes down, so will GDP. Now we'll add a new wrinkle. When there is any change in spending, that is, in C, I, G, or X_n, it will have a multiplied effect on GDP.

When money is spent by one person, it becomes someone else's income. And what do we *do* with most of our income? We spend it. Once again, when this money is spent, someone else receives it as income and, in turn, spends most of it. If a dollar were initially spent, perhaps someone who received that dollar would spend 80 cents, and of that 80 cents received by the next person, perhaps 64 cents would be spent. If we add up all the spending generated by that one dollar, it will add up to four or five or six times that dollar. Hence, we get the name *the multiplier.*

Any change in spending (C, I, or G) will set off a chain reaction, leading to a multiplied change in GDP. How *much* of a multiplied effect? A $10 billion increase in G might increase GDP by $50 billion. In that case, the multiplier is 5. If a decline of $5 billion in I causes GDP to fall by $40 billion, then the multiplier would be 8.

First we'll concentrate on calculating the multiplier, for which we'll use the formula:

$$\frac{1}{1 - MPC}$$

$$\text{Multiplier} = \frac{1}{1 - MPC}$$

Then we'll see how it is used to predict changes in GDP. (A reminder: MPC is marginal propensity to consume.)

The formula above is the same as 1/MPS, or $\dfrac{1}{\text{marginal propensity to save}}$. Remember, MPC + MPS = 1 (or 1 − MPC = MPS). Because the multiplier (like C) deals with spending, $1/(1 - MPC)$ is a more appropriate formula.

The MPC can thus be used to find the multiplier. If the MPC were 0.5, find the multiplier. Work this problem out in the space below. Write down the formula first, then substitute and solve.

Solution:

$$\text{Multiplier} = \frac{1}{1 - MPC} = \frac{1}{1 - 0.5} = \frac{1}{0.5} = 2^1$$

---

[1]Many students get lost at the third step. How do we get 0.5? How come 1 − 0.5 = 0.5? Look at it this way:

$$\begin{array}{r} 1.0 \\ -0.5 \\ \hline 0.5 \end{array}$$

If it's still not clear, then think of 1 as a dollar and 0.5 (or .50) as 50 cents. How much is a dollar minus 50 cents?

Step four is just as easy. How many times does 50 cents go into a dollar? Or, you can just divide 0.5 into 1.0. Either way, it comes out to 2.

Let's try another problem. When the MPC is 0.75, how much is the multiplier?

Solution:

$$\text{Multiplier} = \frac{1}{1 - \text{MPC}} = \frac{1}{1 - 0.75} = \frac{1}{0.25} = 4^2$$

Applications of the Multiplier

The multiplier is used to
calculate the effects of changes
in C, I, and G on GDP.

Knowing the multiplier, we can calculate the effect of changes in C, I, and G on the level of GDP. If GDP is 2,500, the multiplier is 3, and C rises by 10, what is the new level of GDP?

A second formula is needed to determine the new level of GDP:

New GDP = Initial GDP + (Change in spending × Multiplier)

Note the parentheses. Their purpose is to ensure that we multiply before we add. In arithmetic you must always multiply (or divide) before you add (or subtract). Always. The parentheses are there to make sure we do this.

Copy down the formula, substitute, and solve.

Solution:

(1) New GDP = Initial GDP + (Change in spending × Multiplier)

(2)   = 2,500 + (10 × 3)

(3)   = 2,500 + (30)

              = 2,530

Here are a few variations of this type of problem. Suppose that consumer spending rises by $10 billion and the multiplier is 3. What happens to GDP?

(See solution on the next page.)

---

[2]After you've substituted into the formula, think of 1 as a dollar and 0.75 as 75 cents. From there (1/0.25) we divide 0.25 into 1, or a quarter into a dollar.

Solution: It rises by $30 billion: $10 billion $\times$ 3.

Try this one: Government spending falls by $5 billion with a multiplier of 7.

Solution: $-$5 billion $\times$ 7 = $-$35 billion. In other words, if government spending falls by $5 billion with a multiplier of 7, GDP falls by $35 billion.

Two more multiplier applications and we're through. First, how big is the multiplier in Figure 1? If you're not sure, guess. What's your answer? Is it 2? We can find the multiplier by using deductive logic. We know the recessionary gap is $1 trillion. We also know that equilibrium GDP is $2 trillion less than full-employment GDP. (Equilibrium GDP is $5 trillion and full-employment GDP is $7 trillion.) Suppose we were to raise G by $1 trillion. What would happen to the gap? It would vanish! And what would happen to equilibrium GDP? It would rise by $2 trillion and become equal to full-employment GDP.

Still not convinced? Let's redraw Figure 1 as Figure 3 and add $C_1 + I_1 + G_1 + X_{n_1}$. You'll notice that $C_1 + I_1 + G_1 + X_{n_1}$ is $1 trillion higher than $C + I + G + X_n$. You'll also notice that the recessionary gap is gone. And that equilibrium GDP equals full-employment GDP.

One more question: How big is the multiplier in Figure 2? Again, if you're not sure, guess. Is your answer 2.5? How do we get 2.5? OK, we know that the inflationary gap is 200, and we know equilibrium GDP is 500 greater than full-employment GDP. So if we lower G by 200, the inflationary gap disappears. And now equilibrium GDP falls by 500 and is equal to full-employment GDP.

Here's a formula you can use to find the multiplier whether you have an inflationary gap or a recessionary gap:

$$\text{Multiplier} = \frac{\text{Distance between equilibrium GDP and full-employment GDP}}{\text{Gap}}$$

In Figure 4 the distance is 500 and the inflationary gap is 200. So 500/200 = 2.5. You can also use this formula to find the multiplier if there is a recessionary gap. For example,

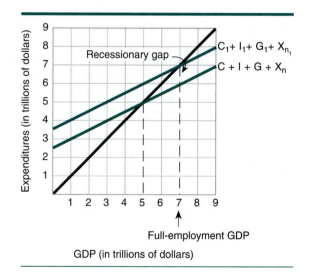

Figure 3

Removing the Recessionary Gap

Let's start with an aggregate demand of $C + I + G + X_n$ and an equilibrium GDP of $5 trillion. To remove the recessionary gap, we raise aggregate demand to $C_1 + I_1 + G_1 + X_{n_1}$. This pushes equilibrium GDP to $7 trillion and removes the recessionary gap.

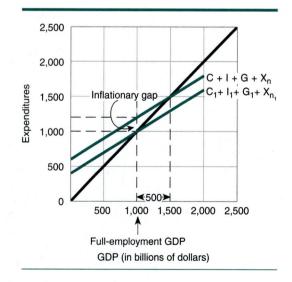

Figure 4

Removing the Inflationary Gap

We'll start with an aggregate demand of $C + I + G + X_n$ and an equilibrium GDP of 1,500. To remove the inflationary gap, we lower aggregate demand to $C_1 + I_1 + G_1 + X_{n_1}$. This pushes equilibrium GDP down to 1,000 and removes the recessionary gap.

Finding the Multiplier

Let's assume that the full-employment GDP is $4 trillion in Figure 3 (use the $C + I + G + X_n$ line; ignore the $C_1 + I_1 + G_1 + X_{n_1}$ line). See if you can answer these three questions:

1. Is there an inflationary gap or a recessionary gap?
2. How much is the gap?
3. How much is the multiplier?

Solution:

1. There is an inflationary gap because full-employment GDP is less than equilibrium GDP. If aggregate demand, or total spending, is greater than the spending necessary to attain full employment, that excess spending will cause inflation.

2. The inflationary gap is measured by the vertical distance between the 45-degree line and the $C + I + G + X_n$ line

at full-employment GDP. It appears to be half a trillion, or $500 billion, which we can write as 500.

3. Multiplier = $\dfrac{\text{Distance between equilibrium GDP and full-employment GDP}}{\text{Gap}}$

$= \dfrac{1,000}{500} = 2$

Now let's assume that full-employment GDP is $6 trillion. Please answer the same three questions.

Solution:

1. There is a recessionary gap.
2. It is $500 billion, or 500.
3. Multiplier = $\dfrac{1,000}{500} = 2$

in Figure 3 the distance between equilibrium GDP and full-employment GDP is $2 trillion, which we can express as 2,000. And the recessionary gap is $1 trillion, or 1,000. Using the formula:

$$\text{Multiplier} = \frac{\text{Distance between equilibrium GDP and full-employment GDP}}{\text{Gap}} = \frac{2,000}{1,000} = 2$$

If you are still a bit uncertain and want a little more practice, then do the work in the Extra Help box, "Finding the Multiplier." The box on the paradox of thrift also provides some insight on how the multiplier works.

One qualifying note is needed here. A significant part of our money supply ends up outside the country, mainly because of our huge trade imbalance. This leakage of currency somewhat lowers the effectiveness of the multiplier. So a multiplier calculated to be, say, 8, might be, in effect, perhaps 7. While we don't know exactly how large this leakage is, we *can* say that it somewhat diminishes the actual size of the multiplier.

Part III: The Automatic Stabilizers

Have you ever been on an airborne plane when the pilot took a stroll through the cabin and you asked yourself, Who's flying the plane? Let's hope it's the copilot. Or, if there's no turbulence, maybe the plane is flying on automatic pilot. If it does get turbulent, then the pilot takes over the manual controls.

An analogy can be made with our economy. Our automatic stabilizers enable us to cruise along fairly smoothly, but when we hit severe economic turbulence, then we hope the president and Congress take the controls. Right now, we'll examine our automatic stabilizers, and in Part IV, we'll talk about discretionary fiscal policy, which is our manual control system.

The automatic stabilizers protect us from the extremes of the business cycle.

In the 1930s the government built a few automatic stabilizers into the economy, mainly to prevent recessions from becoming depressions. Today, when the country hits

ADVANCED WORK

The Paradox of Thrift*

Since childhood we have been taught that saving is good. Benjamin Franklin once said, "A penny saved is a penny earned." Franklin, it turns out, never followed his own advice. It also turns out that if we all try to save more, we'll probably end up with a really bad recession, and we'll all end up saving less. This outcome is explained by the paradox of thrift.

You have probably heard that the sum of the parts does not necessarily add up to the whole. Consider, for example, what you would do if you were in a room full of people and that room suddenly burst into flames. Would you politely suggest to your companions that everyone file out of the room in an orderly fashion? Or would you bolt for the door?

What if the door opened inward (that is, into the room)? Whoever got there first would attempt to pull open the door. But if everyone made a dash for the door, they would all arrive at just about the same time. The person trying to pull open the door wouldn't have space to do this because everyone else would be pushing him against the door. Several people would get injured in the crush. Unless they backed off, no one would get out of the room.

We call this an example of the fallacy of composition. What makes perfect sense for one person to do—rush to the door and pull it open—makes no sense when everyone tries to do it at the same time.

The paradox of thrift is a variant of the fallacy of composition. *If everyone tries to save more, they will all end up saving less.* Let's say that every week you save an extra $10 from your paycheck. At the end of a year, you will have saved an extra $520. Right? Right! Now, what if everyone tries saving an extra $10 a week? At the end of a year, we should have tens of billions in extra savings. Right? Wrong!

How come? Because what makes sense for one person to do does not make sense for everyone to do. If everyone tries to save more, everyone is cutting back on consumption. Business sales fall by hundreds of millions of dollars a week. If 140 million people each cut back by $10 a week, that comes to a weekly reduction of $1.4 billion. Over the course of a year, this will add up to $72.8 billion!

This $72.8 billion decline in consumption will have a multiplied effect on GDP. If the multiplier is 4, GDP will decline by $291.2 billion; if it is 6, GDP will decline by $436.8 billion. So we'd be in a recession.

When retailers get the idea that business will be off over the next few months, they do two things: lay off employees and let their inventory run down. The workers who lose their jobs cut back on their consumption. Meanwhile, the retailers have begun canceling their orders for new inventory, prompting factories to lay off people and lower their orders for raw materials.

As the recession spreads, more and more people get laid off, and each will cut back on his or her consumption, further aggravating the decline in retail sales.

Now we come back to saving. Millions of people have been laid off and millions more are on reduced hours. Still others no longer get overtime. Each of these people, then, has suffered substantially reduced income. Each is not able to save as much as before the recession. Savings decline.

However, there is one big problem with the paradox of thrift. During nearly all the recessions since World War II, people not only tried to save more, but they actually succeeded. While their increased savings did mean less consumption, and consequently, worse recessions, the fact remains that savings *did* rise during these recessions. Let's take the Great Recession of 2007–09 as an example. During 2005–07 our annual savings rate averaged less than 2 percent of disposable personal income. But it rose to 4.6 percent in 2009.

So if everyone *does* try to save more, will they all end up saving less? Evidently not. Still, the logic behind the paradox of thrift remains sound: A rising savings rate during a recession makes that recession worse than it would have otherwise been.

---

*The paradox of thrift is not relevant today because, as a nation, we actually have a negative rate of personal saving. That is, we spend more than we earn. Then why talk about it? Because it does a great job of illustrating how the multiplier works.

routine economic turbulence, Congress does not need to pass any laws, and no new bureaucracies have to be created. All the machinery is in place and ready to go.

Each of these stabilizers protects the economy from the extremes of the business cycle—from recession and inflation. They are not, by themselves, expected to prevent booms and busts, but only to moderate them. To do still more, we need discretionary economic policy, which we'll discuss in the next section.

Personal Income and Payroll Taxes

During recessions the government collects less personal income tax and Social Security tax than it otherwise would. Some workers who had been getting overtime before the

During recessions, tax receipts decline.

recession are lucky to be hanging on to their jobs even without overtime. Some workers are less lucky and have been laid off. That's the bad news. The good news is that they don't have to pay any personal income tax or payroll tax because they have no income.

During inflations, tax receipts rise.

During prosperous times our incomes rise, and during times of inflation our incomes tend to rise still faster. As our incomes rise, we have to pay more taxes. These taxes tend to hold down our spending, relieving inflationary pressures.

During recessions, as incomes fall, federal personal income and Social Security tax receipts fall even faster. This moderates economic declines by leaving more money in taxpayers' pockets.

Personal Savings

As the economy moves into a recession and people lose their jobs, most will be forced to dig into their savings to pay their bills. And as the economy picks up again and the unemployed find jobs, they may replenish their savings. Still, it has been our experience that during recessions, the savings rate generally rises. (See box, "The Paradox of Thrift.")

Credit Availability

Credit availability helps get us through recessions.

Because most Americans now hold bank credit cards, mainly MasterCard and VISA, we may think of these as automatic stabilizers that work in the same way that personal savings does. During good times, we should be paying off the credit card debts that we run up during bad times.

Although many of us are quite good at running up credit card debt during good times as well as bad, our credit cards, as well as other lines of credit, may be thought of as automatic stabilizers during recessions because they give us one more source of funds with which to keep buying things. You may have lost your job and have no money in the bank, but your credit cards are just as good as money—although, of course, you'll be charged a very high rate of interest.

Most Americans can take out home equity loans if they're short of cash. Even if you've lost your job, the bank may not care since they've got your home as collateral. Best of all, you'll pay a much lower interest rate than you would on your credit card debt.

Unemployment Compensation

During recessions, more people collect unemployment benefits.

During recessions, as the unemployment rate climbs, hundreds of thousands and then millions of people register for unemployment benefits. The tens of billions of dollars of unemployment benefits being paid out establish a floor under purchasing power. People who are, they hope, only temporarily out of work will continue spending money. This helps keep retail sales from falling much, and even without further government help, the economy has bought some time to work its way out of the recession. As the economy recovers and moves into the prosperity phase of the cycle, people find jobs more easily and unemployment benefit claims drop substantially.

Reason to study economics: When you are in the unemployment line, at least you will know why you are there.

Just 40 percent of those out of work can qualify for benefits in the United States, compared to 90 percent in Germany and 98 percent in France. While the usual limit for collecting unemployment benefits here is 26 weeks—except during some recessions, when they have been extended—German unemployed workers can collect for at least five years, and in Britain, unemployed people can collect practically forever. In 2009, the average weekly benefit was about $325 including a $25 federal subsidy. Average benefits varied from state-to-state, from $628 in Massachusetts to just $230 in Mississippi. Other countries are much more generous. Swedes, Danes, and Norwegians, for example, receive as much as 90 percent of prior earnings for up to a year after losing a job. In the United States, by contrast, unemployment insurance replaces less than one-third of prior earnings and eligibility is so restricted that nearly two-thirds of unemployed workers receive no benefits at all.

The Corporate Profits Tax

Perhaps the most countercyclical of all the automatic stabilizers is the corporate profit (or income) tax. Corporations must pay 35 percent of their net income above $18.3 million to the federal government. During economic downturns, corporate profits fall much more quickly than wages, consumption, or real GDP; and, of course, during expansions, corporate profits rise much more rapidly.

> During recessions, corporations pay much less corporate income taxes.

Part of this decline is cushioned by the huge falloff of federal tax collections from the corporate sector. This leaves more money to be used for investment or distribution to shareholders in the form of dividends. And when corporate profits shoot up during economic booms, the federal government damps down economic expansion by taxing away 35 percent of the profits of the larger corporations.

Other Transfer Payments

Some people think that when a recession hits, the government automatically raises Social Security benefits. This might make sense, but it doesn't happen. Congress would have to pass special legislation to do so.

Three important payments do rise automatically because of laws on the books. Each is aimed at helping the poor. These are welfare (or public assistance) payments, Medicaid payments, and food stamps.

> A safety net for the poor

These programs are important for two reasons. Not only do they alleviate human suffering during bad economic times, but they also help provide a floor under spending, which helps keep economic downturns from worsening.

The automatic stabilizers smooth out the business cycle, keeping the ups and downs within a moderate range. Since the Great Depression, we have had neither another depression nor a runaway inflation. But the stabilizers, by themselves, cannot altogether eliminate economic fluctuations. The latter part of the expansions are held down in the hypothetical business cycle with stabilizers in place, and the contractions are less severe. Basically, then, the automatic stabilizers smooth out the business cycle but don't eliminate it.

The automatic stabilizers may be likened to running our economy on automatic pilot—not well suited for takeoffs and landings, but fine for the smooth part of the flight. However, when the going gets rough, the economy must resort to manual controls. Discretionary policy is our manual control system.

Figure 5 shows the workings of the stabilizers. The solid line shows real GDP in an economy with no automatic stabilizers. The dotted line shows real GDP in an economy such as ours, which does have automatic stabilizers. The latter part of the expansions are held down in the hypothetical business cycle with stabilizers in place, and the contractions are less severe. Basically, then, the automatic stabilizers smooth out the business cycle but don't eliminate it.

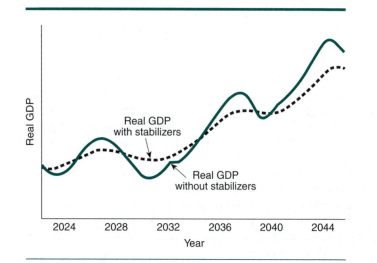

Figure 5

Hypothetical Business Cycles
Without the automatic stabilizers, real GDP would fluctuate much more widely. But you'll note that, while the stabilizers do smooth out the cycle, they do not eliminate it.

Part IV: Discretionary Fiscal Policy

Among the first words of this chapter were *Fiscal policy is the manipulation of the federal budget to attain price stability, relatively full employment, and a satisfactory rate of economic growth.* The automatic stabilizers, which swing the federal budget into substantial deficits during recessions and tend to push down those deficits during periods of inflation, would appear to be part of fiscal policy. Because they are built into our economy, one might call them a passive fiscal policy. But our automatic stabilizers are now taken for granted; therefore we consider fiscal policy to be purely discretionary. Let's now consider the discretionary fiscal policy tools that are available to the federal government.

Making the Automatic Stabilizers More Effective

One problem with unemployment benefits is that they run out in six months while a recession can drag on for more than a year and its effects can last still longer. After the 1990–91 recession ended, the unemployment rate continued rising and did not begin to decline until a full year after the start of the recovery. Extending the benefit period is an example of discretionary fiscal policy because benefits are not extended automatically. In the wake of the Great Recession, unemployment insurance benefits were extended for as long as 99 weeks in states with the highest rates of unemployment. Benefits have been extended in every recession except one since the 1950s. An increase in the benefit ceiling or a widening of eligibility standards are other ways of making this stabilizer more effective.

Public Works

The main fiscal policy to end the Depression was public works.

During the Great Depression, the Roosevelt administration set up several so-called alphabet agencies to provide jobs for the long-term unemployed. Among them, the Works Progress Administration (WPA), the Civilian Conservation Corps (CCC), and the Public Works Administration (PWA) put millions of people to work doing everything from raking leaves to constructing government buildings.

One of the problems in getting these public works projects off the ground was a lack of plans. Not only did the government lack ready-to-go blueprints, but it did not even have a list of the needed projects. If the country is ever again to institute a public works program, it needs to be much better prepared than it was in the early 1930s. If not, by the time the program gets started, the recession will be over.

Although criticized as "make-work projects," the public works projects gave jobs to millions of the unemployed. These workers spent virtually their entire salaries, thereby creating demand for goods and services in the private sector, thus creating still more jobs. Public works is probably not the answer to recessions unless the downturns last so long that the projects can be carried out. Yet one might ask, if public works are so necessary, why wait for a recession to carry them out?

It seems ideally conceivable that the state . . . should undertake public works, that must be executed some time, in the slack periods when they can be executed at least expense, and will, at the same time, have a tendency to counteract a serious evil.

—Philip H. Wicksteed,
The Common Sense of Political Economy

During good times and bad, whether fiscal stimulus is needed or not, the political pressure within Congress for federal spending on local projects is a constant. Referred to as "pork barrel spending," these projects, perhaps most notably Alaska Representative Don Young's "Bridge to Nowhere," cost the taxpayer over $60 billion a year, but their main benefit is to help Congress members get reelected by claiming to bring home the bacon. "The Bridge to Nowhere," which is the current issue of Chapter 3, is a $231 million project that will connect Anchorage with a swampy undeveloped port. This spending, which might have made sense during a time of high unemployment, could hardly be considered a wise fiscal policy measure when the nation's unemployment rate was below 5 percent. During the Congressional elections of 2006, the Democrats attacked the Republicans, who had controlled the House of Representatives for the previous 12 years, of wasting tens of billions of dollars a year of the taxpayers' money on pork barrel projects. Can you guess what *they* did when they won enough seats to take over the House? That's right! Even though the unemployment rate remained below 5 percent, the Democrats continued pork barrel spending at the same pace as their predecessors. The only difference was that now many of those projects were in Democratic majority districts rather than in Republican majority districts.

Changes in Tax Rates

So far, the discretionary policy measures have dealt exclusively with recessions. What can we do to fight inflation? We can raise taxes.

This was done in 1968 when Congress, under President Lyndon Johnson, passed a 10 percent income tax surcharge. If your income was $15,000 and your federal income tax was listed in the tax table as $2,300, you had to pay a $230 surcharge, which raised your taxes to $2,530.

In the case of a recession, a tax cut would be the ticket. The recession of 1981–82 was somewhat mitigated by the Kemp-Roth tax cut, which called for a 5 percent cut in personal income taxes in 1981 and a 10 percent cut in July 1982. However salutary its effects, Kemp-Roth was seen by its framers as a long-run economic stimulant rather than an antirecessionary measure. Similarly, President George W. Bush billed his $1.35 trillion tax cut in 2001, which was spread out over a 10-year period, as both an immediate economic stimulus to fight the current recession as well as a long-term boost to economic growth. And during the jobless recovery that followed, he referred to the tax cuts of 2001 and 2003 as a "jobs program."

Corporate income taxes, too, may be raised during inflations and lowered when recessions occur. The investment tax credit, first adopted by the Kennedy administration, is another way of using taxes to manipulate spending.

A key advantage to using tax rate changes as a countercyclical policy tool is that they provide a quick fix. We have to make sure, however, that temporary tax cuts carried out during recessions do not become permanent cuts.

During the recession of 2001, at the behest of President George W. Bush, Congress passed a one-time tax refund of $300 to individuals and $600 to married couples who filed jointly. Everyone got their checks within months, providing the economy with a much needed stimulus.

Similarly, in early 2008, as it was becoming increasingly apparent that our economy might be in the early stages of a recession, Congress passed an economic stimulus bill whose main feature was the provision of income tax rebate checks, generally in the range of $300–$1,200 to tens of millions of Americans.

Changes in Government Spending

Discretionary fiscal policy dictates that we increase government spending and cut taxes to mitigate business downturns, and that we lower government spending and raise taxes to damp down inflation. In brief, we fight recessions with budget deficits and inflation with budget surpluses.

Who Makes Fiscal Policy?

Making fiscal policy is like driving a car. You steer, you keep your foot on the accelerator, and occasionally you use the brake. Basically, you should not go too fast or too slow, and you need to stay in your lane.

Would you mind letting someone else help you drive? Suppose you had a car with dual controls, like the ones driving schools have. Unless you and the other driver were in complete agreement, not only would driving not be much fun, but you'd be lucky to avoid having an accident.

So, if making fiscal policy is like driving a car, let's ask just who is doing the driving. Is it the president? Or is it Congress? The answer is yes to both questions. In other words, the conduct of our fiscal policy is a lot like driving a dually controlled car. Further complicating maneuvers, sometimes one political party controls Congress while the president belongs to the other party. In October 1990 the federal government all but shut down while President George H. W. Bush struggled with Congress in an effort to pass a budget. And in 1993, even though President Bill Clinton and a substantial majority of members of both houses were Democrats, each house passed a budget by just one vote. In a sense there really *is* no fiscal policy, but rather a series of political compromises within Congress and between the president and Congress. The reason for this lies within our political system, especially the way we pass laws.

To become a law, a bill introduced in either house of Congress must get through the appropriate committee (most bills never get that far) and then receive a majority vote from the members of that house. It must get through the other house of Congress in the same manner. Then a House–Senate conference committee, after compromising on the differences between the two versions of the bill, sends the compromise bill to both houses to be voted on once again. After receiving a majority vote in both houses, the bill goes to the president for his signature.

If the president does not like certain aspects of the bill, he can threaten to veto it, hoping Congress will bend to his wishes. If he gets what he wants, he now signs the bill and it becomes law. If not, he vetoes it. Overriding a veto takes a two-thirds vote in both houses—not an easy task.

Fiscal policy is indeed a powerful tool that may be used to promote full employment, stable prices, and a satisfactory rate of economic growth. But no one seems to be in charge of *making* fiscal policy. Nor is there widespread agreement among economists as to what effect any given fiscal policy measure has on our economy.

At the beginning of the chapter we mentioned that fiscal policy did not even exist before the 1930s. Since then most presidents and Congresses made substantial efforts to attain price stability, relatively full employment, and a satisfactory rate of economic growth. By the late 1930s we also had in place some fairly powerful automatic stabilizers. Figure 6 provides a record of our economic stability from the 1870s through 2007. As you'll notice, we have enjoyed considerably more economic stability since the close of World War II than before it.

Can we then attribute the stability of the last 60-odd years to our discretionary fiscal policy and to the automatic stabilizers? Not entirely. While much, or even most, of this stability is certainly due to these two factors, we need to also consider the role of monetary policy, which is conducted by the Federal Reserve. We'll get to that in just a couple of chapters.

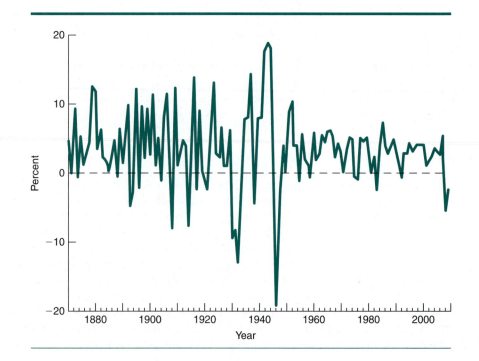

Figure 6

U.S. Economic Growth Rate, 1871–2009

Clearly the decades since 1945 have been much more stable than those preceding that year. You'll notice that our growth rate dropped by almost 20 percent in 1945, a sharper decline than in any previous year, even including those of the Great Depression. The decline in 1945 was due to our shifting from wartime production to peacetime production. That recession was deep, but very, very short. Most people barely felt it.

Sources: Angus Maddison, *Dynamic Forces in Capitalist Development* (New York: Oxford University Press, 1991); *Economic Report of the President,* 2010.

Part V: Fiscal Policy Lags

Defining the Lags

The effectiveness of fiscal policy depends greatly on timing. Unfortunately, it is subject to three lags: the recognition, decision, and impact lags.

Suppose our economy enters a recession and the government provides a counteracting stimulus. What if this stimulus does not have much impact until recovery has set in? The end result of this well-intentioned government policy will be to destabilize the economy by making the recovery and subsequent prosperity far too exuberant. Similarly, if the government were to try to damp down an inflation, but the effects of its policy were not felt until the economy had already entered a recession, the policy would end up making the recession that much worse.

The recognition lag is the time it takes for policy makers to realize that a business cycle's turning point has been passed, or that either inflation or unemployment has become a particular problem. The decision lag is the time it takes for policy makers to decide what to do and to take action. And finally, the impact lag is the time it takes for the policy action to have a substantial effect. The whole process may take anywhere from about nine months to more than three years.

The lengths of the three lags under fiscal policy are not well defined. First, the recognition lag is the time it takes the president and a majority of both houses of Congress to recognize that something is broken and needs fixing—either an inflation or a recession. You would be amazed at how long this can take. In August 1981 we entered a recession, but in the spring of the following year President Reagan still could not bring himself to admit that we were actually in a recession (which, incidentally, proved to be the worst downturn since the Great Depression).

First, the president and Congress must recognize that there is a problem.

Congress, which at the time was divided between a Republican Senate and a Democratic House, also took some time to recognize the problem. This state of affairs was similar to that of 1967; inflation was beginning to get out of hand, but the president and Congress were reluctant to recognize the obvious.

Once the president *and* Congress recognize that something needs to be done about the economy, they must decide what action to take. After investigating the problem with his advisers, the president may make a fiscal policy recommendation to Congress. This recommendation, among others, is studied by appropriate subcommittees and committees, hearings are held, expert witnesses called, votes taken. Eventually bills may be passed by both houses, reconciled by a joint House–Senate committee, repassed by both houses, and sent to the president for his or her signature. This process usually takes several months.

Next, they must decide what to do about it.

All this delay is part of the decision lag. We still have the impact lag. Once a spending bill, say a highway reconstruction measure, has been passed for the purpose of stimulating an economy that is mired in recession, a year may pass before the bulk of the appropriated funds is actually spent and has made a substantial economic impact. By then, of course, the country may already have begun to recover from the recession.

Finally, it will take time for their action to have an impact.

Chronology of the Lags in 2008

The Recognition Lag   Although there were strong signs of an economic slowdown during the fall of 2007—most notably the mortgage lending crisis and the decline in the index of leading economic indicators—Bush administration officials never uttered the "r" word, nor did many members of Congress. But the announcement of the December employment figures on January 4, 2008 was a jarring wake-up call. The unemployment rate had jumped from 4.7 percent to 5.0 percent, and our economy had apparently stopped creating new jobs.

The Decision Lag   It took just a few weeks for President Bush, Treasury Secretary Henry Paulson, and the Democratic and Republican leaders of the House of Representatives to reach agreement on a $168 billion economic stimulus package whose main feature was taxpayer rebates generally ranging from $300 to over $1,200. Its purpose was to put money into people's pockets so they could spend it. By stimulating consumption, these officials hoped to minimize the severity of the recession, if not to avert it completely. One could argue that the true decision lag was from the start of the Great Recession in December 2007 until the passage of the Economic Stimulus Act of 2009—a lag of 14 months.

The Impact Lag   At the time the stimulus package was agreed to, the economy had already been slowing for at least two months, and it was not yet clear whether or not we had gone into an actual recession. Internal Revenue Service officials warned that because February, March, and April were at the peak of the income tax season, they would not be able to begin mailing out rebate checks until May. By then it would be several months too late for the stimulus package to help us avert a recession, though still soon enough to lessen its severity.

Did this stimulus package work? Given the severity of the recession, it was clearly much too small to have much of an impact. While it did put some money into people's pocket, most of it was used to pay down debt, rather than being used for its intended purpose—to be spent.

Perhaps the words of Robert J. Gordon lend just the right perspective:

> Unfortunately, policymakers cannot act as if the economy is an automobile that can quickly be steered back and forth. Rather, the procedure of changing aggregate demand is much closer to that of a captain navigating a giant super-tanker. Even if he gives a signal for a hard turn, it takes a mile before he can see a change, and 10 miles before the ship makes the turn.[3]

Part VI: The Economic Stimulus Package of 2009

The two worst recessions we had had since the Great Depression itself were in 1973–75 and in 1981–82. Both lasted 16 months. According to the National Bureau of Economic Research, the current recession began in December 2007; in April 2009 it became the longest economic downturn on record since the early 1930s.

The Economic Stimulus Act of 2009

The $787 billion stimulus package included $287 billion in tax cuts and $500 billion in government spending. Here are its major items:

- $233 billion in tax cuts for individuals and families: up to $400 tax credit for individuals in 2009 and 2010 (cost: $116 billion) and alternate minimum tax patch (cost: $70 billion)[4]

- $106 billion for education and job training: help for states to prevent cutbacks and layoffs, mostly in education (cost: $54 billion), and additional financing for special education and low-income children (cost: $25 billion)

- $87 billion to states in increased federal contribution to Medicaid costs

- $78 billion for jobless people: expand unemployment benefits (cost: $36 billion) and help for laid-off workers to keep group health insurance (cost: $25 billion)[5]

- $48 billion for highway and bridge construction, and mass transit

---

[3]Robert J. Gordon, *Macroeconomics* (Boston: Little, Brown, 1978), p. 334.

[4]This tax was intended to collect income tax from very rich families who had been paying no taxes. But in recent years it was imposed on millions of upper middle class families. Each year Congress passed legislation that enabled these families to pay little or none of the alternative minimum tax. Since this "patch" is passed every year, it is misleading to count it as part of the economic stimulus package.

[5]The law increases unemployment benefits by $25 a week and allows states to extend those benefits through the end of 2009. It also provides jobless workers with an additional 20 weeks in unemployment benefits, and 13 weeks on top of that if they live in what's deemed a high-unemployment state, of which there were more than 30 in the spring of 2009. Several governors, led by Mark Sanford of South Carolina, refused to accept at least part of these funds because they believed that at the end of the year their states would then be obligated to continue paying the higher weekly benefits.

- $44 billion for energy, including modernizing the electric grid
- $41 billion for infrastructure, water, and the environment
- $29 billion for health, science, and research
- $21 billion for energy investments: expand incentives for renewable energy production facilities (cost: $14 billion)
- $20 billion to expand food stamp benefits

How Effective Was the Stimulus Package?

The stimulus program was enacted in February 2009, and the Great Recession ended at least by the author's estimation—just four months later. Did all this spending and tax cutting end the recession? Well, like chicken soup, it surely didn't hurt.

The Obama Administration has taken credit for creating or saving some 3 million jobs. The Congressional Budget office in the spring of 2010 estimated that the stimulus program saved 1.4 million to 3.4 million jobs. One might ask, "*What* jobs?" After all, employment continued to fall for the rest of the year. Still, all that money—especially the money sent to the states—may well have averted the layoffs of hundreds of thousands of state and municipal employees.

Aid to states and cities may have been the most effective form of stimulus. This money—totalling about $200 billion—has helped teachers, fire fighters, police officers, and health care workers hold on to their jobs.

Although over $100 billion in stimulus spending has been added—including a $34 billion measure passed in July 2010 to provide continued benefits to 2.5 million of the long-term unemployed—nearly 3 out of every 4 Americans believed the economic stimulus had no positive impact.

Was the Deficit Too Big?

Budget deficits rise automatically during recessions because tax receipts fall and some government spending programs rise. But the huge economic stimulus program pushed up the deficit to $1.4 trillion (or $1,400 billion) in fiscal year 2009, more than triple the record $459 billion deficit we ran in fiscal year 2008.

In the long run deficits this big would drive our government into bankruptcy, because we could not continue borrowing such huge sums of money indefinitely. But we ran much larger deficits during wartime—most recently during the Second World War. The 2009 deficit was 9.8 percent of GDP; in 1944 it was 24.5 percent. The previous peacetime record was set in 1983, when the deficit was 5.9 percent of GDP.

Was the 2009 deficit too big? Newsweek columnist Daniel Gross, answered the question *this* way: "Being obsessed with deficits during a downturn is like being obsessed with water conservation when your house is on fire."[6]

The question we need to ask is this: What would have happened to the economy had we *not* run such a large deficit? My own opinion—which is shared by most economists—is that the recession would have been even worse.

The Chinese Stimulus Plan

Rivaling the size of our economic stimulus plan, China, with an economy perhaps 30 percent of the size of ours, created a $586 billion fiscal stimulus program—about 15 percent of its GDP. It was launched in November 2008 and, unlike the American plan, most of its funding was intended to expand the economy's infrastructure—mainly railways, airports, power plants, and highways. In addition, the government made it much easier for banks to extend business loans, which more than doubled between the spring of 2008 and the spring of 2009. Significantly, China clearly averted the worldwide recession, although its annual growth rate dipped from 10 percent to about 8 percent. By late 2009 the Chinese economy was again growing at an annual rate of 10 percent.

---

[6]Daniel Gross, "A Birder's Guide to D.C.," *Newsweek*, November 16, 2009, p. 22.

Part VII: The Deficit Dilemma

Deficits, Surpluses, and the Balanced Budget

A deficit is created when the government is paying out more than it's taking in.

A billion here, a billion there, and pretty soon you're talking about real money.

—Everett Dirksen,
U.S. Senator from Illinois
in the 1960s and 1970s

To understand how fiscal policy works, we need to nail down three basic concepts. First, the deficit. *When government spending is greater than tax revenue, we have a budget deficit.* The government is paying out more than it's taking in. How does it make up the difference? It borrows. Deficits have been much more common than surpluses. In fact, the federal government ran budget deficits every year from 1970 through 1997.

Second, budget surpluses are the exact opposite of deficits. They are prescribed to fight inflation. *When the budget is in a surplus position, tax revenue is greater than government spending.*

Finally, *we have a balanced budget when government expenditures are equal to tax revenue.* We've never had an exactly balanced budget; in many years of the 19th and early 20th centuries, we had small surpluses or deficits. Perhaps if the deficit or surplus were less than $20 billion, we'd call that a balanced budget.

Deficits and Surpluses: The Record

Back in Chapter 7, we talked about federal government spending and federal government tax receipts. Let's put all that data together and focus on how well the government has covered its spending with tax revenue. Let's look at the record since 1970 (see Figure 7).

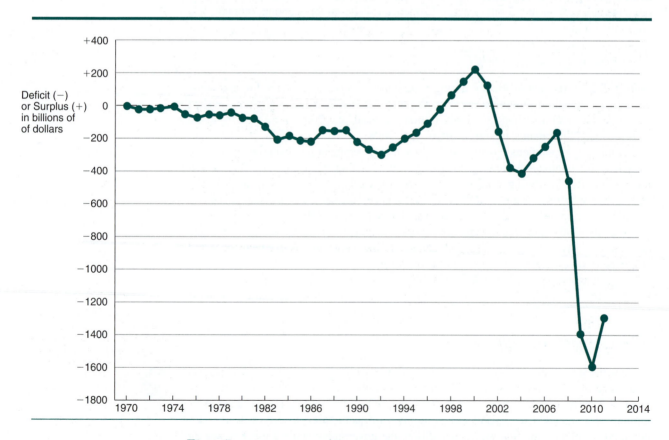

Figure 7

The Federal Budget Deficit, Fiscal Years 1970–2011

There were mounting deficits through most of the 1980s and early 1990s, followed by steadily declining deficits beginning in 1993. Finally in 1998 we had our first surplus since 1969. The 2010 and 2011 deficits are the March 2010 estimates of the Office of Management and Budget.

Sources: Economic Report of the President, 2010; www.whitehouse.gov/omb

How do we interpret the data? On the surface, it's obvious that the deficit went through the roof in the 1980s. Indeed during the late 1940s the government ran three surpluses, in the 1950s it ran four, it ran just one in the 1960s, and it ran none between 1970 and 1997. We ran surpluses from 1998 through 2001, but we've returned to deficits since 2002.

What brought the deficit down after 1992? Congress passed two huge deficit reduction packages in 1990 and in 1993. To secure the spending cuts he wanted in 1990, George ("Read my lips: No new taxes") H. W. Bush agreed with the Democratic leaders of Congress to a tax increase, which probably cost him reelection in 1992. The $492 billion five-year deficit reduction package had a major impact. Then, three years later, President Clinton pushed a five-year $433 billion deficit reduction package through Congress. About half this package was tax increases and half was government spending reductions. From 1993 through 1997 the deficit fell every year, and in 1998 we had our first federal budget surplus since 1969. By 2000 we were running a record surplus of $236 billion. What, then, accounts for our spectacular fall from budgetary grace after 2000?

There were several major causes: the bursting of the high-tech bubble and the subsequent stock market crash of 2000–2001; the March–November 2001 recession; the events of 9/11; our weak and slow recovery from that recession; the economic disruption caused by the war in Iraq; higher military spending for that war, its aftermath, and the war on terror; and the massive tax cuts of 2001 and 2003.

What jumps out at you from Figure 7 is the huge increase in the deficit since fiscal year 2008. Although most Americans seem to accept trillion dollar deficits as an unpleasant economic reality, millions of Tea Party supporters are extremely upset about them. They have argued forcefully that federal spending needs to be drastically reined in, and that the economic role of the federal government should be drastically reduced, to the degree that these advocates of smaller government succeed—especially in the 2010 congressional election and the congressional and presidential elections of 2012—we may see fiscal policy become a less potent economic weapon.

As the economy grew and the unemployment rate was pushed below 5 percent, the deficit was reduced from $413 billion in fiscal year 2003 all the way down to $162 billion in fiscal year 2007. Through the next two decades nearly all of the 77-million-strong baby boom generation (those born between 1946 and 1964) will join the Social Security and Medicare rolls. (See "Current Issue 2: Trillion-Dollar Deficits as Far as the Eye Can See," at the end of this chapter.)

How does our deficit compare with those of other relatively rich nations? As you can see by glancing at Figure 8, each of the nations shown here ran a large deficit relative to its GDP. While ours was over 9 percent, Britain's and Greece's deficits both exceeded 12 percent of their GDPs.

A budget tells us what we can't afford, but it doesn't keep us from buying it.

—William Feather

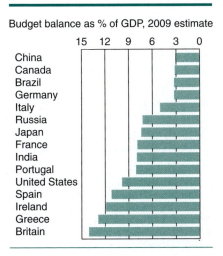

Budget balance as % of GDP, 2009 estimate

Figure 8

Budget Deficit as a Percentage of GDP, Selected Countries, 2009

During 2009 nearly all nations ran substantial budget deficits. While that of the United States was relatively high, other nations, most notably Britain and Greece, ran much larger deficits as percentages of GDP.

Source: The Economist, February 13, 2010, p. 71.

Why Are Large Deficits So Bad?

Let us count the ways. Number one: They tend to raise interest rates, which, in turn, discourages investment. The Bush administration, which ran large deficits, disputed whether these deficits raised interest rates. In early 2003, the mortgage rate as well as a few other rates were at 20-year lows. However, the last word on the effect of deficits on interest rates seems to be a paper by William Gale and Peter Orszag, which is based on 58 earlier studies.[7] Their conclusion: A projected rise in the budget deficit of 1 percent of GDP raises long-term interest rates by 0.4 to 0.6 percentage points. Since we are predicting deficits of about 4 percent of GDP, Gale and Orszag would project a rise in long-term interest rates of about 2 percent.

Number two: The federal government has become increasingly dependent on foreign savers to finance the deficit. How likely is it that foreigners might suddenly sell hundreds of billions of dollars worth of U.S. government securities because they disagreed with some of our foreign policy measures? When France opposed our 2003 war with Iraq, some Americans were so angry with the French they even renamed french fries "freedom fries" and French's mustard found it necessary to proclaim that only its name was French. Fortunately French, German, and other foreign investors did not dump their portfolios of U.S. government securities. Had they done so, interest rates would have shot up.

Number three: The deficit sops up large amounts of personal savings in this country, making that much less savings available to large corporate borrowers seeking funds for new plant and equipment. We'll talk about this when we discuss the crowding-out effect in one more page.

Number four: Because deficits are tacked on to the national debt (which we'll look at in Part IX of this chapter), the higher our deficits, the more interest we will have to pay on the national debt. This money might otherwise have gone to pay for other government services such as education, health care, infrastructure, national parks, and public transportation.

Must We Balance the Budget Every Year?

In a word, "no!" First of all, we couldn't, even if we tried. During recessions, the budget will automatically go into deficit. And as we saw after 9/11, events well beyond our control will force the federal government to spend great sums of money to deal with unforeseen problems.

But there are those who believe that, barring national emergencies and possibly recessions, the government should be legally bound to balance its budget every year. During the 1990s, several attempts were made to pass a constitutional amendment which would have required just that. None was successful.

Part VIII: The Crowding-Out and Crowding-In Effects

Welcome to a debate we are sponsoring between the monetarists and the Keynesians. In this debate the monetarists will argue in favor of the crowding-out effect, while the Keynesians will take the side of the crowding-in effect.

The monetarists maintain that Keynesian deficits designed to raise aggregate demand will have little, if any, positive effect. First, budget deficits drive up interest rates, thus discouraging investment. Second, the more money the government borrows to finance the deficit, the less will be available to private borrowers.

If the proper fiscal policy during recessions is a large budget deficit, one would wonder where the Treasury will get all this money. Presumably it will go out and borrow it. But from whom?

---

[7]William Gale and Peter Orszag, "The Economic Effects of Long-Term Fiscal Discipline," available at www.brookings.edu/papers/2002/1217taxes_gale.aspx

Was the Federal Government Crowding Out Private Borrowers?

In the late 1980s and early 1990s the government was running massive budget deficits, although the unemployment rate was hovering around 5 percent. The Treasury was sopping up over half of all personal saving just to finance these deficits. But foreigners were also financing just over half of the deficit. Because virtually all our personal savings was indeed available to private borrowers, it could be argued that there was no crowding-out effect.

However, had the Treasury not been borrowing so heavily from foreigners, *that* money would have been available to American corporations seeking funds to replace and expand their plant and equipment. Furthermore, because of the huge deficits the Treasury was financing, real interest rates were much higher than they would have otherwise been. These high rates further discouraged private borrowing.

In sum, there definitely *was* a large crowding-out effect in the late 1980s. But it would have been a lot larger had it not been for the great inflow of foreign funds.

In the aftermath of the recession of 1990–91, not only did the government run the two largest budget deficits in U.S. history until then, but the Federal Reserve tried to accommodate private borrowers by pushing interest rates down to 15-year lows. And still the first President Bush was forced to term the recovery "anemic." One of the problems was that many banks were happy to pay only 2 or 3 percent interest for deposits and then buy U.S. government securities of varying maturities paying more than 5 percent interest. What we had here was a classic crowding-out effect at a time when it clearly hurt our economy.

So in the late 1980s and early 1990s, the conservative critics of an expansionary fiscal policy could point to a tangible crowding-out effect.

If it borrows funds from individuals who would have otherwise made this money available for business investment, won't business borrowers be "crowded out" of the financial markets by the government? And won't interest rates be driven up in the process, further discouraging investment? Won't increased government spending financed by borrowing be replacing private investment spending?

The answer is yes to all three questions. Yes—but to what degree?

During recessions business firms cut back on their investing, so the government would be tapping a relatively idle source of funds, and during recessions interest rates tend to fall.

Even during relatively prosperous times, such as the mid-1980s, there is enough money to go around if the Federal Reserve allows the money supply to grow at a fairly rapid clip and if foreign investors are willing to make a few hundred billion dollars available each year to major corporations as well as to the U.S. Treasury.

Nevertheless, the crowding-out effect cannot be dismissed out of hand, particularly during times of tight money, such as the late 1970s and early 1980s. That any borrower as big as the U.S. government crowds other borrowers out of financial markets is a fact (see the box, "Was the Federal Government Crowding Out Private Borrowers?"). And as the late Israeli defense minister Moshe Dayan once put it, "You can't argue with a fact."

Let's take a closer look at the Keynesian position. When there is substantial economic slack, one would not expect increased government borrowing to have much impact in financial markets. Not only would there be little effect on interest rates, but the Treasury would be sopping up funds that would otherwise go unclaimed. When orthodox Keynesian fiscal policy is followed, it is precisely during times of economic slack that large budget deficits are incurred.

One might also mention a possible "crowding-in" effect caused by deficit financing. This results from the stimulative effect that the deficit has on aggregate demand. If a massive personal income tax cut causes the deficit, consumption will rise, pulling up aggregate demand and inducing more investment. Similarly, increased government spending will raise aggregate demand, also inducing more investment. In other words, any rise in aggregate demand will induce a rise in investment.

This leaves us with one last question: which is larger, the crowding-in or the crowding-out effect? It doesn't really matter. The point is that as long as there is a sizable crowding-in effect, every dollar the government borrows will not crowd out a dollar of private borrowing. Thus, all we need to demonstrate is that there is a substantial crowding-in effect.

It appears that if we accept one fact—that the total amount of loanable funds is not fixed—there probably will be a substantial crowding-in effect. If there is indeed a fixed pool of saving, then it follows that every dollar the government borrows is one less dollar available to private savers. But *is* this total pool of saving fixed? If aggregate demand, stimulated by massive budget deficits, *does* rise, won't people save more money (as well as spend more)?

Therefore, as more saving becomes available, not every dollar borrowed by the government will actually be taken from private borrowers. Furthermore, as aggregate demand rises, more investment will be stimulated. If the crowding-in effect dominates the crowding-out effect, not only will government borrowing rise but so will private borrowing and investing. All we need to show is that total borrowing—government and private—rises.

You can see for yourself if there is much of a crowding-in effect. At the behest of President George W. Bush, Congress passed massive tax cuts in 2001 and in 2003. Although huge budget deficits were expected, Bush administration economists predicted that the tax cuts would stimulate eco nomic growth, push up tax revenue, and actually shrink the deficits. They called this process "dynamic scoring." Were they right?

What do *you* think? Are the monetarists right in saying that government borrowing crowds out private borrowing? Or are the orthodox Keynesians correct in saying that the crowding-in effect may dominate the crowding-out effect? The betting here is that the truth lies somewhere between these two extremes.

Part IX: The National Debt[8]

> The debt is like a crazy aunt we keep down in the basement. All the neighbors know she's there, but nobody wants to talk about her.
>
> –Ross Perot–

The attractiveness of financing spending by debt issue to the elected politicians should be obvious. Borrowing allows spending to be made that will yield immediate payoffs without the incurring of any immediate political cost.

—James Buchanan,
The Deficit and
American Democracy

The national debt is the amount of currently outstanding federal securities that the Treasury has issued. It is what the federal government owes to the holders of U.S. government securities.

In 1981 the national debt went over the $1 trillion mark. Do you remember how much money $1 trillion is? Write it out with all the zeros right here:

Written out, it looks like this: $1,000,000,000,000. In 1986 the national debt broke the $2 trillion mark. That means it took the federal government just five years to accumulate as much debt as it had accumulated between 1776 and 1981. On July 1, 2010, our national debt stood at $ 13.1 trillion. (see Figure 9).

Exactly what is the
national debt?

Exactly what is the national debt? It is *the cumulative total of all the federal budget deficits less any surpluses.* Much of it was run up during recessions and wars. It is owed to the holders of Treasury bills, notes, certificates, and bonds. For example, if you own any of these, you are holding part of the national debt.

Who holds the national debt? First we need to differentiate between the publicly held debt and the debt held by U.S. government agencies[9]. The lower part of each bar in Figure 9 shows the portion of the national debt held by the public, while the upper part

---

[8]The national debt is sometimes called the public debt.

[9]The Social Security trust fund holds a little more than half. Other large holders include the Federal Housing Administration, and the Federal Saving and Loan Corporation's Resolution Fund.

[10]Included in the public's holdings are those of the Federal Reserve. Although we tend to think of it as a government agency, technically the Federal Reserve is privately owned. The operations of the Federal Reserve are the subject of Chapter 14.

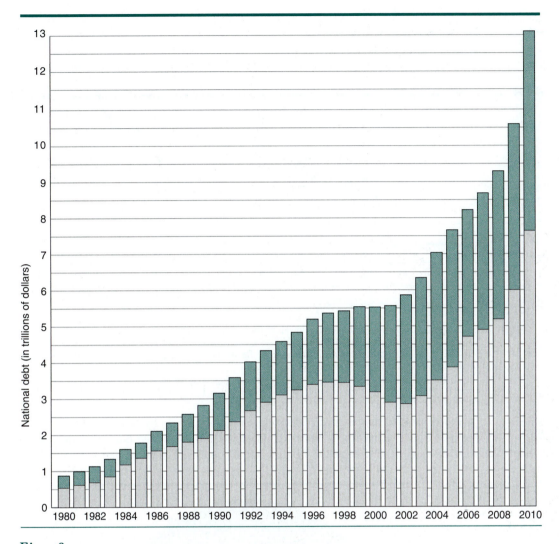

Figure 9
National Debt, 1980–2010*

The steady rise in the national debt through the 1980s and almost the entire 1990s was caused by the federal budget deficits that we ran each year. And when we finally began running surpluses in the late 1990s, we were able to start paying down the debt. Then deficits reappeared in 2002, and once again the national debt began to rise. The lower part of each bar in Figure 9 shows the portion of the national debt held by the public, while the upper part shows the portion that is held by U.S. government agencies. In July 2010 41.7 percent was held by U.S. government agencies, and 58.3 percent by the public.

*Debt on January 1 of each year.

Source: Economic Report of the President, 2010.
www.whitehouse.gov/omb

shows the portion that is held by U.S. government agencies. In July 2010 41.7 percent was held by U.S. government agencies, and 58.3 percent by the public.[10]

Although the national debt has been increasing at an alarming pace since 2002, is this really something we should worry about? After all, don't we owe it to ourselves? Until the 1970s foreigners owned no more than 5 percent of the publicly held debt, but today they hold over 50 percent. Figure 10 shows that their holdings rose sharply in the early 1970s and again since the mid-1990s. How much more of our debt will foreigners need to buy up before we allow that perhaps we don't really owe it to ourselves?

Let's take a closer look at the publicly held debt. As you'll notice in the pie chart shown in Figure 11, 41.7 percent of the national debt is held by U.S. government agencies. Of the publicly held debt, foreigners own exactly half, while American citizens and the Federal Reserve own the other half. The Federal Reserve, although a quasi-governmental agency, is actually composed of 12 privately owned banks. So its share of the national debt is considered publicly held. The Federal Reserve is the subject of Chapter 14.

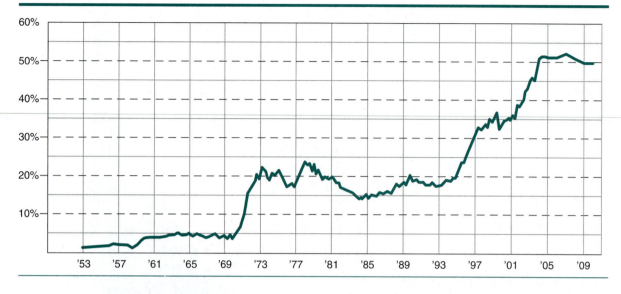

Figure 10

Percentage of Outstanding National Debt Held by Foreigners, 1953–2010

Before the early 1970s, foreigners held no more than about 5 percent of the outstanding (publicly held) debt; today they hold 50 percent. China and Japan are by far the largest foreign holders of our national debt. Together they hold 44 percent of the foreign-held debt.

Source: Haver Analytics; Floyd Norris, "More Than Ever, the U.S. Spends and Foreigners Lend," *The New York Times*, October 1, 2005, p. C4; Federal Reserve Board, Statistical Supplement to the Federal Reserve Bulletin, April 2010.

Blessed are the young, for they shall inherit the national debt.
—Herbert Hoover

Is the national debt a burden that will have to be borne by future generations? As long as we owe it mainly to ourselves, the answer is no. If we did owe it mainly to foreigners, and if they wanted to be paid off, it could be a great burden.

Figure 11

Percentage of National Debt Publically Held and Held by U.S. Government Agencies, July 1, 2010

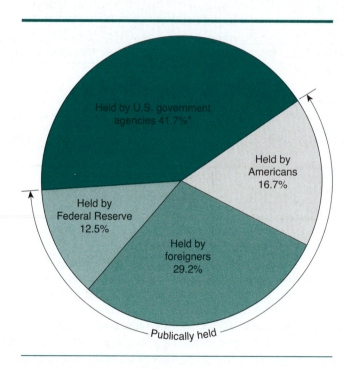

*Figures don't add to 100.0% because of rounding.

The national debt rose substantially during wars. We paid for these wars partly by taxation and partly by borrowing. In wartime a nation will invest very little in plant and equipment; all available resources must go toward the war effort. As a result, during the first half of the 1940s, we built virtually no new plant, equipment, and residential housing. Had there been no war, hundreds of billions of dollars' worth of plant, equipment, and housing would have been built. The generation that came of age after the war inherited less capital and housing than it would have had no war been fought. To that degree, a burden was placed on their shoulders.

Those who would point at the huge increase in the national debt during the war as the cause of our having less plant and equipment have misplaced the blame. It was the war, not the increase in the debt, that prevented wartime construction of capital goods.

When do we have to pay off the debt? We don't. All we have to do is roll it over, or refinance it, as it falls due. Each year about $4 trillion worth of federal securities fall due. By selling new ones, the Treasury keeps us going. But there is no reason why the national debt ever has to be paid off. Besides, as long as we continue running huge deficits, any discussion of paying off the debt is moot.

When do we have to pay off the national debt?

To the degree that the debt is being held increasingly by foreigners, we can no longer say we owe it (only) to ourselves. In the future, even if we never pay back one penny of that debt, our children and our grandchildren will have to pay foreigners hundreds of billions of dollars a year in interest. At least to that degree, then, the public debt *will* be a burden to future generations.

By the end of 2010 our national debt was 15 times as large as it was in 1980. But some of the increase in the debt is really due to inflation. So let's deflate today's debt and compare it with the 1980 debt in dollars of constant purchasing power. When we do that, it turns out that the current debt is about six times as large as it was back in 1980.

A nation is not in danger of financial disaster merely because it owes itself money.
—Andrew W. Mellon,
Secretary of the Treasury
in the 1920s

We can also look at the debt as a percentage of GDP, which is what we do in Figure 12. After rising steadily through the 1980s and the first half of the 1990s, the national debt, as a percentage of GDP, peaked in 1995 at 67 percent of GDP. It declined over the next five years, bottoming out at 57 percent in 2000 and 2001. And then, as our surpluses turned into deficits, the debt as a percentage of GDP began rising again. By mid-2010 it reached 89 percent (see Figure 12).

If you think that *we* have problems, just consider the national debt dilemmas faced by Japan, Italy, and Greece. In 2009, Japan's national debt was more than twice its GDP. The national debts of Italy and Greece were each larger than their GDPs. So, interestingly, even as our national debt continues to rise at a clip of over $1 trillion a year, it remains more manageable than the debts of these other nations.

Indeed, during the spring of 2010, Greece—whose national debt was 115 percent of its GDP, and whose budget deficit was 12.7 percent of GDP—was on the verge of defaulting on its debt, most of which was held by other members of the European Union. This threat set off a financial crisis comparable in scope to the one we experienced in the late summer of 2008—a topic we'll discuss in the next chapter.

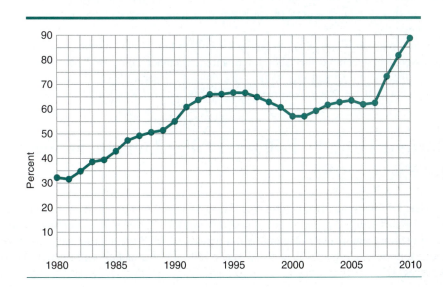

F*igure* 12

The U.S. National Debt as a Percentage of GDP, 1980–2010
Since 1980 our debt has doubled as a percentage of GDP.
Source: See Figure 10.

While the debt picture is hardly rosy, it is not nearly as bad as it might first appear. But let's take things a step further and consider that a substantial debt can actually be viewed in a positive light. Holding U.S. Treasury securities is considered a very safe investment, notwithstanding the dire warnings of a certain economics textbook author. When we began running budget surpluses in the late 1990s, many economists thought that these surpluses would stretch far into the future, and that the national debt would eventually shrink away to nothing. Alan Greenspan, then at the height of his powers as the chairman of the Federal Reserve, mused that investors would increasingly be denied a safe haven for their funds. Of course this has become almost a moot point since most of the funds now being invested in U.S. treasuries come from abroad.

on the web

You can find out exactly how much the national debt is right now by going to either of these websites: brillig.com/debt_clock or www.treasurydirect.gov/govt/reports/pd/pd.htm and click on "Debt to the Penny."

Which is worse—a jobless recovery or huge federal budget deficits? There's no correct answer to this question: both are extremely serious problems. There is a current issue at the end of each chapter, but given the importance of these two topics, you're now getting two current issues for the price of one.

Current Issue 1: A Jobless Recovery?

Although output (as measured by real GDP) has been rising since the third quarter of 2009, not only did the unemployment rate continue to rise, but total employment continued to fall. Before the year's end, there was a growing belief that we were in a "jobless recovery."

Between December 2007, when the Great Recession began, and early 2010, a half year after it ended, total employment fell by 8.4 million. So the big question is: How long will it take to put all these people back to work? During most of the post-World War II recoveries, it took less than a year to put everyone back to work, but it took 23 months after the 1990–91 recession and 39 months after the 2001 recession.

Through the first half of 2010 the pace of new job creation—especially in the private sector—was disappointingly slow. Even more alarming, nearly half the unemployed had been out of work for more than 6 months—the highest rate of long term unemployment since we began keeping records in the early 1940s.

With the pace of the recovery slowing markedly in the late spring and early summer of 2010, many people wondered whether we might plunge back into the recession. And with a June unemployment rate of 9.5 percent—and half the unemployed out of work for more than 6 months—even the prospect of a jobless recovery seemed the best we could hope for.

How long will it take, then, to create 8.4 million jobs—plus millions more for those who entered or reentered the labor force since December 2007. And how long will it take for the unemployment rate to fall back down to 5 percent, which we consider full employment? I'll bet that as you read these words, we *still* won't know.

Current Issue 2: Trillion-Dollar Deficits as Far as the Eye Can See

Just three or four years ago, trillion-dollar deficits were beyond the realm of our imagination. Now, sadly, they have become commonplace. In general, economists believe that in the long run, deficits of more than 3 percent of GDP are unsustainable. And yet, as you'll notice in Figure 13, in fiscal years 2009–11, our deficit will average nearly 10 percent.

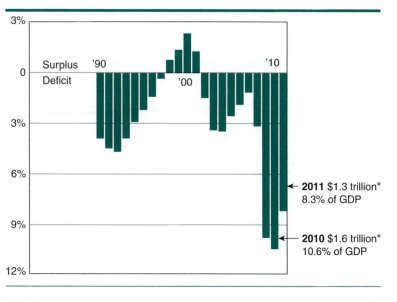

F*igure* 13
Federal Budget Surplus or
Deficit as Percentage of GDP,
1990–2011
*OMB estimate
Source: Office of Management and
Budget

*Projection

As you know, our deficits are so high now because of the high cost of dealing with the financial crisis and the Great Recession. But as our recovery continues, won't the deficit go back down? Yes it will. The real question is: how far and how fast? Obama administration economists are projecting deficits of over 4 percent of GDP for the rest of the decade. But they may well be too optimistic.

There are three reasons why the deficit will not fall more quickly: (1) a slow, jobless recovery; (2) the retirement of the baby boom generation; (3) rising interest payments of the publicly held national debt.

Because it will probably take more than five years for our economy to generate enough jobs to bring us even close to full employment (i.e., an unemployment rate of 5 percent), we can expect government expenditures on transfer programs—especially unemployment insurance benefits and food stamps—to remain very high. More importantly, tax receipts will also lag.

From 1930 through 1945 we averaged just 1 million births a year. But from 1946 through 1964, this average shot up to 3 million. How do you explain this change?

OK, *I'll* explain it. In the 1930s, couples could not afford to have many children because of the Great Depression. And the birthrate stayed low for the first half of the 1940s because so many married men were sent abroad during World War II. But as soon as the war ended, 12 million men came home. I'll let you take it from there.

We called the period of high birthrates from the mid-1940s through the mid-1960s the "baby boom." Now fast forward to the second and third decades of the current century. The baby boomers will be retiring, and when they do, the federal government is going to have to shell out hundreds of billions in additional Social Security and Medicare payments. So if you think the federal budget deficits are big—you ain't seen nothin' yet.

In 2008 we took in $190 billion more in Social Security taxes than we paid out in Social Security benefits. But because Social Security tax revenue fell so sharply during the recession, in 2010 benefits paid may have exceeded taxes collected. Once the recovery has more fully taken hold, much more will be paid in than paid out. However, by 2017 this positive cash flow will turn negative—unless Congress takes decisive action well before then—and we can expect federal budget deficits to stay above the trillion dollar mark.

In 2009 we paid about $260 billion in interest to the owners of the publicly held national debt. As this debt continues to climb, and as interest rates, which are now extremely low, begin to rise—so too will interest payments on the national debt. These rising interest payments, in turn, will further push up the debt.

In the second decade of this century huge and growing Social Security and Medicare expenditures along with rising interest payments will drive up the deficit. Each year's deficit will be tacked on to the national debt. A higher debt will mean still higher interest payments. So we can look forward to a vicious spiral of rising debt and deficits, each feeding off the other. Ten years from now we'll still be looking back at the good old days of $400-billion deficits.

Questions for Further Thought and Discussion

1. Describe the differences between an inflationary gap and a recessionary gap.
2. Explain why large deficits are so bad.
3. It can be argued that there really is no fiscal policy. How would you make this argument?
4. To what degree is the public debt a burden to future generations?
5. Explain how, in general, the automatic stabilizers work. Then use one automatic stabilizer to illustrate this.
6. Suppose income taxes and unemployment compensation were cut by an equal amount. How would aggregate demand be affected?
7. Right now is there an inflationary gap or a recessionary gap?
8. Can you remember the last good or service you purchased? Explain how the money you spent will lead to a multiplied chain of increased income and spending.
9. As late as 1992 we were running budget deficits of nearly $300 billion. How do you explain the decline in the deficits through the rest of the decade of the 1990s?
10. Explain the crowding-in and crowding-out effects. How valid are these two concepts?
11. *Practical Application:* If you had a job as a financial counselor and a bad recession hit, what advice would you give your clients to enable them to keep their heads above water?
12. *Web Activity:* How much are the projected total deficits for fiscal years 2013 and 2014? Go to www.cbo.gov and click on The Budget and Economic Outlook: An Update, and then click on Budget Projections (pdf).
13. *Web Activity:* How much is the national debt right now? Go to www.brillig.com/debt_clock. At the same time tomorrow, check to see by how much it went up.

Workbook for Chapter 12

McGraw Hill **connect** | ECONOMICS

Name _____   Date _____

Multiple-Choice Questions

Circle the letter that corresponds to the best answer.

1. Which one of these would be the most accurate statement? _____. (LO6)
   a) There was a very short fiscal policy decision lag in 2008.
   b) There was virtually no fiscal policy impact lag in 2008.
   c) In 2008 rebate checks were sent out within weeks after the beginning of the economic slowdown.
   d) President George W. Bush and the leaders of Congress were very slow to act after recognizing that there was an economic slowdown in early 2008.

2. When equilibrium GDP is too small, we have _____. (LO1)
   a) a recessionary gap   c) an inflationary gap
   b) a depression   d) none of these

3. There is an inflationary gap when _____. (LO1)
   a) equilibrium GDP is equal to full-employment GDP
   b) equilibrium GDP is smaller than full-employment GDP
   c) equilibrium GDP is larger than full-employment GDP
   d) none of these occur

4. Fiscal policy and monetary policy are _____. (LO1)
   a) different means used to attain different goals
   b) different means used to attain the same goals
   c) the same means to attain the same goals
   d) the same means to attain different goals

5. Budget surpluses are most appropriate during _____. (LO5)
   a) depressions
   b) recessions
   c) inflations

6. Each of the following is an automatic stabilizer except _____. (LO3)
   a) unemployment compensation
   b) direct taxes
   c) welfare payments
   d) Social Security benefits

7. The crowding-out effect is _____. (LO7)
   a) much stronger during a recession than during prosperity
   b) much stronger during prosperity than during a recession
   c) equally strong during a recession and prosperity

8. When there is a recession, the biggest decline is in _____. (LO3)
   a) Social Security tax receipts
   b) personal income tax receipts
   c) consumer spending
   d) corporate aftertax profits

9. The automatic stabilizers _____. (LO3)
   a) help smooth out the business cycle
   b) make the business cycle worse
   c) eliminate the business cycle

10. Each of the following is an example of discretionary fiscal policy except _____. (LO4)
    a) public works spending
    b) making the automatic stabilizers more effective
    c) changes in tax rates
    d) the unemployment insurance program

11. Which of the following is an example of crowding out? (LO7)
    a) Federal government spending causes changes in state and local government spending.
    b) Government spending reduces private spending.
    c) Tax changes perceived as temporary are largely ignored.
    d) Government spending causes the price level to rise.

12. Fiscal policy is made by _____. (LO1)
    a) the president only
    b) Congress only
    c) both the president and Congress
    d) neither the president nor Congress

13. The requirement to override a presidential veto is _____. (LO4)
    a) a majority vote in each house of Congress
    b) a two-thirds vote in each house of Congress
    c) a three-quarters vote in each house of Congress
    d) a majority vote of both houses of Congress combined

14. The crowding-out effect cancels out at least part of the impact of _____. (LO7)
    a) expansionary fiscal policy
    b) expansionary monetary policy
    c) restrictive fiscal policy
    d) restrictive monetary policy

15. If equilibrium GDP is $5.5 trillion and full employment GDP is $5 trillion, there is _____. (LO1)
    a) definitely an inflationary gap
    b) probably an inflationary gap
    c) definitely a recessionary gap
    d) probably a recessionary gap

16. Statement 1: A tax cut will have the same impact on the recessionary gap as an increase in G only if people spend the entire tax cut. (LO1)
    Statement 2: The paradox of thrift is more relevant today, when savings are so low, than it was back in the 1950s and 1960s.
    a) Statement 1 is true and statement 2 is false.
    b) Statement 2 is true and statement 1 is false.
    c) Both statements are true.
    d) Both statements are false.

17. The fiscal policy recognition lag (LO6)
    a) is always very short.
    b) is always very long.
    c) is always longer than the decision and impact lags combined.
    d) can very considerably in length.

18. Which statement is true? (LO9, 11)
    a) About one-third of the national debt is rolled over (or refinanced) every year.
    b) The national debt is doubling every 10 years.
    c) Unless we balance the budget within the next five years, the United States stands a good chance of going bankrupt.
    d) None of these statements is true.

19. Since 2001 the federal budget deficit _____ and the national debt _____. (LO4)
    a) increased, increased
    b) decreased, decreased
    c) increased, decreased
    d) decreased, increased

20. Which statement is true? (LO9, 11)
    a) The national debt is larger than GDP.
    b) The national debt will have to be paid off eventually.
    c) Most of the national debt is held by foreigners.
    d) None of these statements is true.

21. If the federal government attempts to eliminate a budget deficit during a depression, this will _____. (LO4)
    a) alleviate the depression
    b) contribute to inflation
    c) make the depression worse
    d) have no economic effect

22. During times of inflation, we want to _____. (LO4, 5)
    a) raise taxes and run budget deficits
    b) raise taxes and run budget surpluses
    c) lower taxes and run budget surpluses
    d) lower taxes and run budget deficits

23. Which statement is true? (LO9)
    a) The public debt is larger than our GDP.
    b) The public debt is the sum of our deficits minus our surpluses over the years since the beginning of the country.
    c) We have had budget deficits only during recession years and wartime.
    d) None of these statements is true.

24. The main feature of the 2008 economic stimulus package was **(LO6)**

    a) taxpayer rebates.

    b) an across-the-board tax cut.

    c) an increase in spending on food stamps and unemployment benefits.

    d) a large highway building program.

25. A major advantage of the automatic stabilizers is that they _____. **(LO3)**

    a) simultaneously stabilize the economy and tend to reduce the size of the public debt

    b) guarantee that the federal budget will be balanced over the course of the business cycle

    c) automatically produce surpluses during recessions and deficits during inflations

    d) require no legislative action by Congress to be made effective

26. The most valid argument against the size of the national debt is that it _____. **(LO9)**

    a) will ruin the nation when we have to pay it back

    b) is owed mainly to foreigners

    c) leaves future generations less plant, equipment, and housing than would be left had there been a smaller debt

    d) will bankrupt the nation because there is a limit as to how much we can borrow

27. Your best estimate of our national debt on January 1, 2015 would be _____. **(LO9, 11)**

    a) $9 trillion   d) $18 trillion

    b) $12 trillion   e) $21 trillion

    c) $15 trillion

28. In 2006 and 2007 we had _____. **(LO1)**

    a) a recessionary gap

    b) neither an inflationary gap nor a recessionary gap

    c) an inflationary gap

29. Between 1998 and 2000 the federal budget surplus _____ and the publicly held national debt _____. **(LO5, 9)**

    a) rose, rose   c) rose, fell

    b) fell, fell   d) fell, rose

30. Dynamic scoring is closely related to _____. **(LO7)**

    a) the crowding-out effect

    b) the crowding-in effect

    c) both the crowding-out and crowding-in effect

    d) neither the crowding-out nor crowding-in effect

31. The automatic stabilizers _____. **(LO3)**

    a) moderate the extremes of the business cycle

    b) make the business cycle more extreme

    c) have virtually no effect on the business cycle

32. Compared to the federal budget deficit in fiscal year 2008, the 2009 deficit was _____. **(LO5)**

    a) about the same size

    b) a little larger

    c) twice the size

    d) four times the size

33. Each of the following is a reason why the deficit is bad *except* that _____. **(LO5)**

    a) this money might otherwise have gone to pay for other government services

    b) like the national debt, we owe it to ourselves

    c) we have become increasingly dependent on foreigners to finance it

    d) it tends to raise interest rates

34. The $787 billion stimulus package _____. **(LO8)**

    a) had little effect on ending the Great Recession

    b) ended the Great Recession almost immediately

    c) was basically a Keynesian strategy to end the recession

    d) had little effect on the federal budget deficit

35. Which is the most accurate statement? **(LO8)**

    a) The Chinese stimulus package was more successful than the American stimulus package.

    b) The American stimulus package was more successful than the Chinese stimulus package.

    c) The Chinese and American stimulus packages were equally successful.

36. We had a "jobless recovery" after each of the following recessions *except* the recession of _____. **(LO10)**

    a) 1957–1958   c) 2001

    b) 1990–1991   d) 2007–2009

Fill-In Questions

1. The means that fiscal policy uses to attain its goals are the manipulation of _____ and _____. (LO4)

2. We could eliminate inflationary gaps and recessionary gaps by making _____ GDP equal to _____ GDP. (LO1)

3. The two ways of eliminating an inflationary gap are

   (1) _____

   and (2) _____. (LO1)

4. The two ways of eliminating a recessionary gap are

   (1) _____

   and (2) _____. (LO1)

5. Welfare spending, unemployment compensation, and direct taxes are all examples of _____. (LO3)

6. The crowding-out effect states that when the Treasury borrows a lot of money to finance a budget deficit,

   _____. (LO7)

7. Perhaps the most countercyclical of all the automatic stabilizers is the _____. (LO3)

8. In addition to the automatic stabilizer, we have

   _____ fiscal policy. (LO3, 4)

9. Fiscal policy was invented by _____. (LO4)

10. When equilibrium GDP is equal to full-employment GDP, we have an inflationary gap equal to

    _____. (LO1)

11. The Great Recession began in _____

    (month and year). (LO8)

Problems

1. (a) In Figure 1, is there an inflationary gap or a recessionary gap? (b) How much is it? (c) How much is the multiplier? (LO1, 2)

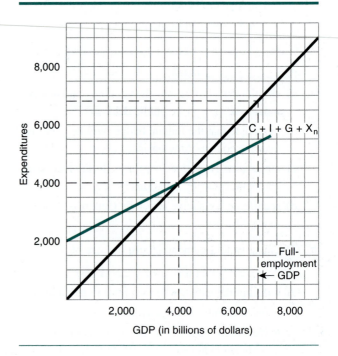

Figure 1

2. To remove the gap in Figure 1, what two fiscal policy measures would you recommend? (LO1)

3. When the MPC is .8, how much is the multiplier? (LO2)

4. If the MPC is .6, how much is the multiplier? (LO2)

5. If C rises by $10 billion and the multiplier is 4, what happens to the level of GDP? (LO2)

6. If I falls by $20 billion and the multiplier is 5, what happens to the level of GDP? (LO2)

7. If GDP is 3,400, the multiplier is 5, and I rises by 15, what is the new level of GDP? (LO2)

8. If GDP is 3,900, the multiplier is 8, and G falls by 10, what is the new level of GDP? (LO2)

9. Suppose that Derek Bowman and Nicole Bowman each have MPCs of .5. If Derek receives one dollar of income, how much of that dollar would he be expected to spend? If Nicole receives all of the money that Derek spent, how much would Nicole be expected to spend? (LO2)

10. If equilibrium GDP is $400 billion greater than full-employment GDP and there is an inflationary gap of $50 billion, how much is the multiplier? (LO2)

11. If the full-employment GDP is $1 trillion greater than equilibrium GDP and the multiplier is 5, how much is the recessionary gap? (LO2)

12. If Guy Barnes receives $1,000 from his newly created government job and gives $900 to Jingles Althaus for writing him a speech, and then Jingles gives $810 to Alayna Noel for installing a computer system, assuming everyone else in the nation has the same spending pattern: (a) How much is the multiplier? (b) If $10 billion of new investment had been made, by how much would our GDP rise? (LO2)

13. Suppose that in the year 2020 our national debt were $10 trillion and our budget deficit were $300 billion. If a plan to gradually reduce the deficit and to balance

the budget in the year 2030 were successful, make an estimate of the national debt in 2030. (LO9, 11)

15. In fiscal year 2029 there is a budget deficit of $1 trillion. The fourth Bush administration, which believes in dynamic scoring, gets Congress to pass a tax cut of $500 billion a year for the next 20 years. How much will the Bush administration's economists predict the deficit will be in fiscal year 2034? (LO7)

14. In Figure 2: (a) Is there an inflationary gap or a recessionary gap? (b) How much is it? (c) How much is the multiplier? (LO1, 2)

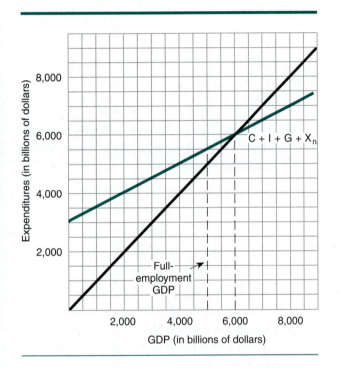

Figure 2

Chapter 13

Money and Banking

Why would it be a dumb idea to keep your money under your mattress, especially during times of inflation? What backs up our money supply? How much is a dollar worth today? What would happen if everyone tried to get their money out of the bank at the same time? By the time you've gotten to the end of the chapter, you'll know the answers to these questions.

Banks create money. The rate of monetary growth itself is controlled by the Federal Reserve, which serves as our nation's central bank. In this chapter we'll look at our country's money supply and banking system, and in the next, at the Federal Reserve System.

First we'll talk about the money supply in the United States and the jobs it does. Next we'll work in a little monetary theory; we'll look at the demand for money and how interest rates are set. Then we'll turn to banking, beginning with its origins in medieval times; moving right along, we'll look at modern banking. So fasten your seat belt; in the words of the late Jackie Gleason, "And away we go!"

LEARNING OBJECTIVES

After reading this chapter you should be able to:

1. List and discuss the three jobs of money.
2. Explain what money is.
3. Distinguish among M1, M2, and M3.
4. Analyze the demand for money.
5. Discuss the origins of banking.
6. Define and discuss branch banking and bank chartering.
7. Summarize the savings and loan debacle.
8. Describe and analyze the 2008 financial meltdown.
9. Discuss overdraft privileges.

Money

Through the ages many different kinds of things have been used as money—corn, beads, whales' teeth, shells, stones, feathers, salt, and even cocoa beans, the main ingredient of chocolate. In some time and place, each of these items was accepted as payment for a good or service. So we can define money as *any asset that can be used to make a purchase.*

The Three Jobs of Money

How important *is* money? Imagine trying to get by without any. How well would you manage if you were dropped off in some strange town with no money, no credit cards, and no friends or family? What if there were no such thing as money? If you were

Any commodity to be called "money" must be generally acceptable in exchange, and any commodity generally acceptable in exchange should be called money.

—Irving Fischer

The three jobs of money are
(1) medium of exchange,
(2) standard of value,
(3) store of value.

hungry, maybe you could find a place where you'd be able to trade your wristwatch for a meal. But then, how would you pay for your *next* meal? And where would you sleep that night? And the next?

So wouldn't you agree that money is pretty important? Sometimes we don't know quite *how* important until we're caught without it. Money is important to us as individual consumers, and it is also essential to our economy. It performs three important jobs that enable our economy to function smoothly and productively.

Medium of Exchange

Money's most important job

Money is a terrible master but an excellent servant.

—P. T. Barnum,
Circus owner

By far the most important job of money is to serve as a medium of exchange: When any good or service is purchased, people use money.

Money makes it much easier to buy and to sell because money is universally acceptable. With money I can go out and buy whatever I want—provided, of course, I have enough of it. Similarly, a seller will sell to anyone who comes along with enough money; he won't have to wait for a buyer who's willing to trade something the seller needs.

Money, then, provides us with a shortcut in doing business. By acting as a medium of exchange, money performs its most important function.

Money doesn't need to have any inherent value or use—like salt, or corn, or cocoa beans—to serve as a medium of exchange. As long as we feel confident that people will accept it in exchange for their goods and services, then money is functioning very well as a medium of exchange.

Standard of Value

A currency, to be perfect, should be absolutely invariable in value.

—David Ricardo,
Works

Wanna buy a brand name DVD player? A new sports car? A Swiss watch?

"Sure," you say. "How much?"

Thus money performs well at its second job—as a standard of value. If I told you that I got gasoline at $1 a gallon, you'd want to know the exact location of that gas station. But if I said that I bought a cheeseburger at a fast-food place for $10, you might wonder whether I have both oars in the water. A clerical job that pays $2 an hour would be nearly impossible to fill, while one paying $50 an hour would be swamped with applicants.

Does money work well as a standard of value? You tell *me*.

Is money a good standard of value?

Store of Value

I measure everything I do by the size of a silver dollar. If it don't [sic] come up to that standard, then I know it's no good.

—Thomas A. Edison

Imagine that in 1988 you put $100 under your mattress and took out that same hundred dollars in 2008. How much was that $100 worth?

In other words, if you could buy 100 units of goods and services with your $100 in 1988, how many units could you buy with $100 in 2008? Eighty? No, fewer. Seventy? No, but very close. OK, I'll put you out of your misery. You could have bought just 55 units.

Did someone sneak into your bedroom in the middle of the night and steal most of your money? No; but over the years, inflation took its toll. During this 20-year period, inflation robbed the dollar of almost half of its purchasing power.

Is money a good store of value?

This brings us back to the third job of money. Is money a good store of value or wealth? Over the long run, and particularly since World War II, it has been a very poor store of value. However, over relatively short periods of time, say, a few weeks or months, money does not lose much of its value. More significantly, during periods of price stability, money is an excellent store of value. Of course, the best time to hold money is during deflation because the longer you hold it, the more it's worth. For example, if you held money under your mattress from late 1929 to early 1933, it would have doubled in value during those years.

Other Useful Properties of Money

For thousands of years gold and silver have served as money, but not iron or wood. Iron and wood are not *scarce* enough to serve as money. Imagine *this* transaction: How much are those ox carts? Five pounds of wood? Great! I'll take ten of them.

Money versus Barter

Imagine living in a country with no money. Every time you needed something, you would have to find someone who had what you wanted and was willing to trade for something that you had.

But if there were money, a widely accepted medium of exchange, you wouldn't need to barter. You could just go out and buy what you wanted without having to find someone willing to trade.

Money also provides a standard of value. Every good and service has a price that's expressed in terms of dollars and cents. If there were no money, then everything we traded would be valued in terms of what we traded for. For example, a haircut might trade for three movie tickets.

Suppose there were just four goods and services in our economy—haircuts, hamburgers, movie tickets, and shoes. The price of haircuts would be expressed in terms of hamburgers, movie tickets, and shoes. The price of hamburgers would be expressed in terms of movie tickets and shoes. And the price of movie tickets would be expressed in terms of

shoes. If you add up these exchanges, you see that four goods and services would have six prices in a barter economy.

As the number of goods and services in a barter economy increases, the number of prices increases exponentially (see the table below). It sure is hard to do business when you have to keep track of so many prices.

Number of Goods and Services	Number of Prices in a Money Economy	Number of Prices in a Barter Economy
2	2	1
3	3	3
4	4	6
10	10	45
100	100	4,950
1,000	1,000	499,500

Relative to wood and iron, gold is scarce. But not that scarce that there isn't enough of it to be used as money. It there were, for example, just one pound of gold in the entire kingdom, there wouldn't be enough of it to serve as a money supply.

A second useful property of money is *divisibility,* which definitely helps when you're trying to make change. Imagine trying to do business with just hundred dollar bills. Of course with paper money that problem doesn't arise because the government prints up plenty of ones, fives, tens, twenties, and fifties, and also mints plenty of coins. But a country that uses cattle as money would run into a serious problem of divisibility.

Finally, money needs to be *portable.* Imagine going on a business trip and paying for your rental car, hotel, and meals with sacks of corn. Our paper currency is quite portable. But coins—even silver dollars—are *not* very portable. Just try carrying $100 in coins in your handbag or your pocket.

Money versus Barter

Try to imagine how hard it would be to do business without money. Whenever you shopped, you'd have to have something to trade that the shopkeeper wanted. Your employer would have to pay you with something that you could trade for at least some of the things you needed. You'd have to find a way to make your car payments and your rent or mortgage payments, and pay for electricity, gasoline, food, clothing, appliances, and anything else you needed. In short, to carry out every transaction, you would need to find someone with whom you had a double coincidence of wants.

Without money, the only way to do business is by bartering. "How many quarter sections of beef do you want for that car?" or "Will you accept four pounds of sugar for that 18-ounce steak?"

For barter to work, I must want what you have and you must want what I have. This makes it pretty difficult to do business. (See the Advanced Work box, "Money versus Barter.")

Everything, then, must be assessed in money; for this enables men always to exchange their services, and so makes society possible.

—Aristotle,
Nicomachean Ethics

Our Money Supply

What does our money supply
consist of?

What does our money supply consist of? Gold? No! U.S. government bonds? No! Diamonds? No! Money consists of just a few things: coins, paper money, demand (or checking) deposits, and checklike deposits (sometimes called NOW—or negotiable order of withdrawal—accounts) held by the nonbank public. Coins (pennies, nickels, dimes, quarters, half-dollars, silver dollars, and other dollar coins) and paper money (dollar bills, fives, tens, twenties, fifties, and hundreds) together are considered currency. (By the way, where did the *dollar* come from? See the box on this topic.)

Nearly five out of every 10 dollars in our money supply are demand deposits and other checkable deposits. Virtually all the rest is currency. We have to be careful, however, to distinguish between checks and demand (or checking) deposits. Jackie Gleason used to tell a story about two guys who get into an argument in a bar about who is more miserly (or cheaper). Suddenly one of them pulls out a dollar bill and a book of matches, lights the bill on fire, and lets it burn to a crisp. Not to be outdone, the other guy pulls out a five, lights it, and watches it burn to a crisp. So then the first guy does the same thing with a $10 bill. Well, the other guy doesn't want to look bad, so he reaches into his pocket, pulls out his checkbook, writes out a check for $1,000, lights it, and watches it burn to a crisp.

Checks are *not* money. Checkable deposits *are*. Previously known as checking deposits, checkable deposits are essentially demand deposits.

Incidentally, demand deposits are so named because they are payable "on demand." When you write a check, your bank must honor it, provided, of course, that you have enough money in your account to cover the check. Banks also insist that a certain number of business days go by before they will cash a specific check. It is usually 5 days for a local check and 7 to 10 days for an out-of-town check. Banks call this waiting period the time it takes for a check to clear. But any money in your checking account that has been cleared is available to depositors on demand.

Our currency is legal tender for all debts, public and private. But don't take *my* word for it. You'll find those words written just to the left of George Washington's portrait on the one dollar bill, or to the left of Abraham Lincoln's on the five. So the government says that your money must be accepted for payment of all debts. Does the government say that about checks and credit cards? No! (See the accompanying box.) Now what does it say on the back of each dollar just below "THE UNITED STATES OF AMERICA"? It says, "IN GOD WE TRUST." And as many people say: "In God we trust—all others pay cash."

Where Did the Dollar Come From?

The U.S. dollar traces its roots back to the old Spanish-milled silver dollar. You didn't think it was based on the old British system, did you? You'd really have to be crazy to try to copy a system that uses pence, shillings, guineas, and pounds.

Are you any good at trivia questions? In Robert Louis Stevenson's *Treasure Island,* there was a parrot who, as parrots will do, kept repeating the same phrase over and over. OK, what was the phrase? You have eight seconds to answer the question. What was the phrase that the parrot, who, by the way, was acquainted with Long John Silver, kept repeating? Did you guess? Sorry—time's up.

The answer is "Pieces of eight. Pieces of eight." See that? You learn something every day.

By the way, how much money is two bits? It's a quarter. And four bits? That's right—50 cents. Eight bits? A dollar.

What was that parrot getting at with his "Pieces of eight. Pieces of eight"? He was talking dollars, Spanish-milled silver dollars. Those dollars were milled in such a way, that eight pieces—or bits—could be torn from each dollar, like perforated slices in a metal pie. That way, if you had a dollar and wanted to spend just 25 cents, you tore off two pieces or bits. To this day, some South American countries have coins worth 12½ centavos.

on the web

If you'd like to learn more about our supply of currency, the Federal Reserve Bank of Atlanta has a very interesting website: www.frbatlanta.org/pubs/dollarscents and click on "Dollars and Cents brochure."

How Do We Pay Our Bills?

There are many ways to pay for things—cash, check, credit card, debit card, prepaid or stored-value cards, and electronic fund transfers. Checks had been most important before the new millennium, but we have been moving rapidly toward a relatively check-less economy.

Credit cards, and especially debit cards (see box, "Are Credit and Debit Cards Money?"), increasingly are used to pay for goods and services. And prepaid cards, which have long been issued by phone companies, are now issued by nearly all major retailers as well as by credit card companies.

More and more people are paying their bills with electronic fund transfers—movements of funds directly from one bank account to another. Many people have arrangements with the phone and electric companies to have their bills automatically deducted from their bank accounts. Similarly, some employers deposit paychecks electronically. And every month, the Social Security Administration sends out tens of millions of benefit payments electronically. Today three-quarters of all financial transactions are electronic.

M1 and M2

Our money supply includes currency, demand deposits, traveler's checks, and what the Federal Reserve terms "other checkable deposits," which include the NOW accounts and "share draft accounts," or checking accounts issued by credit unions.

According to the Federal Reserve there is over $750 billion in currency in the hands of the public (see Figure 1). But the U.S. Treasury estimates that between two-thirds

M1 = currency, demand deposits, traveler's checks, and other checkable deposits

Are Credit and Debit Cards Money?

No—neither credit cards nor debit cards is a form of money. But both *do* enable us to buy a huge range of goods and services without needing cash. Because they look alike and are issued mainly by VISA and Master-Card, when you present your card, you will be asked, "Credit or debit?"

Credit cards enable you to borrow thousands of dollars, depending on the size of your credit line. What the issuing bank would really like you to do is run up a large balance and make just the minimum payment each month, year-after-year. That way they can keep charging you 18 or 20 percent interest (or possibly even higher rates) on your outstanding balance. Today American households, on average, possess 14 credit cards, some of which were issued by banks, and others by stores, oil companies, and other retailers.

Both credit and debit cards are very important forms of ID. Not only can you travel and make major purchases without having to carry hundreds or thousands of

dollars in cash, but you won't be able to rent a car, stay in some hotels, or transact certain types of business without such a card. But remember, they're only pieces of plastic—not money.

Debit cards look like credit cards. They're not money either. When you buy something, the sales clerk asks you, "Credit or debit?" If you have a debit card, the money comes right out of your checking account. Suppose you've got $1,000 in your checking account and use your debit card to pay for a $200 purchase. Before you've left the cash register, your checking account balance has already gone down to $800.

Credit cards first became widely used in the 1960s, while debit cards came into their own in the late 1990s. Today, debit cards account for over 35 billion purchase transactions a year; credit cards account for 25 billion. But the total dollar amount of credit card purchases, $2.2 trillion, is still much greater than the $1.4 trillion in purchases made by debit cardholders.

Figure 1

M1 and M2, April 5, 2010
By adding savings deposits, small-
denomination time deposits, and
money market mutual funds held
by individuals to M1, we get M2.
Percentages may not add to
100.0 percent due to rounding.
*Source: Federal Reserve Statistical
Release,* April 5, 2010.

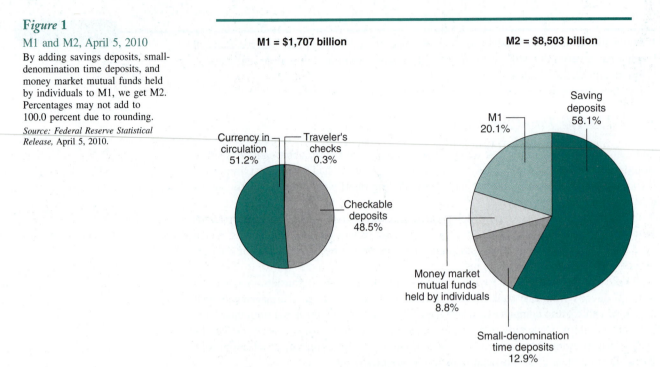

M1 = $1,707 billion

M2 = $8,503 billion

Currency in
circulation
51.2%

Traveler's
checks
0.3%

Checkable
deposits
48.5%

Saving
deposits
58.1%

M1
20.1%

Money market
mutual funds
held by individuals
8.8%

Small-denomination
time deposits
12.9%

and three-quarters of U.S. currency is held outside the United States. Foreigners, especially Russians, consider American dollars—particularly one hundred dollar bills—as a
much better medium of exchange and standard of value than their own currencies. So
the bottom line is that our money supply, M1, may be as much as $500 billion lower
than the official figure shown in Figure 1.

M1 is shown along with M2 in Figure 1. As of April 2010, our money supply totaled
$1,707 billion. Nearly everyone considers M1 our money supply, but we're also going
to consider a broader measure of money, M2.

*By adding savings deposits, small-denomination time deposits, and money market
mutual funds held by individuals to M1, we get M2.* You know what savings deposits
are. Time deposits hold funds that must be left in the bank for a specified period of
time—a week, a month, three months, a year, five years, or even longer.

Remember the bank ads that warn, "There is a substantial penalty for early withdrawal"? These warnings are another way of saying that under the conditions of a
time deposit, you are legally required to leave your money in the bank for a specified
period of time. And so, unlike a demand deposit, time deposits are not payable until
a certain date.

Technically, the money held in time and savings deposits does not have to be paid
to the depositors "on demand." When you fill out a withdrawal slip to take money
out of your savings account, you are completely confident that you will walk out of
the bank with your money. Legally, however, your bank can require up to 30 days'
written notice before giving you these funds. In practice, of course, no bank ever does
this. Although nearly every bank in the country is insured by the Federal Deposit
Insurance Corporation, it is quite possible that, if a 30-day waiting period were
enforced, many nervous depositors would rush into their banks to get their money
while they could. Money market mutual funds are issued by stockbrokers and other
institutions, usually pay slightly higher interest rates than banks, and offer check-writing
privileges.

As you'll notice in Figure 1, M2 is five times as large as M1. That's because M2
includes not just M1 but also savings deposits, small-denomination time deposits, and
money market mutual funds held by individuals.

M1 + savings, small-
denomination time deposits, and
money market funds = M2

M2 + large-denomination time
deposits = M3

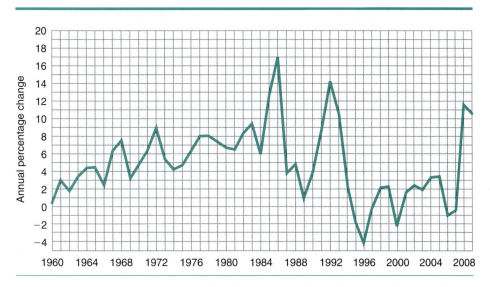

Figure 2

Annual Percentage Change in the Money Supply, M1, 1960–2009

Between 1960 and 1983, there was a fairly steady upward trend in the annual growth of M1 from less than 1 percent to just over 9 percent. But since then there have been extremely sharp fluctuations, ranging from an annual increase of 17 percent to a decrease of about 4 percent.

Sources: Economic Report of the President, 2010; *Federal Reserve Bulletin,* March 2010.

A strong case can be made to designate M2 as our basic money supply rather than M1. First, it is the monetary measure most closely watched by the Federal Reserve, the agency that controls the growth of our money supply. Second, with the enormous growth of money market deposit accounts, time deposits, and money market mutual funds, which people can quickly convert into cash, attention has shifted to M2. But I'm enough of a traditionalist to keep calling M1 our basic money supply—at least until the next edition of this text.

Our Growing Money Supply

Our money supply grows from year to year as the amount of currency in circulation goes up and as our checking deposits and checklike deposits go up as well. How fast does the money supply grow? Figure 2 shows monetary growth from the 1960s through 2009.

Monetary growth has not been smooth. You'll notice huge jumps, for example, in the mid-1980s and early 1990s. The Federal Reserve controls the rate of monetary growth. How? Read all about it in the next chapter.

The Demand for Money

How much of *your* assets do you hold in the form of money? A typical middle-class family might own a home, two cars, several thousand dollars' worth of corporate stock, and perhaps one or two U.S. Treasury bonds. Of course, none of that is money. But the same family may also have a couple of bank accounts and $800 in cash. Let's consider the reasons why people hold some of their assets in the form of money.

Economists recognize that people hold money for a variety of purposes. John Maynard Keynes noted that people had three reasons for holding money: to make transactions, for precautionary reasons, and to speculate. After we discuss the Keynesian motives for holding money, we shall look at the influences that shape the demand for holding money.

Why do people hold money?

The Keynesian Motives for Holding Money   Instead of holding their assets in other forms—stocks, bonds, real estate, commodities—everyone opts to hold at least some of their assets in the form of currency or demand deposits. John Maynard Keynes observed that people hold money not just to buy things, but also for precautionary and speculative reasons. But the transactions motive is, by far, the most important motive for holding money.

Transactions motive

Individuals have day-to-day purchases for which they pay in cash or by check. You take care of your rent or mortgage payment, car payment, monthly bills, and major purchases by check. Cash is sometimes needed for groceries, gasoline, restaurant meals, the movies, and nearly every other small purchase. Businesses, too, need to keep substantial checking accounts to pay their bills and to meet their payrolls. Individuals and businesses, then, both need to hold a certain amount of money for regular expenses. Keynes called this the transactions motive for holding money.

Precautionary motive

Next we have the precautionary motive. People will keep money on hand, sometimes called a rainy-day fund, just in case some unforeseen emergency arises. They do not actually expect to spend this money, but they want to be ready if the need arises.

Speculative motive

Finally, there is the speculative motive for holding money. When interest rates are very low—as they were during the Great Depression when Keynes was writing—you don't stand to lose much by holding your assets in the form of money. Alternatively, by tying up your assets in the form of bonds, you actually stand to lose money should interest rates rise, because you'd be locked into very low rates. In effect, the speculative demand for money is based on the belief that better opportunities for investment will come along and that, in particular, interest rates will rise.

These three Keynesian motives, especially the transactions motive, explain why people want to hold some of their assets in the form of cash. But how *much?* That depends on the four influences on the demand for money.

Four Influences on the Demand for Money　　The amount of money we hold is influenced by four factors: (1) inflation, (2) income, (3) interest rates, and (4) credit availability. Changes in these factors change how much money we hold.

(1) Inflation　　During periods of inflation, as prices rise, we need to hold an increasing amount of money to meet our day-to-day needs. When the price of a hot dog rose from a nickel to a dime during the late 1940s, hot dog lovers needed to carry twice as much money to satisfy their craving. Fifty years ago a family of four could eat out and go to the movies for about $10; doing that today might cost six times as much. So they would need to have six times as much money.

Money is the poor people's credit card.

　　—Marshall McLuhan

(2) Income　　Poor people seldom carry around much money. Check it out. The more you make, the more you spend, and the more you spend, the more money you need to hold as cash or in your checking account. Even if you use a credit card, you still have to pay your bill at the end of the month. As income rises, so does the demand for money balances.

(3) The Interest Rate　　So far we've had two positive relationships: the quantity of money demanded rises with the level of prices and income. Are you ready for a negative relationship? All right, then. The quantity of money demanded goes down as interest rates rise.

Until recently people did not receive interest for holding money. Cash that you keep in your wallet or under your mattress still pays no interest, and until the late 1970s neither did checking deposits. Even today nearly all checking deposits pay less than 2 percent interest, and some don't pay any interest whatsoever. Alternatives to holding your assets in the form of money are to hold them in the form of bonds, money market funds, time deposits, and other interest-bearing securities. As interest rates rise, these assets become more attractive than money balances. Thus, there is a negative relationship between interest rates and money balances.

Do you remember the concept of opportunity cost, which was introduced in Chapter 2? What is the opportunity cost of holding money? It's the interest that you forgo.

(4) Credit Availability　　If you can get credit, you don't need to hold so much money. Forty years ago most Americans paid cash for their smaller purchases and used checks for big-ticket items. The only form of consumer credit readily available was from retail merchants and manufacturers. The last four decades have seen a veritable explosion in consumer credit in the form of credit cards and bank loans. Over this period increasing credit availability has been exerting a downward pressure on the demand for money.

We can now make four generalizations:

1. As interest rates rise, people tend to hold less money.
2. As the rate of inflation rises, people tend to hold more money.
3. As the level of income rises, people tend to hold more money.
4. People tend to hold less money as credit availability increases.

Banking

A Short History of Banking

There are 6,800 commercial banks in the United States. These are defined as banks that hold demand deposits, but other banks—mutual savings banks, savings and loan associations, credit unions, and mutual money market funds—also issue checking accounts. The distinction between commercial banks and other savings institutions is blurring.

We'll talk about the origins of banking before we discuss how banking is conducted today in the United States. The first banks were run by goldsmiths back in the Middle Ages. We'll see that these fellows invented not only banking, but paper money as well.

In medieval times, about the only secure place for your money was in the safes of the goldsmiths, so anybody who was anybody kept his money with the local goldsmith. These gentlemen would give receipts that possibly looked a little like the hatcheck slips you get at some of the fancier restaurants. If you left 10 gold coins with the smith, he wrote 10 on your receipt. If you happened to be rich, it was very important to be able to count past 10.

The origins of banking

Although no one is quite sure who was the first to accept paper money—that is, goldsmiths' receipts—it might well have happened this way:

A knight was having his castle completely redone—new wallpaper, new bearskin rugs, new dungeon, new drawbridge—the works! When the job was finally completed, the contractor handed him a bill for 32 gold pieces.

The knight told the contractor, "Wait right here. I'll hitch up the team and take the oxcart into town. I'll get 32 gold coins from the goldsmith. I shouldn't be gone more than three days."

"Why bother to go all the way into town for the 32 gold coins?" asked the contractor. "When you give them to me, I'll have to ride all the way back into town and deposit the coins right back in the goldsmith's safe."

"You mean you're not going to charge me for the job?" The knight, while able to count past 10, came up short in certain other areas.

"Of course I want to get paid," replied the contractor. "Just give me your receipt for 32 gold coins."

It took the knight a little while to figure this out, but after the contractor went over it with him another six or eight times, he was finally able to summarize their transaction: "If I give you my receipt, we each save a trip to the goldsmith." And with that, paper money began to circulate.

The goldsmiths were not only able to count higher than anyone else in town, but they generally had a little more upstairs as well. Some of them began to figure out that they could really start to mint money, so to speak. First, they recognized that when people did come in to retrieve their gold coins, they did not insist on receiving the identical coins they had left. Second, they noticed that more and more people were not bothering to come in at all to get their money because they were paying their debts with the receipts. And so, the goldsmiths were struck with this evil thought: Why not lend out some of these gold coins just sitting here in the safe?

Moment at which modern
banking was born

This was the moment modern banking was born. As long as the total number of receipts circulating was equal to the number of gold coins in the safe, there was no banking system, but when the number of receipts exceeded the number of coins in the safe, a banking system was created. For example, if a goldsmith had 1,000 coins in his safe and receipts for 1,000 coins circulating, he wasn't a banker. What if he knew that his depositors would never all come at the same time for their money and he decided to lend out just 10 gold coins? He would then still have receipts for 1,000 coins circulating, but he'd have only 990 coins in his safe.

The "paper money" issued by the goldsmith is no longer fully backed by gold, but there's really nothing to worry about because not everyone will show up at the same time for their gold. Meanwhile, the goldsmith is collecting interest on the 10 gold pieces he lent out.

"But why stop there?" asks the goldsmith. "Why not lend out 100 gold coins, or even 500?" And so he does. With 500 coins lent out, he still has 500 in his safe to cover the 1,000 receipts in circulation. And what are the chances that half his depositors will suddenly turn up demanding their coins?

Now we have 500 coins backing up 1,000 receipts, or a reserve ratio of 50 percent. As long as no panics occur, 50 percent is certainly a prudent ratio. As the ratio declines (from 100 to 50 percent), let's see what happened to the money supply, the gold coins, and the goldsmith's receipts in the hands of the public (Figure 3).

Let's go a step further and have the goldsmith lend out an additional 250 gold coins. See if you can figure out the reserve ratio and the size of the money supply.

Because there are now 250 coins backing 1,000 receipts, the reserve ratio is 25 percent. Meanwhile the money supply has grown from 1,500 to 1,750, because in addition to the 1,000 receipts, 750 coins are in the hands of the public.

If the goldsmith were to continue lending out gold coins, he would end up with none in his safe. His reserve ratio would sink to zero, and the money supply would be 2,000 (1,000 receipts and 1,000 coins).

Being such a clever fellow, the goldsmith has noticed that his receipts circulate as easily as gold coins. And so, long before he has lent out all his coins, which he really needs as reserves (or backing for his receipts), he begins to make loans in the form of his receipts. For example, suppose you need to borrow 10 gold coins. The goldsmith merely writes up a receipt for 10 gold coins and off you go with your money.

If the goldsmith so chose, he could even print up 10,000 receipts, which would bring about a reserve ratio of 10 percent (1,000 coins backing 10,000 receipts) and a money supply of 10,000 receipts. Or he could lend out 100,000, bringing the reserve ratio down

Figure 3

Goldsmith's Receipts and Reserves

Three questions: What is the goldsmith's reserve ratio when there are (a) 1,000 receipts in circulation and 1,000 coins in his safe? (b) 1,000 receipts in circulation and 500 coins in his safe? (c) 1,000 receipts in circulation and 250 coins in his safe? Answers: (a) 100 percent; (b) 50 percent; (c) 25 percent.

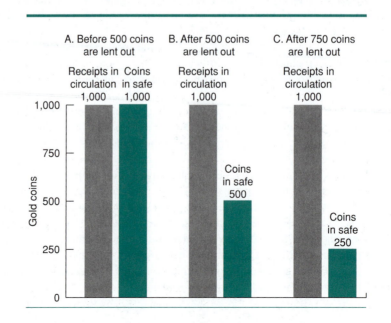

to 1 percent (1,000 coins backing up 100,000 receipts) and creating a money supply of 100,000 receipts.

The system worked as long as the goldsmiths did not get too greedy and as long as the depositors maintained their confidence in their goldsmith's ability to redeem his receipts in gold coins. From time to time, however, individual goldsmiths went too far in lending out money, whether in the form of gold coins or receipts. When depositors began to notice so many receipts in circulation, they asked themselves whether the goldsmith could possibly have enough coins in his safe to redeem them all. And when they thought he might not, they rushed into town to withdraw their gold coins before everyone else tried to.

If too many people reached the same conclusion, a panic ensued and the goldsmith could not possibly meet the demands of his depositors. In effect, then, he went bankrupt, and those left holding his receipts found them worthless. Of course, that was all before the days of the Federal Deposit Insurance Corporation (FDIC), so there was no one to whom depositors could turn.

The system worked as long as the goldsmiths did not get too greedy.

Modern Banking

Like the early goldsmiths, today's bankers don't keep 100 percent reserve backing for their deposits. If a bank kept all its deposits in its vault, it would lose money from the day it opened. The whole idea of banking is to borrow money at low interest rates and then lend out that same money at high interest rates. The more you lend, the more profits you make.

Banks would like to keep about 2 percent of their deposits in the form of vault cash. As long as depositors maintain confidence in the banks—or at least in the FDIC—there is really no need to keep more than 2 percent on reserve.

Unhappily for the banks, however, they are generally required to keep a lot more than 2 percent of their deposits on reserve. All the nation's commercial banks, credit unions, savings and loan associations, and mutual savings banks now have to keep up to 10 percent of their checking deposits on reserve. (See Table 1 of Chapter 14.)

Let's take a closer look at our banks. A bank as a financial institution accepts deposits, makes loans, and offers checking accounts.

Commercial Banks These 6,800 banks account for the bulk of checkable deposits. Until the passage of the Depository Institutions Deregulation and Monetary Control Act of 1980, which is outlined near the end of the next chapter, only commercial banks were legally allowed to issue checking deposits, and they were the only institutions clearly recognized as "banks." Usually they have the word "bank" in their names. Traditionally, banks lent money for very short-term commercial loans, but in the last few decades they have branched out into consumer loans, as well as commercial and residential mortgages, and many offer brokerage services.

Savings and Loan Associations Although originally established to finance home building, these associations also offer most of the services offered by commercial banks. The 800 S&Ls invest more than three-quarters of their savings deposits in home mortgages. Later in the chapter we'll cover the savings and loan debacle of the 1980s, which ultimately reduced the number of S&Ls by almost two-thirds.

Mutual Savings Banks Mostly operated in the northeastern United States, these institutions were created in the 19th century to encourage saving by the "common people." They traditionally made small personal loans, but today, like savings and loan associations, they offer the same range of services as commercial banks. There are about 1,200 mutual savings banks, all of which are located in New York, Massachusetts, Connecticut, Pennsylvania, and New Jersey.

Credit Unions Although there are close to 8,000 credit unions in the United States, they hold less than 5 percent of total savings deposits. While these banks, like the others we've mentioned, do offer a full range of financial services, they specialize in small consumer loans. They are cooperatives that generally serve specific employee, union, or community groups.

The Banking Act of 1980 blurred the distinctions between commercial banks and the three other depository institutions. The main distinction—before 1980 only commercial banks were legally allowed to issue checking accounts—was swept away in 1980.

The Big Banks   Figure 4 lists our country's top 10 banks by size of assets in 2009. Nearly all are familiar names. You may notice that two of the top three, Citigroup and JPMorgan Chase, are located in New York City. Although it remains the financial capital of America, New York is no longer the preeminent financial center of the world.

The top 10 banks hold about $3.2 trillion of America's $7.7 trillion of deposits. That's certainly a lot of money in the hands of a relatively small number of institutions. There has been a trend toward consolidation of financial institutions over the last 25 years. And that consolidation means a lot less competition in the industry. Since competition is what drives firms to be efficient, we certainly have cause for concern.

Consolidation has also brought about huge economies of scale—most notably ongoing computerization and the spreading network of ATMs—efficiencies that are necessary for American banks to compete in global markets. Considering the trend toward financial supermarkets providing one-stop shopping, the efficiencies from consolidation may even outweigh the efficiency losses resulting from diminished competition.

Figure 4

The Top Ten American Banks, Ranked by Assets, 12/31/09

Source: www.ffiec.gov/nicweb/
Top50form.aspx

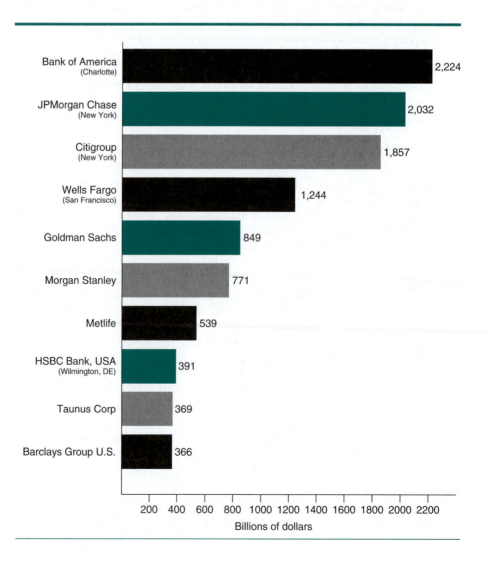

TABLE 1	The World's Top Ten Banks, Ranked by Assets, December 31, 2009	
Bank	Country	Total Assets (in billions)
Royal Bank of Scotland	United Kingdom	$3,483
Deutsche Bank	Germany	3,069
Barclays	United Kingdom	2,977
BNP Paribas	France	2,892
Crédit Agricole	France	2,303
Bank of America	United States	2,224
JPMorgan Chase	United States	2,032
UBS	Switzerland	1,881
Sociéte Générale	France	1,574
Bank of Tokyo-Mitsubishi	Japan	1,494

Source: www.bankersalmanac.com

How do the banks listed in Figure 4 rank internationally? Of the top 10 commercial banks (ranked by size of assets), 3 are French, 2 are British and 2 are American. The top 10 American banks are listed in Figure 4, and the world's top 10 banks in Table 1.

While banking is consolidating in the United States, and most of the money lent out goes to very large corporations, the opposite trend is taking place in many of the world's poorest countries. Microlending—loans of no more than a few hundred dollars—has enabled millions of business owners to set up shop. This development is described in the accompanying box.

Bank Lending   Banking is based on one simple principle: Borrow money at low interest rates and lend that money out at much higher interest rates. Even when interest rates are very low, as they have been in recent years, banks charge their borrowers a lot more

A banker is a fellow who lends his umbrella when the sun is shining and wants it back the minute it begins to rain.

—Mark Twain

Microlending*

In the United States and in other developed economies, bank loans to business generally range between a few thousand dollars and a few billion dollars. But in very poor countries, there is a large need for very small business loans—usually for less than $500, and, in many cases, even less than $100. Nobel Prize winner Mouhammad Yunus created the Grameen Bank of Bangladesh, which, in the words of the Nobel Prize selection committee, was created to bring to reality something that "had appeared to be an impossible idea," namely loans to people who lacked collateral.

Since its founding in 1974, Grameen has extended over $8 billion in loans. The average loan is about $100 and approximately 99 percent are paid back in full. Rather than follow the traditional path of growing banks, and catering to the relatively wealthy members of society, Grameen continued making small loans just to poor business owners. Although the bank charges about 20 percent interest, this is an extremely low rate

for poor entrepreneurs with no collateral. Widespread microlending has been around for many decades, but Grameen took it to a much higher level. And while it has barely made a dent in the abject poverty of countries like Bangladesh, microlending has certainly enabled millions of budding entrepreneurs to create growing businesses.

Nicholas D. Kristof and Sheryl WuDunn describe how a very poor Pakistani woman name Siama took out a $65 loan to set up an embroidery business, selling to the merchants of Lahore. Eventually she was able to employ 30 families. She had received her loan from the Kashf Foundation, which lends almost exclusively to women, in groups of 25. "The women guarantee one another's debts and meet every two weeks to make payments. . . ."[†]

---

*See "Macro credit," in *The Economist,* October 21, 2006, p.78.

[†]Nicholas D. Kristof and Sheryl WuDunn, "The Women's Crusade," *The New York Times Magazine,* August 23, 2009, pp. 29–30.

"Welfare Banks"

Most of us take for granted the services provided by our neighborhood banks. They cash our paychecks; they operate 24-hour cash machines; and, if we need the money to buy a new car or even a house, they lend it to us.

But where do poor people do their banking? Chances are, they go to the "welfare bank," which is what the check-cashing stores are called. You'll find at least one in virtually every poor neighborhood. Where did the name come from? Well, on "check day," which almost always falls on the 1st and the 16th of every month, 6 million Americans receiving public assistance get their checks in the mail. Why don't they cash them at their neighborhood banks? First of all, many poor neighborhoods don't have banks. Second, you usually need to have a minimum balance of at least $1,500 or the bank will charge you some pretty stiff fees for its services. Third, people receiving public assistance are not allowed to have bank accounts; they have no choice but to find someplace else to cash their checks.

The check-cashing outlets not only cash checks but also sell money orders. Who pays their bills by money order? Poor people do. And, of course, a money order may cost $1, or $2, or even more. To cash a check, you usually pay a fee of $5 or 1 to 6 percent of the value of the check, but some check-cashing stores will charge you as much as 20 percent.

You may ask why banks almost always require a minimum balance on checking accounts in the first place. The reason is that every banking transaction—depositing money, withdrawing money, processing checks, even posting interest—costs the banks money. However, the poor, especially those on welfare, can least afford to pay the fees charged by check-cashing services. Congress, as well as state legislatures, has considered passing laws requiring banks to cash welfare and Social Security checks, and to provide other banking services to people who cannot afford to keep the stipulated minimum balances, but the American Bankers Association, one of the nation's most powerful special interest groups, has easily beaten back this legislation.

In the 1990s the number of check-cashing outfits tripled to 7,000 and reached 11,000 in 2006. These outfits charged poor people between 4 and 10 times what they would have paid for the same services at a bank. And yet most poor people are unaware that several states (including Illinois, Massachusetts, New Jersey, New York, Rhode Island, Vermont, and Minnesota) have laws that require banks to offer accounts with minimum deposits of $100 or less and monthly fees of no more than $3. Although banks are often required to post information about low-cost checking accounts, few actually do, because these laws are rarely enforced.

than they pay their depositors. Just look at the rates that banks post in their windows or in their lobbies. They come right out and admit that they pay either zero or up to maybe 3 percent interest on most deposits—and perhaps 1 or 2 points more if you leave your money on deposit for a few years—but they charge about 7 percent for fixed-rate mortgages, a bit more for most business loans, and about 18 percent on credit card loans. (See the box, "Welfare Banks.")

Financial Intermediaries   Financial intermediaries channel funds from savers to borrowers. Basically they repackage the flow of deposits, insurance premiums, pension contributions, and other forms of savings into larger chunks—$10,000, $1 million, $50 million, or even more—for large business borrowers. And, of course, they pay relatively low rates of interest to their lenders and charge relatively high rates to their borrowers. We're all familiar with banks, but this function is performed by a variety of other financial intermediaries (see the box, "Nonbank Financial Intermediaries").

Sometimes business borrowers dispense with financial middlemen altogether by borrowing directly from savers. The U.S. Treasury does this every month by issuing new bonds, certificates, notes, and bills. And increasingly, large business borrowers are doing the same thing by issuing relatively short-term commercial paper and long-term bonds.

One way that banks and other financial intermediaries differentiate between the relatively well off and the less fortunate is in the home mortgage market. Just over two-thirds of all American families own their home, nearly all of which have outstanding mortgages.

There are two distinct mortgage markets: the conventional market, in which commercial banks, savings banks, savings and loan associations, and credit unions provide middle

Nonbank Financial Intermediaries

Banks offer their customers checking deposits that are included in M1. Some nonbank financial intermediaries may come close, but no cigar. Money market mutual funds, for instance, often allow their investors to write checks on their balances, but usually only a few a month, and for at least $500 or $1,000.

Pension funds, generally set up by large corporations, are another major form of financial intermediary. TIAA-CREF, which nearly all college professors have joined, is the largest, with a stock and bond portfolio worth several hundred billion dollars. Where did it get all this money? From our paychecks, with matching contributions from our employers.

Insurance companies collect billions of dollars in premiums every year, which they invest in real estate, stocks and bonds, and mortgages. Consumer finance companies—such as Beneficial Finance and Household Finance—borrow at very low rates, because they have excellent credit ratings, and charge their customers 25, 30, or even 40 percent interest rates. Why are these people willing to pay so much? Because they don't have much choice—if their credit ratings had been better, they could have borrowed from a bank.

class and relatively well off homeowners conventional mortgages, and the subprime market, which caters to poorer homeowners and has interest rates that are double what they are in the conventional market. Banks generally do not lend directly to homeowners in the subprime market, but they either provide the funds to consumer lending companies like Countrywide Credit or Household International, that provide the actual mortgages, or else huge banks, such as Bank of America and Citicorp own these subprime lenders outright.

There have been moves on the local, state, and federal levels to more closely regulate these subprime lenders. Their defenders point out that without this market, millions of relatively poor families would be unable to own homes. However, the high interest rates and other financial charges have caused hundreds of thousands of families to lose their homes each year. The case of Veronica Harding, which was reported in *The New York Times,* illustrates the plight of relatively poor homeowners. Ms Harding ". . . bought a row house in North Philadelphia for $7,500 in 1980, but now owes about $35,000 after refinancing five times in four years. The last loan generated $5,600 in fees, or 16 percent of the loan value.[1]

In 2002 Household International paid a record $484 million fine to settle allegations that it had misled borrowers in more than a dozen states into paying mortgage rates that in some cases were almost twice what was promised. Household also agreed to stop allowing loan officers to persuade customers to refinance home loans to take advantage of lower rates without advising them about other fees they would have to pay.[2]

Bank Regulation

Branch Banking and Bank Chartering

Branch Banking versus Unit Banking Banking is legally defined as accepting deposits. Branch banking, therefore, would be the acceptance of deposits at more than one location. Branch banking rules are set by the state in which a bank is located. Bank

---

[1]Richard A. Oppel, Jr. and Patrick McGeehan, "Lenders Try to Fend Off Laws on Subprime Loans," *New York Times,* April 4, 2001, p. C17.

[2]Subprime lending is discussed more extensively in the chapter, "Rent, Interest, and Profit," in *Economics* and *Microeconomics.* It is also the main part of the Current Issue at the end of the next chapter.

of America, for example, is subject to North Carolina banking law, while Citibank and JPMorgan Chase are regulated by New York banking law.

Three types of branch banking have evolved under various state laws. First is unrestricted branch banking, under which a bank may open branches throughout the state. Golden West Financial and Wells Fargo have branches all over California.

A second variation is restricted, or limited, branch banking. For example, a bank may be allowed to open branches only in contiguous communities. What is permissible varies from state to state.

> The three types of branch banking are
> (1) unrestricted branching,
> (2) limited branching,
> (3) unit banking.

Finally, there is unit banking, in which state law forbids any branching whatsoever. A bank that opens an office that receives deposits at a particular location cannot open any other branches. This obviously restricts the size of banks in those states. In fact, banks in unit banking states are, on the average, about one-fifth the size of banks in states that permit unrestricted branching.

Right now two out of five states, nearly all in the East and Far West, have unlimited branching. Another two out of five states, mainly in the Midwest and the South, allow limited branching. And finally, the remaining states, mostly in the Midwest, permit only unit banking.

There are 95,000 bank branches throughout the nation—an increase of 13,000 since 1996—but some banks are closing branches and replacing them with automated teller machines. Why the shift to ATMs? Processing a teller transaction costs more than double what an ATM transaction costs. By the end of 2009 there were about 425,000 ATMs in the United States, about 40 percent privately owned. These are typically found in convenience stores, bars, restaurants, grocery stores, and check cashing establishments. Many are owned by the same person who owns the business in which they are located.

The ATM Wars   Should banks be allowed to charge fees—usually $1 to $2—to noncustomers? Virtually all bankers and most economists (including the author) would answer "yes!"

First, there's the issue of fairness. Six out of seven ATM users don't pay surcharges. The fees hit only users who go to "foreign" ATMs—machines not owned by their own bank. Why should a bank's customers underwrite the noncustomers who demand access to cash wherever they are? And why should a bank provide a free service to people who do not otherwise patronize it? Indeed, after Santa Monica and San Francisco banned the fees, Bank of America and Wells Fargo briefly stopped allowing noncustomers in those cities to use their machines.

Second, we need to think of an ATM as a convenience. We pay more to shop at a "convenience store" than at a supermarket. We pay more for soda from a vending machine than at a grocery. Why not charge people for the convenience of withdrawing cash at an airport, at a shopping mall, or even in another state?

And finally, banning the surcharges would leave consumers with fewer choices. It would presumably become unprofitable to operate the machines in some out-of-the-way places that didn't have them before the fees. Perhaps banks won't continue to serve out-of-town travelers. We'll all have to make do with fewer cash machines and longer lines.

> Most banks have state charters.

State and Nationally Chartered Banks   To operate a bank, you must get a charter. More than two-thirds of the nation's banks have state charters; the rest have national charters. National charters are issued by the comptroller of the currency and are generally harder to obtain than state charters. Each of the 50 states issues state charters.

To get a bank charter you need to demonstrate three things: (1) that your community needs a bank or an additional bank; (2) that you have enough capital to start a bank; and (3) that you are of good character.

Most large banks are nationally chartered. Often the word *national* will appear in their names, for example, First National City Bank or Mellon National Bank. Incidentally, all nationally chartered banks must join the Federal Reserve. About three-quarters of all banks have state charters.

To summarize, all nationally chartered banks must join the Federal Reserve System. All Federal Reserve member banks must join the FDIC. Only a small percentage of the state-chartered banks are members of the Federal Reserve. Nearly all banks are members of the FDIC.

Interstate Banking   Until 1994 interstate banking was technically illegal, although banks managed to engage in the practice by buying banks in other states and operating them as separate entities. But the passage of the Riegle-Neal Interstate Banking and Branching Efficiency Act of 1994 swept away the last barriers to opening branches in different states. Until this law was passed, for example, a customer of a bank branch in North Carolina was not permitted to make a deposit at one of the same bank's South Carolina branches.

The Federal Deposit Insurance Corporation

After the massive bank failures of the 1930s, Congress set up the FDIC—another case of closing the barn door after the horses had run off. The amount insured has progressively been raised, reaching a ceiling of $100,000 in 1980. But in response to the financial crisis of 2008, the ceiling was raised to $250,000 per depositor. For example, if you have a checking account balance of $200,000 and a $300,000 CD, a total of just $250,000 is insured. On January 1st, 2014, the insurance ceiling will be returned to $100,000.

The whole idea of the FDIC is to avert bank panics by assuring the public that the federal government stands behind the bank, ready to pay off depositors if it should fail. The very fact that the government is ready to do this has apparently provided enough confidence in the banking system to avoid any situation that could lead to widespread panic.

The whole idea of the FDIC

The FDIC would rather have another bank take over an ailing institution than be forced to pay off its depositors. Often, to encourage such takeovers, the FDIC will actually give the cooperating bank up to several hundred million dollars to take certain white elephants off its hands.

The FDIC prefers takeovers to payoffs.

By law, the FDIC is required to maintain a rainy-day fund equal to at least 1.15 percent of the level of insured deposits, which now total $4.8 trillion. The fund is financed by an annual assessment on their deposits. Through 2010, that assessment was 12 to 16 cents on every $100 in deposits, but on January 1, 2011, it will rise by 3 cents.

Is the FDIC in any danger of running out of money? Not really. The Congress, the Federal Reserve, the Treasury, and all the financial resources of the U.S. government are committed to the preservation of this institution.

Will the FDIC run out of money?

That said, in the fall of 2009, the FDIC actually *did* run out of money. Its reserves, which totaled over $50 billion in April 2008, had fallen steadily for the next year and a half, because of a sharp rise in bank failures (see Figure 5). Rather than go to the Treasury for a loan, the FDIC ordered its member banks to prepay their assessments that would have otherwise been due through 2012.

More than 99 percent of all banks are members of the FDIC. If you want to make sure that yours is, first check to see whether there's a sign in the window attesting to this fact. If there isn't, ask inside, and if the answer is no, then very calmly walk up to the teller and withdraw all your money. Membership in the FDIC means that your money is safe and that we will probably never have a repetition of what happened back in the 1930s when there were runs on the banks, culminating in the Great Depression.

The financial crisis of 2008 and the accompanying recession took a heavy toll on the nation's banks. Bank failures shot up from just 3 in 2007 to 25 in 2008, and then to 140 in 2009 (see Figure 5). By late July 2010 over 100 more banks had gone under; before the year's end the total would surpass the 140 failures of 2009.

Figure 5

U.S. Bank Failures, 2000–2009
From the beginning of the new
century through 2007, we never had
more than 10 bank failures in one
year. But failures shot up in 2008
and 2009 because of the financial
crisis and the recession.
Source: www.fdic.gov/bank/individual/
failed/banklist.html

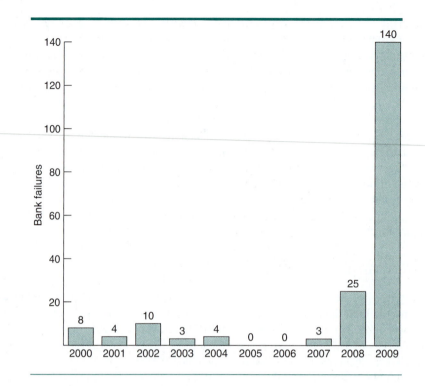

The Savings and Loan Debacle

While the rate of bank failures was quite high in 2009 and 2010, they did not come close to the level of failures two decades earlier. In 1989 alone 534 savings and loans were seized.

The origins   In early 1990 the financial press was calling this the greatest financial scandal in the history of the United States. How could it have happened? How bad *was* it? The roots of the problem date to the 1950s and 1960s, when the nation's 3,000 savings and loan associations were handing out millions of 30-year mortgages at 4, 5, and 6 percent fixed interest rates. This was good business—at that time—because the S&Ls were paying just 2 or 3 percent interest to their shareholders.[3]

When interest rates went through the roof from the late 1970s through the early 1980s, the shareholders rushed in to withdraw their money. But their money wasn't just sitting there in the vaults. It was already lent out to homeowners. It was being paid back, a little each month, over a 30-year period.

Why did the shareholders want to take their money out? Because they could get much higher interest rates by purchasing Treasury bills, certificates of deposit, money market mutual funds, corporate bonds, or other financial instruments. Why didn't the savings and loan associations simply pay them more interest? Because they were legally barred from doing so.

In 1980 the law was changed to allow the savings and loan associations to pay much higher rates of interest.[4] In addition, they were freed from making primarily home mortgage loans. What the S&Ls did, then, with their newfound freedom was go out and borrow funds at very high interest rates and lend them out at still higher interest rates. The only trouble was that the loans they tended to make were very risky ones.

Dangerous speculation   Money was lent to farmland speculators in the Midwest and to people buying up oil properties in the Southwest. These seemed like reasonably safe loans because the prices of this land had been rising very rapidly. But what goes up must come down. At least it did during the severe recession of 1981–82. And what was a bad situation nationwide got

---

[3]Technically, people who deposit their money in savings and loan associations are shareholders, but if you'd rather call them depositors, that's fine with me.

[4]Insurance coverage was raised at that time from $40,000 to $100,000 on savings and loan shares and on bank deposits.

to be a worse situation in the Southwest and the Midwest as declining oil prices and drought depressed land prices still further. Borrowers defaulted on their loans, and the S&Ls were stuck with large holdings of real estate, which they had to sell in a depressed market. In short, scores of S&Ls—most notably in Texas and Oklahoma—lost their shirts.

And that was just *part* of the problem. Real estate developers, many of them based in California, Florida, and Texas, bought control of many S&Ls and poured billions of dollars into shopping malls, office parks, condos, and other ventures of dubious merit (dubious during a time of sinking real estate prices, anyway). And so another wave of S&Ls was taken to the cleaners.

Still another aspect of the S&L debacle revolved around junk bonds, which were   Junk bonds
used extensively to finance corporate takeovers or, alternatively, to stave off hostile take-overs. To raise billions of dollars quickly, corporate raiders—or the boards of the corporations facing hostile bids—would issue bonds given very low credit ratings. Why did anyone want to buy them? Because they paid relatively high interest rates.

Among the biggest buyers of these junk bonds were failing S&Ls. And so, using their shareholders' money, they helped feed the speculative corporate takeover frenzy that dominated Wall Street during the 1980s. When the prices of many of these bonds plunged steeply in the late 1980s, in the wake of the stock market crash of October 1987, several hundred more S&Ls were ruined.

The federal government ended up paying hundred of billions of dollars to clean up the mess. Depositors were paid off, hundreds of failed S&Ls were shut down, and the surviving S&Ls were now more closely supervised.

on the web

Every Friday the FDIC lists any bank that has failed during that week. During 2009 2 or 3 were usually listed. www.fdic.gov/bank/individual/failed/banklist.html

Current Issue: Overdraft Privileges

When you don't have enough money in your account to cover a check you wrote, your check will bounce. This can be very embarrassing, so banks and credit unions now grant overdraft privileges to their depositors. If you overdraw your account, your check won't bounce, but you *will* have to pay an overdraft fee.

Each time a person overdraws her account, she's charged a fee of $10 to $38 according to a 2008 FDIC study, and she must pay back the overdraft within a week or two. When an overdraft occurs as a result of a debit card or ATM transaction, banks generally don't immediately inform their customers or give them the option of reversing the transaction. Instead they mail out a notice. So a person may incur several overdrafts before realizing how many fees she's incurred.

Here's what happened to one college student who took advantage of his overdraft privileges:

> Chris Keeley went on a shopping spree last Christmas Eve, buying $230 in gifts with his debit card. But the New York University student's holiday mood soured a few days later when he received a notice from Pittsburgh's PNC Bank that he had overdrawn the funds in his checking account. While PNC allowed each of his seven transactions to go through, it charged him $31 for each overdraft—or a hefty $217 in fees for his $230 worth of purchases.[5]

Would *you* agree to pay $217 in interest on a two-week $230 loan? Did Chris Keeley know how much he would be paying for overdrawing his checking account? It all comes down to the issue of truth-in-lending, and the banks could certainly be more forthcoming about the cost of the overdraft privileges they so freely extend.

---

[5]See *BusinessWeek,* May 2, 2005, p. 68.

About three-quarters of all banks and credit unions automatically enroll their customers in overdraft programs. The rapidly growing use of debit cards—whose transactions surpassed credit card transactions in 2004—has become the main means by which depositors unwittingly overdraw their accounts. In 2009 banks and credit unions earned over $40 billion in overdraft fees—about three-quarters of their total service charge income.

According to a study by the FDIC, it was the practice of more than three-quarters of all banks to automatically sign customers up for overdraft privileges. A large number of those customers erroneously assumed that somehow they would be instantaneously informed by their bank if they were about to overdraw their checking account. A Federal Reserve regulation, which took effect on July 1, 2010, prohibits banks from charging overdraft fees on ATMs or debit cards, unless a customer has agreed to pay extra charges for exceeded account balances.

If you *do* have overdraft privileges, you'll need to keep very careful track of your balance. If that balance is low, then every check, debit charge, or ATM withdrawal puts you at risk of racking up substantial finance charges. Overdrafts may be a privilege, but it comes at a price you don't want to pay.

Questions for Further Thought and Discussion

1. When would you expect to find barter used instead of money?

2. What happens to the demand for money as (a) the price level rises; and (b) the availability of credit rises? Explain your answers.

3. Describe the conditions that were necessary for modern banking to be born.

4. What were the conditions that led to the savings and loan debacle?

5. How could rapid inflation undermine money's ability to perform each of its four basic jobs?

6. What distinguishes money from other assets, such as corporate stock, government bonds, and expensive jewelry?

7. Our money supply is defined as M1. But the Board of Governors of the Federal Reserve and many others believe M2 would better define our money supply. Can you think of one reason to support M1 and one reason to support M2?

8. Why do most interest rates go up and down together over time?

9. Financial intermediaries perform an important job. What is that job, and how do they perform it?

10. What percentage of your money balance do you hold for transactions purposes, precautionary purposes, and speculative purposes?

11. What percentages of your or your family's bills are paid by cash, by check, and by credit card?

12. *Practical Application:* How would you change the current system of bank overdraft fees to make it more equitable, but still profitable to banks?

13. *Web Activity:* If you would like to make your own microloan of as little as $25 to someone setting up a small business, with an extremely high likelihood of being repaid, go to www.kiva.org This website is recommended by *New York Times* columnists Nicholas D. Kristof and Sheryl WuDunn (see box in chapter, "Microlending").

14. *Web Activity:* How much is M1 and M2? You can find out at http://federalreserve.gov/releases/h6/Current.

Workbook for Chapter 13 — connect ECONOMICS

Name _____ Date _____

Multiple-Choice Questions

Circle the letter that corresponds to the best answer.

1. Each of the following except _____ is a job of the money supply. **(LO1)**
   a) medium of exchange
   b) store of value
   c) standard of value
   d) receipt for gold

2. Which is the most important job of money? **(LO1)**
   a) Medium of exchange
   b) Store of value
   c) Standard of value
   d) Receipt for gold

3. The basic alternative to money in the United States would be _____. **(LO2)**
   a) gold
   b) barter
   c) stealing
   d) the underground economy

4. Barter involves _____. **(LO2)**
   a) money
   b) specialization
   c) a double coincidence of wants
   d) demand deposits

5. Which one of the following is not part of our money supply? **(LO2)**
   a) Dollar bills
   b) Demand deposits
   c) Traveler's checks
   d) Gold

6. Which statement is true? **(LO3)**
   a) M1 is larger than M2.
   b) M1 is equal to M2.
   c) M2 is larger than M1.
   d) M1 is sometimes larger than M2 and sometimes smaller than M2.

7. Which statement is true? **(LO2)**
   a) Checks are not money.
   b) A small part of our money supply is silver certificates.
   c) Most of our money supply is in the form of currency.
   d) None of these statements is true.

8. The U.S. dollar is based on _____ currency. **(LO2)**
   a) British   b) French
   c) Dutch   d) Spanish

9. Which is not in M2? **(LO3)**
   a) Currency
   b) Demand deposits
   c) Small-denomination time deposits
   d) Large-denomination time deposits

10. Which statement is true? **(LO3)**
    a) Credit cards are a form of money.
    b) Debit cards are a form of money.
    c) M2 is about six times the size of M1.
    d) M1 is about six times the size of M2.

11. When you buy something with a credit card _____ and when you buy something with a debit card _____. **(LO3)**
    a) you owe money; you owe money
    b) you owe money; money is taken out of your checking account
    c) money is taken out of your checking account; money is taken out of your checking account
    d) money is taken out of your checking account; you owe money

12. In April 2010 M1 was more than $ _____ billion. **(LO3)**
    a) 600   b) 900
    c) 1,300   d) 1,700

13. Over the last three decades our money supply _____. (LO3)

    a) grew steadily at about the same rate

    b) fell steadily at about the same rate

    c) rose steadily through the 1970s and fell steadily through the 1980s and 1990s

    d) fell steadily through the 1970s and rose steadily through the 1980s and 1990s

    e) grew most years, but at widely varying rates

14. The interest rate on business loans _____ the interest rate that banks pay their depositors. (LO4)

    a) is higher than

    b) is lower than

    c) has no relationship to

15. The most important way of paying for goods and services is _____. (LO2)

    a) electronic fund transfers

    b) gold

    c) checks

    d) cash

    e) prepaid or stored-value cards

16. Which one of the following would be the best definition of money? (LO2)

    a) Any asset that can be used to make a purchase.

    b) A precious commodity such as gold or silver.

    c) A credit or debit card.

    d) A commodity that has an inherent value or use.

17. John Maynard Keynes identified three motives for holding money. Which motive listed below did Keynes not identify? (LO4)

    a) Transactions   b) Precautionary

    c) Psychological   d) Speculative

18. As the price level rises, the amount of money demanded for transactions purposes _____. (LO4)

    a) rises

    b) falls

    c) remains about the same

19. As the interest rate rises, the quantity of money demanded _____. (LO4)

    a) rises

    b) falls

    c) remains about the same

20. People tend to hold more money as _____. (LO4)

    a) incomes rise and credit availability rises

    b) incomes fall and credit availability falls

    c) incomes rise and credit availability falls

    d) incomes fall and credit availability rises

21. The distinction between commercial banks and other banks is _____. (LO5, 6)

    a) very clear   b) becoming blurred

    c) nonexistent   d) none of these

22. Which statement is true? (LO3)

    a) Most U.S. currency is held by foreigners.

    b) We have greatly underestimated the amount of currency circulating in the U.S.

    c) Russians hold virtually no U.S. currency.

    d) About 10 percent of our currency is held by foreigners.

23. What led to the bankruptcy of many goldsmiths was that they _____. (LO5)

    a) had a reserve ratio that was too high

    b) had a reserve ratio that was too low

    c) lent out gold coins instead of receipts

    d) lent out receipts instead of gold coins

24. Which statement is false? (LO6)

    a) About 99 percent of all banks are members of the FDIC.

    b) If the FDIC runs out of money, the federal government will supply it with more funds.

    c) The FDIC would rather have another bank take over an ailing institution than be forced to pay off its depositors.

    d) None of these statements is false.

25. Which statement is true? (LO6)

    a) Most states allow only unit banking.

    b) Most states allow unlimited branching.

    c) Most banks have national charters.

    d) None of these statements is true.

26. To get a bank charter, you need to demonstrate each of the following, except _____. (LO6)

    a) that your community needs a bank or an additional bank

    b) that you have sufficient banking experience

    c) that you have enough capital to start a bank

    d) that you are of good character

27. Each of the following is a useful property of money

   except _____. (LO1)

   a) portability   b) scarcity

   c) divisibility   d) held only by the rich

28. Which seems to be the most appropriate way to lend money to small business borrowers in poor nations? (LO5)

   a) Loans by conventional banks requiring collateral

   b) Loans by conventional banks not requiring collateral

   c) Loans by microlenders requiring collateral

   d) Loans by microlenders not requiring collateral

29. Which one of the following is the most accurate statement about Internet banking? (LO5)

   a) It will never happen because depositors would never trust a bank that has no branches, checkbooks, or ATMs.

   b) It is attractive to some depositors because Internet banks usually pay higher interest rates than conventional brick and mortar banks.

   c) It is less attractive than conventional brick and mortar banks because Internet banks charge depositors higher fees and require large minimum deposits.

   d) By the year 2020 Internet banks will hold more than half of all U.S. deposits.

30. Suppose you had no money in your checking account and your bank granted you overdraft privileges. You then went out and charged $20 on your debit card. How much would your bank charge you in fees for using your overdraft privileges? (LO6, 7)

   a) 0

   b) $5

   c) $10–$15

   d) $15–$35

   e) $50

31. Which statement is true? (LO5)

   a) Citigroup, JPMorgan Chase, and Bank of America each hold over $1 trillion in deposits.

   b) Citigroup, JPMorgan Chase, and Bank of America hold just over one quarter of all bank deposits in the U.S.

   c) Citigroup, JPMorgan Chase, and Bank of America are the three largest banks in the world, when ranked in terms of deposits.

   d) No American bank holds more than 5 percent of all U.S. bank deposits.

32. Which one of the following is the most accurate statement? (LO9)

   a) Banks usually extend overdraft privileges only to their largest depositors.

   b) Bankers know that if they extend overdraft privileges, virtually all their depositors will end up having to pay substantial finance charges.

   c) Using overdraft privileges are a great way to borrow money, because you won't have to pay any finance charges if you pay off your balance before the end of the month.

   d) If you have a low checking deposit balance and your bank has extended you overdraft privileges, then every check, debit charge, or ATM withdrawal puts you at risk of racking up substantial finance charges.

33. Our worst financial crisis since the Great Depression was _____. (LO8)

   a) the financial meltdown in 2008

   b) the savings and loan debacle of the 1980s

   c) the stagflation of the 1970s

   d) the shortage of currency during World War II

Fill-In Questions

1. The most important job of money is as _____. The other two jobs of money are _____ and _____. (LO1)

2. The alternative to money would be _____. To do this, you would need a _____. (LO2)

3. The U.S. dollar is based on the _____. (LO2)

4. The basic function of credit cards is _____. (LO3)

5. To get from M1 to M2, we add _____. (LO3)

6. M2 is _____ times the size of M1. (LO6)

7. About _____ percent of the states allow only unit banking. (LO6)

8. About _____ percent of all banks have state charters. (LO6)

9. The world's first bankers were the _____. (LO5)

10. Modern banking was born when the first bankers noticed two things: (1) _____ and (2) _____. (LO5)

11. The world's first paper money was in the form of _____. (LO1, 2)

12. If a goldsmith had 100 gold coins sitting in his safe and lent out 50 of them, this would imply a reserve ratio of _____ percent. (LO5)

13. The bankruptcy of the goldsmiths who lent out part of the gold they were safekeeping was caused by _____. (LO5)

14. Banks are very heavily regulated. The main reason for this is that _____. (LO6)

15. The FDIC insures all bank deposits of up to $_____. (LO6)

16. Rather than pay off depositors of a failed bank, the FDIC would prefer that _____ _____. (LO6)

Problems

1. (a) A goldsmith has 1,000 gold coins in his safe and 1,000 receipts circulating. How much are his outstanding loans and what is his reserve ratio? (b) The goldsmith then lends out 100 of the coins. What is his reserve ratio? (LO5)

2. A goldsmith has 100 gold coins in his safe. If there are 500 receipts in circulation, how much is his reserve ratio? (LO5)

3. How much would M2 be if M1 were 500; small-denomination time deposits, savings deposits, and money market mutual funds held by individuals totaled 1,200; and large-denomination time deposits were 300? (LO3)

4. Initially M1 is 1,000 and M2 is 4,000. Find the size of M1 and M2 if demand deposits rise by 100. (LO3)

5. State numerically what would happen to M1 if:
(a) Ashley Whittingham brought $1,000 to her bank and deposited it in her checking account;
(b) Nicolas Gindorff took $500 out of his checking account and put it in his savings account;
(c) Richard Barnett bought $700 of traveler's checks for which he paid by check. (LO3)

Chapter 14

The Federal Reserve and Monetary Policy

Who wields the most power over our economy? Congress? The president? For many years some believed it was a man named Alan Greenspan, who served as Federal Reserve chairman from 1987 to 2006. When things were not working out, some people asked, "Who elected that guy?" It turns out that no one elected Dr. Greenspan. He was appointed by four presidents and confirmed by the Senate.

In the first part of the chapter, we'll examine the organization and management of the Federal Reserve System (the Fed), especially how it uses open-market operations, changes in the federal funds and discount rates, and changes in reserve requirements to control the rate of growth of the money supply.

Monetary policy is the manipulation of the money supply. The Federal Reserve determines how much money should be circulating in our economy. The goals of monetary policy are price stability, relatively full employment, and a satisfactory rate of economic growth. If you go back to the first page of Chapter 12, you'll see that the goals of fiscal and monetary policy are identical. The melodies are the same, but the lyrics are quite different. Fiscal policy is the use of government spending and taxation to affect the overall economy, while monetary policy controls the growth of the money supply.

LEARNING OBJECTIVES

After reading this chapter you should be able to:

1. Understand the organization of the Federal Reserve System.
2. Explain reserve requirements.
3. Apply the deposit expansion multiplier.
4. Explain the creation and destruction of money.
5. List and apply the tools of monetary policy.
6. Discuss the Fed's effectiveness in fighting inflation and recession.
7. Examine the Banking Acts of 1980 and 1999.
8. List and discuss monetary policy lags.
9. Summarize the housing bubble and the subprime mortgage mess.
10. Explain how a normally functioning financial system was restored.
11. Discuss whether Ben Bernanke should have been reappointed to a second term.

The Federal Reserve System

Unlike most other industrial nations, the United States was without a central bank until 1913.[1] While the Bank of England and the Bank of France acted, respectively, as England's

---

[1]There had been a First United States Bank (1791–1811) and a Second United States Bank (1816–36), but the charters of both had been allowed to lapse, mainly for political reasons.

and France's central banking authority, Americans were left defenseless when financial panics set in. Every few years in the 1880s, 1890s, and early 1900s, financial crises developed and eventually receded until, finally, we had the Panic of 1907.

During this panic, people rushed to their banks to take out their money, and business was severely disrupted. The public demanded that the government take steps to prevent this from ever happening again. After six years of intermittent debate, Congress finally passed the Federal Reserve Act of 1913. One of the hopes of its framers was that the 12 Federal Reserve District Banks would, at times of crisis, act as a "lender of last resort." In other words, if U.S. bankers were caught short of funds, someone now stood ready to give them a little time to get their affairs back in order.

In the very first paragraph of the Federal Reserve Act, Congress outlined its main objectives:

> An Act to provide for the establishment of Federal reserve banks, to furnish an elastic currency, to afford means of rediscounting commercial paper, to establish a more effective supervision of banking in the United States, and for other purposes.

What's an elastic currency? It's a money supply that expands when the economy is growing rapidly and businesses need more money. Rediscounting, which we'll talk about later in the chapter, is a way for the Federal Reserve to lend money to banks, which, in turn, would lend that money to businesses.

The Federal Reserve has five main jobs:

1. Conduct monetary policy, which is, by far, the most important job. Monetary policy is the control of the rate of growth of the money supply to foster relatively full employment, price stability, and a satisfactory rate of economic growth.

2. Serve as a lender of last resort to commercial banks, savings banks, savings and loan associations, and credit unions.

3. Issue currency (see the box, "Who Issues Our Currency?").

4. Provide banking services to the U.S. government.

5. Supervise and regulate our financial institutions.

The Federal Reserve District Banks

The 12 Federal Reserve District Banks

There are 12 Federal Reserve District Banks, one in each of the nation's Federal Reserve districts. These are shown in the map in Figure 1. Each of these banks issues currency to accommodate the business needs of its district.[2] (To learn who actually issues our currency, see box.)

You'll notice in Figure 1 that the Federal Reserve District Banks are concentrated in the East and Midwest, which reflects the concentration of banks and business activity in 1913. Each Federal Reserve District Bank is owned by the several hundred member banks in that district. A bank becomes a member by buying stock in the Federal Reserve District Bank, so the Fed is a quasi public–private enterprise, not controlled by the president or by Congress. However, effective control is really exercised by the Federal Reserve Board of Governors in Washington, D.C.

The Board of Governors

The seven members of the Federal Reserve Board

The seven members of the Board of Governors are nominated by the president, subject to confirmation by the Senate. Each is appointed for one 14-year term and is ineligible to serve a second term. The terms are staggered so that vacancies occur every two years. That way, in every four-year term, a president appoints two members of the Board of Governors.

---

[2]The Bureau of Engraving in Washington does the actual printing, but why be picky?

Who Issues Our Currency?

The U.S. Treasury issues it, right? Wrong! Our currency is issued by the 12 Federal Reserve District Banks.* Check it out. Pull a dollar out of your wallet and look at it. What does it say right near the top, about a half inch above George Washington's picture? That's right— "Federal Reserve Note."

If you thought the Treasury issues our currency, it used to (and the Secretary of the Treasury still signs every bill). The last paper currency it issued, until the mid-1960s, was $1 and $5 silver certificates. These certificates are now out of circulation, snapped up by collectors. The Treasury still issues our pennies, nickels, dimes, quarters, half dollars, and metal (no longer silver) dollars, but that's just the small change of our money supply.

And what about the backing for the dollar? Look on the back of the bill just above the big "ONE." What's the backing for our currency? That's right—"In God We Trust." Actually, there is backing for our currency—the government's word, as well as its general acceptability.

---

*As noted in footnote 2, the actual printing is done by the Federal Bureau of Engraving.

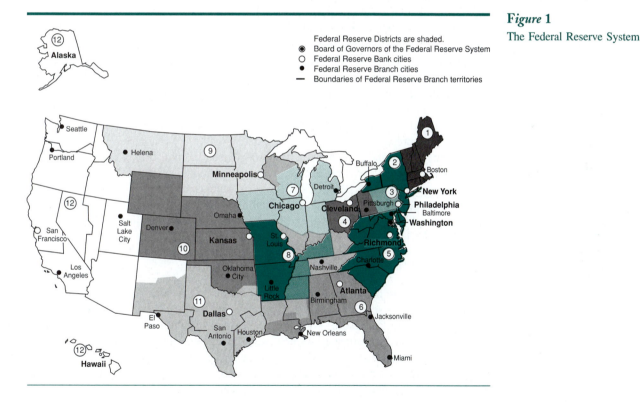

Federal Reserve Districts are shaded.
- ◉ Board of Governors of the Federal Reserve System
- ○ Federal Reserve Bank cities
- ● Federal Reserve Branch cities
- — Boundaries of Federal Reserve Branch territories

Figure 1
The Federal Reserve System

Usually, however, a president gets to appoint three or even four members during a single executive term because many governors do not serve their full 14-year terms. Why not? Mainly because they could make much more money "on the outside." All seven members of the Board that were serving in January 2009 when President Barack Obama took office had been appointed by President George W. Bush, and five had PhDs in economics. During his first year and a half, Obama made three appointments. In addition he nominated Ben Bernanke for a second term as chair.

The chairman of the Board, who generally exercises considerable influence, serves a 4-year term, which is part of his or her 14-year tenure as a member of the Board. He or she is also appointed by the president and may serve more than one term as chairman.

Independence of the Board of Governors

Should the Board of Governors be controlled by or answerable to anyone else?

Does the president "control" the Board of Governors and its chairman? The answer is, generally, no. First, unless there is a vacancy caused by death or resignation, the president would have to serve two terms to appoint four members to the Board. In practice, though, many governors do not serve their full terms. Second, once someone is appointed to the Board, there is no reason to expect that person to do the president's bidding.

The president does get to appoint a chairman sometime during his or her term. There have been proposals that the president be allowed to appoint his own chairman at the beginning of the executive term so that monetary and fiscal policy can be coordinated, but no action has been taken thus far.

Once a Board member or chairman is confirmed by the Senate, she or he is not answerable to the president or Congress. Some feel that for a group of unelected officials, the members of the Board have too much power. When interest rates soar or inflation rages out of control, these rascals cannot be turned out of office by an angry electorate. About all we can do is hope that better people will eventually be appointed to the Board.

Others feel that the difficult, unpopular decisions of monetary policy must be made by those who are insulated from the wrath of the voters. Tight money is hardly a popular policy, but when the Federal Reserve Board members think it will help control inflation, why should they be inhibited by fears of political reprisal?

How independent is our central bank in comparison to other leading central banks? The Bank of England has relatively little independence from political control. The British government sets a specific numerical target for inflation each year which the bank tries to hit. Consequently, the bank is often under pressure to increase the money supply and stimulate the economy, leading to relatively high inflation rates.

The Bank of Canada and the Bank of Japan are in the middle rank of central banks in terms of independence. Both enjoy considerable independence but still come under some political pressure.

You may recall the 12-member European Monetary Union from Chapter 8. Its common currency, the euro, has replaced each member nation's currency. The euro is issued by the European Central Bank, which coexists with Deutsche Bundesbank, La Banca d'Italia, and each of the other nations' central banks. The ECB is perhaps the most independent central bank in the world, and has been very effective in limiting inflation.

Legal Reserve Requirements

The Federal Reserve's most important job

The Federal Reserve has various jobs, the most important of which is to control the money supply. When it was set up in 1913, the framers of the Federal Reserve Act envisaged the Fed as a "lender of last resort." Obviously, the record of widespread bank failures in the early 1930s is a sad commentary on how well the Fed was able to do that job.

Before we consider how the Fed works today, we will look at the focal point of the Federal Reserve's control of our money supply–legal reserve requirements. Every financial institution in the country is legally required to hold a certain percentage of its deposits on reserve, either in the form of deposits at its Federal Reserve District Bank or in its own vaults (see Table 1).

TABLE 1	Legal Reserve Requirements for Checking Accounts,* January 1, 2010**
$0 million − $10.7 million	0%
$10.7 million − $55.2 million	3
over $55.2 million	10

*Time deposits have a 0% reserve requirement.
**The numerical boundaries of these limits are revised annually.
Source: http://www.federalreserve.gov/monetarypolicy/reservereq.htm

We'll be using some technical terms, so let's be very clear about their meanings. *Required reserves* is the minimum amount of vault cash and deposits at the Federal Reserve District Bank that must be held by the financial institution. *Actual reserves* is what the bank is holding. If a bank is holding more than required, it has excess reserves. Therefore, *actual reserves − required reserves = excess reserves.*

If a bank had $100 million in checking deposits, how much reserves would it be required to hold? Work it out right here, using the information in Table 1:

Solution:

First $10.7 million of deposits: 0% reserve requirement

Next $44.5 million: $44,500,000 × .03 = $1,335,000

Next $44.8 million: $44,800,000 × .10 =   4,480,000

Required reserves $5,815,000

If this bank happened to be holding reserves of $9 million, find its excess reserves.

Solution:

Actual reserves − Required reserves = Excess reserves

$9,000,000 − $5,815,000 = $3,185,000

Because banks have traditionally earned no interest on their reserves, (since October 2008, the Fed *has* been paying interest on excess reserves) they have tried to keep them down to a bare minimum. In fact, a bank has ideally held no excess reserves whatsoever; its goal was zero excess reserves.

Let's try another question. If a bank had demand deposits of $1 billion and held $120 million in actual reserves (in the form of deposits at the Federal Reserve District Bank and vault cash), calculate (1) its required reserves and (2) its excess reserves.

Solution:

(1) 0% of 10.7 million =   0

3% of $44.5 million = $1,335,000

10% of remaining $944.8 million =   94,480,000

Required reserves = $95,815,000

(2) Actual reserves − Required reserves = Excess reserves

$120,000,000 − $95,815,000 = $24,185,000

Can a bank ever end up with negative excess reserves? Think about it. Time's up: what do you think? If actual reserves are less than required reserves, then excess reserves are negative. Or, in simple English, the bank is short of required reserves. If a bank does find itself short, it will usually borrow reserves from another bank that has some excess reserves. The reserves it borrows are called *federal funds,* and the interest rate charged for them is called the *federal funds rate.* A bank short of reserves may also borrow at the discount window of its Federal Reserve District Bank, a process we'll discuss later in the chapter.

The Monetary Control Act of 1980 (which will be discussed in detail toward the end of this chapter) called for uniform reserve requirements for all financial institutions—commercial banks, savings banks, savings and loan associations, money market mutual funds, and credit unions. You'll notice in Table 1 that the reserve requirement for time deposits is zero. Because time deposits, by definition, are held for relatively long periods of time, the Federal Reserve Board eliminated reserve requirements for all time deposits in 1992.

Primary and Secondary Reserves

A bank's *primary reserves are its vault cash and its deposits at the Federal Reserve District Bank.* Bankers are, if nothing else, prudent. Their main aims, other than making high profits, are to protect their depositors and to maintain liquidity. Liquidity is the ability to convert assets quickly into cash without loss.

What are the three main aims of bankers?

Even without legal reserve requirements, bankers would keep some cash on reserve to meet the day-to-day needs of their depositors as well as to meet any unforeseen large withdrawals. The cash that banks do keep on hand, together with their deposits at the Federal Reserve District Banks, is usually called primary reserves. In addition, every bank holds secondary reserves, mainly in the form of very short-term U.S. government securities.

Treasury bills, notes, certificates, and bonds (that will mature in less than a year) are generally considered a bank's secondary reserves. These can quickly be converted to cash without loss if a bank suddenly needs money, whether because of increased withdrawals or perhaps a shortage of primary reserves. Generally, in the case of a shortage of primary reserves, a bank will borrow on a daily basis from other banks in the federal funds market.

The Creation and Destruction of Money

The Creation of Money

Money consists of checking deposits, checklike deposits, and currency in the hands of the public. To create money, banks must increase either currency held by the public or checkable deposits. The way banks do this is by making loans.

Banks create money by making loans.

A businessperson walks into Bank of America and requests a loan of $10,000. Later that day she calls the bank and finds out that her loan is granted. Because she already has a checking account at Bank of America, the bank merely adds $10,000 to her balance. In return she signs a form promising to pay back the loan with interest on a specified date. That's it. Money has been created. Checking deposits have just increased by $10,000.

If, for some reason, the businessperson had asked to be paid in cash, the public would have held $10,000 more in currency. And the bank? The $10,000 it loaned out was merely inventory; it was not counted as part of our money supply.

The point is that the bank just created $10,000. Whether checkable deposits or currency held by the public rose by that amount, our money supply rose by $10,000.

This may sound like a license to print money. It is, but it's a very restricted license. A bank may make loans only if it has some available reserves. And who determines whether banks have these reserves? You guessed it—the Federal Reserve. So we really have three parties involved in the creation of money: the person who wants to borrow the money, the bank that creates the money, and the Federal Reserve, which allows this creative act to take place.

The Destruction of Money

Whoever creates can usually destroy as well. That's what happens when the business-person pays back her loan. She'll probably write a check on her account for $10,000 plus the interests she owes, and when the bank deducts that amount from her account, down goes the money supply. Or if she pays back the loan in cash, again—down goes the money supply. In this case the currency leaves the hands of the public (literally) and goes into the bank's inventory. The bank will stamp the loan agreement form "paid," and the transaction is completed.

> Money is destroyed when a loan is repaid to the bank.

The creation and destruction of money is a major function of banking. The basic way this is done is through loans. The most important commercial bank loans are commercial and industrial loans, although consumer loans have grown considerably in importance since the 1970s.

Limits to Deposit Creation

Most bank loans involve giving the borrower an additional deposit in his or her checking account; therefore, it would appear that banks can create all the money they wanted by doing this. All you need is a simple bookkeeping operation. A $20,000 loan means you increase that customer's account by $20,000 by a computer entry.

Remember the goldsmith who kept writing receipts until there were 1,000 gold coins in his safe backing 100,000 receipts? Why can't bankers keep issuing loans by increasing the checking accounts of their customers?

The first limit would be prudence. Most banks would try to keep about 2 percent of their demand deposits on reserve in the form of vault cash; in case some of their depositors came in to cash checks, there would be enough money on hand to pay them. But no banker has that choice. The Federal Reserve sets legal requirements to which the banks must adhere, and, as I've already mentioned, these limits are substantially higher than those that might be set by the most prudent of bankers.

Deposit Expansion

How Deposit Expansion Works

To see how deposit expansion works, we'll assume a 10 percent reserve ratio because that's an easy number with which to work. And we'll assume everyone uses just one bank. Suppose someone comes into a bank and deposits $100,000.

We know that banks don't like to have idle reserves because they don't earn any interest on them. So what does the bank do with the $100,000? It lends out as much as it can. Let's assume it lends $90,000 to a single business firm.

Normally, the bank would need an additional $9,000 in reserves to cover the new $90,000 demand deposit. But why did the company borrow $90,000? Obviously it was needed for certain business expenses; no one pays interest on borrowed money just to sit on it.

Again, keeping things simple, suppose this company wrote a check for $90,000 to pay for additional inventory. The company receiving the check deposits it in its bank, and the process is repeated. The bank keeps the required 10 percent ($9,000) on reserve and lends out the remaining $81,000. This money is spent and eventually deposited in a third bank, which keeps 10 percent ($8,100) on reserve and lends out $72,900.

We could go on and on. Indeed, we have in Table 2. Were we to continue the process with an infinite number of banks, we would eventually end up with $1 million in deposits and $100,000 in reserves.

TABLE 2	Hypothetical Deposit Expansion with 10 Percent Reserve Requirement

Deposits	Reserves
$100,000.00	$10,000.00
90,000.00	9,000.00
81,000.00	8,100.00
72,900.00	7,290.00
65,610.00	6,561.00
59,049.00	5,904.90
53,541.00	5,354.10
48,186.90	4,818.69
43,368.21	4,336.82
—*	—*
—	—
—	—
$1,000,000.00	$100,000.00

*To save space, the rest of the calculations are omitted.

The Deposit Expansion Multiplier

Remember the multiplier in Chapter 12? Now we'll look at the deposit expansion multiplier, which is based on the same principle and nearly the same formula.

Any new money injected into the banking system will have a multiplied effect on the money supply. How large this multiplied effect will be depends on the size of the multiplier. In general, when the reserve ratio is low, the multiplier will be high and vice versa.

The formula for the deposit expansion multiplier is:

$$\text{Deposit expansion multiplier} = \frac{1}{\text{Reserve ratio}}$$

$$\frac{1}{\text{Reserve ratio}}$$

If the reserve ratio is .10, we substitute and solve to find the multiplier:

$$\frac{1}{\text{Reserve ratio}} = \frac{1}{.10} = 10$$

Remember, how many dimes are in a dollar?

If the reserve ratio is .25, find the deposit expansion multiplier. Do it right here.

Using the formula, we get:

$$\frac{1}{\text{Reserve ratio}} = \frac{1}{.25} = 4$$

How many times does .25 go into 1? How many times does a quarter go into a dollar?

Three Modifications of the Deposit Expansion Multiplier

Not every dollar of deposit expansion will actually be redeposited and lent out repeatedly. Some people may choose to hold or spend some of their money as currency. For example, an individual receiving a $300 check may deposit $200 and receive $100 back as cash.

This cash leakage tends to cut down on the deposit expansion multiplier because not all the money lent out is redeposited. For example, if $90,000 is lent out but only $81,000 is redeposited, this would have the same effect on the multiplier as a 10 percent increase in the reserve ratio.

It is also possible, although unlikely in times of inflation, for banks to carry excess reserves. To the degree that they do, however, this cuts down on the deposit expansion multiplier. Why? Because it, in effect, raises the reserve ratio. For example, if the reserve ratio rose from .20 to .25 because banks were carrying a 5 percent excess reserve, the multiplier would fall from 5 ($\frac{1}{.2} = 5$) to 4 ($\frac{1}{.25} = 4$). These leakages take place during times of recession and low interest rates, when banks may carry excess reserves. One might also keep in mind that during recessions, banks might carry excess reserves because of a scarcity of creditworthy borrowers.

Finally, there are leakages of dollars to foreign countries caused mainly by our huge foreign trade imbalance. Our imports far exceed our exports, so there is a large drain of dollars to foreigners. And then, too, there is all the currency that American tourists spend abroad, plus the tens of billions sent covertly to international drug traffickers. Some of these dollars return to the United States in the form of various investments (particularly in U.S. government securities, corporate securities, and real estate), but there is a definite net outflow of dollars, which, in turn, depresses still further the deposit expansion multiplier.

Where does all this leave us? It leaves us with the conclusion that the deposit expansion multiplier is, in reality, quite a bit lower than it would be if we based it solely on the reserve ratio. In other words, if the reserve ratio tells us it's 10, perhaps it's only 6.

Now that I've made you do these calculations, a confession is in order. The deposit expansion multiplier is a bit less wonderful than I led you to believe. It's just too big. You can probably get on with your life just accepting this fact, but if you happen to be from Missouri (the Show Me State), then you can check out the Advanced Work box, "Three Modifications of the Deposit Expansion Multiplier."

Cash, Checks, and Electronic Money

One of the jobs of the Federal Reserve is called check clearing. Through this process, once the checks you write are deposited by the people you gave them to, they make their way through our financial system, facilitated by the Fed, and eventually wind up photocopied on the back of your monthly bank statement.

In 2004 Congress passed the Check Clearing for the 21st Century Act, often called Check 21, which is intended to hasten the adoption of electronic check processing. One important effect of this law will be that bank statements will carry photocopies of checks, not originals, saving banks from having to fly checks across the country. The new system allows the bank that first receives the check to create an electronic image for transmission through the system. Will this law ultimately lead to the elimination of paper checks? Maybe, but probably not for quite a few years.

A second important effect of the law is that you can no longer give someone a check and plan on having three or four days for it to clear. It may clear now within a day, or even less, so you need to have sufficient money in your account when you write a check.

If your company in Boston needs to pay $937,042.91 to my company in St. Louis, does it send a check? Chances are, it will wire the money. To pay your phone bill, do you still send a check, or have the payment deducted electronically from your bank account? An increasing number of Americans no longer receive paychecks. Instead their pay is deposited electronically into their bank accounts. And when you buy things and pay with your debit card, a few seconds after your card is swiped by the sales clerk, the amount of your purchase has been deducted from your checking account.

Increasingly, money is changing hands electronically rather than in the form of checks. The Fed runs the system under which more than $1.4 trillion a day are transferred electronically—90 percent of the total payments made worldwide in dollars. About one-third of these transfers are carried out by the Federal Reserve's electronic network, while most of the other two-thirds are done by the Clearing House Interbank Payments System (CHIPS), which is owned by 10 of the world's largest banks.

The Tools of Monetary Policy

The most important job of the Fed is to control the growth of the money supply; its most important policy tool to do that job is open-market operations.

How Open-Market Operations Work

What are open-market operations?

Open-market operations are the buying and selling of U.S. Treasury bills, notes, and bonds. The Fed does not market new securities.[3] That's the Treasury's job. Rather, the Fed buys and sells securities that have already been marketed by the Treasury, some of which might be several years old.

The total value of all outstanding U.S. government securities was about $6 trillion as of mid-2010. The Fed held an additional $800 billion. What open-market operations consist of, then, is the buying and selling of chunks of the national debt. The Fed does this by dealing with government bond houses, which are private U.S. securities dealers. If the Fed wants to buy $900 million of Treasury notes that will mature within the next three months, it places an order with a few of these bond houses, which then buy up the securities for the Fed. When the Fed wants to sell securities, it again goes to the government bond houses and has them do the actual selling.

How the Fed increases the money supply

When the Fed wants to increase the money supply, it goes into the open market and buys U.S. government securities. You might ask, "What if people don't want to sell?" Remember the line from *The Godfather,* "I'll make you an offer you can't refuse"? Well, that's exactly what the Fed does. It tells the government bond houses, "Buy us 30,000 Treasury bills no matter what the price."

Question: What do you get when you cross the Godfather with an economist? Answer: An offer you can't understand.

If the Fed goes on a buying spree in the open market, it will quickly drive up the prices of U.S. government securities. All this buying will push down interest rates. Let's see why.

Suppose a bond is issued by the Treasury with a face value of $1,000 and an interest rate of 8 percent. This means the bond costs the initial buyer $1,000 and pays $80 interest a year. The price of the bond will fluctuate considerably over its life; but when it matures, the Treasury must pay the owner $1,000, its face value. And every year the Treasury must pay the owner $80 interest.

Using the formula

$$\text{Interest rate} = \frac{\text{Interest paid}}{\text{Price of bond}}$$

$$\text{Interest rate} = \frac{\text{Interest paid}}{\text{Price of bond}}$$

we can observe that a $1,000 bond paying $80 interest pays an interest rate of 8 percent:

$$\frac{\$80}{\$1.000} = 8 \text{ percent}$$

This is sometimes called the stated rate or face rate.

We have been talking about the Fed going into the open market and buying government securities. Suppose the Fed bought enough securities to bid up their price to

---

[3]The Fed is legally limited to buying no more than $5 billion in newly issued government securities a year, which is less than 1 percent of what the Treasury issues.

$1,200. Remember, these securities still pay $80 interest a year. Let's calculate their new interest rate:

$$\text{Interest rate} = \frac{\text{Interest paid}}{\text{Price of bond}} = \frac{\$80}{\$1,200} = 6\frac{2}{3} \text{ percent}$$

You see that, as previously noted, when the Fed goes into the open market to buy securities, it bids up their price and lowers their interest rates. In the process, as we shall soon see, this also expands the money supply.

The $6\frac{2}{3}$ percent is the effective, or market, rate of interest. Although the U.S. Treasury is still paying 8 percent ($80) on the face value ($1,000) of the bond, the Federal Reserve has effectively lowered the market rate of interest to $6\frac{2}{3}$ percent. Incidentally, if the Treasury were to issue new bonds that day, it would need to pay an interest rate of just $6\frac{2}{3}$ percent (that is, $66.67 on a $1,000 bond).

When the Fed wants to contract the money supply, or at least slow down its rate of expansion, it goes into the open market and sells securities. In the process, it lowers bond prices and raises interest rates. How the Fed contracts the money supply

When selling securities, the Fed also uses the "Godfather principle." Again, it makes an offer that can't be refused (in this case, an offer to sell securities at low enough prices to get rid of a certain amount).

If the Fed bids bond prices down to $800, we use the same formula to find that the interest rate has risen to 10 percent.

$$\text{Interest rate} = \frac{\text{Interest paid}}{\text{Price of bond}} = \frac{\$80}{\$800} = 10 \text{ percent}$$

When the Fed sells securities on the open market to contract the money supply, bond prices fall and interest rates rise. Falling bond prices and rising interest rates generally accompany a tightening of the money supply.

You should note that although the Fed deals only with U.S. government securities, interest rates and bond prices move together in a broad range. When the Fed depresses the prices of U.S. government securities, all government and corporate bond prices tend to fall. And when the Fed pushes up the interest on U.S. government securities, all interest rates tend to rise.

Let's try another interest rate problem. Find the interest rate on a bond that pays $100 a year in interest and is currently selling for $800. Work it out right here:

Solution:

$$\text{Interest rate} = \frac{\text{Interest paid}}{\text{Price of bond}} = \frac{\$100}{\$800} = 12.5 \text{ percent}$$

Figure 2A and Figure 2B show how open market operations affect interest rates. We'll begin at equilibrium point E_1 in Figure 2A. If the Fed buys a huge amount of U.S. Treasury securities on the open market, this purchase raises the money supply from MS_1 ($3 trillion) to MS_2 ($4 trillion) pushing the equilibrium point from E_1 to E_2, and driving down the interest rate from 8 percent to 6 percent.[4]

Figure 2B illustrates what happens when the Fed sells a huge amount of U.S. Treasury securities on the open market. Money supply falls from MS_1 ($3 trillion) to MS_2

---

[4]The Fed rarely increases or decreases the money supply by more than 1 or 2 percent at a time. The huge changes shown in Figures 2A and 2B are used to show graphically how changes in the money supply cause changes in the interest rate.

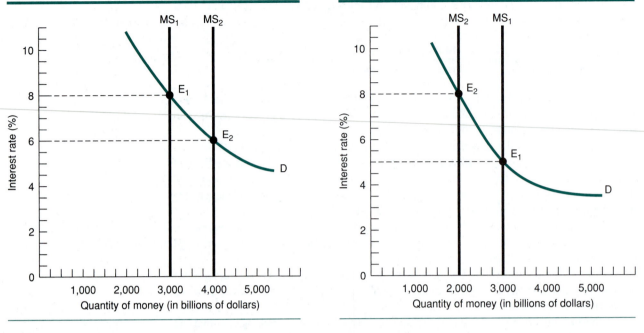

Figure 2A
Increase in Money Supply

Figure 2B
Decrease in Money Supply

($2 trillion) pushing the equilibrium point from E_1 to E_2, and driving the interest rate up from 5 percent to 8 percent.

The Federal Open-Market Committee

How the open-market operations are conducted

Open-market operations are conducted by the Federal Open-Market Committee (FOMC), which consists of 12 people. Eight are permanent members—the seven members of the Board of Governors and the president of the New York Federal Reserve District Bank (he or she is a permanent member because nearly all open-market purchases are made in the New York federal securities market). The other four members of the FOMC are presidents of the other 11 Federal Reserve District Banks; they serve on a one-year rotating basis.

The FOMC meets eight times a year to decide what policy to follow. This is not to say that every six weeks the committee changes directions from buy to sell to buy again.

To fight recessions, the FOMC buys securities.

Assume the FOMC decides to ease credit a bit, perhaps because of the threat of a recession. It might decide to buy $700 million of securities on the open market. The New York Bank, as agent of the Federal Reserve, places an order with several government bond houses. The bonds are paid for by checks written on various Federal Reserve District Banks. Each government bond house deposits the checks in its own commercial bank. From there the checks are sent to the New York Federal Reserve District Bank, which adds the amount of the checks to the banks' reserves.

Say, for example, the Fed gives a $100 million check to bond house number one, which deposits it in its account at Commerce Bank. From there the check is sent a few blocks away to the New York Federal Reserve District Bank, which adds $100 million to the reserves of Commerce Bank.

What does Commerce Bank do with $100 million of reserves? Assuming it now has excess reserves of $100 million, it will lend most of it out. Up goes the money supply! As we have noted, banks seldom keep excess reserves because they don't earn interest. Thus we have a multiple expansion of deposits.

The process works the same way if the government bond houses are not the ultimate sellers of the securities. Usually those sellers are individuals, corporations, or banks. If an individual sells a $10,000 bond to a government bond house, which, in turn, sells it to the Fed, the government bond house is only the middleman. When the Fed pays the government bond house, this money will be turned over to the person who sold the bond. When she deposits her check at her local bank, say the National State Bank of New Jersey, the check will still be sent to the New York Federal Reserve District Bank. Ten thousand dollars will be added to the reserves of the National State Bank, which is now free to lend it out.

When banks lend out money, the money supply increases. When the Fed buys $700 million of securities, it is making $700 million of reserves available to the banking system. Most of this money will be lent out, and through the deposit expansion multiplier, it will create a multiplied deposit amount. For example, if the reserve ratio were 10 percent, the multiplier would be 10 (Multiplier = 1/Reserve ratio = $\frac{1}{10}$ = 10). However, allowing for currency leakages and bank holdings of some excess reserves, we'll say that the multiplier is actually only 6. A $700 million open-market purchase will lead to about a $4.2 billion expansion of deposits (and, therefore, a $4.2 billion expansion of the money supply).

During periods of inflation, when the FOMC decides to sell securities, we have exactly the opposite set of events. If the FOMC were to give the government bond houses $700 million of securities with orders to sell them at whatever the market will bring, we can easily trace the steps.

To fight inflation, the FOMC sells securities.

Customers will be found, and they will pay by check. For example, a corporation with an account at SunTrust Bank in Atlanta might buy $50,000 of securities. When its check reaches the Atlanta Federal Reserve District Bank, $50,000 is deducted from the reserves of SunTrust Bank. Similar reserve deductions occur around the country. Soon reserves for the entire banking system are reduced by $700 million.

That's just the first step. The banks will probably be short of reserves as they carry little, if any, excess. Where do they get the money? They can borrow from their Federal Reserve District Bank's discount windows, but this will only tide them over temporarily, and they're reluctant to do this anyway. They can go into the federal funds market, which is an overnight market in which banks borrow from each other on a day-to-day basis if they are short of reserves. But because most banks are short because of FOMC sales, this source of funds has constricted.

Ultimately, the banks will have to curb their loans, which is what the FOMC wanted all along. Initially, then, we would expect that $700 million less reserves will mean $700 million less in loans. But *had* those loans been made, with a multiplier of six, there would have been some $4.2 billion worth of loans, and the money supply would have been $4.2 billion higher.

We're saying that if reserves are reduced by $700 million, this will, with a multiplier of six, ultimately reduce the money supply by $4.2 billion. Or, put slightly differently, when reserves are reduced, the money supply will end up being lower than it would otherwise have been.

Are you ready to apply your knowledge of the monetary multiplier to determine the potential effect of the sale of some securities on the open market? Suppose the Fed buys $200 million of securities and the monetary multiplier is 5. By how much could our money supply increase?

Solution:

$$\begin{array}{ccc} \text{Excess} \\ \text{reserves} \end{array} \times \begin{array}{c} \text{Monetary} \\ \text{multiplier} \end{array} = \begin{array}{c} \text{Potential expansion of} \\ \text{the money supply} \end{array}$$

$$\$200 \text{ million} \times 5 = \$1,000,000,000$$

You can get the latest official pronouncement by the FOMC by going to www.federalreserve. gov and clicking on News and Events.

Discount Rate and Federal Funds Rate Changes

The discount rate is the interest rate paid by member banks when they borrow at the Federal Reserve District Bank. The main reason today's banks borrow is that they are having trouble maintaining their required reserves.

The original intent of the Federal Reserve Act of 1913 was to have the District Banks lend money to member banks to take care of seasonal business needs. In the busy period before Christmas, firms would borrow money from their banks, which would, in turn, borrow from the Federal Reserve District Banks. Borrowing, then, was really note discounting. You technically borrowed $1,000, but if the interest rate was 8 percent, the interest—$80 for a one-year loan—was deducted in advance. All you got was $920; you paid back $1,000.

How discounting works

This was called discounting. When the commercial banks took these IOUs or commercial paper to the Federal Reserve District Bank, they would borrow money to cover these loans. This was called rediscounting.

Today banks no longer rediscount their commercial paper. Instead, they borrow directly from the Federal Reserve and call the interest they pay the discount rate. On any given day, banks rarely owe the Fed more than a couple of hundred million dollars. But remember that the Fed does stand ready in times of emergency, as a lender of last resort. One such emergency was set off by the terrorist attacks of 9/11. On September 12, 2001, banks borrowed $45.5 billion from the Fed. Had those funds not been available, there is no telling if a financial panic might have taken place, possibly with depositors all over the country rushing to their banks to withdraw their money.

Rather than borrow from the Fed, banks usually borrow excess reserves from each other, usually for no more than a few days at a time. The interest rate they pay is called the Federal funds rate. Kathleen Madigan of *BusinessWeek* describes what happens when the Fed changes the discount rate and the Federal funds rate simultaneously:

> The Fed can also change the discount rate when it alters the Federal funds rate, a one-two punch called "banging the gong" because it reverberates across global markets. The discount rate is charged when a member bank borrows from the Fed, a move done when the bank can't borrow anywhere else. The discount rate is usually set equal to or a half-point below the funds rate.[5]

Figure 3 provides a record of the Federal funds rate between 1954 and June 2010. Why did the Fed lower the rate 13 times between the beginning of 2001 and mid-2003? Because the economy had entered a recession and had lost more than two and a half million jobs since January 2001.

The Federal funds rate hit 20 percent twice in the late 1970s and early 1980s. At that time the Fed was worried mainly about double digit inflation, so it pursued a very stringent tight money policy. Consequently the economy had back-to-back recessions in 1980 and 1981–82. When the Fed was convinced it had broken the back of the inflation, it eased money growth in late 1982, the Federal funds rate—and all other interest rates— fell sharply, and the recession ended.

The Federal funds rate is actually set by the forces of supply and demand, but the Federal Open-Market Committee sets a Federal funds rate target and then makes sure that target is hit. When the committee raised the Federal funds rate target from 3 percent to 3.25 percent in July 2005, it sold billions of dollars worth of U.S. government securities. Setting the target Federal funds rate is the FOMC's primary policy instrument. Indeed, setting that target rate *is,* in effect, monetary policy.

---

[5]Kathleen Madigan, *BusinessWeek,* February 7, 2000, pp. 124 and 126.

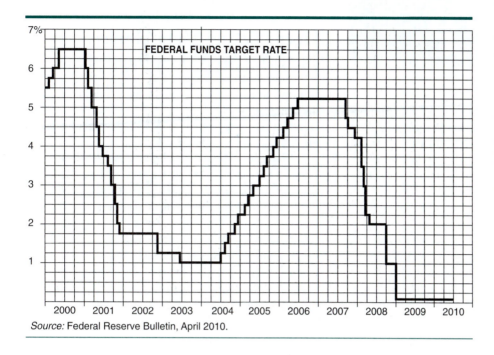

Source: Federal Reserve Bulletin, April 2010.

Figure 3

The Target Federal Funds Rate 1954–2010

This rate was pushed to a 45-year low of just 1 percent on June 25, 2003. In June 2004 the Open Market Committee began raising the rate in quarter of a percent increments. By July 2006 it had reached 5.25 percent. As our economy began sinking into a recession in late 2007 the Federal funds target rate was steadily lowered until January 2009 when it was set at a historic low of 0%–0.25%.

Between September 2007, when the economy began to show signs of weakening, and May 2008, the target rate was lowered from 5.25 percent to 2.00 percent, as the Fed bought huge quantities of U.S. government securities. As the recession worsened and the full effects of the financial crisis were felt, the rate was pushed down to 1 percent in November 2008 and to a historic low of 0 percent–0.25 percent in January 2009.

Paying Interest on Reserve Deposits

In the wake of the strenuous measures taken by the Fed to deal with the financial crisis of 2008, the nation's banks were left sitting on over $1 trillion in excess reserves in early 2010. Through the recession and the early stages of the recovery, bankers were reluctant to provide loans to any but the most creditworthy borrowers, while many potential borrowers feared taking on new debt until they were more confident that business would be improving.

This huge overhang of excess reserves was perceived by many economists—as well as by the members of the FOMC—as having great inflationary potential. What would happen if, as the recovery picked up steam, these funds were quickly lent out? Our money supply would shoot up, setting off a new round of inflation. In reaction, the Fed might be forced to once again tighten credit, cutting off the recovery, and pushing us into another recession.

To have some control over the rate at which the banks would be lending out their excess reserves as the recovery proceeded, in October 2008 the Fed began paying interest on the reserves that the banks had on deposit at their Federal Reserve District Bank. Initially this rate was set at just 0.25 percent, but as the target federal funds rate eventually rose, so too would the interest rate paid on reserves.

As the recovery proceeds, this new monetary policy tool might eventually rival the target Federal funds rate in importance. While the Fed can only *influence* that rate, it unilaterally sets the interest rate it pays on excess reserves. By raising that rate, it will discourage the banks from lending out their excess reserves. As you read these words, the chances are that banks will be earning a lot more than one-quarter percent on their excess reserves.

Does Printing More Money Increase Our Money Supply?

When the Federal Reserve Banks issue currency, doesn't this increase our money supply? Surprisingly, the answer is no, Now I'm going to prove it.

What is the money supply? It's currency, demand deposits, and other checkable deposits held by the public. So the question is, When the Fed prints currency, how does it get into the hands of the public?

Suppose the Federal Reserve Bank of San Francisco issues 10 one-hundred-dollar bills and gives them to Security Pacific Corp., which pays by having its reserves lowered by $1,000. (Actually, its reserves stay the same, because this money goes into its vault.) Next, a local businesswoman writes a check for $1,000 on her account at Security Pacific and walks out of the bank with the 10 one-hundred-dollar bills.

Did that transaction increase the money supply? What do you think? On the one hand, when the teller gave the woman the cash, that increased the amount of money in the hands of the public by $1,000. But what the bank gave with that one hand, it took away with the other by decreasing her checking account by $1,000.

To recap: When the Federal Reserve Bank of San Francisco issued $1,000 in currency, did that lead to an increase in the money supply? No, it did not. When the Fed prints money, it does so to accommodate the needs of the public. If the public wishes to hold more of its money in the form of currency—and, parenthetically, less in the form of checking deposits—the Fed will accommodate these wishes. So the next time someone walks up to you on the street and asks you whether the Fed increases the money supply by issuing currency, tell him no.

Changing Reserve Requirements

The Fed's ultimate weapon

A changing of reserve requirements is really the ultimate weapon of the Federal Reserve System. Like nuclear weapons, which are rarely—if ever—used, it can be nice to know that the mechanism is there.

The Federal Reserve Board has the power to change reserve requirements within legal limits, but in practice it does this perhaps once in a decade. The limits for checkable deposits are between 8 and 14 percent.[6]

The basic reserve rate was set at 12 percent in 1980 for most checking deposits; in 1992 it was lowered to 10 percent. The Board of Governors took this strong measure to help the economy recover from the lingering effects of the 1990–91 recession. In banking circles this 10 percent rate is often referred to as the *reserve ratio,* ignoring the fact that there is, in effect, a 0 percent reserve requirement for the first $10.7 million of checking deposits and a 3 percent requirement on the next $44.5 million (see Table 1 on page 340).

This weapon is so rarely used because it is simply too powerful. For example, if the Federal Reserve Board raised the reserve requirement on demand deposits by just one half of 1 percent, the nation's banks and thrift institutions would have to come up with nearly $4 billion in reserves.

Why does the Fed rarely change reserve requirements?

Reserve requirements, then, are raised reluctantly by the Board of Governors, and only after all else fails. However, when the economy is gripped by recession, the Fed becomes less reluctant to turn to its ultimate weapon; but even then, reserve requirement changes are a last resort.

The Fed has three ways of increasing our money supply: lowering reserve requirements, lowering the discount rate, and buying government securities on the open market. What about printing currency? Does *this* raise our money supply? If you think the answer is yes, then you definitely should read the box, "Does Printing More Money Increase Our Money Supply?"

---

[6]If five members of the Board deem it desirable, the maximum can be raised to 18 percent, and if conditions are extraordinary, any rate whatsoever may be set.

Margin Requirements

The Federal Reserve Board has the power to set margin requirements in the stock market. In Chapter 1 we talked about how in the 1920s stock market speculators could borrow 90 percent of the price of a stock from a stockbroker and put up just 10 percent of their own money. If the stock went up, they made a lot of money. But when the market crashed in 1929, not only were these speculators wiped out but so were their stockbrokers, who were not repaid. They, in turn, could not repay the banks all they had borrowed.

Today the margin requirement is set by the Federal Reserve Board, which has pegged it at 50 percent since 1974. Which means that, if you wanted to invest $10,000 in the stock market, you would need to put up $5,000 of your own money. When Alan Greenspan, who had repeatedly expressed concern about the "irrational exhuberance" of the stock market, was asked why he didn't raise the margin requirement, he replied that an increase would be unfair to small investors. Perhaps, but margin debt has grown at an alarmingly rapid rate since 1990. In that year margin debt was just over 4 percent of all consumer debt. By the end of 2000 it was more than 16 percent.

If—or perhaps one should say when—the market turns down sharply, the stockbrokers will ask their margin customers to put up more money, or else they will sell their stocks. Some won't have the money, so their stocks will be sold, driving stock prices down still further. Although we are not nearly as vulnerable as we were in 1929, the huge and growing overhang of margin debt makes it increasingly likely that a sharp decline in stock prices could lead to a stock market crash.

Favorite test question: Of the three main monetary policy instruments, which is the most important?

The correct answer is "open-market operations." It has the advantage of flexibility, since government securities can be bought or sold in large or small amounts. In addition, its impact on bank reserves is prompt. So the buying and selling of U.S. government securities is, by far, the most important monetary policy weapon in the Fed's arsenal.

A relatively minor Federal Reserve policy tool is raising and lowering the stock market margin requirement, which is discussed in the accompanying box.

Summary: The Tools of Monetary Policy

What three things can the Fed do to fight a recession? List them right here:

1.

2.

3.

The answers are (1) lower the discount rate, (2) buy securities on the open market, and, ultimately, if these two don't do the job, (3) lower reserve requirements.

What three things can the Fed do to fight inflation? List them here:

1.

2.

3.

The answers are (1) raise the discount rate, (2) sell securities on the open market, and, ultimately, if these two don't do the job, (3) raise reserve requirements. (For further results of monetary policy, see the Advanced Work box, "The Effectiveness of Monetary Policy in an Open Economy.")

What is the current Federal funds target rate? Go to www.moneycafe.com/library/fedfundsrate.htm

The Effectiveness of Monetary Policy in an Open Economy

 Suppose the Fed tightens money and interest rates rise. Investors all over the world will be attracted to the higher interest rates they can earn by purchasing U.S. bonds, corporate bonds, and other assets. But in order to invest, they will need to exchange their money for U.S. dollars.

This will drive up the dollar relative to foreign currencies. In other words, you will now be able to get more euros, yen, and pounds for your dollars. Foreign goods will become cheaper to Americans and our imports will soar. Meanwhile, foreigners will be getting fewer dollars for their euros, yen, and pounds, so they will find American goods more expensive. And they will cut back on their purchases of those goods.

Let's recap: Tight money drives up interest rates, making American investments more attractive to foreigners.

They will bid up the dollar, thus lowering our exports and raising our imports. So tight money works to lower our net exports (exports minus imports).

Did you get all that? We've really gotten a bit ahead of ourselves, because the effects to exchange rate changes on foreign trade are not analyzed until the last chapter of this book. But while we're at it, how would an expansionary monetary policy affect our net exports?

It would have just the opposite effect of a contractionary policy. Monetary expansion would lower our interest rates. Lower interest rates are not attractive to foreign investors, whose demand for U.S. dollars will drop. If the dollar falls relative to foreign currencies, that makes our exports cheaper and our imports more expensive. Thus, an expansionary monetary policy will raise our net exports and further stimulate our economy.

The Fed's Effectiveness in Fighting Inflation and Recession

A Summing Up: The Transmission Mechanism

How does monetary policy affect GDP? In general, when the Federal Reserve raises the rate of monetary growth, this tends to raise GDP growth. This cause and effect relationship is described by the transmission mechanism shown in Figure 4. What happens when

Figure 4
The Transmission Mechanism: Expansionary Monetary Policy

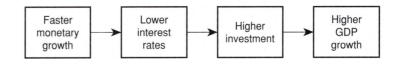

the Fed lowers the rate of monetary growth? As you probably guessed, this has the oppose effect: lower monetary growth tends to lower GDP growth. This relationship is shown in Figure 5.

Figure 5
The Transmission Mechanism: Contractionary Monetary Policy

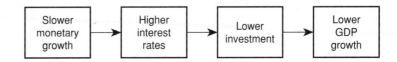

The Fed is more effective in fighting inflation than recession.

Federal Reserve policy in fighting inflation and recession has been likened to pulling and then pushing on a string. Like pulling on a string, when the Fed fights inflation, it gets results—provided, of course, it pulls hard enough.

Fighting a recession is another matter. Like pushing on a string, no matter how hard the Fed pushes, it might not get anywhere.

First we'll consider fighting inflation. Assume all three basic policy tools have been used: Securities have been sold on the open market, the discount and federal funds target rates have been raised, and, ultimately, reserve requirements have been raised. The results are that bond prices have plunged, interest rates have soared, and money supply growth has been stopped dead in its tracks. Banks find it impossible to increase

Figure 6

The Prime Rate of Interest Charged by Banks on Short-Term Business Loans, 1978–2010

Although the prime rate is set by the nation's largest banks, it is strongly influenced by the actions of the Federal Reserve Board of Governors. It has been 3.25 percent since January 2009.

Source: Federal Reserve Bulletin, 1978–2010; http://research.stlouisfed.org/fred2/data/PRIME.txt

their loan portfolios. There's a credit crunch and there's credit rationing. Old customers can still borrow, but their credit lines are slashed. (My own line of credit, for example, was cut by Citibank during the 1980 credit crunch from $3,500 to $500.) Nearly all new customers are turned away. During the first half of 2008 major lenders—including Washington Mutual, IndyMacc Bank, and Capital One—sent out letters to many of their borrowers saying that declining property values were prompting the decision to cut off credit.

During times like these, the rate of inflation has got to decline. It's hard to raise prices when no one is buying anything. No one can buy because no one has any money. Of course, the Fed is somewhat reluctant to tighten up too much or for too long because such a policy generally brings on recessions. Indeed the back-to-back recessions we suffered in 1980 and 1981–82 were caused primarily by the Fed's tight money policy, which pushed interest rates above 20 percent (see Figure 6).

The government fighting inflation is like the Mafia fighting crime.
—Laurence J. Peter

The prime rate rose steadily from 4 percent in June 2003 to 8.25 percent in July 2006. But as the real estate market began to tank the prime rate was lowered from 8.25 percent in September 2007 to 3.25 percent in January 2009. It has remained at that level well into 2010. The Fed was reluctant to push up interest rates until the economic recovery was on firm footing. But when you read these words, the chances are that the prime will be well above 3.25 percent.

The Fed has a far harder time dealing with a recession. Again, assume the standard tools have been used: Securities have been purchased on the open market, the discount and federal funds target rates have been lowered, and reserve requirements have been lowered. All this creates excess reserves for the banks. But now the $1,000,000 question: What do they *do* with these reserves?

Do they lend them out? Is that your final answer? Yes! To whom should they lend them? To a businessowner who needs a loan to keep going? To a firm that can't meet its next payroll without a loan? To an individual who has just lost her job and can't meet her car payments?

Businesses that were good credit risks during prosperity become poor risks during recessions. Individuals, too, lose creditworthiness during recessions, particularly if they've just been laid off. So the very segment of the economic community most in need of help during recessions is least likely to be accommodated.

Meanwhile, many of the top credit-rated corporations are not coming in to borrow large sums of money. During recessions the companies to whom the banks will lend money are not borrowing. Why? Because business isn't so great for them either. Would you borrow to buy more equipment—even at low interest rates—if your equipment was one-third idle? Would you expand your factory if sales were down 20 percent—even if the interest rate fell to 4 percent?

The recession of 2001 provides a good example of the unresponsiveness of the economy to strong monetary stimulation. Between March 2001 (when we went into a recession) and April 2003, the Federal funds target rate was cut from 5 percent all the way down to 1 percent. And yet real investment lagged for years. It sank from a peak of $1,689 billion (in constant 2000 dollars) in the fourth quarter of 2000 and did not get that high again until the fourth quarter of 2003. While the Fed's actions should be credited with keeping the recession relatively mild, our lagging rate of investment showed the limits of monetary policy in stimulating investment during recessions.

All of this said, may we conclude that easy money has little or no effect in ending a recession? Not at all! It's like the adage "You can lead a horse to water, but you can't make him drink." But if that horse happens to be thirsty, just try to *stop* him from drinking.

The Fed was able to help end the recessions of 1980 and 1981–82 by relaxing credit and driving down interest rates. However, the excruciatingly slow and halting recovery of 1991–92 was not very responsive to the lowest interest rates in 15 years. Furthermore, even though the banks had plenty of money that they could have loaned out to individuals and business firms, many banks preferred to purchase short-term U.S. government securities.[7]

The Liquidity Trap

John Maynard Keynes determined that at very low interest rates people would not lend out their money, would not put it in the bank, would not buy bonds with it, but would simply hold it. That's right—they'd sit on it, they'd hoard it, but they wouldn't spend it or make it available to anyone else.

> At very low interest rates, people don't lend out their money.

Why should they? When the interest rate declines to, say, 2 percent, why would people risk their money for such a low rate of return? And why would they tie it up at such a low interest rate when within a few months the interest rate might rise? *Then* they would sink it into interest-bearing assets, but not now.

Suppose that during a severe recession the Fed purchased billions of dollars of U.S. Treasury securities on the open market, creating huge excess reserves. What if these reserves were not lent out, but just sat there? This is exactly what happened in Japan from the mid-1990s into the new millennium. The Bank of Japan pushed interest rates down to virtually 0, while Japanese citizens just sat on personal savings of over $1 trillion. Japan was caught in a *liquidity trap*, a situation in which people believe that interest rates are much more likely to rise than to fall. Why tie up your money in fixed interest assets such as corporate or government bonds? When interest rates rise, they'll be stuck with assets whose prices are falling. When a nation's economy has fallen into a liquidity trap, the central bank has little power to set things right.

on the web

What is the current prime rate of interest? Go to www.moneycafe.com/library/primerate.htm.

---

[7]Do you recall the crowding-out effect discussed in Chapter 12? It shows how private borrowers are crowded out of financial markets by the U.S. Treasury, thus offsetting some of the effects of an expansionary fiscal policy.

The Depository Institutions Deregulation and Monetary Control Act of 1980

Economic historians will mark the 1970s and 1980s as decades of swift and significant change in American banking. During this period, the distinction between commercial banks and thrift institutions (savings banks, savings and loan associations, and credit unions) became blurred to the point where it was hard to tell what was a bank and what wasn't.

What is a bank and what isn't?

Until 1980 there was a clear legal line of demarcation between commercial and thrift institutions. Banks (meaning commercial banks) could issue checking deposits; savings banks, savings and loan associations, and credit unions could not. The only problem was that more and more of the thrifts were doing just that. The way they got around the law was to call those checking deposits something else—namely, negotiable order of withdrawal accounts (or NOW accounts). Thus, technically, people who had deposits at these thrift institutions were not writing checks; they were writing negotiable orders of withdrawal.

While Federal Reserve regulation prohibited commercial banks from paying any interest on checking deposits, the thrifts were paying their depositors about 5 percent interest on their NOW accounts. Because these were technically savings accounts rather than checking accounts, it was OK to pay interest. Therefore, the thrifts had it both ways: They were able to give their depositors checking accounts and pay interest on them— which gave them a considerable competitive advantage over commercial banks.

The commercial banks complained to the Fed and to anyone else who would listen, but to little avail. Finally Congress took matters into its own hands and passed the Depository Institutions Deregulation and Monetary Control Act of 1980. It had three key provisions:

The three key provisions of the Banking Act of 1980

1. All depository institutions are now subject to the Fed's legal reserve requirements. Before this act, only those commercial banks that were members of the Federal Reserve—about one-third of all commercial banks were members—were subject to these requirements. The other commercial banks and thrift institutions were subject to state reserve requirements, which were substantially lower.

2. All depository institutions are now legally authorized to issue checking deposits. Furthermore, they may be interest bearing. Previously, commercial banks were forbidden to pay interest on checking accounts, while the thrift institutions claimed to be paying interest on savings accounts.

3. All depository institutions now enjoy all the advantages that only Federal Reserve member banks formerly enjoyed—including check clearing and borrowing from the Fed (discounting).

Remember that the main job of the Federal Reserve is to control the money supply. By bringing all depository institutions—especially the nonmember commercial banks and the savings banks that had NOW accounts—under the Fed's control, the Monetary Control Act made this job a lot easier.

Another important consequence of this law is that by the end of the 1990s, intense competition reduced the 40,000-plus financial institutions that existed at the beginning of the 1980s to just 20,000 today. The lifting of the prohibition against interstate banking, combined with further advances in electronic banking, will create greater consolidation, with perhaps just 30 or 40 giant financial institutions doing most of the business.

The number of financial institutions is shrinking quickly.

The Banking Act of 1999

In 1980 the jurisdiction of the Federal Reserve had been extended to all commercial banks and thrift institutions. In 1999 it was further extended to insurance companies, pension funds, investment companies, securities brokers, and finance companies.

The new law repealed sections of the Glass-Steagall Act of 1933, which was based on the premise that America's financial house could best be restored if bankers and brokers stayed in separate rooms. It was thought that this could reduce the potential conflicts of interest between investment banking[8] and commercial banking, which had contributed to the speculative frenzy leading to the stock market crash of 1929. Under Glass-Steagall, commercial banks could receive no more than 10 percent of their income from the securities markets, a limit so restrictive that most simply abandoned business on Wall Street selling stocks and bonds to their customers. Over time, Federal judges and regulators chipped away at Glass-Steagall and other restrictions on cross-ownership of banks, insurance companies, and securities firms, enabling, for instance, Citibank to merge with Travelers in 1998 to form Citigroup, which, for the next decade, was the world's largest financial services company. Indeed, this merger helped secure the scrapping of Glass-Steagall.

One purpose of the 1999 law was to give all financial firms, including banks, the chance to sell all sorts of investments. In this way they would be similar to banks in other countries that already provide such services. According to *The Economist,* "Banks in America and Japan—where laws based on Glass-Steagall were imposed by the Americans during the post-war occupation—suffered from a lack of diversification compared with 'universal' banks in continental Europe."[9] The law allows banks, securities firms, and insurance companies to merge and to sell each other's products, and has enabled a wave of mergers as companies compete to build financial supermarkets offering all the services customers need under one roof. Clearly, the Banking Act of 1999 was a major contributory factor to the financial crisis of 2008.

Monetary Policy Lags

As with fiscal policy, which we discussed in Chapter 12, the effectiveness of monetary policy also depends greatly on timing. And then too, monetary policy is also subject to the recognition, decision, and impact lags. Here's a brief summary of the lags.

The recognition lag is the time it takes for policy makers to realize that a business cycle turning point has been passed. The decision lag is the time it takes for policy makers to decide what to do and to take action. And finally, the impact lag is the time it takes for the policy action to have a substantial effect.

Recognition lag is usually shorter for monetary than for fiscal policy.

One would expect monetary policy time lags to be somewhat shorter than fiscal policy time lags. The Board of Governors, which always has at least three or four professional economists among its membership, continually monitors the economy. Furthermore, because the Federal Open Market Committee has just 12 members, with the chair playing the dominant role, a consensus with respect to policy changes is reached far more easily than it is under our political method of conducting fiscal policy. While the legislative wrangling among the members of each house of Congress, between the two houses, and between the president and Congress may take several months, consensus among the members of the Federal Open Market Committee is reached relatively quickly. The decision lag is thus fairly short.

How long is the impact lag—the time until monetary policy changes have a substantial effect? Economists estimate this time as anywhere from nine months to about three years. Further, there is some agreement that a tight money policy will slow down an inflation more quickly than an easy money policy will hasten a recovery. Still, there is no general agreement on whether monetary policy or fiscal policy is faster—or more effective.

While the goals of monetary policy and fiscal policy are identical—low unemployment, stable prices, and a satisfactory rate of economic growth—the effects of each are felt in different economic sectors. Fiscal policy is generally directed toward the consumer sector

---

[8]Investment banks sell new stock and new bonds for existing companies and help arrange corporate mergers.
[9]"The Wall Falls," *The Economist,* October 30, 1999, p. 79.

(tax cuts) or the government sector (spending programs). Monetary policy, however, has its strongest impact on the investment sector. In brief, tight money discourages investment, and a rapidly growing money supply has the opposite effect. The only question, then, is how long it takes before the investment sector feels the impact of monetary policy changes.

Corporate investment does not fall off precipitously when the interest rate rises, nor does it shoot up when the interest rate falls. Although investment in plant and equipment becomes more attractive when the interest rate declines, as a rule large corporations take months, and sometimes years, to formulate investment plans. Therefore, transitory changes in the availability of investment funds or the rate of interest do not have a substantial impact on the level of investment in the short run. However, over a two- or three-year period, it's another story.

During a period of inflation, the proper monetary policy for the Fed to pursue is to slow down or even halt the growth of the money supply. But what if, by the time this is done and has had any impact, the economy has already entered a recession? Clearly it will make that recession even worse.

During a period of recession, what is the proper monetary policy? To speed up the rate of growth of the money supply. But suppose that by the time this policy has had any impact, recovery has begun? Oh no! Now this monetary expansion will fuel the next round of inflation.

To sum up, because of the recognition lag, the decision lag, and especially the impact lag, monetary policy is too slow to have its intended effect. By the time the monetary brakes are working to halt an inflation, the economy may have already entered a recession; and when an expansionary monetary policy is pursued to bring the economy out of a recession, recovery has already set in. Thus, because of the time lags, monetary policy may actually destabilize the economy. The Fed surely did not intend to have that effect, but the road to economic instability is often paved with good intentions.

The financial crisis of 2008, and the speculative real estate bubble that led up to it, present a special case with respect to monetary policy lags. Surely the Fed—under the leadership of Alan Greenspan, and then, since January 2006, Ben Bernanke—was very slow to recognize the problem. But once it did, in early 2008, the Fed quickly sprang into action.

Contrast that with the actions—or lack thereof—of Japan's central bank, which did not adopt a zero-percent interest rate policy until 1999, more than eight years after its economy had tanked. At least it took the Fed "just" 20 months to recognize the gathering financial crisis.

The Housing Bubble, the Subprime Mortgage Mess, and the Financial Crisis of 2008

During the first years of the new millennium, our economy went through the traumas of the bursting of the dot-com bubble, a recession, and the terrorist attacks of 9/11. Chairman Alan Greenspan induced the Open Market Committee to push down the Federal funds rate to the extremely low level of just 1 percent. Despite this stimulation, our economy continued to stagnate well into 2003. But one sector which *did* quickly benefit from low interest rates was the housing industry, giving rise to another economic bubble.

Taking advantage of low short-term interest rates, mortgage brokers began to grant record numbers of adjustable rate mortgages to millions of buyers with lower and lower incomes and credit ratings. Rather than lock into somewhat higher fixed rate mortgages, these buyers opted to pay initially lower interest rates in the hope that these rates would stay low. As long as interest rates stayed low, their mortgage payments remained low.

These conditions created a speculative home buying frenzy which continued through 2006, Ben Bernanke's first year as Fed chairman. As long as interest rates remained low and the price of homes continued rising, the housing bubble could keep growing. Both Greenspan, and then Bernanke, ignored the warning signs that the bubble would soon burst. Mortgage brokers, taking advantage of these conditions, vastly expanded the pool of home buyers by financing millions of subprime loans to families that could not have otherwise qualified for home ownership. These borrowers were relatively poor people who typically paid a low interest rate (called a "teaser rate") for two or three years, and then a much higher rate. They would not have ordinarily qualified for loans, either because their income was too low to meet the anticipated payments, or because of a poor credit history. Indeed about 60 percent of subprime loans required either no income verification or only the most cursory check.

After making these loans, mortgage companies usually sold them off to investment banks, which, in turn, combined them into securities known as collateralized debt obligations (CDOs). Between 2001 and 2006 subprime loans rose from just $50 billion to over $1 trillion. With perfect hindsight, it was not hard to see the approaching train wreck. Two things would make this inevitable. First, hundreds of thousands of subprime borrowers would default on their mortgages, many of them losing their homes. And then too, real estate prices would not only stop rising, but would begin to fall.

Ben Stein put this in more personal terms:

> John Jones wanted to buy a home. He had poor credit. He went to his local mortgage lender, George Smith, and secured a mortgage with a low interest rate at first but a much, much higher rate down the line.
>
> Time passed. It turned out that Mr. Jones bit off more than he could chew. He looked at his mortgage payment. Maybe it had been reset to a higher rate. He saw the housing market deteriorating around him. His house was worth less than he paid for it, and he was paying more—maybe a lot more—than he could afford or than he would have had to pay for a comparable rental. He moved out and mailed the keys to the local lender, Mr. Smith.[10]

Mr. Smith, however, had long since gone out of business. So Mr. Jones's keys, along with those from all the other defaulting borrowers, were forwarded to the investment bank that purchased the subprime mortgages issued by Mr. Smith's company. But the investment bank no longer held these loans. They were packaged as CDOs and sold to large banks (such as Citigroup or JPMorgan Chase), hedge funds, insurers, and to other financial institutions. In early 2008, before all these losses were sorted out, it was clear that they would amount to hundreds of billions of dollars.

An expert on the massive bank failures of the 1930s, Bernanke was determined that history not repeat itself. He and his fellow governors, as well as the presidents of the other Federal Reserve Banks, may have been somewhat slow to smell the smoke, but once they did, they acted very quickly and forcefully to put out the fire.

Although some of our huge banks—most notably Citigroup and JPMorgan Chase—took huge mortgage losses, the bulk of the losses were incurred by an array of investment banks, hedge funds, brokerage houses, and other unregulated firms. Since the new millennium there had been a veritable explosion in complex derivative instruments, such as collateralized debt obligations and credit default swaps, which were intended primarily to transfer risk. Thus was born what has been termed, "the shadow banking system."

In March 2008 the Fed announced a series of short-term (28- to 90-day) loans totaling up to $400 billion—and even more, if needed—mainly to commercial and investment banks. Its most widely publicized loan was a $30 billion credit line to help JPMorgan Chase acquire a virtually bankrupt Bear Stearns, a Wall Street investment bank which had lost tens of billions in the mortgage market. In addition, some 20 large investment banks, which had long relationships with the Fed buying and selling U.S. government securities, would be lent up to a few hundred billion dollars if needed.

Until early 2008 lending had been confined to Federal Reserve member banks. Now other financial intermediaries would be extended credit if that's what it took to

---

[10]Ben Stein, "The Unending Allure of the Free Lunch," *The New York Times,* February 10, 2008, Business Section, p.6.

avert a financial meltdown. In addition, a wide variety of investments could serve as collateral, including $1.25 trillion of hard-to-sell securities backed by mortgages.

What caused the credit crisis? Many people would guess it was the subprime mortgage mess, but that may have been just the last straw. For several years investment banks and other firms were making huge leveraged bets that the prices of real estate, as well as a multitude of other investments, would continue to rise. Borrowing as much as $100 for every $1 of capital, these firms were up to their ears in debt. To make things worse, because of the complex web of debt, if even one large firm—Bear Stearns, for example—were to default, the ripple effect might bring down our entire financial house of cards. Because few of these firms were subject to regulation by the Fed, the FDIC, or any other government authority, no one knew how much was owed to whom. Indeed, we shall probably never know.

What would have happened if Bear Stearns had failed? Very possibly the wholesale dumping of mortgage securities and other assets into a market that was frozen, where buyers were nowhere to be found. One failure would have led to the next, until hundreds—or even thousands—of hedge funds, banks, and brokerage firms would have gone belly up. The bailout was great for the big investors most responsible for the financial crisis, but what about the millions of Americans who stood to lose their homes?

In the long run we need to ask what kind of message this massive bailout has sent to our financial markets. If, during times of financial crisis, the Fed will always stand ready to provide a massive bailout, then won't this just encourage people to take foolish risks, since they will be protected from the consequences of their decisions? Central banks have long been sensitive to the problem of "moral hazard," the danger that rescuing investors from their mistakes will simply encourage others to be more reckless in the future. Alan Blinder summarized the Fed's dilemma: "These kinds of crisis prevention measures always have to balance potential moral hazard costs down the line against the clear and present danger that something is going to happen right now." That something, in early 2008, was a financial crisis that was threatening to sprial out of control, possibly bringing down our entire financial structure, and with it, those of the rest of the world.

Restoring a Normally Functioning Financial System

In the fall of 2008 our economy was beset by two increasingly severe economic problems—a financial meltdown, and what was looking more and more like a long and deep recession. These problems called for a two-pronged attack—getting our financial institutions functioning normally again and preventing the recession from getting much worse.

The $700,000,000,000 TARP Bailout

With our financial institutions holding trillions of dollars in collateralized debt obligations as well as in other securities of dubious value, they had no choice but to write down the value of what were now termed "toxic assets." Because of the intertwined ownership of many of these securities, it was unclear who owed what to whom. There was a great danger that a large part of our financial sector would soon be toppled like falling dominos, possibly setting off a worldwide financial meltdown. So, in late September 2008, in the heat of the national election campaign, enormous pressure was brought to bear on Congress to do something big—and to do it fast.

After two weeks of political maneuvering, on October 3, 2008, Congress passed, and President George W. Bush signed into law, the $700 billion Troubled Assets Relief Program. This gave the Treasury the power to purchase illiquid assets from banks and other financial institutions and even to buy their stock.

Much of the impetus for the passage of the bailout was built around a plea for compassion for the millions of homeowners facing foreclosure. Included in the wording of the law was a requirement that the Treasury "develop a plan that seeks to maximize assistance for homeowners." But the legislation allowed the Treasury to spend the first $350 billion almost entirely at its own discretion. In what some considered a "bait and switch" scheme, Treasury officials were soon saying that funding to forestall home foreclosures would not be productive; the TARP funds would be better spent buying up troubled banks and helping healthy banks buy failing banks and other financial institutions. The hope was that this in-flow of cash would get banks to start lending again. But most bankers receiving these funds were reluctant to lend them out, afraid that if economic conditions continued to deteriorate, these new loans would go bad. Mostly, the first $350 billion of the bailout was used as an insurance policy against the possibility of a prolonged recession. In January 2009, at the behest of President Bush and President-elect Obama, Congress voted to release the second $350 billion of the bailout funds to the Treasury. Ultimately just $125 billion was disbursed.

Although TARP clearly helped avert a financial meltdown, critics pointed out three major flows: (1) The money was not used for its expressed purpose—to help millions of homeowners who might be forced out of their homes; (2) There was no requirement that the banks use the money to expand lending; and (3) There was no prohibition that the banks use the money to pay huge executive bonuses.

By mid-2010 almost 90 percent of the money had been paid back to the U.S. Treasury with interest. Having sold its equity stakes in several financial institutions, the government actually made a profit from some of these transactions. It might be years before it was clear whether all of the TARP loans would be recovered, but from the standpoint of averting a financial meltdown, the $475 billion was money well invested.

Although most of the public's eventual anger about the government's Wall Street bailout was focused on TARP, in addition to the $475 billion aid package, the Federal Reserve, the Treasury, and the FDIC had incurred at least another $17 trillion in direct and indirect financial obligations. For example, the Treasury guaranteed payment for more than $300 billion of Citigroup's liabilities. And the Federal Reserve issued over $1.7 trillion in emergency loans to troubled corporations and financial institutions.

Stopping Mortgage Foreclosures

By early 2009 one out of 11 homes was in foreclosure. During this process, which on average takes about 18 months, the homeowner typically makes no mortgage payments and no repairs. In addition, abandoned homes are often stripped and vandalized. Mortgage lenders lose about half the outstanding loan amount. As more than 2 million foreclosed homes are put back on the market each year, they continue to drive down housing prices.

In February 2009, President Obama announced a $275 billion plan to help as many as nine million American homeowners refinance their mortgages to avert foreclosure. The plan, which went into effect in March, had three main parts:

(1) Assist some four million families who were at risk of losing their homes by providing incentives to lenders who altered loan terms to make them more affordable.[11]

(2) Help about five million homeowners who were current in their payments, but did not have enough equity in their homes to be able to refinance their mortgages to take advantage of lower interest rates.

(3) Provide Fannie Mae and Fredie Mac with $200 billion of additional financing to help shore up their mortgages.

---

[11]A year later the plan had permanently lowered the mortgage payments of less than 100,000 homeowners. Critics contended that the plan did more harm than good. As New York Times columnist, Peter S. Goodman, observed, the program ". . . has raised false hopes among people who simply cannot afford their homes. As a result, desperate homeowners have sent payments to banks in often-futile efforts to keep their homes, which some see as wasting dollars they could have saved in preparation for moving to cheaper rental residences." See Peter S. Goodman, *The New York Times,* January 2, 2010, p.1.

Did the plan work? At the end of May 2010, just 340,000 homeowners held permanently modified mortgages. About half were expected to be in default within the next 12 months.

While this plan has helped a few hundred thousand families keep their homes, it did nothing to help the 15 million families whose homes were "underwater"—that is, their mortgage debt is considerably more than the market value of their homes. Why keep sinking even more money into your home if you're not building up equity? Why pay, say, $2,000 a month in mortgage payments, heating, and real estate taxes, when you could rent a comparable home or apartment for half as much?

Every month, hundreds of thousands of these homeowners were simply walking away from their homes. Given a monetary incentive—namely a substantial reduction in their mortgage debt—most of these families would have a much greater incentive to remain in their homes and continue making their mortgage payments. Still, by helping hundreds of thousands of homeowners avoid foreclosure, the Obama plan did help stem the decline in the prices of homes. That, in turn, has provided some relief to those whose homes were under water.

Last Word: Financial Regulatory From

It took a bitterly divided Congress almost two years to finally enact a law designed to help avert future financial meltdowns. Here are the main provisions of the *Dodd-Frank Wall Street Reform and Consumer Protection Act,* passed in July 2010:

- It sets up a Consumer Financial Protection Bureau, with broad authority to write new rules for mortgages, credit cards, payday loans, and other consumer products.

- It grants power to federal officials to break up firms whose failure would cause financial havoc.

- A Financial Services Oversight Council would be established to provide an early warning system to detect potential trouble in the financial services markets. It would be empowered to issue "cease and desist" order to firms engaged in financially risky behavior.

- Banks will be restricted to investing no more than 3 percent of their capital in hedge and private equity funds. In addition, most of the complex financial risk swaps known as derivatives will be traded through public exchanges.

- Loose mortgage lending practices—such as not reviewing the income and credit histories of mortgage applicants to ensure they can afford payments—would end. Firms bundling mortgages into pooled investment instruments would need to keep 5 percent of these instruments on their books.

Before signing the new legislation, President Obama declared that "because of this law, the American people will never again be asked to foot the bill for Wall Street's mistakes. . . . There will be no more taxpayer-funded bailouts. Period."

The multi-trillion dollar question is whether the new law will achieve the stated purpose of its Congressional sponsors—to create a regulatory apparatus that will avert future financial crises. My own view is that it takes a big step in the right direction, but largely addresses the factors that created the near meltdown of 2008, rather than crises which may develop in the future. Whatever else might be said, our financial services industry does not lack the creative talent to cause future disasters.

Chapter Issue: Should Ben Bernanke Have Been Given a Second Term?

Ben Bernanke was nominated for a second term by President Obama, and, in January 2010, he was confirmed by the Senate. The 70 to 30 vote—by far the closest vote for a Fed chair—indicated a great deal of dissatisfaction with his stewardship of our monetary policy. So let's ask: Did he deserve a second term?

Just a day before the Senate vote, Alan Blinder, Bernanke's colleague from Princeton, and a former Fed vice chairman, wrote an op ed article in *The New York Times,* offering these words of support:

> Mr. Bernanke led the Fed to lower its interest rates to virtually zero in December 2008, and then to hold them there. The central bank also invented approaches to lending and purchasing assets that breathed some life into moribund markets like commercial paper and mortgage-based securities.[12]

One of the most important jobs of the Fed is to act as a lender of last resort. During the early years of the Great Depression, when the nation's banks desperately needed help, the Federal Reserve Board just sat on its hands. But in 2008 and 2009, the Fed extended some $7 trillion in loans to a wide variety of financial institutions and other large corporations.

A fair criticism of these actions would be that Bernanke, who was in a strong position to demand concessions from these institutions, asked for absolutely nothing in return, except that the loans be repaid. He might easily have demanded that the financial institutions use some of the funds to extend commercial and mortgage loans, and to end their practice of granting huge bonuses to their top executives.

Nearly all his critics have conceded that Bernanke acted creatively and decisively once he and his colleagues at the Fed understood that we were facing a financial meltdown. While he was partially responsible for the problem, he was largely responsible for the solution. When all the economic and financial historians have sent in their grades, Ben Bernanke's GPA for his first term will be a solid B. He won't make dean's list, but he certainly deserves to stay in school for at least another term.

Questions for Further Thought and Discussion

1. Should the Federal Reserve Board of Governors remain independent? What is the strongest argument on either side?

2. Is the Federal Reserve more effective in fighting recessions or inflations? Explain your answer, if possible, using a flow chart.

3. What is the most important job of the Federal Reserve? What makes it so important?

4. What are open-market operations? How are they conducted to fight inflation and recession?

5. Draw a diagram showing the impact on bond prices, interest rates, and the level of investment of (a) an expansionary monetary policy; (b) a contractionary monetary policy.

6. Why has the power to set the discount rate become a less effective monetary policy tool over the last eight decades?

7. In 1980 and in 1999 two major banking laws were passed. Explain how each law affects bank consolidation.

8. What is the current macroeconomic situation in the United States? What should the Fed do about it?

9. What monetary policy tools should the Fed use to achieve the result you recommended in question 8?

10. How is money created and destroyed? Explain the concept of the money multiplier, and discuss the factors that influence its size.

11. *Practical Application:* How well has the Fed done in pursuing its main policy goals since Ben Bernanke became chairman in January 2006?

12. *Web Activity:* What is the current interest rate paid by the Fed on reserves held at Federal Reserve District Banks? Go to www.federalreserve.gov/monetarypolicy

---

[12]Alan S. Blinder, "The Fed's Best Man," *The New York Times,* January 28, 2010, p. A33.

Workbook for Chapter 14

Name _____   Date _____

Multiple-Choice Questions

Circle the letter that corresponds to the best answer.

1. Fiscal and monetary policy have _____. (LO1)
   a) the same means and ends
   b) different means and ends
   c) the same means and different ends
   d) different means and the same ends

2. Which statement is true? (LO1)
   a) The United States has always had a central bank.
   b) The United States has never had a central bank.
   c) The United States had a central bank until 1913.
   d) The United States has had a central bank since 1913.

3. The most important Federal Reserve policy weapon is _____. (LO1, 2)
   a) changing reserve requirements
   b) changing the discount rate
   c) moral suasion
   d) open-market operations

4. To restrict monetary growth, the Federal Reserve will _____. (LO2)
   a) raise the Federal funds rate and sell securities
   b) raise the Federal funds rate and buy securities
   c) lower the Federal funds rate and sell securities
   d) lower the Federal funds rate and buy securities

5. Monetary policy is conducted by _____. (LO1)
   a) the president only
   b) Congress only
   c) the president and Congress
   d) the Federal Reserve

6. A liquidity trap most likely will occur when _____. (LO4)
   a) there is a severe recession and interest rates are relatively high
   b) there is a severe recession and interest rates are relatively low
   c) there is great prosperity and interest rates are relatively high
   d) there is great prosperity and interest rates are relatively low

7. Control of the Federal Reserve System is vested in _____. (LO1)
   a) the president
   b) Congress
   c) the Board of Governors
   d) the District Banks

8. Basically the Board of Governors is _____. (LO1)
   a) independent
   b) dependent on the president and Congress
   c) powerless
   d) on a par with the District Banks

9. Legal reserve requirements are changed _____. (LO2)
   a) very often
   b) on rare occasions
   c) never
   d) none of these

10. Which of these is a secondary reserve? (LO2)
    a) Treasury bills
    b) gold
    c) vault cash
    d) deposits at the Federal Reserve District Bank

11. The larger the reserve requirement, the _____. (LO2)
    a) smaller the deposit expansion multiplier
    b) larger the deposit expansion multiplier
    c) easier it is for banks to lend money

12. Each of the following is a leakage from the deposit expansion multiplier except _____. (LO3)

   a) cash

   b) the foreign trade imbalance

   c) excess reserves

   d) all of these are leakages

13. Check clearing is done by _____. (LO1, 2)

   a) the bank where a check is deposited

   b) the bank on which a check is written

   c) the Federal Reserve System

   d) the comptroller of the currency

14. Open-market operations are _____. (LO5)

   a) the buying and selling of U.S. government securities by the Fed

   b) borrowing by banks from the Fed

   c) the selling of U.S. government securities by the U.S. Treasury

   d) raising or lowering reserve requirements by the Fed

15. When the Fed wants to increase the money supply, it _____. (LO5)

   a) raises the Federal funds rate

   b) raises reserve requirements

   c) sells securities

   d) buys securities

16. To buy securities, the Fed offers _____. (LO5)

   a) a low price and drives up interest rates

   b) a low price and drives down interest rates

   c) a high price and drives up interest rates

   d) a high price and drives down interest rates

17. Which statement is the most accurate? (LO5)

   a) The Federal funds rate and the discount rate rise and fall together.

   b) The prime rate of interest is usually about a half percentage point below the Federal funds rate.

   c) The Federal funds rate did not change at all during the late 1990s.

   d) The Federal Reserve has little influence on interest rates.

18. Which one of the following is the most accurate statement? (LO8)

   a) The impact lag of monetary policy is considerably shorter than the impact lag of fiscal policy.

   b) The recognition lag of monetary policy is often shorter than the recognition lag of fiscal policy.

   c) The impact lag of monetary policy is anywhere from three to six months.

   d) The level of corporate investment is very responsive to even slight changes in the interest rate.

19. Which statement is true? (LO6)

   a) The Fed is more effective at fighting inflation than fighting recession.

   b) The Fed is more effective at fighting recession than fighting inflation.

   c) The Fed is effective at fighting both recession and inflation.

   d) The Fed is effective at fighting neither inflation nor recession.

20. The Depository Institutions Deregulation and Monetary Control Act of 1980 had three key provisions, one of which was _____. (LO7)

   a) uniform reserve requirements for all financial institutions

   b) zero reserve requirements for all time deposits

   c) that no interest may be paid on checking deposits

   d) that vault cash would no longer count toward reserves

21. The main job of the Fed is to _____. (LO6)

   a) control the rate of growth of the money supply

   b) manage the national debt

   c) provide low-interest loans to all financial institutions

   d) raise and lower tax rates

22. One of the main results of the Depository Institutions Deregulation and Monetary Control Act of 1980 may be to _____. (LO7)

   a) lessen the number of financial institutions in the United States

   b) increase the number of financial institutions in the United States

   c) discourage the formation of big, nationwide, all-purpose financial institutions

   d) make it easier for the member banks to borrow money from the Federal Reserve District Banks

23. Reserve requirements are changed _____. (LO2)
    a) once a week
    b) three or four times a year
    c) once every two or three years
    d) once every ten or fifteen years
    e) only if Congress passes a new law

24. Suppose that the deposit expansion multiplier were 7. After taking into account its three modifications, we might estimate the true deposit multiplier to be

    _____. (LO3)
    a) 14   d) 4
    b) 9   e) 1
    c) 7

25. Statement 1: Currency leakages take place especially during times of recession and low interest rates. Statement 2: The process of check clearing is being partially replaced by the electronic transferring of money. (LO3)
    a) Statement 1 is true and statement 2 is false.
    b) Statement 2 is true and statement 1 is false.
    c) Both statements are true.
    d) Both statements are false.

26. Which is the most accurate statement? The Federal

    Reserve _____. (LO5)
    a) markets new Treasury bills, notes, certificates, and bonds
    b) runs a check clearing operation for U.S. government checks, but does not handle checks written by private individuals or business firms
    c) Open-Market Committee is part of the U.S. Treasury
    d) buys and sells chunks of the national debt

27. The limits set by law for reserves on checking

    accounts are between _____. (LO2, 5)
    a) 0% and 9%   b) 3% and 12%
    c) 8% and 14%   d) 12% and 18%

28. Which of the following is the most accurate statement? (LO5)
    a) We will have a checkless economy before 2012.
    b) Your bank must return the checks you wrote with your monthly statement.
    c) The Fed uses open-market operations to hit its target Federal funds rate.
    d) When the Fed pushes up the money supply, interest rates tend to rise.

29. The repeal of Glass-Steagall in 1999

    _____. (LO7)
    a) had the objective of allowing banks, securities firms, and insurance companies to merge and to sell each others' products
    b) will result in a huge expansion in the number of financial institutions doing business in the United States
    c) will result in the same abuses that led to the passage of the original act in 1929
    d) will make it much harder for U.S. financial institutions to merge

30. If the equilibrium rate of interest is 7 percent and market price of a U.S. government bond is $1,000, what is the most likely interest rate and bond price if the Fed increases the money supply by a substantial amount? (LO5)
    a) 8 percent; $1,100
    b) 8 percent; $1,000
    c) 8 percent; $900
    d) 6 percent; $1,100
    e) 6 percent; $1,000
    f) 6 percent; $900

31. Faster monetary growth tends to _____. (LO4)
    a) lower interest rates, leading to lower investment
    b) lower interest rates, leading to higher investment
    c) raise interest rates, leading to lower investment
    d) raise interest rates, leading to higher investment

32. Which would be the most accurate statement? (LO1)
    a) The Federal Reserve Board of Governors has more power than the monetary authorities of any other country.
    b) The Deutsche Bundesbank has more power than the Federal Reserve.
    c) The Bank of England and La Banca d'Italia are two of the most powerful central banks.
    d) The European Central Bank is one of the most powerful central banks in the world.

33. The subprime lending mess was caused by (LO9)
    a) the lowered lending standards of mortgage brokers.
    b) the Federal Reserve's lowering of interest rates.
    c) both the lowered lending standards of mortgages brokers and the Federal Reserve's lowering of interest rates.
    d) neither the lowered lending standards of mortgage brokers nor the Federal Reserve's lowering of interest rates.

34. A decrease in the rate of growth in the money supply will tend to _____ interest rates and _____ the level of investment. (LO4)
    a) raise, raise
    b) lower, lower
    c) lower, raise
    d) raise, lower

35. Money is created when someone _____. (LO4)
    a) takes out a bank loan
    b) pays back a bank loan
    c) spends money
    d) saves money

36. Bank deposit creation is limited by _____. (LO4)
    a) reserve requirements
    b) the interest rate
    c) whether a bank is nationally or state chartered
    d) whether a bank is in a large city or a rural area

37. The primary objective of the Fed in mid–2008 was to _____. (LO9)
    a) avert a financial meltdown
    b) enable millions of subprime borrowers to keep their homes
    c) tamp down inflation
    d) prevent a recession

38. The main players in the shadow banking system are _____. (LO9)
    a) the large commercial banks
    b) the smaller banks
    c) investment banks, hedge funds, and brokerage houses
    d) foreign investors

39. To deal with the financial crisis of 2008 the Fed resorted primarily to _____. (LO9)
    a) traditional policy weapons used to fight inflation
    b) traditional policy weapons used to fight recessions
    c) extraordinary measures that broke new policy ground
    d) urging the large financial intermediaries to do the right thing

40. Which is the most accurate statement? (LO9)
    a) The Fed's actions in dealing with the 2008 financial crisis may encourage future risky financial behavior, since a future crisis will be met with another bailout.
    b) Although the Fed managed to avert a financial meltdown in 2008, it will not have the resources to deal with future financial crises.
    c) The Fed was not at all responsible for the recent housing bubble.
    d) From a long-run perspective, the massive financial bailout carried out by the Fed did much more harm than good.

41. Who should be held the least responsible for the real estate bubble and the subsequent financial crisis? (LO9, 10, 11)
    a) Alan Greenspan
    b) Ben Bernanke
    c) President George W. Bush
    d) President Barack Obama

42. Which one of following is the most accurate statement? (LO10, 11)
    a) Ben Bernanke was much more effective in averting a financial meltdown than in preventing the real estate bubble.
    b) Ben Bernanke was much more effective in preventing the real estate bubble than in averting a financial meltdown.
    c) Ben Bernanke was very effective in preventing the real estate bubble and in averting a financial meltdown.
    d) Ben Bernanke was not effective in preventing the real estate bubble and in averting a financial meltdown.

43. TARP _____. (LO10)
    a) saved millions of homeowners from defaulting on their mortgages
    b) provided funds which enabled banks to expand their lending
    c) provided a much needed infusion of funds to hundreds of financial institutions
    d) was of little help in averting a financial meltdown

44. Which one of the following was a major initiative of the Obama administration to deal with home mortgage foreclosures? (LO10)

   a) TARP

   b) A federal funds rate of virtually zero

   c) A $275 billion program to lower mortgage payments, help mortgage refinancing, and provide $200 billion to Freddie Mac and Fannie Mae

   d) A massive tax cut to the middle class and working class

45. The main reason why the Fed began paying interest on bank reserves was to _____. (LO6)

   a) provide the banks with an incentive to continue holding excess reserves on deposit at their Federal Reserve District Bank.

   b) encourage banks to lend out more money.

   c) prevent deflation.

   d) prevent bank failures.

Fill-In Questions

1. Our paper currency is issued by _____. (LO1)

2. Our currency is backed by _____. (LO1)

3. According to Keynes's liquidity trap, at very low interest rates, people would _____. (LO4)

4. Control of the Federal Reserve is held by _____. (LO1)

5. At the present time, nearly all checking deposits are subject to a legal reserve requirement of _____ percent. (LO2, 5)

6. Time deposits are subject to no reserve requirement because _____ _____. (LO2)

7. All reserves pay an interest rate of _____ percent. (LO2)

8. If the Fed wants to increase the money supply, it will follow these two steps: (1) _____ _____; (2) _____ _____; and if these do not prove sufficient, it may _____. (LO5)

9. It has been much easier for the Fed to fight _____ than _____. (LO6)

Problems

1. If you ran a bank with checking deposits of $20 million, you would need to hold reserves of how much? (Use Table 1 on page 340.) (LO2)

2. If you ran a bank with checking deposits of $400 million, you would need to hold reserves of a little less than how much (assuming you don't remember the cutoff point)? (LO2)

3. If the reserve requirement were 15 percent, how much would the deposit multiplier be? (LO2)

4. Using your answer from the previous problem, if the Federal Reserve increased bank reserves by $100 million, by how much would the money supply rise? (LO2)

5. How much is the effective, or market, interest rate on a bond that has a face value of $1,000 and a selling price of $1,200 and that pays $120 interest? (LO5)

6. If a bank has reserves of $21 million and demand deposits of $200 million, how much are the bank's: (a) required reserves? (b) excess reserves? (LO2)

7. Approximately how much in reserves does a bank with $5 billion in demand deposits have to hold? (LO2)

8. If a bank has reserves of $100 million and checking deposits of $700 million, how much are the bank's: (a) required reserves? (b) excess reserves? (LO2)

9. How much reserves would a bank have to hold on: (a) $1 billion of time deposits that will mature in less than 18 months? (b) $1 billion of time deposits that will mature in more than 18 months? (Hint: see Table 1 on page 340.) (LO2)

10. Use the information in Table 1 to find this bank's required reserves. (LO2)

TABLE 1

Checking deposits: $1 billion
Time deposits: $300 million

*C*hapter 15

A Century of Economic Theory

The First Law of Economics: For every economist, there exists an equal and opposite economist.
The Second Law of Economics: They're both wrong.

Economists are not easy to follow when they talk about familiar, day-to-day events like unemployment rate changes and the rising consumer price index. But when they talk theory, sometimes even their fellow economists have difficulty understanding what they are saying to each other. I'll repeat the words of George Bernard Shaw: "If all economists were laid end to end, they would not reach a conclusion."

John Maynard Keynes put all of this into perspective much more elegantly:

> The ideas of economists and political philosophers, both when they are right and when they are wrong, are more powerful than is commonly understood. Indeed, the world is ruled by little else. Practical men, who believe themselves to be quite exempt from any intellectual influences, are usually slaves of some defunct economist.

What conclusion will you reach at the end of this chapter? If you're like my fellow economists, you will choose one school of economic thought to defend, while attacking each of the others. I hope you'll take each economic theory with a grain of salt, disregarding what you can't accept while appreciating the cogency of the arguments that have been advanced. No attempt is being made to do more than outline some of the underlying ideas of each of the five main schools of the last one hundred years.

An economist is someone good with numbers who didn't have the personality to become an accountant.

—Anonymous

LEARNING OBJECTIVES

After reading this chapter you should be able to:

1. Discuss the equation of exchange.
2. Explain the quantity theory of money.
3. Analyze classical economics.
4. Analyze Keynesian economics.
5. Apply the policy prescription of the monetarist school.
6. Describe supply-side economics.
7. Judge the rational expectations theory.
8. Apply behaviorist economics.
9. Assess the use of conventional macropolicy to fight recession and inflation.

The Equation of Exchange

Much of the Keynesian-Monetarist debate revolves around the quantity theory of money, which itself is based on the equation of exchange. So in the first two sections let's look at these two concepts before we deal specifically with any of the schools of economic thought. The equation of exchange and the quantity theory of money are easily confused, perhaps because the equation of exchange is used to explain the

Don't get the equation of exchange mixed up with the quantity theory of money.

quantity theory. I warn my students every term about how easily the unwary test taker writes down the equation of exchange when asked for the quantity theory, or vice versa. Still, many of them remain faithful to the tradition of confusing the two concepts on the next exam.

The equation of exchange is

MV = PQ

$$MV = PQ$$

What do these letters stand for? M represents the number of dollars in the nation's money supply—the currency, demand deposits, and checklike deposits.

The velocity of circulation, or the number of times per year that each dollar in our money supply is spent, is represented by V. If we were to multiply M times V, or MV, that would be our money supply multiplied by the number of times per year each dollar is spent—in other words, total spending. Total spending by a nation during a given year is GDP. Therefore:

$$MV = GDP$$

Now for the other side of the equation. P represents the price level, or the average price of all the goods and services sold during the year. Finally, there's Q, the quantity of goods and services sold during the year. Multiplying P times Q, we get the total amount of money received by the sellers of all the final goods and services produced by the nation that year. This is also GDP. Things equal to the same thing are equal to each other (MV = GDP; PQ = GDP); therefore MV = PQ.

We'll get a better idea of how this equation works by replacing the letters with numbers. For M we can substitute $900 billion, and we'll give V a value of 9.

$$MV = PQ$$
$$900 \times 9 = PQ$$
$$8,100 = PQ$$

This gives us a GDP of 8,100, or $8.1 trillion. As a form of shorthand, economists write billions of dollars without the dollar sign. The money supply of $900 billion becomes 900, and the GDP of $8,100 billion becomes 8,100.

So far we have MV = 8,100; therefore, PQ also = 8,100. How much are P and Q? We don't know. All we do know is that P $\times$ Q = 8,100.

What we'll do, so we can fool around with this equation, is arbitrarily assign values to P and Q. That might not be very nice or proper, but let me assure you that people do this sort of thing every day. Let's take P. Who can guess what the average price of all the final goods and services sold actually is? In other words, could you guess the average price of all those cars, houses, hot dogs, pairs of shoes, haircuts, cans of beer, cavity fillings, and so on? As there's no way of even guessing, we'll make the number $81. Why $81? Because it will be easy to work with. But perhaps $61.17 or $123.98 is the actual value of P. We'll never know.

Now we'll consider Q. How many final goods and services were sold during the year? 23 billion? 345 billion? Again, we can't possibly know, so we'll assign a number. If we've already picked $81 for P, and PQ = 8,100, then Q must equal 100 (meaning, in economists' shorthand, 100 billion). Therefore:

$$MV = PQ$$
$$900 \times 9 = 81 \times 100$$
$$8,100 = 8,100$$

That's the equation of exchange. It must always balance, as must all equations. If one side rises by a certain percentage, the other side must rise by the same percentage. For example, if MV rose to 9,000, PQ would also rise to 9,000.

The Quantity Theory of Money

The quantity theory of money has both a crude version and a more sophisticated version. The crude quantity theory of money holds that when the money supply changes by a certain percentage, the price level changes by that same percentage. For example, if the money supply were to rise by 10 percent, the price level would rise by 10 percent. Similarly, if M were to double, then P would double. Using the same figures we assigned to the equation of exchange, let's see what happens if M and P double.

The crude version of the quantity theory

$$MV = PQ$$
$$900 \times 9 = 81 \times 100$$
$$1{,}800 \times 9 = 162 \times 100$$
$$16{,}200 = 16{,}200$$

If we double M, then MV doubles, and if we double P, PQ doubles. Because both sides of the equation must be equal, it appears that the crude quantity theory of money works out.

There are only two problems here. We are assuming V and Q remain constant. Do they? If they do, the crude quantity theory is correct. But what if they don't? For example, what if M, P, and Q all double? For the equation to balance, V would have to double. Similarly, what if M doubles and V declines by 50 percent? In that case, the rise in M would be canceled by the decline in V. If M doubles and MV stays the same, can we expect an automatic doubling of P?

Let's take a closer look at V and then at Q. Since 1950 V has risen fairly steadily from about three to over ten. In other words, individuals and businesses are spending their dollars much more quickly. Alternatively, they are making more efficient use of their money balances.

During a period of very tight money in the late 1970s and early 1980s, V rose to nearly seven.

There are several explanations for the rise of V. First, there's inflation. Why hold large money balances when they lose their value over time? Second, why hold idle cash balances when they could be earning interest? Finally, the use of credit cards, debit cards, and automatic teller machines (ATMs), especially during the last 15 years, has allowed people to carry less cash. As a result, V has more than tripled since the mid-1950s.

Now let's see about Q, the quantity of final goods and services produced. During recessions, production, and therefore Q, will fall. For example, during the 1981–82 recession Q fell at an annual rate of about 4 percent during the fourth quarter of 1981 and the first quarter of 1982. During recoveries, production picks up, so we go from a declining Q to a rising Q.

Obviously, then, we cannot consider V or Q to be constants. Therefore, the crude version of the quantity theory is invalid.

The real problem with the early quantity theorists is that they overstated their case. Clearly, rapid monetary growth will invariably lead to inflation. But does a given rate of increase in the money supply lead to precisely the same rate of growth in the price level? Not in *my* book, nor in any other economics text.

Today's modern monetarists, those who believe the key economic variable is changes in M, have come up with a more sophisticated quantity theory. They assume any short-term changes in V are either very small or predictable. The situation with Q, however, is another story.

The sophisticated version of the quantity theory

Let's say M rises by 10 percent and V stays the same: MV will rise by 10 percent and PQ will rise by 10 percent. So far, so good. In fact, so far the crude and sophisticated quantity theories are identical. But what happens next is entirely up to the level of production, Q.

If there's considerable unemployment and we increase M, most, if not all, of this increase will be reflected in an increase in production, Q. Money flowing into the economy will lead to increased spending, output, and employment. Will it lead to higher prices as well? Probably not. It is reasonable to expect most of the rise in M to be reflected in a rise in Q.

The value of money . . . varies inversely as its quantity; every increase of quantity lowering the value, and every diminution raising it, in a ratio exactly equivalent.

—John Stuart Mill,
Principles of Political Economy

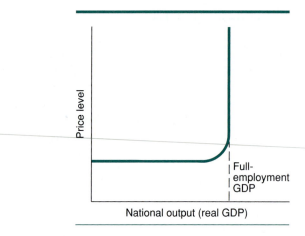

***Figure* 1**

Hypothetical Aggregate Supply Curve

Moving from the extreme left side of the aggregate supply curve, we can raise output without raising prices until we begin to approach full-employment GDP. After continuing to raise output, accompanied by a rising price level, we reach full-employment GDP, at which point any further movement along the aggregate supply curve will raise prices without increasing output.

Sophisticated quantity theory in brief

As we approach full employment, however, further increases in M will begin to lead, more and more, to increases in P, the price level (see Figure 1). And it is there that the sophisticated quantity theory becomes operative. We therefore can make two statements summarizing the sophisticated quantity theory:

1. If we are well below full employment, an increase in M will lead mainly to an increase in Q.

2. If we are close to full employment, an increase in M will lead mainly to an increase in P.

That's the sophisticated quantity theory of money. Please don't confuse it with the crude quantity theory, and don't confuse either quantity theory with the equation of exchange.

What is the sophisticated quantity theory supposed to do? Like most theories, it makes a prediction. In its least rigorous version, it says that changes in M's rate of growth lead to similar changes in PQ's rate of growth. If M is increasing slowly, PQ will increase slowly; rapid growth in M leads to rapid growth in PQ. Although no precise mathematical relationship is claimed (as under the crude quantity theory), the monetarists say changes in M lead to predictable changes in PQ.

Classical Economics

The American economy suffered very bad recessions, even depressions, in the 1830s, 1870s, and 1890s, but eventually we always did manage to recover. If the government tried to get the country out of a recession, said the classicals, it only made things worse.

Recessions cure themselves.

The classical school of economics was mainstream economics from roughly 1775 to 1930. Adam Smith's *The Wealth of Nations,* a plea for laissez-faire (no government interference), was virtually the economics bible through most of this period. The classicals believed our economy was self-regulating. Recessions would cure themselves, and a built-in mechanism was always pushing the economy toward full employment.

Say's law

As we saw at the beginning of Chapter 11, the centerpiece of the classical system was Say's law: Supply creates its own demand. Everything produced gets sold. Why? Because people work so that they can spend.

Savings will be invested.

What if people save some of their incomes? No problem, said the classicals, because that savings will be invested. With that, they pointed to Figure 2, which shows a graph of saving and investment. The two are equal at an interest rate of 10 percent.

What if the amount of money people wanted to save at 10 percent interest were greater than the amount businesspeople wanted to invest? Still no problem, said the classicals. The interest rate would fall automatically. People would be inclined to save less

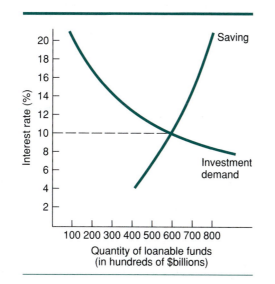

Figure 2
The Interest Rate Mechanism
An interest rate of 10 percent is
found at the intersection of the
saving curve and the investment
demand curve.

at lower interest rates, and businesspeople would be inclined to invest more. Eventually, the interest rate would fall far enough so that savings and investment would be equal.

Interest rate mechanism

The classicals also assumed downwardly flexible wage rates and prices. If there happened to be a temporary recession and business firms could not sell their entire inventories, they would simply lower their prices until their inventories were depleted. Similarly, if some workers were unemployed, they would offer to work for lower wages and would find new jobs.

Flexible wages and prices

Another basic classical tenet was the quantity theory of money. Stated in its crudest version, when the money supply changes by a certain percentage, the price level changes by that same percentage. Thus, when the money supply is increased by 5 percent, the price level rises by 5 percent.

Quantity theory of money

Resorting once again to the equation of exchange:

$$MV = PQ$$

If M rises by 5 percent and P rises by 5 percent, that means V and Q remain constant. In the six decades since World War II V has generally been stable during nonrecession years and during peacetime. How stable has Q been? Q, the quantity of output of goods and services, rises during nonrecession years and falls during recession years.

V and Q are constant.

Q: How many conservative economists does it take to screw in a light bulb?
A: None. If the government would just leave it alone, it would screw in itself.

Where does all this leave us as regards the quantity theory? In its crude version, which the classicals espoused, we could hardly expect V *and* Q to stay constant from year to year. So much, then, for the crude quantity theory.

Finally, let's take a closer look at the classical contention that recessions are temporary phenomena, which, with the help of Say's law, the interest rate mechanism, and downwardly flexible wages and prices, cure themselves. This leads to the basic classical macroeconomic policy when there is a recession: Do nothing!

If the government attempted to cure a recession by spending more money or cutting taxes, these measures would not get the economy out of the recession. Why not? Because the recession would cure itself. Government intervention could not help, and it might even hurt.

Government can't cure recessions.

What about monetary policy? If there were a recession, the standard monetary policy would be to increase the rate of growth of the money supply. What would this accomplish? Ask the classicals. Because the recession would be curing itself, output, Q, would go up automatically. Because V would be stable, a rise in M would simply be translated into a rise in P, so the attempt to cure the recession by means of monetary policy would only cause inflation.

The classical school dominated economic thought until the time of the Great Depression. If recessions cure themselves automatically, asked John Maynard Keynes in the 1930s, why is the entire world economy dragging along from year to year in unending depression? And if the economy isn't curing itself, said Keynes, government intervention is in order.

Keynesian Economics

John Maynard Keynes wrote his landmark work *The General Theory of Employment, Interest, and Money* during the depths of the Great Depression. While President Herbert Hoover (perhaps the last political leader to uphold the theories of classical economics) was telling everyone who would listen that recovery was just around the corner, things were going from bad to worse. As the unemployment rate mounted, production plummeted, and soup kitchens proliferated, more and more Americans demanded that the federal government do something. When Franklin Roosevelt defeated Hoover by a landslide in 1932, he had a mandate to do whatever was necessary to bring about recovery.

Keynes: The problem with recessions is inadequate aggregate demand.

Keynes provided a blueprint. The problem, he said, was inadequate aggregate demand. People were just not buying enough goods and services to employ the entire labor force. In fact, aggregate demand was so low that only the government could spend enough money to provide a sufficient boost.

Keynes defined aggregate demand as consumer spending, investment spending, and government spending (plus net exports, which at that time were negligible). Consumption is a function of disposable income. When disposable income is low, said Keynes, consumption is low. And during the Great Depression disposable income was extremely low.

The cure for recession is government spending.

Investment, which is largely a function of the marginal efficiency of investment, or the expected profit rate, was not just low, but even negative. So we could not hope that an upturn in investment would lead the way out of the Depression. The only hope was for the government to spend enough money to raise aggregate demand sufficiently to get people back to work.

What type of spending was necessary? Any kind, said Keynes. Quantity is much more relevant than quality. Even if the government employed some people to dig holes, said Keynes, and others to fill up those holes, it would still be able to spend the country out of these economic woes.

Where would the government get the money? There were two choices: print it or borrow it. If the government printed it, wouldn't that cause inflation? Keynes thought this unlikely; during the Depression, the country had been experiencing *de*flation, or falling prices. Who would even *think* of raising prices when she was having trouble finding customers?

In a campaign speech in Brooklyn in the fall of 1932, Roosevelt castigated Hoover for not balancing his budget.

What about budget deficits? Nothing improper about these, said Keynes. Although the common wisdom of the times was that the government must balance its budget, there was absolutely nothing wrong with deficits during recessions and depressions. It was necessary to prime the pump by sucking up the idle savings that businesses were not borrowing and using those funds to get the economy moving again.

Once government spending was under way, people would have some money in their pockets. And what would they do with that money? You guessed it—they'd spend it. This money would then end up in other people's pockets, and they, in turn, would spend it once again. This is the fabled multiplier effect that we introduced in Chapter 12.

That money would continue to be spent again and again, putting more and more people back to work. As they began paying taxes, the deficit would melt away. The government could cut back on its spending programs while tax receipts swelled, so we could view the budget deficits as a temporary expedient to get the economy off dead center.

But what of the classical automatic mechanism that ensured that the economy always moved toward full employment? In the long run, Keynes conceded, maybe it really *did* work. But in the long run, noted Keynes, "we are all dead."

Why invest in new plant and equipment when most of your capacity is idle?

Why didn't the classical mechanism work in the short run? Keynes observed that interest rates fell to about 2 percent during the Great Depression, but business firms still were not borrowing all that much to build new plant and equipment. After all, who in his right mind would invest in new plant and equipment when his factory was operating at only 30 or 40 percent of capacity? Besides, said Keynes, at an interest rate of 2 percent, many people would not be willing to lend out their savings. Why tie up their money at such a low interest rate? Why not just sit on this money until interest rates rose again?

So much for the interest rate mechanism. With respect to downwardly flexible wages and prices, there were institutional barriers. Labor unions would oppose lowered wage rates, while highly concentrated industries would tend to prefer output decreases to price cuts during recessions.

Keynes also raised some objections to the quantity theory of money. Most significant, he asked what would happen to the money that would be printed if the government did increase the money supply. The classicals had assumed it would be spent, thus pushing up the price level. This could happen, conceded Keynes, but during a bad recession perhaps people would just hold their money, waiting for interest rates to rise before they lent it out.

If M rises, what if people don't spend additional money, but just hold it?

Wouldn't they spend it, as the classicals suggested? Poor people would. But if they were poor, what would they be doing with money in the first place? If the money supply were increased during a bad recession, said Keynes, that money would simply be held as idle cash balances by relatively well-to-do people. Nothing would happen to the money until the economy was well on its way toward recovery, interest rates rose, and more investment opportunities became available.

By the mid-1930s the classical school of economics had lost most of its adherents. Not everyone became a Keynesian. Conservative economists in particular could never fully reconcile themselves to the vastly increased economic role that the Keynesians awarded to the federal government. In fact, the remaining economic schools to be considered here—the monetarists, the supply-siders, and the rational expectationists—would all rail against the evils of big government.

But big government was here to stay. Although the massive spending programs of Franklin Roosevelt's New Deal did not get the country out of the Depression, the much bigger defense spending during World War II certainly did. There was no question that Keynes had been right, but since the war Americans had been plagued not just by periodic recessions but by almost unending inflation. There was growing feeling among economists that perhaps Keynesian economics was just recession and depression economics, that it could not satisfactorily deal with curbing inflation.

Is Keynesian economics valid just during recessions?

As you know, Keynesian economics enjoyed a revival in early 2009 when the Obama administration modeled its $787 billion economic stimulus package (described in Chapter 12) largely on Keynesian policy prescriptions. So for at least a few years, this school of economics will be back in fashion.

The Monetarist School

The Importance of the Rate of Monetary Growth

Monetarism begins and ends with one obsession: the rate of growth of the money supply. According to monetarists, most of our major economic problems, especially inflation and recession, are due to the Federal Reserve's mismanagement of our rate of monetary growth.

Monetarists are obsessed with the growth rate of M.

Milton Friedman, an economist who did exhaustive studies of the relationship between the rate of growth of the money supply and the rate of increase in prices, reached a couple of not surprising conclusions. First, the United States has never had a serious inflation that was not accompanied by rapid monetary growth. Second, when the money supply has grown slowly, the country has had no inflation.

In a study of the monetary history of the United States during the period of nearly a century after the Civil War, Friedman and his longtime collaborator Anna Jacobson Schwartz reached this conclusion: "Changes in the behavior of the money stock have been closely associated with changes in economic activity, money income, and prices."[1]

---

[1]Milton Friedman and Anna Jacobson Schwartz, *A Monetary History of the United States, 1867–1960* (Princeton, NJ: Princeton University Press, 1971), p. 676.

Monetarists modified crude
quantity theory.

Building on the quantity theory of money, the monetarists agreed with the classicals that when the money supply grows, the price level rises, albeit not at exactly the same rate. But they refuted Keynes's argument that if the money supply were raised during a recession, people might just hold on to these added funds. Like the classicals, the monetarists assumed that to get it is to spend it—not necessarily on consumer goods, but on stocks, bonds, real estate, and other noncash assets.

If people *did* spend this additional money, the prices of what they bought would be bid up. In other words, the monetarists were saying that the quantity theory basically holds true.

Monetarists' analysis has been borne out by the facts.

So far, so good. Now for recessions. What causes them? When the Federal Reserve increases the money supply at less than the rate needed by business—say, anything less than 3 percent a year—the economy is headed for trouble. Sometimes, in fact, the Fed does not let it grow at all and may even cause it to shrink slightly.

By and large the facts have borne out the monetarists' analysis. Without a steady increase in the money supply of at least 3 percent a year, there is a high likelihood of a recession.

The Basic Propositions of Monetarism

(1) The Key to Stable Economic Growth Is a Constant Rate of Increase in the Money Supply

Has our economic history been one of stable growth? No inflation? No recessions? Since World War II alone, we've had four waves of inflation and 10 recessions.

The Fed is blamed for our economic instability.

The monetarists place almost the entire blame on the Federal Reserve Board of Governors. If only they had been increasing the money supply by a steady 3 percent a year, we could have avoided most of this instability.

Let's trace the monetarist reasoning by analyzing the Fed's actions over the course of a business cycle. As a recession sets in, the Fed increases the rate of growth of the money supply. This stimulates output in the short run, helping to pull the economy out of the recession. In the long run, however, this expanded money supply causes inflation. So what does the Fed do? It slams on the monetary brakes, slowing the rate of growth in the money supply. This brings on a recession. And what does the Fed do in response? It increases the rate of monetary growth.

Stop-go monetary policy

"Is this stop-go, stop-go monetary policy any way to run an economy?" ask the monetarists. This type of policy inspires about as much confidence as the student driver approaching a red light. First he hits the brakes about 100 yards from the corner. Then, overcompensating for his error, he hits the accelerator much too hard. When the car lurches forward, he hits the brakes again, bringing the car to a dead stop about 50 yards from the corner. Then he repeats the whole process.

In the late 1960s, an accelerating rate of monetary growth was accompanied by a rising rate of inflation, which, in the early 1970s, reached double-digit proportions. In 1973 the Federal Reserve Board put on the brakes, and we went into the worst recession we had suffered since World War II. In 1975 the Fed eased up and we recovered. Then, in late 1979, the brakes were applied. The prime rate of interest soared to more than 20 percent, and in January 1980 we went into a sharp six-month recession. What happened next? You guessed it. The Fed eased up again. Interest rates came down, and economic recovery set in. But in 1981 the Fed, alarmed at the rising inflation rate, slammed on the monetary brakes, and we entered still another recession in August 1981. The prime once again soared to more than 20 percent. This recession proved even deeper than that of 1973–75. In summer 1982 the Fed once again eased up on the brakes; sure enough, by November of that year the recession had ended.

(2) Expansionary Monetary Policy Will Only Temporarily Depress Interest Rates

In the short run, when the Fed increases the rate of monetary growth, interest rates decline. If the interest rate is the price of money, it follows that if the money supply is increased and there is no change in the demand for money, then its price (the interest rate) will decline.

The monetarists tell us that in the long run an increase in monetary growth will not lower interest rates; the increased money supply causes inflation. Lenders will demand higher interest rates to compensate them for being repaid in inflated dollars.

In the long run, a rise in M pushes up inflation and interest rates.

Let's say, for example, there's no inflation and the interest rate is 5 percent. This is the real rate of interest. The rate of inflation then rises to 8 percent; that means if it cost you $10,000 to live last year, your cost of living is now $10,800. If lenders can anticipate the rate of inflation, they will insist that they be paid not just for the real interest rate of 5 percent but also for the anticipated inflation of 8 percent. This raises the interest rate from 5 percent to a nominal rate of 13 percent.

When the Federal Reserve allows the money supply to grow quickly, interest rates are kept down for a while until lenders realize the rate of inflation (caused by faster monetary growth) is rising. They will then demand higher interest rates. Thus, a higher rate of monetary growth in the short run will keep interest rates low, but in the long run it will lead to higher interest rates.

(3) Expansionary Monetary Policy Will Only Temporarily Reduce the Unemployment Rate   The first two basic propositions partially explain the third. First, when monetary growth speeds up, output is expanded, but in the long run only prices will rise. Because rising output would lower the unemployment rate, in the short run unemployment is reduced. But in the long run, an increase in the rate of monetary growth will raise prices, not output, so the unemployment rate will go back up. We'll come back to why this happens.

The second basic proposition states that expansionary monetary policy only temporarily depresses interest rates. In the short run, more money means lower interest rates. These lower interest rates encourage more investment and, consequently, less unemployment.

But in the long run the added money in circulation causes inflation, which, in turn, raises interest rates. As interest rates rise, investment declines and the unemployment rate goes back up.

The monetarists have explained the temporary reduction in the unemployment rate more directly. As labor union members begin to anticipate inflation, they will demand higher wage rates. New labor contract settlements will reflect the higher cost of living, but these higher wage settlements will price some workers out of the market, thus raising the unemployment rate.

(4) Expansionary Fiscal Policy Will Only Temporarily Raise Output and Employment   Here we have another conflict—this time a basic one—between the monetarists and the Keynesians. The Keynesians believe fiscal policy, particularly heavy government spending, will pull us out of a recession. But how is this spending going to be financed? By borrowing. The Treasury goes into the market for loanable funds and borrows hundreds of billions of dollars to finance the deficit.

The monetarists point out that such huge government borrowing comes directly into conflict with the borrowing of business firms and consumers. Not only will it be harder for these groups to borrow, but interest rates will be driven up. This crowding-out effect represents, according to the monetarists, a substitution of public for private spending. All we're really doing is spending more on government goods and services and less on consumer and investment goods and services. Aggregate demand is not increased.

Crowding-out effect

How well would a budget surplus restrain inflation? Not very, say the monetarists. The Treasury would be repaying part of the national debt, which would tend to push down interest rates and make borrowing easier. Private borrowing would replace public borrowing. The hoped-for restraint would not materialize because private borrowers would now be spending these borrowed funds on goods and services. In effect, then, we would still have the same level of spending.

The Monetary Rule

The policy prescription of the monetarists is simply to increase the money supply at a constant rate. When there is a recession, this steady infusion of money will pick up the economy. When there is inflation, a steady rate of monetary growth will slow it down. So one size of monetary growth fits all economic occasions.

You might ask why the money supply should be increased at all during inflation. There are two answers. First, the monetarists would tell you that if we didn't increase the money supply at all, we would be going back to the old, failed discretionary monetary policies of the past—the start-and-stop, start-and-stop policies that only made the business cycle worse. Second, over the long run the economy does need a steady infusion of money to enable economic growth.

The monetarists' steady monetary growth prescription is analogous to the feeding policy of the American Army. Every day, in every part of the world, at every meal, the soldiers walk along the chow line and receive, in addition to the main course and dessert, two pieces of white bread, two pats of butter, and one pint of whole milk. The main course is also dished out in equal portions. The food servers do not dole out portions whose sizes vary with that of the eater. They look from the serving pan to the eater's tray, slopping out serving spoonfuls of whatever it is that the Army decided to cook that day.

So, we have a 6-foot 6-inch 300-pound person getting the same size portion as does a 5-foot 6-inch 130-pound person. My theory is that the Army wants everyone to be the same size—a theory that also seems to be borne out by the single uniform size that is issued. If everyone eats the same portion, presumably they will all end up this same size.

Perhaps the monetarists got the idea of increasing the money supply by a constant percentage by observing Army chow lines. They believe our economic health will be relatively good—if not always excellent—if we have a steady diet of money. No starts and stops, no extreme ups and downs, and, to complete the analogy, no very fat years and no very lean years.

The Decline of Monetarism

It's interesting that when the Fed really began to pay attention to what the monetarists were saying, this may have led to the ultimate decline of the monetarist school. In October 1979 Federal Reserve Chairman Paul Volcker announced a major policy shift. No longer would the Fed focus only on keeping interest rates on an even keel. From now on the Fed would set monetary growth targets and stick to them.

This new policy was followed for most of the next three years. The double-digit inflation that prevailed in 1979 and 1980 was finally brought under control by late 1982—but not until we had gone through a period of sky-high interest rates, very high unemployment, and back-to-back recessions.

Even though the Fed had finally followed the advice of the monetarists—at least to a large degree—and even though the nagging inflation of the last 15 years had finally been wrung out of the economy, people began to look elsewhere for their economic gurus. They looked to the White House, which had become a stronghold of the latest school of economics, the supply-side school.

Supply-Side Economics

Supply-side economics came into vogue in the early 1980s when Ronald Reagan assumed the presidency. Supply-siders felt that the economic role of the federal government had grown much too large and that high tax rates and onerous government rules and regulations were hurting the incentives of individuals and business firms to produce goods and services. President Reagan suggested a simple solution: get the government off the backs of the American people. How? By cutting taxes and reducing government spending and regulation.

The objective of supply-side economics, then, is to raise aggregate supply, the total amount of goods and services the country produces. The problem, said the supply-siders, is that high marginal tax rates are hurting the incentive to work and to invest. All the government needs to do is cut tax rates, and *voilà!* Up goes production.

Many of the undesirable side effects of high marginal tax rates are explained by the work effect, the savings and investment effect, and the elimination of productive market exchanges, which we shall take up in turn.

The Work Effect

People are often confronted with work–leisure decisions. Should I put in that extra couple of hours of overtime? Should I take on a second job? Should I keep my store open longer hours? If you answer yes to any of these, you'll have to give the government a pretty big slice of that extra income. At some point you may well conclude, "I'd have to be nuts to take on any extra work; I'd only be working for the government."

At what point do *you* start working for the government? When it takes 20 cents out of each dollar of extra income (a marginal tax rate of 20 percent)? When it takes 30 cents? Or 40 cents? If you are a wage-earner, you will have to pay Medicare and Social Security tax, federal income tax, and, probably, some state income tax. Back in 1980, before the passage of the Kemp-Roth tax cut and the tax cuts that came under the Tax Reform Act of 1986, people earning more than $50,000 a year often had marginal tax rates of more than 50 percent. If you paid more than half of your overtime earnings in taxes, would you consider yourself to be working for the government?

Facing high marginal tax rates, many people refuse to work more than a certain number of hours of overtime or take on second jobs and other forms of extra work. Instead, they opt for more leisure time. In sum, high marginal tax rates rob people not only of some potential income but of the incentive to work longer hours. People working shorter hours obviously produce less, so total output is lower than it might have been with lower marginal tax rates.

The Saving and Investment Effect

When people save money, they earn interest on their savings. But a high marginal tax rate on interest income will provide a disincentive to save, making less savings available for investment purposes.

Similarly, people who borrow money for investment purposes—new plant and equipment and inventory—hope that this will lead to greater profits. But if those profits are subject to a high marginal tax rate, once again there is a disincentive to invest.

Supply-side economists point to the economic stagnation of the late 1970s and early 1980s as proof of the basic propositions of their theory. On the other hand, the economic record during the Reagan years, particularly with respect to saving, investment, and economic growth, was nothing to write home about.

The Elimination of Productive Market Exchanges

Most people have jobs at which they are good; if an accountant, a carpenter, an automobile mechanic, and a gourmet chef are all relatively good at their professions, that's probably why they chose those lines of work to begin with—and all that on-the-job training didn't hurt either.

When you need your taxes prepared—especially if you stand to save several thousand dollars—you go to an accountant. When you need your transmission fixed, unless you're a skilled mechanic, you'll certainly be better off going to someone who is. In fact, one of the main reasons our standard of living is so high in the United States is because a large proportion of our labor force is composed of individuals with specialized skills.

What happens when your roof must be reshingled? Do you hire a roofer, or do you do it yourself? Do you do it yourself because it's cheaper?

Well, maybe it's cheaper and maybe it isn't. Suppose you can reshingle your roof in 100 hours and a roofer can do the job in 60 hours. If the roofer charges you $12 an hour (in addition to materials), it will cost you $720. How many hours would you have to work to earn $720? Suppose your clerical job pays $10 an hour and you are in the 40 percent marginal tax bracket. You take home only $6 an hour (that is, 60 percent of $10).

Do you hire the roofer or do it yourself? If you do it yourself, it will take you 100 hours. If you hire the roofer, you must pay him $720. How many hours would you have to work to bring home $720? Figure it out: $720/$6 = 120 hours. I think even *I* would rather spend 100 hours on my roof than 120 hours in front of a class. And I'm afraid of heights!

There is a serious misallocation of labor when the productive market exchange—your clerical work for your roofer's labor—is eliminated; but because of the high marginal tax rate, it pays for you to work less at your regular job (at which you are presumably good) and more at household tasks (at which you are not so good). When you add up all the productive market exchanges short-circuited by high marginal tax rates, you may well be talking about hundreds of billions of dollars in misallocated resources.

High tax rates discourage productive market exchanges.

Policy prescription: Cut taxes!

The Laffer Curve

Supply-side economists have one basic policy prescription: Cut tax rates! Won't federal tax revenue fall precipitously? But Arthur Laffer, an orthodox supply-side economics professor, said that cutting marginal tax rates could lead to an increase in government revenue. (See the box, "The Laffer Curve.")

Let's see how this works by looking at the case of a specific individual. Suppose this person pays $50,000 on an income of $100,000. If this person's tax rate were lowered to 40 percent, she would pay $40,000. Right? Wrong, say the supply-siders. She would now have an incentive to work harder. How *much* harder? Hard enough, say, to earn $130,000 by working every available hour of overtime or taking on a second job.

How much is 40 percent of $130,000? It comes out to exactly $52,000. How much did the government collect from her before the tax cut? Only $50,000. So by cutting tax rates, say the supply-siders, the government will end up collecting more revenue. But when the government cut tax rates in 1981 and 1982, tax revenue actually declined. Of course, there was a recession going on.

During the last two years of the Reagan administration, it had become apparent that supply-side economics was an idea whose time had gone. Although inflation had been brought under control and interest rates had declined as well (largely because of the efforts of the Federal Reserve), the supply-side policies had not yielded the rapid rate of economic growth that the public had been led to expect. Perhaps the greatest legacies of supply-side economics were huge budget deficits.

Arthur Laffer, American economist

Waiting for supply-side economics to work is like leaving the landing lights on for Amelia Earhart.

—Walter Heller

Andrew Mellon: Our First Supply-Side Economist

Long before the term *supply-side economics* was even coined, it was being practiced by our longest serving secretary of the treasury, Andrew Mellon, who held this post under Presidents Warren Harding, Calvin Coolidge, and Herbert Hoover. Over time he was able to oversee a series of personal income tax cuts which were especially beneficial to our nation's highest income citizens. More than five decades before supply-side economics became popular, here is what Mellon wrote:

> Any man of energy and initiative in this country can get what he wants out of life. But when that initiative is crippled by legislation or by a tax system which denies him the right to receive a reasonable share of his earnings, then he will no longer exert himself and the country will be deprived of the energy on which its continued greatness depends.[2]

---

[2]Andrew W. Mellon, *Taxation: The People's Business* (New York: Macmillan, 1924), p. 12.

The Laffer Curve

Imagine that we're at point A on the Laffer curve drawn in Figure A. We cut the marginal tax rate from 50 percent to 40 percent, and lo and behold, tax revenue rises from $1,200 billion to nearly $1,400 billion. Is this sophistry? (That's Greek for "pulling a fast one.")

What if we were at, say, point C on the Laffer curve and we cut tax rates? What would happen to federal tax revenue? Obviously, it would decline.

The problem is to figure out where we are on the Laffer curve, or what the parameters of the curve itself are, before we start cutting taxes. There really *is* a Laffer curve out there. The trouble is we don't know exactly where, so when we try to use it as a policy tool, it's kind of like playing an economic version of pin the tail on the donkey. When you play a game blindfolded, you run the risk of looking a lot like the six-year-old kids who miss the donkey completely. And this game is for somewhat higher stakes.

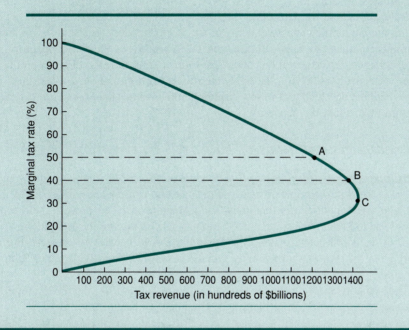

Figure A

The Laffer Curve

At a marginal tax rate of 0, tax revenues are 0. Tax revenue can be increased by raising the marginal tax rate to point C, at which they will be maximized. If marginal tax rates are raised still higher, tax revenue will decline. And, if the marginal tax rate were 100 percent, no one would work, and tax revenue would be 0. The rationale of the Laffer curve is that, when the marginal tax rate is too high, say, at 50 percent (see point A), we can raise tax revenue by lowering it to 40 percent (see point B).

Rational Expectations Theory

Whatever else you have learned about economic policy, you know that economists don't all agree on what policies we should follow. But most economists would more or less agree on two sets of policies. To fight inflation, you want to lower the rate of growth of the money supply and reduce federal government budget deficits. And to fight recessions, you want to do the opposite: increase the rate of growth of the money supply and increase the size of the deficits. But prominent among those who would disagree with these policies are the rational expectationists.

Most economists agree on two sets of policies.

You probably never saw *Monty Python and the Holy Grail,* but in that movie there was a group of knights who distinguished themselves solely by saying "Neee." No matter what questions they were asked, they would always answer "Neee." Assuming "Neee" was Middle English for nay or no, those knights were the rational expectations theorists, or the new classical economists of their day.

Like the "old" classical economists, today's rational expectationists say no to any form of government economic intervention. Such intervention, no matter how well intentioned, would do a lot more harm than good. In fact, they maintain that anti-inflationary and antirecessionary policies, at best, would have no effect whatsoever. More likely, say the new classical economists, these policies would end up making things worse.

It would be best for the government to do nothing, even if there were a recession or a substantial amount of inflation. The economy will automatically and quickly right itself, ending up again with full employment and little or no inflation. The reason that fiscal and monetary policy would have little effect, according to the rational expectationists, is that they affect mainly aggregate demand but that the prime economic mover is aggregate supply.

They argued that at any given time there was a natural level of real GDP, toward which the economy gravitated. The recessionary and inflationary gaps that so perplexed policymakers during the 1970s weren't gaps at all.[3] Instead they reflected changes in the economy's own natural level of output. When oil prices went through the roof in 1973 and again in 1979, said the rational expectationists, they created declines in aggregate supply, lowering the natural level of GDP. There was nothing the government could do about these new economic facts, except to keep out of the way and let our economy quickly adjust to them as it moved to its new natural level of output.

The view of Robert Lucas

Robert Lucas of the University of Chicago, a 1995 Nobel Prize winner, is clearly top gun among the new classical economists. Lucas believes that people can anticipate government policies to fight inflation and recession, given their knowledge of policy, past experience, and expectations about the future. Consequently, they act on this anticipation, effectively nullifying the intended effects of those policies. What, then, should the government do? It should follow strict guidelines rather than try to use discretionary policy to tinker with the economy.

The Three Assumptions of Rational Expectations Theory

Rational expectations theory is based on three assumptions: (1) that individuals and business firms learn through experience to anticipate the consequences of changes in monetary and fiscal policy; (2) that they act instantaneously to protect their economic interests; and (3) that all resource and product markets are purely competitive.

Now we'll translate. Imagine the Federal Reserve decides to increase the money supply's rate of growth sharply. Why would the Fed do this? To stimulate output and raise employment.

An economist is someone who doesn't know what he's talking about—and makes you feel it's your fault.
                    —Anonymous

The scenario, according to the Fed, would be as follows: (1) the money supply rises; (2) business firms order more plant and equipment and more inventory; (3) more jobs are created and output rises; (4) wages do not rise right away, but prices do; (5) because prices rise and wages stay the same, profits rise; (6) eventually wages catch up to prices, profits go back down, and the expansion comes to an end.

This may have happened in the old days, say the rational expectations theorists, but surely people have learned something from all this experience. Everybody knows that when the Fed sharply increases the monetary growth rate, inflation will result. Business firms, of course, will raise prices. But what about labor? Anticipating the expected inflation, wage-earners will demand wage increases now. No more playing catch-up after the cost of living has already risen.

If wage rates are increased along with prices, do profits increase? No! If profits are not rising, there goes the main reason for increasing output and hiring more people—which, of course, was why the rate of monetary growth was raised in the first place.

Let's return to the rational expectations theorists' three assumptions. The first one is plausible enough—that through experience, we learn to anticipate the consequences of changes in monetary and fiscal policy. So, if a sharp increase in the rate of growth of the money supply always leads to inflation, eventually we will all learn to recognize this pattern. (See the box, "Rational Expectations versus Adaptive Expectations.")

It would follow from the next two assumptions that the intended results of macroeconomic policy shifts will be completely frustrated. Why? If you knew that prices would be increasing, would you be willing to sit back and passively accept a decline in your standard of living? Wouldn't you demand a higher wage rate to keep pace with rising

---

[3]The recessionary and inflationary gaps are discussed in Parts I and II of Chapter 12.

Rational Expectations versus Adaptive Expectations

How do we predict the future? The simplest way is to assume that past trends will continue. The *adaptive expectations hypothesis* is based on the assumption that the best indicator of the future is what happened in the past.

Suppose the price level has been rising at an annual rate of 6 percent for the last three years. Under adaptive expectations, people will expect prices to rise about 6 percent in year 4. Now let's add a wrinkle. Suppose that in year 4 the rate of inflation rises to 9 percent. So what rate of inflation do people now predict for year 5? They predict 9 percent. Well, suppose that in year 5 it rises to 14 percent. What will everyone predict for year 6? Fourteen percent? Fine. Except that in year 6 it goes down to 10 percent. So for year 7 everyone predicts 10 percent. But in year 7 the inflation rate falls to just 5 percent.

Under adaptive expectations, forecasts of the future rate of inflation may be right on the money, but they may also exhibit systematic error. When inflation is accelerating, forecasts will tend to be too low. And when inflation is decelerating (that is, disinflation is taking place), then forecasts will tend to be too high.

The *rational expectations hypothesis* makes the assumption that people do not keep making the same mistakes over and over again when predicting future events. After getting burned once or twice, they do not systematically keep assuming that past trends will necessarily continue into the future.

The rational expectations hypothesis assumes that future expectations are based not just on past trends but on an understanding of how the economy works. For example, to form their expectation of the inflation rate, decision makers will use all available information, including past inflation rates, the impact of expected policy actions and their knowledge of macroeconomic relationships within our economy.

So which hypothesis is right—rational expectations or adaptive expectations? To the degree that people have a sense of how our economy operates—and to the degree that they don't just blindly assume that past trends will continue into the future—the rational expectations hypothesis appears to have greater validity. But it falls far short of its adherents' claim that it is so powerful that it nullifies descretionary monetary and fiscal policy.

prices? The rational expectations theorists say people can always be expected to promote their personal economic interests, and furthermore, in a purely competitive market, they are free to do so.

Most macroeconomic policy changes, say the rational expectations theorists, are readily predictable. When there's inflation, there are extended debates in Congress, demands for cuts in government spending and tax increases, and a slowdown in the rate of monetary growth. Both Congress and the Federal Reserve generally telegraph policy moves, often months in advance. So when these moves are made, no one is surprised. And because the public anticipates these policy changes, their intended effects are canceled out by the actions taken by individuals and business firms to protect their economic interests. In the case of policies aimed at raising output and employment, all the government gets for its efforts is more inflation.

Most macroeconomic policy changes are predictable.

What should the government do? It should do, say the rational expectations theorists, as little as possible. Like the classical economists and the monetarists, they believe the more the government tries to be an economic stabilizing force, the more it will destabilize the economy.

What should the government do?

Basically, then, the federal government should figure out the right policies to follow and stick to them. What *are* the right policies? As you might expect, they've taken up the conservative economists' agenda: (1) steady monetary growth of 3 to 4 percent a year (the monetarists' monetary rule) and (2) a balanced budget (favored by the classical economists, among others).

Is it reasonable to expect individuals and business firms to predict the consequences of macroeconomic policy changes correctly when economists themselves come up with widely varying predictions, most of which are wrong? Economists place little faith in each other's rationality; is it rational for them to ascribe a greater prescience to the general population than they give themselves?

Criticism of the rational expectations school

In a world of constant change, is it possible for people to accurately predict the economic consequences of policy changes? Indeed, when a continually changing cast of policy makers, each with his or her own economic agenda, seems to be calling for entirely new economic approaches every few years, it's awfully hard to tell the players without a scorecard. It's even harder to predict the final score.

A second criticism of the rational expectations school is that our economic markets are not purely competitive; some are not competitive at all. Labor unions are not an economist's idea of purely competitive labor market institutions. Nor would industries such as those that produce automobiles, petroleum, cigarettes, and breakfast cereals, each of which has just a handful of firms doing most of the producing, be considered very competitive. How much competition does Microsoft Windows have?

Finally, critics raise the question of the rigidities imposed by contracts. The labor union with the two- or three-year contract cannot reopen bargaining with employers when greater inflation is anticipated because of a suddenly expansionary monetary policy. Nor can business firms that have long-term contracts with customers decide to charge higher prices because they perceive more inflation in the future.

An economist is someone who cannot see something working in practice without asking whether it would work in theory.
—Walter Heller

But this school is correct in calling their attention to how expectations may affect the outcome of macroeconomic policy changes. In recent years, then, economists have become more aware that to the degree policy changes are predictable, people will certainly act to protect their economic interests. Because they will succeed to some degree, they will partially counteract the effect of the government's macroeconomic policy.

This leaves us with a major economic policy disagreement: What should the government do when there's a recession? "Nothing," say the monetarists because policy makers are too incompetent to make the right decision. "Nothing," say the classical economists and the rational expectationists, since the economy will quickly and automatically move back to full employment. But this is definitely a minority view. Most economists today would agree that, since it might take years for our economy to work its way out of a recession, some monetary and fiscal policy actions would need to be taken.

In the event of inflation, this same policy dichotomy would be apparent. Although the monetarists might be somewhat amenable to a large degree of monetary restraint, the classical economists and rational expectationists would again suggest that the government do nothing. But the large majority of economists would again advocate some monetary and fiscal policy actions.

21st Century Economic Theory

In the first few years of the new century we've already had a mild revival of the supply-side school, and the rise of a completely new school of economic thought—economic behaviorism. Here are some preliminary observations.

The Supply-Side Revival?

Despite the fact that he [Labor Secretary John Dunlop] is an economist, basically I have great confidence in him.
—George Meany

By mid-2003 President George W. Bush had signed legislation passed by razor-thin Republican Congressional majorities which cut taxes by at least $2 trillion by the end of the decade. Just as in 1981 when Ronald Reagan signed the massive Kemp-Roth tax cut, the president maintained that the tax cut would spur economic growth, raise tax revenues, and consequently, shrink the federal budget deficit. Is this a resurrection of supply-side economics? Bush administration officials aren't *calling* it supply-side economics, but these tax cuts certainly do pass the smell test.

The basic premise of supply-side economics is that lower marginal tax rates would give people a greater incentive to work. Under President Bush's plan, for example, the top marginal tax rate of 39.6 percent would be cut to 35 percent, while taxpayers in each of the lower brackets—36 percent, 33 percent, 28 percent, and 15 percent—would also receive substantial tax cuts.

The question is: If your marginal tax rate is lowered (enabling you to keep more of your earnings), would you work more hours? The supply-siders say "Yes!"

The Economic Behaviorists

In economics, like in popular music, we often ask ourselves, who's hot and who's not? There's a hot new group of young economists, many of whom are barely out of graduate school and are complete newcomers to the economic theory scene. Their work is just beginning to appear in some of the big economics journals, so it may be a while yet before they work their way up to the top of the charts. They call themselves economic behaviorists, and they're definitely going to hit it big.

Until the behavioral economists arrived upon the scene, a core belief among economists of all schools of thought was that people's actions were guided by rational, unemotional self-interest. So if you won the lottery, you would put most of this money aside for the rest of your life. The behavioral economists observed that most lottery winners quickly spent most or all of their winnings. Maybe not very rational behavior, but very *human* behavior.

The behaviorist view of the business cycle also departs from mainstream economic thinking. When the good times are rolling, most people seem to think that they will continue indefinitely. Remember the stock market boom in the 1990s? People kicked themselves for not putting more of their money in the market. Then, when the market tanked, those who were most heavily invested were the ones kicking themselves.

Economics is the only field in which two people can share a Nobel Prize for saying opposing things.

—Roberto Alazar

Of course the same pattern was repeated during the real estate bubble, which began in 2000 and lasted until 2006. You were surely a genius if you invested in a new home, especially in a part of the Sunbelt where home prices more than doubled. But if you hadn't sold before the bubble burst, you might have gotten stuck with a home that was worth a lot less than your mortgage.

One of the two 2002 Nobel Prize winners in economics was Daniel Kahneman, who is not even an economist. A cognitive psychologist, Kahneman described humans as shortsighted, overconfident in their predictive skills, and irrationally prone to buying insurance on cheap home appliances. The next time a salesperson tries to sell you a three-year warranty on an air conditioner, a vacuum cleaner, or a microwave oven, take Daniel Kahneman's advice and just say no.

Two University of Chicago professors, Richard Thaler and Cass Sunstein, have written a very provocative book that makes behavioral economics very accessible to the general reader. Their main contention is that while people often don't act in their own economic self-interest, they can sometimes be quite easily "nudged" to do so. One of their main contentions is that if we can harness the power of inertia, we can get people to act in their own self-interest, rather than against it.

Suppose that when you were hired to begin work at a new company, your employer asked if you would like to enroll in a retirement plan (such as a 401k). Thaler and Sunstein note that "Contributions are tax deductible, accumulations are tax deferred, and in many plans the employer matches at least part of the contributions of the employee."[4] So, you may ask, "What's not to like?"

Surely it is in almost every new employee's economic self-interest to join this plan.[5] But often they don't. Why not? For nearly all, it's simply inertia. For some, it's just the bother of filling out the necessary paperwork.

Thaler and Sunstein cite a study from the United Kingdom of data from 25 retirement plans that actually don't require any contributions from employees, since their employers put in all the money. But the employees did need to opt into the retirement plan by filling out the requisite forms. Just 51 percent did so. The rest forfeited all that "free money."

How do we get employees to act in their own economic self-interest? Thaler and Sunstein suggest that the default rule be changed from nonenrollment to enrollment. "When an employee first becomes eligible, she receives a form indicating that she will be enrolled in the plan . . . unless she fills out a form asking to opt out."[6] In other words,

---

[4]Richard H. Thaler and Cass R. Sunstein, *Nudge: Improving Decisions About Health, Wealth, and Happiness* (New York: Penguin, 2008), p. 109.

[5]Those especially young workers just starting out and with pressing financial needs would find it sensible not to enroll.

[6]Thaler and Sunstein, *op. cit.*, p. 111.

the default is you're automatically in unless you take action to opt out. By nudging employees to act in their self-interest, nearly all will do so.

BusinessWeek columnist Peter Coy provides an apt summary of the behaviorists' contribution:

> The new idea is to drag into economics the common-sense observation that people are often short-sighted, emotional, and irrational—even acting against their own best interests. Such things as addiction, procrastination, and spitefulness, which don't fit comfortably into the traditional paradigm of economics, are the meat of this new area of behavioral economics.[7]

In sum, the behavioral economists are not challenging the mainstream beliefs that rational behavior and economic self-interest are important motivators of economic behavior. But they *are* challenging the belief that these are the *only* motivating factors. Their goal is to apply a wider range of psychological concepts to economic theory.

Conventional Macropolicy to Fight Recessions

Is it possible, then, to formulate conventional economic policy to fight recessions and inflation? As you know, it would be impossible to obtain unanimous agreement for *any* given policy. But a majority of economists, with varying degrees of enthusiasm, would go along with the conventional fiscal and monetary policies summarized below.

Fighting Recessions

We're going to talk about the conventional fiscal and monetary policies that are advocated by most economists. But a significant minority opinion—especially among the monetarists and rational expectationists—runs counter to the majority opinion on macropolicy. So if you happen to disagree with conventional fiscal and monetary policy, just grit your teeth, work your way through the next few pages, and be thankful that they will be short.

Run deficits to fight recessions.

The most conventional fiscal policy for fighting a recession is to run a budget deficit. Indeed, given the automatic stabilizers as well as our tax laws, deficits are virtually inevitable during recessions. We would also cut taxes, raise government spending, or some combination of the two.

Speed up M growth to fight recessions.

Were we to enter a recession, the conventional monetary policy would be to speed up the rate of growth of the money supply. Here we need to be careful: If we were to speed it up too much, we would have to worry about an inflation and possibly rising interest rates, which, in time, would kill off any recovery.

Two Policy Dilemmas

1. Huge budget deficits are financed by massive borrowings by the Treasury. As the economy begins to recover, business and consumer borrowing picks up as well. What does all this loan demand do to interest rates? It drives them up. And when interest rates, which were high even during the recession, rise still higher in the early stages of recovery, what happens next? The recovery collapses.

   Thus, a budget deficit, designed to stimulate the economy, necessitates massive Treasury borrowing, driving up interest rates and ultimately choking off recovery. Is there any way to resolve this dilemma? How about gradually reducing the deficit as the recovery progresses? This may happen automatically as government payments decline for public assistance, food stamps, and unemployment benefits, and as personal and corporate income tax payments pick up.

---

[7]Peter Coy, "More Oddball Tales for *Freakonomics* Fans," *BusinessWeek*, November 2, 2009, p. 74.

2. Let's consider rapid monetary growth. It stimulates recovery, making funds available to business firms and consumers. Interest rates may decline. So far, so good. But when we increase the money supply this rapidly, we also court inflation, and with inflation, people will demand more interest for their savings. With inflation and higher interest rates, it won't be long before the recovery sputters to a stop.

Can you think of a way out of this dilemma? We could try to reduce the rate of monetary growth as recovery begins to set in.

Fighting the Great Recession

The presidential administrations of George W. Bush and Barack Obama, the Congress, and the Federal Reserve all employed conventional macropolicy to combat the Great Recession. By fiscal year 2009 the deficit shot up to $1.4 trillion, and short-term interest rates were reduced to close to 0. At the time I am writing these words—in June 2010—it is too soon to tell if rising interest rates will eventually choke off the recovery. Or whether the huge deficits and the flood of money in the hands of the banks will set off an inflationary spiral.

Conventional Macropolicy to Fight Inflation

To fight inflation, we would immediately want to try to reduce the size of the federal budget deficit—if we happen to be running one. It would be too much of a shock to reduce it too quickly, but in the face of persistent inflation, we would need to reduce the deficit year by year and ultimately run budget surpluses.

To fight inflation, reduce the deficit.

The obvious policy move here would be to slow down the rate of growth of the money supply, indeed; if inflation were beginning to rage out of control, not only would the Fed have to stop the money supply from growing, but it would have to cause it to contract slightly.

To fight inflation, slow the rate of M growth.

Fighting Inflationary Recessions

Some people think of inflations and recessions as separate problems. They once were. However, beginning with the recession in 1957–58, the price level has risen during every recession. To add insult to injury, during three of the most recent recessions, 1973–75, 1980, and 1981–82, inflation was of double-digit proportions.

Let's review conventional fiscal policy to fight recession and inflation. To fight recession, we run budget deficits; to fight inflation, we run surpluses. Very well, then, what do we do to fight an inflationary recession? That's one dilemma.

We'll go on to the second dilemma. What is the conventional monetary policy to fight a recession? It's to speed up the rate of monetary growth. And to fight an inflation? Slow it down.

Here's the million-dollar question: How do we fight an inflation and a recession simultaneously using conventional fiscal and monetary policy? The answer: We can't.

Don't give up; there *is* hope.

One approach would be to try a combination of tight money to fight the inflation and a large budget deficit to provide the economic stimulus needed to fight the recession. We kind of stumbled onto this combination during the recession of 1981–82, but not until the Fed eased up on the tight money part did the economy finally begin to recover. By then, much of the inflation had been wrung from the economy.

This suggests a second approach. First deal with the inflation, then cure the recession. In the early 1950s the United States suffered from a surge of inflation brought on by the Korean War. Three recessions occurred over the course of just eight years. By the end of the third recession, the consumer price index was virtually stable. Then, through almost the entire decade of the 1960s, the economy went through a recession-free expansion.

Conventional monetary and fiscal policy tools are sufficient to deal with simple recessions or inflations, but inflationary recessions pose additional problems. Conventional macropolicy cannot cure them without a great deal of suffering, especially by those who lose their jobs, their businesses, and even their homes.

Conventional policies are not ideal for fighting inflationary recessions.

The Limits of Macropolicy

There is no question that the federal government can easily alter the course of our economy; but during the last couple of decades, substantial changes took place that sharply limited its power. The internationalization of our economy has completely altered the rules of the macroeconomic policy game.

Marc Levinson noted these changes:

> International capital flows . . . have made it much more difficult for the central bank to plot the nation's monetary course.
>
> Suppose, for example, that the Fed wants to boost the economy's growth rate. When international capital flows were small, the central bank could stimulate borrowing by pumping up the money supply or cutting the discount rate. But now, lower real interest rates will spur investors to move their capital out of dollar-denominated investments. Economists can't even begin to estimate the likely extent of those capital flows.[8]

Levinson's analysis is supported by that of Kenichi Ohmae, who reasons that if the Fed tightens the money supply and pushes up interest rates, money will flow in from abroad, attracted by our relatively high interest rates. This will frustrate the tight-money and high-interest-rate objectives of the Fed, and, in effect, render the traditional instruments of monetary policy obsolete.[9]

As our economy becomes even more closely integrated into the world economy—a topic we'll pursue in the last two chapters in this book—it is clear that macropolicy will become less important. Still, while macropolicy may no longer be the only economic game in town, it is still, by far, the biggest game.

There is another limitation to macropolicy: our huge and growing deficits. Should we need to fight a new recession, can we cut taxes still further and push federal government spending even higher? When the previous recession struck in early 2001, we actually had been running a budget surplus. It was a lot easier in 2001 to cut taxes and raise government spending than it would be when the deficit is over $1 trillion. Such a large deficit will limit our fiscal policy options when the next recession begins.

Conclusion

Murray Weidenbaum, who served as chairman of President Reagan's Council of Economic Advisors, puts a lot of what we've been talking about in this chapter into perspective:

> Each of the major schools of economic thought can be useful on occasion. The insights of Keynesian economics proved appropriate for Western societies attempting to get out of deep depression in the 1930s. The tools of monetarism were powerfully effective in squeezing out the inflationary force of the 1970s. Supply-side economics played an important role in getting the public to understand the high costs of taxation and thus to support tax reform in the 1980s. But sensible public policy cannot long focus on any one objective or be limited to one policy approach.[10]

---

[8]Marc Levinson, "Economic Policy: The Old Tools Won't Work," *Duns Business Month,* January 1987, pp. 30–33.

[9]Kenichi Ohmae, *The Borderless World* (HarperCollins, 1990), p. xi.

[10]Murray Weidenbaum, *Rendezvous with Reality* (New York: Basic Books, 1988), p. 23.

Current Issue: True Believers

Presidents do not often declare themselves members of any particular economic school, although Richard Nixon did once proclaim, "I am a Keynesian," and Ronald Reagan was a firm adherent of supply-side economics. While President George W. Bush never said so in as many words, he clearly placed most of his economic bets on the workings of supply-side economics by presiding over two massive tax cuts during his first term.

You'll recall that John Maynard Keynes advocated spending whatever it takes to bring us out of economic downturns. The Great Recession and the accompanying financial crisis presented our nation with its worst economic situation since the 1930s. As we saw in Chapter 12, Keynesian economics did provide the fiscal policy tools to help end the recession. But an extremely expansionary monetary policy, together with a few unprecedented financial measures carried out by the Federal Reserve, the Federal Deposit Insurance Corporation, and the U.S. Treasury not only helped fight the recession, but may well have staved off a financial meltdown.

Just as there are said to be no atheists in foxholes, when faced with financial crises, our presidents, representatives in Congress, and Federal Reserve officials, when faced with serious economic problems, become true believers in at least one of the leading schools of economic thought.

Questions for Further Thought and Discussion

1. According to the classical economists, how did Say's law, the interest rate mechanism, and downwardly flexible wages and prices ensure that recessions would cure themselves?

2. According to John Maynard Keynes, what was the basic problem during recessions, and what was his solution?

3. What is the monetary rule and why is it favored by the monetarists?

4. What is the Laffer curve? How do supply-siders use it with respect to tax rates?

5. What are the three basic assumptions of the rational expectations theorists? Are they valid?

6. Is there any consensus among at least some of the different schools of economic thought with respect to the effectiveness of monetary and fiscal policy?

7. How does the crude quantity theory of money differ from the modern, sophisticated version?

8. When a recession begins, if the federal government spent tens of billions of dollars on a highway building program and consequently ran a large deficit, how would this fiscal policy measure be judged by each of the five main schools of 20th century economic thought?

9. *Practical Application:* Outline the conventional monetary and fiscal policies for fighting an inflation. Then outline the conventional monetary and fiscal policies for fighting a recession. Why would an inflationary recession pose a dilemma for those who would attempt to apply conventional monetary and fiscal policies?

10. *Practical Application:* As academic dean, you have full control of your college's registration process. Using what you've learned from the book *Nudge* by Thaler and Sunstein, how would you get newly registering freshmen to enroll in a free 5-hour driver safety course?

11. *Practical Application:* As the last living believer in the crude quantity theory of money, you need to deal with a ruinous annual deflation rate of 10 percent. What simple economic measure would you take to end the deflation?

Workbook for Chapter 15 connect | ECONOMICS

Name _____ Date _____

Multiple-Choice Questions

Circle the letter that corresponds to the best answer.

1. Say's law states that _____. (LO3)
   a) supply creates its own demand
   b) demand creates its own supply
   c) demand will always exceed supply
   d) supply will always exceed demand

2. According to the classical economists, if the quantity of money that people wanted to save was greater than the amount that people wanted to invest,

   _____. (LO3)
   a) there would be a recession
   b) there would be inflation
   c) the interest rate would fall
   d) the interest rate would rise

3. The classical economists believed _____. (LO3)
   a) both wages and prices were downwardly flexible
   b) neither wages nor prices were downwardly flexible
   c) wages, but not prices, were downwardly flexible
   d) prices, but not wages, were downwardly flexible

4. The classicals believed recessions were

   _____. (LO3)
   a) impossible
   b) potential depressions
   c) temporary
   d) hard to end without government intervention

5. The problem during recessions, said John Maynard

   Keynes, was _____. (LO4)
   a) inadequate aggregate supply
   b) inadequate aggregate demand
   c) too much inflation
   d) too much government intervention

6. According to Keynes, _____ was necessary to get us out of a depression. (LO4)
   a) investment spending
   b) consumer spending
   c) foreign spending
   d) any kind of spending

7. Keynes believed budget deficits were

   _____. (LO4)
   a) to be avoided at all costs
   b) bad during recessions
   c) good during recessions
   d) good all the time

8. The key to investment spending, said Keynes, was

   _____. (LO4)
   a) the interest rate
   b) the expected profit rate
   c) foreign spending
   d) government spending

9. Classical economics lost most of its popularity in

   _____. (LO3)
   a) the 1920s   c) the 1960s
   b) the 1930s   d) the 1980s

10. Big government was ushered in during the

    _____. (LO4)
    a) 1920s   c) 1960s
    b) 1930s   d) 1980s

11. To the monetarists, the most important thing was

    _____. (LO5)
    a) the rate of growth of the money supply
    b) balancing the federal budget
    c) raising the federal government's tax base
    d) giving the Federal Reserve free reign

12. During a recession, if the money supply were increased _____. (LO4, 5)
    a) the Keynesians and the monetarists agree that people would probably just hold on to these funds
    b) the Keynesians and the monetarists agree that people would spend this money on assets of one kind or another
    c) the Keynesians believe people would probably just hold on to these funds, while the monetarists believe people would spend this money on assets of one kind or another

13. Which of the following is a basic proposition of monetarism? (LO5)
    a) The key to stable economic growth is a constant rate of increase in the money supply.
    b) Expansionary monetary policy will permanently depress the interest rates.
    c) Expansionary monetary policy will permanently reduce the unemployment rate.
    d) Expansionary fiscal policy will permanently raise output and employment.

14. The monetary rule states that _____. (LO5)
    a) the federal budget must be balanced every year
    b) the money supply must increase at the same rate as the price level
    c) the money supply must remain a constant from year to year
    d) the money supply must be increased at a constant rate

15. The monetarists criticized _____. (LO5)
    a) the stop-and-go policies of the Federal Reserve
    b) the ineffectiveness of monetary policy at fighting inflation
    c) the importance given to money by the Keynesians
    d) the Fed for keeping a heavy foot on the monetary brake and allowing the money supply to rise by only 3 percent a year

16. Supply-siders felt _____. (LO6)
    a) the federal government played too large an economic role
    b) the federal government played too small an economic role
    c) tax rates were too low
    d) the federal government was not spending enough to meet the needs of the poor

17. According to the supply-siders, each of the following resulted from high marginal tax rates except _____. (LO6)
    a) the work effect
    b) the savings-investment effect
    c) the elimination of productive market exchanges
    d) lagging demand for imported goods and services

18. According to the Laffer curve, when very high marginal tax rates are lowered, tax revenue will _____. (LO6)
    a) decline considerably
    b) decline slightly
    c) stay the same
    d) increase

19. The rational expectations theorists said anti-inflationary policy will _____. (LO7)
    a) generally work
    b) definitely do more harm than good
    c) either do no good or do harm

20. According to the rational expectations theorists, everyone learns that when the Fed sharply increases monetary growth _____. (LO7)
    a) inflation will result and people must move to protect themselves
    b) a recession will result and people must move to protect themselves
    c) people will continue to make the same mistakes over and over again

21. The effects of most macroeconomic policy changes, say the rational expectations theorists, are _____. (LO7)
    a) very hard to predict
    b) very easy to predict
    c) slow—that is, they take place over a period of many years
    d) irrational

22. The advice the rational expectations theorists give the federal government is to _____. (LO7)
    a) change macropolicy often
    b) figure out the right policies to follow and stick to them
    c) figure out what the public is expecting and then do the opposite

23. Which school would advocate government spending to end a recession? (LO4)
    a) Classical
    b) Keynesian
    c) Monetarist
    d) Supply-side
    e) Rational expectations

24. Which school would consider cutting tax rates as the cure for all our economic ills? (LO6)
    a) Classical
    b) Keynesian
    c) Monetarist
    d) Supply-side
    e) Rational expectations

25. MV = PQ _____. (LO1)
    a) all the time
    b) most of the time
    c) some of the time
    d) never

26. If MV rises, PQ _____. (LO1)
    a) must rise
    b) may rise
    c) must stay the same
    d) must fall

27. The crude quantity theory of money states that if M rises by 20 percent, P will _____. (LO2)
    a) fall by 20 percent
    b) fall
    c) stay the same
    d) rise
    e) rise by 20 percent

28. The modern monetarists believe _____. (LO5)
    a) V is very unstable
    b) V never changes
    c) any changes in V are either very small or predictable
    d) if M rises, V will fall by the same percentage

29. As we approach full employment, what will probably happen? (LO1, 2)
    a) V will fall
    b) Q will fall
    c) Q will rise
    d) P will rise
    e) P will fall

30. Each of the following explains why wages are not downwardly flexible *except* _____. (LO4)
    a) the efficiency wage theory
    b) the law of diminishing returns
    c) the insider-outsider theory
    d) labor contracts
    e) the minimum wage

31. The rational expectationists believe that fiscal and monetary policy are _____. (LO7)
    a) most effective fighting recessions
    b) most effective fighting inflation
    c) more effective in influencing aggregate supply than aggregate demand
    d) not effective

32. The behaviorial economists believe that economic behavior is guided _____. (LO7)
    a) entirely by rational, unemotional self-interest
    b) entirely by emotions
    c) by both rational self-interest and emotions
    d) by neither rational self-interest nor emotions

33. The main point made by Richard Thaler and Cass Sunstein in *Nudge* was that _____. (LO8)
    a) most people almost always act in their own economic self-interest
    b) most people almost never act in their own economic self-interest
    c) by changing the default, you can induce more people to act in their own economic self-interest
    d) the strongest inducement to get people to do what is good for the economy is to offer them "free money"

34. The conventional fiscal policy to fight a recession would be to _____. (LO9)
    a) increase the rate of monetary growth
    b) decrease the rate of monetary growth
    c) run budget deficits
    d) run budget surpluses

35. The conventional monetary policy to fight inflation would be to _____. (LO9)
    a) increase the rate of monetary growth
    b) decrease the rate of monetary growth
    c) run budget deficits
    d) run budget surpluses

36. One problem or dilemma we might face in fighting a recession is that _____. (LO9)
    a) we might end up with budget surpluses
    b) output might rise too quickly
    c) interest rates might fall
    d) interest rates might rise

37. During recessions, we want _____. (LO9)
   a) budget deficits and faster monetary growth
   b) budget deficits and slower monetary growth
   c) budget surpluses and faster monetary growth
   d) budget surpluses and slower monetary growth

38. During inflations, we want _____. (LO9)
   a) budget deficits and faster monetary growth
   b) budget deficits and slower monetary growth
   c) budget surpluses and faster monetary growth
   d) budget surpluses and slower monetary growth

39. Which statement is true? (LO9)
   a) In recent years inflation and recession have become separate problems.
   b) In recent years inflation and recession have become related problems.
   c) Inflation and recession have never been related problems.
   d) Inflation and recession have always been related problems.

40. In recent years macropolicy has _____. (LO9)
   a) become more powerful
   b) become less powerful
   c) remained about as powerful as it was 15 years ago

Fill-In Questions

1. According to the classical economists, if there is a recession, the government should _____. (LO3)

2. The classicals, applying Say's law, believed all our income would be _____; all our production would be _____; and all our savings would be _____. (LO3)

3. The classicals said if the amount of money people wanted to save was greater than the amount businesspeople wanted to invest, _____ _____. (LO3)

4. According to Keynes, the main institutional barriers to downward wage and price flexibility were (1) _____ and (2) _____. (LO4)

5. Milton Friedman is a leader of the _____ school. (LO5)

6. John Maynard Keynes said that during recessions and depressions, the main problem was _____ _____. (LO4)

7. To solve that problem, Keynes suggested _____ _____. (LO4)

8. Monetarism begins and ends with one obsession: _____. (LO5)

9. Milton Friedman concluded that we have never had a serious inflation that was not accompanied by _____. (LO5)

10. The monetarists believed that if the money supply were raised during a recession, people would _____. (LO5)

11. According to the monetarists, recessions are caused by _____. (LO5)

12. The key to stable economic growth, according to the monetarists, is _____. (LO5)

13. The monetarists say expansionary monetary policy will _____ depress interest rates and the unemployment rate. They further say expansionary monetary policy will _____ raise output and employment. (LO5)

14. The objective of supply-side economics is to _____ _____. The problem, said the supply-siders, was that _____ were hurting the incentive to work and invest. (LO6)

15. The way to get people to work more, say the supply-siders, is to _____. (LO6)

16. According to the Laffer curve, reducing very high marginal tax rates will result in _____ federal tax revenue. (LO6)

17. Most macroeconomic policy changes, say the rational expectations theorists, are _____ _____. (LO7)

18. The main criticism leveled at the rational expectations theorists is that _____ _____. (LO7)

19. The three main goals of macropolicy are

   (1) _____; (2) _____

   _____; and (3) _____. (LO9)

20. The conventional fiscal policy to fight a recession is

   to _____ while the conventional

   monetary policy is to _____. (LO9)

21. The conventional fiscal policy to fight an inflation is

   to _____, while

   the conventional monetary policy is to _____

   _____. (LO9)

22. One problem with both expansionary monetary and
   fiscal policies used to fight recessions is that they

   could lead to _____

   _____. (LO9)

23. The dilemma of fighting an inflationary recession

   with conventional fiscal policy would be _____

   _____. (LO9)

24. The dilemma of fighting an inflationary recession

   with conventional monetary policy would be _____

   _____. (LO9)

Problems

1. If M were 600 and V were 10, how much would
   PQ be? (LO1)

2. According to the crude quantity theory of money, if
   M were to increase by 10 percent, what would
   happen to V, P, and Q? (LO2)

3. If M were 800, P were 20, and Q were 400, how
   much would V be? (LO1)

4. Initially M = 600, V = 8, P = 16, and Q = 300.
   According to the crude quantity theory of money, if
   M rose to 720, how much would P be? (LO1)

5. If P were 7 and Q were 800, how much would MV
   be? (LO1)

Chapter 16

Economic Growth and Productivity

The American worker has long been among the most productive in the world, turning out relatively large amounts of goods or services per hour. Our hourly output has been growing rapidly since the mid-1990s. The McKinsey Global Institute breaks the economy down into 60 sectors. U.S. workers are the most productive on Earth in at least 50 sectors. This, in turn, has driven our rate of economic growth, making us among the fastest growing mature economies in the world.

But there have been some very serious problems. Our extremely low savings rate has forced us to borrow almost $2 billion a day from foreigners to finance not just our federal budget and trade deficits, but also much of our investment in new plant and equipment. The quality of our labor force has declined in recent decades, which reflects a failing educational system. And as globalization proceeds, there is growing concern about the migration of high-skilled, well-paying jobs, mainly to China, India, and other developing countries.

Our problems pale in comparison with those of the less developed countries of Asia, Africa, and Latin America. They are just beginning the journey to development that we undertook more than two centuries ago. But, unlike us, they are beginning from a base of such abject poverty that many of them may not have the resources needed to build developing economies.

LEARNING OBJECTIVES

After reading this chapter you should be able to:

1. Summarize the causes of economic growth in the United States.
2. Examine and explain the role played by productivity.
3. List and explain the reasons why our productivity growth has varied in recent decades.
4. Assess the roles of savings, capital, and technology.
5. List and examine the factors slowing our economic growth.
6. Discuss and analyze economic growth in the less developed countries.
7. Judge the Malthusian theory of population.
8. Analyze Baumol's Disease.

The Industrial Revolution and American Economic Development

Prior to the Industrial Revolution, about two and a half centuries ago, one generation lived about as well as the next—or as badly. Except for a few rich families, almost everyone was poor. Throughout the world, you were lucky if you had the basics—three

Economic Growth during the Last Millennium

For most of the last millennium, growth in world output per head averaged little more than 0.1 percent a year. But that growth accelerated to 1.2 percent a year around 1800. The accompanying chart shows that world GDP today is more than 60 times as great as it was 1,000 years ago.

The Industrial Revolution set off this great burst of sustained economic growth. But until the mid-20th century nearly all this growth was confined to Europe, the United States, Canada, Australia, New Zealand, and Japan. Since the early 1980s most of the growth has come from the emerging economies of Asia.

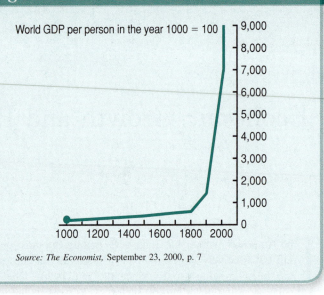

World GDP per person in the year 1000 = 100

Source: The Economist, September 23, 2000, p. 7; extention from 2000–2008 based on author's calculations.

Source: The Economist, September 23, 2000, p. 7

---

square meals a day, some homespun clothes on your back, and a thatched roof over your head.

If you were *really* lucky, you might live to see your old age, which began around your 40th birthday. You lived and died within a few miles of where you were born, you spent most of your time farming, and you were illiterate. About the only good thing in life before the Industrial Revolution was that you never had to worry about finding a parking space.

The Industrial Revolution made possible sustained economic growth and rising living standards for the first time in history.

The Industrial Revolution made possible sustained economic growth and rising living standards for the first time in history (see the accompanying box, "Economic Growth during the Last Millennium"). The steam engine, the factory system, mass production, the mechanized cotton spindle, the blast furnace (for smelting iron), railroads, and scores of other innovations ushered in a massive increase in productivity and output.

Although living standards in the industrializing nations of Western Europe and in the United States rose steadily, not until the 1920s did the age of mass consumption truly arrive. Homes were electrified; electric appliances, telephones, and cars became commonplace; and most working people were even beginning to enjoy increasing amounts of leisure time. After the Great Depression and World War II, the industrialized nations were able to pick up where they had left off in 1930, and by 1990 living standards in most of these countries had tripled. Chapter 1 of this book traced American economic development over the last two centuries.

Starting in 1780, England needed 58 years to double its per capita GDP. The American Industrial Revolution following the Civil War was a bit faster, with per capita output doubling in 47 years. Beginning in 1885, Japan doubled its per capita GDP in 34 years.

But borrowing heavily on earlier technology and making use of a great influx of Japanese capital, South Korea doubled its per capita output in just 11 years, starting in 1966. And now, China is roaring along with its own industrial revolution, doubling its per capita output every 10 years.

The Industrial Revolution, which began in England around the middle of the 18th century, entered its second phase in America in the early years of the 20th century. It was based on the mass production of cars, electrical machinery, steel, oil, and chemicals. But in the last three decades, the third phase of the Industrial Revolution has taken hold in Japan, Western Europe, and newly industrialized countries of Southeast Asia, as well as in the United States. This phase is based largely on consumer electronics, computer systems, communications systems, computer software, and advances in manufacturing processes. Since the early 1990s we have been in the fourth phase of the Industrial

Revolution—the information age. During this period nearly all business firms and most homes in the world's richest countries have been computerized.

on the web

How fast is the U.S. economy growing? Go to www.bea.gov and then click on "U.S. economy at a glance" in the upper left corner. You'll see a bar graph showing the quarterly growth of real GDP.

The Record of Productivity Growth

What factor or factors determine an economy's growth rate? One of the foremost growth theorists, Edward Denison, identified three key factors. In an extensive study of American economic growth over the 1929–82 period, Denison attributed about half our growth to added inputs of labor and capital and the rest to increased productivity.[1] The main source of productivity growth was advances in knowledge obtained through research and development. A second major source was improvements in the quality of labor, primarily the consequence of improvements in education and training.

Productivity is output per unit of input. For example, a telephone switchboard operator handles 100 calls per hour. So the output is 100 calls handled, and input is one hour of labor. If, one year later, the switchboard operator handles 103 calls per hour, his productivity has grown 3 percent.

The faster our productivity grows, the faster our output, or real GDP will grow. (This relationship is shown in Figure 1.) New ways of doing things can sometimes drastically boost productivity. Before we began shipping freight in standard-sized containers in the 1960s, it would take 300 longshoremen 10 days to unload a large freighter. Today it takes 30 longshoremen just one and a half days to do the same job. Another example: I'm old enough to remember the photocopy machines that looked liked elongated toasters. You'd place the page to be copied in one slot and about 30 seconds later it would emerge from the other slot. And your copy would emerge from a third slot at

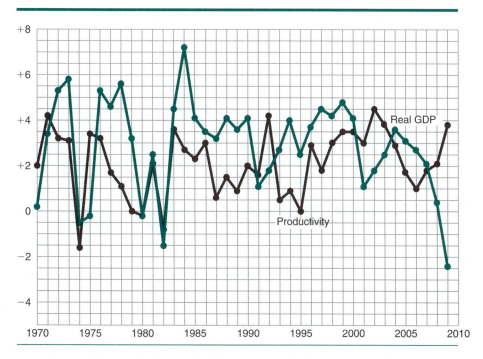

Figure 1

Annual Percentage Change in Productivity and Real GDP, 1970–2009

Source: Economic Report of the President, 2010; www.bls.gov/news.release/prod2t01.htm.

---

[1]Edward S. Denison, *Accounting for Slower Economic Growth* (Washington, D.C.: Brookings Institution, 1979).

Figure 2

Annual Productivity Percentage
Increase, by Decade,
1950–2009

*Source: Economic Report of the
President,* 2010; www.whitehouse.gov/
omb/budget/fy2009/economy.html

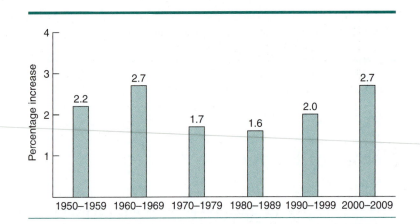

the same time. Of course you'd have to wait another minute or so for that copy to dry. And if you weren't careful, you'd get chemicals all over your original. That happened to my friend when he tried to make a copy of a ten-dollar bill and it turned brown. Today, machines make hundreds of copies in a minute. So we could say that the productivity of photocopy machines—and longshoremen as well—has improved by several thousand percent since the 1950s.

Figure 2 provides a summary of productivity growth since 1950. As you'll notice, it lagged considerably in the 1970s and 1980s.

One may question whether our measure of productivity is all that accurate to begin with. Since 1990 the average workweek has been virtually constant, never rising above 34.5 hours, nor falling below 33.0 hours. But with the advent of laptops, cell phones, and personal digital assistants, many information workers are on call 24/7. If the Labor Department is ignoring these extra, out of the office, hours that so many millions of workers are putting in, then it is overestimating productivity growth.

This leaves us with two questions. First, why was our rate of productivity growth so low from the 1970s through the 1980s? And second, why did it pick up again in the 1990s?

You can find the latest quarterly figures on productivity growth at www.bls.gov/lpc/home. htm. First click on "Get Detailed Productivity and Costs Statistics," then click on "Major Sector Productivity and Costs," and finally, check the box, "Business Output per Hour."

How Saving and Investment Affect Productivity Growth

We're looking for the factors that depressed our productivity growth from the mid-1970s through the early 1990s, and we're looking for those factors that pushed up our productivity growth beginning in the mid-1990s.

Low savings rate means low productivity growth.

Our Low Savings Rate   There is no one clear reason why our rate of productivity increase slowed in the 1970s and 1980s, but a reason singled out by many economists is our low savings rate. Americans have been poor savers for generations, but through most years of the 1950s, 1960s, and 1970s, we still managed to put away around 7 to 8 percent of disposable income. This changed in the 1980s, however, when savings averaged just 5.4 percent of disposable income. In the second half of the 1990s it declined steadily, and has averaged a little more than 2 percent since 2005.

As a nation, we're spending more than we're earning. We made up the difference by borrowing from foreigners, taking out home equity loans, running up credit card debt, or digging in our savings. It boggles the mind that in a relatively poor country like China, people can save as much as 40 percent of their income, but in our own relatively rich country, we can barely make ends meet.

Figure 3

U.S. Gross Savings Rate: Gross Saving as a Percentage of GDP, 1960–2009

There has been a downward trend in gross savings from the late 1970s when it was over 20 percent of Gross National Income to just 10 percent in 2009.

Source: Economic Report of the President, 2010; Survey of Current Business, March 2010.

Why do Americans save so little? Much of the blame is placed on the generations that came of age over the last few decades, whose rallying cries were, "Shop till you drop," "Born to Shop," and "I want it all and I want it now!" Their sense of entitlement was fostered by indulgent parents who did not want their children to go without. And, of course, the parents, themselves, did not go without either. The members of the baby-boom generation, unlike their middle-aged predecessors, have saved very little of their disposable incomes.

The generations that came of age in the 1980s and 1990s have not done as well as their parents' generations.

Although their savings rate is extremely low, Americans are putting away hundreds of billions for their retirement in the form of 401Ks, IRAs, and mutual funds, as well as the purchase of individual corporate stocks and bonds. Most of this does not count as personal savings, but a large chunk of these funds find their way into corporate investment.

Personal savings is just one part of the total amount saved by Americans, which we call *gross saving* (see Figure 3). Businesses save as well as does the government (I'm lumping together the federal, state, and local governments). Businesses save money through retained earnings (that is, profits plowed back into the business), but most of their savings is in the form of depreciation (or capital consumption) allowances (which we talked about in Chapter 6). These funds are used to replace the plant and equipment that have worn out or become obsolete, and they are also used to purchase additional plant and equipment.

Gross saving = personal + business + government saving

The federal government ran budget deficits from 1970 through 1997, while the state and local governments generally ran surpluses. Beginning in the late 1970s, the federal deficits far outweighed the state and local surpluses, so the government contribution to the gross savings rate became a big minus.

As we noted back in Chapter 7, the large federal budget deficits of the early 1990s fell during the rest of the decade, and by 1998 we were running surpluses. But soon after the new millennium began things took a turn for the worse. In short order the stock market tanked, the telecommunications-led boom became a bust, a recession set in, and, of course, there were the terrorist attacks of 9/11. Although the economy did slowly recover from the recession, the federal, state, and local government surpluses disappeared, and with the advent of the Great Recession, our combined deficit in 2009 was about $1.5 trillion.

What does our gross savings rate look like? In Figure 3 you can see an unmistakable downward trend from the late 1970s to the early 1990s, and then an apparent reversal beginning in 1993. But since the beginning of the new millennium there has been another downward trend. Not only are we running huge and growing federal budget deficits but our lagging personal savings rate has averaged just slightly over 2 percent since 2005.

Because we save so little, we generate a very low flow of funds for investment. Since the late 1990s we've been running huge trade deficits and foreigners have been recycling most of the dollars we sent them by making investments in the United States. Our investment is consequently much higher than it would otherwise have been due to this influx of dollars from abroad. For foreigners, the key attraction of investing in the United States is the relatively high interest rates that we pay.

Foreign investors have been attracted by our high interest rates.

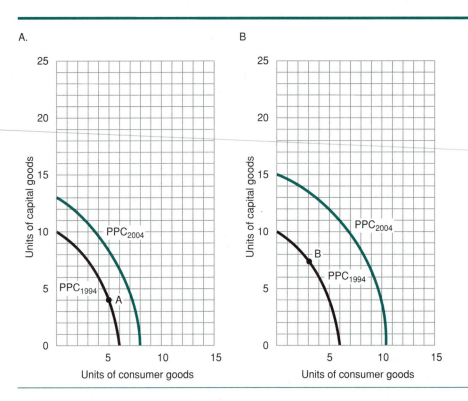

Figure 4

Capital Spending and Economic Growth

Panels A and B show identical production possibility curves in 1994. If a nation allocates its production of capital goods and consumer goods at point A of panel A, in 10 years it will be at PPC$_{2004}$. If it allocates its production of capital goods and consumer goods at point B of panel B, in 10 years it will be at much higher PPC$_{2004}$.

Our Low Rate of Investment   To increase our output at a satisfactory rate, we need to keep replacing worn-out and obsolete capital with the most up-to-date and technologically advanced plant, equipment, and software. And we need not only to replace the capital that we've cast off, but also to keep increasing our capital stock.

Do you recall the production possibilities curves from Chapter 2? Figure 4 reproduces a few of them. The production possibilities curve provides a snapshot of our economy at full employment producing just two types of goods. Here they're capital goods and consumer goods. A country that devotes a higher proportion of its resources to capital goods than to consumer goods will grow faster than another country that initially has the same production possibilities curve but emphasizes consumer goods.

As you can see, the country shown in Figure 4B has a much higher rate of growth than the one in Figure 4A. And the reason why it has enjoyed this relatively high growth should be obvious. Perhaps the two countries in question are the United States and China (leaving aside the fact that China's economy is just a fraction of the size of ours). The lesson our nation must learn is that until we begin to devote more resources to capital goods production and less to consumer goods production, our growth rate will be lower than it would have otherwise been.

We have depended on foreign investors to provide us with some of *their* savings. And where did they get all those dollars? We supplied them ourselves by running massive trade deficits in recent years. As long as foreigners are willing to accept our dollars in payment for these trade deficits and to send most of them back to us in the form of investment, we can keep our financial heads above water. But as long-time former Federal Reserve chairman Alan Greenspan has repeatedly warned, foreigners will not be willing to accommodate us forever.

How Labor Force Changes Affect Productivity Growth

In 1870, American, German, French, Japanese, and British workers averaged nearly 3,000 hours a year on the job. Now it is less than 2,000 hours, with much of the decline having come since World War II. How does our labor force stack up against those of the rest of the industrial world? Are we growing flabby and complacent? Some things

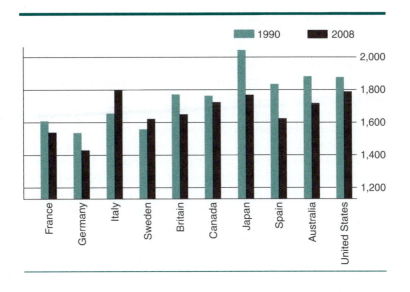

Figure 5

Average Number of Hours per Employed Person in Selected Countries, 1990 and 2008

Two things stand out here. First, in each of these countries—with the exception of Italy—the average person worked fewer hours in 2008 than in 1990. And second, Americans worked longer hours than workers of each of the other countries—again, with the exception of Italy. Indeed, the average American worker put in 360 hours a year more than the average German worker.

Source: OECD

are easier to measure than others, so we'll start with the easiest: the declining average workweek.

(1) The Average Workweek and Workyear In 1900 the average workweek was 60 hours, and less than 2 percent of Americans took vacations. Today most people put in the standard nine-to-five (or eight-to-four) with an hour for lunch. Until the 1920s most Americans were putting in a six-day week. From there we went to a standard Monday-to-Friday plus half a day on Saturday, and finally, by the late 1940s, we got it down to the five-day week.

In the 1950s, if George Washington's birthday fell on a Saturday, you had to celebrate on your own time. But today his birthday (as well as several other holidays) is celebrated on Monday, ensuring that almost everyone not only has the day off but also gets to enjoy a three-day weekend. In fact, most full-time workers are guaranteed 10 paid holidays. When you figure in vacation time, paid sick leave, and personal leave, it's a wonder anyone ever has to show up to work at all. And if you run out of sick leave, you can always call in dead.

I really don't mean to give you the impression that Americans are a nation of slackers, because the average American works longer hours than her counterpart in nearly every other large industrialized nation (see Figure 5). There was a significant drop-off in hours worked in most of these nations since 1990, but it is clear that Americans are among the world's hardest working people. While Americans average just two weeks of paid vacation a year, Western Europeans average five or six weeks. And then there are all those off-the-clock hours on company business that so many workers put in on the phone and at their home computers.

What is the effect of all these long working hours on productivity? Employers may be aware that after working more than a certain number of hours their employees becomes less productive. But in these times of fierce global competition, many employers squeeze their workers well beyond that point.

(2) Our Failing Educational System *"I didn't meet the bar. But I think truly and honestly it has no relevancy to what I do every day."*—Wilfredo Laboy, the school superintendent of Lawrence, Mass., on failing a basic literacy test for the third time.

Because we were the first nation to provide free universal public education, our well-trained and educated labor force gave us a huge competitive advantage in the emerging global economy during the first decades of the 20th century. But in the decades after World War II, not only were the educational systems of other developed nations improving, but ours was getting a lot worse. In 1982 the National Commission on Excellence in Education, which was appointed by President Ronald Reagan, reported that the United

States was failing to meet the needs of the competitive workforce. It most famously said that a "rising tide of mediocrity" was threatening our nation. That was then. And now? Now our public educational system has gotten still worse. Here's one fact that says it all: Less than half of our high school graduates can function at an eighth grade level.

Business firms are having trouble finding secretaries who can spell and put together grammatically correct sentences. Law firms spend millions of dollars teaching their attorneys how to write. And fast-food restaurant chains have found it necessary to place pictures of burgers, fries, sodas, and other items on their cash registers because so many of their clerks are numerically challenged.

More people are going to college, but our labor force is less educated.

It is truly paradoxical that at a time when more people than ever are attending college and millions of them are graduating every year, our labor force is less well-educated than those of previous generations. So I'll resolve the paradox. Our educational leaders figured out that they could get more students through the educational system by lowering standards every 10 or 15 years—kind of like a reverse game of limbo. They kept lowering the limbo stick and letting people step *over* it instead of having to squeeze *under* it. Peer pressure ("Don't appear too smart, or we won't accept you"), television (watching sitcoms rather than reading books), and less parental supervision (one-parent families or two parents holding down jobs) have also taken a toll. Did I leave out video games?

Given the product of our educational system, it is no great surprise that the quality of our labor force has been derided, especially in comparison with those of other leading industrial nations. In an age when literacy, numerical skills, and problem-solving ability are crucial in the workplace, our schools are failing us.

Let no child be left behind.
—President George W. Bush

There is something very wrong with the way our children learn. By the time they reach high school, most of them still cannot do simple arithmetic without a calculator, and when they enter college, more than one out of three freshmen must enroll in at least one remedial course (at some community colleges, it's 9 out of 10). If this is called higher education, one shudders to think of what is happening on the lower levels.

A large and growing number of 18-year-olds are entering an increasingly high-tech labor market, unable to find jobs that pay much more than the minimum wage rate of $7.25 an hour. This is the other half—those who don't go to college. Several Western European nations, most notably Germany, have work-study programs for most teenagers who are not planning to enroll in college. They are awarded certificates of competence upon completing these programs, which often lead to relatively high-paying technical jobs.

Basically the dominant competitive weapon of the 21st century will be the education and skills of the work force.

—Lester Thurow, former dean, MIT Sloan School of Management

On the plus side, despite their lagging academic performance, our high school students have not suffered any loss of self-esteem. Our 12th graders rank in the 10th percentile (i.e., the lowest 10 percent) in math globally, but first in their opinion of their own math skills.

Despite all our educational problems, however, the United States must be doing something right. Although the United States has less than 5 percent of the world's population, since 2000 Americans won over 90 percent of the Nobel Prizes in economics, over 60 percent in physics, and over half in medicine. And the United States has captured sizable world leads in many knowledge industries—computers, telecommunications, and finance. Clearly, the upper stratum of our work force is very smart and well educated. But what about the rest of us? (See the box, "The Best and the Brightest.")

The key to maintaining our technological edge is in continuing to produce sufficient numbers of engineers. American colleges award 70,000 undergraduate degrees in engineering, compared with 600,000 in China and 350,000 in India. About half of our graduating engineers are foreign-born. And American universities award 25 percent of all their PhDs in science and engineering to Chinese citizens, and an additional 35 percent to citizens of other countries.

Over the last 10 years many states have abolished automatic promotion, and several have introduced competency exams at various grade levels. Many school systems have gone "back to basics," a movement which stresses mastering reading, writing, and arithmetic in the early grades. The charter school movement (which provides autonomy from local school boards for individual schools) and the growing popularity of private schools

The Best and the Brightest

The Intel Science Talent Search is an annual competition among the nation's brightest high school seniors. Ten of the 40 finalists in 2005 had perfect 1600 scores on their SATs. Of course those who made it into the final 40 did not receive even one-tenth of 1 percent of the media coverage of the NCAA basketball tournament's final four. But hey! This is America, where the jocks trump the nerds every day of the year. Not that I'm criticizing.

Craig R. Barrett, CEO of Intel, notes that even after decades of lamenting America's relatively poor skills in math, science, and engineering, "we still do a very, very poor job of educating our kids." Comparing high school graduates in the world's top 25 countries, he says, "an American kid is, on average, near the bottom 10 percent."*

Over the last decade about one-quarter of the Intel finalists were immigrants, and half were the children of immigrants. Research by the National Foundation for American Policy in Arlington, Virginia, indicates that 60 percent of the nation's top science and math students are children of immigrants. So, if you want to do well in these subjects, you would do well to be born in a foreign country, or at least have parents who were.

At the elite high schools around the country we have thousands of students doing research with atom smashers, fiber-optics, DNA, stem-cells, and nanotechnology. But what about the rest of us? What about the fact that half of all high school math and science teachers are unqualified to teach their subjects? And that about one-half of all American 18-year-olds cannot do simple arithmetic?

*Otis Port, with John Clary, "Meet the Best and Brightest," *BusinessWeek*, March 22, 2005, p. 88. See also, www.businessweek.com/go/sts.

(most notably the Edison project) are promising developments. There is also growing support for school vouchers—a very controversial initiative—which would give parents a range of choices of public and private schools, rather than having to send their children to the local public school. Whatever the results of these reforms, there is virtual agreement that an improving educational system holds the key to high productivity growth, and ultimately, to a high rate of economic growth.

(3) The Permanent Underclass: Poverty, Drugs, and Crime

One of the major factors holding down our growth rate is a permanent underclass of nearly 10 percent of our population. Most of these people are supported by our tax dollars, and many are members of third- and fourth-generation welfare families. No other industrialized nation in the world has such a large dependent population.

We have a permanent underclass constituting 10 percent of our population.

Closely associated with poverty are drugs and crime. Although poor people are much more likely than any other population group to be afflicted by both drugs and crime, these problems have affected the life of nearly every American. No community is free of either drugs or crime, and they have taken an enormous toll, both economically and socially. Although we cannot quantify how the related problems of poverty, drugs, and crime have affected our rate of economic growth, they have clearly played a major role in lowering productivity and output, as well as our quality of life.

Poverty amidst plenty is an apt description of America today. Although we try to avoid making value judgments in economics, it is amazing that so few Americans feel an urgent need to alleviate the poverty that is all around us. The homeless, especially in the downtown areas of large cities, have become invisible to most of us as we pass them by.

Poverty amid plenty

Just to begin to wipe out poverty and eradicate the epidemics of drugs and crime would take a massive effort. Somehow these 25 million Americans must be rewoven into our social fabric and become fully integrated, self-supporting members of our labor force. But there are signs since the mid-1990s that some of these disturbing trends have been reversed. The welfare rolls have been cut by more than 60 percent and the crime rate has fallen substantially all across the country.

(4) Restrictions on Immigration

To say this country was literally built by immigrants would be no exaggeration. Immigration has been a tremendous source of strength to our nation. Even though immigrant families were always willing to start out on the

This country was built by immigrants.

bottom rung of the economic ladder and work their way up, the rise of "native American" groups eventually led to severe restrictions on the number of people allowed into this country.

The Daughters of the American Revolution, many of whom trace their ancestry back to the Mayflower, used to invite the president of the United States to address them every year. In 1933 Franklin Roosevelt, whose forebears arrived in New York while it was still a Dutch colony, was invited to speak. His first words were, "Fellow immigrants." Needless to say, the Daughters never asked him back.

Roosevelt's point, of course, was that we are indeed a nation of immigrants—regardless of when our families arrived. And each new wave of immigrants—whether from Europe, Africa, Latin America, or Asia—worked hard so that their children would have a better life. Hard work and deferred gratification were the hallmarks of each immigrant group.

Before the early 1920s, when a series of increasingly restrictive immigration laws were passed, virtually anyone who wanted to come here was welcome.[2] In the early years of the 20th century, close to a million people came here each year, mostly from eastern and southern Europe. The prime motivation in restricting their numbers was to prevent further dilution of our vaunted northern European stock.

Immigrants are usually in their 20s or 30s, and they tend to be more adventurous, ambitious, and upwardly mobile than those who stay behind. As an added bonus, their educations have already been completed, so we reap the benefits while their native countries bear the costs. This phenomenon has been termed the *brain drain*.

Immigrants are often willing to work 14 to 16 hours a day, seven days a week. Within a couple of years, an immigrant has typically saved enough to open a small business. They may never get rich, but their children will go to college.

Until the 1920s immigrants were a tremendous source of economic strength. Not only did they help build the railroads, settle the West, staff the factories, and set up businesses, but they provided the energy, the ambition, and the drive that were often lacking in native-born Americans.

Today, with legal immigration restricted to slightly over 800,000 people a year, we are deprived of much of what made our economy go. There is no way to quantify how much this has cost us in terms of economic growth, but a remark overheard in the giant Hunts Point produce market in the Bronx sums it up well. An older man pointed at a hard-working Korean vegetable store owner and said to his friend, "*He* works like our *grandfathers* used to work."

Today nearly one-third of the entrepreneurs and higher-level employees in Silicon Valley come from overseas. Indians started some of the Valley's most famous companies—Vinod Khosla of Sun Microsystems and Sabeer Bhatia of Hotmail, for example—and together with Chinese entrepreneurs were responsible in 2008 for nearly one-third of the Valley's new start-ups, creating 60,000 jobs.

Because of much tighter entry restrictions since 9/11, people seeking to visit the United States have faced much longer waits for approval, and many more are refused visas. In the year 2000, we gave almost 300,000 temporary visas to people working and studying in scientific and technical areas; that number is down to half that today.

But our basic problem with respect to immigration dates back to 1965, when immigration policy became heavily titled toward reunited families. Since then more than 70 percent of each year's immigrant visas are granted to reunify families, while only 20 percent are reserved for professionals and other skilled workers. Still, there had been a temporary hike to 195,000 visas in 2001 for technical and professional workers for jobs that Americans could not fill, but by 2007 the cap dropped back to 65,000. If we are determined to restrict immigration, we would do well to follow Canada's example; 54 percent of its immigrants are skilled workers. New Zealand allows some companies to hand out work visas along

---

[2]Everyone, that is, except people from China and Japan. Fewer than 100 a year were allowed in under law and by the so-called Gentlemen's Agreement as well as the Chinese Exclusion Act of 1882. Just to be even-handed (I'm saying this tongue-in-cheek), Congress enacted the Immigration Act of 1924, whose quotas tried to limit Italian and Jewish immigration. From 1924 until after World War II, no one from Japan or China was allowed to enter the United States.

with job offers. And Britain gives graduates of the world's top 50 business schools an automatic right to work in the country for a year.

Testifying before the U.S. Senate in 2007, Microsoft chairman Bill Gates told the lawmakers that, "It makes no sense to tell well-trained, highly skilled individuals—many of whom are educated at our top universities—that the U.S. does not welcome or value them." After his plea for increasing the number of H-1B visas fell upon deaf ears, Gates's company opened an office just a few miles over the Canadian border in Richmond, British Columbia, and went about hiring hundreds of workers who had been unable to obtain American visas.

The Role of Technological Change

Way back in Chapter 2, we saw that there are two basic ways to attain economic growth: (1) more inputs of capital and labor and (2) technological change. So far we've been talking about capital and labor. Now we'll turn to technological change.

Economic growth rate is largely determined by the rate of technological change.

The rate of technological change may well be the single most important determinant of a nation's rate of economic growth. Technological change enables us to produce more output from the same package of resources or, alternatively, to produce the same output with fewer resources. Technological change could be the creation of new or better goods and services. It also includes greater efficiency in market processes, improvements in the qualities of resources, improved knowledge about how to combine resources, and the introduction of new production processes.

A nation's educational system plays a basic role in promoting a high rate of technological change. How well trained are its scientists and engineers, and how many graduate each year? How well trained are its workforce, its industrial managers, and its marketing people?

Over the last 20 years computer literacy has increased exponentially. Today more than four-fifths of all American homes have at least one personal computer and most ten-year-olds can use computers for a multitude of activities. And so, as basic reading, writing, and math skills have declined, computer skills have increased dramatically.

How has computerization affected productivity? Two statements by Nobel Prize–winner Robert Solow may lend some insight. In 1987 he said, "You can see the computer age everywhere but in the productivity statistics." In 2000 he said, "You can now see computers in the productivity statistics." Between 1973 and 1995 the annual rate of productivity growth was about 1.5 percent, and it has since almost doubled. But how much of this increase was due to computerization? The most comprehensive study of this question was conducted by two economists at the Federal Reserve, Stephen Oliner and Daniel Sichel, who concluded that computers were responsible for as much as two-thirds of this increase.[3]

What is the tangible impact of the computer and the Internet? Many industries are benefiting: airlines and theaters through ticket sales on the Web, retailers through e-commerce, Wall Street through online trading. Internet retail sales have been growing at double-digit rates and by 2009 made up 7 percent of overall retail revenue. Perhaps most significant is business-to-business (B2B) commerce on the Internet, which has cut purchasing costs of some firms by as much as one-third. B2B transactions have risen from just $45 billion in 1998 to over $7 trillion in 2009.

Here are a few tangible examples of how information technology has boosted productivity:

- It costs FedEx $2.40 to track a package for a customer who calls by phone, but just 4 cents for one who visits its website. The company now gets more than 3 million online tracking requests a day, compared with only 20,000 to 30,000 by phone.

- Walmart developed a system for tracking inventories for every store and automatically restocking the shelves.

---

[3]"Economic Focus: Productivity on Stilts," *The Economist*, June 10, 2000, p. 86.

- The airlines have installed ATM-like machines at airports that deliver boarding passes, making do with fewer counter clerks, while cutting the cost of ticket processing from $10 to just $1.
- Bar codes save customers, retailers, and manufacturers $40 billion a year in the supermarket and mass-merchandise sectors.
- In 1970 some 421,000 telephone and switchboard operators were employed by the telecommunications industry when Americans made 9.8 billion calls. Today, thanks to advances in switching technology, we need less than 60,000 operators to handle over 120 billion calls.

What took so long for the introduction of computers to have such a major impact on productivity? For one thing, it wasn't enough for a company to just buy a bunch of computers. Employees needed time to learn how to use them, and whole computer networks needed to be built up. The Internet, which has been so vital to computerization, was not all that widely used until the mid-1990s, when productivity growth doubled. Referring to the introduction of a new technology such as computerization, Thomas Friedman observed, ". . . it always takes time for all the flanking technologies, and the business processes and habits needed to get the most out of them, to converge and create that next productivity breakthrough."[4]

Globalization, of course, has had a profound effect on productivity. As lower-priced technology flooded the marketplace, it helped generate new jobs, as companies that snapped up computers suddenly required software and workers who could adapt the products to their needs. Furthermore, in order to continue to live and prosper in a global economy, American firms had to become much leaner and meaner. Their very survival depended on significantly boosting productivity.

Our Inefficient Transportation System

For most of our history, we have had a first-rate transportation system. The early 19th century was the era of canal building, and during the last third of the century we built a transcontinental railroad system, which made possible our mass production and mass consumption economy. Before the century was over, every large urban area had a well-run mass transit system of trains and trolleys.

Well into the 1900s, ours was the world's best transportation system, enabling people to travel quickly, comfortably, and cheaply, not just within urban areas, but all the way across our vast country. Freight, too, was moved quickly and economically by rail.

But then, in the decades after World War II, our nation suburbanized. Housing, shopping malls, factories, and office parks were scattered across the suburban landscape. Consequently, the only way to get around was by car. And because factories and shopping districts were no longer concentrated in the downtowns of our large cities, trucking replaced the rail transportation as our primary shipper of freight.

We let our world-class railways deteriorate, while our economic competitors built up their own systems. Today, we are the only advanced economy without a high-speed rail system.

Our oil production, which peaked in 1970, has been declining for the last four decades, while our demand for oil has risen exponentially. We now must import two thirds of our oil. Had we maintained our excellent public transportation system, we would still be exporting oil instead of having to import so much of it.

How has our inefficient transportation system held down our economic growth? We need to devote a much larger percentage of our GDP to transportation than any of our global competitors. These resources, which we expend on oil, cars, highway building and maintenance, as well as on the paving of millions of acres of parking lots, could have been put to much better use in other sectors of our economy.

---

[4]Thomas Friedman, *The World Is Flat* (New York: Farrar, Straus and Giroux, 2005), p. 177.

Our Bloated Health Care System

We have the greatest health care system in the world.
— Senator Richard Shelby, Republican, Alabama

America arguably has the best health care system in the world, and clearly the most expensive. But are we getting the maximum bang for our health care buck? Not even close.

We rank at or near the bottom in terms of life expectancy, infant mortality, and overall medical coverage. Not only do we spend more than any other country per person for health care, but we are the only rich country that doesn't provide universal health care. Some 49 million Americans have no medical insurance. But we do lead the world in administrative costs and in hours spent filling out medical forms.

- In 1950 the country spent less than $500 in today's dollars on the average person's medical care, compared to nearly $7,000 today.
- Since the year 2000, health care costs have been rising more than four times the rate of inflation.
- We have fewer doctors per capita than most other rich countries.
- The United States spends almost twice as much per capita on health care as most other wealthy countries.

Our rapidly rising health care costs impose a tremendous burden on taxpayers, who foot the bill for Medicare and Medicaid, on private employers, who must shell out hundreds of billions of dollars in medical insurance premiums, and on individual Americans who pay the balance.

The United States spends much more on health care per capita (see Figure 6) than any other economically advanced nation, but the quality of that care has come under heavy criticism. One out of every six dollars of our GDP goes toward health care, but we are clearly getting less per dollar than the citizens of every other industrial country (see Figure 6). Again, while there is no way of quantifying how much the inefficiencies of our health care system have slowed our economic growth, they have clearly played a major role (see the box, "A Visit to the Doctor's Office").

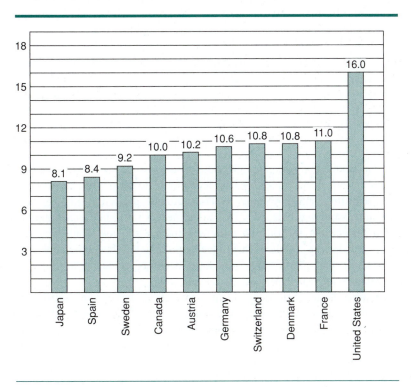

Figure 6

Health Care Spending as a Percentage of GDP, the Top Ten Countries, 2008
Source: World Trade Organization, 2009

A Visit to the Doctor's Office

Are you ready for another "I am old enough to remember" story? When I was a kid, Dr. Rubinstein was our family doctor, and his nurse was Mrs. Plotkin. Perhaps every other year, the third week in September, I would have such a bad asthma attack that I could barely breathe. My mother would be on the phone with Mrs. Plotkin, and within an hour, Dr. Rubinstein would come by, give me an injection, and in seconds I was able to breathe again. I think he charged around $10 for house calls.

Today, of course, few doctors make house calls. You have two options—drag yourself to the emergency room of the closest hospital, or call the EMS and go to the hospital by ambulance. Of course, if you're poor, you might well consider the hospital emergency room to be your family doctor's office.

Doctors' offices have changed radically in recent decades. No longer do you have just a doctor and nurse in a three-room office, with a reception area, an examination room, and the doctor's private office with all her diplomas. Now you've got three or four additional employees, who spend nearly all of their time filling out insurance forms or talking on the phone with insurance companies.

When you call for a doctor's appointment, what's the first question you're asked? You're asked, "What kind of insurance do you have?"

And when you're sitting there in the waiting room, you can hear someone on the phone talking to someone at Oxford, Blue Cross, or another insurance company discussing coverage and reimbursement. Multiply this conversation by the hundreds of thousands that are taking place between doctor's offices and insurance companies all over the country and think of the resources being used to fill out an unending stream of insurance forms. Back in the good old days, none of these jobs even existed and there were no forms to fill out, and no claims to be submitted. It was just the patients, the doctor, and the nurse in a quiet three-room office.

So exactly what's going on here? Why is medical care so different from back in the good old days? Why are doctors so harried, rushing from one examination room to another? Indeed, when did medical practices come to resemble factory assembly lines?

More than anything else, the advent of medical insurance has driven health care costs through the roof. Many doctors need to pay over $100,000 a year for malpractice insurance. But more visible to the patient, every medical office must employ people to deal with insurance companies. This necessitates not only putting more people on the payroll, but paying a higher rent for more office space. Because of this huge overhead, doctors are driven to work much longer hours and to see more patients per hour.

Think about just covering the rent. Fifty years ago, a doctor charged about $10 for an office visit and paid, say, $200 a month rent. So he could cover his rent by seeing 20 patients. Today, that doctor might get $100 per patient (including insurance company reimbursement and a patient's co-payment), but pays $4,000 in rent. And the doctor must also pay the salaries and health care insurance costs of all his employees. Do the math.

Back in the 1950s, before Medicare, Medicaid, and before the rise of the huge private insurance bureaucracies, medical care was on a pay-as-you-go basis. Now, an operation or even a simple medical procedure unleashes a flood of paperwork. As you get older and your medical problems increase, you may need a secretary to handle all your insurance claims. That would free up more of your time to spend in your doctor's waiting room.

When labor and management negotiate a new collective bargaining agreement, the most contentious issue is usually who is responsible for paying the workers' health insurance premiums. By 2009 the average annual premium employers paid for employee family coverage was $13,000. Since health insurance premiums have been rising much faster than the rate of inflation, employers have been very anxious to contain this cost. Indeed, medical insurance premiums have become such a large cost of doing business that many employers have become increasingly reluctant to hire new employees.

Health care costs are high today not just because of high administrative costs. Since insurance providers pay doctors on a fee-for-service-provided basis, the more procedures and tests they provide, the more they are paid. So there is a very strong incentive to do more tests and procedures—whether or not they are needed. And then too, the fear of being sued for malpractice if they don't provide every possible treatment—whether medically necessary or not—further inflates our health care bill.

Finally, most patients, who have some kind of insurance, treat their medical care as if it were a free service. Like the customer at an all-you-can-eat buffet, we consume a lot more than we would if we had to pay for each item. And why *not?* It's *free,* isn't it?

The Shift to a Service Economy

Through the 1970s and 1980s most of our productivity growth was in the manufacturing sector, which was being pushed to the wall by foreign competition. But productivity growth in services was low to nonexistent. Can you think of a service worker whose productivity has not grown at all over time? In a *New Yorker* piece, James Surowiecki observed that:

> In a number of industries, workers produce about as much per hour as they did a decade or two ago. The average college professor can't grade papers or give lectures any faster today than he did in the early nineties. It takes a waiter just as long to serve a meal, and a car-repair guy just as long to fix a radiator hose.[5]

New York University Professor William Baumol has argued that any service—health care, law, education, social work—is inherently labor intensive. He used as an example the playing of Mozart's string quartets, which have been performed countless times since the composer's death in 1791. Playing one of his quartets still requires four instruments and four players and the same number of minutes. No way has ever been found to make this process more efficient. Similarly, despite all the medical advances in recent decades, doctors still examine just one patient at a time, while surgeons perform just one operation at a time.

This phenomenon has been named "Baumol's Disease." He believed that because productivity growth in the labor-intensive service sector tends to lag behind manufacturing productivity growth, costs in service-related businesses end up increasing over time. Baumol predicted that the share of GDP spent on health care would rise from 11.6 percent in 1990 to 35 percent in 2040. By 2009, health care's share had already reached 17 percent. While the cost of many manufactured goods have declined, the cost of health care has increased much faster than the rate of inflation. Indeed, since 1948 the cost of a day in the hospital has risen 700 percent in dollars of constant purchasing power. If a cure is not found for Baumol's Disease, then the not-too-distant future shock of the baby boomers' health care needs may drag down productivity gains in the coming decades.

As you may have noticed, college tuition, like the cost of health care, has been increasing much faster than the rate of inflation. College administrators have come up with a great way to increase productivity: pack more students into each class. The most efficient producers, then, would be the professors who teach hundreds of students in huge lecture halls. There are students who not only have never met their professors, but are sitting so far back that they can barely *see* them either. A few years ago I may have hit upon a new way to increase professorial productivity. When our academic vice president asked me how I intended to make up for a class I missed, I said that for the rest of the semester I would talk faster. Can you think of any other jobs in the service sector subject to Baumol's Disease?

Additional Factors Affecting Our Rate of Growth

Since the early 1970s various other factors retarding our rate of economic growth have come into play: higher energy costs, environmental protection requirements, health and safety regulations, high military spending, the effects of 9/11, and the

Factors retarding our growth rate are higher energy costs, environmental protection requirements, health and safety regulations, rising health care costs, the effects of 9/11, military spending, and others.

---

[5]James Surowiecki, "What Ails Us," *The New Yorker,* July 7, 2003, p. 27.

influence of special interest groups. When the OPEC nations quadrupled the price of oil in 1973, this not only set off a severe inflationary recession, but it permanently raised the cost of doing business and somewhat retarded our rate of growth. Similarly, environmental protection legislation requiring the expenditure of tens of billions of dollars to reduce air and water pollution also slowed economic growth. And then, too, new health and safety regulations—some of which were relaxed in the 1980s—ate up billions of dollars that would have otherwise been invested in plant and equipment or research and development.

None of this is to say that environmental protection and health and safety measures were not needed. Indeed, they probably reduced medical expenses and sick time significantly, while substantially improving the quality of our lives. But they did divert resources from investment, consequently slowing our rate of growth perhaps by as much as 1 percent a year.

The effect of military spending

Like soaring health care and transportation costs, high military spending has been a drag on our economic growth. Between the close of World War II in 1945 and the end of the cold war in 1990, we devoted about 6 percent of our GDP to defense. Japan, whose economy grew much more rapidly during this period, held military spending to less than 1 percent. Resources that would have otherwise been used to produce capital goods and consumer goods and services were instead expended on military salaries, weapons systems, guns, bullets, and bombs. With the collapse of the Soviet Union and its satellite empire in Eastern Europe, we were finally able to cut defense spending to just 3 percent of GDP by the start of the new millennium. But after 9/11 when the terrorists struck, our defense spending began going right back up again. In 2009 we devoted more than 5 percent of our GDP to military spending.

Perhaps one-third of our military spending is directed towards ensuring an uninterrupted flow of oil to our shores. Because our transportation system is fueled mainly by oil, and our domestic production has been declining for the last 40 years, we must now import two thirds of the oil we consume. To safeguard the flow of oil to the United States, our navy patrols the major shipping routes, while our armed forces maintain military bases around the globe. Many argue that the two wars we fought with Iraq since 1990 were largely about oil. In sum, our tremendous need for imported oil largely explains why we spend as much on defense as the rest of the world put together.

Emblematic of our heavy dependency on oil was the tragic Deepwater Horizon explosion on April 20, 2010, which killed 11 crew members, and set off an environmental disaster. More than two months later BP (formerly British Petroleum) had not yet been able to cap the well, which continued to spew millions of gallons of oil into the Gulf of Mexico.

Perhaps the worst oil spill in history, it is not only destroying marine life, fishing, and bathing across a wide swath of the Gulf, but its effects will linger for decades. While there is no shortage of blameworthy villains, perhaps the most guilty party is the American driver, who consumes huge quantities of gasoline. This dependency, in turn, can be traced to our post-World War II suburbanization, which was based on a cheap and reliable supply of oil. Perhaps the only salutary effect of this disaster is that we will no longer be subjected to the idiotic mantra, "Drill, baby, drill!"

Most developed nations have experienced an eventual slowing of their growth rate. Mancur Olson, in his study titled *The Rise and Decline of Nations,* concludes that special interest groups—particularly labor unions, farmers' cooperatives, and employers' associations—become stronger as the economy grows.[6] These groups then make it more difficult to introduce new technologies that could continue to increase growth. For example, the International Longshoremen's Union prevented the containerization of freight for years until the shippers offered them an extremely lucrative retirement plan. And the farmers have persuaded Congress to provide them with $19 billion a year in price supports and subsidies.

Labor unions, corporate political action committees (PACs), trade associations, as well as myriad other groups all have their own special interests to promote. Teachers want generous pay increases and tenure protection, agribusinesses want crop subsidies,

---

[6]Mancur Olson, *The Rise and Decline of Nations* (New Haven, CT: Yale University Press, 1982).

Global Warming and Economic Growth

As former Vice President Al Gore has put it, global warming is "an inconvenient truth." During the last century the temperature of the earth's surface warmed by about 1 degree Fahrenheit. This warming was caused by an accumulation in the atmosphere of carbon dioxide and other gas emissions from cars and trucks, power plants, factories, and anything else that involved the burning of fossil fuels such as oil and coal.

These atmospheric gases created a greenhouse effect, which is trapping heat on our planet the same way a greenhouse traps heat. The warming rays of the sun are let in, but their heat is retained. By mid-century, average temperatures may be 2 or 3 degrees higher.

The polar ice caps will continue to melt, ocean levels will rise by perhaps 2 feet, and many coastal areas will be flooded. There may be fairly drastic climatic changes as well as more violent hurricanes and tornadoes. Global warming may incur huge worldwide economic costs, perhaps amounting to hundreds of billions—or even trillions—of dollars a year.

All of this raises the question: what can we *do* about global warming? The short—and very alarming—answer is that it's already too late. Even if all carbon emissions were stopped today, the earth would continue to warm for at least another century. So the best we could do, then, is to begin to curb these emissions and limit the damage.

Among the ways to accomplish this are a carbon tax, a system of trading emissions permits, a shift to nuclear energy, stricter automobile fuel efficiency standards, and more subsidized public transportation. We could employ our best scientists to seek out new solutions just as we employed our best physicists to build an atomic bomb during the Second World War.

All of these solutions, as well as dozens of others, would be very costly. But do we really have any choice? If we take no action, then in the decades ahead, our lives will be very unpleasantly impacted by the effects of global warming.

I can't help being reminded of a classic Jack Benny joke. Benny was a very popular comedian in the 1940s and 1950s, who had a well known reputation for cheapness. One day a robber pulled a gun on him and demanded, "Your money or your life!" When Benny didn't immediately reply, the robber stated even more emphatically, "Your *money* or your *life!*" After a couple of seconds, Benny replied, "I'm *thinking, I'm thinking.*"

Although we are the world's leading producer of harmful emissions, China, which is building one new coal burning power plant a week, will soon surpass us. In the coming years, China, India, Brazil, Indonesia, and other industrializing nations are on their way to becoming the dominant producers of greenhouse gases for decades to come. And so, any plans to curb their emission must include these nations as well as the more economically advanced nations.

and defense contractors want multibillion dollar weapons spending programs. When Congress debated health care reform in late 2009, thousands of lobbyists descended upon the Capitol. Meanwhile, pharmaceutical companies, medical associations, hospitals, health care insurers, and other special interest groups spent over $1 million a day trying to influence wavering members of Congress.

Finally we'll consider the effects of global warming and how dealing with it would affect economic growth (see box). For decades, political leaders around the world denied that there was such a thing as global warming, and then, when the scientific evidence of its existence became overwhelming, they hesitated to take the necessary measures because of their economic cost. But, like rock 'n' roll, global warming is here to stay, and whether we deal with it or not, it will have an increasingly important effect on worldwide economic growth.

Summary

We've talked about a multitude of factors affecting our productivity, but we need a more integrated explanation of why our productivity growth was so low from the 1970s to the 1980s and why it picked up again.

1. *Our low savings rate*   In addition to our low personal savings rate, the federal government ran huge deficits until the mid-1990s. Since 2001 we have had mounting federal deficits and extremely low personal savings.

2. *Our low rate of investment*   Net domestic investment trended downward from the late 1960s until 1992, when it began to rise sharply. So the downward trends in both savings and investment tended to depress productivity growth in the 1970s, 1980s, and the early 1990s.

3. *The rising quantity of labor*   The average workweek, which had been declining in the 1950s and 1960s, stopped falling in the 1970s. Today Americans work more hours per year than their counterparts in every other economically advanced nation.

4. *The declining quality of labor*   Although more people than ever before are going to college, our educational standards today—from the first grade through college—are well below the standards we maintained 40 or 50 years ago. I realize that this viewpoint is controversial (there are many people who disagree with me), but we all agree that a good education is crucial to performing most jobs in today's high-tech economy. Although computer literacy is extremely high in this country, more than half of those entering the labor force are profoundly weak in reading, writing, and arithmetic—skills that are required in the workplace. So the declining quality of labor has had a long-term depressing effect on our productivity growth.

5. *The growth of the permanent underclass and its attendant problems of poverty, drugs, and crime*   This factor has also tended to depress productivity growth in the 1970s and 1980s. However, sharp declines in welfare dependency and crime since the early 1990s may have contributed to productivity growth over the last decade.

6. *Restrictions on immigration*   Immigration restrictions dating back to the 1920s may have lowered productivity growth. In recent decades we have been allowing a fairly large flow of relatively low-skilled immigrants into the country. Today Congress is debating what to do about the estimated 11 million illegal immigrants living here.

7. *Computerization*   The United States was computerized in the 1990s, and the long-awaited accompanying rise in productivity growth began to materialize in the second half of that decade. We may eventually conclude that computers have had an increasingly salutary effect on productivity since the mid- to late-1980s. The 1999 *Economic Report of the President* noted that "although the electric dynamo was invented well before the turn of the century, it did not seem to fuel large gains in productivity until many years later."[7] Productivity growth actually slowed between 1890 and 1913, but it increased rapidly between 1919 and 1929. If history repeats itself we should experience rapid productivity growth well into the first decades of the 21st century because of computerization.

8. *Military and other security spending*   A large and growing share of our resources is being spent not just on weaponry and research, past, current, and future wars, and homeland security, but on private security as well. The loss of these resources, which would otherwise have been used to raise economic growth, is holding down productivity gains.

9. *Globalization*   The spur of foreign competition forced manufacturing companies into being much more efficient, especially in the 1970s and 1980s, and more recently it has boosted efficiency in those service industries that were vulnerable.

10. *Our inefficient transportation system*   Since World War II, we have let our once excellent public transportation system deteriorate, while becoming almost completely dependent on automobiles. In addition, we are now moving most of our freight by truck rather than by rail. Consequently we have had to devote a much higher percentage of our GDP to moving people and freight than we did 60 years ago. Those resources might otherwise have been put to much more productive use.

11. *Our bloated health care system*   We spend almost double per capita what most of our global competitors spend on health care, but without better results. This is because of our exceedingly high administrative costs and the prescription and consumption of a huge amount of unneeded care. Had these wasted resources found

---

[7]Page 77.

more productive uses, our economic growth would have been much higher these past four or five decades.

12. *Global warming*   As the greenhouse effect becomes more pronounced, climate changes, rising ocean levels, and increasingly violent hurricanes and tornadoes will do huge amounts of economic damage. And then too, the cost of measures to mitigate global warming will slow economic growth by one- or two-tenths of a percent.

Why did productivity growth slow in the early 1970s? Was this slowdown caused by the oil price shock of 1973? The tens of millions of young baby boomers who were entering the labor force? The decline of manufacturing and the accompanying rise of the service sector? There is certainly no shortage of theories, and consequently, there is no clear consensus among economists. Although we don't know for sure why productivity growth declined in 1973, there is fairly widespread agreement about the causes of the sharp rise in productivity growth since 1995.

By 1995 the forces depressing our productivity growth were overwhelmed by the gains wrought by computerization and global competition. Computerization had reached the necessary critical mass to finally produce the long awaited burst in efficiencies. A large majority of adults had become computer proficient, and as the price of personal computer systems and other equipment such as smart cash registers fell sharply, nearly every business firm could afford them.

By the mid-1990s global competition, which had been confined mainly to manufacturing, was now affecting many of our service industries. In later chapters we'll discuss how scientific, engineering, clerical, legal, financial, medical, and customer service work has been flowing overseas. Like manufacturing firms in earlier decades, many service firms were now forced to compete, thus boosting their productivity.

But economists, by definition, are a pessimistic lot. Many of us look at rising military and other security spending, as well as the coming retirement of the baby boom generation and the projected rise in health care costs, and we think that these factors, among others, may slow productivity growth in future decades. But on the other hand, perhaps new innovations in such fields as nanotechnology, communications, medical research, or in some fields not yet imagined, will create the next wave of productivity growth.

Output per Employee: An International Comparison

Despite all the factors I've cited that have tended to hold down the productivity of our economy, by most measures, the American worker continues to be the most productive in the world. Figure 7 provides a comparison of the output of employees of the United States and four other nations. These five nations have the highest value added per employee in the world.

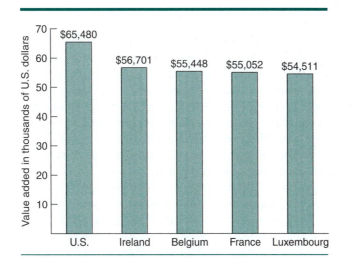

Figure 7

Value Added per Person Employed, U.S. and Other Leading Countries, 2008*

Source: International Labor Organization: www.ilo.org/global

*In 1990 U.S. dollars

As you've noticed, we're number one, and we have a substantial lead over the other four leading nations. There are two reasons why our workers have such a high output. Not only do we have a very high output per hour (which is the conventional measure of productivity), but we also work longer hours than the workers of nearly any other developed economy (glance back at Figure 5).

How do we rank in the world in terms of output per hour? It turns out that our workers, with an average output of $36.54, are in a virtual tie with those of Norway ($36.38) and France ($35.96).

Economic Growth in the Less Developed Countries

Well, enough about *our* problems. Now let's talk about other people's problems. Let's talk about people who *really* have problems—those who live in less developed countries (LDCs).

The world can be divided into three groups of countries: the industrialized nations, the newly industrializing countries (NICs), and the less developed countries (LDCs). The big question, then, is how to get from LDC to NIC and, ultimately, to industrialized. And, parenthetically, at what cost?

The only way to industrialize

The only way to industrialize is to build up capital in the form of new plant and equipment. There are two main ways of doing this: working more and consuming less. As some of the poor nations of the world are barely at subsistence level, it's pretty hard for them to consume less. And because there is often a great deal of unemployment in preponderantly agricultural economies, those who want to work more have a hard time finding work.

Each of the LDCs shown in Table 1 has a per capita GDP of less than $352. As it happens, the world's six poorest countries are in Africa. Not all the LDCs have per capita incomes as low as that, but nearly one-third of the world's population lives on less than $2 a day.

TABLE 1	The Poorest Countries in the World
Country	GDP Per Capita, 2009 ($ U.S.)
Congo, Dem. Rep.	$171
Burundi	174
Liberia	210
Guinea-Bissau	244
Zimbabwe	303
Malawi	352

Source: www.economywatch.com

Thomas Robert Malthus, English cleric and economist

Compounding the problems of the LDCs are rapidly growing populations. More than 200 years ago, an English economist named Thomas Robert Malthus predicted that the world's growth of food production would not be able to keep up with the growth of population (see the box, "The Malthusian Theory of Population"). The Malthusian dilemma—a food supply growing at an arithmetic rate and a population growing at a geometric rate—is becoming a reality in some of the nations of sub-Saharan Africa, as well as in a few countries in Asia and in Latin America. Hundreds of millions face starvation, with virtually no chance to substantially raise their food output. The recurrent famines in sub-Saharan Africa may be mere dress rehearsals for a future crisis of much greater dimension.

Even more alarming in the long run, the birthrates of less developed nations show little indication of declining. And unless they decline, the emergency shipments of foodstuffs from the rest of the world are merely postponing the inevitable.

More than three-quarters of the world's poor try to squeeze out a living on small family farms. In addition to their small plots of land, the main assets of these farmers

ADVANCED <u>WORK</u>

The Malthusian Theory of Population

Economics is called the "dismal science" largely because of the Malthusian theory. As it was originally formulated, the theory predicted that famine and warfare would, within perhaps a few generations, beset the world. This was inevitable because of a tendency for the world's population to double every 25 years.

Let's place the Malthusian theory in its historical context. At the end of the 18th century, Europe had grown very crowded. Since the amount of land that could be farmed was limited, what would happen as the population continued to increase?

The Reverend Thomas Robert Malthus wrote the first edition of the *Essay on the Principle of Population* in 1798. His two main points were that population tended to grow in a geometric progression—1, 2, 4, 8, 16, 32—and that the only ways to stop population from growing this rapidly were the "positive checks" of pestilence, famine, and war. Not a very pleasant outlook.

In his second edition, Malthus held out slightly more hope for holding down the rate of the population increase. It could be contained by the "preventive check" of "moral restraint," which meant not getting married until one could support a family (and, it went without saying, no fooling around before you got married).

Malthus also noted that the food supply could not increase as rapidly as population tended to because the planet was limited in size and there was only a fixed amount of arable land. He felt the food supply would ultimately tend to grow in an arithmetic progression—1, 2, 3, 4, 5, 6—and it would not take a mathematical genius to conclude that we would be in trouble within a few generations. The relevant figures are shown in the table below.*

Year	Food Production	Population
1800	1	1
1825	2	2
1850	3	4
1875	4	8
1900	5	16
1925	6	32

The Malthusian theory is a variant of the law of diminishing returns. As increasing amounts of labor are applied to a fixed amount of land, eventually marginal output will decline.

Was Malthus right? Surely not in the industrialized countries, particularly the United States, Canada, and Australia, which are major exporters of wheat and other farm products. Two things happened in these countries to ward off Malthus's dire predictions. First, because of tremendous technological advances in agriculture—tractors, harvesters, better fertilizer, and high-yield seeds—farmers were able to feed many more people.[†] Second, as industrialization spread and more and more people left the countryside for the cities, the birthrate fell.

However, the less developed countries are caught in a double bind. The Malthusian positive check of a high death rate has been largely removed by public health measures, such as malaria control, smallpox vaccine, and more sanitary garbage disposal. But because these countries have not yet been able to industrialize and urbanize their populations, birthrates remain high. In most of Asia, Africa, and Latin America, populations are doubling every 30 to 35 years, putting hundreds of millions of people in peril of starvation. Famine is a reality in these countries, and it may well become even more widespread in the coming decades.

Many see the AIDS epidemic, which has swept through much of sub-Saharan Africa, as a fulfillment of the Malthusian prophecy. In some countries as many as one in five people is infected with the HIV virus and may eventually die of AIDS. Even if the governments of the developed world and the major pharmaceutical companies make cheap or free vaccines available and somehow bring this epidemic under control, according to the Malthusian theory people in these same countries will eventually die of starvation. The only long-term solution, according to the followers of Malthus, would be to somehow bring down the extremely high birthrates in these countries.

---

*Malthus did not use actual years in his predictions; the years in the table are purely hypothetical to illustrate his theory. Also, Malthus did not predict that this would actually happen. Rather, he indicated that these were the tendencies, but that population increases could be checked by war, pestilence, famine, or moral restraint.

[†]Some observers have been encouraged by the so-called Green Revolution, which has enabled many large growers to double and triple yields by using better seeds and fertilizer. However, the prime beneficiaries have been the wealthy farmers and a few multinational agribusinesses, such as Dole, Del Monte, and Ralston Purina. They have profited by producing for export such crops as sugar, soybeans, bananas, and peanuts. But they have also forced millions of small farmers off the land and actually caused the production of indigenous food staples to decline, making these countries even more dependent on food imports.

are their children, who not only provide a ready supply of labor, but also the main source of support when the parents are too old to work. It follows, then, that the more children you have, the richer you are.

A family might have eight children, four of whom survive to adulthood—let's say, two sons and two daughters. But now we run into problems. While the two daughters will marry and move to other farms, the two sons stand to inherit the farm. Over generations, the farms are subdivided, until the typical farm is not large enough to support the people trying to live on it.

One way out of this dilemma may be the family planning programs that have been attempting to lower birthrates in the LDCs. Supported by government funding as well as grants from the Population Council, the International Planned Parenthood Federation, and the United Nations, the programs have had great success in lowering birthrates. In 1970 families in LDCs had an average of six children. Today that average is just three. With fewer mouths to feed, these countries now have more savings available for development.

Even *with* family planning programs, the populations of most LDCs continue to grow between 2 and 3 percent a year, and these countries must struggle to increase their food supplies at that rate just to keep pace. To industrialize, they would need to attain a high enough economic growth rate to be able to produce capital goods as well as the basic consumer necessities. Thus many LDCs clearly will never be able to begin industrializing without outside help.

Grants and loans from industrialized nations

There *is* one additional source of capital: grants and loans from the industrialized nations. Over the last four decades hundreds of billions of dollars have been provided by the United States, the Soviet Union, Western Europe, and Japan. But now that many LDCs are deeply in debt (some have defaulted on their loans), it is unlikely that more credit will be extended. In fact, the interest that must be paid out each year by the LDCs has become a tremendous burden.

During the 1980s some nations *did* attain the status of NIC. The "four tigers" of Asia—South Korea, Taiwan, Hong Kong, and Singapore—as well as Malaysia, Brazil, Indonesia, and Thailand have done this, largely through foreign investment.

Military spending and wars

Still another problem is that virtually all LDCs spend a major part of their budgets on armaments, which diverts desperately needed funds from development. Warfare in Southeast Asia, Afghanistan, the Congo, Ethiopia, Sudan, Peru, Somalia, and the Persian Gulf has further exacerbated the situation. The United States, the former Soviet Union, China, and several European nations have encouraged this unfortunate tendency by selling—or even giving—arms to developing nations.

China and India, the world's most populous nations, have made impressive strides toward development. Today almost one-half of the people in the world live in LDCs, and in those countries nearly half live at or near the subsistence level. Most live out their lives in abject poverty, with no hope that they or their children will have better lives.

Current Issue: Health Care Costs in the Coming Decades

It is said that we have the greatest health care system in the world, but maybe we need to take another look. Leaving aside our skyrocketing medical bills, let's compare the results of our system with those of other industrialized countries.

- American life expectancy is lower than average.
- Childhood immunization rates in the U.S. are lower than average.
- Infant mortality rates are higher than in 80 percent of the other countries.
- We have fewer doctors per capita and have fewer doctor visits per year.
- We are admitted to the hospital less frequently.
- Two-thirds of adults are overweight; one-third are obese.

Does *this* sound like better medical care? The next question: Do we get what we pay for? Not really. The U.S. spends more than $1,000 per year per capita just for health care-related paperwork and administration. Canada, where medical care is provided by the government, spends just $300 per person. And, of course, every other industrialized country insures all its citizens. Although we spend a lot more per capita on medical care, more than 46 million Americans are uninsured.

But that's the *good* news. The *bad* news begins when the baby boom generation enters retirement over the next two decades. That's when our health care bill will *really* go through the roof. And if you think we need to worry about the Social Security trust fund going bust, just wait till you see what happens to the Medicare trust fund.

An inefficient health care system and escalating health care costs are a tremendous drag on productivity growth, and consequently, on our economic growth. Unless we fix this malfunctioning system, our economic growth rate will continue to lag.

Here's my own suggestion for a partial quick fix. By introducing what's called a single payer system, we could eliminate most of the wasteful paperwork, phone calls, and the multitude of forms. That single payer would replace the hundreds of private insurance companies, managed care organizations, and government agencies. It could be a private company, or, more likely, a government agency.

This would relieve private employers of a tremendous financial obligation—insurance premiums that now average $13,000 for each employee's family. Not only are huge and growing health care premiums a disincentive to hiring additional employees, but they create a tremendous competitive disadvantage to American companies. By adding $1,500 to the cost of building every car, health care costs were a major cause of the bankruptcies at General Motors and Chrysler.

Questions for Further Thought and Discussion

1. How has our educational system affected the quality of our labor force?
2. Explain the Malthusian theory of population. Is it relevant today anywhere in the world? Explain where and why.
3. How does the American savings rate compare to that of other leading industrial nations? What accounts for the difference?
4. What changes took place during the Industrial Revolution that made possible sustained economic growth?
5. Why did our rate of productivity growth slow from the mid-1970s through the mid-1990s?
6. Why did our rate of productivity growth speed up in the late 1990s? Is this higher growth rate just temporary, or will it be sustained over the next 10 or 15 years?
7. Should we remove all barriers to immigration into the United States? What would be the consequences?
8. If we could let in an extra hundred thousand immigrants every year, should we favor certain immigrants over others? Why?
9. *Practical Application:* If you were hired as an efficiency consultant by a large corporation, list the measures you might take to raise the productivity of the workers.
10. *Practical Application:* In this chapter we have given some examples of Baumol's Disease. Can you think of two more examples that you have observed?
11. *Practical Application:* Looking at Figure 7 (on page 417), you'll see that the average output of American workers is more than $10,000 greater than that of French workers. Yet the average output per hour of French and American workers is about the same. Can you explain how this can be? Hint: Look at Figure 5 (on page 405).

Workbook for Chapter 16

Name _____   Date _____

Multiple-Choice Questions

Circle the letter that corresponds to the best answer.

1. Our rate of productivity increase in the 1980s was

   _____ the rate of productivity increase in the
   1960s. (LO2)
   a) faster than
   b) about
   c) slower than

2. Which one of the following statements is
   true? (LO5)
   a) America's immigration policies are much less
      restrictive today than they were 100 years ago.
   b) The fewer immigrants we let into the United
      States, the better off we'll be.
   c) The colleges in the United States graduate fewer
      engineers than those in China, India, and Japan.
   d) The United States and Canada have virtually
      identical immigration policies.

3. Each of the following except _____ slowed our

   rate of economic growth in the 1970s. (LO4)
   a) research and development spending
   b) pollution regulations and requiring pollution
      reduction
   c) health and safety regulations
   d) rising energy costs

4. The key to productivity growth is _____. (LO2)
   a) an increasing labor force
   b) technological change
   c) expansion of land under cultivation
   d) the use of deteriorating and obsolete capital

5. Rising productivity could be each of these except

   _____. (LO2)
   a) more units of output from more units of input
   b) more output per unit of input
   c) the same output from fewer units of input

6. Edward Denison attributes about _____ percent
   of our economic growth to increases in
   productivity. (LO2)
   a) 10   b) 30
   c) 50   d) 70
   e) 90

7. Almost half of the people in the world live in

   _____. (LO6)
   a) LDCs
   b) NICs
   c) industrialized countries

8. The Malthusian theory appears to be coming true in

   _____. (LO6)
   a) sub-Saharan Africa
   b) the United States
   c) China
   d) the entire world

9. Which one of the following factors contributed most
   to our economic growth between 1995 and
   today? (LO4)
   a) Our high rate of savings
   b) Our educational system
   c) Technological change
   d) Our high rate of investment

10. Sustained economic growth did not begin anywhere

    in the world until around _____. (LO1)
    a) 1450   b) 1600
    c) 1750   d) 1900

11. Which is the most accurate statement? (LO3, 4)
    a) We are spending more on defense (as a percentage
       of our GDP) than at any previous time in our
       history.
    b) We are spending less on defense (as a percentage
       of GDP) than at any previous time in our history.
    c) Defense spending (as a percentage of GDP) is
       declining.
    d) Defense spending (as a percentage of GDP) is
       rising.

12. Which statement is true? (LO5)

   a) Immigration has long been a tremendous drain on our economy and has slowed our rate of economic growth.

   b) Hundreds of thousands of immigrants come here every year on work visas.

   c) Our immigration policies in the 19th century favored Chinese immigrants.

   d) Very few immigrants have found employment in California's Silicon Valley.

13. Which is the most accurate statement? (LO5)

   a) Americans work fewer hours per year than the citizens of virtually every other developed country.

   b) Americans work about the same number of hours as French and German workers.

   c) Americans work more hours than the citizens of virtually every other developed country.

14. The events of 9/11 had _____. (LO2)

   a) the long-term effect of raising our rate of productivity growth

   b) the long-term effect of lowering our rate of productivity growth

   c) virtually no effect on our rate of productivity growth

15. All other things remaining equal, which country in the figure below would you expect to have a higher growth rate? (LO4)

   a) Country A

   b) Country B

   c) They would have the same growth rate.

   d) There is no way of telling which would have the higher growth rate.

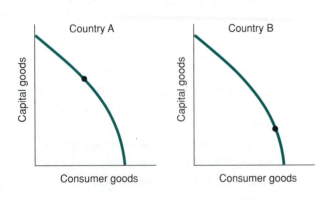

16. Which one of the following has *not* slowed our productivity growth? (LO3, 4)

   a) High military spending

   b) High health care costs

   c) Immigration

   d) Low savings

   e) Technological change

17. Which statement best reflects the role of our educational system in preparing students for the workforce? (LO5)

   a) More people than ever are attending college, so our labor force is better educated than at any time in our history.

   b) Business firms are having trouble finding secretaries who can spell and put together grammatically correct sentences.

   c) Most people in our labor force are unable to perform their jobs because of their educational shortcomings.

   d) Increased spending on teachers' salaries, science labs, and computer facilities will completely solve any educational problems this nation has.

18. Which statement is true? (LO5)

   a) The permanent underclass is basically an economic asset because it is a cheap source of labor.

   b) The permanent underclass has slowed our rate of economic growth.

   c) About 2 percent of all Americans are members of the permanent underclass.

   d) Because the United States is a socially mobile society, there is no such thing as a permanent underclass.

19. Which is the most accurate statement? (LO5)

   a) The tremendous surge of immigrants into the United States has slowed our economic growth.

   b) Most high-tech employers oppose increasing immigration quotas.

   c) In the late 1990s the flood of immigrants willing to take low-paying jobs has caused millions of Americans to be unemployed.

   d) Very few businesses are owned by immigrants.

20. A major reason why health care costs are so high is _____. (LO3)
    a) doctors must not only pay high malpractice insurance premiums, but employ people just to deal with health care insurance payments
    b) doctors have become very greedy
    c) Medicaid and Medicare have forced up doctors' fees
    d) doctors are spending so much time with each patient.

21. Mancur Olson suggests that the best remedy for overcoming the economic influence of special interest groups is _____. (LO3)
    a) bringing down the barriers to international trade
    b) having the federal government curb the influence of special interest groups
    c) raising tariffs on all imports that are putting American workers out of work
    d) having the federal government nationalize all industries dominated by special interest groups

22. Which of the following statements is true? (LO3)
    a) The American health care system is run very efficiently.
    b) About one out of every six dollars of our GDP goes toward health care.
    c) The United States spends less per person on health care than most other developed nations.
    d) Health insurance premiums are an insignificant cost of doing business for most large companies.

23. Rapid population growth _____ the economic development of LDCs. (LO6)
    a) severely hampers
    b) slightly hampers
    c) slightly helps
    d) greatly helps

24. Malthus may have been correct in his predictions for _____. (LO7)
    a) at least some industrial countries and some LDCs
    b) at least some industrial countries but no LDCs
    c) at least some LDCs but no industrial countries
    d) neither the LDCs nor the industrial countries

25. Since 1995 our productivity rose by more than 2.5 percent in _____. (LO2)
    a) just one year
    b) two years
    c) three years
    d) more than three years

26. FedEx, Walmart, and the airlines have (LO3)
    a) not taken advantage of the information technology revolution.
    b) used the information technology revolution mainly to lay off employees.
    c) used the information technology revolution to cut costs.
    d) all experienced lower productivity growth due to the information technology revolution.

27. Which statement is true? (LO5)
    a) Americans are the most productive workers in the world.
    b) In most economic sectors Americans are less productive than workers in other mature economies.
    c) The official average workweek for most American information workers greatly overestimates the hours they really work.
    d) Productivity growth in the United States has slowed since the mid-1990s.

28. Each of the following countries except _____ is extremely poor. (LO6)
    a) Liberia
    b) Brazil
    c) Burundi
    d) Zimbabwe

29. Which one of the following statements would you agree with? (LO3)
    a) By the mid-1990s computerization had reached the critical mass necessary to significantly raise our rate of productivity growth.
    b) Globalization has slowed our rate of productivity growth.
    c) High military and homeland security spending since 9/11 has helped raise our rate of productivity growth.
    d) Since 2001 the United States has been able to meet nearly all its financial needs from government and individual savings.

30. Which one of the following is the most accurate statement? (LO8)
   a) Baumol's Disease explains most of our loss of manufacturing jobs to foreign competitors.
   b) The productivity of many workers in the service sector cannot be increased.
   c) William Baumol believes that the expansion of the health care industry will greatly increase our productivity growth rate in the coming decades.
   d) The sharp increase in productivity growth since 1995 proves that Baumol's Disease has been cured.

31. Which statement is true? (LO3)
   a) Americans unquestionably receive the best health care in the world.
   b) Americans have the highest life expectancy and the lowest infant mortality rate in the world.
   c) More than $1,000 per capita in the U.S. is spent on health care-related paperwork and administration.
   d) The U.S. has more doctors per capita than any other nation.

32. The most likely effect of a worldwide effort to slow greenhouse gas emissions would be to _____ the rate of economic growth. (LO5)
   a) substantially lower   c) slightly raise
   b) slightly lower   d) substantially raise

33. Which one of these statements best describes our transportation system? (LO5)
   a) It is the most efficient in the world.
   b) It is very heavily dependent on public transportation.
   c) It is largely responsible for our dependency on foreign oil.
   d) It spurs our economic growth by freeing up large quantities of resource to be used by other economic sectors.

Fill-In Questions

1. Productivity is defined as _____ _____. (LO2)

2. Most Americans, French, Germans, Japanese, and British work less than _____ hours a year. (LO5)

3. The Industrial Revolution began over _____ centuries ago in _____. (LO1)

4. Edward Denison attributes about _____ percent of our economic growth to increases in labor and capital and about _____ percent to increases in productivity. (LO3)

5. Sustained economic growth was made possible by the _____. (LO1)

6. The threat of terrorist attacks has tended to _____ our rate of productivity growth. (LO3)

7. Compared to the 1970s and 1980s, our rate of productivity growth is _____. (LO2)

8. By the year 2015 we may be spending about _____ percent of our GDP on health care. (LO3)

Problem

1. Given the information in Table 1, fill in Malthus's predictions for the years 2025, 2050, and 2075. (LO7)

TABLE 1		
Year	Food Production	Population
2000	1	1
2025	_____	_____
2050	_____	_____
2075	_____	_____

2. If real GDP rose by 4 percent and the productivity rate rose by 2 percent, by how much would employment rise? (LO2)

3. Productivity has been rising by about 3 percent a year. By how much would real GDP need to rise to increase employment? (LO2)

Chapter 17

Income Distribution and Poverty

The economic history of the United States has been one of tremendous growth, a rising standard of living, and a home in the suburbs for most American families. But income has not been distributed evenly, and tens of millions of Americans have been left far behind. Indeed, poverty amid plenty has been one of the basic failures of our society.

Fifth Avenue is the eastern border of New York's Central Park. More than a dozen billionaires have Fifth Avenue addresses, living in duplexes and triplexes with great views of the park. Many homeless people also have Fifth Avenue addresses, but they live in cardboard boxes just inside the park.

Visit any welfare office and you'll see dozens of very poor children waiting with their mothers for a worker to see them about their cases. But these children are rich compared to the children you'll find picking through garbage in the outlying areas of most large South American cities. Go out at night and you'll find children sleeping on the sidewalks.

This chapter is divided into two parts: income distribution and poverty. If income were distributed evenly, every American would have an income of $40,000 a year—that's every man, woman, and child—and there would be no poverty. In fact, if income were distributed evenly, there would be virtually nothing to say about income distribution and poverty, and this chapter would not have been written.

> *The forces of a capitalist society, if left unchecked, tend to make the rich richer and the poor poorer.*
>
> —Jawaharlal Nehru

LEARNING OBJECTIVES

After reading this chapter you should be able to:

1. Measure the inequality of income distribution in the United States.
2. Distinguish between the distribution of income and the distribution of wealth.
3. List and discuss what determines how income is distributed.
4. Define and discuss poverty in the United States.
5. Name and discuss the groups of people who are poor.
6. List the main government transfer programs to help the poor.
7. Explain the main causes of poverty.
8. Differentiate between the liberal and conservative theories of poverty.
9. Discuss and assess the solutions to poverty.
10. Judge whether welfare reform has been successful.
11. Assess your chances of ever being poor.

Income Distribution in the United States

The Poor, the Middle Class, and the Rich

How unequal is income distribution in the United States? To answer this question, we must first answer three subsidiary questions: How unequal are the incomes of (1) the poor and the rich, (2) blacks, whites, and Hispanics and (3) males and females? There are no big surprises here. The rich make more money than the poor; whites make more than blacks; and men make more money than women. The question is, How *much* more?

Do you know what a quintile is? I'll bet no one ever asked you *that* before. A quinquennial is an event that occurs every five years; a quintuplet is one of five babies born at the same time. A *quintile* is one-fifth, just like a quarter is one-fourth. We'll use this term to measure income distribution.

Who is rich, who is middle class, and who is poor?

The poor are in the lowest quintile, the middle class in the next three quintiles, and the rich in the upper quintile. Is it accurate to say that 20 percent of our population is poor, 60 percent is middle class, and 20 percent is rich? Probably not. But because social scientists can't agree about where to draw the dividing lines between the poor and the middle class and between the middle class and the rich, this arbitrary arrangement is as good as any other. And besides, we get to deal with nice round numbers—20, 60, and 20.

Table 1 lists the dividing lines between quintiles. If your family's income is below $20,712, then it is in the lowest quintile of household income. If it's above $100,240, it's in the highest quintile. And just in case you're interested, if your family's income is above $180,000, then it's in the top 5 percent.

TABLE 1	U.S. Household Income, by Quintile, 2006
	Upper Income Limit
Lowest quintile	$20,712
Second quintile	37,400*
Third quintile	59,500*
Fourth quintile	100,240
Top quintile	

*Author's estimates
Source: **www.census.gov**

The Lorenz curve

Now we're going to analyze a Lorenz curve, named for M. O. Lorenz, who drew the first one in 1905. Let's begin by looking at the axes of Figure 1. On the horizontal axis we have the percentage of households, beginning with the poor (0 percent to 20 percent), running through the middle class (20 percent to 80 percent), and ending with the rich (80 percent to 100 percent). The vertical axis shows the cumulative share of income earned by these households.

Figure 1 has just two lines. The straight line that runs diagonally from the lower left to the upper right is the line of perfect equality. You'll notice that the poorest 20 percent of the households receive exactly 20 percent of the income, and that 40 percent of the households receive exactly 40 percent of the income. In other words, every household in the country makes exactly the same amount of money.

The curve to the right of the straight diagonal line is the Lorenz curve, which tells us how income is actually distributed. What percent of income does the poorest 20 percent of all households receive? And how much does the next poorest 20 percent receive? Put your answers here:

Lowest fifth:

Second fifth:

Finding the Percentage of Income Share of the Quintiles in Figure 1

The lowest quintile receives 5 percent of all income. Right? How much does the second quintile get? It gets 7.5 percent. Where did we get that number? What is the percentage share of income earned by the lowest 40 percent of households? It looks like 12.5 percent—right? Now if the bottom quintile earns 5 percent, and the lowest two quintiles earn a total of 12.5 percent, how much do households in the second-lowest quintile earn? They earn 7.5 percent (12.5 percent − 5 percent).

Next question: How much is the cumulative percentage share of income of the lower 60 percent of households? It comes to 25 percent. So how much is the third quintile's income share? It's 12.5 percent (25 percent − 12.5 percent). In other words, we take the lower 60 percent of households' share (25 percent) and subtract from it the combined share of the lower two quintiles (12.5 percent).

The lower 80 percent receives 40 percent of income. From that, we subtract the income share of the lower 60 percent (25 percent), which leaves the fourth quintile with a 15 percent income share. One more quintile to go—the highest quintile. If 100 percent of all households receive 100 percent of all income and the lowest 80 percent of all households receive a total of 40 percent, what's left for the top quintile? You got it—60 percent.

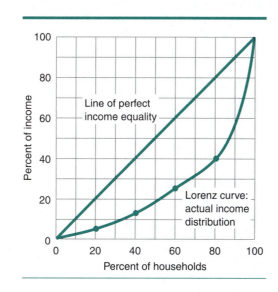

Figure 1

Hypothetical Lorenz Curve
The line of perfect income equality shows that any given percent of households receives that same percent of income. For example, the lowest 20 percent of all households would receive 20 percent of the income. Every household would receive the same income: There would be no rich or poor. The Lorenz curve shows the actual income distribution. In this particular example, the poorest 20 percent of all households receive about 5 percent of all income, while the richest fifth receives 60 percent.

Third fifth:

Fourth fifth:

Highest fifth:

The lowest fifth receives just 5 percent of all income; the second fifth receives 7.5 percent; the third fifth receives 12.5 percent; the fourth fifth receives 15 percent; and the highest fifth receives 60 percent. (If you don't know how I got these numbers, please read the box, "Finding the Percentage of Income Share of the Quintiles in Figure 1.")

What do you think of *that* income distribution? Not very equal, is it? You'll notice the Lorenz curve is pretty far to the right of the diagonal line. That diagonal is the line of perfect equality, so the farther the Lorenz curve is from it, the less equal the distribution of income becomes.

Do you know what I forgot to do? I forgot to define the Lorenz curve. Do *you* want to take a stab at a definition? Here's mine: *A Lorenz curve shows the cumulative share of income earned by each quintile of households.*

Definition of the Lorenz curve

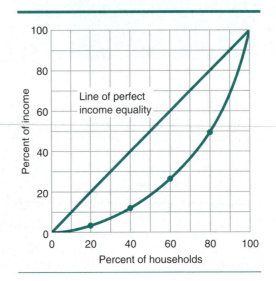

Figure 2

Lorenz Curve of Income Distribution of the United States, 2008

Would you say that the United States has an equal distribution of income? No? I would agree. OK, what percentage of all income is received by those in the poorest 20 percent of all households, and what percentage of all income is received by those in the richest 20 percent of all households? The poorest 20 percent received 3.4 percent of all income; the richest 20 percent received over 50 percent of all income.

Source: U.S. Bureau of the Census, *Current Population Reports, Series P-60.* Issued August 2009.

How does our own income distribution look? It's plotted for you in Figure 2. Once again, figure out the distribution of income, and write your answers here:

Lowest fifth:

Second fifth:

Third fifth:

Fourth fifth:

Highest fifth:

Check your answers against those in the right-hand column of Table 2. Your figures don't have to match mine exactly because we're both making our own observations from the graph.

It doesn't take a rocket scientist to figure out that income distribution was more uneven early in the 21st century than it was in the late 1960s. We know that changes in our tax laws have been a major factor. Income tax rates and taxes on capital gains were cut, especially for the rich, while payroll tax rates were raised, taking a large bite out of the incomes of the working poor, the working class, and the lower middle class. Indeed, about 75 percent of all Americans pay more today in payroll taxes than they do in personal income tax.

The rich also reaped huge capital gains since the 1980s, largely from increases in stock prices, real estate, and investments in their own businesses. During this same period the average hourly wage rate (adjusted for inflation) has not risen. Meanwhile the relatively high-

TABLE 2	Percentages of Total Income before Taxes Received by Each Fifth of American Families, 1968 and 2008	
Income Rank	1968	2008
Lowest fifth	5.6%	3.4%
Second fifth	12.4	8.6
Third fifth	17.7	14.7
Fourth fifth	23.7	23.3
Highest fifth	40.5	50.0

Note: 1968 figures don't add to 100.0 because of rounding.
Source: See Figure 2.

paying manufacturing sector has been shedding hundreds of thousands of jobs almost every year, while employment in the relatively low-paying service sector has been rising rapidly.

Now, let's compare the distribution of income in 2008 with that in 1968. Has income become *more* evenly distributed or *less* evenly distributed? A society in which the poorest fifth of the population gets just 3.4 percent of the income and the richest fifth gets half has a very uneven distribution of income. Since 1968, the top fifth's share of income rose from 40.5 percent to 50.0 percent, whereas the share of the lower three-fifths declined from 35.7 percent to 26.7 percent. In short, then, the rich are getting richer and the poor are getting poorer.

When it is said that our income is unevenly distributed, we need to ask: relative to what standard? Obviously it is unevenly distributed relative to the line of perfect income equality in Figure 2. It is less evenly distributed relative to its distribution in the late 1960s.

How well off is the typical American family? Probably the best way to measure that is by finding the median, or middle income, of all families. Imagine if we could list all American household incomes in ascending order. Half of all families would have incomes above the median and the other half would have incomes below the median. How much would the median income be? By glancing at the left bar in Figure 3 you'll find the answer for our median income in 2008. How much was it?

Has income become more equally distributed since 1968?

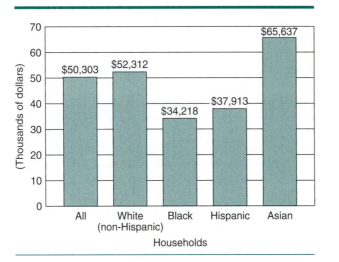

Figure 3

Median Household Income, by Selected Characteristics, 2008
The median household income in 2008 was $50,303. Half of all households earned less than $50,303 and half earned more than $50,303. Median household income for white and Asian households was higher than the overall median; it was lower for black and Hispanic households than the overall median.
Source: See Figure 2.

It came to exactly $50,303. Of course some folks did better than others. Asian-American families did the best, with a median income of $65,637; black families did the worst, earning a median income of just $34,218.

Now let's see how our overall median income fared over time. The record since 1967 is presented in Figure 4. You'll notice from its title that we're looking at "Real Median Household Income," which is measured in 2008 dollars (in other words, dollars of constant purchasing power). So the typical family earned $40,300 in 1967, and just over $50,000 in 2008—an increase of about 20 percent.

Between 1967 and 2008 median family income increased by nearly one quarter. At the beginning of this period, just one-third of all married women with children were working. By 2008 nearly two-thirds of them had jobs. Indeed, the increase in median family income between 1967 and 2008 is explained entirely by the fact that tens of millions of married women with children went out and got jobs.

We know, of course, that over this period, the quality of goods and services improved substantially, and many new ones became available. So the typical American family is much better off than it was back in 1968.

If you glance again at Figure 4, you'll notice the shaded areas designating periods of recession. It's no surprise that during each of the recessions over the last 40 years, real median household income declined. But take a look at the years immediately following the previous two recessions. It appears likely, then, that real median family income will decline from 2007—when the Great Recession began—perhaps through 2010 or even 2011. As you'll notice, real median income continued to fall well after every previous recession ended.

Figure 4

Real Median Household Income: 1967 to 2008, in 2008 Dollars

Median household income—the level at which half of all households earn more money and half earn less—was about 25 percent higher in 2008 than it was in the late 1990s.

Note: The data points are placed at the midpoints of the respective years. Median household income data are not available before 1967.

Source: U.S. Census Bureau, Current Population Survey, 1968 to 2009 Annual Social and Economic Supplements.

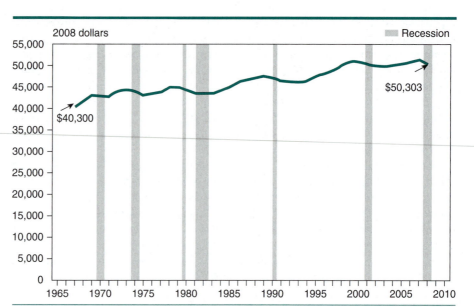

The global divide between the rich and the poor is much more apparent in the area of consumption spending. The richest 20 percent of humanity consumes 86 percent of all goods and services, while the poorest fifth consumes just 1.3 percent. In other words, when we look at the consumption rate of all the people on this planet, someone in the richest fifth consumes about 66 times as much as someone in the poorest fifth.

Distribution of Wealth in the United States

The rich are different from you and me.

—F. Scott Fitzgerald

Yes, they are different. They have more money.

—Ernest Hemingway

Every year *Forbes* magazine compiles a list of America's richest 400 men and women. To have made this list in 2009 you needed a net worth, or total wealth, of at least $950 million—down from $1.3 billion in 2007.

Who made *Forbes* magazine's top 10 list of American billionaires? It's shown in Table 3. It should come as no surprise that Bill Gates heads the list, and some of the other names should also be familiar.

Let's make sure we're clear on the difference between wealth and income. Your income this year includes your annual wages or salary, as well as any interest, dividends, profits,

TABLE 3 The Forbes 2009 Top 10 List of American Billionaires*		
Name and Rank	Main Source of Income	Net Worth (in $ billions)
1. William H. Gates, III	Microsoft (cofounder)	$53
2. Warren E. Buffett	Berkshire Hathaway / Stock market	47
3. Lawrence J. Ellison	Oracle (founder)	28
4. Christy Walton & family	Walmart (inheritor)	22.5
5. Jim C. Walton	Walmart (inheritor)	20.7
6. Alice Walton	Walmart (inheritor)	20.6
7. S. Robson Walton	Walmart (inheritor)	19.8
8. Michael Bloomberg	Bloomberg LP (founder)	18.0
9. Sergey Brin	Google (cofounder)	17.5
Larry Page	Google (cofounder)	17.5
Charles Koch	Koch Industries inheritor	17.5
David Koch	Koch Industries inheritor	17.5
10. Steven Ballmer	Microsoft	14.5

*One thing stands out when we look at this list of the nation's richest people. Six of them inherited their wealth.
Source: www.forbes.com/lists/2010/10/billionaires-2010_The-Worlds-Billionaires_Rank.html

rent, and government transfer payments you received (for example, Social Security benefits, unemployment insurance benefits). Wealth includes housing and other real estate, checking and savings accounts, certificates of deposit, stocks and bonds, and other valuable assets. One reason for the greater concentration of wealth in the hands of the rich is the slashing of federal income tax rates paid by the very rich. In 1981 the top tax bracket was 70 percent; today it is 35 percent. But the main reason why the distribution of wealth in America is becoming less equal is because the distribution of income is becoming less equal. In summary, the rich are getting richer and the poor are getting poorer.

There is inherited wealth in this country and also inherited poverty.
—President John F. Kennedy

Here's *Forbes* magazine's list of the 400 richest Americans: www.forbes.com/richlist Each year *Forbes* updates this list. If you keep looking, who knows? Maybe your name will turn up.

Distribution of Income: Equity and Efficiency

First we'll consider what a fair and just distribution of income would be, and then we'll talk about how income distribution affects the efficient operation of our economy.

Is it fair that some people earn hundreds of millions of dollars a year while others don't make enough to put food on the table and a roof over their heads? Shouldn't we be a more egalitarian society, where no one is superrich or dirt poor? Or should we go even further and ensure that we all earn approximately the same income?

There is widespread agreement that it's good for the rich to give some of their money to the poor. After all, the tens of millions of Americans who give to charity each year can't all be wrong. And if the government uses some of our tax dollars to help the truly needy, that too is something that most of us could support.

OK, so would it be such a bad thing for a rich guy to fork over a buck or two to a poor guy? After all, that money would mean a whole lot more to the poor guy, while the rich guy would hardly miss it. But what if we carry this redistribution scheme to its logical conclusion? Let's have everyone who's earning more than the average income give his surplus to those earning less. When we've finished, we'll all have exactly the same income. I have just stated the utilitarian case for equality.

What do *you* think? Is this fair? What about the people who worked hard for their money, putting in hours of overtime, holding down two jobs, and never seeing their families or friends? And what about the lazy bums who don't even bother looking for a job because they know they'll have exactly the same income as the working stiffs?

So much for a fair and just distribution of income. How does income distribution affect our economic efficiency? Well, for starters, what would an equal distribution of income do to work incentives? Would *you* work hard if you'd end up with exactly the same income as a lot of people who just sat at home and waited for their checks? Two of the things that make our economy go are the carrot and the stick. The carrot is all the money you can make by working hard. And the stick is that if you don't work, you don't eat.

Another incentive that would suffer is the incentive to save. Considering that the interest you'd get from your savings would be divided among everyone, why bother to save at all? Why invest, for that matter? Why bother to engage in any productive activities whatsoever, when we'll all end up with the same income no matter what we do?

Of course, if we were to pursue this reasoning to its logical conclusion, we would end up with very little output (because only a few workaholics would still be producing) and therefore very little real income.

So what should we do? Neither extreme seems desirable. Complete income equality would rob us of our productive incentives. And substantial income inequality would mean a great deal of human suffering, because many of the poor would not be able to afford even the basic necessities of life.

Whatever the means of income redistribution, the ends are always the same—to take from the rich and give to the poor. Robin Hood may not have won favor with the Sheriff of Nottingham or with the rich people he robbed, but most folks agree that the

Poverty is an anomaly to rich people; it is very difficult to make out why people who want dinner do not ring the bell.
—Walter Bagehot

Short of genius, a rich man cannot imagine poverty.
—Charles Péguy

How does income distribution affect our economic efficiency?

rich—*and* the middle class—should give some of their money to the poor. The only question is, how much?

What Determines Income Distribution?

About two-thirds of all personal income is earned in wages and salaries, so we'll concentrate on the factors causing these incomes to vary so widely. And then we'll take a look at property income, which accounts for a little less than one-quarter of all personal income. Finally, we'll look at government transfer payments, which account for the rest.

Differences in Wages and Salaries　We saw in the chapter, "Labor Markets and Wages Rates," that wage rates are determined by the forces of supply and demand. Demand is the marginal revenue product schedule for a particular line of work, and supply is the people willing and able to do this work.

Intelligence, skills, education, and training all enhance the demand for particular individuals. But increasingly, members of our labor force are competing not only against one another, but against workers all over the world. In a widely used example, hospitals are electronically sending MRIs to India where they are read and interpreted by Indian physicians, who work for just a fraction of the wages paid to American doctors. Our high-tech, globalizing world is enlarging the supply of labor for certain jobs, and consequently, depressing wage rates.

Property Income　As you might have suspected, most property income goes to the rich. These payments are in the form of rent, interest, dividends, and profits (which include capital gains). The two largest sources of wealth, exclusive of inheritance, have been the fortunes made in the stock market and the starting up of new companies (see Table 3).

Property income may also be derived from ownership of stocks, bonds, bank deposits, and other assets. Because the poor and the working class hold little property, little (if any) of their income comes from this source. The Tax Policy Center has determined that families with incomes of less than $50,000 derived just 3 percent of their income from capital gains and dividends; families with incomes in excess of $10 million received 61.4 percent of their incomes from those sources.

Income from Government Transfer Payments　In addition to wages, salaries, and property income, some people receive government transfer payments. For retirees, Social Security benefits may be their main means of support. For most people collecting unemployment benefits, these checks are usually their sole means of support. And public assistance recipients all depend on these benefits plus food stamps for most or all of their income.

As you can see in Figure 5, Social Security, Medicare, and Medicaid are the big three of federal income transfer programs. Although the poor benefit from all three, only Medicaid spending is "means tested."

Why do some people earn more than others?

Why does a college graduate earn more than a grade school dropout?

Some people's money is merited. And other people's money is inherited.

　　　　　　—Ogden Nash

Figure 5

Federal Income Transfer Programs, Fiscal Year 2009
Social Security, Medicare, and Medicaid account for nearly 80 percent of all federal transfers. Welfare benefits are just 4 percent.
Source: Office of Management and Budget.

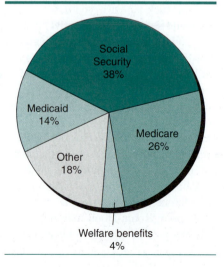

Poverty in America

I still have the audacity to believe that people everywhere can have three meals a day.
—The Reverend Martin Luther King, Jr.—

The poor will never cease out of the land.
—Moses, *Deuteronomy*, 15:11

Poverty Defined

There are two basic ways to define poverty—as a relative concept and as an absolute concept. By defining the poor as the lowest income quintile (that is, the lowest 20 percent) in the nation, we're saying that this group of people is poor relative to the rest of the population.

The relative concept of poverty

There are a couple of problems with this definition. First, suppose everyone's standard of living quadrupled from one year to the next. We'd *still* be calling those in the lowest quintile poor, even though most of the "poor" would be living better this year than the entire middle class lived last year. Although Jesus *did* say, "For ye have the poor always with you" (Matthew 26:11), *these* poor people would be driving late-model cars, living in nice houses, and eating in fancy restaurants three or four nights a week.

Viewed over time, poverty is clearly a relative concept. Nearly 90 percent of Americans living in 1900 would fall below the poverty line as it is defined today.

A second difficulty with the concept of relative poverty is that the lowest income quintile in the United States and other relatively rich countries is infinitely better off than the average citizens of the world's poorest nations. In Bangladesh, Ethiopia, Mali, and Zambia, most people struggle to survive on maybe $200 or $300 a year. Even our homeless population fares considerably better than that.

What about the absolute concept of poverty? Well, there's one basic problem here, too. Who gets to determine the dividing line between poor and not poor, and how is that determination reached? The best approach is to set up a minimum basic standard of living and figure out how much it costs to maintain that standard from year to year. So far, so good. Who gets to set up this basic living standard, and what goods and services should go into it?

The absolute concept of poverty

Just how bad is the problem of poverty in the rest of the world? One-third of the world's people have no access to electricity and nearly two-thirds have never made a phone call (see box, "The Price of Safe Drinking Water"). Almost half of the world lives on less than $2 a day. There is general agreement that the world's greatest concentration of poverty is in sub-Saharan Africa. According to Cornell's International Labour Organization more than three-quarters of the population in 14 countries lives on less than $2 a day—Nigeria, Mali, Madagascar, Zambia, India, Burkina Faso, Niger, Pakistan, Gambia, Central African Republic, Nepal, Mozambique, Bangladesh, and Ethiopia.

A better measure of economic well-being for the poor would be their level of consumer spending. In the Labor Department's latest Consumer Expenditures Survey (2003), the average reported income for the bottom quintile of households was just $8,201, but reported consumption outlays were $18,492. How do we explain how the poor can spend more than twice their incomes? Clearly, most poor people don't report their entire incomes. And then, too, they are going deeper into debt each year. Whatever the full explanation, the poor are obviously better off than the official poverty level would indicate.

The most widely used poverty standard in the United States is the official poverty line calculated each year by the U.S. Bureau of the Census. Its estimate is based on the assumption that poor families spend about one-third of their incomes on food. Each year it calculates the minimum food budget for a family of four for one week, multiplies that figure by 52 for the family's annual food budget, and then triples that figure to get the official poverty line. In 2008 that line was set at $22,025 for a family of four.[1]

Can a family of four live on $22,000? It all depends on what you mean by "live." Is it enough to put food on the table, clothes on your back, and a roof over your head?

The official poverty line

---

[1] When this method of calculating poverty was devised in the early 1960s, food accounted for 24 percent of the average family budget (not 33 percent); today food accounts for just 10 percent.

The Price of Safe Drinking Water

Americans, on average, drink over 25 gallons of bottled water a year. And globally, bottled water is now a $50-billion industry. At the other end of the economic spectrum, more than one billion of the world's poor people lack reliable access to safe drinking water. Writing in *The New York Times,* Tom Standage noted that "The World Health Organization estimates that at any given time, around half the people in the developing world are suffering from diseases associated with inadequate water or sanitation, which kill around a million people a year."*

Newsweek reports that "More than one billion people worldwide lack access to safe drinking water and 6,000 people die each day of waterborne diseases like typhoid, cholera, and dysentery."†

So while the world's relatively affluent folks think nothing of shelling out a dollar for a bottle of water—rather than drink perfectly adequate tap water—over one billion people don't have any safe drinking water at all. What would it take to provide them with clean water? The International Water Management Institute estimates that clean water could be provided to everyone on earth for an outlay of $1.7 billion a year beyond current spending on water projects. But despite the best efforts of rock star Bono and hundreds of other advocates, the world's rich countries have not given sufficient help.

Perhaps $1.7 billion seems like a lot of money, so let's break that down to nickels. Worldwide we buy 50 billion bottles of water. How much money would we raise if we paid a nickel deposit on each bottle of water we purchased? Go ahead and do the math.

We would raise $2.5 billion. Wouldn't *you* be willing to pay a nickel each time you bought a bottle of water for such a worthy cause? Still, you may remember the response of Queen Marie Antoinette during the days just before the French Revolution when told that the people had no bread. "Let them eat cake!" she declared. And so, when we're told that over one billion poor people don't have safe drinking water, we say, "Let them drink *bottled* water!"

---

*Tom Standage, "Bad to the Last Drop," *The New York Times,* August 1, 2005. See online at www.globalpolicy.org/component/article/218-injustice-and-inequality/46547.html

†Jennie Yabroff, "Water for the World," *Newsweek,* June 18, 2007, p. 20.

In some parts of the country, the answer is yes. In the more expensive cities such as New York, Boston, and San Francisco, as well as in many suburban communities, especially in the Northeast, $22,000 won't provide even the bare necessities, largely because of relatively high rents.

Once the poverty line has been established, we can find the poverty rate by dividing the number of poor people by the total population of the country. So the poverty rate is the percentage of Americans who are poor. In 2008 our poverty rate was 13.2, which means that 13.2 percent of Americans were poor.

The Census Bureau has been tracking the poverty rate since 1959. As you can observe in Figure 6, there was a sharp decline throughout the 1960s and early 1970s. In 1973 the rate bottomed out at about half the 1960 rate. The main causes of the decline were the prosperity of the 1960s and the War on Poverty conducted by the administration of President Lyndon Johnson. The federal government spent tens of billions of dollars on education, job training, and the creation of government jobs for millions of poor people.

You'll notice the shaded parts of Figure 6, which indicate periods of recession. Usually the poverty rate rises during recessions and falls again once we've recovered. Because of the Great Recession, our poverty rate in 2008 hit an 11-year high.

The poverty rate would be substantially lower if we counted the value of in-kind benefits.

Some conservative critics point out that the poverty rate would be substantially lower if we counted the value of noncash, or in-kind, benefits given to the poor by the government. These include Medicaid, housing subsidies, low-rent public housing, food stamps, and school lunches. If these in-kind benefits were counted, the poverty rate would have been about 3 percentage points lower than the reported rate of 13.2 percent.

Poverty is a relative term. When compared to the average American, those living below the poverty line have a much lower standard of living. But that standard of living usually includes at least one large screen TV and, very possibly, a cell phone and a computer. Over 70 percent of the poor own cars and 46 percent own their own homes. Not only do the American poor live much, much better than the poor in Africa, Asia, and Latin America, but they also live about as well as the average American did just

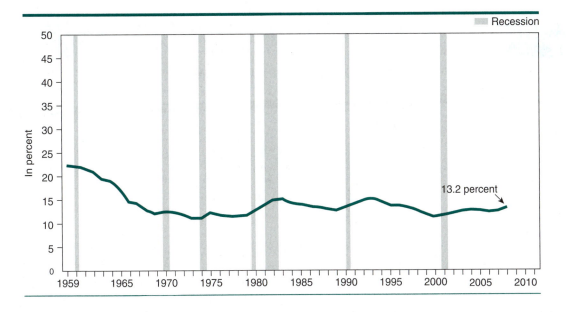

Figure 6

U.S. Poverty Rate: Percentage of Individuals below the Poverty Line, 1959–2008

The poverty rate was cut in half between 1960 and 1973, largely because of President Lyndon Johnson's war on poverty, much of which was continued and even expanded under President Richard Nixon. It remained above 12 percent from 1980, began falling steadily since 1993, and finally got below 12 percent in 1999. However, it began rising again in 2001, reaching 12.7 in 2004, then falling to 12.3 in 2006, and rising to 13.2 in 2008.

Note: The data points are placed at the midpoints of the respective years.

Source: U.S. Census Bureau, Current Population Survey, 1960 to 2007 Annual Social and Economic Supplements. U.S. Census Bureau, Current Population Reports, PV 60–233 Income, Poverty, and Health Insurance Coverage in the United States: 2006, issued August 2007.

decades ago. Michael Cox, of the Dallas Federal Reserve Bank, found that the material possessions of Americans at the poverty line in 2000 roughly equaled those of middle-income Americans in 1971.[2]

on the web

How does your income compare with those of the other 6.7 billion people in the world? Go to www.globalrichlist.com, type in your annual income (without the dollar sign) and make sure it's classified in the appropriate currency.

Who Are the Poor?

Who *are* the poor? Old people? Traditionally, people older than 65 have had a much higher poverty rate than the general population, but the advent of Medicare, higher Social Security benefits, and supplementary Social Security benefits over the last three decades has reduced the poverty rate for older Americans to well below the overall rate. The proportion of retirees living in poverty has fallen from 35 percent in 1960 to just 9.7 percent in 2008.

Are most poor people black? No, most poor people are white. It *is* true that almost one out of four blacks is poor, but only 13 percent of our population is black. So about one quarter of the poor is black. Figure 7 shows the relative poverty rates for white, black, Hispanic, and Asian Americans. The poverty rates for both blacks and Hispanics is almost triple the poverty rate for non-Hispanic whites.

If you happen to be a member of a female-headed household with children, your chances of being poor are more than two out of five. But if your family has any children

Most poor people are white.

God must love the poor—he made so many of them.

—Abraham Lincoln

[2]See W. Michael Cox and Richard Alms, "Defining Poverty Up," *Wall Street Journal*, November 2, 1999, p. A26.

Figure 7

Poverty Rates by Race, 2008
The poverty rates of blacks and
Hispanics are both more than
double that for whites.
Source: U.S. Bureau of the Census.

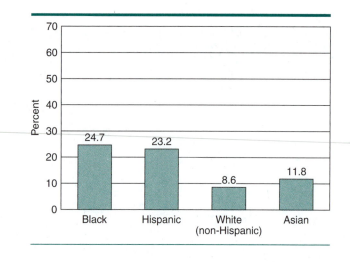

The working poor

The long-term unemployed

under six (with no husband present) then you have a better than one chance in two of living below the poverty line.

Where do the poor live? Although they are scattered throughout the nation, until recently the largest concentration of poor people was in large- and medium-sized cities. But according to the results of a 2005 Brookings Institution survey, there were 1.2 million more poor people living in the suburbs than in the cities. Most of the suburban poor live in the Midwest and the South.[3]

All the people employed at or just above the minimum wage could be considered the working poor. Most of them receive little or no government benefits, yet somehow manage to make ends meet from paycheck to paycheck. But even if they don't get one cent from the government, they are still part of our poverty problem.

Finally, there are the chronically (long-term) unemployed and the discouraged workers. Although the U.S. unemployment rate was relatively low from the mid-1990s until the Great Recession of 2007–2009, this measure does not take into account the millions of Americans who have been out of work for years. The official unemployment statistics count only those who have actively sought employment; people who have given up looking for jobs are not included. And at the very bottom of the economic barrel are the homeless (see the box, "The Homeless").

Child Poverty

Perhaps the most striking thing about poverty in America is how it affects children. Particularly hard hit by poverty are black children and Hispanic children (see Figure 8). Of children who grew up in long-term poverty—those poor for a least nine years during their childhood—about 80 percent were black. "Children are our future" may be a cliché, but they are nevertheless a future that we neglect at our peril.

It is said that a society may be judged by how it treats its children. In 2008 19 percent of American children lived in poverty. It is astounding that a nation as rich as ours can permit this to happen.

The Organization for Economic Cooperation and Development (OECD) is a group of 24 of most of the world's richest nations. UNICEF (the United Nations Children's Fund) did a study in 2008 which measured the degree of child poverty in each of the OECD countries. Child poverty was defined as the percent of children under 18 in households with earnings of less than 50 percent of the national median income. For the United States, that came to under $24,100.

How well did we do? Would you believe that the United States had a child poverty rate of 22.5 percent—by far the highest rate among all 24 OECD countries?

[3]See Peg Tyre and Matthew Philips, "Poor Among Plenty," *Newsweek*, February 12, 2007, p. 54.

The Homeless

The law, in its majestic equality, forbids the rich as well as the poor to sleep under bridges, to beg in the streets, and to steal bread.

—Anatole France—

We've created a lot of $6-an-hour jobs and not much $6-an-hour housing.

—John Donahue—

Chicago Coalition for the Homeless

There have always been homeless people in America—the hobo jungles of the Depression era, the skid rows (or skid roads, as they are known in the West), and, of course, the isolated shopping-bag ladies and other folks who lived out on the street, in doorways, or in train stations. But now there are literally millions of them. In a nation of some 310 million people, between 2 and 3 million are homeless.

A convergence of four trends has multiplied the number of homeless people who congregate in all our large cities. Since World War II the number of entry-level factory jobs almost disappeared from every large city. Meanwhile, the availability of cheap housing (basically furnished rooms) has also declined as the cities' more dilapidated neighborhoods were demolished to make way for urban renewal projects.

A third trend has been gentrification, which has pushed rents through the roof, so to speak, in New York, San Francisco, Boston, Chicago, and most other major cities. Finally, the deinstitutionalization of the mentally ill over the last two and a half decades (without the promised halfway houses to treat and shelter them) has further added to the homeless population.

The U.S. Department of Health and Human Services estimates that one-third of the homeless are mentally ill and that half of the homeless are alcoholics or drug addicts. The Veteran's Administration estimates that nearly 200,000 veterans of various wars are homeless on any given night, many as a result of substance abuse. "Veterans, who represent only 11% of the civilian adult population, comprise 26% of the homeless population," says a report by the Homelessness Research Institute.*

Interestingly, about one-quarter of the homeless work full time, according to the U.S. Conference of Mayors. The problem for them is being trapped between jobs that pay too little and housing that costs too much.

*See *Time*, November 19, 2007, p. 21.

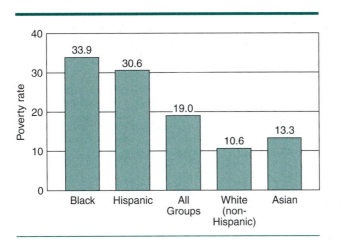

Figure 8

Children under 18 below Poverty Level by Race and Hispanic Origin, 2008
The child poverty rate is more than three times as high for black children as for white children. More than 1 in 3 black children live in poverty.
Source: Bureau of Labor Statistics and Bureau of the Census, *CPS Annual Demographic Survey.*

(See Figure 9.) Four nations—Belgium, Finland, Norway, and Sweden—had rates well under 5 percent. And another four—Denmark, the Czech Republic, France, and the Netherlands—all were well below 10 percent.

How do we interpret these results? While we cannot conclude that poor American children are much worse off than poor children in *all* of the OECD countries, they certainly are worse off than those in *most* of them. Because our median family income is higher than those of most other OECD countries, it would be reasonable to assume that poor American children are no worse off than poor children in countries like Poland, Spain, Greece, or the Czech Republic.

Figure 9

Child Poverty Rates in Selected Countries: Children Living in Households with Income Less than 50 Percent of the National Median Income, 2007–2008
Of the countries shown here, the United States has the highest rate of child poverty. Note that this measure is somewhat different from defining the childhood poverty rate as the percentage of children in families living below the official poverty line shown in Figure 8.
Source: UNICEF.

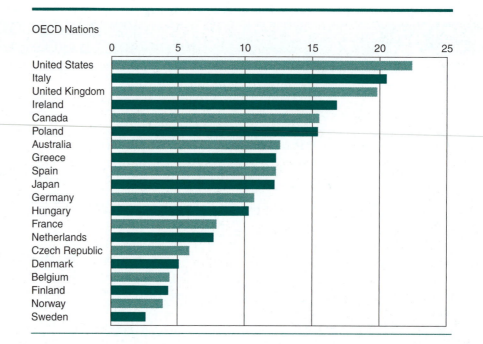

A decent provision for the poor is a true test of civilization.
        —Samuel Johnson

But this study actually highlights a strong dichotomy within our country. If 22.5 percent of our children are members of families earning less than $24,100, then clearly the standard of living of poor American children is very low compared to that of middle-class and rich American children.

Perhaps the most troubling statistic is that 53.3 percent of all American children under six in a family headed by a female lived in poverty in 2008. But just 11.0 percent of the children under six living in married-couple families are poor. Using this information, Katherine Boo draws an interesting conclusion: ". . . for children a two-parent household is the most effective antipoverty program we know. Three out of four white children are born to such households. Only one in three black children is."[4]

Large-scale, high-rise, low-income public housing projects have been especially good breeding grounds for this culture of poverty. In these neighborhoods at least three-quarters of the families are on welfare, most of the girls get pregnant before they are 18, and there is a great degree of drug dependency and an extremely high rate of violent crime. The gangs are the real authority in the ghetto, according to Nicholas Lemann. The gang "forces kids through physical terror, to give up school and work and become professional criminals."[5] To some degree this phenomenon has evolved in poor Hispanic and non-Hispanic white neighborhoods as well.

The Main Government Transfer Programs

Until the 1930s, the poor depended on help from friends and family, and failing that, from private charities. But when millions of otherwise respectable middle class and working class Americans were thrown out of work during the Great Depression, they demanded that the federal government provide them with some means of support, whether jobs, welfare payments, or any other programs that would keep the wolf from the door. Today, of course, the government continues to provide most of the help given to the poor, but private charities also continue to help as well.

---

[4]Katherine Boo, "The Black Gender Gap," *The Atlantic Monthly,* January/February 2003, p. 107.

[5]Nicholas Lemann, "The Origins of the Underclass," *The Atlantic Monthly,* June 1986, p. 39.

Support Our Troops

We have noted how our military bases were surrounded by payday lenders, only too happy to extend our service men and women and their spouses short-term loans at exorbitant interest rates. But these companies are just symptoms of an underlying problem, not the cause. The problem is that we don't pay our troops enough to keep their heads above water. Hundreds of thousands of military families live from paycheck to paycheck, leaving them at the mercy of these predatory lenders.

In a book describing hunger in America, Loretta Schwartz-Nobel wrote a chapter entitled, "From Front Lines to Food Lines." Here's how she explains why so many military families run into financial problems:

> Advocates for the military families consistently point out that the acute problem comes when an enlisted man marries and has children. That is partly because there is no additional food allowance for the family of an enlisted man, and also because housing allowances are never enough to cover the costs of housing, food and all the other added expenses of families. In fact, they usually aren't even enough to cope with housing expenses alone. As a result, families who are living in areas with high rents often end up moving forty or fifty miles away from their duty stations to areas where housing is less expensive and more available. But even that has a downside, because it means that now they have to maintain both a car and costly insurance.
>
> If they live in military housing, the government pays for their utilities, but if they live off base, the utilities are often a large additional expense. Unfortunately, many bases have very little housing and extremely long waiting lists.*

Most of those joining the military are hoping for a step up on the economic ladder. How well paid *are* the members of our armed forces? In 2008 a private first class with less than two year's active service earned $1,534.20 a month before taxes ($18,410.40 on an annual basis). That income leaves a family of four well below the poverty line of $22,025.

Here's an excerpt from an article entitled, "Thousands of US Military Families Live in Poverty," by Brian Mann.

> Ms. Levesque runs a food pantry in Watertown, New York, a short drive from the Fort Drum Army base. She says Army families make up 20 percent of the people who come in, looking for free meals and supplies. "The military kind of has a 'we take care of our own' motto, which you realize that they kind of don't," she said. "And there are a lot of people who fall through the cracks and need the assistance who aren't getting it."
>
> Ms. Levesque speaks from experience, as a social service worker, but also as the wife of a soldier. Her husband, an army specialist, brings home roughly $1,300 a month after taxes—not enough to pay for rent, food, utilities and other necessities. "I have always worked two jobs," said Amy Levesque. "And my husband, he's in the military plus he has a nighttime job. Luckily we don't have any children. With children, it would be very difficult."[†]

There's another side to this issue. Since the draft was ended in 1974, almost 90 percent of the volunteers have been members of poor and working-class families. For these youngsters, joining the military usually provides more promising economic prospects than they would have enjoyed in civilian life. "Be the best you can be," is presumably better than you could have been "on the outside." So despite the shortcomings just enumerated in this box, for most new recruits, joining the service actually raises their economic well-being.

---

*Loretta Schwartz-Nobel, *Growing Up Empty: The Hunger Epidemic in America* (New York: HarperCollins, 2002), pp. 99–100.

[†]*Source:* www.globalpolicy.org/component/article/218-injustice-and-inequality/46509.html

---

The poor are not invisible. The people lined up outside food pantries or inside check cashing stores are usually living below the poverty line or pretty close to it, but you might be surprised to learn that some of them are in military families. Their economic situation is described in the box, "Support Our Troops."

The Social Security Act of 1935 set up three major programs: Social Security, unemployment insurance, and public assistance. Taxes paid by workers and their employers financed the first two programs. Public assistance, which was intended to help families experiencing temporary economic distress, was the only means-tested program. To obtain public assistance (or relief, as it was then called), you needed to demonstrate that your income or means of support was insufficient to cover your basic needs.

The Social Security Act of 1935

Helping the Poor Get Money Back from the IRS

In a column in *Newsweek*, Bob Burke tells how he organized a program to help poor families get substantial tax refunds.

> One day I had an idea. I knew the federal government had tax credits to ease the burden on working-poor families, but the process for claiming these credits was simply too complicated for most to get the assistance they had coming. I came up with a plan: I would gather a group of business professionals to offer free tax-preparation services. We'd meet at the school on Saturday mornings and get the word out in the community that we were there to help.
>
> . . .
>
> After about an hour, these volunteers usually had the pleasant task of informing a hardworking,

> low-income family that they would receive thousands of dollars back from the Internal Revenue Service. All that without a commercial tax-preparation service's taking out a big chunk.
>
> I vividly remember when a single mother of two, who hadn't earned enough in three years to file a return, burst into tears when I told her that the IRS had withheld too much from her paychecks and owed her $10,000. She said she would use the money to fix the leaky roof on her house. Others were equally emotional, making plans to pay overdue bills, buy clothes and school supplies for their children or even move to a safer neighborhood.

Source: Bob Burke, "Helping the Needy Crack the Tax Code," *Newsweek*, April 26, 2004, p. 15.

Can you name our biggest antipoverty program? The one that lifts more people out of poverty than any other government program?

Amazingly, the correct answer is Social Security. After all, Social Security is *not* an antipoverty program, but that's just being picky. The fact is, if it were not for Social Security, close to one out of every two Americans over 65 would be living below the poverty line. And for two-thirds of the elderly, Social Security supplies more than half their income. So we can say that while Social Security is not an antipoverty program per se, it certainly has that effect.

Medicare and Medicaid

Two major programs, Medicare and Medicaid, were added in the mid-1960s under President Johnson's Great Society program. Medicare, which is really a supplement to Social Security, provides retirees and their families with free or very low-cost medical care. Free medical care is provided to the poor under Medicaid.

The food stamp program, which also began in the 1960s, enabled the very poor as well as the working poor to buy enough food. Like Medicare and Medicaid, it has expanded tremendously since the late 1960s. But until the mid-1990s, just 40 percent of those eligible were actually on the rolls. This changed as the presidential administrations of Bill Clinton and George W. Bush helped erase the program's stigma and made the enrollment process easier. Today, one in eight Americans, and one in four children receive food stamps.

About two-thirds of those eligible are now covered. Benefits average about $130 a month for each person in a household. During the recession of 2007–2009, the number of people receiving benefits rose from 26 million to 39 million. About half of all Americans receive food stamps, at least briefly, by the time they turn 20. Among black children, the figure is 90 percent.

Still another very important form of aid to the working poor is the earned income tax credit, which is written into our Internal Revenue Code. Those eligible, instead of *paying* income tax, actually receive what amounts to a refund check from the Internal Revenue Service. The purpose of the earned income tax credit is to encourage the poor to work by supplementing their earnings. The program supplements their earnings by as much as $2 an hour. Some of the recipients of the earned income tax credit not only get a full refund on the income taxes that were withheld from their paychecks all year but, in addition, they may receive a once-a-year payment of up to a couple of thousand dollars. Over 20 million Americans receive the credit, with about 5 million gaining enough to rise above the poverty line (see the box, "Helping the Poor Get Money Back from the IRS").

Still, millions of eligible low-wage workers are either unaware of this program or cannot figure out how to apply. The earned income tax credit is popular with liberals because it provides a substantial amount of income to the poor, and it is also popular with conservatives because only families with a working member are eligible. Today it is, by far, the biggest single federal policy targeting the poor. In addition, about a dozen states have also introduced their own EITC programs that supplement the federal credit.

Have these programs worked? Yes, they have. Each has accomplished what it was set up to do. But there are three major problems: (1) their costs have gone through the roof; (2) they have fostered a permanent dependency on government support among millions of poor families; and (3) they have not ended poverty.

Public assistance has been the greatest disappointment. Intended to provide "temporary relief," public assistance instead engendered a permanent dependence in millions of families.

One misconception about welfare mothers is that they keep having more and more children so that they can collect bigger checks. Indeed, many states no longer increase the size of a welfare grant if more children are born into a family. In actuality, 72 percent of all welfare families have only one or two children.

A welfare culture evolved over decades, giving rise to second-, third-, and fourth-generation welfare families. Typically, teenage girls become pregnant, keep their babies, go on welfare, do not marry, and have no hope of becoming self-supporting. In a sense, the young mothers are provided with surrogate husbands in the form of public assistance checks. Eventually their children grow up, become teenage parents themselves, and continue the welfare pattern through another generation.

The welfare culture

The number of people receiving public assistance remained remarkably steady—at about 11 million—from 1975 through 1992, but the welfare rolls shot up from 11 million in mid-1993 to a peak of 14.4 million in March 1994 (see Figure 10 near the end of this chapter). The main reason for this increase was the recession of 1990–91. By early 1994, the benefits of the subsequent economic expansion finally began to reach people at the bottom of the economic ladder, and the welfare rolls began to decline. Another important factor was that many states have restricted eligibility for welfare. And then, too, the passage of the Welfare Reform Act—which we'll discuss near the end of the chapter—was perhaps the main reason why so many mothers found work and left welfare.

The words of one welfare mother are especially poignant: "I'm sorry I got myself into this and my children into this. And I don't know how to get them out of it. If I don't get them away from here, they're going to end up dead, in jail, or like me."[6]

Theories of the Causes of Poverty

Any theory of poverty must take into account our entire socioeconomic system, how it is set up, how it is run, and who gets what. Poor people live on the margin or even beyond the system. They are basically superfluous and rarely have much impact on the system. They are an unfortunate presence, by-products that have been discarded but are grudgingly tolerated by society's "productive" members.

At least a dozen theories of poverty have attracted support, and each has at least *some* apparent validity. But because there are so many different poverty groups, no single theory can have universal applicability. We'll begin by briefly outlining a few theories, and then we'll look at the two with the largest number of adherents: the conservative and liberal theories.

The Poor Are Lazy   This theory was popular through most of the 19th century and right up to the time of the Great Depression. God's chosen people, who were destined to go to heaven, worked hard all their lives and were rewarded by attaining great earthly

---

[6]See Celia W. Dugger, "On the Edge of Survival: Single Mothers on Welfare," *The New York Times,* July 6, 1992, p. B6.

riches. And the poor? Well, you can figure out for yourself where they were headed. This theory went down the tubes when the Great Depression hit and millions of relatively affluent Americans were thrown out of work, lost their life savings, and had to ask the government for handouts.

The Heritage of Slavery   Because blacks were brought here in chains and held back for three centuries by slavery and a feudal sharecropping system in the South, the current poverty of many blacks can be explained by centuries of oppression. Not only were blacks systematically excluded from all but the most menial jobs, but they were denied the educational opportunities open to almost all other Americans. Mortgage loans, restaurant meals, hotel and motel lodging, union membership, and apartment rentals were routinely denied. In effect, then, blacks were systematically excluded from the nation's economic mainstream until the 1960s. Is it any wonder, ask adherents of this theory, that after so many years of oppression both during and after slavery, so many blacks still find themselves mired in poverty?

Employment Discrimination   Employment discrimination has been especially strong in holding down the incomes of women, blacks, Hispanics, and other minorities. The fact that women working full-time have generally earned about three-quarters of what their male counterparts have earned clearly points toward discrimination. Similar figures for blacks and Hispanics arouse the same suspicion.

Full-time working women have earned 60 percent of what full-time working men earned.

But other factors have also contributed to these wage differentials—education, training, and experience, and, in the case of many women, the years taken off work to raise children. Social scientists generally believe that about half of these wage differentials result from employment discrimination and the other half from other factors. As more employment opportunities become available to women and to minorities, we may see a narrowing of wage differentials. Meanwhile, employment discrimination has obviously been playing a major role in the poverty of women, blacks, Hispanics, and other minorities.

Black Male Joblessness   Back in 1970, about 33 percent of all black families were headed by women. By the mid-1990s, the number had jumped to over 60 percent. The growing perception of a permanent welfare population of single black mothers and their children has raised the question of where are the young black males who got them pregnant? In college? Playing major-league ball? Probably not.

Only half of all black males aged 16 to 64 are employed.

While more than four-fifths of all white males aged 20 to 44 are employed, only about half of their black counterparts have jobs. What are the rest of them doing? Some are officially unemployed, and some are "discouraged workers" who have stopped looking for work. And where are the rest of these guys? Some may be working in the underground economy—in either the legal or illegal sector. And others have just slipped through the cracks.

William A. Darity, Jr., and Samuel L. Myers, Jr., argue that "black men are being excluded from the emerging economic order; they are socially unwanted, superfluous, and marginal." Consequently there is a shrinking pool of marriageable black men. This growing marginality has led to drug abuse, violent crime, incarceration, and a high death rate, further depleting the ranks of marriageable young black men. Cutting welfare benefits, Darity and Myers observe, will do nothing to lower the number of black female-headed households, because the underlying problem is finding meaningful employment for millions of black men.[7]

The absence of eligible males does explain why there are so many single young black women, but it doesn't explain why these women are having so many children.

---

[7]William A. Darity, Jr., and Samuel L. Myers, Jr., "Family Structure and the Marginalization of Black Men: Policy Implications," presented at the American Economic Association Meetings, Washington, DC, January 1995.

Some conservatives, most notably Charles Murray,[8] believe that they allow themselves to get pregnant because they want to get on welfare. However, substantial research indicates that although public assistance is the main source of support once these girls give birth, peer pressure, the wish to go through the rite of passage into womanhood, and the desire for something to love are the real motivating factors.[9]

Let's pause here for a minute to catch our breath. We've been talking for a while about the causes of what is mainly black poverty. Keep in mind that most poor people are white. But when we distinguish between short-term poverty and a permanent underclass, we are talking mainly about a problem that has affected blacks, who constitute about 60 percent of the long-term poor.

Poverty Breeds Poverty   Poverty itself generally breeds poverty. Before birth an infant may suffer from poor prenatal care or even acquire an addiction to drugs, particularly crack. During childhood inadequate nutrition and a lack of medical and dental care also take their tolls. An unsafe—or even violent—environment, emotional deprivation, and a broken home also militate against a good childhood. This situation makes it extremely difficult to do well in school, so the easiest course is to give up.

Inadequate Human Capital   Human capital is defined as the acquired skills of an individual—education, training, and work habits. People who grew up poor usually had poor home learning environments, attended poor schools, dropped out before graduation, acquired little useful work experience, did not develop good work habits, and have poorly developed communication skills. In sum, they are virtually unemployable in today's economy.

The Conservative View versus the Liberal View

Now we're ready for the Super Bowl of poverty theory debate—the conservatives versus the liberals. Representing the conservative view will be Charles Murray, whose book *Losing Ground* depicts overly generous public assistance programs as perpetuating a dependent underclass. William Julius Wilson is perhaps the most prominent of Murray's liberal critics, so he'll represent their view.[10]

The conservatives and the liberals agree completely on ends—getting the long-term poor off welfare and into self-supporting employment—but they disagree completely on the appropriate means. Basically, the liberals favor the carrot approach, while the conservatives advocate the stick.

> The conservatives and liberals agree on ends but disagree on means.

During the Great Depression, President Franklin Roosevelt's New Deal program attempted to lift one-third of all Americans out of poverty. Poverty wasn't rediscovered until the 1960s,[11] and the response was President Lyndon Johnson's Great Society program. Did this program and its extension through the 1970s actually help alleviate poverty? Here's Murray's response:

> Did the Great Society program help alleviate poverty?

In 1968, as Lyndon Johnson left office, 13 percent of Americans were poor, using the official definition. Over the next 12 years, our expenditures on social welfare quadrupled. And, in 1980, the percentage of poor Americans was—13 percent.[12]

---

[8]Charles Murray, *Losing Ground: American Social Policy, 1950–1980* (New York: Basic Books, 1984).

[9]P. Cutright, "Illegitimacy and Income Supplements," *Studies in Public Welfare,* paper no. 12, prepared for the use of the Subcommittee on Fiscal Policy of the Joint Economic Committee. Congress of the United States (Washington, DC: Government Printing Office, 1973); C. R. Winegarden, "The Fertility of AFDC Women: An Economic Analysis," *Journal of Economics and Business* 26 (1974), pp. 159–66; William Julius Wilson, *When Work Disappears* (New York: Knopf, 1996), pp. 107–9.

[10]Wilson would probably reject any label, but his views are supported by nearly all liberals.

[11]Interest was sparked by Michael Harrington's book, *The Other America* (New York: MacMillan, 1962).

[12]Murray, *Losing Ground,* p. 8.

Charles Murray, American economist

Murray draws this conclusion: By showering so much money on the poor, the government robbed them of their incentive to work. Using the archetypal couple, Harold and Phyllis, showed how in 1960 Harold would have gone out and gotten a minimum-wage job to support Phyllis and their newborn baby. But 10 years later the couple would be better off receiving public assistance and food stamps, living together without getting married, and having Harold work periodically. Why work steadily at an unpleasant, dead-end job, asks Murray, when you can fall back on welfare, food stamps, unemployment insurance, and other government benefit programs?

All of this sounds perfectly logical, but Murray's logic was shot full of holes by his critics. We'll start with welfare spending. Although payments *did* increase from 1968 to 1980, when we adjust them for inflation these payments actually decreased between 1972 and 1980. William Julius Wilson really lowers the boom:

> The evidence does not sustain Murray's contentions. First, countries with far more generous social welfare programs than the United States—Germany, Denmark, France, Sweden, and Great Britain—all have sharply lower rates of teenage births and teenage crime.
>
> Second, if welfare benefits figured in the decision to have a baby, more babies would be born in states with relatively high levels of welfare payments. But careful state-by-state comparisons show no evidence that [public assistance] influences childbearing decisions; sex and childbearing among teenagers do not seem to be a product of careful economic analysis.[13]

Another problem with Murray's analysis is that the unemployment rate doubled between 1968 and 1980, yet the poverty rate remained constant. Why? Because of all the social programs that were in place—unemployment insurance, public assistance, food stamps, and Medicaid, among others. Although there was substantial economic growth throughout most of the 1970s, this growth was insufficient to absorb all of the housewives and baby boomers who had entered the labor market.

Murray blamed the antipoverty programs for increasing poverty. Liberals would say he really had it backward: These programs prevented a bad situation from getting worse. During a time of rising unemployment, particularly among black males, it was actually a triumph of social policy to keep the poverty rate from rising.

All of this said, Murray's thesis should not be dismissed out of hand. There *are* plenty of people out there who choose welfare as the easy way out. Even more to the point, a culture of poverty *has* developed during the last four decades. Had he said that the largesse of the federal government had induced a sizable minority of the poor to succumb to the joys of living on the dole, he would have had a valid point. Murray simply overstated his case.

Decades ago, when I was a case worker for the New York City Welfare Department, I saw hundreds of thick case folders documenting the lives of second-, third-, and fourth-generation welfare families, consisting of scores of people, virtually all of whom had spent most or all of their lives dependent on public assistance. Had Murray confined his theory to this group, he would have had the support of the large majority of those working directly with the welfare population. Again, there *is* no valid general theory of the causes of welfare dependency.

In his landmark work *The Truly Disadvantaged*, Wilson begins by describing the black ghettos as they were more than 40 years ago. Sure there was crime, but it was still safe to walk the streets at night. And sure there was joblessness, but nothing like what there has been these last 30 years. Then he goes on to describe other social problems:

Forty years ago the ghettos were a lot kinder and gentler places to live.

> There were single-parent families, but they were a small minority of all black families and tended to be incorporated within extended family networks and to be headed not by unwed teenagers and young adult women but by middle-aged women who usually were widowed, separated, or divorced. There were welfare recipients, but only a very small percentage of

---

[13]William Julius Wilson, Introduction to Lisbeth B. Schorr and Daniel Schorr, *Within Our Reach* (New York: Doubleday, 1989), p. xxv.

the families could be said to be welfare-dependent. In short, unlike the present period, inner-city communities prior to 1960 exhibited the features of social organization— including a sense of community, positive neighborhood identification, and explicit norms and sanctions against aberrant behavior.[14]

So what happened? What happened was the civil rights revolution led by Martin Luther King, Jr., in the early 1960s and the subsequent legislation that lowered racial housing and employment barriers. Until then the big-city ghettos had been socioeconomically integrated. But this quickly changed by the late 60s as millions of blacks, who had been penned up in the ghettos, were finally able to move out. They moved into the houses and apartments that had been vacated by the whites who had fled to the suburbs.

How did this outward migration affect those who were left behind?

William Julius Wilson, American sociologist

The exodus of middle- and working-class families from many ghetto neighborhoods removes an important "social buffer" that could deflect the full impact of the kind of prolonged and increasing joblessness that plagued inner-city neighborhoods in the 1970s and early 1980s. . . . Even if the truly disadvantaged segments of an inner-city area experience a significant increase in long-term joblessness, the basic institutions in that area (churches, schools, stores, recreational facilities, etc.) would remain viable if much of the base of their support comes from the more economically stable and secure families. Moreover, the very presence of these families during such periods provides mainstream role models that help keep alive the perception that education is meaningful, that steady employment is a viable alternative to welfare, and that family stability is the norm, not the exception.[15]

The outward migration of middle- and working-class blacks had a significant impact on those left behind.

This isolation makes it harder to find a job; few ghetto dwellers are tied into the job network. And because few relatives or neighbors have steady work, tardiness and absenteeism are not considered aberrant behavior. Consequently, those who do find jobs seldom hold them very long.

So the key is jobs—or rather the lack of them:

Lack of jobs is the key.

The black delay in marriage and the lower rate of remarriage, each associated with high percentages of out-of-wedlock births in female-headed households, can be directly tied to the employment status of black males. Indeed, black women, especially young black women, are confronting a shrinking pool of "marriageable" (that is, economically stable) men.[16]

The migration of black middle- and working-class families from the ghettos removed the key social constraint against crime. And the erection of huge, high-rise, low-income public housing projects further destroyed the remaining sense of community. Place together a large number of female-headed families with a large number of teenage children (who commit more crime than any other population group) and you've got the recipe for not only high crime rates but almost complete social breakdown.

Wilson's thesis is a direct repudiation of Murray's, which blames public assistance and other social programs for the emergence of the permanent black underclass. Wilson finds no evidence to support that contention. Instead, he blames a whole range of social and economic forces, including past employment discrimination.

Solutions

All poor people have one thing in common: They don't have nearly enough money. Or, in the words of the great wit, Finley Peter Dunne, "One of the strangest things about life is that the poor, who need the money the most, are the very ones that never have it."

The best way to help poor people is to not be one of them.

—Reverend Ike,
New York City preacher

---

[14]William Julius Wilson, *The Truly Disadvantaged* (Chicago: University of Chicago Press, 1987), p. 3.

[15]Ibid., p. 56.

[16]Ibid., p. 145.

The basic liberal solution—in addition to combating employment discrimination—is to provide the poor with better education and training, and with millions of government jobs. The conservatives have placed their faith in providing the poor with jobs mainly in the private sector. But the basic strain running through conservative thought about welfare recipients may be summed up in just three little words: Cut 'em off. A solution with widespread support, workfare, combines the liberal carrot of training and jobs with the conservative stick of cutting off the benefits of those who refuse to seek training or work.

The Conservative Solutions   To end the poor's dependency on government largesse, Charles Murray would simply pull the plug on the life-support system:

> [Scrap] the entire welfare and income-support structure for working-aged persons, including [public assistance], medicaid, food stamps, unemployment insurance, workers' compensation, subsidized housing, disability insurance, and the rest. It would leave the working-aged person with no recourse whatsoever except the job market, family members, friends, and public or private locally funded services.[17]

The Liberal Solutions   While the conservatives claim the government has done too much for the poor, the liberals believe much too little has been done. Barbara Ehrenreich, for example, points out that an increasing number of jobs do not pay enough to subsist on.[18] The solution? Government jobs.

Jobs, jobs, jobs

Government jobs doing what? Jobs rebuilding the nation's crumbling highways and bridges, and staffing hospitals, schools, libraries, and day care centers. Jobs rebuilding dilapidated inner-city housing and cleaning up toxic waste dumps. In the 1930s, the Works Progress Administration (WPA) of the New Deal employed millions of Americans building highways, airports, bridges, parks, and school buildings. Much of this infrastructure is badly in need of repair. In addition we need millions of people to staff day care centers, libraries, and after-school programs. Why not create a labor-intensive, minimum-wage public service jobs program of last resort for today's low-skilled and jobless workers?[19]

But some liberals acknowledge that even a massive jobs program won't get *all* of the poor off the dole. Remember that nearly all people receiving public assistance are women with young children.

Our country will need to go beyond providing jobs if we are to succeed in greatly reducing poverty. The lives of those in the permanent underclass are filled with hopelessness and despair. The lack of jobs put most of these families into this predicament, but it will take more than jobs, three or four generations later, to get them out of it.

More is needed than providing jobs.

Dr. David Rogers, president of the Robert Wood Johnson Foundation, remarked that "human misery is generally the result of, or accompanied by, a great untidy basketful of intertwined and interconnected circumstances and happenings"[20] that all need attention if a problem is to be solved. This point was amplified by Lisbeth and Daniel Schorr in their landmark work *Within Our Reach:*

> The mother who cannot respond appropriately to a child's evolving needs while simultaneously coping with unemployment, an abusive husband or boyfriend, an apartment without hot water, insufficient money for food, and her own memories of past neglect—even a mother who is stressed to the breaking point can be helped by a neighborhood agency that provides day care, counseling, and the support that convinces her that she is not helpless and alone.[21]

---

[17]Murray, *Losing Ground,* pp. 227–28.

[18]Barbara Ehrenreich, *Nickel and Dimed* (New York: Henry Holt, 2001); Beth Schulman, *The Betrayal of Work* (New York: The New Press, 2003).

[19]See William Julius Wilson, *When Work Disappears* (New York: Knopf, 1996), pp. 225–38; and Sheldon Danziger and Peter Gottschalk, *America Unequal* (Cambridge, MA: Harvard University Press, 1995), p. 174.

[20]Robert Wood Johnson Foundation, *Annual Report,* 1984.

[21]Lisbeth B. Schorr and Daniel Schorr, *Within Our Reach* (New York: Doubleday, 1989), p. 151.

Welfare Reform: The Personal Responsibility and Work Opportunity Reconciliation Act of 1996

This was the most significant piece of welfare legislation since the Social Security Act of 1935. These are its main provisions:

- The federal guarantee of cash assistance for poor children is ended.

- The head of every welfare family would have to work within two years or the family would lose benefits.

- After receiving welfare for two months adults must find jobs or perform community service.

- Lifetime welfare benefits would be limited to five years. (Hardship exemptions would be available to 20 percent of families. These families would continue receiving public assistance.)

- Each state receives a lump sum to run its own welfare and work programs.

- Up to 20 percent of those on public assistance—the ones who are least employable—will be allowed to remain on the rolls beyond the time limit.

For the first time since 1935 the federal government no longer guaranteed support to all of America's children. Critics have pointed out that the law required some 4 million mothers, nearly all with little education and poor job skills, to somehow go out and find jobs that would support their families. And most significantly, the law created no new jobs, paid for no training programs, and made no provision for additional free or low-cost day care facilities.

Around the time that Congress had passed and President Clinton had signed the Welfare Reform Act there were dire predictions that when families were thrown off public assistance, we would see children starving in the streets. But a study by Kathryn Edin and Laura Lein found that virtually all poor single mothers—whether working or receiving public assistance—were supplementing their income with money from a support network of relatives, boyfriends, or the absent fathers of their children.[22]

Has welfare reform been successful? The answer is yes—and no. In March 1994, the welfare rolls stood at a peak of 14.4 million recipients. (See Figure 10.) The rolls,

Workfare is now the law of the land.

We have ended welfare as we know it.

—President Bill Clinton

The trouble with being poor is that it takes up all your time.

—Willem de Kooning

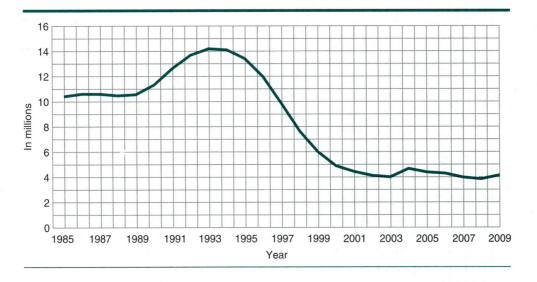

Figure 10

Recipients of Temporary Assistance for Needy Families, 1985–2009

After climbing from 1989 through 1993, the welfare rolls declined every year. The decline was especially sharp between 1994 and 1999.

Source: Statistical Abstract of the United States, 2009; U.S. Department of Health & Human Services, www.hhs.gov.

---

[22]Kathryn Edin and Laura Lein, *Making Ends Meet* (Ithaca, NY: Cornell University Press, 1997).

Going the Extra Mile

President Ronald Reagan used to refer to "Welfare Queens"—women who lived high off the hog on their welfare checks and made no effort to support themselves or their children. While there are indeed still some "Welfare Queens," most of the women on welfare are either working, very actively looking for work, or are being trained for some form of work. In order to work, poor single mothers not only have to find jobs, find transportation to those jobs, but they have to arrange child care as well. This is what six Greenwood Mississippi women must go through every working day:

Six Leflore County mothers are picked up in vans at 3 a.m. for a ride to jobs in faraway chicken

processing plants where they earn about $6 an hour, or $12,000 a year. With stops to deliver children to sitters, the trip takes three or four hours.

The women still collect a welfare check because the pay does not lift them above the poverty line, and the state pays for their child care and the van, and gives them $5 a day for lunch and a $3,000 bonus for working for two years. *

_____

*Peter T. Kilborn, "Recession Is Stretching the Limit on Welfare Benefits," *The New York Times,* December 9, 2001.

which began falling in 1994, continued to fall steadily through the next 9 years, reaching 4 million in 2003. (See the box, "Going the Extra Mile.") Since then between 3.8 and 4.8 million Americans have been receiving public assistance.

The current mantra is "work first," the policy of putting people to work without detours through training and education. So far, the state strategies appear to be paying off, since recipients have fled the welfare rolls in record numbers, but there have been serious problems. The wages earned by former welfare mothers average about $8 an hour, and 75 percent of them also lacked medical benefits. About one-third of those who left the rolls were back on welfare within a year.

Douglas J. Besharov, who teaches at the University of Maryland School of Public Policy and is a resident scholar at the conservative American Enterprise Institute, has summarized what has happened to the single mothers who left the welfare roles in the wake of welfare reform:

> . . . the best estimates are that only about 40 percent to 50 percent of mothers who left welfare have steady, full-time jobs. Another 15 percent or so work part time. According to surveys in various states, these mothers are earning about $8 an hour. That's about $16,000 a year for full-time employment. It is their story that the supporters of welfare reform celebrate, but $16,000 is not a lot of money, especially for a mother with two children.[23]

Despite the worst job market in 70 years, millions of single mothers are expected to find jobs that will support their families. Among families living below the poverty level with working mothers, child care absorbs about one third of household income.

Recognizing the need for subsidized childcare, the federal government now provides $7 billion a year to be used in state run programs. But in a time of tremendous budgetary pressure, about half the states cut hundreds of thousands of subsidized child-care slots in 2008, 2009, and 2010. Today just 1.6 million children—a small fraction of those eligible—receive subsidized child care.

Unable to secure affordable child care, thousands of single working mothers have been pushed out of the labor force and onto the public assistance rolls. It would appear then that welfare reform without adequate provision for child care has left many poor families between a rock and a hard place.

_____

[23]Douglas J. Besharov, "End Welfare Lite As We Know It," *The New York Times,* August 15, 2006, p. A19.

Current Issue: Will You Ever Be Poor?

What are the chances that your income will fall below the poverty line for at least a year? Most Americans experience more than a year of poverty sometime after their 20th birthday. We're not talking about college or graduate student poverty. Indeed you can greatly increase your chances of experiencing some poverty if you don't have a high school diploma. And if you're black, then you stand more than 9 chances out of 10 of being poor for more than a year sometime during your adulthood.

Where do these numbers come from? They come from an ongoing study, the Panel Study of Income Dynamics, which has been following the same individuals and households every year since 1968. These 18,000 individuals from 4,800 households are tracked annually, and children born into these families are also included. Any dropouts are replaced by families with similar characteristics.[24]

TABLE 4	The Cumulative Percentage of Americans Who Experience at Least a Year of Poverty, by Race	
	Cumulative Percentage	
Age	Black	White
20	29.7	6.9
35	61.6	25.6
55	79.3	38.3
75	91.0	52.6

Source: Data from Panel Study of Income Dynamics. Computations from Rank, op. cit., p. 96.

Table 4 shows the cumulative percentage of poverty by race for various age groups. Interestingly a majority of whites experiences a bout of poverty by the age of 75. But some 91 percent of all blacks spend at least a year of their lives below the poverty line.

See if you happen to know the answer to *this* question: Who would more likely be poor—a black person or a high school dropout? You can figure out the answer for yourself by glancing at Tables 4 and 5.

TABLE 5	The Cumulative Percentage of Americans Who Experience at Least a Year of Poverty, by Education	
	Cumulative Percentage	
Age	Less than 12 years	12 years or more
20	12.4	8.6
35	41.5	29.1
55	60.5	39.2
75	75.3	48.0

Source: Data from Panel Study of Income Dynamics. Computations from Rank, op. cit., p. 96.

Comparing the cumulative percentages at each age, you should note that the chances of a black person being poor are much greater than that of a high school dropout. In

---

[24]See Mark Robert Rank, *One Nation, Underprivileged* (New York: Oxford University Press, 2004), pp. 90–91.

other words race is a much better predictor of one's lifetime prospects of being poor than a high school diploma.

Despite the fact that your income may fall below the poverty line, you probably won't ever be truly poor. The reason is that you'll be able to fall back on your accumulated wealth, especially your home. As you know, tens of millions of Americans have taken out home equity loans, which they use to finance their children's educations, major consumption purchases, and sometimes just to maintain a lifestyle that requires spending more than their current income. So if your income *does* fall below the poverty for a year or two, or possibly even longer, you will probably manage quite well by taking out a home equity loan, digging into your savings, borrowing from your retirement plan, or, if worst comes to worse, maxing out your credit cards.

Middle class people generally have a built-in safety net to help them through bad times. But the truly poor, who were described in great detail through most of this chapter, have few resources to fall back on in bad times. Indeed, for most of them, the bad times may well be the norm. So over the next 50 years, I'd like you to keep a record of how many years your income falls below the poverty line. If that never happens, then you've beaten the odds.

Questions for Further Thought and Discussion

1. What's the difference between the distribution of income and the distribution of wealth? Describe the distribution of income and the distribution of wealth in the United States.

2. Discuss the basic determinants of income distribution.

3. Who are the poor in the United States? A few population groups have very high incidences of poverty. Explain why people in each of these groups tend to be poor.

4. There are several theories of the causes of poverty. Why can't a single theory explain all the poverty in the United States?

5. Compare and contrast the conservative and liberal views of poverty.

6. What has happened to the welfare rolls since the mid-1990s? What are the causes of this trend?

7. *Practical Application:* What steps would you take to cut our poverty rate in half?

8. *Web Activity:* Are you eligible for the Earned Income Tax Credit? Find out at www.hrblock/taxes/tax_tips/calculators/index.html and click on Earned Income Credit or www.wwwebtax.com/credits/earned_income_credit.htm

9. *Web Activity:* Do you want to be a billionaire? Aside from inheriting money, in which three industries or economic sectors have our 100 richest billionaires made their fortunes? Go to www.forbes.com/richlist

Workbook for Chapter 17 ![McGraw Hill] connect | ECONOMICS

Name _____   Date _____

Multiple-Choice Questions

Circle the letter that corresponds to the best answer.

1. Most social scientists define the poor as being the lowest _____ percent of our income recipients. **(LO4)**
   a) 10   d) 40
   b) 20   e) 50
   c) 3

2. Which is the most accurate statement? **(LO7)**
   a) Although there are several theories of poverty, it is possible to formulate just one theory which completely explains 99 percent of all poverty in the United States.
   b) There are at least a dozen theories of poverty, and each has at least some apparent validity.
   c) Poverty can be explained largely by employment discrimination.
   d) Poverty is no longer a major socioeconomic problem in the United States.

3. The Darity-Myers thesis is an attempt to explain _____. **(LO7)**
   a) black poverty
   b) the poverty of the elderly
   c) worldwide poverty
   d) the permanent underclass

4. An equal distribution of income would _____. **(LO1)**
   a) hurt both the work incentive and the incentive to save
   b) hurt neither the work incentive nor the incentive to save
   c) hurt the work incentive but not the incentive to save
   d) hurt the incentive to save but not the work incentive

5. Doctors earn more than people in other professions basically because _____. **(LO2, 3)**
   a) they need to be compensated for all those years they spent in school
   b) they are in short supply relative to the demand for their services
   c) it costs a lot more to be a doctor—office expenses, support staff, and malpractice insurance—than it does to be in almost any other profession
   d) doctors put in longer hours than most other people

6. To keep a family of four at the poverty line a person working a 40-hour week would need to earn about _____ an hour. **(LO4)**
   a) $7   d) $13
   b) $9   e) $15
   c) $11

7. Compared to their levels in 2003, the poverty line has _____ and the minimum hourly wage has _____. **(LO4)**
   a) gone up, gone up
   b) stayed the same, stayed the same
   c) gone up, stayed the same
   d) stayed the same, gone up

8. Women working full-time earn a little more than _____ percent of what is earned by their male counterparts. **(LO1, 2)**
   a) 33   c) 75
   b) 50   d) 100

9. Each of the following is a major source of great wealth except _____. **(LO2)**
   a) earning large salaries
   b) starting up new companies
   c) real estate
   d) inheritance

10. Which is not aimed solely at the poor? (LO6)
    a) Food stamps
    b) Public assistance
    c) Social Security
    d) Medicaid

11. Which statement is true? (LO7, 9)
    a) Very few poor people hold jobs.
    b) The main reason for poverty is that some people refuse to work.
    c) A person holding a minimum wage job could raise her family out of poverty.
    d) There are millions of people whose jobs don't pay enough to support their families.

12. Which statement is false? (LO5)
    a) About three-fourths of the poor are single mothers and their children.
    b) About half of the poor are elderly.
    c) People living in the South are more likely to be poor than those living in the rest of the country.
    d) None of these statements is false.

13. About _____ million Americans are homeless. (LO5)
    a) 2 to 3   d) 20 to 25
    b) 6 to 8   e) 40 to 50
    c) 12 to 15

14. Which statement is true? (LO5)
    a) Most poor people are black.
    b) Most black people are poor.
    c) People over age 65 have a higher poverty rate than the overall rate for Americans.
    d) None of these statements is true.

15. Darity and Myers predict that _____. (LO7)
    a) welfare reform will lead to a sharp decline in the number of black families living below the poverty line
    b) cutting welfare benefits will increase the ranks of marriageable young black men
    c) the underlying cause of poverty is too much government intervention
    d) there will be an increasing number of black families headed by females

16. "The exodus of middle- and working-class families from many ghetto neighborhoods removes an important 'social buffer'" was said by _____. (LO7)
    a) Nicholas Lemann
    b) Charles Murray
    c) Barbara Ehrenreich
    d) William Julius Wilson

17. Which statement is true? (LO5)
    a) Virtually none of the homeless have jobs.
    b) Many of the homeless are mentally ill.
    c) The homeless are concentrated in a few large cities.
    d) None of these statements is true.

18. Nearly one out of every _____ children lives in poverty. (LO5)
    a) two   c) five
    b) three   d) nine

19. Social scientists believe _____ the differential between what women and men earn can be explained by employment discrimination. (LO3)
    a) almost all of
    b) about half of
    c) only a small part of

20. Which statement is false? (LO7, 9)
    a) Poverty breeds poverty.
    b) Poor people have low human capital.
    c) The liberals and conservatives disagree on how to get people off the welfare rolls and into self-supporting jobs.
    d) None of these statements is false.

21. It would not be reasonable to say that poor people are _____. (LO5)
    a) grudgingly tolerated by society's "productive" members
    b) largely superfluous to our socioeconomic system
    c) basically self-supporting
    d) poor for a variety of reasons

22. Which one of the following statements is false? (LO6, 7)

   a) The poor pay higher prices to buy groceries, furniture, and appliances.

   b) Low-income families can pay over $500 more for the same car bought by a higher-income household.

   c) The poor pay higher interest rates than people with higher incomes.

   d) Very few poor people can claim the earned income tax credit.

23. The earned income tax credit is _____. (LO6)

   a) a form of welfare

   b) a refund check paid to the working poor by the Internal Revenue Service

   c) a very minor form of government aid to the poor

   d) opposed by both liberals and conservatives

24. The superrich get most of their income from _____. (LO3)

   a) rent, interest, and profits

   b) wages

   c) illegal transactions

   d) real estate investments

25. The richest fifth of all American families receives _____ percent of our total income. (LO1)

   a) almost 35   c) more than 60

   b) about 50   d) more than 75

26. Which of the following is the most accurate statement? (LO5)

   a) The standard of living of poor American children is very low compared to that of middle-class American children.

   b) Poor children in the United States are much worse off than poor children in virtually all other OECD countries.

   c) Poor children in the United States are much better off than poor children in virtually all other OECD countries.

   d) There is no way to compare the degree of child poverty in the United States with the degree of child poverty in other economically advanced countries.

27. Between 1968 and 2008, the percentage share of total income grew for the _____. (LO1, 3)

   a) lowest two quintiles

   b) the middle three quintiles

   c) the highest quintile

   d) the highest quintile and the lowest quintile

28. Between 1968 and 2008, our income distribution has _____. (LO1)

   a) became more equal

   b) stayed about the same

   c) became less equal

29. Real median family income in the U.S. has _____. (LO1, 2)

   a) grown each year since 2000

   b) declined each year since 2000

   c) risen by about 20 percent since the late 1960s

   d) become lower today than it was in 1975

30. Which of the following statements is the most accurate? (LO5, 6)

   a) The welfare rolls today are much lower than they were in 1996.

   b) About 1 in 8 Americans lives below the poverty line.

   c) Without Social Security benefits, at least 75 percent of all senior citizens would be poor.

   d) The Welfare Reform Act of 1996 has cut the poverty rate by almost 60 percent.

31. Which statement is true? (LO2)

   a) All of the 10 richest Americans inherited their fortunes.

   b) In order to make the top ten list of American billionaires, you need a fortune of over $15 billion.

   c) The two richest families in the United States today are the Rockefellers and the Fords.

   d) Most of the 10 richest Americans own large manufacturing companies.

32. Which is the most accurate statement? (LO4, 5)

   a) Although there are poor children in the U.S., our child poverty problem is not nearly as bad as that of most other rich countries.

   b) The reason so many people in poor countries still don't have safe drinking water is that it would cost at least $50 billion a year to provide it.

   c) Poor people in the U.S. spend more than double their reported incomes.

   d) Although some war veterans are poor, virtually none is homeless because of the efforts of the Veteran's Administration to find them housing.

33. Which statement is true? (LO1, 2)
    a) If we redistributed income every year so that everyone would get the same amount, this would hurt the efficiency of our economy.
    b) Virtually everyone agrees that we should redistribute most of the income received by the rich to the poor.
    c) The poor get a great deal more satisfaction from each additional dollar of income than the rich.
    d) There is no relationship between the distribution of income and economic incentives.

34. The largest government program aimed exclusively at helping the poor is _____. (LO6)
    a) the earned income tax credit
    b) public assistance
    c) food stamps
    d) Social Security

35. Which one of the following people would most likely experience at least a year of poverty after her or his 20th birthday? (LO5)
    a) A high school dropout
    b) A black person
    c) A white person
    d) A college dropout

36. Which statement is true? (LO6, 10)
    a) Most of the nation's poor receive welfare benefits.
    b) Since the Welfare Reform Act of 1996, no new welfare cases have been accepted.
    c) More people than ever are receiving welfare benefits.
    d) Most single mothers who have recently left the welfare rolls remain poor.

37. Which statement is true? (LO6, 9)
    a) Over 90 percent of the families receiving public assistance are headed by people who are employed.
    b) Nearly 90 percent of those in the workforce earn at least $10 an hour.
    c) The welfare rolls are much lower today than they were in 1994.
    d) If every adult on welfare were willing to work, we could cut the number of welfare families by over 75 percent.

38. Which one of the following is the most accurate statement? (LO4)
    a) Our poverty rate is somewhat higher today than it was in 1999.
    b) Our poverty rate is over 15 percent.
    c) If it were not for the 2007–2009 recession, our poverty rate would probably be below 10 percent.
    d) Our poverty rate is currently at an all-time low.

39. What would be the most effective way of raising people out of poverty? (LO9)
    a) Cut off welfare payments to every family with at least one adult member between the ages of 18 and 64.
    b) Raise the minimum hourly wage.
    c) Eliminate the earned income tax credit.
    d) Have the government put welfare recipients to work at minimum wage jobs.

40. Which one of the following statements is the most accurate? (LO9)
    a) Our nation provides cradle-to-grave security for our military personnel and their families.
    b) Because of the relative high pay and benefits provided by the military, very few military families run into financial problems.
    c) No military family lives below the poverty line.
    d) Some military families depend on food pantries.

41. Which one of these is the most accurate statement about real median family income? (LO1, 2)
    a) It has declined steadily over the last five years.
    b) It has fallen during nearly every recession since the 1960s.
    c) It is about twice as high as it was in 1970.
    d) It increased steadily since 2000.

42. Which is the most accurate statement? (LO6)
    a) Because of the efforts of the Veterans Administration, only a handful of veterans are homeless.
    b) Most military families have to get by on food stamps and help from food pantries and soup kitchens.
    c) Military pay is high enough to keep virtually all military families well above the official poverty line.
    d) Although nearly all of our leading politicians wear American flag lapel pins, they do not provide enough economic support to our troops, so many military families are in severe financial difficulty.

43. Who made this statement? "I still have the audacity to believe that people everywhere can have three meals a day." (LO4, 8)
    a) Charles Murray
    b) William Julius Wilson
    c) Barbara Bush (mother of President George W. Bush)
    d) Martin Luther King, Jr.
    e) Lisbeth B. Schorr

44. Which one of the following statements is *false?* (LO5)
    a) Nearly half of all poor Americans own their own homes.
    b) A poor person today has roughly the same standard of living as a middle-income person 30 years ago.
    c) The reported consumption spending of people in the lowest income quintile is about twice their reported income.
    d) The standard of living of American's poor is comparable to that of most of the rest of the world's poor people.

45. Who would most likely receive food stamps before the age of 20? (LO6)
    a) A white person
    b) A black person
    c) An Asian-American person
    d) A person who grew up in a two-parent household

46. Which is the most accurate statement? (LO6, 10)
    a) Most poor people receive public assistance (formerly called welfare).
    b) Public assistance has been discontinued.
    c) The number of people receiving public assistance is less than one-third as high as it was in 1993.
    d) Because of the 2007–2009 recession, the public assistance rolls have reached an all-time high.

47. Which statement best reflects the views of Charles Murray? (LO8)
    a) The main cause of poverty can be traced to the heritage of slavery.
    b) Poverty is caused largely by government antipoverty programs.
    c) Poverty can be substantially reduced by providing government jobs to all who want to work.
    d) The prime cause of poverty is that poor people are basically lazy.

48. Which one of the following people would stand the least chance of being poor during her or his lifetime? (LO 11)
    a) Someone with less than 12 years of education
    b) Someone with more than 12 years of education
    c) Someone white
    d) Someone black

Fill-In Questions

1. The richest 1 percent of our population owns over _____ percent of our wealth. (LO2)

2. The two biggest benefit programs aimed solely at the poor are _____ and _____. (LO6)

3. About one out of every _____ black Americans is poor. (LO4)

4. About _____ percent of all poor people are black. (LO4)

5. The basic problem with the absolute concept of poverty is finding the _____. (LO4)

6. The poverty line is set by the _____. (LO4)

7. The richest quintile of humanity spends about _____ times as much on consumption as the world's poorest quintile. (LO1)

Problems

Use Figure 1 to answer problems 1 through 4. (LO1)

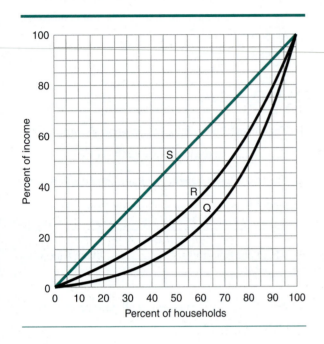

Figure 1

1. How much is the percentage of income received by the lowest quintile on line R?

2. How much is the percentage of income earned by the highest quintile on Lorenz curve Q?

3. How much is the percentage of income received by the highest quintile on line R?

4. How much is the percentage of income received by the middle three quintiles on line S?

Chapter 18

International Trade

> More and more of our imports come from overseas.
>
> —President George W. Bush

Huge container ships steam into Seattle every day loaded with shoes, clothing, textiles, furniture, TVs, and cameras that were made in Asia. On their return trip these same ships leave half empty, bearing chemicals, meat, grain, as well as hay, scrap metal, and scrap paper. These cargoes vividly illustrate our relationship with our Asian trading partners: We buy what they make, but they don't buy that much of what we make.

Trillions of dollars' worth of business in international trade is conducted every year. Certain trading nations—Japan, the United Kingdom, Singapore, the Netherlands, Korea, and Taiwan among them—draw their economic lifeblood from foreign trade, while others, such as the United States, France, Germany, Russia, and China, are relatively self-sufficient. Yet even the United States has become increasingly dependent on imported TVs, apparel, textiles, steel, compact cars, oil, and other goods.

How this trade is conducted is the subject of this chapter; how it is financed is the subject of the next. The thread that runs through international trade and finance is specialization and exchange. If all the nations of the world were self-sufficient, there would be no international trade and little need for international finance. But if that were to happen, the world would have a much lower standard of living.

LEARNING OBJECTIVES

After reading this chapter you should be able to:

1. Summarize the history of U.S. trade.
2. Explain the relationship between specialization and exchange.
3. Define and differentiate between absolute advantage and comparative advantage.
4. List and evaluate the arguments for protection.
5. Compare the advantages and disadvantages of tariffs versus quotas.
6. List and discuss the causes of our trade imbalance.
7. Compare the causes of our trade deficits with Japan and China.
8. Differentiate between free trade in word and in deed.
9. Explain how we can reduce our trade deficit.
10. Evaluate the pros and cons of a "Buy American" policy.
11. List and discuss the effects of globalization on our economy.

America is being flooded with imports, and millions of workers are being thrown out of work. Americans are buying not just foreign-made cameras and DVD players, but also foreign-made steel, textiles, apparel, personal computers, cars, and toys. But why worry? After all, the world is now a global village, and we all buy from and sell to each other. Why should we buy something from an American firm when we can get a better deal from a foreign firm?

459

International trade is really good for everyone. As consumers, we are able to purchase a whole array of goods and services that would not have otherwise been available—at least, not at such low prices. Hence, we can thank international trade for much of our high standard of living. As producers, we are able to sell a great deal of our output abroad, thereby increasing our employment and profits. So far, so good. The only trouble is that during the last two decades or so, we have been buying a lot more from foreigners than they have been buying from us.

So what do we *do?* Do we throw up protective tariff barriers to keep out lower-priced foreign imports? Or, like the old Avis rent-a-car commercials, do we just try harder? After a brief history of U.S. trade, in Part II of the chapter we'll consider the theory of international trade, why such trade is so wonderful, and why we should not do anything to impede its flow. In Part III we'll take a closer look at the practice of international trade and try to zero in on the causes of our trade imbalance and what we can do to redress it. And then, in Part IV, we'll look at why we've been running huge trade deficits with Japan and China.

Part I: A Brief History of U.S. Trade

The United States did not always run large trade deficits. Indeed, we ran surpluses for virtually the entire first three-quarters of the 20th century. Let's look at that record, and at U.S. government trade policy over the years.

U.S. Trade before 1975

We ran trade surpluses before 1975 and deficits after 1975.

Why 1975? Because that's the last year we ran a trade surplus. Until 1971 the United States had run a surplus nearly every year of the 20th century.

Until the early 1900s we were primarily an agricultural nation, exporting cotton and grain to Europe in exchange for manufactured goods. These included not just consumer goods—shoes, clothing, books, and furniture—but also a great deal of machinery and equipment for our growing industrial sector. We ran relatively small trade deficits through most of the 19th century.

But once we had become a powerful industrial nation, by the turn of the 20th century, we had not only less need of European manufactures but we were now exporting our own manufactured goods. With the outbreak of World War I in 1914, we added armaments to our growing list of exports, as our trade surpluses mounted. In the 1920s we inundated the world with Model T Fords, as well as a host of other American vehicles, along with radios, phonographs, toasters, waffle irons, and other consumer appliances.

The Great Depression of the 1930s depressed not only worldwide production of goods and services but their export as well. Our trade surpluses increased in the 1940s, with the advent of World War II, when, once again, we shipped huge quantities of food and armaments to England, the Soviet Union, China, and our other allies. It took 15 years for the world's other leading industrial powers to recover from the devastation of the war, during which time we supplied the world from our cornucopia of manufacturing and agricultural products. During this period, and well into the 1960s, we continued running substantial trade surpluses.

U.S. Trade since 1975

We faced increasing trade competition in the 1960s.

By the early 1960s Japan and the industrial nations of Western Europe had rebuilt their factories and stemmed the flood of American imports. Later in that decade these nations, especially Japan, were exporting cars, TVs, cameras, and other consumer goods to the United States and going head-to-head with American manufacturers throughout the world. By the late 1970s our trade deficits were mounting (see Figure 1). Although these deficits rose and fell over the years, by 1984 they crossed the $100 billion mark.

In the late 1990s, our trade deficit really took off. Some of the contributing factors were the high U.S. dollar (which made our exports more expensive and our imports cheaper), our rapid economic growth, which expanded our demand for foreign goods and services, and our insatiable appetite for foreign consumer goods.

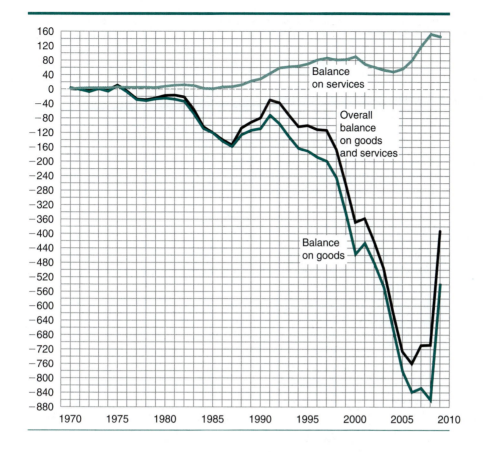

Figure 1

U.S. Balance of Trade in Goods and Services, and Overall Balance, 1970–2009 (in billions of dollars)

Since the late 1980s we have been running a large and growing surplus on services. Our balance on goods, which has been negative since the mid-1970s, has grown much worse since 1991.

Sources: Economic Report of the President, 1985–2010; Economic Indicators, April 2010.

Our service sector has had a positive balance since the mid-1980s, but it has been increasingly overwhelmed by our huge and growing negative balance of trade in goods. The major contributors to our positive service balance include education, financial, travel, medical, and legal services, royalties and license fees, operational leasing, and film and television video rentals and sales.

Back in 1960 just 4 percent of the cars Americans purchased and 6 percent of our TVs, radios, and other consumer electronics were built outside the United States. Also, we imported just 5 percent of our steel and 3 percent of our machine tools. Today all of our TVs, nearly all of our other consumer electronics, and over one-quarter of our cars are imported. And today we import two thirds of our oil, compared to just 15 percent in 1960.

Table 1 provides a snapshot view of our imports, exports, and balance of trade in 2009. As you can see, we imported $537 billion more in goods than we exported. Services

TABLE 1	U.S. Balance of Trade, 2009*
	(in billions of dollars)
Goods	
Imports	−$1,572
Exports	+ 1,035
Balance of goods	− 537
Services	
Imports	−$380
Exports	+ 525
Balance of services	+ 145
Balance of trade*	− 392

*Numbers may not add up exactly because of rounding.

continued to be the one bright spot of our trade balance, since we exported $145 billion more than we imported.

The Effect of the Great Recession on Our Balance of Trade

As you'll notice from the middle line in Figure 1, our trade deficit—the overall balance on goods and services—fell by over $300 billion from 2008 to 2009. Why did it fall so sharply, and—even more important—will this be a permanent decline? As we shall see, the answer to the first question will help answer the second.

The Great Recession of 2007–2009 affected not just our own country, but nearly all our major trading partners. As consumption and production fell, all these nations curbed their imports. And, of course, by definition, as worldwide imports fell, worldwide exports fell by exactly the same amount.

Consumption and production declined somewhat faster in the United States than it did in the rest of the economically advanced nations. Consequently our demand for imported goods and services fell more than the demand for our exports. What happened, then, in 2009, was that our imports fell much more than our exports, and our trade deficit declined substantially.

Our trade deficit also fell during the recessions of 1990–91and 2001, but during the Great Recession of 2007–2009 it fell much more sharply. In the late spring of 2010, with a financial crisis brewing in Europe—and with the fall of the euro—it appeared that for the rest of the year our exports to Europe would lag. If our own economic recovery continued, then it appeared likely that our trade deficit would shoot back up again.

So how likely will our relatively low trade deficits be permanent? As the world continues to recover from the Great Recession, our imports and our exports will increase. And unless our recovery is relatively slow—compared to those of our trading partners—we can expect that our trade deficit will climb steadily over the next few years.

---

on the web

How big was our trade deficit last month? Go to www.census.gov/indicator/www/ustrade.html

---

U.S. Government Trade Policy

We can get a snapshot view of this policy over the last two centuries by glancing at Figure 2. The relatively high tariffs through most of the 19th century and during the Great Depression reflected the political climate of those times.

A century of high protective tariffs

Back in Chapter 1 we talked about the high protective tariff being a cause of the Civil War. How did that come to be? Initially the tariff was purely a revenue-raising device, but after the War of 1812 war-born industries found it impossible to meet British competition, and the tariff took on a protective tinge. In 1816 the first protective tariff was adopted, followed in 1828 by the "Tariff of Abominations." But to whom was this tariff so abominable? To the South, which was primarily an agrarian economy, exporting cotton and importing manufactured goods. Of course the industrial Northern manufacturers wanted the South to buy their own goods rather than import them from Europe. However the South, allied with the Western states joining the union, was able to induce Congress to progressively lower tariffs until the Civil War. Note that, in 1861, when the 11 states of the Confederacy withdrew from the union, tariffs went right back up once more. Business-oriented Republican administrations kept them high until the Underwood Tariff of 1913, which, incidentally, was passed by a Southern-dominated Democratic Congress.

Again, during the Great Depression, virtually every industrial power, beset with massive unemployment, raised its tariffs to keep out foreign goods. Of course, since everyone was doing this, world trade dwindled to a fraction of what it had been in the 1920s. While certain jobs were protected, others, mainly in the export sector, were lost. Economists believe that these high tariffs, especially the Smoot-Hawley Tariff of 1930, made the depression a lot worse than it might have otherwise been.

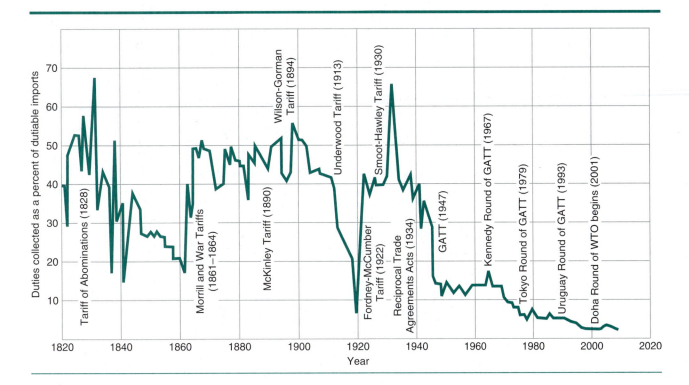

F*igure* 2

U.S. Tariffs, 1820–2009

Although tariffs fluctuated widely from the 1820s through the early 1930s, there has been a strong downward trend. Today tariffs average less than 5 percent of the price of our imported durable goods.

Source: U.S. Department of Commerce.

The GATT (General Agreement on Trade and Tariffs) treaty of 1947 began a downward trend in tariffs all around the world, leading to the formation of the World Trade Organization, which was set up to further facilitate world trade. GATT and the World Trade Organization were discussed in Chapter 8 of *Economics* and *Macroeconomics*.

A downward trend in tariffs since 1947

You can find our imports, exports, and trade deficit for the most recent three years at www.bea.gov. Click on "Survey of Current Business" at the left, then go to "National Data," "National Income and Product Accounts," NIPA tables, and finally, "Gross Domestic Product." It's much less complicated than it sounds.

Part II: The Theory of International Trade

Since 1992 our trade deficit has ballooned from just $30 billion to hundreds of billions. What can we do to reverse this trend? Should we restrict this profusion of imports, or should we listen to the reasoning of the economics profession, which is nearly unanimous in arguing for free trade?

If we will not buy, we cannot sell.
—President William McKinley

Specialization and Trade

The basis for international trade is specialization. Different nations specialize in the production of those goods and services for which their resources are best suited. An individual who attempts to be entirely self-sufficient would have to make her own nails, grow her own food, spin her own cloth, sew her own clothes, make her own tools, ad

Specialization is the basis for international trade.

infinitum. It is much easier and a lot cheaper to work at one particular job or specialty and use one's earnings to buy those nails, food, clothes, and so on.

It pays for nations to specialize, just as it pays for individuals.

What makes sense individually also makes sense internationally. Thus, just as it pays for individuals to specialize and trade, it pays for nations to do so. And that's exactly what we do: On a national basis we specialize and trade. But it would be impossible to do this unless there were a big enough market in which to buy and sell the goods and services we produce. Of course, the United States has long been the world's largest national market.

Adam Smith recognized the advantages of foreign trade more than two centuries ago when he wrote:

> If a foreign country can supply us with a commodity cheaper than we ourselves can make it, better buy it of them with some part of the produce of our own industry, employed in a way in which we have some advantage. The general industry of the country . . . will not thereby be diminished . . . but only left to find out the way in which it can be employed with the greatest advantage.[1]

Smith's argument provides the basis for international trade. Country A specializes in making the products that it can make most cheaply. Country B does the same. When they trade, each country will be better off than they would have been if they didn't specialize and trade.

Absolute Advantage

Let us say that workers in Brazil can produce more cell phones per hour than workers in Argentina. But Argentinian workers can turn out more PlayStations per hour than can Brazilian workers. We would say, then, that Brazilian workers have an absolute advantage in producing cell phones, while Argentinian workers have an absolute advantage in producing PlayStations. *Absolute advantage is the ability of a country to produce a good using fewer resources than another country.*

Common sense tells us that Brazil should trade some of its PlayStations for some of Argentina's cell phones. But the basis for trade is not absolute advantage, but comparative advantage. This concept shows us just how much two countries can gain by trading.

The propensity to truck, barter and exchange one thing for another is common to all men, and to be found in no other race of animals.

—Adam Smith

Comparative Advantage

Back in Chapter 2 we introduced production possibility curves, which showed how much a country could produce if its output were limited to just two goods. Now we'll look at the production possibilities frontiers of Peru and Pakistan (see Figure 3).

Notice that the production possibilities frontiers of Peru and Pakistan are straight lines, rather than the curves we had in Chapter 2. To keep things simple, let's assume that the resources used to produce corn are equally suitable for producing cameras. That enables us to have straight-line production possibility frontiers, which will help us demonstrate the law of comparative advantage.

Peru can produce two bushels of corn for every camera it makes. And Pakistan can produce one bushel of corn for every two cameras it makes. Are you ready for the million dollar question? OK, here's the question: Should Pakistan and Peru trade with each other?

What's your answer? If you said "yes," then you're right! That's because both nations are better off by trading than by not trading. Pakistan gains by trading cameras to Peru for corn; Peru gains by trading corn to Pakistan for cameras. So both nations gain by trading.

Let's go back to the concept of opportunity cost. What is Pakistan's opportunity cost of producing two cameras? In other words, to produce two cameras, what does Pakistan give up?

The answer is one bushel of corn. Now what is the opportunity cost of growing two bushels of corn for Peru?

---

[1]Adam Smith, *The Wealth of Nations*, vol. 1, ed. Edwin Cannan (London: University Paperbacks by Methuen, 1961), pp. 478–79.

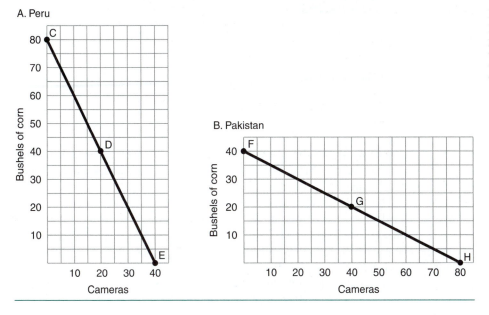

Figure 3

Production Possibilities Curves

Peru, operating at full capacity, can produce 80 bushels of corn or 40 cameras. Pakistan, operating at full capacity, can produce 40 bushels of corn or 80 cameras.

Peru's opportunity cost is one camera. Now we're ready for the law of comparative advantage. *The law of comparative advantage states that total output is greatest when each product is made by the country that has the lowest opportunity cost.* If the relative opportunity costs of producing goods (what must be given up in one good in order to get another good) differ between two countries, there are potential gains from trade.

Please glance back at Figure 3. You'll notice that Peru produces at point D (40 bushels of corn and 20 cameras). Pakistan is at point G (20 bushels of corn and 40 cameras). Table 2 restates points D and G.

TABLE 2	Production and Consumption of Corn and Cameras before Specialization and Trade	
	Pakistan	Peru
Bushels of corn	20	40
Cameras	40	20

We know that Pakistan can gain by trading cameras for corn, while Peru can gain by trading corn for cameras. So let's have Pakistan specialize in the production of cameras, placing it at point H of Figure 3. Meanwhile Peru, which now specializes in growing corn, will produce at point C of Figure 3. Table 3 restates points C and H.

Now Peru and Pakistan can trade. Let's assume the terms of trade are one camera for one bushel of corn. Pakistan will send Peru 40 cameras in exchange for 40 bushels of corn. This brings us to Table 4.

TABLE 3	Production of Corn and Cameras after Specialization	
	Pakistan	Peru
Bushels of corn	0	80
Cameras	80	0

TABLE 4	Consumption of Corn and Cameras after Trade	
	Pakistan	Peru
Bushels of corn	40	40
Cameras	40	40

It should be pretty obvious that both countries gained by specializing and trading. Just compare the numbers in Table 2 with those in Table 4. Pakistan gained 20 bushels of corn and Peru gained 20 cameras.

Let's work out another comparative advantage example. If France used all its resources, it could turn out 10 cars or 20 flat screen TVs, while Spain, using all its resources could turn out 5 cars or 15 TVs.

Which country has a comparative advantage in building cars, and which country has a comparative advantage in building TVs? Write your answers here:

_____ has a comparative advantage building cars.

_____ has a comparative advantage building TVs.

Solution: The opportunity cost to France of producing one car would be two TVs. The opportunity cost to Spain of producing one car would be three TVs. So France has a comparative advantage building cars and Spain has a comparative advantage building TVs.

Suppose the terms of trade were five TVs for two cars. Why would it pay for France to trade two cars in exchange for five TVs?

Solution: If France produced both cars and TVs, for every five TVs it made, it would be making two and a half less cars. But if France traded with Spain, she could produce just two cars and get five TVs in exchange.

Next question: Why would it pay for Spain to trade five TVs for two cars?

Solution: If Spain produced both cars and TVs, for every two cars she made, Spain would be making six less TVs. But if Spain traded with France, she could produce just five TVs and get two cars in exchange. If you'd like a little more practice, see the box, "How Comparative Advantage Leads to Gains from Specialization and Trade."

You probably never heard of the renowned facelift surgeon Dr. Khorsheed, but he is a legend in his own country, not just for his splendid work, but because of the great illustration he provides of the law of comparative advantage (see the box, "To Facelift or to File: *That* Is the Question").

Absolute Advantage versus Comparative Advantage

One of the things economists are fond of saying is that you can't compare apples and oranges. Here's a corollary: You can't compare absolute advantage and comparative advantage. The words may not exactly trip off your tongue, but still they ring true. Let's see why.

First, what *is* absolute advantage? It means that one country is better than another at producing some good or service (that is, it can produce it more cheaply). For example, the United States enjoys an absolute advantage over Japan in building commercial aircraft. But the Japanese enjoy an absolute advantage over the United States in making cameras. They can turn out cameras at a lower cost than we can, while we can build planes at a lower cost than the Japanese can.

So absolute advantage is a comparison of the cost of production in two different countries. What about comparative advantage? Let me quote myself: "The law of comparative advantage states that total output is greatest when each product is made by the country that has the lowest opportunity cost."

EXTRA
HELP

How Comparative Advantage Leads to Gains from Specialization and Trade

Just glance at Figure A and answer this question: Which country should specialize in producing telescopes and which country should specialize in producing microscopes?

Solution: If Canada used all its resources, it could produce either 60 telescopes or 30 microscopes. The opportunity cost of producing one microscope would be two telescopes. If Belgium used all its resources it could produce either 30 telescopes or 90 microscopes. The opportunity cost of producing one telescope would be three microscopes.

Clearly, then, Canada should specialize in making telescopes and Belgium should specialize in making microscopes.

If one microscope could be traded for one telescope, let's see how Canada would gain by trading its telescopes for Belgium's microscopes.

If Canada didn't specialize and trade, the opportunity cost for every microscope it produced would be not producing two telescopes. But it can now trade one telescope and receive in return one microscope. It's better to give up one telescope in exchange for one microscope than to give up two telescopes for one microscope (by producing both rather than specializing and trading).

Now let's see how Belgium gains from trading its microscopes for Canada's telescopes. If Belgium didn't trade, the opportunity cost of producing one telescope would be three microscopes. But if Belgium specialized in making microscopes, it would give up just one microscope in exchange for one telescope.

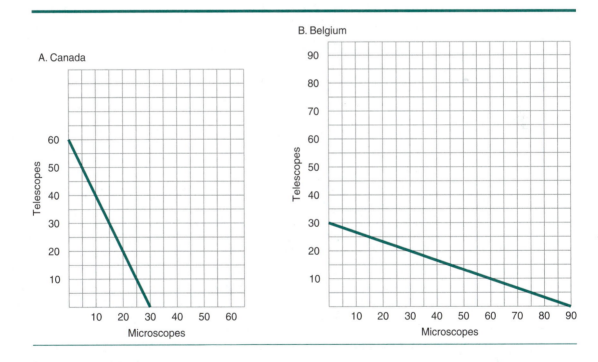

Figure A

Production Possibilities Curves

Operating at full capacity, Canada can produce 60 telescopes or 30 microscopes. Operating at full capacity, Belgium can produce 30 telescopes or 90 microscopes.

So we can say that as long as the relative opportunity costs of producing goods differ among nations, there are potential gains from trade even if one country has an absolute advantage in producing everything. Therefore *absolute* advantage is not necessary for trade to take place, but *comparative* advantage is.

To Facelift or to File: That *Is the Question*

Fereydoon Khorsheed is known in his country as the Michaelangelo of facelifts. He can do two a day at $3,000 a pop. The only problem is that he has to spend half the day doing paperwork, leaving him time to perform just one operation. So he hires Ashok Desai for $200 a day to deal with insurance companies, to do billing, filing, scheduling, and to keep the books. Now he is free to spend his entire working time doing facelifts, and his earnings double to $6,000 a day.

A perfectionist, Dr. Khorsheed soon discovers that it takes Mr. Desai a full day to do what he, Dr. Khorsheed, did in just half a day.

Question: Who has an absolute advantage in doing paperwork and who has an absolute advantage in doing facelifts?

Answer: Dr. Khorsheed has an absolute advantage in both endeavors. Mr. Desai can't do facelifts at all, and Dr. Khorsheed is twice as fast at paperwork.

Next question: Should Dr. Khorsheed fire Mr. Desai and do the paperwork himself?

Answer: Clearly not. He now earns $6,000 doing facelifts, pays Mr. Desai $200, leaving a net income of $5,800. If Dr. Khorsheed did paperwork for half the day, he'd have time for only one facelift and earn just $3,000.

So while Dr. Khorsheed is both a better facelifter and a better paperworker, it pays for him to specialize in facelifting, in which he has a comparative advantage, and leave the paperwork to Mr. Desai.

"The Gains from Trade" box summarizes most of what we've covered over the last 5 pages. I guarantee that when you have worked your way through this discussion, you will have become a great advocate of free trade.

The Arguments for Protection

> *America's gargantuan trade deficit is a weight around American workers' necks that is pulling them into a cycle of debt, bankruptcy and low-wage service jobs.*
>
> –Richard Trumka–
> AFL–CIO secretary-treasurer

As America continues to hemorrhage manufacturing jobs, there is a growing outcry for protection against the flood of foreign imports. But American consumers are virtually addicted to Japanese cars, South Korean TVs, Chinese microwave ovens, and hundreds of other manufactured goods from all over the world. How do we justify taxing or excluding so many things that so many Americans want to buy?

Four main arguments for protection

Four main arguments have been made for protection. Each seems plausible and strikes a responsive chord in the minds of the American public. But under closer examination, all four are essentially pleas by special interest groups for protection against more efficient competitors.

Does our dependence on foreign suppliers make us vulnerable in time of war?

(1) The National Security Argument   Originally this argument may have been advanced by American watchmakers, who warned the country not to become dependent on Swiss watchmakers because in the event of war Americans would not be able to make the timing devices for explosives without Swiss expertise. Yet during one long, drawn-out war, World War II, the United States was able to develop synthetics, notably rubber, to replace the supplies of raw materials that were cut off. And the Germans were able to convert coal into oil. It would appear, then, that the Swiss watch argument may have been somewhat overstated.

If our country were involved in a limited war, it is conceivable that our oil supplies from the Mideast might be cut off (although no American president would stand by passively while this happened), but we could probably replace these imports by producing more oil ourselves and by drawing on our strategic oil reserve. When Iraqi forces invaded Kuwait in 1990 President George Bush was able to put together an international coalition that quickly

The Gains from Trade

Let's look at the gains from trade, this time from a somewhat different prospective. By just glancing at Table A, you should easily be able to answer these questions:

1. Which country has an absolute advantage in producing shoes and which country has an absolute advantage in producing soybeans?

2. Which country has a comparative advantage in producing shoes and which country has a comparative advantage in producing soybeans?

Did you write down your answers? Please do that now. OK, let's see if we got the same answers:

1. The United States has an absolute advantage in producing both shoes and soybeans.

2. The United States has a comparative advantage in producing soybeans, while China enjoys a comparative advantage in producing shoes.

So it will pay for the United States to trade soybeans for Chinese shoes. And, of course, it will pay for the Chinese to trade their shoes for our soybeans.

I'd like to take credit for this example, but it actually appeared in the Federal Reserve Bank of Dallas's 2003 annual report. As we'll see, trade expands the economic pies of both China and the United States, leaving the consumers of both nations much better off than before they traded. That, indeed, is the reason why economists love free trade.

Table B shows China and the U.S. before and after trade. Before trade, China produced 500 pairs of shoes and the United States produced 300 pairs. After trade, China produced all the shoes—all 2,000 pairs. So total shoe production after trade rose from 800 pairs to 2,000 pairs.

Now let's see what happened to soybean production, which is shown in Table B. Before trade, the U.S. produced 4,000 bushels, while China produced 3,000. After trade the U.S. produced 10,000 bushels, while China did not produce any soybeans. So total output of soybeans rose from 7,000 before trade to 10,000 after trade.

Because trade enabled the U.S. to specialize in soybean production, and China to specialize in shoe production, the total output of both goods rose very substantially.

At the bottom of Table B, we have consumption of shoes and soybeans in both countries. Trade enabled China to increase its consumption of shoes from 500 pairs

Table A Hypothetical Labor Force and Output, U.S. and China*

	CHINA	UNITED STATES
Labor Force	500	100
Output per Worker		
Shoes (pairs)	4	5
Soybeans (bushels)	8	100

Table B Hypothetical Employment, Production, and Consumption, U.S. and China*

	CHINA		UNITED STATES	
Employment	No Trade	Free Trade	No Trade	Free Trade
Shoes	125	500	60	0
Soybeans	375	0	40	100
Production				
Shoes	500	2,000	300	0
Soybeans	3,000	0	4,000	10,000
Consumption				
Shoes	500	1,500	300	500
Soybeans	3,000	5,000	4,000	5,000

to 1,500 pairs. In the U.S., shoe consumption rose from 300 pairs to 500. Similarly, soybean consumption rose from 3,000 bushels to 5,000 in China, while in the U.S. it rose from 4,000 to 5,000.

Let's sum up. China enjoyed a comparative advantage in producing shoes, while the U.S. had a comparative advantage in producing soybeans. By specializing in the good each nation produced most efficiently, and then trading for the other good, both nations were much better off.

---

*Table A and Table B are reproduced from the 2003 Annual Report of the Federal Reserve Bank of Dallas, p. 16.

Sweatshop Labor

Sweatshop employees put in very long hours under very poor working conditions for very low pay. Most of the clothing and footwear we import is produced by sweatshops. Reebok, Nike, Liz Claiborne, the Gap, J.C. Penney, Sears-Kmart, Walmart, Disney, and Target are some of the leading sellers of goods made in sweatshops in Asia and Latin America.

In El Salvador alone, 200 factories make clothing for the American market. In 1995, conditions were so bad in her factory, a contractor for the Gap, Abigail Martinez, helped lead a strike that got the Gap's attention. This is a *New York Times* then-and-now account:

Six years ago, Abigail Martinez earned 55 cents an hour sewing cotton tops and khaki pants. Back then, she says, workers were made to spend 18-hour days in an unventilated factory with undrinkable water. Employees who displeased the bosses were denied bathroom breaks or occasionally made to sweep outside all morning in the broiling sun.

Today, she and other workers have coffee breaks and lunch on an outdoor terrace cafeteria. Bathrooms are unlocked, the factory is breezy and clean, and employees can complain to a board of independent monitors if they feel abused.

The changes are a result of efforts by Gap, the big clothing chain, to improve working conditions at this independent factory, one of many that supply its clothes.

Yet Ms. Martinez today earns 60 cents an hour, only 5 cents more than six years ago.

But consider the alternative. If Abigail Martinez quits, will she get a better job? And if wages in El Salvador were to rise, the Gap and other foreign clothing firms would move to another low-wage country.

In 2003 *BusinessWeek* reported that a dozen companies belonging to the Fair Labor Association (www.fairlabor.org) made public labor audits of the overseas factories that produce their products. Among their findings were that workers were forced to do overtime and work seven straight days, there were arbitrary firings, very limited drinking water, widespread sexual harassment, dirty toilets, no sick leave, and no pay stubs.

Sources: Leslie Kaufman and David Gonzalez, "Labor Standards Clash with Global Reality," *The New York Times,* April 24, 2001, p. A1; Aaron Bernstein, "Sweatshops: Finally, Airing the Dirty Linen," *Business-Week,* June 23, 2003, p. 100.

---

defeated Iraq. And if there were a third world war we would certainly not have to worry about a cutoff of needed war material because the war would last only a few minutes.

If the national security argument is applied only to limited or local wars rather than to worldwide wars, it is possible that we do need to maintain certain defense-related industries. A justification that the United States should make its own aircraft, ordnance (bombs and artillery shells), and nuclear submarines might well be valid on a national security basis. But these industries have done extremely well in international markets and are hardly in need of protection.

Are American industries still infant industries?

(2) The Infant Industry Argument　In the late 18th century American manufacturers clamored for protection against "unfair" British competition. British manufacturers were "dumping" their products on our shores. By pricing their goods below cost, the British would drive infant American manufacturers out of business. Once their American competition was out of the way, the British companies would jack up their prices.

Whatever validity this reasoning once had has long since vanished. American manufactured products are no longer produced by infant industries being swamped by foreign giants. About the best that can be said is that some of our infant industries never matured, while others went well beyond the point of maturity and actually attained senility. Perhaps a senile industry argument might be more applicable to such stalwarts as steel, textiles, clothing, and automobiles.

How can the United States compete against countries that pay sweatshop wages?

(3) The Low-Wage Argument　The reasoning here is best summed up by this question: How can American workers compete with foreigners who are paid sweatshop wages (see box)? Certain goods and services are very labor intensive (that is, labor constitutes most or nearly all of the resource costs). Clothing manufacturing, domestic work, rice cultivation, most kinds of assembly-line work, and repetitive clerical work are examples. There is no reason for American firms to compete with foreign firms to provide these goods and services.

Why *are* certain workers paid higher wage rates than others? Why *are* some countries high-wage countries, while others are low-wage countries? In general, high-wage workers produce more than low-wage workers. The main reason workers in high-wage countries produce more is that they have more capital with which to work than do workers in low-wage countries.

Why are some countries high-wage countries, while others are low-wage countries?

And so labor was paid more in the United States than almost anywhere else in the world during the three decades following World War II because we had more capital (plant and equipment) per worker than any other country. But as other countries succeeded in rebuilding and adding to their capital, our advantage disappeared.

The low-wage countries of Asia, Africa, and Latin America have a competitive advantage. So do the high-capital countries of Japan, the United States, Canada, and the European Union. Why not combine the best of both worlds—low wages and high capital?

That's just what multinational corporations have done around the world. Just across the Rio Grande in northern Mexico, thousands of factories churn out everything from cars and refrigerators to water beds and garage-door openers; they then ship most of these goods back into the United States. The factories are called *maquiladoras,* from the Mexican word for handwork. The workers are seldom paid much more than $1 an hour, less than a quarter of the U.S. minimum wage of $7.25.

The question, then, is how to deal with low-wage competition. The answer is to deal with it the way we always have. We have always imported labor-intensive goods—sugar, handmade rugs, wood carvings, even Chinese back scratchers—because they were cheap. By specializing in the production of goods and services in which we excel, we can use the proceeds to buy the goods and services produced by people who work for very low wages.

(4) The Employment Argument

Hasn't the flood of imports thrown millions of Americans out of work? There is no denying that hundreds of thousands of workers in each of the industries with stiff foreign competition—autos, steel, textiles, clothing, consumer electronics, and petroleum—have lost their jobs due to this competition. If we had restricted our imports of these goods by means of tariffs or quotas, most of these jobs could have been saved.

But the governments of our foreign competitors would have reciprocated by restricting our exports. Furthermore, a nation pays for its imports by selling its exports. By curbing our imports, we will be depriving other nations of the earnings they need to buy our exports. In sum, if we restrict our imports, our exports will go down as well.

If we restrict our imports, our exports will decline.

The jobs we save in steel, autos, textiles, clothing, consumer electronics, and petroleum will be lost in our traditional export industries—machinery, office equipment, aircraft, chemicals, computer software, and agricultural products. From an economic standpoint, this would involve a considerable loss because we would be shifting production from our relatively efficient export industries to our relatively inefficient import industries. Is that any way to run an economy?

Nevertheless, you may ask about the human cost. What happens to the workers who are thrown out of work by foreign competition? Should their employers help them or should the government? And what can be done to help them? Ideally, these displaced workers should be retrained and possibly relocated to work in our relatively efficient industries. Those who cannot be retrained or cannot move should be given some form of work, if only to keep them off the welfare rolls.

What about the workers who lose their jobs because of imports?

Who should help these displaced workers adjust? In a sense, their employers are responsible because these people were loyal and productive employees for perhaps 20 or 30 years. Often, however, the companies that should bear most of the responsibility for helping their employees are hardly in a position to do so. After all, they wouldn't be laying off workers if business were good to begin with.

Does the United States Win or Lose from Globalization?

There is no question that the forces of globalization have raised the living standards of all trading nations. Worldwide competition has forced every trading nation to become much more efficient. American firms must compete not only against each other, but increasingly against their counterparts based all over the world.

Ask yourself this question: Am I better off today than my parents were when they were my age? Just look at the huge array of consumer goods the average person enjoys today that did not even exist 25 or 30 years ago. Nearly all of them—personal computers, cell phones, DVD players, iPods, PlayStations, BlackBerry devices, for example—are imported from abroad. Had globalization not progressed as quickly, some of these goods would not have been available to the average American.

No one has ever disputed that globalization has made some people winners and others losers. As consumers, of course, we're all winners, but how many of us have already lost our jobs or will lose them over the next few years?

So far most of the work sent abroad has been labor-intensive and lower skilled, so the job losses were limited to blue-collar factory workers. As long as we're specializing in high skilled work, and have plenty of it, the job losses are confined to our most poorly educated and low skilled workers.

But now we are seeing more and more offshoring of so-called white-collar jobs, which are performed by nearly half our workforce. Today that brainpower can zip around world at low cost, and a global labor market for skilled workers seems to be emerging for the first time—and has the potential to upset traditional notions of national specialization.

What if blue- and white-collar employees alike are thrown into the global labor pool? Tens of millions of workers could end up losing more than they gain in lower prices.

Let's take a closer look at globalization's job losers. Just 30 percent of laid-off workers earn the same or more after three years. In fact only 68 percent even hold a job at that point, while the rest are unemployed, retired, or just not in the labor force. On average, those reemployed earn 10 percent less than they did on their old jobs.

You might not even need to lose your job to be adversely affected by globalization. What if you found yourself competing against much lower-paid foreign professionals, like many of today's radiologists, programmers, and software writers? Or what if you found yourself in a profession being crowded by thousands of laid-off Americans? All you would need would be a simple supply and demand graph to show you that your wage rate would be going down.

Ten years ago economists were virtually unanimous in extolling the advantages of globalization. But now, a growing minority is not so sure. While there's no holding back the tide of globalization, one can wonder if there isn't more we could do to ensure that all of our economic boats rise with the tide.

That leaves the party of last resort: the federal government. What does the federal government do for workers who are displaced by foreign competition? Not very much. These workers receive extended unemployment benefits, are eligible for job retraining, and may receive some moving expenses. But the bottom line is that a middle-aged worker who loses her $20-an-hour job will probably not find another one that pays close to that, and government programs will not begin to compensate for this loss (see box, "Does the United States Win or Lose from Globalization?").

Tariffs or Quotas

Although economists are loathe to be in such a situation, suppose it came down to choosing between the two main forms of protection: tariffs and import quotas. Which would be better? Or, more accurately, which is the lesser of two evils?

A tariff is a tax on imports.

A tariff is a tax on imports. Throughout most of U.S. history until World War I, the tariff was our main source of federal revenue. The United States, which has lower tariffs than most other countries, charges less than 5 percent of the value of most imports.

A quota is a limit on the import of certain goods.

A quota is a limit on the import of certain goods. Sometimes this is a legal limit (as in the case of steel, apparel, textiles and sugar), and sometimes it is a "voluntary" limit (as was the case with cars from Japan). In the early and mid-1980s the Japanese limited their export of cars to the United States to fewer than 2.5 million a year, but only because of the threat of more stringent legal limits in the form of higher tariffs.

We have long maintained textile import quotas, which, in recent years, have been especially effective in keeping out low-priced Chinese textiles. Although the quotas on Chinese textiles were ostensibly removed on New Year's day of 2005, American textile producers were able to get nearly half reinstated later in the year. In addition we persuaded the Chinese to voluntarily adhere to quotas.

Both tariffs and quotas raise the price that consumers in the importing country must pay. However, there are three important differences in the effects of tariffs and quotas.

First, the federal government receives the proceeds of a tariff. Under import quotas there *are* no tax revenues.

Second, a tariff affects all foreign sellers equally, but import quotas are directed against particular sellers on an arbitrary basis. For example, in 1986 various Japanese car manufacturers had widely varying quotas, but the import of South Korean Hyundais was unrestricted.

A third difference involves relative efficiency. Efficient foreign producers will be able to pay a uniform tariff that less efficient producers will not be able to meet. But arbitrary import quotas may allow relatively inefficient foreign producers to send us their goods while keeping out those of their more efficient competitors. This comes down to somewhat higher prices for the American consumer because less efficient producers will charge higher prices than more efficient producers.

Figure 4 illustrates the effects of a tariff. A $50 tariff on cameras raises the price of a camera from $200 to about $245. And it causes the quantity purchased to fall from 2.25 million to 2.1 million.

Incidentally, a tariff, like any other excise tax, causes a decrease in supply—that is, a smaller quantity is supplied at every possible price. The effect of taxes on supply was discussed at length near the end of the elasticities of demand and supply chapter in *Economics* and *Microeconomics*.

To summarize, tariffs are better than quotas, but free trade is best. In the long run, the American consumer must pay for trade restrictions in the form of higher prices.

Tariffs are better than quotas, but free trade is best.

Conclusion

The case for free trade is one of the cornerstones of economics. (See the box, "Petition of the Candlemakers to Shut Out the Sun.") Economics is all about the efficient allocation of scarce resources, so there is no reason why this efficient allocation should not be

No nation was ever ruined by trade.

—Benjamin Franklin

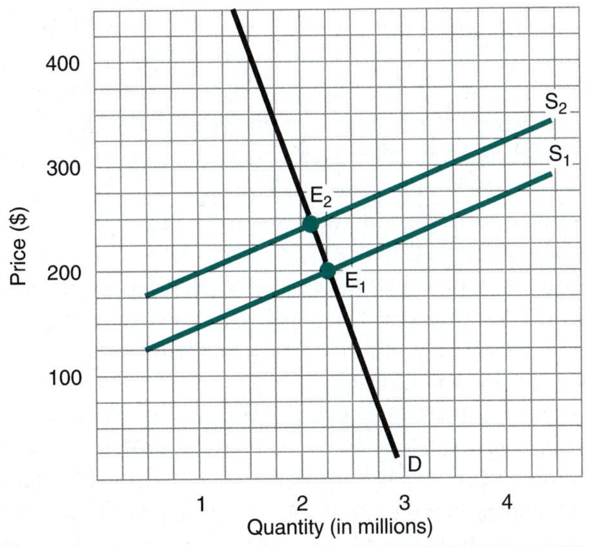

Figure 4

A Tariff Lowers Supply
This $50 tariff lowers supply from S_1 to S_2. Price rises from $200 to about $245, and quantity purchased falls from 2.25 million to 2.1 million. We move from equilibrium point E_1 to E_2. The tariff of $50 is the vertical distance between S_1 and S_2.

Petition of the Candlemakers to Shut Out the Sun

The case of protection against "unfair" competition was extended to its absurd conclusion by Frédéric Bastiat, a mid-19th-century French economist who wrote an imagined petition to the Chamber of Deputies. Parts of that petition follow.

We are suffering from the intolerable competition of a foreign rival, placed, it would seem, in a condition so far superior to ours for the production of light, that he absolutely inundates our national market with it at a price fabulously reduced. The moment he shows himself, our trade leaves us—all consumers apply to him, and a branch of native industry, having countless ramifications, is all at once rendered completely stagnant. This rival . . . is no other than the Sun. What we pray for is, that it may please you to pass a law ordering the shutting up of all windows, skylights, dormerwindows, outside and inside shutters, curtains, blinds, bull's eyes; in a word, of all openings, holes, chinks, clefts, and fissures, by or through which the light of the sun has been in use to enter houses . . .*

Frédéric Bastiat,
19th-century French economist

*Frédéric Bastiat, *Economic Sophisms* (Edinburgh: Oliver and Boyd, Tweeddale Court, 1873), pp. 49–53.

---

applied beyond national boundaries. A baseball team that has more pitchers than it knows what to do with but needs a good-hitting shortstop will trade that extra pitcher or two for the shortstop. It will trade with a team that has an extra shortstop but needs more pitching. This trade will help both teams.

International trade helps every country; we all have higher living standards because of it. To the degree that we can remove the tariffs, import quotas, and other impediments to free trade, we will all be better off.

It has been estimated that lower-priced imports kept the rate of inflation one or two points below what it would otherwise have been since the mid-1980s. This is still another important reason for not restricting imports.

Imports pressure American companies to become more efficient. It is obvious, for example, that Toyota, Nissan, Honda, and the other Japanese automakers drove Detroit to make far better cars with far fewer workers than it used to. Indeed, our annual productivity gains of 10 percent would have been inconceivable without the spur of Japanese competition. Our chemical, steel, pharmaceutical, computer, textile, apparel, commercial aircraft, machine tool, paper copier, and semiconductor industries have all been spurred to much higher levels of efficiency by their foreign competitors.

None of this is to deny that there are problems. The millions of workers who have lost their jobs due to foreign competition cannot be expected to cheerfully make personal sacrifices in the interest of the greater national economic well-being. In the long run we may all be better off if there is worldwide free trade, but, as John Maynard Keynes once noted, "In the long run we are all dead."

The economics profession nearly unanimously backs free trade.

While the economics profession is nearly unanimous in advocating free trade, there is nearly complete disagreement over what to do about our huge trade deficit. If we do nothing, as fervent free traders advocate, can we count on our trade imbalance to eventually correct itself? Or will foreigners—especially the Japanese and Chinese—continue to outsell us? These are just two of the questions I'll try to answer in the third part of this chapter.

Part III: The Practice of International Trade

What Are the Causes of Our Trade Imbalance?

Here are the top five reasons for our huge and growing trade imbalance.

(1) We Have Become a Nation of Consumption Junkies   The United States is the world's greatest consumption superpower. Today we are borrowing over $2 billion a day from foreigners to finance our consumption habit. Most Americans believe that somehow we're entitled to all these goods and services, even if we need to borrow to pay for them.

We are consuming more than we are producing, borrowing more than we are saving, and spending more than we are earning.

—Murray Weidenbaum

We are notoriously poor savers. Indeed since 2005 we have not been able to save even 1 percent of our disposable personal income. If you're not saving, it's hard to invest. Luckily foreign savers have been picking up the slack by lending us hundreds of billions of dollars a year. But this windfall will not continue indefinitely.

(2) Huge Oil Imports   Because we are so dependent on gasoline for transportation, we import two thirds of our oil. And yet, we pay just a fraction of what the citizens of other industrial nations pay for gasoline. As our domestic production of oil continues to decline, our dependency on oil imports will keep growing. In 2009 the cost of our oil imports, driven by tight global supplies and high prices, reached a record high of $350 billion, accounting for nearly our entire trade deficit.

Why are we so dependent on oil imports? Until the 1960s, as the world's leading producer, we needed to import no more than 15 percent of our oil. But American production peaked in 1970, and as our need for oil grew rapidly with suburbanization, we had to import more and more. Today we must get two-thirds of our oil from abroad.

Other major industrial countries, most notably Japan and the members of the European Union, were better able to deal with their need for oil, even though few produced much of their own. None had anything like the suburban sprawl of the United States, so their citizens were not nearly as dependent on automobile transportation. And then too, unlike Americans, their citizens were willing to pay $3 or $4 a gallon in taxes, which provided a powerful incentive to conserve gasoline.

(3) Our Failing Educational System   The American educational system, once second to none, is now second to practically everyone's. The illiterate high school graduate is no longer the rare exception, and about one-third of all college freshmen need remedial work in the three Rs—reading, writing, and arithmetic. Nearly every college—even the Ivy League schools—has special classes for students unprepared to do college work. In test after test, Americans rank at or near the bottom of the industrial countries.

Our schools are turning out students who cannot read or write.

Half our high school math and science teachers are unqualified to teach those subjects. In Florida and in Massachusetts, thousands of teachers failed exams testing them on the very subject matter they had been hired to teach. No wonder that our educational system turns out one million functional illiterates every year—not exactly job candidates for today's high-tech economy.

An attempt to correct some of the problems of our failing educational system was made by President George W. Bush when he got Congress to pass the "Leave No Child Behind" law, which mandated testing of children at different grade levels to ensure that all children would meet certain national educational standards. Though this legislation was passed with widespread bipartisan support, its implementation has proven very controversial, and widespread opposition has arisen from state and local educational establishments.

While we're on the subject, what do you think of *this* educational reform? Every teacher must pass an 8th grade reading test and every math teacher must pass a test covering the math that she or he teaches. Whenever this idea is proposed, you can't imagine the opposition it generates from teachers' unions and other interest groups.

Most of the science, math, and computer graduate students receiving PhDs in our universities are foreigners, more and more of whom are returning home, mainly to China, India, and other Asian countries. As our manufacturing base erodes, we are losing our cutting-edge intellectual superiority in product design, software engineering, and other vital fields. Today, most patent applications are made by foreigners, and in the not too distant future, the term "Made in America" may become an anachronism.

(4) The Role of Multinationals   Before the 1960s the vast low-wage workforces of the world's poorer nations were no threat to the workers in the high-wage economies like the United States. Our workers were many times more productive than those in the poorer nations because they had so much more capital to work with.

More capital, higher productivity, and higher wages

All of this began to change in the 1960s as multinational corporations began to move their manufacturing operations offshore to take advantage of this low-wage labor pool. By providing these workers with sufficient plant and equipment, the multinationals were able to increase their productivity to the level of American assembly-line workers.

The hollow corporation

The term *hollow corporation* gained currency in the last two decades as more and more companies put their names on imported goods. These companies' sole function is to sell such goods as the Dodge Colt or the Panasonic TV, both of which are made in Japan. Yet our import business is not dominated by firms that market goods for foreign producers, but rather by our own multinational corporations that have shifted most of their production overseas. Joel Kurtzman describes their operations:

> These multinationals have transformed themselves from producers of goods to importers and marketers of goods made overseas by their foreign divisions and affiliates. Because so many of our imports come to us in the form of trade between the different divisions of American multinationals, the balance-of-payments deficit has become structurally integrated into our economy.[2]

(5) Relative Growth Rate   So far we've talked about all our deficiencies contributing to our balance of trade deficit. But even our virtues seem to contribute to that deficit. Between 1995 and 2007 we have had one of the highest rates of economic growth in the industrialized world. Countries with high economic growth rates import more goods and services than they would have if they had low growth rates.

(6) Our Shrinking Manufacturing Base   Still another reason for our huge and growing trade imbalance is that since the 1960s we've lost a good part of our manufacturing base as American companies shipped production and jobs abroad. Cars, steel, consumer electronics, computers, textiles, and clothing were once among our leading exports, but millions of jobs in those industries have disappeared. Still, for decades, our chemical industry seemed largely immune from foreign competition. No more. Although that industry will certainly not disappear any time soon, it may be fighting a losing battle against foreign competitors who can undersell us (see the box, "The Chemical Industry in Decline").

In recent years the U.S. dollar has been high relative to the currencies of our trading partners—most notably to the Chinese yuan. Consequently the prices of our exports have been higher, and we sold less to foreigners than if the dollar had been lower. Similarly, the prices of our imports have been higher, and we have been buying more from foreigners than if the dollar were lower. We'll address this issue at length in the next chapter.

---

[2]Joel Kurtzman, *The Decline and Crash of the American Economy* (New York: W. W. Norton, 1988), p. 131.

The Chemical Industry in Decline

Through the late 1990s, the United States led the world in making chemicals, with the largest market, the latest technology, and the best know-how. And U.S. plants had a natural advantage thanks to an abundant supply of cheap natural gas, a building block for plastics, fertilizers, and even pharmaceuticals. Today none of that is true. U.S. natural gas prices are the highest in the world, while the bigger, faster growing markets are overseas. And new facilities in the developing world are as sophisticated and productive as those in the United States.

Some 120 chemical plants are being built around the world with price tags of $1 billion or more. Only one of those plants will be in the United States, but 50 are being built in China. The reason: It's becoming much too costly to produce chemicals in the United States.

As chemical production facilities close across the United States—Dow Chemical has closed over 25 percent of its plants since the new millennium—the next casualty will be the engineers and scientists doing workaday research. In 2004, Du Pont opened a lab in Shanghai that has grown into a basic research center with 200 scientists.

Our balance of trade in chemicals had long been one of our economic mainstays. As recently as 1997 we had a $20 billion surplus. But just six years later that surplus became a $10 billion deficit.

Our $500 billion chemical industry will not disappear overnight, but its demise is emblematic of the decline and fall of the entire American manufacturing sector. And with respect to our trade deficit, our chemical industry, instead of holding down the deficit, is becoming a major contributor.

Part IV: Our Trade Deficit with Japan and China

For most of the 1980s and 1990s, Japan was our fiercest trade competitor. In addition, year after year we ran huge trade deficits with that country. In the long run, however, our largest trade deficits are with China, which overtook Japan in 2000. (See Figure 5.)

Many goods once made elsewhere in Asia—in Japan, Taiwan, Singapore, South Korea—are now produced in foreign-owned factories that have been moved to China. So our growing deficit with China is partially offset by declining deficits with other Asian nations.

Japanese Trading Practices

The American economy has long been, by far, the largest in the world. But in the years after World War II, as the only major nation with an undamaged economy, we produced half the world's manufactured goods. Our economy had been built on the dual foundations of mass production and mass consumption. Basically we mass produced consumer goods, which were then sold to the vast American market.

The Japanese economic infrastructure had been largely destroyed by our relentless bombings during the war. And even if the Japanese had somehow been able to produce low-cost consumer goods, their market was not only much smaller than the American market, but much, much poorer. So the Japanese government and business leaders developed a strategy to rebuild their economy. They would flood the rich American market with very cheap, low-end consumer goods, and then move up the economic feeding chain, eventually producing black and white TVs, color TVs, motorcycles, and cars.

The Japanese compete not just on the basis of price but on the basis of product quality. They have taken our system of mass production one step further, turning out a wide range of customized variations, while we continue to concentrate largely on single standardized products.

The Japanese compete on the basis of price and quality.

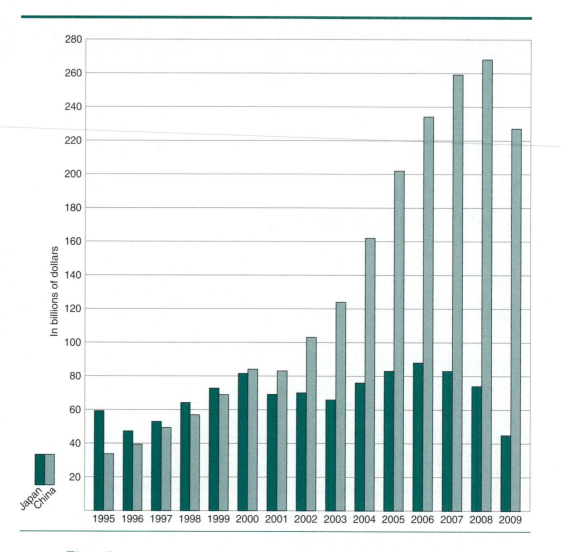

Figure 5

U.S. Trade Deficit with Japan and China, 1995–2009
Our deficit with China grew steadily since 1990 and has surpassed our deficit with Japan.
Source: U.S. Dept. of Census.

Our Trade Deficit with China

When we began trading with China in the mid-1970s, after President Richard Nixon's historic trip to open relations with that nation, American exporters had great hopes that the world's most populous nation would eventually become the world's largest consumer market. Three decades later, toys, athletic shoes, clothing, textiles, and other relatively low-price manufactured goods are flooding into the United States, along with an increasing stream of higher-priced goods such as tools, auto parts, electronic gear, microwave ovens, and personal computers. Although U.S. exports to China are growing rapidly, our exports are less than one-fourth of our imports.

Why are we importing so much from China? Mainly because U.S. retailers are seeking the cheapest goods available and finding them in China. Walmart Stores imported $27 billion worth of goods in 2009; and Target, Sears-Kmart, Toys 'R' Us, and other giant retailers also found that the price was right in China.

One of the big trade issues between China and the United States is that thousands of Chinese factories, many controlled by top officers of the Chinese army, have been making unauthorized, or knock-off, copies of American movies, CDs, and most important, computer software. Days after the premier of the latest *Terminator* film in the U.S., pirate copies were on sale throughout China. More than 90 percent of the movies, music, and software are illegal copies sold at a fraction of the original price.

It's bad enough that the Chinese are pirating American goods and services and selling them in their own country. But now they're taking their piracy a step further. In 2005, the U.S. Patent and Trademark Office said that 66 percent of the counterfeit goods seized at American borders now come from China, up from just 16 percent five years before. Indeed Chinese-made fakes are so good that bogus Duracell batteries, Oral-B toothbrushes, and pretend Prestobarba disposable razors are sold all over the world. And the U.S. Chamber of Commerce says that Chinese piracy and counterfeiting have cost American industry over $200 billion a year.

Our trade deficits with China have been running over $200 billion a year since 2005. These are the largest deficits ever recorded by one country with another country. But closer inspection reveals that our trade deficit with China is grossly overstated. Most often "made in China" is actually made elsewhere—by multinational companies in Japan, South Korea, Taiwan, and the United States, that are using China as the final assembly station in their vast global production networks. Indeed, about 60 percent of this country's exports are controlled by foreign companies. A Barbie doll may cost $20, but China gets only about 35 cents of that. In recent years, however, the Chinese government has insisted that increasing proportions of its manufactured goods actually be made in China. For example, solar panels—of which China is the leading producer—must have at least 75 percent Chinese content.

While China had a huge trade surplus with the United States, it also had a huge trade deficit with the rest of Asia in 2009. What were the Chinese importing? Much of their imports were components of television sets, cars, refrigerators, microwave ovens, and other consumer electronics. When these products were assembled and shipped out as final products, China's exports appeared to be much greater than they actually were. Consequently its trade surplus with the United States was greatly exaggerated.

Since the beginning of the new millennium we have lost over 5 million manufacturing jobs. Some of these losses may be attributed to China, but probably other nations and certainly the huge multinational corporations—many of which are based in the United States—should bear much more of the blame. And it is the American consumer who has benefited the most from the flood of low-cost goods that were assembled, if not made, in China.

Trading with China and Japan: More Differences than Similarities

There is one striking similarity between the Japanese and Chinese development models. Both were pulled by the engine provided by the huge American market. After World War II, the only consumers who had the money to buy Japanese exports were the Americans. So the Japanese economic recovery plan was, essentially, a no-brainer. Close the much smaller Japanese home market to American producers, while selling the bulk of their manufactures to the rich Americans.

When the Chinese launched their industrial development plan in the early 1980s, they followed a similar strategy—create an export platform on the East China coast to sell cheap manufactured goods to the rich Americans, and, to a lesser degree, to the rich consumers of Western Europe and Japan. The Chinese, unlike the Japanese before them, had a relatively open economy. Foreign manufacturers were more than welcome to set up shop in China.

Was the Chinese market closed to foreigners? *What* market? Few Chinese consumers had the money to buy relatively expensive imported goods. But as Chinese economic development really began to take off, and relatively cheap Chinese manufactured products flooded the world, the American consumer could no longer finance this expansion. No problem. The Chinese government simply lent Americans much of the money we needed each year to finance our huge and growing trade deficit.

During the Japanese industrial revival of the 1950s and 1960s, their manufacturers went head-to-head with ours. In the production of black and white TVs, and later, color TVs, the Japanese built on our technology, undersold American manufacturers in the vast American market, while the Japanese market remained closed to American TVs. As a result, American TV manufacturers were driven out of business.

Our trading position with Japan is very much like a colony and a colonial power. Our trading relationship with the Chinese is very different. We send airplanes, computers, movies, compact disks, cars, cigarettes, power-generating equipment, and computer software in exchanges for toys, clothing, shoes, and low-end consumer electronics. Much of what they're sending to us used to come from Japan back in the 1950s. "Made in Japan" has been replaced by "Made in China."

Our huge trade deficit with China will probably continue to grow, but even more importantly, its entire nature is rapidly evolving. We have long assumed this division of labor: The Chinese would focus on lower-skill sectors, while the United States would dominate the knowledge-intensive industries. But as Harvard economist Richard B. Freeman observed, "What is stunning about China is that for the first time we have a huge, poor country that can compete both with very low wages and in high tech. Combine the two, and America has a problem."

So far the hardest hit industries have been those that were destined to migrate to low-cost nations anyway. But now China is moving into more advanced industries where America remains competitive, adding state-of-the-art capacity in motor vehicles, specialty steel, petrochemicals, and microchips. In other words, the United States has been losing its lead in the knowledge economy, while China evolves from our sweatshop to our competitor.

Japanese gains in the production of semiconductors, machine tools, steel, autos, TVs, and VCRs led directly to the loss of millions of well-paying American jobs. Although Chinese products may compete on a broader scale with American goods in the future, Chinese exports so far have generally not translated into major job losses in the United States. China's leading exports are products that have not been produced in large quantity by American factories for more than a decade.

The Chinese, like the Japanese before them, have insisted on licensing agreements and large-scale transfer of technology as the price for agreeing to imports. These agreements, of course, lead to the eventual elimination of imports from the United States. However, the Chinese have taken this process one step further. Sometimes, instead of entering into licensing agreements, Chinese factories simply manufacture pirated versions, or knock-offs, of American videos, CDs, computer software, and designer apparel.

From the mid-1980s through the mid-1990s we engaged in a good deal of Japan-bashing, blaming that country for our growing trade deficit. To a large degree our complaints were justified. Not only were our manufacturing jobs migrating to Japan, but the Japanese market was largely closed to American exports.

In recent years we have shifted much of the blame to China, with whom we now run our largest trade deficit (see Figure 5). But the nature of our trade deficit with China today is not, in any sense, like our deficit with Japan two decades ago. Japan was competing in businesses that were at the heart of the American economy. But our imports from China—clothing, toys, shoes, textiles, TVs, and consumer electronics—are mainly merchandise we stopped making here decades ago. Furthermore, China is remarkably open to trade. Between 1995 and 2005, our exports to China almost quadrupled. In coming years, this rapid growth will continue as the Chinese consumer market continues its rapid expansion.

My own prediction is that by 2015, not only will we be running still larger trade deficits with China, but we will be importing more than a million very low-priced Chinese cars each year. By then China bashing may have been elevated from an art form to the national sport.

Final Word

Two major issues have been raised in this chapter. First, that there are clear advantages to free trade. And second, that the United States, which has been a strong free trade advocate, has been running large and growing trade deficits. Let's take one more look at both issues.

Free Trade in Word and Deed

Going back to the early 1980s, every president has strongly advocated the principle of free trade and has helped reduce tariffs and other trade barriers throughout the world. Robert Zoellick, the chief trade negotiator during the first term of President George W. Bush, pushed various proposals within the World Trade Organization to lower tariffs and export subsidies, as well as to remove all barriers to the free flow of goods and services across national borders. European Union members, most notably France, have refused to lower subsidies.

Members of the European Union called our free trade advocacy hypocritical when in March 2002, President Bush raised tariffs on imported steel. In fact they brought a case against the United States before the World Trade Court. In December 2003, President Bush rescinded the tariffs.

Like his immediate predecessor, President Barack Obama has advocated free trade, at least in principle. But just eight months after taking office, he imposed a 35 percent tariff on Chinese tires. This was done at the behest of the United Steelworkers Union after the U.S. International Trade Commission ruled that a huge increase in tire imports had cost an estimated 5,000 workers their jobs.

A second deviation from our free trade policy is our huge agricultural subsidies—averaging almost $20 billion a year. The world's poorer nations, where up to 90 percent of the labor force is engaged in agriculture, have demanded that the United States, the European Union, and other rich nations abolish these subsidies, which, clearly, make it impossible for the poorer nations to sell their agricultural goods on the world market (see the box, "Farm Subsidies and the Poorer Nations").

On balance, the United States has long been a free trading nation. Zoellick was very active in negotiating free trade agreements with Singapore, Chile, South Africa,

---

Farm Subsidies and the Poorer Nations

The world richest countries provide over $300 billion in subsidies to their farmers. These subsidies enable farmers from the United States, the European Union, Canada, and Australia to export much of their output at artificially low prices. The farmers of the world's poorer nations cannot match these low prices, so they are largely shut out of world agricultural markets. Consequently these nations cannot export their agricultural surpluses and get foreign exchange.

Mexico is the world's birthplace of corn. But after the signing of the North American Free Trade Agreement (NAFTA) in 1994, American farmers flooded the Mexican market with low-priced corn. Since then, the price of Mexican corn fell more than 70 percent, severely reducing the incomes of the 15 million Mexicans who depend on corn for their livelihood.

Of the $20 billion a year that American taxpayers shell out in farm subsidies, more than $10 billion goes to corn farmers. This allows them to sell their corn at prices far below what it cost them to produce it. In effect, then, the American taxpayer has subsidized the shipment of cheap corn to Mexico, where it has pushed the poorest farmers out of business.

Japan's subsidies are 59 percent of the value of production, while those of the European Union are 34 percent of production and in the United States they are 21 percent. Will these nations agree to lower or eliminate these subsidies? Probably not in *our* lifetime. It would be political suicide. Imagine what would happen to all those senators and representatives from the farm states, not to mention all those presidential electoral votes.

and other countries. Our $20 billion in agricultural subsidies are just 6 percent of the annual subsidies provided to farmers in the world's richest countries.

Reducing Our Trade Deficit

To reduce our overall trade deficit we need to make a combination of four things happen. First, we need to maintain our high rate of productivity growth and keep improving the quality of American goods and services. Second, we need to lower our dependence on oil imports, perhaps by raising the federal tax on gasoline. Third, we must reduce our rapidly rising deficit with China. And finally, we need to face up to the fact that we are a nation of consumption junkies. In sum, we consume much more than we produce, and have done so by running up a multitrillion dollar tab.

Perhaps our best hope to reduce our trade deficit lies with the rapidly expanding Internet, which makes it much easier to provide services of all types—banking, education, consulting, retailing, and even gambling—through websites that are globally accessible. Since the United States has long had a positive trade balance in services, there is good reason to expect the Internet to continue pushing up our export of services.

Current Issue 1: Buy American?

Our nation has long been committed to free trade, but a growing number of Americans believe that we need to curb our imports, largely to keep jobs from being offshored as well as to preserve our economic independence. For much of the time since World War II, Japanese consumers willingly paid more for domestically produced goods than they would have for foreign imports. They did this not just to help Japanese manufacturers through their long recovery from the devastation caused by American bombing during the war, but also in the sometimes misguided belief that somehow Japanese products better met their needs. This practice was best exemplified by the widely accepted claim that Japanese-made skis were better suited than imported skis for the unique Japanese snow.

But the American consumer has never been very susceptible to calls for patriotic buying. Even during the era of bad national feeling toward the French for opposing our 2003 invasion of Iraq, about the best we could do to punish the French was to refer to french fries as "freedom fries." Take *that,* you ingrates! And after all we did for you during World War II! More significantly, during 2003 our imports from France actually went up.

Perhaps a better case for economic nationalism could be made against Saudi Arabia. We now import two thirds of our oil, and that country has long been one of our largest suppliers. Although 15 of the 19 plane hijackers on 9/11 were Saudis, we never considered curbing oil imports from that country, let alone going to war.

Today there's a good deal of China bashing for running $200 billion trade surpluses with us, flooding our stores with low-cost TVs, DVD players, microwave ovens, toys, furniture, and textiles. But all that bad feeling toward the Chinese has not hurt business at Walmart, which sells more Chinese exports than any other company in the world. Back in the early 1970s, when we began running large trade deficits with Japan, our leading Japan basher was Treasury Secretary John Connally, who declared that as far as he was concerned, the Japanese could sit in their Toyotas on the docks of Yokohoma, watching their Sony TVs. Still, through the next two decades, our trade deficit with Japan continued to mount.

The bottom line is that Americans are consumers first, while paying just lip service to economic nationalism. No nation of economic nationalists would run up our long string of record-setting trade deficits. So pass the freedom fries and, in the words of the old Beach Boys song, "I better turn on the lights, so we can ride my Honda tonight."

Current Issue 2: Globalization

While globalization is a relatively new term, it is a process which has been going on for hundreds of years. But it has sped up over the last three decades as we have been moving from hundreds of national economies to a worldwide economy.

A decline in shipping costs, vast improvements in communications, the opening and development of the Chinese economy, and the end of the Cold War have all accelerated the pace of globalization. As a result, billions of people around the globe have become active participants in a free enterprise world economy.

We can define globalization as the unimpeded flow of goods and services, labor, and capital across national borders. It ensures a more efficient allocation of resources, which is what economics is all about.

What makes globalization so controversial is the offshoring of millions of jobs and the decimation of our manufacturing base. In theory, these jobs will be replaced by others—mainly high value-added and high-tech jobs. There's just one problem: we are still waiting for those jobs to be created. And in the meanwhile, hundreds of thousands of high-tech jobs have been offshored.

Those living in the Midwest have seen firsthand how our industrial heartland turned into a rust belt. But that rust belt extends well beyond the borders of Wisconsin, Michigan, Illinois, Indiana, and Ohio. It also runs through most of western and central Pennsylvania, much of upstate New York, as well as the old textile towns of the southeastern states and the steel mills of Birmingham.

Trying to reverse the forces of globalization would be no more successful than trying to hold back the tides. The American consumer buys imported goods if they are at least as good as domestic goods and are cheaper. American business firms shift production overseas if they can cut costs. And finally, foreign savers invest their money in the United States when they can earn a higher return here than elsewhere.

But globalization is one tide that has not raised all boats. As Senator John McCain told Michigan voters during his 2008 presidential campaign: all those automotive industry jobs would not be coming back. Indeed, just a few months later General Motors and Chrysler went bankrupt.

The question we must answer is not how to stop, or even slow, globalization; rather, it is how to best deal with its consequences. Clearly we cannot bring back the millions of manufacturing jobs that have migrated to low-wage countries.

Perhaps the most promising effort so far is sending hundreds of thousands of laid-off blue collar workers to local community colleges to be trained for jobs in expanding industries such as renewable energy and health care. For example, three out of five nurses are educated at community colleges. But until hiring picks up, perhaps in 2011, it won't be clear if retraining will have much of an impact.

One may ask if, on the whole, globalization has been good or bad for the American economy. The easy answer is that it has been a great boon to consumers, but a disaster to workers whose jobs have been offshored. My view is that while most Americans are better off because of globalization, it has contributed substantially to our long-term economic decline. I believe that America is a fading economic power, and, at the end of the next—and last—chapter, I've summed up the reasons for such a pessimistic prognosis.

Questions for Further Thought and Discussion

1. Explain what comparative advantage is. Make up an example to illustrate this concept.
2. What is wrong with having tariffs and quotas? Which is the lesser of the two evils, and why?
3. Explain why globalization is good for the United States. What are the drawbacks of globalization for our economy?

4. What would you suggest we do to reduce our trade deficit?

5. We run huge trade imbalances with two countries. Explain the cause of the imbalances.

6. Should we be worried about our trade deficit? Explain why or why not.

7. What is the economist's case for free trade?

8. *Practical Application:* Can you think of any valid reason for tariff protection? Try to make a case for it.

9. *Web Activity:* How much were our imports, exports, and trade deficit during the last year? Go to www.bea.gov, click on "Survey of Current Business" at the left, then go to "National Data," "National Income and Product Accounts," NIPA tables, and finally, "Gross Domestic Product."

Workbook for Chapter 18 connect ECONOMICS

Name _____ Date _____

Multiple-Choice Questions

Circle the letter that corresponds to the best answer.

1. Our balance of trade _____. (LO2)
   a) has always been positive
   b) turned negative in the mid-1970s
   c) turned negative in the mid-1980s
   d) has always been negative

2. Which makes the most sense economically? (LO2)
   a) Individual self-sufficiency
   b) National self-sufficiency
   c) National specialization
   d) None of these

3. Which statement do you agree with? (LO6, 9)
   a) There are several problems causing our huge trade deficit; there are no easy solutions to these problems.
   b) We could quickly eliminate our trade deficit by raising tariffs.
   c) The main reason we have a large trade deficit is that foreigners refuse to buy American goods and services.
   d) The main reason for our large trade deficit is our relatively low rate of economic growth.

4. The Chinese economic expansion since the early 1980s and the Japanese economic expansion from the late 1940s through the 1980s were _____. (LO7)
   a) virtually identical
   b) both dependent on the American market
   c) based in the economic principles of Karl Marx
   d) based on closing their domestic markets to American goods and services

5. Which statement is false? (LO3)
   a) No nation will engage in trade with another nation unless it will gain by that trade.
   b) The terms of trade will fall somewhere between the domestic exchange equations of the two trading nations.
   c) Most economists advocate free trade.
   d) None of these statements is false.

6. Our largest trade deficit is with _____. (LO7)
   a) Japan   d) Mexico
   b) Canada   e) Germany
   c) China

7. Which one of the following does NOT contribute to our huge trade deficit? (LO6)
   a) Our failing educational system
   b) Our high defense spending
   c) Our high saving rate
   d) Our huge oil imports

8. The least applicable argument for protecting American industry from foreign competition would be the _____ argument. (LO4)
   a) national security   c) low-wage
   b) infant industry   d) employment

9. Imports would be lowered by _____. (LO5)
   a) tariffs only
   b) import quotas only
   c) both tariffs and import quotas
   d) neither tariffs nor import quotas

10. Of these three choices—tariffs, quotas, and free trade—economists like _____ the most and _____ the least. (LO5)
    a) tariffs, quotas   d) free trade, quotas
    b) tariffs, free trade   e) quotas, free trade
    c) free trade, tariffs   f) quotas, tariffs

11. Our biggest annual trade deficit in our history was more than _____ billion. (LO2)

   a) $300
   b) $400
   c) $500
   d) $600
   e) $700

12. Which country regularly counterfeits American goods and services, a practice which costs American industry over $200 billion a year? (LO6)

   a) Mexico
   b) Canada
   c) China
   d) Japan

13. Which would be the most accurate statement with respect to our chemical industry? (LO6)

   a) It is on the decline and now contributes to our balance of trade deficit.
   b) It is large and growing.
   c) It generally provides a trade surplus of about $20 billion a year.
   d) It will almost completely disappear by the year 2015.

14. Which one of these statements is the most accurate? (LO8)

   a) Globalization, on balance, has been very bad for the U.S. economy.
   b) All the effects of globalization have been very good for the U.S. economy.
   c) The best way to reduce our trade deficit is for Congress to pass a law requiring that we buy only American products.
   d) Each of our recent presidents has basically supported the concept of free trade.

15. Our trade deficit with China in 2009 was _____. (LO7)

   a) under $100 billion
   b) between $100 billion and $150 billion
   c) between $150 billion and $200 billion
   d) over $200 billion

16. Statement 1: Our trade deficit with China is larger than our trade deficit with Japan.
   Statement 2: Americans pay lower taxes on gasoline than do the citizens of most of the nations in Western Europe. (LO7)

   a) Statement 1 is true, and statement 2 is false.
   b) Statement 2 is true, and statement 1 is false.
   c) Both statements are true.
   d) Both statements are false.

17. Of the following, our imports of _____ contribute most to our trade deficit. (LO6)

   a) oil
   b) clothing
   c) textiles
   d) consumer electronics

18. Which of the following would best describe our trading relationship with China five years from now? (LO7)

   a) Our trade deficit will be higher and we will be importing a higher proportion of "low-skill" products.
   b) Our trade deficit will be higher and we will be importing a higher proportion of "high-skill" products.
   c) Our trade deficit will be lower and we will be importing a higher proportion of "low-skill" products.
   d) Our trade deficit will be lower and we will be importing a higher proportion of "high-skill" products.

19. Which statement is the most accurate? (LO1, 2)

   a) Globalization has made some people winners and others losers.
   b) Globalization has been good for everyone involved.
   c) Globalization has been bad for everyone involved.
   d) Virtually all economists believe that globalization has almost no downside.

20. Which statement is true about how globalization has affected American workers? (LO4, 1)

   a) The only jobs that have been lost or will be lost are blue-collar factory jobs.
   b) Most workers who have lost their jobs because of globalization have ended up in better paying jobs.
   c) Until now a relatively high proportion of Americans perform high-skill, well paying jobs, while a relatively high proportion of Chinese perform low-skill, poorly paying jobs.
   d) Globalization cannot be considered a threat to the livelihoods of highly-skilled, well paid American workers.

21. Which is the most accurate statement? (LO1)

a) The United States can be described as a purely free trading nation.

b) The United States is one of the most protectionist nations in the world.

c) The rich nations provide hundreds of billions of dollars in agricultural subsidies to the poorer nations.

d) The United States provides smaller agricultural subsidies than does Japan and the European Union.

22. Which statement is true? (LO3)

a) Comparative advantage is not necessary for trade to take place, but absolute advantage is.

b) Absolute advantage is not necessary for trade to take place, but comparative advantage is.

c) Both absolute and comparative advantage are necessary for trade to take place.

d) Neither absolute nor comparative advantage are necessary for trade to take place.

23. Which statement is true? (LO4)

a) There are basically no arguments that can be made on behalf of trade protection.

b) The arguments for trade protection are more valid than the arguments for free trade.

c) The United States has had a record of fully supporting free trade since the early 20th century.

d) Much of what we import has been produced by "sweatshop labor."

24. In order for trade between two countries to take place, _____. (LO3)

a) absolute advantage is necessary

b) comparative advantage is necessary

c) both absolute and comparative advantage are necessary

d) neither absolute nor comparative advantage is necessary

25. Which of the following is the most accurate statement? (LO2, 10)

a) Americans are very willing to buy domestically produced goods, even if they are more expensive than imported goods.

b) We import more foreign goods than we did 40 years ago, but merchandise imports are still about the same percentage of our GDP.

c) In the decades following World War II, the Japanese consumer has strongly favored domestically manufactured goods over imports.

d) France paid a high economic price when many Americans switched from french fries to freedom fries.

26. Which one of the following statements is the most accurate? (LO11)

a) Our economy would be much better off if the entire globalization process were reversed.

b) The globalization process creates billions of winners and no losers.

c) The process of globalization could easily be reversed if Congress and the president were willing to act.

d) Globalization ensures a more efficient allocation of resources throughout the world.

27. What accounts for the sharp fall in our trade deficit in 2009? (LO1)

a) Our imports fell more than our exports.

b) Our exports fell more than our imports.

c) The recession was much worse in the rest of the world than in the U.S.

d) The American consumer made a much greater effort to buy American products to keep jobs in the United States.

Fill-In Questions

1. The basis for international trade is _____. (LO2)

Use Figure 1 to answer questions 2 and 3.

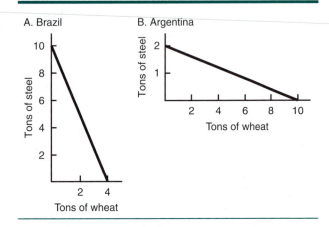

A. Brazil   B. Argentina

Figure **1**

2. Brazil is better at producing _____ than at producing _____.
   Argentina is better at producing _____ than at producing _____. (LO3)

3. If 1 ton of steel could be traded for 1 ton of wheat, Brazil would trade its _____ for Argentina's _____. (LO3)

4. _____ is the country with which we have the largest trade imbalance. (LO6, 7)

5. It would greatly reduce our trade deficit the most if we could curb our import of _____. (LO6)

6. Our trade deficit in 2009 was $ _____. (LO2, 6)

7. If our trade deficit with China and Japan were 0, our total trade deficit would be reduced by almost $ _____ billion.

8. The law of comparative advantage states that total output is greatest when each product is made by the country that has the _____. (LO3)

9. A tariff is a tax on _____; a quota is a limit on _____. (LO5)

10. _____ was the last year in which we ran a trade surplus. (LO2)

Problems

Assume Bolivia and Chile use the same amount of resources to produce tin and copper. Figure 2 represents their production possibilities curves. Use it to answer problems 1 through 4.

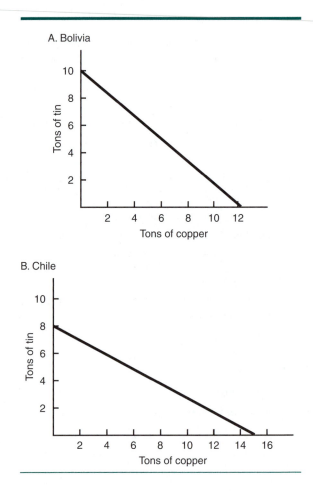

A. Bolivia

B. Chile

Figure **2**

1. Bolivia has a comparative advantage in the production of which metal? (LO3)

2. Chile has a comparative advantage in the production of which metal? (LO3)

3. Bolivia will trade _____ for _____. (LO3)

4. Chile will trade _____ for _____. (LO3)

Chapter 19

International Finance

The United States is the world's largest economy and the world's largest trading nation. We import more than any other nation and we also run the world's largest negative trade balance—averaging over $700 billion between 2005 and 2008.

How do we finance all this trading, and how do we finance our negative balance in trade? International trade is just one part of international finance. The other part encompasses foreign investment, capital inflows and outflows, exchange rates, and other international transactions, as well as the finance of international trade.

One consequence of our mounting trade deficits is that foreigners are buying up American assets. How much of America is foreign owned today, and will most of this country one day be owned by foreigners? Will foreigners soon have enough financial leverage to influence—or even dictate—our economic and foreign policies? Stay tuned, and by the end of the chapter you will learn the answers to these important questions.

LEARNING OBJECTIVES

After reading this chapter you should be able to:

1. Explain how international trade is financed.
2. Define and measure our balance of payments.
3. List and discuss the different exchange rate systems.
4. Summarize how we became a debtor nation.
5. Explain American exceptionality from a historical perspective.

The Mechanics of International Finance

Think of international trade and finance as an extension of our nation's economic activities beyond our borders. Instead of buying microchips from a firm in California, we buy them from a firm in Japan. Instead of selling Cadillacs in Miami, we sell them in Rio de Janeiro. And rather than building a factory in Chicago, we build one in China.

Financing International Trade

When an American importer buys $2 million of wine from a French merchant, how does she pay? In dollars? In euros? In gold? Gold is used only by governments, and then only on very rare occasions, to settle international transactions. Dollars, although sometimes acceptable as an international currency, are not as useful as euros to the

TABLE 1	U.S. Balance of Payments, 2009*
	*(in $ billions)**

Current Account	(billions of dollars)
Exports of goods and services	+1,560
Imports of goods and services	−1,952
Net investment income	+ 89
Net transfers	− 118
Current account balance	− 421

Capital Account	
Foreign investment in the U.S.	+435
U.S. investment abroad	−237
Statistical discrepancy	−184
Capital account balance	+421

*Numbers may not add up due to rounding.
Source: *Survey of Current Business,* April 2010; *Economic Indicators,* April 2010.

French wine merchant. After all, the merchant will have to pay his employees and suppliers in euros.

There's no problem exchanging dollars for euros in either the United States or France. Many banks in New York have plenty of euros on hand, and virtually every bank in the country can get euros (as well as other foreign currencies) within a day or two. In Paris and every other French city, dollars are readily available from banks and storefront foreign exchange dealers. On any given day—actually, at any given minute—there is a market exchange rate of euros for dollars; all you need to do is find the right teller and you can exchange your dollars for euros or euros for dollars within minutes.

Financing international trade is part of the economic flow of money and credit that crosses international boundaries every day. For the rest of this chapter we'll see where these funds are going and, in particular, how the United States is involved. We'll begin with the U.S. balance of payments, which provides an accounting of our country's international financial transactions.

The Balance of Payments

Often our balance of payments is confused with our balance of trade. Actually, the balance of trade is a major part of the balance of payments. *The entire flow of U.S. dollars and foreign currencies into and out of the country constitutes the balance of payments,* while the trade balance is just the difference between our imports and our exports.

The balance of payments consists of two parts. First is *the current account, which summarizes all the goods and services produced during the current year that we buy from or sell to foreigners.* The second part is *the capital account, which records the long-term transactions that we conduct with foreigners.* The total of the current and capital accounts will always be zero; that is, our balance of payments never has a deficit or a surplus. When we look at these accounts in more detail, the picture should become clearer.

The balance of payments has two parts: the current account and the capital account.

Table 1 shows the U.S. balance of payments in 2009. The great villain of the piece is our huge trade deficit. Next we have income from investments. From the early 20th century to the early 1980s the United States had a substantial net investment income because Americans invested much more abroad than foreigners invested in the

Sending Money Home

My maternal grandmother, the oldest of eight children, grew up in a small town in Russia, not far from the Black Sea. While still a teenager she was sent to America where she would work in a garment factory, saving up money to send for her younger siblings, one-by-one. Together, they earned enough within a few years to bring the entire family to America. This was a familiar family saga in the decades before the restrictive immigration laws were passed in the 1920s, intended to restrict the influx of "undesirables" from Eastern and Southern Europe.

Today recent immigrants cannot easily send for their families, but they do provide them with substantial support by regularly wiring them money. If you'll glance at Table 1, you'll notice that $118 billion in net transfers was sent abroad in 2009. About three-quarters of those funds were remittances sent by recent immigrants to their families back home.

Here's the deal: We hire immigrants to harvest our crops, tend our lawns, take care of our children, staff our restaurants, clean our offices and homes, and pay them minimum, or even sub-minimum wages, often off the books. They live as cheaply as possible, scrimping and saving so they can send money home to their parents and children, often providing the sole means of support for their families. To sum up: These folks perform low-wage work that most Americans won't do themselves, and then send home a large part of their wages.

United States. Since then foreigners have been investing more in the U.S. than we have been investing abroad, so eventually those investments will earn more income than ours. In other words, in the not-too-distant future, net investment income will turn negative. Finally, we have net transfers, which include foreign aid, military spending abroad, remittances to relatives living abroad, and pensions paid to Americans living abroad.

I think that our net unilateral transfers abroad may be even larger than the −$118 billion listed in Table 1. (See the box, "Sending Money Home.") This was sent mainly by recent immigrants to their families in Mexico, the Caribbean, and to Central and South America.

Our balance on the current account is a clear indicator of how we're doing. A negative balance on the current account of −$421 billion means that we went $421 billion deeper into debt with foreigners.

When we add up the numbers that go into our current account, it is easy to see why this figure is negative and why our current account deficit has been growing in recent years. (See Figure 1.) But what international finance takes away with one hand, it pays back with the other. Thus, by definition, our current account deficit is balanced by our capital account surplus.

Although our balance of payments every year, by definition, is zero, foreigners are buying up more and more of our country. So it is tempting to refer to our current account deficit as our balance of payments deficit (I've slipped a few times myself). Please remember that our huge current account deficit is offset by our capital account surplus.

The way it works is that we buy much more from foreigners than they buy from us. In effect, they lend or give us the money to make up the difference between our imports and our exports. It would not be an exaggeration to say that we borrow so much from foreigners to finance our current account deficits that we sell them pieces of the American rock, so to speak. Those pieces consist mainly of corporate stock and real estate, but they also lend us hundreds of billions of dollars each year in the form of purchases of corporate and government bonds and other debt instruments. Unless we can reduce our deficit in the trade of goods and services, our current account deficit will keep growing, and foreigners will have little choice but to keep sending most of those dollars back here to buy up more and more of our assets.

As you can see from Figure 2, our current account deficit as a percentage of GDP has been rising very rapidly since the early 1990s. In 2006 we were borrowing 6.2 percent of our GDP from foreigners, but by 2009 it has fallen back to just 2.9 percent. The main

Our current account deficit is balanced by our capital account surplus.

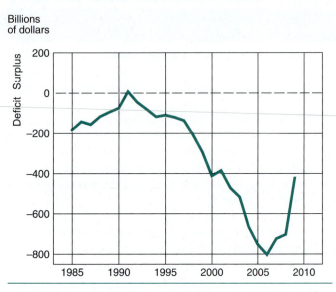

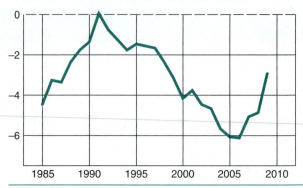

Figure 2

U.S. Current Account Deficit or Surplus as a Percentage of GDP, 1985–2009

In 1991 we ran a tiny surplus—$3 billion—on our current account. But in subsequent years we ran mounting deficits. By 2005 our current account deficit was 6.3 percent of GDP.

Source: Economic Report of the President, 2006.

Figure 1

U.S. Current Account Surpluses and Deficits, 1985–2009

Since 1991 our negative balance on current account grew steadily, topping $800 billion in 2006. But it peaked in 2006 and fell precipitously in 2009, to just $421 billion.

Source: Economic Report of the President, 2009; Economic Indicators, March 2010.

reason for this decline was that our trade deficit fell sharply in 2009—a byproduct of the Great Recession.

Figure 3 shows how our current account deficit as a percentage of GDP compared with that of other major trading nations. China and Germany had huge current account surpluses. But the United States, along with Australia, ran relatively large deficits as a percentage of GDP.

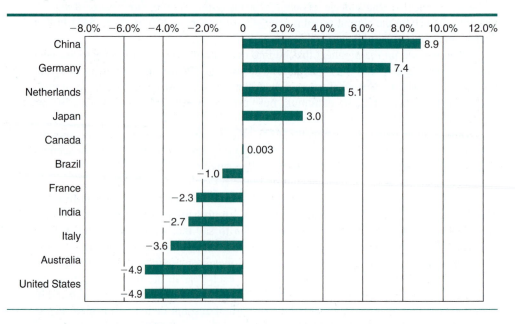

Figure 3

Current Account Deficit or Surplus as Percentage of GDP, Selected Countries, 2008

Among these countries, the United States and Australia are running the largest current account deficits relative to their GDPs.

Source: OECD.

Exchange Rate Systems

The basis for international finance is the exchange of well over 100 national currencies. Until the 1930s the world's currencies were based on gold. Since then a relatively free-floating exchange rate system has evolved. Under this system exchange rates are determined largely by the forces of supply and demand. In other words, how many yen, yuan, euros, or pounds you can get for your dollars is determined largely by the impersonal forces of the market.

An exchange rate is the price of a country's currency in terms of another currency. If you received 100 Japanese yen for $1, then you could say that a yen is worth one cent. And if a British pound were exchanged for $2, then you could say that a dollar is worth half a pound. In April 2010, you needed about 75 euros (the euro is the official currency of Germany, France, Italy, and nine other European countries) to get $100. So a euro was worth about $1.33.

There are three fairly distinct periods in the recent history of exchange rates. First, we'll examine the period before 1944, when most of the world was on the gold standard. Second, we'll look at the period from 1944 to 1973, when international finance was based on fixed exchange rates. Finally, we shall review the period from 1973 to the present, when we have had relatively freely floating exchange rates.

Three distinct periods

The Gold Standard

There has been some talk in recent years about a return to the gold standard, but it's not going to happen. Exactly what *is* the gold standard, what are its advantages, and what are its disadvantages? Funny you should ask.

Exactly what is the gold standard?

A nation is on the gold standard when it defines its currency in terms of gold. Until 1933 the U.S. dollar was worth 1/23 of an ounce of gold. In other words, you could buy an ounce of gold from the Treasury for $23 or sell this department an ounce for $23. Paper money was fully convertible into gold. If you gave the Treasury $23, you would get one ounce of gold—no ifs, ands, or buts. In 1933, we raised the price of gold to $35 an ounce, which meant a dollar was worth 1/35 of an ounce of gold.

To be on the gold standard, a nation must maintain a fixed ratio between its gold stock and its money supply. That way, when the gold stock rises, so does the money supply. Should gold leave the country, the money supply declines.

That brings us to the third and last requirement of the gold standard: There must be no barriers to the free flow of gold into and out of the country.

When we put all these things together, we have the gold standard. The nation's money supply, which is based on gold, is tied to the money supply of every other nation on the gold standard. It is the closest the world has ever come to an international currency. This system worked quite well until World War I, when most of the belligerents temporarily went off the gold standard because many of their citizens were hoarding gold and trying to ship it off to neutral nations.

Ideally, here is how the gold standard works. When Country A exports as much as it imports from Country B, no gold is transferred. But when Country A imports more than it exports, it has to ship the difference, in gold, to the trading partners with whom it has trade deficits.

How the gold standard works

Suppose the United States had to ship 1 million ounces of gold to other countries. This would lower our gold stock and, consequently, our money supply. When our money supply declined, so would our price level. This would make our goods cheaper relative to foreign goods. Our imports would decline and our exports would rise because foreigners would find American imports cheaper than their own goods.

What we had, then, was a self-correcting mechanism. A negative balance of trade caused an outflow of gold, a lower money supply, lower prices, and ultimately, fewer

A self-correcting mechanism

imports and more exports. Thus, under the gold standard, negative trade balances eliminated themselves.

After World War I the nations that had left the gold standard returned to the fold, but some nations' currencies were overvalued (relative to their price in gold) while others' currencies were undervalued. Adjustments were difficult because the nations whose currency was overvalued would have faced a gold drain and, consequently, lower prices and lower wages. But wages and prices are rarely downwardly flexible.

An alternative was to devalue—that is, lower the price of money in relation to gold. For example, a 10 percent devaluation would mean that instead of getting 10 British pounds for an ounce of gold, you now get 11. As the Great Depression spread, one nation after another devalued, and within a few years virtually everyone was off the gold standard.

Evaluation of the gold standard

Let's step back for a moment and evaluate the gold standard. It *did* work for a long time, automatically eliminating trade surpluses and deficits. And it *did* stimulate international trade by removing the uncertainty of fluctuating exchange rates.

But the gold standard has a downside. First, it will work only when the gold supply increases as quickly as the world's need for money. By the early 20th century this was no longer the case. Second, it will work only if participating nations are willing to accept the periodic inflation and unemployment that accompany the elimination of trade imbalances. In today's world political leaders must pay far more attention to their domestic constituencies than to their trading partners. Finally, strict adherence to the gold standard would render monetary policy utterly ineffective. If gold were flowing into the United States, the Federal Reserve would be powerless to slow the rate of monetary growth and the ensuing inflation. And if there were an outflow of gold, the Federal Reserve would be unable to slow the decline in the money supply and thereby prevent the advent of a recession.

With the breakdown of the gold standard in the 1930s, protectionism returned as one nation after another raised tariff barriers higher and higher. Devaluation followed devaluation until the entire structure of international trade and finance was near complete collapse. Then came World War II—and with it, a great revival of economic activity. While the war was still raging, the Bretton Woods conference was called to set up a system of international finance that would lend some stability to how exchange rates were set.

The Gold Exchange Standard, 1944–73

Fixed exchange rates

The Bretton Woods (New Hampshire) conference set up the International Monetary Fund (IMF) to supervise a system of fixed exchange rates, all of which were based on the U.S. dollar, which was based on gold. The dollar was defined as being worth 1/35 of an ounce of gold, so gold was $35 an ounce, and dollars were convertible into gold at that price.

Other currencies were convertible into dollars at fixed prices, so these currencies were indirectly convertible into gold. But this was short of a gold standard because the money supplies of these nations were not tied to gold and no longer would trade deficits or surpluses automatically eliminate themselves. If a nation ran consistent trade deficits, it could devalue its currency relative to the dollar. A devaluation of 10 percent or less could be done without the IMF's permission (larger cuts required permission).

The new system functioned well for 25 years after World War II. The United States ran almost continual balance-of-payment deficits during the 1950s and 1960s, which eventually led to an international financial crisis in 1971. But until that year these deficits contributed to international liquidity. This is because U.S. dollars as well as gold were held as reserves for international payments by virtually every country in the world but the United States.

Why were U.S. dollars so acceptable?

Why were U.S. dollars acceptable to other nations? First, the United States held the largest stock of gold in the world and stood ready to sell that gold at $35 an ounce to the central banks of all nations. Second, the American economy was by far the largest and strongest in the world.

By the late 1960s, as our gold stock dwindled and as foreign governments found themselves with increasing stocks of dollars, these nations began to ask some embarrassing questions. If the United States continued to run balance-of-payments deficits, would we be able to redeem the dollars they were holding for gold at $35 an ounce? Would the United States be forced to devalue the dollar, thus making other countries' dollar holdings less valuable?

The Freely Floating Exchange Rate System, 1973 to the Present

To return to 1971, when our payments deficits finally forced us to abandon the gold exchange standard—and forced the rest of the world off as well—the IMF needed to set up a new system fast, and that system was, in computer terminology, a default system.

We were back to the old system that economists fondly refer to as the law of supply and demand. How does it apply to foreign exchange? The same way it applies to everything else.

We were back to the law of supply and demand.

Figure 4 shows hypothetical supply and demand curves for British pounds. Inferring from these curves, you can get 2 dollars for 1 pound.

Who sets this exchange rate? Basically, the forces of supply and demand do. The question then is, Where does the supply and demand for pounds come from?

The demand curve for pounds represents the desire of Americans to exchange their dollars for pounds. Why do they want pounds? To buy British goods and services, stocks, bonds, real estate, and other assets.

Likewise, the supply curve of pounds represents the desire of British citizens to purchase American goods, services, and financial assets.

Now we get to the beauty of the law of supply and demand. The point at which the two curves cross tells us the exchange rate of pounds and dollars. In Figure 4 we have a rate of 2 dollars for 1 pound.

With freely floating exchange rates, currencies will sometimes *depreciate* in value relative to other currencies. If the pound, for instance, depreciates with respect to the euro, it may fall from one pound equals 1.5 euros to one pound equals 1.4 euros. *Depreciation of a currency occurs when one currency becomes cheaper in terms of another currency.* Similarly, a currency can *appreciate* in value relative to another currency. Before appreciation 125 yen equaled one euro, but after the yen appreciated 120 yen

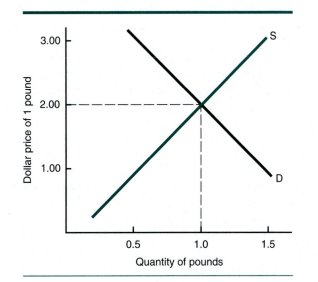

Figure 4

Hypothetical Demand for and Supply of British Pounds
How is the exchange rate set between dollars and pounds? It is set by the forces of demand and supply.

We don't have completely free-
floating exchange rates.

equaled one euro. *Appreciation of a currency occurs when one currency becomes more expensive in terms of another currency.* Whenever one currency depreciates, another currency must appreciate.

If we had completely free-floating exchange rates (that is, no government interference), the market forces of supply and demand would set the exchange rates. To a large degree, this is what happens; but governments do intervene, although usually for just a limited time. In other words, government intervention may temporarily influence exchange rates, but exchange rates are set by the forces of supply and demand in the long run.

China is the big exception to the freely floating exchange rate system. For many years the Chinese government tied its currency to the dollar at the rate of 8.28 yuan to the dollar. By the new millennium it was clear that the yuan was undervalued and that if it was allowed to float freely, fewer yuan would be exchanged for each dollar. Finally, since the summer of 2005 the Chinese government has allowed the yuan to very slowly appreciate against the dollar—a topic we'll return to later in this chapter. But it does not appear that future appreciations of the yuan will substantially reduce our trade deficit with China. Indeed it reached an all-time world record of $268 billion in 2008. As *The Economist* observed:

> America's trade deficit is due mainly to excessive spending and inadequate saving, not to unfair Chinese competition. If China has contributed to America's deficit it is not through its undervalued exchange rate, but by holding down bond yields and so fuelling excessive household borrowing and spending. From this point of view, global monetary policy is now made in Beijing, not Washington.[1]

How have the Chinese managed to manipulate the exchange rate of the yuan against the dollar? Because it runs huge trade surpluses with the United States, the Chinese government uses its surplus dollars to buy dollar-denominated securities, largely U.S. government bonds. Maintaining an undervalued yuan, it has been able to make Chinese exports more attractive to American consumers by keeping down their prices.

Three factors influence the exchange rates between countries. The most important factor is the relative price levels of the two countries. If American goods are relatively cheap compared to German goods, there will be a relatively low demand for euros and a relatively high supply of euros. In other words, everyone—Germans and Americans—wants dollars to buy American goods.

A second factor is the relative growth rates of the American and German economies. Whichever is growing faster generates a greater demand for imports. If the American economy is growing faster, it will raise the demand for euros (to be used to buy imported goods from Germany) while decreasing the supply of euros (the Germans will hold more euros and fewer dollars because they are not buying many American goods).

The third and final factor is the relative level of interest rates in the two countries. If the interest rates are higher in Germany than they are in the United States, American investors will want to take advantage of the higher rates by buying German securities. They will sell their dollars for euros, driving up the price of euros. In effect, then, the demand for euros will rise and their supply will decline.

Figure 5 shows five important exchange rates. If the weighted-average exchange value of the U.S. dollar in Panel A confuses you, then help is on the way. You'll find it in the box, "Interpreting the Top Line in Figure 5."

Because of our record trade deficits with China, officials of the Bush and Obama administrations, as well as many members of Congress, demanded that the Chinese government allow the yuan to appreciate at a faster pace against the dollar. At its present pace, the dollar will not depreciate to 6 yuan before the end of 2013.

---

[1]*The Economist*, July 30, 2005, p. 11.

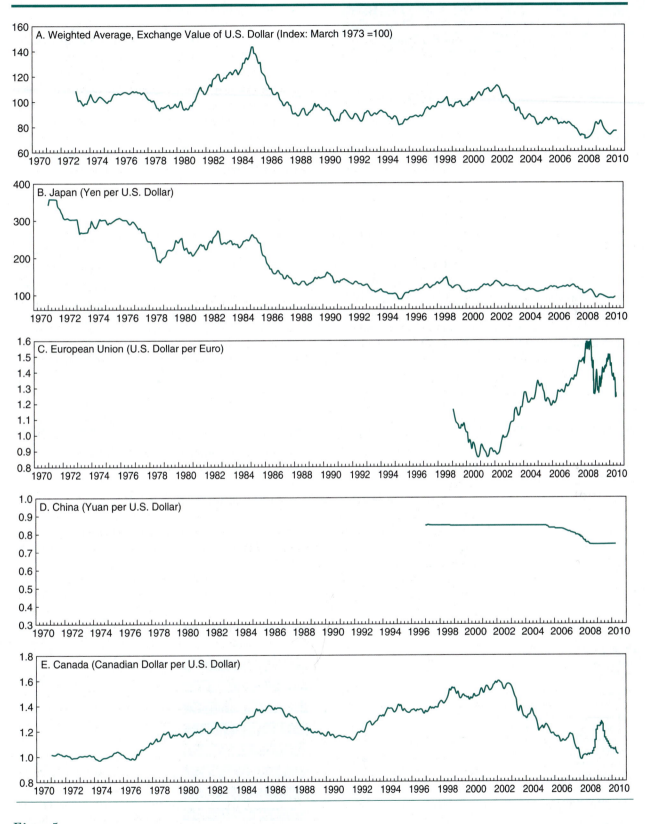

Figure 5

International Exchange Rates, 1972–2010

The value of the U.S. dollar in relation to the yen, the yuan, and other currencies has fluctuated rather widely over the last four decades. To a large degree the dollar has appreciated and depreciated relative to all other major currencies, moving up in value in the early 1980s, down in the later 1980s, up in the late 1990s, and down again in the new millennium.

Source: Business Cycle Indicators, April 2010.

The graph line in Panel A of Figure 5 shows how the U.S. dollar has fluctuated against other major currencies since 1972. When the line rises, that means the dollar has risen in value against a weighted average of 10 major foreign currencies. What does this mean in plain English?

First, a weighted average of currencies is similar to your grade point average. If you're really curious about how weighted averages are constructed, look at the box "Construction of the Consumer Price Index" in Chapter 10 in *Economics* and *Macroeconomics*.

Figure 5 charts an index of the dollar's relationship to other major currencies, with a base of March 1973. Let's say that in March 1973 a dollar traded for 50 francs. We set that base year at 100. Suppose the index rose to 200 a few years later. Then you might be able to get 100 francs for your dollar.*

The index did rise from 95 in 1980 to just over 140 in 1985; so the dollar rose by about 60 percent. What did this mean to American consumers? It meant that on the average they could get about 60 percent more foreign currency for their dollars than they could have just five years before.

Interpreting the Top Line in Figure 5

Suppose a Honda Accord cost 1,000,000 yen in 1985. If 250 yen exchanged for one dollar, the car cost an American $4,000 (1,000,000/250). By 1988 you could get only 125 yen for your dollar. If that new Accord still cost 1,000,000 yen, how many dollars did you need to buy it? Don't wait for me to tell you. I'd like you to work out the answer here:

Here's the solution: 1,000,000/125 = $8,000.

When the dollar rises in value, foreign goods become cheaper; at the same time American goods become more expensive to foreigners. What do you think this does to our trade balance? That's right—it makes it worse. Since the late 1980s the index has generally fluctuated within a range of 80 to 100.

---

*This is, of course, an oversimplification, because the dollar will not have risen by 100 percent against every currency during this period. It will have risen by more than 100 percent against some and by less than 100 percent against others.

Let's see how the dollar stacks up against the currencies of our leading trading partners as of April 8, 2010. Figure 6 tells us how many euros, pounds, yen, and other foreign currencies we could have gotten for a dollar.

Suppose you bought a Volkswagen Beetle for 9,500 euros. How much would that come to in dollars and cents?

Solution: First, note that, since the exchange rate in Figure 6 is 0.75 euros for a dollar, the number of dollars you need to pay is more than the number of euros. To find the answer (to the nearest dollar), divide the 9,500 euros by the exchange rate of 0.75.

$$\frac{9,500}{0.75} = \$12,667$$

Figure 6

Exchange Rates: Foreign Currency per American Dollar, April 8, 2010

How many Mexican pesos would you get for a dollar? You would get 12.2 pesos. Can you figure out how many dollars (actually how many cents) you would get for a peso? You would get 8.2 cents. Exchange rates fluctuate from minute to minute, and they are usually calibrated to hundredths, or even thousandths of a cent.

Source: The Federal Reserve, www. federalreserve.gov

$1 Will Buy

1.77 Brazilian reals

0.65 British pounds

1.00 Canadian dollars

6.83 Chinese yuan

0.75 euros

44.4 Indian rupees

93.4 Japanese yen

12.2 Mexican pesos

7.27 South African rand

1121.0 South Korean won

1.07 Swiss francs

on the web

To convert U.S. dollars into euros, yen, yuan, and other currencies, go to www.x-rates.com/calculator.html

How Well Do Freely Floating (Flexible) Exchange Rates Work?

Until 1973 most countries had fixed exchange rates because they feared flexible rates would fluctuate wildly. Has that happened since 1973? While there certainly have been some ups and downs, most notably with the dollar, we can still say so far, so good.

So far, so good.

The Euro

On January 1, 1999, most of Western Europe introduced a single currency, the euro. (See Panel C, Figure 5.) The European Monetary Union has 17 members—Austria, Belgium, Cyprus, Estonia, Finland, France, Germany, Greece, Ireland, Italy, Luxembourg, Malta, Netherlands, Portugal, Slovakia, Slovenia, and Spain. Flying into Spain from Finland now involves no more hassle than the hop from Chicago to New York. No need to show a passport and—thanks to the euro—no need for the traveler to change money or grapple with baffling prices.

Imagine if the United States were divided into 50 states, each with its own currency. Think how hard it would be to do business. Not only would exchange rates change, literally from minute to minute, but, since business payments are often made 30 or 60 days after delivery, you might end up paying 5 or 10 percent more—or less—than the contractual price. This added element of uncertainty would make it much harder to do business. So, what the members of the euro area are doing, then, is attempting to move toward a unified market with a single currency, just like the one we've long enjoyed in the United States.

The Yen and the Yuan

As we noted in the previous chapter, our two biggest trade deficits are with China and Japan. And, as it happens, the Chinese and Japanese monetary authorities have kept the value of their currencies low against the dollar. Indeed the Chinese yuan (also called the renminbi) has been pegged at 8.28 from 1998 until mid-2005 when it was finally allowed to appreciate, albeit at a very slow pace (see Figure 5, Panel D). It was estimated that in the spring of 2010 the yuan was still artificially undervalued by as much as 40 percent against the dollar. This has made Chinese goods and services cheaper to American consumers and American goods and services more expensive to Chinese consumers. Between mid-2005 and mid-2008 the yuan rose 21 percent against the dollar. But then, in July 2008, China informally repegged the yuan at 6.83 to the dollar. After almost two years of intense pressure from the United States and its other major trading partners, at the end of June 2010 the Chinese central bank announced that it would once again allow the yuan to appreciate against a basket of other currencies, including the dollar. However, it was expected that the ensuing appreciation would be no faster than it had been from 2005 through 2008.

Japan, too, extremely concerned about falling exports, has kept the yen artificially low against the dollar, making its exports to the U.S. cheaper and American imports more expensive. Japan has long been one of our major trading partners, so the exchange rate between the yen and the dollar is very closely watched. What would happen to the number of yen you could get for a dollar if the supply of dollars rose and the demand for dollars fell?

You should be able to figure that out very easily. In Figure 7, we show the question in graphic form, and as we can see, in this particular case, the dollar fell from 100 yen to 80 yen.

Figure 7

Hypothetical Supply of and
Demand for Dollars Relative
to Yen

If the supply of dollars outside the
United States were to go up from
S_1 to S_2 while the demand for
dollars went down from D_1 to D_2
what would happen to the price of
the dollar relative to yen? It would
go down, in this case from 100 yen
to 80 yen.

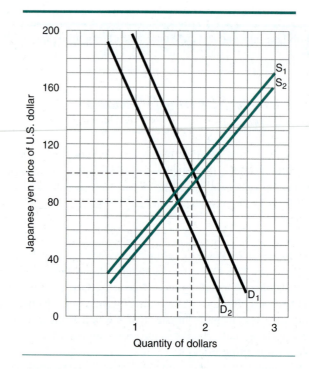

The chances are you've never heard of the hamburger standard or the Big Mac index, but you're about to. Begun by *The Economist* as a tongue-in-cheek effort to see if the dollar was undervalued or overvalued, the hamburger standard has actually taken on a life of its own (see the box, "The Hamburger Standard").

The Falling Dollar and the U.S. Trade Deficit

If foreigners have to pay higher prices, they will buy fewer of our exports. For example, if the dollar appreciates against the euro, from say, 0.8 euros to the dollar to 1.2 euros to the dollar, that would make our goods and services 50 percent more expensive to the French, the Germans, the Italians, and all the other Europeans buying our exports. So an appreciating dollar would tend to lower our exports.

Similarly, an appreciating dollar would tend to raise our imports from France, Germany, Italy, and other countries using the euro. Before the dollar appreciated, you might have had to pay $10 for a bottle of European wine; but after it appreciated from 0.8 euros to 1.2 euros, you would pay just $6.67. As the law of demand tells us, *when the price of a good is lowered, more of it is demanded.*

So if the U.S. dollar appreciates, our exports tend to fall and our imports tend to rise. And what happens when the dollar depreciates? You *guessed* it! Our exports tend to fall and our imports tend to rise.

So what has been happening to the dollar since January 2002? Let's go to the video tape—or, in this case, the top chart in Figure 5. From January 2002 through March 2008, the dollar depreciated 37 percent against a weighted average of currencies.

OK, so others things being equal, what would you expect to have happened to our trade deficit over this period? You would have expected it to fall. *Did it?* The answer is yes and no. Table 2 (on page 502) lists our trade deficits from 2001 through 2009. You'll notice that our trade deficit more than doubled between 2001 and 2006, and then, in 2007 it finally declined.

Apparently the lower dollar eventually *did* push down our trade deficit in 2007, making our exports cheaper and our imports more expensive. But why did our depreciating dollar take so long to reduce our trade deficit? There are two fairly obvious answers. First, two of our leading trading partners, China and Japan, were very actively buying up U.S. Treasury securities to prop up the dollar, all the while holding down the value of their

The Hamburger Standard

Suppose you were addicted to Big Macs, so no matter where you were in the world, you would rush to MacDonald's for dinner. If you did this in the United States in January 2010, a Big Mac would have cost you, on average, $3.58. If you had been in China, after you changed your dollars into yuan, that same Big Mac would have cost you just $1.83 (see chart). But in Switzerland, after changing your dollars into Swiss francs, you would have had to shell out $6.30—and in Norway, you would have had to shell out seven dollars and two cents in Norwegian krone.

The Big Mac index was created by *The Economist* to determine whether or not the dollar was overvalued or undervalued. If it were overvalued with respect to another currency, then you would be getting a bargain when you exchanged your dollars for that currency. You'd certainly have gotten a bargain in China when you exchanged your dollars for yuan and bought that Big Mac for the equivalent of just $1.83. That same hamburger would have cost you $3.58 in the United States. Indeed, we could say that the yuan was undervalued with respect to the dollar. By the same logic, you would not have gotten your money's worth in Norway, paying the equivalent of $7.02 for your Big Mac. We could say that the Swiss franc was overvalued with respect to the dollar.

See if you can figure out by what percent the Norwegian krone is *over*valued relative to the dollar. Be sure to write down your answer.

Solution: It's overvalued by 93 percent. Here's the math: You're overpaying by $3.44 ($7.02 − $3.58).
$$\frac{\$3.44}{\$3.58} = 0.93 = 93\%$$

One last question. By what percent is the Chinese yuan *under*valued relative to the dollar?

Solution: It's undervalued by 49 percent.
You're underpaying by $1.75. $\dfrac{\$1.75}{\$3.58} = 0.49 = 49\%$

Published two or three times a year by *The Economist,* The Big Mac index is intended as a light-hearted guide to whether currencies are at their "correct level."

> . . . in the long run, exchange rates should move toward rates that would equalise the prices of an identical basket of goods and services in any two countries. To put it simply: a dollar should buy the same everywhere. Our basket is a MacDonald's Big Mac, produced locally to roughly the same recipe in 118 countries.*

---

*"Economic focus/McCurrencies," *The Economist,* June 11, 2005.
Source: *The Economist,* February 1, 2007.

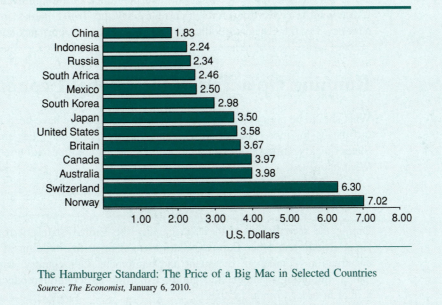

The Hamburger Standard: The Price of a Big Mac in Selected Countries
Source: The Economist, January 6, 2010.

own currencies relative to the dollar. In other words, while the dollar was depreciating against the euro, the British pound, and the Canadian dollar, it was not depreciating against the yuan and the yen.

The second reason why the depreciating dollar did not push down our trade deficit before 2007 was that foreign sellers were willing to accept lower prices and profits in

TABLE 2 U.S. Trade Deficit, 2001–2009

(in billions of dollars)

Year	Deficit
2001	$371
2002	427
2003	504
2004	619
2005	723
2006	769
2007	714
2008	708
2009	392

Source: *Economic Report of the President*, 2010; *Survey of Current Business*, March 2010.

order to protect their share of the world's largest consumer market. This view is summarized by *New Yorker* financial columnist, James Surowiecki:

> But what's most interesting is that foreign companies have essentially chosen to protect U.S. consumers from the effects of the weak dollar. They have resisted increasing prices here, accepting lower profit margins in order to maintain their market share. The American market is too big and too important for them to run the risk of losing customers, and, because it's so competitive, they generally can't raise prices without losing market share. So high-end television sets, foreign beer, and luxury cars have all remained relatively affordable, even though the dollars we buy them with are worth much less than they were a few years ago.[2]

on the web

How much can you get for one U.S. dollar in yen, yuan, euros, and other currencies? Go to www.federalreserve.gov/releases and then click on foreign exchange rates—daily. If you want to convert one foreign currency, say the British pound, into another foreign currency, say the Canadian dollar, go to http://oanda.com/currency/converter

Running Up a Tab in the Global Economy

What should be pretty clear by now is that, as a nation, we have been living well beyond our means for more than 25 years—and that the party can't last forever. The United States quickly shifted from being the world's largest creditor nation to the largest debtor. What happened?

From Largest Creditor to Largest Debtor

During the second half of the 19th century the United States borrowed heavily from Great Britain and other European nations to finance the building of railroads and the construction of much of our plant and equipment. Our country was a classic debtor nation, importing manufactured goods, exporting agricultural products, and borrowing capital in order to industrialize.

During World War I the United States became the world's leading creditor nation.

On the eve of World War I with the process of industrialization largely completed, we finally became a creditor nation. In 1914 foreigners owed us more than we owed them. The assets Americans held in foreign countries—factories, real estate, office buildings, corporate stock and bonds, and government bonds—were greater than the

---

[2]James Surowiecki, "The Financial Page Greenback Blues," *The New Yorker*, October 8, 2007, p. 38.

assets foreigners held in the United States. Our creditor status rose substantially during the war as we loaned the Allies billions of dollars. We became the world's leading creditor nation, a position we held until 1982.

How did we lose this position and fall into debt, quickly becoming the world's largest debtor? How could the largest, most productive economy in the world—a nation with low unemployment and stable prices—manage to run up such a huge tab?

The main reason for this turnaround was our large and growing trade deficits. As a nation we are living for today and not worrying about what will happen tomorrow. To say that, as a people, Americans are world-class consumers would not be an exaggeration. "Born to shop" and "shop till you drop" are apt descriptions of tens of millions of American consumers.

You can see the trend in foreign assets in the United States and U.S. assets abroad by looking at Figure 8. In 1985 we became a net debtor nation, and since that year,

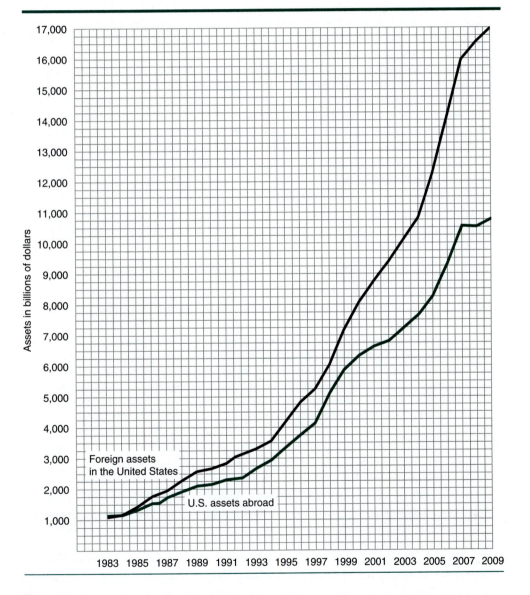

Figure 8

U.S. Assets Abroad and Foreign Assets in the United States, 1983–2009

In the mid-1980s we went from being a creditor nation to a debtor nation. Almost each year since 1985 the gap between foreign assets in the United States and U.S. assets abroad has kept growing. By the end of 2009 this gap had reached over $6 trillion.

Sources: Economic Report of the President, 2009; Survey of Current Business, March 2010.

foreign investment in the United States has far outstripped our investment abroad. These trends will continue into the foreseeable future as foreigners continue accumulating dollars—mainly because of our huge trade deficits—and using them to buy up our assets.

And yet, American investors are earning more interest, dividends, and profits on their investments abroad than were foreigner investors on their investments in the United States. How could that be? William Cline provides a succinct explanation:

> The large and liquid U.S. asset market, with its legal guarantees and (despite Enron) transparency, make the United States the natural place for foreign investors to place the lower-risk spectrum of their portfolios. Conversely, U.S. investors will tend to seek foreign assets to obtain the higher-risk, higher-return spectrum of their portfolios.[3]

If we add up all the assets that Americans own abroad and subtract the assets that foreigners own in the United States we would get the U.S. stock of net foreign assets. Looking at Figure 8, you can see that the U.S. stock of net foreign assets has been negative since the mid-1980s, and that it began to grow very rapidly at around the beginning of the 21st century.

In 2000 Americans owned about $6.2 trillion in foreign assets, while foreigners owned about $8 trillion in American assets—a gap of $1.8 trillion. By 2009 this gap grew to $6.3 trillion, when the American stock of assets held abroad was $10.7 trillion and the stock of assets foreigners held in the U.S. was nearly $17 trillion. So during this nine-year period, our stock of net foreign assets shot up from −$1.8 trillion to −$6.3 trillion. Even if our current account deficit were to keep falling over the next 10 years, the gap between what we own abroad and what foreigners own in the United States will continue to rise.

Something's gotta give. Most likely the dollar's decline, which began in 2002, will continue, perhaps for years. This will make our exports cheaper, so foreigners will buy more from us. Similarly, the lower-valued dollar will make imported goods and services more expensive, so we'll import less. As the dollar falls—note that I said "as" and not "if"—our exports will rise, our imports will fall, and so our trade deficit will shrink.

But a declining dollar, as Paul Krugman notes, makes foreign investment in dollar-denominated assets much less attractive, thereby slowing the inflow of foreign investment:

> Right now foreign investors are willing to hold 10-year U.S. government bonds, even though they pay only a slightly higher interest rate than their European counterparts. Those investors seem to believe, in other words, that today's strong dollar will persist for another 10 years. But the size of our trade deficit makes that unlikely. So foreign investors, and therefore the value of the dollar, are arguably doing a Wile E. Coyote—one of these days they will look down, realize that they have already walked over the edge of the cliff, and plunge.[4]

Well over $1 trillion of our currency remains abroad where it circulates as a medium of exchange. The Federal Reserve estimates that over two-thirds of all the U.S. currency being printed is eventually used as unofficial legal tender in China, Russia, Mexico, Romania, Bolivia, the Philippines, Tajikistan, Vietnam, and dozens of other countries. Lithuania, Argentina, and Brazil have formally pegged their currencies to the dollar, while many others have done so informally. In effect, then, much of the world is unofficially on the dollar standard.

The U.S. dollar is actually the official currency of more than two dozen countries, the largest of which are Ecuador, El Salvador, Guatemala, and Panama. And several others, including Mexico and Argentina, have been considering dollarization.

---

[3]William R. Cline, *The United States as a Debtor Nation* (Washington, DC: Institute for International Economics, 2005).

[4]Paul Krugman, "Deficit Attention Disorder," *The New York Times*, March 26, 2000, section 4, p. 17.

The Role of Drug Money

There are no hard figures or even reliable estimates on the amount of money sent abroad to pay for cocaine and heroin imports. But considering that the United States is clearly the world's leading drug importer, it is reasonable to say that more than $30 billion a year is sent abroad to drug growers and traffickers. The transfer of funds is done by cash or electronically through the worldwide banking network and is not easy to trace.

How does this affect our balance-of-payments deficit? It doesn't, except that we often run "statistical discrepancies" that sometimes run to over $80 billion. Now where could all that money be coming from? And where could it be going?

Some of it is coming back into the United States to purchase legitimate businesses, some to buy luxury condominiums along South Florida's "Gold Coast," and some may even be going to buy up part of the national debt. The point is, however reprehensible the drug dealers are, the economic effect of their transactions is similar to the effects of any other imports. The bottom line is that Americans are buying today's pleasures with tomorrow's income.

Laura D'Andrea Tyson, Dean of the London Business School, explains how the de facto dollar standard works:

> In a dollar-standard world, global growth fuels the demand for liquid dollar assets, and the United States can provide these assets, whether in the form of currency, government securities, or private securities, with no well-defined time frame for net repayment. As a result, the United States seems to enjoy a virtually unlimited line of credit denominated in its own currency with the rest of the world. This credit finances America's large and growing current-account deficit. The United States benefits from this arrangement because it can consume much more than it produces. But the rest of the world also benefits both because it gets the dollar holdings it requires and because the United States uses the credit to import goods and services and serve as the world's growth engine.[5]

Laura D'Andrea Tyson, Dean of the London School of Economics

As long as we can maintain a low inflation rate and currency stability, the world may continue to accept our dollars in exchange for a multitude of goods and services. We're certainly getting a great deal. We get to buy hundreds of billions of dollars' worth of stuff each year and pay for it just by printing money.

The foreign saver has a strong voice in setting the interest rates—not just for U.S. government securities but indirectly for other interest rates as well. As our dependence on funds from abroad grows, we are abdicating not just our role as the world's leading economic power but our economic sovereignty. As time goes by, decisions affecting the American economy will be made not in New York and Washington but in Tokyo, London, Beijing, Frankfurt, and other financial capitals outside the United States.

The U.S. Treasury depends on the foreign saver to finance the deficit.

As a nation we are living for today and not worrying about what will happen tomorrow. "America has thrown itself a party and billed the tab to the future," says Harvard economist Benjamin Friedman.[6] But all parties must end sometime, and someone is going to be left with a mess to clean up. (See the box, "The Role of Drug Money," for a discussion of another aspect of our living for today.)

We are living for today and not worrying about tomorrow.

Living beyond Our Means

The root cause of our problems has been that we as a nation have been consuming more than we have been producing, spending more than we have been earning, or, in short, living for today without providing for tomorrow. In the 19th century, when this country also

---

[5]Laura D'Andrea Tyson, "In the Dollar We (and All Other Nations) Trust," *BusinessWeek*, October 28, 2002, p. 26. Dr. Tyson was Chair of the President's Council of Economic Advisors, 1993–95.

[6]Benjamin M. Friedman, *Day of Reckoning* (New York: Random House, 1988), p. 4.

ran up a large international debt, we were financing capital expansion. This investment in the future enabled us to vastly expand our production and quickly pay off our debt.

Today we are following a radically different course. We are not borrowing from abroad to finance capital expansion but rather to pay for a massive spending spree. What are we buying? We're buying consumer electronics, cars, designer clothes, and oil.

America has become a nation of consumption junkies. This is not, in itself, such a terrible thing if we supported our habit. But we can't. So we ask foreigners to indulge us. And so far they have—at a price. We've been giving them IOUs in the form of U.S. dollars, and more and more, foreigners have been cashing them in for pieces of America. It seems as though everyone—the British, the Japanese, the Dutch, the Canadians, the Chinese, the Germans—owns a piece of the rock.

Since the early 1980s we've seen a massive recycling of dollars. As our trade deficits rose, the dollars we sent abroad were lent back to us as foreigners took advantage of our relatively high interest rates to purchase Treasury securities and corporate bonds. But they have increasingly been using their dollar stash to buy up pieces of America in the form of real estate and corporate stock. One might say foreigners are now not just America's creditors but its owners as well. *The Economist* summed up our current account dilemma:

> Just as an individual cannot pile on credit-card debt forever, so a country cannot increase the burden of its foreign debt indefinitely. Eventually, interest on the accumulated debt would use all the economy's resources, leaving nothing for domestic spending.[7]

A Codependent Relationship

China, and to a lesser degree, Japan and a few other East Asian countries, are locked into a codependent relationship with the United States. As long as we keep buying from them, even though we're running huge bilateral trade deficits, they continue to finance those deficits by lending us money. Indeed, China and Japan alone not only finance over half our trade deficit, but over half our federal budget deficit as well.

This is a great deal for us, because we get to consume much more than we produce. Why are these nations so nice to us? Because the huge American market enables them to expand production and job creation beyond what their own populations can consume. In addition, these Asian nations are so eager to keep their goods inexpensive, that they are willing to buy hundreds of billions of dollars in U.S. Treasury securities each year to prevent the dollar from depreciating too quickly.

Had the central banks of China, Japan, and America's other major Asian trading partners not made these purchases, the market forces of supply and demand would have driven the dollar well below its current level. A lower dollar would have made our imports more expensive and our exports cheaper, helping to reduce our trade deficit. But our codependent relationships with these nations precluded that from happening.

The Economist summarized the consequences of our codependent relationships with our Asian trading partners:

> The Asian central banks are masking market signals; America's current-account deficit reflects insufficient saving by households and an excessive budget deficit. Normally, investors would demand higher bond yields to compensate them for the increased risk, thereby giving the government a warning as well as an incentive to borrow less. But Asia's buying of Treasury bonds, with little regard for risk and return is keeping yields artificially low, which makes pruning the budget seem less urgent. At the same time low interest rates prolong America's unhealthy consumer spending and borrowing binge.[8]

The United States borrows almost $2 billion a day from foreigners, largely to finance our trade deficit, but much of this money is also used to finance the federal budget

We are a nation of consumption junkies.

We are selling off the rock—piece by piece.

---

[7]"The Price of Profligacy," *The Economist,* September 20, 2003, p. 7.
[8]"A Fair Exchange?" in *The Economist,* October 2, 2004, p. 16.

deficit as well. The Japanese and Chinese governments are the largest holders of U.S. government securities. Together they are keeping us financially afloat.

This arrangement has operated smoothly as we began running larger and larger trade and budget deficits, with the salutary effect of holding down our interest rates. Presumably it will continue into the foreseeable future because we, the Chinese, and the Japanese have too much to lose by upsetting the financial apple cart. But the time may come, perhaps five or ten years down the road, when our foreign creditors strongly disagree with some policy of the American government.

I won't even speculate as to what might set off such a conflict, but increasingly, we will have to take into account the opinions of our creditors. Most alarming, each year, we are digging ourselves into a deeper and deeper financial hole.

Why We Need to Worry about the Current Account Deficit

Ours is the world's largest economy, our rate of productivity growth is quite high, and we are on the cutting edge of the latest technology. So why worry about our current account deficit?

Countries that use American dollars for their currency as well as countries that hold U.S. government securities as assets have somewhat limited needs and will reach a point when they don't need any more dollars or U.S. Treasury debt. And as we continue selling off our nation's assets and debt to foreigners, they will reach the limit of how much they are willing to hold.

When that happens, foreigners will demand fewer dollars, the dollar will depreciate in value, foreigners holding American assets will suffer tremendous losses, and Americans will find that they have to pay a lot more for imported goods. Our living standard will fall, and we'll probably have a really bad recession or even a depression.

Today we still have a choice. We can bring our current account deficit under control or we can pay the consequences a few years from now. My guess is that we'll let things keep drifting until it's too late. In the meanwhile, keep your eye on the current account deficit.

Editorial: American Exceptionality

Toward the end of the main section of daily newspapers, you'll find the editorial page. Here's where the editors get a chance to say what they *really* think. This may surprise readers, who find plenty of opinions expressed in news articles. But economics textbook authors are held to a higher standard. We are expected to present both sides of most controversial economic issues. So while our personal viewpoints may well show through, we really do make a strong effort to be, in the words of Fox News, "fair and balanced."

In this last section of the last chapter, I'd like to shift gears, going from neutral to fast forward. Let me tell you what I *really* think about the American economy and where it's headed.

For a century we've been the world's largest economy, and for most of this time we have enjoyed the highest standard of living in history. There has long been a strong belief in American exceptionalism, perhaps best expressed by this line from our hymn, *America the Beautiful,* "God shed his grace on thee."

Since the implosion of the Soviet Union in 1991, we have been the world's only superpower. Indeed we spend nearly as much on armaments as the rest of the world combined. There are some who see parallels between our recent military record and those of the Roman, the Spanish, and the British empires. In fact, one can easily make the case that our empire is not only in decline, but may soon begin to fall apart.

There are many people, both in this country and abroad, who believe that, like the Romans, the Spanish, and the British before them, the Americans have built a huge empire to serve its economic interests. And like the *Pax Britannica* that lasted a century from the end of the Napoleonic Wars in 1815 to the beginning of World War I in 1914, we too have used our military might to impose what has been termed a "New World Order." And what would be the coin of our realm? You *guessed* it! The U.S. dollar! Bill Bonner and Addison Wiggin describe the economic workings of this American empire, and how it differs from its predecessors.

> America provides a *pax dollarium* for nearly the entire world. But the United States does not take direct tribute from its vassal states and dependent territories for providing this service. Instead, it borrows from them. Living standards rise in the United States. But they are rising on borrowed money, not on stolen money. The big difference is that America's vassal states can stop lending at any time. If they care to, they can even dump their current loans on the open market destroying the U.S. dollar and forcing interest rates so high that a recession—or depression—is practically guaranteed. What is worse, the longer the present system continues, the worse off Americans are.[9]

Let's look at the facts:

- Our federal budget deficits are well over $1 trillion.
- We have been running huge trade deficits for over a decade.
- Our defense spending is growing at an unsustainable pace, while our military is stretched to the breaking point.
- We are living well beyond our means, depending on the kindness of foreigners.
- We have lost most of our manufacturing base and are now losing our innovative edge as well.
- Americans have one of the lowest savings rate of all nations.
- American students have among the lowest scores on international tests.
- We import two-thirds of our oil.
- We spend almost twice as much per capita on health care than most other economically advanced nations.
- The United States is the only economically advanced nation without a high-speed railway system.

Considered individually, none of these facts is too alarming, but what conclusions do you reach when you look at the entire package? What trends do you see? Do you think our nation can sustain this course indefinitely?

No one disputes that by early in the 20th century we had built the greatest economy in the history of the world. Six factors, reinforcing one another, and unique to our nation, largely accounted for the rise of our economy:

1. Universal free public education.
2. A world-class local, interurban, and national public transportation network.
3. The development of mass production.
4. The development of mass consumption.
5. The building of a huge manufacturing base.
6. Maintaining our cutting-edge technology.

Today, not only are these factors no longer unique to our nation, but some of our economic rivals have caught up to, and surpassed us. Less than a century ago we were a lean and mean rising industrial power. We ran the world's most efficient economy. Today, we still are, by far, the world's largest economic power. But unless we begin to make far more efficient use of our resources, we will quickly become a fading economic superpower.

By nature economists are usually pessimists. That's why economics has long been called "the dismal science." So here we have the United States at the top of its economic

---

[9]Bill Bonner and Addison Wiggin, *Empire of Debt* (Hoboken, NJ: John Wiley and Sons, 2005), p. 40.

game, the unchallenged leader of the world, and I'm suggesting that our game is almost up, that we've been building up to a great fall.

One of the endearing characteristics of economics is that different people can look at the same set of facts and reach diametrically opposed conclusions. I've concluded that we are headed for an economic collapse—a collapse that will certainly come sometime in the next two or three decades. But you might have looked at these same facts and concluded that the best is yet to come. Hopefully we'll both live long enough to see which one of us is right.

Questions for Further Thought and Discussion

1. What is meant by our balance of payments? Explain what current account and capital account are.

2. What is the gold standard? How does it work?

3. Why does the dollar fluctuate with other currencies?

4. How did the United States go from being the world's largest creditor nation to the world's largest debtor?

5. Can there be a deficit on Current Account and a deficit on Capital Account at the same time? Explain.

6. For several months before your vacation trip to Germany you find that the exchange rate for the dollar has increased relative to the euro. Are you pleased or saddened? Explain.

7. If the dollar depreciates relative to the Japanese yen, will the Sony DVD player you wanted become more or less expensive? What effect will this have on the number of Sony DVD players that Americans buy?

8. Explain why a currency depreciation leads to an improvement in a nation's balance of trade.

9. What is a foreign exchange rate? Provide a few examples.

10. How is the exchange rate determined in a freely floating rate system?

11. Who demands Japanese yen? Who supplies yen?

12. *Practical Application:* Foreigners are buying up hundreds of billions of dollars a year in American assets. In what ways should this be a matter of concern to Americans?

13. *Practical Application:* Anne Hilbert has been hired by a Washington think tank to predict the trend over the next decade in the weighted average exchange value of the U.S. dollar. Its record from 1972 through early 2010 is shown in Figure 5 (A); she needs to provide evidence to back up her conclusion.

14. *Web Activity:* Jennifer Saxton bought a microwave oven made in China for $200. How much would she have paid in Chinese yuan? Go to www.x-rates.com/calculator.html

15. *Web Activity:* Melissa Larmon bought a German camera for 300 euros. How much would she have paid in U.S. dollars? Go to www.x-rates.com/calculator.html

Workbook for Chapter 19

Name _____   Date _____

Multiple-Choice Questions

Circle the letter that corresponds to the best answer.

1. We became a debtor nation in _____. (LO4)

   a) 1975   c) 1985

   b) 1980   d) 1990

2. In 2009 our net foreign debt was over $ _____

   trillion. (LO4)

   a) two   c) six   e) ten

   b) four   d) eight

3. Which one of the following is the most accurate
   statement? (LO5)

   a) The American empire, like the Romans, the
      Spanish, and the British before us, uses its
      military might to force other nations to provide
      us with low-cost goods.

   b) No one would ever suggest that there is such a
      thing as an American empire.

   c) We have become very dependent on our trading
      partners, who have been willing to accept U.S.
      dollars to finance our trade deficits.

   d) Although our international trade position has
      deteriorated in recent years, we can continue on
      this course indefinitely.

4. During the 1980s, _____. (LO4)

   a) both American investment abroad and foreign
      investment in the United States increased

   b) both American investment abroad and foreign
      investment in the United States decreased

   c) American investment abroad increased and
      foreign investment in the United States decreased

   d) American investment abroad decreased and
      foreign investment in the United States increased

5. The world's leading debtor nation is

   _____. (LO4)

   a) Argentina   c) Mexico

   b) Brazil   d) the United States

6. Which statement is true? (LO4)

   a) Foreigners own most of the assets in the United
      States.

   b) We own more assets in foreign countries than
      foreigners own in the United States.

   c) Foreigners are driving up interest rates in the
      United States.

   d) None of these statements is true.

7. Which one of the following statement is the most
   accurate? (LO4)

   a) As a percentage of GDP, the United States has the
      highest current account surplus of any nation.

   b) As a percentage of GDP, the United States has the
      highest current account deficit of any nation.

   c) As a percentage of GDP, our current account
      deficit is roughly the same as it was 10 years ago.

   d) Our current account deficit is rising at an
      unsustainable pace.

8. An American importer of Italian shoes would pay in

   _____. (LO1)

   a) dollars   c) euros

   b) gold   d) lira

9. The total of our current and capital accounts

   _____. (LO2)

   a) will always be zero

   b) will always be negative

   c) will always be positive

   d) may be positive or negative

10. In recent years we bought _____ from

    foreigners than they bought from us, and we invested

    _____ in foreign countries than foreigners

    invested in the United States. (LO2, 4)

    a) more, more   c) less, more

    b) less, less   d) more, less

11. Today international finance is based on

    _____. (LO3)

    a) the gold standard
    b) mainly a relatively free-floating exchange rate system
    c) fixed rates of exchange

12. The international gold standard worked well until

    _____. (LO3)

    a) World War I   c) 1968
    b) 1940   d) 1975

13. If we were on an international gold standard,

    _____. (LO3)

    a) inflations would be eliminated
    b) recessions would be eliminated
    c) trade deficits and surpluses would be eliminated
    d) no nation would ever have to devaluate its currency

14. Which of the following is false? (LO3)

    a) The gold standard will work only when the gold supply increases as quickly as the world's need for money.
    b) The gold standard will work only if all nations agree to devaluate their currencies simultaneously.
    c) The gold standard will work only if participating nations are willing to accept periodic inflation.
    d) The gold standard will work only if participating nations are willing to accept periodic unemployment.

15. The gold exchange standard was in effect from

    _____. (LO3)

    a) 1900 to 1944   c) 1955 to 1980
    b) 1944 to 1973   d) 1973 to the present

16. The United States began to consistently run current

    account deficits since _____. (LO1, 4)

    a) 1961   d) 1991
    b) 1971   e) 2001
    c) 1981

17. Today currency exchange rates are set mainly by

    _____. (LO3)

    a) the International Monetary Fund
    b) the U.S. Treasury
    c) bilateral agreements between trading nations
    d) supply and demand

18. The most important influence on the exchange rate

    between two countries is _____. (LO3)

    a) the relative price levels of the two countries
    b) the relative growth rates of the two countries
    c) the relative level of interest rates in both countries
    d) the relative wage rates of both countries

19. Devaluation would tend to _____. (LO3)

    a) make the devaluating country's goods cheaper
    b) make the devaluating country's goods more expensive
    c) have no effect on the value of the devaluating country's goods

20. Which is the most accurate statement? (LO3, 4)

    a) Since the euro was introduced it has lost almost half its value.
    b) The euro has facilitated trade among the members of the euro zone.
    c) The euro is now the world's most important reserve currency.
    d) The euro circulates as currency in most of the countries of the world.

21. The main reason why we are the world's largest

    debtor nation is _____. (LO4)

    a) our military spending
    b) our trade deficit
    c) inflation
    d) high taxes

22. Which is the most accurate statement? (LO2)

    a) Since our current account deficit is matched by our capital account surplus, we have no problem with respect to our international transactions.
    b) Foreigners invest all the dollars they receive from our capital account deficit to buy American assets.
    c) Our current account deficits are declining and should disappear before the year 2015.
    d) A declining dollar makes foreign investment in dollar-denominated assets much less attractive to foreigners.

23. Which of these is the most accurate statement? (LO4)

    a) There is no basis for the claim that the United States is living beyond its means.
    b) Our current account deficit is not a serious problem.
    c) Our trade deficit is a major economic problem.
    d) Since 2002 the dollar has been rising against most major currencies.

24. If you were going to spend time in Italy, France, and Germany, you would be paying for things with

_____. (LO1)

a) lira, francs, and marks

b) dollars

c) euros

d) gold

25. Which is the most accurate statement? (LO2)

a) Our balance on the current account is negative.

b) Since our balance of payments is always zero, there is little to worry about.

c) The income Americans receive from their foreign investments is much greater than the income foreigners receive for their American investments.

d) Because our imports are much greater than our exports, the federal government is forced to make up the difference.

26. Suppose the world was on the gold standard. If Peru ran persistent trade deficits, _____. (LO3)

a) Peru would be able to continue doing so with no consequences

b) Peru's money stock would decline, its prices would fall, and its trade deficit disappear

c) Peru would soon suffer from inflation

d) Peru would raise tariffs and prohibit the shipment of gold from the country

27. Suppose that in the year 2014 we run a trade deficit of $900 billion. Our current account deficit would be

about _____ billion. (LO4)

a) $600   d) $1,000

b) $800   e) $1,200

c) $900

28. The most accurate statement would be: (LO4)

a) The current account deficit is high, but falling.

b) The current account deficit will bankrupt us by 2020.

c) If our trade deficit begins falling, the current account deficit will fall.

d) Our trade deficit is much higher than our current account deficit.

29. According to the "Big Mac Index,"

_____. (LO3)

a) the U.S. dollar is too highly valued relative to virtually all other currencies

b) the U.S. dollar is valued too low relative to virtually all other currencies

c) you will be able to buy a Big Mac much more cheaply in China or Russia than in the United States

d) you will have to pay much more for a Big Mac in China or Russia than you would in the United States

30. Which is the most accurate statement? In early 2008 there was strong evidence that the _____. (LO3)

a) yuan and yen were overvalued against the dollar

b) yuan and yen were undervalued against the dollar

c) yuan was undervalued against the yen

d) yen was undervalued against the yuan

31. Running mounting current account deficits is

analogous to _____. (LO4)

a) running up debt on a credit card

b) taking money out of one pocket and putting it in another

c) owing money to ourselves

d) borrowing money that never has to be repaid

32. If a Japanese DVD player priced at 12,000 yen can be purchased for $60, the exchange rate is (LO3)

a) 200 yen per dollar.   d) 200 dollars per yen.

b) 20 yen per dollar.   e) none of the above.

c) 20 dollars per yen.

33. Suppose that last month the U.S. dollar was trading on the foreign-exchange market at 0.85 euros per dollar. Today the U.S. dollar is trading at 0.88 euros per dollar. (LO3)

a) The dollar has depreciated and the euro has appreciated.

b) The euro has depreciated and the dollar has appreciated.

c) Both the euro and the dollar have appreciated.

d) Neither the euro nor the dollar have depreciated.

Fill-In Questions

1. The entire flow of U.S. dollars and foreign currencies into and out of the country constitutes our

   _____. (LO2)

2. Most all the dollars that foreigners have earned from trading with the United States have been

   _____ in the form of

   _____

   _____. (LO2)

3. The basis for international finance is the exchange of

   _____. (LO1)

4. A nation is on the gold standard when it _____

   _____. (LO3)

5. To be on the gold standard, a nation must maintain a fixed ratio between its gold stock and _____

   _____. (LO3)

6. Under the gold standard, if country J imports more than it exports, it has to ship _____

   _____ to the trading partners with whom it has trade deficits. This will depress country J's _____, and its price level will _____. (LO3)

7. Under the gold standard, if country K's price level declines, its imports will _____

   and its exports will _____. (LO3)

8. Today exchange rates are set by _____

   and _____. (LO3)

9. If Tim Matray wanted to buy wine from a French merchant, he would pay her with _____. (LO1)

10. The main difference between our being a debtor nation in the 19th century and our being a debtor nation since the early 1980s was that in the 19th century we ran up a debt by buying _____ goods; since the early 1980s we have run up a debt buying _____ goods. (LO4)

Problems

Use the exchange rates listed in Figure 6 of the chapter to find how much it would cost in U.S. dollars and cents to make the purchases listed in problems 1–4.

1. A Toyota Corolla priced at 1.4 million yen. (LO3)

2. A carton of Canadian paper priced at $9.00 Canadian. (LO3)

3. A British book priced at 12 pounds. (LO3)

4. A German camera priced at 250 euros. (LO3)

Use the exchange rates listed in Figure 6 to find how much it would cost in the currency specified to make the purchases listed in problems 5–8.

5. A DVD priced at $10 is sold in Mexico City. (LO3)

6. Windows Vista priced at $100 is sold in China. (LO3)

7. A Cadillac priced at $20,000 is sold in London. (LO3)

8. A bottle of Viagra priced at $40 is sold in Berlin. (LO3)

9. A country had exports of $100 billion, imports of $90 billion, net transfers from abroad of −$10 billion, and −$5 billion of net income from foreign investments. What is the country's current account balance? (LO3)

10. Brazil ran a current account deficit of $55 billion. What is its balance on the capital account? (LO3)

11. If you could buy a market basket of goods and services in the United States for $1,000 and those same goods and services cost you $1,200 after you converted your dollars into euros, (a) is the euro undervalued or overvalued relative to the dollar? (b) by what percent? (LO3)

12. If you could buy a market basket of goods and services in the United States for $10,000 and those same goods and services cost you $7,000 in Russia after you converted your dollars into rubles, (a) is the ruble undervalued or overvalued relative to the dollar? (b) by what percent? (LO3)

Glossary

a

Ability-to-Pay Principle   The amount of taxes that people pay should be based on their ability to pay (that is, their incomes).

Absolute Advantage   The ability of a country to produce a good at a lower cost than its trading partners.

Accelerator Principle   If sales or consumption is rising at a constant rate, gross investment will stay the same; if sales rise at a decreasing rate, both gross investment and GDP will fall.

Accounting Profit   Sales minus explicit cost. Implicit costs are not considered.

Aggregate Demand   The sum of all expenditures for goods and services.

Aggregate Demand Curve   Curve showing planned purchase rates for all goods and services in the economy at various price levels.

Aggregate Supply   The nation's total output of goods and services.

Aggregate Supply Curve   Curve showing the level of real GDP produced at different price levels during a time period, *ceteris paribus*.

Allocative Efficiency   Occurs when no resources are wasted; it is not possible to make any person better off without making someone else worse off.

Anticipated Inflation   The rate of inflation that we believe will occur; when it does, we are in a situation of fully anticipated inflation.

Antitrust Laws   These laws, including the Sherman and Clayton acts, attempted to enforce competition and to control the corporate merger movement.

Appreciation   An increase in the value of a currency in terms of other currencies.

Arbitration   An arbitrator imposes a settlement on labor and management if they cannot reach a collective bargaining agreement.

Asset   Something that is owned by or owed to an individual or a business firm.

Asset Demand   Holding money as a store of value instead of other assets such as stocks, bonds, savings accounts, certificates of deposit, or gold.

Automatic Stabilizers   Programs such as unemployment insurance benefits and taxes that are already on the books to help alleviate recessions and hold down the rate of inflation.

Autonomous Consumption   The minimum amount that people will spend on the necessities of life.

Average Fixed Cost   Fixed cost divided by output.

Average Propensity to Consume   The percentage of disposable income that is spent; consumption divided by disposable income.

Average Propensity to Save   The percentage of disposable income that is saved; saving divided by disposable income.

Average Tax Rate   The percentage of taxable income that is paid in taxes; taxes paid divided by taxable income.

Average Total Cost (ATC)   Total cost divided by output.

Average Variable Cost (AVC)   Variable cost divided by output.

b

Backward-Bending Labor Supply Curve   As the wage rate rises, more and more people are willing to work longer and longer hours up to a point. They will then substitute more leisure time for higher earnings.

Balanced Budget   When federal tax receipts equal federal government spending.

Balance of Payments   The entire flow of U.S. dollars and foreign currencies into and out of the country.

Balance of Trade   The difference between the value of our imports and our exports.

Balance on Capital Account   A category that itemizes changes in foreign asset holdings in one nation and that nation's asset holdings abroad.

Balance on Current Account   A category that itemizes a nation's imports and exports of goods and services, income receipts and payments on investment, and unilateral transfers.

Bank   A commercial bank or thrift institution that offers checkable deposits.

Bank Run   Attempts by many depositors to withdraw their money out of fear that that bank was failing, or that all banks were failing.

Barrier to Entry   Anything that prevents the entry of new firms into an industry.

Barter   The exchange of one good or service for another good or service; a trade.

Base Year   The year with which other years are compared when an index is constructed: for example, a price index.

Benefits-Received Principle   The amount of taxes people pay should be based on the benefits they receive from the government.

Board of Governors   The Federal Reserve System's governing body.

Bonds   (See Government Bonds or Corporate Bonds.)

Boom   Period of prolonged economic expansion.

Break-Even Point   The low point on the firm's average total cost curve. If the price is below this point, the firm will go out of business in the long run.

Budget Deficit   When federal tax receipts are less than federal government spending.

Budget Surplus   When federal tax receipts are greater than federal government spending.

Business Cycle   Increases and decreases in the level of business activity that occur at irregular intervals and last for varying lengths of time.

Business Firm   A company that produces goods and services for sale to individual consumers, other firms, or the government.

C

CPI   (See Consumer Price Index.)

Capital   All means of production (mainly plant and equipment) created by people.

Capital Account   The section of a nation's international balance of payments statement in which the foreign purchases of that nation's assets and that nation's purchases of assets abroad are recorded.

Capitalism   An economic system in which most economic decisions are made by private owners and most of the means of production are privately owned.

Capital/Output Ratio   The ratio of capital stock to GDP.

Cartel   A group of firms behaving like a monopoly.

Central Bank   A bank whose chief function is the control of the nation's money supply.

Certificate of Deposit (CD)   A time deposit (almost always of $500 or more) with a fixed maturity date offered by banks and other financial institutions.

Change in Demand   A change in the quantity demanded of a good or service at at least one price that is caused by factors other than a change in the price of that good or service.

Change in Supply   A change in the quantity supplied of a good or service at at least one price that is caused by factors other than a change in the price of that good or service.

Checkable-Deposit   Any deposit in a commercial bank or thrift institution against which a check may be written.

Check Clearing   The process by which money is transferred from the checking accounts of the writers of checks to the checking accounts of the recipients of the checks.

Circular Flow Model   Goods and services flow from business firms to households in exchange for consumer expenditures, while resources flow from households to business firms in exchange for resource payments.

Classical Economics   Laissez-faire economics. Our economy, if left free from government interference, tends toward full employment. The prevalent school of economics from about 1800 to 1930.

Closed Economy   An economy which does little or no trading, or has any other interactions with other economies.

Closed Shop   An employer may hire only union members; outlawed under the Taft-Hartley Act.

Collective Bargaining   Negotiations between union and management to obtain agreements on wages, working conditions, and other issues.

Collusion   The practice of firms to negotiate price and/or market share decisions that limit competition in a market.

Commercial Bank   A firm that engages in the business of banking, accepting deposits, offering checking accounts, and making loans.

Communism   An economic system characterized by collective ownership of most resources and central planning.

Comparative Advantage   Total output is greatest when each product is made by the country that has the lowest opportunity cost.

Competition   Rivalry among business firms for resources and customers.

Complementary Goods   Goods and services that are used together; when the price of one falls, the demand for the other rises (and conversely).

Concentration Ratio   The percentage share of industry sales by the four leading firms.

Conglomerate Merger   Merger between two companies in unrelated industries.

Constant-Cost Industry   An industry whose total output can be increased without an increase in long-run-per-unit costs; an industry whose long-run supply curve is flat.

Constant Dollars   Dollars expressed in terms of real purchasing power, using a particular year as the base of comparison, in contrast to current dollars.

Constant Returns to Scale   Cost per unit of production are the same for any output.

Consumer Price Index   The most important measure of inflation. This tells us the percentage rise in the price level since the base year, which is set at 100; represented by CPI.

Consumer Surplus   The difference between what you pay for some good or service and what you would have been willing to pay.

Consumption   The expenditure by individuals on durable goods, nondurable goods, and services; represented by C.

Consumption Function   As income rises, consumption rises, but not as quickly.

Consumption Schedule   A schedule of the amounts that people plan to spend for consumer goods and services at different levels of disposable income.

Contraction   The downturn of the business cycle, when real GDP is declining.

Contractionary Fiscal Policy   To fight inflation, the federal government raises taxes and/or cuts spending.

Contractionary Monetary Policy   To fight inflation, the Federal Reserve decreases the money supply.

Corporate Bonds   This is a debt of the corporation. Bondholders have loaned money to the company and are its creditors.

Corporate Stock   Share in a corporation. The stockholders own the corporation.

Corporation   A business firm that is a legal person. Its chief advantage is that each owner's liability is limited to the amount of money he or she invested in the company.

Cost-of-Living Adjustments (COLAs)   Clauses in contracts that allow for increases in wages, Social Security benefits, and other payments to take account of changes in the cost of living.

Cost-Push Inflation   Rising costs of doing business push up prices.

Craft Unions   Labor unions composed of workers who engage in a particular trade or have a particular skill.

Credit Unions   Financial institution cooperatives made up of depositors with a common affiliation.

Creeping Inflation   A relatively low rate of inflation, such as the rate of less than 4 percent in the United States in recent years.

Cross Elasticity of Demand   This measures the responsiveness of the demand for good A to a change in the price of good B, indicating how much more or less of good A is purchased as the price of good B changes.

Crowding-In Effect   An increase in private sector spending stimulated by federal budget deficits financed by U.S. Treasury borrowing.

Crowding-Out Effect   Large federal budget deficits are financed by Treasury borrowing, which then crowds private borrowers out of financial markets and drives up interest rates.

Crude Quantity Theory of Money   The belief that changes in the money supply are directly proportional to changes in the price level.

Currency   Coins and paper money that serve as a medium of exchange.

Current Account   The section of a nation's international balance of payments that records its exports and imports of goods and services, its net investment income, and its net transfers.

Cyclical Unemployment   When people are out of work because the economy is operating below the full-employment level. It rises sharply during recessions.

d

Decreasing Cost Industry   An industry in which an increase in output leads to a reduction in the long-run average cost, such that the long-run industry supply curve slopes downward.

Deficit   (See Budget Deficit.)

Deflation   A decline in the price level for at least two years.

Demand   A schedule of quantities of a good or service that people will buy at different prices; represented by D.

Demand Curve   A graphical representation of the demand schedule showing the inverse relationship between price and quantity demanded.

Demand Deposit   A deposit in a commercial bank or other financial intermediary against which checks may be written.

Demand for Money   This represents the inverse relationship between the level of money balances and the price of holding money balances.

Demand, Law of   When the price of a good is lowered, more of it is demanded; when the price is raised, less is demanded.

Demand-Pull Inflation   Inflation caused primarily by an increase in aggregate demand: too many dollars chasing too few goods.

Demand Schedule   A schedule of quantities of a good or service that people are willing to buy at different prices.

Depository Institutions Deregulation and Monetary Control Act of 1980   This made all depository institutions subject to the Federal Reserve's legal reserve requirements and allowed all depository institutions to issue checking deposits.

Depreciation   A fall in the price of a nation's currency relative to foreign currencies.

Depression   A deep and prolonged business downturn; the last one occurred in the 1930s.

Deregulation   The process of converting a regulated firm or industry into an unregulated firm or industry.

Derived Demand   Demand for resources derived from demand for the final product.

Devaluation   Government policy that lowers the nation's exchange rate so that its currency is worth less than it had been relative to foreign currencies.

Diminishing Marginal Utility   Declining utility, or satisfaction, derived from each additional unit consumed of a particular good or service.

Diminishing Returns, Law of   If units of a resource are added to a fixed proportion of other resources, marginal output will eventually decline.

Direct Tax   Tax on a particular person. Most important are federal personal income tax and payroll (Social Security) tax.

Discounting   The method by which the present value of a future sum or a future stream of sums is obtained.

Discount Rate   The interest rate charged by the Federal Reserve to depository institutions.

Discouraged Workers   People without jobs who have given up looking for work.

Discretionary Fiscal Policy   Changes in government spending and taxes to promote full employment, price stability, and economic growth.

Diseconomies of Scale   An increase in average total cost as output rises.

Disequilibrium   When aggregate demand does not equal aggregate supply.

Disinflation   Occurs when the rate of inflation declines.

Disposable Income   Aftertax income. Term applies to individuals and to the nation.

Dissaving   When consumption is greater than disposable income; negative saving.

Dividends   The part of corporate profits paid to its shareholders.

Division of Labor   The provision of specialized jobs.

Durable Goods   Things that last at least a year or two.

e

E-commerce   Buying and selling on the Internet.

Economic Cost   Explicit costs plus implicit costs.

Economic Goods   Goods that are scarce, for which the quantity demanded exceeds the quantity supplied at a zero price.

Economic Growth   An outward shift of the production possibilities frontier brought about by an increase in available resources and/or a technological improvement.

Economic Problem   When we have limited resources available to fulfill society's relatively limitless wants.

Economic Profit   Sales minus explicit costs and implicit costs.

Economic Rent   The excess payment to a resource above what it is necessary to pay to secure its use.

Economics   The efficient allocation of the scarce means of production toward the satisfaction of human wants.

Economies of Scale   Reductions in average total cost as output rises.

Efficiency   Conditions under which maximum output is produced with a given level of inputs.

Elasticity of Demand   Measures the change in quantity demanded in response to a change in price.

Elasticity of Supply   Measures the change in quantity supplied in response to a change in price.

Entitlement Programs   Government programs such as Social Security, Medicare, Medicaid, and food stamps, that guarantee particular levels of cash or noncash benefits to those who fit the programs' criteria.

Entrepreneurial Ability   Ability to recognize a business opportunity and successfully set up a business firm to take advantage of it.

Equation of Exchange   Shows the relationship among four variables: M (the money supply), V (velocity of circulation), P (the price level), and Q (the quantity of goods and services produced). MV = PQ.

Equilibrium   When aggregate demand equals aggregate supply.

Equilibrium Point   Point at which quantity demanded equals quantity supplied; where demand and supply curves cross.

Equilibrium Price   The price at which quantity demand is equal to quantity supplied.

Equilibrium Quantity   The quantity bought and sold at the equilibrium price.

Euro   The common currency in most of Western Europe.

European Union (EU)   An organization of European nations that has reduced trade barriers among themselves.

Excess Reserves   The difference between actual reserves and required reserves.

Exchange   The process of trading one thing for another.

Exchange Rates   The price of foreign currency; for example, how many dollars we must give up in exchange for marks, yen, and pounds.

Excise Tax   A sales tax levied on a particular good or service; for example, gasoline and cigarette taxes.

Expansionary Fiscal Policy   To fight recessions, the federal government lowers taxes and/or raises spending.

Expansionary Monetary Policy   To fight recessions, the Federal Reserve increases the money supply.

Expected Rate of Profit   Expected profits divided by money invested.

Expenditures Approach   A way of computing GDP by adding up the dollar value at current market prices of all final goods and services.

Explicit Costs   Dollar costs incurred by business firms, such as wages, rent, and interest.

Exports   Goods and services produced in a nation and sold to customers in other nations.

Externality   A consequence of an economic activity, such as pollution, that affects third parties.

f

FDIC   (See Federal Deposit Insurance Corporation.)

Factors of Production   The resources of land, labor, capital, and entrepreneurial ability.

Featherbedding   Any labor practice that forces employers to use more workers than they would otherwise employ; a make-work program.

Federal Deposit Insurance Corporation   Insures bank deposits up to $100,000.

Federal Funds Rate   The interest rate banks and other depository institutions charge one another on overnight loans made out of their excess reserves.

Federal Open Market Committee (FOMC)   The principal decision-making body of the Federal Reserve, conducting open market operations.

Federal Reserve Note   Paper money issued by the Federal Reserve.

Federal Reserve System   Central bank of the United States, whose main job is to control our rate of monetary growth.

Federal Trade Commission (FTC)   Works to prevent false and deceptive advertising and has a role in approving or disapproving mergers.

Fiat Money   Paper money that is not backed by or convertible into any good; it is money because the government says it is money.

Financial Intermediaries   Firms that accept deposits from savers and use those deposits to make loans to borrowers.

Firm   A business that employs resources to produce a good or service for profit and owns and operate one or more plants.

Fiscal Policy   Manipulation of the federal budget to attain price stability, relatively full employment, and a satisfactory rate of economic growth.

Fiscal Year   Budget year. U.S. federal budget fiscal year begins on October 1.

Fixed Costs   These stay the same no matter how much output changes.

Fixed Exchange Rate   A rate determined by government and then maintained by buying and selling quantities of its own currency on the foreign exchange market.

Floating Exchange Rate   An exchange rate determined by the demand for and the supply of a nation's currency.

Foreign Exchange Market   A market in which currencies of different nations are bought and sold.

Foreign Exchange Rate   The price of one currency in terms of another.

Fractional Reserve Banking   A system in which depository institutions held reserves that are less than the amount of total deposits.

Free Trade   The absence of artificial (government) barriers to trade among individuals and firms in different nations.

Frictional Unemployment   Refers to people who are between jobs or just entering or reentering the labor market.

Fringe Benefits   Nonwage compensation, mainly medical insurance, that workers receive from employers.

Full Employment   When a society's resources are all being used with maximum efficiency.

Full-Employment GDP   That level of spending (or aggregate demand) that will result in full employment.

Future Value   The amount of money in the future that an amount of money today will yield, at current interest rates.

g

Game Theory   The study of how people behave in strategic situations.

GATT (General Agreement on Tariffs and Trade)   An agreement to negotiate reductions in tariffs and other trade barriers.

GDP   (See Gross Domestic Product.)

GDP Deflator   A price index used to measure price changes in the items that go into GDP.

GDP Gap   The amount of production by which potential GDP exceeds actual GDP.

Globalization   The integration of national economies into a worldwide economy.

Gold Standard   A historical system of fixed exchange rates in which nations defined their currency in terms of gold, maintained a fixed relationship between their stock of gold and their money supplies, and allowed gold to be freely exported and imported.

Government Bonds   Long-term debt of the federal government.

Government Expenditures   Federal, state, and local government outlays for goods and services, including transfer payments.

Government Failure   Misallocation of resources in the public sector.

Government Purchases   All goods and services bought by the federal, state, and local governments.

Government Transfer Payment   (See Transfer Payment.)

Gross Domestic Product (GDP)   The nation's expenditure on all the goods and services produced in the country during the year at market prices; represented by GDP.

Gross Investment   A company's total investment in plant, equipment, and inventory. Also, a nation's plant, equipment, inventory, and residential housing investment.

h

Herfindahl-Hirschman Index   A measure of concentration calculated as the sum of the squares of the market share of each firm in an industry.

Horizontal Merger   Conventional merger between two firms in the same industry.

Household   An economic unit of one or more persons living under one roof.

Human Capital   The accumulation of knowledge and skills that make a worker productive.

Hyperinflation   Runaway inflation; in the United States, double-digit inflation.

i

Imperfect Competition   All market structures except perfect competition; includes monopoly, oligopoly, and monopolistic competition.

Implicit Costs   The firm's opportunity costs of using resources owned or provided by the owner.

Imports   Goods and services bought by people in one country that are produced in other countries.

Income   A flow of money to households.

Income Approach   Method of finding GDP by adding all the incomes earned in the production of final goods and services.

Income Effect   A person's willingness to give up some income in exchange for more leisure time.

Income Elasticity of Demand   The ratio of the percentage change in the quantity demanded of a good to a percentage change in consumer income. It measures the responsiveness of consumer purchases to changes in income.

Incomes Policy   Wage controls, price controls, and tax incentives used to try to control inflation.

Increasing Costs, Law of   As the output of a good expands, the opportunity cost of producing additional units of this good increases.

Increasing Returns   An increase in firm's output by a larger percentage than the percentage increase in its inputs.

Increasing Returns to Scale   A situation in which a firm's minimum long-run average total cost decreases as the level of output rises.

Indexation   The automatic correction by contract or law to a dollar amount to allow for inflation.

Indirect Tax   Tax on a thing rather than on a particular person; for example, sales tax.

Induced Consumption   Spending induced by changes in the level of income.

Industrial Union   A union representing all the workers in a single industry, regardless of each worker's skill or craft.

Inelastic Demand   A demand relationship in which a given percentage change in price results in a smaller percentage change in quantity sold.

Inelastic Supply   A supply relationship in which a given percentage change in price results in a smaller percentage change in quantity supplied.

Inferior Goods   Goods for which demands decrease when people's incomes rise.

Inflation   A general rise in the price level.

Inflationary Gap   Occurs when equilibrium GDP is greater than full-employment GDP.

Innovation   An idea that eventually takes the form of new, applied technology or a new production process.

Interest   The cost of borrowed funds.

Interest Rate   Interest paid divided by amount borrowed.

Interlocking Directorates   When one person serves on the boards of at least two competing firms.

Intermediate Goods   Goods used to produce other goods.

International Monetary Fund (IMF)   An organization of over 150 nations set up as a lender of last resort, especially to nations that had otherwise been planning to devalue their currency, or were in financial crisis.

Inventories   Goods that have been produced but remain unsold.

Inventory Investment   Changes in the stocks of finished goods and raw materials that firms keep in reserve to meet orders.

Investment   The purchase or construction of any new plant, equipment, or residential housing, or the accumulation of inventory; represented by I.

j

Jurisdictional Dispute   A dispute involving two or more unions over which should represent the workers in a particular shop or plant.

k

Keynesian Economics   As formulated by John Maynard Keynes, this school believed the private economy was inherently unstable and that government intervention was necessary to prevent recessions from becoming depressions.

Kinked Demand Curve   The demand curve for the cutthroat oligopolist, which is based on the assumption that competitors will match a price cut, but will not match a price increase.

l

Labor   The work and time for which employees are paid.

Labor Force   The total number of employed and unemployed people.

Labor Union   Worker organization that seeks to secure economic benefits for its members.

Laffer Curve   Shows that at very high tax rates, very few people will work and pay taxes; therefore government revenue will rise as tax rates are lowered.

Laissez-Faire   The philosophy that the private economy should function without any government interference.

Land   Natural resources used to produce goods and services.

Law of Demand   An increase in a product's price will reduce the quantity of it demanded, and conversely for a decrease in price.

Law of Diminishing (Marginal) Returns   The observation that, after some point, successive equal-sized increases of a resource, added to fixed factors of other resources, will result in smaller increases in output.

Law of Diminishing Marginal Utility   As we consume increasing amounts of a good or service, we derive diminishing utility, or satisfaction, from each additional unit consumed.

Law of Increasing Costs   As the output of one good expands, the opportunity cost of producing additional units of this good increases.

Law of Supply   An increase in the price of a product will increase the quantity of it supplied; and conversely for a decrease in price.

Legal Reserves   Reserves that depository institutions are allowed by law to claim as reserves; vault cash and deposits held at Federal Reserve district banks.

Legal Tender   Coins and paper money officially declared to be acceptable for the settlement of financial debts.

Less Developed Countries (LDCs)   Economies in Asia, Africa, and Latin America with relatively low per capita incomes.

Leveraged Buyouts   A primarily debt-financed purchase of a controlling interest of a corporation's stock.

Limited Liability   The liability of the owners of a corporation is limited to the value of the shares in the firm that they own.

Liquidity   Money or things that can be quickly and easily converted into money with little or no loss of value.

Liquidity Preference   The demand for money.

Liquidity Trap   At very low interest rates, said John Maynard Keynes, people will neither lend out their money nor put it in the bank, but will simply hold it.

Loanable Funds   The supply of money that savers have made available to borrowers.

Long Run   When all costs become variable costs and firms can enter or leave the industry.

Long-Run Equilibrium   The intersection of the AD and LRAS curves, when wages and prices have adjusted to their final equilibrium levels.

Lorenz Curve   Data plotted to show the percentage of income enjoyed by each percentage of households, ranked according to their income.

m

M   The money supply—currency, checking deposits, and checklike deposits (identical to M1).

M1   Currency, checking deposits, and checklike deposits.

M2   M1 plus savings deposits, small-denomination time deposits, and money market mutual funds.

M3   M2 plus large-denomination time deposits.

Macroeconomics   The part of economics concerned with the economy as a whole, dealing with huge aggregates like national output, employment, the money supply, bank deposits, and government spending.

Malthusian Theory of Population   Population tends to grow in a geometric progression (1, 2, 4, 8, 16), while food production tends to grow in an arithmetic progression (1, 2, 3, 4, 5).

Margin Requirement   The maximum percentage of the cost of a stock purchase that can be borrowed from a bank, stockbroker, or any other financial institution, with stock offered as collateral; this percentage is set by the Federal Reserve.

Marginal Cost (MC)   The cost of producing one additional unit of output.

Marginal Physical Product (MPP)   The additional output produced by one more unit of input.

Marginal Propensity to Consume (MPC)   Change in consumption divided by change in income.

Marginal Propensity to Save (MPS)   Change in saving divided by change in income.

Marginal Revenue (MR)   The revenue derived from selling one additional unit of output.

Marginal Revenue Product (MRP)   The demand for a resource, based on that resource's marginal output and the price at which it is sold.

Marginal Tax Rate   Additional taxes paid divided by taxable income.

Marginal Utility   The additional utility derived from consuming one more unit of some good or service.

Market   Any place where buyers and sellers exchange goods and services.

Market Failure   A less than efficient allocation of resources.

Market Period   A period during which sellers are unable to change quantity offered for sale in response to a change in price.

Maximum Profit Point   A firm will always produce at this point; marginal cost equals marginal revenue.

MC = MR Rule   For a firm to maximize its profits, marginal cost must equal marginal revenue.

Measure of Economic Welfare   A measure developed by James Tobin and William Nordhaus that modifies GDP by excluding "economic bads" and "regrettable necessities" and adding household, unreported, and illegal production.

Mediation   A third party acts as a go-between for labor and management during collective bargaining.

Medium of Exchange   Items sellers generally accept and buyers generally use to pay for a good or service; the primary job of money.

Merchandise Trade Balance   The difference between the value of merchandise exports and the value of merchandise imports.

Merger   Two or more firms combining to form a single firm.

Microeconomics   The part of economics concerned with individual units such as firms and households and with individual markets, particular prices, and specific goods and services.

Minimum Wage   An hourly wage floor set by government that firms must pay their workers.

Mixed Economy   An economy in which production and distribution is done partly by the private sector and partly by the government.

Monetarism   A school of economics that places paramount importance on money as the key determinant of the level of prices, income, and employment.

Monetary Policy   Control of the rate of monetary growth by the Board of Governors of the Federal Reserve.

Monetary Rule   The money supply may grow at a specified annual percentage rate, generally about 3–4 percent.

Money   Main job is to be a medium of exchange; also serves as a standard of value and a store of value.

Money Multiplier   The amount of money the banking system generates with each dollar of reserves.

Money Supply   Currency, checking deposits, and checklike deposits (M or M1).

Money Wages   The current dollar amount of a person's wages.

Monopolistic Competition   An industry that has many firms producing a differentiated product.

Monopoly   An industry in which one firm produces all the output. The good or service produced has no close substitutes.

Monopsony   A market in which a single buyer has no rivals.

Moral Hazard   The condition that exists when one party to a transaction changes his behavior in a way that is hidden from and costly to the other party.

Multinational Corporation   A corporation doing business in more than one country; often it owns production facilities in at least one country and sells in many countries.

Multiplier   Any change in spending (C, I, or G) will set off a chain reaction leading to a multiplied change in GDP. Equation is $1/(1 - MPC)$.

n

NDP   (See Net Domestic Product.)

National Debt   (See Public Debt.)

National Income   Net domestic product minus indirect business taxes.

Natural Monopoly   An industry in which a single firm can provide cheaper service than could several competing firms.

Negative Income Tax   Cash payments by the government to the poor—an income tax in reverse. The cash payments decrease as income levels increase.

Net Domestic Product   The sum of consumption, net investment, government purchases, and net exports.

Net Domestic Product (NDP)   The sum of consumption, net investment, government purchases, and net exports. Essentially, GDP minus depreciation.

Net Exports   One country's exports to other countries minus its imports from other countries.

Net Investment   Gross investment minus depreciation.

Net Productivity of Capital   The expected annual profit rate.

Net Worth   The difference between assets and liabilities.

Nominal GDP   The value of the final goods and services produced in a given year valued at that year's prices.

Nominal Interest Rate   The real interest rate plus the inflation rate.

Nominal Wages   (See Money Wages.)

Noncompeting Groups   Various strata of labor that do not compete for jobs; for example, doctors and secretaries, skilled and unskilled workers.

Nondurable Goods   Goods that are expected to last or be used for less than one year.

Normal Good   A good whose demand varies directly with income; nearly all goods are normal goods.

Normal Profits   The return to the businessowners for the opportunity cost of their implicit inputs.

North American Free Trade Agreement (NAFTA)   A free trade area consisting of the United States, Canada, and Mexico.

o

Offshoring   Work that had been performed at home is sent abroad.

Oligopoly   An industry with just a few firms.

Oligopsony   A market in which there are only a few buyers.

Open Economy   An economy linked to the rest of the world through international trade.

Open-Market Operations   The purchase or sale of Treasury securities by the Federal Reserve; main monetary policy weapon.

Open Shop   When no one is forced to join a union even though the union represents all the workers in contract negotiations.

Opportunity Cost   The forgone value of what you give up when you make a choice.

Output Effect   When the price of any resource rises, the cost of production rises, which, in turn, lowers the supply of the final product. When supply falls, price rises, consequently reducing output.

p

P   The price level, or the average price of all goods and services produced during the current year.

Paradox of Thrift   If everyone tries to save more, they will all end up saving less.

Partnership   A business firm owned by two or more people.

Payroll Tax   (See Social Security Tax.)

Per Capita Income   A nation's total income per person.

Per Capita Real GDP   Real GDP divided by population.

Perfect Competition   An industry with so many firms that no one firm has any influence over price, and firms produce an identical product.

Perfectly Elastic Demand Curve   A perfectly horizontal demand curve; the firm can sell as much as it wishes at that price.

Perfectly Elastic Supply Curve   A perfectly horizontal supply curve; the slightest decrease in price causes the quantity supplied to fall to zero.

Perfectly Inelastic Demand Curve   A perfectly vertical demand curve; no matter what the price is, the quantity demanded remains the same.

Perfectly Inelastic Supply Curve   A perfectly vertical supply curve; quantity supplied remains constant no matter what happens to price.

Permanent Income Hypothesis   Formulated by Milton Friedman, it states that the strongest influence on consumption is one's estimated lifetime income.

Personal Income   Income received by household, including both earned income and transfer payments.

Phillips Curve   Curve showing inverse relationship between the unemployment rate and the rate of inflation.

Plant   A store, factory, office, or other physical establishment that performs one or more functions in the production, fabrication, and sales of goods and services.

Poverty   A situation in which the basic needs of an individual or family exceed the means to satisfy them.

Poverty Rate   The percentage of the population with incomes below the official poverty line established by the federal government.

Present Value   The value today of the stream of expected future annual income that a property generates.

Price   The amount of money needed to buy a particular good, service, or resource.

Price Ceiling   Government-imposed maximum legal price.

Price Discrimination   Occurs when a seller charges two or more prices for the same good or service.

Price Elasticity of Demand   (See Elasticity of Demand.)

Price Elasticity of Supply   (See Elasticity of Supply.)

Price Floor   Government-imposed minimum price (used almost exclusively to keep agricultural commodity prices up).

Price Index   An index number that shows how the weighted average price of a market basket of goods changes through time.

Price Leadership   One firm, often the dominant firm in an oligopolistic industry, raises or lowers price, and the other firms quickly match the new price.

Price Level   A measure of prices in a given month or year in relation to prices in a base year.

Price Support   Government-created price floor for a good or service.

Price System   Mechanism that allocates resources, goods, and services based on supply and demand.

Prime Rate   Rate of interest that banks charge their most creditworthy customers.

Producer Surplus   The difference between what sellers receive for a good or service and the minimum price for which they would have sold the good or service.

Product Differentiation   The distinction between or among goods and services made in the minds of buyers.

Production   Any good or service for which people are willing to pay.

Production Function   A technological relationship expressing the maximum quantity of a good attainable from different combinations of factor inputs.

Production Possibilities Curve   The potential total output combinations of any two goods for an economy.

Production Possibilities Frontier   A curve representing a hypothetical model of a two-product economy operating at full employment.

Productivity   Output per unit of input; efficiency with which resources are used.

Profit   The difference between total revenue and total cost.

Progressive Tax   Places greater burden on those with best ability to pay and little or no burden on the poor (for example, federal personal income tax).

Proportional Tax   A tax whose burden falls equally among the rich, the middle class, and the poor.

Proprietorship   An unincorporated business firm owned by just one person.

Protective Tariff   A tariff designed to shield domestic producers of a good or service from the competition of foreign producers.

Public Debt   The amount of federal securities outstanding, which represents what the federal government owes (the accumulation of federal deficits minus surpluses over the last two centuries).

Public Goods   Goods or services produced by the government; they can be jointly consumed by many individuals simultaneously at no additional cost and with no reduction in quality or quantity.

q

Q   Output, or number of goods and services produced during the current year.

Quantity Theory of Money   Crude version: Changes in the money supply cause proportional changes in the price level. Sophisticated version: If we are well below full employment, an increase in M will lead to an increase in output. If we are close to full employment, an increase in M will lead mainly to an increase in P.

Quotas   Numerical limits imposed on the quantity of a specific good that may be imported.

r

Rational Expectations Theory   This is based on three assumptions: (1) that individuals and business firms learn through experience to anticipate the consequences of changes in monetary and fiscal policy; (2) that they act immediately to protect their economic interests; and (3) that all resource and product markets are purely competitive.

Real Balance Effect   The influence a change in household purchasing power has on the quantity of real GDP that consumers are willing to buy.

Real GDP   GDP corrected for inflation; actual production.

Real Income   Income adjusted for price changes.

Real Interest Rate   Nominal interest rate minus inflation rate.

Real Wages   Nominal wages corrected for inflation.

Recession   A decline in real GDP for two consecutive quarters.

Recessionary Gap   This occurs when equilibrium GDP is less than full-employment GDP.

Recovery Phase of business cycle during which real GDP increases from trough level to level of previous peak.

Regressive Tax Falls more heavily on the poor than on the rich; for example, Social Security tax.

Rent (See Economic Rent.)

Rent Control Government-set price ceiling on rent.

Required Reserve Ratio Percentage of deposits that must be held as vault cash and reserve deposits by all depository institutions.

Required Reserves Minimum vault cash or reserves; held at the Federal Reserve District Bank.

Reserves Vault cash and deposits of banks held by Federal Reserve district banks.

Resources Land, labor, capital, and entrepreneurial ability used to produce goods and services.

Retained Earnings Earnings that a corporation keeps for investment in plant and equipment or for other purposes, rather than distributed to shareholders.

Right-to-Work Laws Under the Taft-Hartley Act, states are permitted to pass these laws, which prohibit the union shop. (Union membership cannot be made a condition of securing employment.)

Rule of Reason Mere size is no offense. Market conduct rather than market share should determine whether antitrust laws have been violated.

S

Saving Disposable income not spent for consumer goods; equal to disposable income minus personal consumption expenditures.

Saving Function As income rises, saving rises, but not as quickly.

Say's Law Supply creates its own demand.

Scarcity The inability of an economy to generate enough goods and services to satisfy all human wants.

Seasonal Unemployment Unemployment resulting from the seasonal pattern of work in certain industries, with workers regularly laid off during the slow season and rehired during the busy season.

Secondary Boycott A boycott of products or a company that sells the products of a company that is being struck.

Sherman Act The federal antitrust law enacted in 1890 that prohibited monopolization and conspiracies to restrain trade.

Shortage The amount by which the quantity demanded of a product exceeds the quantity supplied at a particular (below-equilibrium) price.

Short Run The length of time it takes all fixed costs to become variable costs.

Shut Down Cessation of a firm's operations as output falls to zero.

Shut-Down Point The low point on the firm's average variable cost curve. If price is below the shut-down point, the firm will shut down in the short run.

Socialism An economic system in which the government owns most of the productive resources except labor; it usually involves the redistribution of income.

Social Security The U.S. social insurance program financed by a federal payroll tax that provides disability, retirement, and death benefits.

Social Security Tax A tax paid equally by employee and employer, based on employee's wages. Most proceeds are used to pay Social Security retirement and Medicare benefits.

Sole Proprietorship An unincorporated business firm owned by one person.

Specialization Division of productive activities so that no one is self-sufficient.

Stagflation A period of either recession or stagnation accompanied by inflation.

Stock (See Corporate Stock.)

Strike When a collective bargaining agreement cannot be reached, a union calls for a work stoppage to last until an agreement is reached.

Structural Unemployment When people are out of work for a couple of years or longer.

Substitute Goods Products or services that can be used in place of each other. When the price of one falls, the demand for the other falls, and conversely with an increase of price.

Substitution Effect If the price of a resource, say labor, goes up, business firms tend to substitute capital or land for some of their now-expensive workers. Also, the substitution of more hours of work for leisure time as the wage rate rises.

Supply A schedule of quantities that people will sell at different prices.

Supply, Law of When the price of a good is lowered, less of it is supplied; when the price is raised, more is supplied.

Supply-Side Economics Main tenets: economic role of federal government is too large; high tax rates and government regulations hurt the incentives of individuals and business firms to produce goods and services.

Surplus The amount by which the quantity supplied of a product exceeds the quantity demanded at a specific (above-equilibrium) price.

Surplus Value A Marxian term: the amount by which the value of a worker's daily output exceeds the worker's daily wage.

t

Tariff A tax on imported goods.

Terms of Trade The ratio of exchange between an imported good and an exported good.

Time Deposit A deposit in a financial institution that requires notice of withdrawal or must be left for some fixed period of time.

Total Cost The sum of fixed and variable costs.

Total Revenue The price of a good or service multiplied by the number of units sold.

Trade Deficit The amount by which the value of a nation's imports exceed the value of its exports.

Transactions Demand for Money The demand for money by individuals and business firms to pay for day-to-day expenses.

Transfer Payment   Payment by one branch of government to another or to an individual. Largest transfer payment is Social Security.

Transmission Mechanism   The series of changes brought about by a change in monetary policy that ultimately changes the level of GDP.

U

Unanticipated Inflation   A rate of inflation that is either higher or lower than expected.

Underemployment   Failure to use our resources efficiently. A situation in which workers are employed in positions requiring less skill and education than they have or other resources are employed in their most productive use.

Underground Economy   Unreported or illegal production of goods and services that is not counted in GDP.

Unemployment   The total number of people over 16 who are ready, willing, and able to work, who have been unsuccessfully seeking employment.

Unemployment Rate   Number of unemployed divided by the labor force.

Union Shop   All employees must join the union, usually within 30 days after they are hired.

U.S. Treasury Securities   Bonds, bills, and notes that the Treasury issues when it borrows.

Utility   The satisfaction you derive from a good or service that you purchase. How much utility you derive is measured by how much you would be willing to pay.

V

Variable Costs   These vary with output. When output rises, variable costs rise; when output declines, variable costs fall.

Velocity (V)   The number of times per year each dollar in the money supply is spent.

Vertical Merger   The joining of two firms engaged in different parts of an industrial process, or the joining of a manufacturer and a retailer.

W

Wage   The price paid for the use or services of labor per unit of time.

Wage and Price Controls   Rules established by the government that either place a ceiling on wages and prices or limit their rate of increase.

Wealth   Anything that has value because it produces income or could produce income.

Workfare   A plan that requires welfare recipients to accept jobs or to enter training programs.

World Trade Organization (WTO)   The successor organization to GATT, which handles all trade disputes among member nations.

Index

Page numbers followed by n refer to notes.

f

connect™ | ECONOMICS

Less managing. More teaching. Greater learning.

INSTRUCTORS...

Would you like your students to show up for class more prepared?
(Let's face it, class is much more fun if everyone is engaged and prepared...)

Want an easy way to assign homework online and track student progress?
(Less time grading means more time teaching...)

Want an instant view of student or class performance? *(No more wondering if students understand...)*

Need to collect data and generate reports required for administration or accreditation? *(Say goodbye to manually tracking student learning outcomes...)*

Want to record and post your lectures for students to view online?

With McGraw-Hill's *Connect™ Plus Economics,*

INSTRUCTORS GET:

- Simple **assignment management,** allowing you to spend more time teaching.
- **Auto-graded** assignments, quizzes, and tests.
- **Detailed Visual Reporting** where student and section results can be viewed and analyzed.
- Sophisticated **online testing** capability.
- A **filtering and reporting** function that allows you to easily assign and report on materials that are correlated to accreditation standards, learning outcomes, and Bloom's taxonomy.
- An easy-to-use **lecture capture** tool.
- The option to **upload course documents** for student access.

STUDENTS...

Want to get **better grades**? *(Who doesn't?)*

Prefer to do your **homework online**? *(After all, you are online anyway...)*

Need **a better way** to **study** before the big test?

(A little peace of mind is a good thing...)

With **McGraw-Hill's** *Connect*™ **Plus Economics,**

STUDENTS GET:

- **Easy online access** to homework, tests, and quizzes assigned by your instructor.

- **Immediate feedback** on how you're doing. (No more wishing you could call your instructor at 1 a.m.)

- **Quick access** to lectures, practice materials, eBook, and more. (All the material you need to be successful is right at your fingertips.)

- A Self-Quiz and Study tool that **assesses your knowledge** and **recommends** specific readings, supplemental study materials, and additional practice work.*

*Available with select McGraw-Hill titles.